Religion: North American Style

Religion: North American Style SECOND EDITION

EDITED BY

Patrick H. McNamara

University of New Mexico

WADSWORTH PUBLISHING COMPANY

Belmont, California

A Division of Wadsworth, Inc.

Sociology Editor: Sheryl Fullerton
Production Editor: Deborah M. Oren
Managing Designer: Cynthia Bassett
Designer/Cover: Albert Burkhardt
Copy Editor: John Eastman
Technical Illustrator: Albert Burkhardt
Signing Representative: Nancy Tandberg

Printed in the United States of America

1 2 3 4 5 6 7 8 9 10—88 87 86 85 84

ISBN 0-534-02798-9

Library of Congress Cataloging in Publication Data
Main entry under title:

Religion North American style.

    Rev. ed. of: Religion American style. [1974]
    Includes bibliographical references and index.
    1. Religion and sociology—Addresses, essays,
lectures. 2. North America—Religion—Addresses,
essays, lectures.   I. McNamara, Patrick H.
BL60.R35 1984   306.6'097   83-6665
ISBN 0-534-02798-9

CONTENTS

Sources for Correlation Chart

Chalfant, H. Paul; Beckley, Robert E.; and Palmer, C. Eddie. *Religion in Contemporary Society*. Sherman Oaks, Calif.: Alfred, 1981.

Fallding, Harold. *The Sociology of Religion*. Toronto: McGraw-Hill Ryerson, 1974.

Hargrove, Barbara. *The Sociology of Religion: Classical and Contemporary Approaches*. Arlington Heights, Ill.: AHM, 1979.

Johnstone, Ronald L. *Religion in Society: A Sociology of Religion*. Second Edition. Englewood Cliffs, N.J.: Prentice-Hall, 1983.

McGuire, Meredith B. *Religion: The Social Context*. Belmont, Calif.: Wadsworth, 1981.

O'Dea, Thomas F., and Aviad, Janet O'Dea. *The Sociology of Religion*. Second Edition. Englewood Cliffs, N.J.: Prentice-Hall, 1983.

Wilson, Bryan. *Religion in Sociological Perspective*. New York: Oxford, 1982.

Wilson, John. *Religion in American Society: The Effective Presence*. Englewood Cliffs, N.J.: Prentice-Hall, 1978.

Yinger, J. Milton, *The Scientific Study of Religion*. New York: Macmillan, 1970.

CORRELATION CHART

Selected Sociology of Religion Textbooks

Readings in *Religion: North American Style, 2nd Ed.*		Chalfant et al.	Fallding	Hargrove	Johnstone	McGuire	O'Dea/Aviad	B. Wilson	J. Wilson	Yinger
Chapter 1	Durkheim	1	1	1,2	2	1	1,2	1,2	1	5
	Geertz	1	1,3	1,2,3	1,2	1	1,2	2	1	1,4
	Spiro	1	1	1	1	1	1	1,2	1	1
	Kaufmann	1	1,2	1	1	1	2	2	1	1,2
	Brown	2	3,4	3,4	1	1	2	2	1,2	1
	Berger	2	3	4	3	2	1,5	2	1	8,9
	Carnes	2	3	4,7	3	2	4	2	6	8,9
Chapter 2	Malinowski	2	4	3	4,13	6	1,3	2,6	1,9	7
	Geissler	3	4	3,9	4,13	6	3	2,6	9,12	6
	Bellah	7	1,3	5	6,13	6	1	2,6	9	19
	Christenson & Wimberley	7	1,3	5	6	6	1	2,6	9	19
	Fenn	7,14	8	5,7	4,6,13	6,8	1.5	3,6	18	19
Chapter 3	Fallding	4,7	5,6	6,8	5,10,12	5	3,4	3	7,13	13
	Kelley	4	6	13	13	5	3,4	3,4	8,13	13
	Perry & Hoge	4	6	13	4,12	5	3,4	3	8,13	12,13
	Caplow	12,14	8	4	8,13	8	5	2,6	18	21
Chapter 4	Niebuhr	4	5,6	7	5,8,12	5	4	4	4,7	13
	Bainbridge & Stark	4,8	5,6	14	5,8	5	4	4	7	13,14
	Wilson & Clow	2,8	5	7	5,8,12	5,7	4	4,6	5,6,7	13,14
	Earle, Knudsen, & Shriver	8,12	5	7	5,8	5	4	4	4	14
Chapter 5	Fichter	5,6	6	7	12	5	5,6	3,6	3,7	21
	Fee et al.	3,11	6	10	3	8	3	6	6,12,15	4
	Prevallet	3,5	4	4,16	9,13	5,6	2,5	3,6	2,6	12
Chapter 6	Sklare	7	5,7	9	12	5	3	3	9	21

		Chalfant et al.	Fallding	Hargrove	Johnstone	McGuire	O'Dea/Aviad	B. Wilson	J. Wilson	Yinger
	Lazerwitz & Harrison	6,7	5,7	9	12	5	3	3	9,15	21
	Ginsburg	2,3	7,8	4,9	3,12	2,3	5	3	2,12	21
Chapter 7	Marx	11	2	8	7,8	7	1,4	1,2	16	6,10,22
	Westhues	11	5	11	6,7,13	6,7	5,6	2,3,6	16,17	22
	Lorentzen	8,11	5	8,14	6,8,9,10	7	4,6	4,6	14,16	18,22
	Catholic Bishops	5,7,11	7	11	6,13	6,7	5,6	2,6	17	20
Chapter 8	Lefever	12	4,5	8,12	7,8	3,5	4	4	11,14	14,16
	Harding	6,12,13	5	8,13	11	7	5,6	4	15,17	15
	Ruether	5	3	9,13,15	9	4	2,6	5,6	12	15,21
Chapter 9	Bird & Reimer	10	8	15	5,13	5	5	5	19	8,9
	Downton	3,9,10	7	14,15	3,5,13	3,5	4	5	4,6	7,8
	Balch	9,10	8	4,15	3,5,13	2,3	4	5	6,7	7,8
	Richardson et al.	5,9	5	9,15	3,5,9	2,3,5	4	5	4,12	14
	Tipton	3,4,10	8	14	13	2,3,5	4	5	6,16	9,10
	Bromley & Shupe	4,10	8	14,15	5,13	3,5	4	5	6,7	13
Concluding Postscript		14	8	16	13	8	6	6	18,19	22

P R E F A C E

If art and literature primarily express the
realm of inner meaning and are free to explore
even the most aberrant and idiosyncratic
wishes, hopes, and anxieties, religion is always
concerned with the link between subject and
object, with the whole that contains them and
forms their ground. Though religion is not primarily subjective, it is not objective either. It
symbolizes unities in which we participate. . . .[1]

These are the words of Robert N. Bellah, and fifteen years of teaching the sociology of religion leave me in complete agreement with
them. I find myself in full sympathy with Bellah's "symbolic realism," with the concept of religion as both a cognitive and a noncog-
nitive symbolic world. This perspective suggests that one take this
world seriously in conducting both one's life and one's classes, and
that the importance of this world be respected in the developing
consciousness of students. Religion thus becomes a way of appre-
hending and constructing, through symbols, a reality that is both
"inner" to the individual and "outer" in the sense of familiar institutional forms. I do not deny the difficulty of maintaining the
"double vision" of which Bellah speaks—holding fast to canons of
scientific inquiry and analysis, avoiding advocacy of any particular
religious tradition, yet attempting to understand, as a teacher, the
meaning and value of religious understanding and to communicate
that understanding to students.

I intend this reader to aid students in their struggles to grasp the
sociologist's distinctive viewpoint of religion. My teaching experience has convinced me that many, if not most, students are so deeply socialized into the role of believer—or skeptic or unbeliever—that
they resist and find difficult the challenge of the sociological viewpoint: to see religious phenomena in social context, applying concepts such as manifest and latent functions, conflicts of interests,
organizational dilemmas, and role playing. Yet no student who has
made the effort and achieved some success is anything but grateful
for the experience. "I understand my own religion—or religious
background—a lot better now. . . . glad I took the course." "I see
why certain religions appeal to some groups and why they hold the
things they do and act the way they do." Not infrequently, though,
one will add, "But I was kind of lost for a while."

Thus this reader. To get students "into" the sociological viewpoint, I have found readings indispensable. Many of those included
within these covers have proved invaluable to me and my students;

several appeared in a reader I previously edited;[2] others I later introduced into my classes. Two kinds of readings seem helpful to students: the more formal or analytical, which are labeled *readings*, and the more informal and illustrative, called *selections*. Among the readings are excerpts from classical authors such as Durkheim, Malinowski, Marx, and Niebuhr. I have briefly sketched Weber's Protestant Ethic thesis in the introduction to Chapter 8, and used other chapter introductions to summarize research literature not explicitly included in the readings.

I usually employ readings in conjunction with a textbook. Those who have a similar preference will find the preceding correlation chart useful. But I have tried to provide enough background material in each chapter's introduction to enable this reader to be used by itself. Another alternative is to use it with classical works such as those by Durkheim and Weber.

The abundance of excellent material made it a real challenge to select readings. Besides stylistic readability, I also used the criterion that an article lucidly review previous research or at least raise key questions, in either case broadening the student's grasp of sociological issues. The central readings of Chapter 4 (by Bainbridge and Stark, and Wilson and Clow) are fine examples. Later readings by Lazerwitz and Harrison, Lorentzen, Bird and Reimer, and Downton are similarly good examples.

Canadian scholarship is a new addition to this reader, represented in articles as well as suggested additional readings. Although our cultures are similar in many ways, the differences are marked and afford instructive comparisons for students in both countries. Harold Fallding's essay on "mainline" churches in Canada and the United States (Chapter 3) is an example of comparative sociology at its best.

Part One opens with the functionalist viewpoint, which is deeply embedded in the Durkheimian legacy to sociology of religion, and continues in the work of Talcott Parsons and his students, such as Robert N. Bellah. I have found it easier to go from the functionalist to the conflict viewpoint rather than vice versa, complementing the functionalist perspective with that of Peter Berger's reality construction. (I rarely, if ever, teach the course without using Berger's *The Sacred Canopy* with its interplay of functionalism and symbolic interaction.) Chapter 2 is, for all practical purposes, a continuation of Chapter 1. Civil religion has deep roots in Durkheim's work and has generated a sharp critical response in the work of Richard K. Fenn and others. Fenn's critique goes to the heart of the Durkheimian tradition and its subsequent development by Talcott Parsons.

Part Two takes the student into the more or less familiar territory of North American religious bodies and traditions, where much of the theory conveyed in Part One finds application.

Part Three introduces the conflict perspective, which is reiterated to some extent in my Concluding Postscript. To the extent that churches as institutions and groups of committed believers challenge policies and trends of the larger society—particularly those enjoying wide political support—the conflict perspective is certainly useful, if not indispensable. The "life issues" of abortion and the nuclear arms race (the latter well exemplified in the American Catholic Bishops' pastoral statement on war and peace) issues of resource scarcity and environmental damage, the continuing domestic and international economic crises that bring misery to many—all are laden with moral values and thus invite the response of religious bodies. At this writing (early 1983), that response seems forthcoming and may lead to a collision of church and state unprecedented in North American history. Such developments may be among the most fascinating to watch and analyze in the closing decades of this century.

Finally, the so-called "new religions" discussed in Part Four raise the important theoretical issue of secularization, at least in one of its forms. Some sociologists find many of the new religions, to the extent they appeal and minister to private needs and preferences, wholly irrelevant to the larger social structure. Their presence raises the question: Do they push religion even deeper into the cultural periphery of private concerns, or do they generate motivations that promote such prophetic concerns as social justice? Perhaps it is too early to judge. Again, this dynamic is one that bears watching as we move into the late 1980s and 1990s.

In the meantime, I continue to find teaching sociology of religion an exciting experience. Many colleagues with whom I have shared these experiences at regional and national conferences, in settings both formal and highly informal (evenings after those sessions are finished!), feel equally enthusiastic. I welcome their comments and suggestions regarding this book and hope it enriches their teaching experiences as well as the learning experiences of their students.

I wish to thank my students and my colleagues for their encouragement, as well as members of my family who endured the late-night clicking of the typewriter. I wish to thank Edgar W. Mills of the University of Texas at San Antonio, Marion Dearman of California State University, Los Angeles, and Mark Abrahamson of the University of Connecticut for their valuable criticisms. I am also grateful to John Eastman, whose meticulous editing improved this book. Finally, my appreciation goes to Debbie Oren, Wadsworth's fine production editor, and not least, to William H. Oliver, sociology editor, who, with me, saw the need for this volume.

Notes

1. Robert N. Bellah, *Beyond Belief: Essays on Religion in a Post-Traditional World* (New York: Harper & Row, 1970), pp. 154–55.
2. Patrick H. McNamara, ed., *Religion American Style* (New York: Harper & Row, 1974).

One

Religion and Society: Exploring the Relationships

1

Functionalism: Concept and Variations

Try to define religion and you invite an argument. Yet every sociologist of religion uses either a personal definition or someone else's definition with added critical comment. Not that attempts to define religion are only recent. Scholars have historically resembled the blind men describing the elephant in the old fable, pointing to different features of religious belief and practice in offering definitions of religion. Greek and Roman philosophers could simply define religion as the worship of the gods. Medieval theologians, both Christian and Arabic, wrote of knowledge and love of "the True God." Skeptics of the French Enlightenment saw religion as an institution perpetuating ignorance and servitude. Modern psychology, following the lead of Sigmund Freud, views much of religion as a feeling of infantile dependence on a protective father figure; the late philosopher-theologian Paul Tillich preferred the term *ultimate concern* to describe what is essential about religion.

None of these definitions as stated is wholly satisfactory to a sociologist. The relationship of religion to society is central to any sociologist's attempt to define religion. A social scientist searches for the most universal features of religion; that is, those that can be found in most societies.

A functionalist approach is often employed in this search. Its roots lie deep in sociology's history. Functionalism tries to state in comprehensive theoretical terms what religion *does*, what role or roles it performs in human society. Religion's role is deduced from an examination of how it relates to the ongoing, changing social system. (Functionalism is not, however, the only major theoretical approach to religion in society. Conflict theory is also important and will be considered in Chapter 7).

Functionalists acknowledge their debt to French sociologist
Emile Durkheim. Sharing the skepticism of most nineteenth-century
intellectuals about traditional religious beliefs, Durkheim was nonetheless impressed by the universal presence of religion in all world
societies. He refused to believe that religion was purely illusory.
Something so deeply rooted in people's lives had to have *some* basis
in reality. But what was that basis?

The first reading in this chapter, taken from the conclusion of
Durkheim's *The Elementary Forms of the Religious Life*, tells us that
the reality conceived and felt by believers is not the *real* basis for
religion. Religion's real basis is society itself. For society, to Durkheim, exercises a moral force upon its members. The idea of a
superhuman force comes not from mankind's awe at the forces of
nature nor from experiences of a spiritual realm, such as those
evoked by dreams, visions, trances, and death itself, when the principle of life or a "soul" seems to leave the body. Durkheim used
detailed descriptions of the religious rites of Australian aborigines
to show how the tribe, or society itself, gives rise to "collective sentiments" that become external, or supraindividual, realities forming
a constraining influence on individual lives; yet believers are unaware of the true basis of these ritual origins. Society's power is
magnified in the performance of religious rituals in which the participants get "carried away" and feel intensely the "external power"
that makes them "think and act differently than in normal times."
Out of this "effervescence," as Durkheim called the emotional
"high" of ritual participation, "the religious idea seems to be
born."[1]

Over time, the ideas and feelings generated in these ways come
to form a whole world of the *sacred*, symbolized not only in rites
and ceremonies, but in totemic emblems, holy vessels and other objects, special incantations, gestures, dances, and so on. Durkheim
emphasized that the sacred character of something is due *not* to the
thing itself (what, for example, is inherently "sacred" about a cup
used only in religious ceremony?) but is conferred by the society
and sustained by repeated activity and usage. Society generates a
whole world of the sacred, which is distinguished "over against"
the world of the *profane* or not-sacred. Believers hold the world of
the sacred as more deeply real and meaningful than the everyday
world of the profane. But to sustain this belief in and adherence to
the world of the sacred, confirming rituals are necessary. Belief
must be maintained through activity. Durkheim rejected an intellectual or purely idea-based explanation of religion's reality. Belief
and behavior mutually strengthen one another. If ritual performances were to cease, religious belief would atrophy. Reenactment
of ritual is particularly necessary to a society, Durkheim insisted,
when the society is threatened by or actually undergoing a crisis. A
people, a tribe, a nation, a small community all "need" the mutual

reaffirmation of their most central beliefs and values, their core feelings about themselves and their identity, at times of challenge to their continued existence or well-being.

The idea of "needs" lies at the heart of the functionalist viewpoint. Social scientists following Durkheim, while not losing sight of the *societal* needs he emphasized, have postulated sets of *individual* needs that religious belief and behavior fulfill—needs, again, that are considered universal and that are met in collective ways. Again, the importance of the group is emphasized.

Needs also lie at the heart of the second reading from Clifford Geertz's "Religion as a Cultural System." Geertz suggests that ritual is particularly important as a symbolic reminder and reassurance to a society's members in any one of *three* critical and recurring human experiences (or needs) that threaten to "break in" and create doubt, confusion, or even chaos and despair. These three episodes are bafflement, death and suffering, and the inability to make sound moral judgments. Geertz explains what he means by each of these conditions and shows how a religious system attempts to cope with them by defining a symbolic world that appears intellectually and emotionally whole and satisfying for a group of people—a tribe, a clan, a congregation, a nation. Here is Geertz's definition of religion:

(1) a system of symbols which acts to (2) establish powerful, pervasive, and long-lasting moods and motivations in men by (3) formulating conceptions of a general order of existence and (4) clothing these conceptions with such an aura of factuality that (5) the moods and motivations seem uniquely realistic.[2]

Geertz acknowledges the roles of other meaning systems as well. Religion is not the only one that people may employ. Common sense, science, art, all confer meaning in their own right. He contrasts the functions of these meaning systems with the unique function of the religious symbol system.

Geertz reinforces Durkheim's conviction of the importance of ritual. Turning to Navaho curing rites or "sings," he points out that these ceremonies give participants and observers a way of expressing suffering, therefore helping them understand and endure it. Such rites also reidentify the Navaho as a "holy people" and symbolize their place in the larger cosmic order. World-as-lived-in and world-as-imagined are fused together so that "they turn out to be the same world." In this way religion can truly give shape to the daily world in which people live out their lives.

J. Milton Yinger's research, cited in the Additional Readings to this chapter, further explores the questions asked by Durkheim and pursued by Geertz. He has fashioned surveys to find out whether there may exist "common structures" or recurring problems in the human condition to which religions throughout the world—despite their obvious, sometimes dramatic differences—attempt to respond. His approach originally involved only American college students but subsequently reached out to samples of college students from seven other countries. Yinger's statements are designed to tap "non-doctrinal religious attitudes" concerning "meaning, suffering, and injustice" and to discover whether respondents assume a "religious" attitude toward these problems or view them through some other "nonreligious" meaning framework. His respondents were asked their extent of agreement or disagreement with such statements as the following:

1. Suffering, injustice, and finally death are the lot of man, but they need not be negative experiences; their significance and effects can be shaped by our beliefs.
2. In face of the almost continuous conflict and violence in life, I cannot see how men are going to learn to live in mutual respect and peace with one another.
3. Somehow I cannot get very interested in the talk about "the basic human condition" and "man's ultimate problems."
4. Mankind's most difficult and destructive experiences are often the source of increased understanding and powers of endurance.
5. Despite the often chaotic conditions of human life, I believe that there is order and pattern to existence that someday we'll come to understand.[3]

Yinger discovered that a large majority of his respondents claimed "another kind of reality that supersedes or redefines experiences."[4] In other words, extremely few respondents found the cosmos simply meaningless and "just there" to be accepted or endured. Meaninglessness, suffering, and injustice are problems of widespread interest, conceived as part of the human condition, yet viewed as capable of being changed or having their meaning transposed by human world views. The same finding holds for those who profess to be religious within their tradition (Buddhism, Protestantism, and Catholicism were represented in the seven-nation survey) as well as for those who profess no religion or who say they are agnostic or atheist.

Yinger's research suggests that people's "ultimate concerns," as he defines them in his survey items, need involve no explicit reference to God, gods, or the supernatural—though most of his respondents seemed to postulate a superempirical framework. His findings can be integrated into a long-standing discussion in the sociology of religion: the best way of defining religion for purposes of research and clarity of discussion. Yinger is apparently a member of what is called the *inclusivist* camp, those who refer to religion as concerning "ultimate values" or "ultimate concerns" but without reference to the supernatural as essential. Groups not usually regarded as religious, but whose views involve some kind of reflection upon "ultimate" human purposes, can be regarded as religious in this broad, overarching sense. Liberal humanism, communism, or socialism may well qualify for some people at some time in their lives as satisfactory interpretive schemes for the "big questions" seen above: life's meaning, end, suffering, and moral challenges.

Anthropologist Melford E. Spiro dissents vigorously from this inclusive view. He represents those scholars tagged *exclusivist*, who reply that any such broad definition violates the way most people understand religion; that is, as including some kind of supernatural being or force. The inclusive definition, he argues, only breeds confusion. To include secular "isms" of one kind or another as potentially religious blurs a real difference in *substance* of belief, even though the *functions* of secular beliefs, for some of their adherents, may be similar. Exclusivists ask: Why not call secular "isms" something like "surrogate religiosity"? Why not say that if we do *not* take this stance, we have difficulty in clearly defining those commitments held or sought by modern-day persons who are resolutely walking away from traditional religions in which they have been raised. In effect, we say to such persons, "Well, you're still religious, you know."[5]

To handle objections from the inclusivist camp, Spiro usefully distinguishes between beliefs and beings that are *objects* of ultimate concern, on the one hand; and the *value* of such beliefs and beings, on the other, as means or ends in themselves. Superhuman beings, for some (or many) religious adherents, may be objects of ultimate concern in themselves. Or they may be valued for the *ends* (such as money, health, power, or victory) they may assist one in achieving. Spiro follows Durkheim in labeling as *sacred* that which is ultimately valued in itself, or a belief referring to such. Crucial for Spiro is that *both* "religious" (superhuman) and "nonreligious" (denying the superhuman) viewpoints may be designated as sacred, depending on whether one or the other is of ultimate concern to some individual, group, or society. Thus not all ultimate concerns will be religious. Communists investing their beliefs and goals with ultimate significance, committing their lives to this world view, have *sacralized* communism; but communism is *not*, in this view, a religion since it denies the existence and relevance of a superhuman world. (On the other hand, believers in a supernatural world view who use their beliefs and accompanying practices exclusively for worldly gain may be said to be practicing magic—religion has become a means, not a primary or ultimate goal. Both magic and religion place human beings in contact with supraempirical realities; but magic is essentially manipulative in character, for use in "getting what you want").[6]

Carrying out these reflections still further is philosopher Walter Kaufmann, who relentlessly challenges the notion that everyone must have some ultimate commitment or concern. His strictures sharply remind us that no theory of religion should postulate some overarching interpretation of the cosmos of *all* men and women. In the words of Sigmund Freud, modern (and primitive?) human beings may be among those "who go no further, but humbly acquiesce in the small part which human beings play in the great world— such a man is . . . irreligious in the truest sense of the word."[7]

Joseph Epes Brown's "Sun Dance" illustrates elements identified by Durkheim in his classic definition of religion as "a unified system of beliefs and practices relative to sacred things which unite into one single moral community all those who adhere to them."[8] We return to the central role of ritual. The ceremonies of the Plains Indians of North America affirm the power of suffering and celebrate the sacred time of spring and its life-bringing forces.

The foregoing readings introduce us to the problems experienced by many persons in urbanized, industrialized societies, societies so different from the relatively simple, undifferentiated communities of shared beliefs and rituals discussed by Durkheim and illustrated by Brown. Confronted with a variety of options, modern city dwellers find their traditional religious views competing with world views formed in the private spheres of family, friends, and neighbors. To be sure, individuals may borrow from creedal formulations and beliefs of churches to which they belong; but as the sanctions formerly wielded by religious institutions weaken (for how many people is excommunication a serious threat?), individuals become more free to construct an amalgam stemming partly from church traditions and partly from the many sources mentioned in the readings.[9]

In a social setting that teems with what Thomas Luckmann terms an "assortment of religious representations available to potential consumers," how can one *maintain* a world view?[10] Peter Berger addresses this issue in "Plausibility Structures." Berger's *The Sacred Canopy* elaborates a sociopsychological theory of religion's function in society and in individual lives. He uses a kind of sociology-of-knowledge perspective to stress the crucial importance of interaction with "confirming others." According to Berger, without the massive institutional support of the kind that Durkheim and Geertz predicate of simpler societies, religious beliefs and practices stand or fall depending on the answer to one question: How supportive is your community of reference? If those persons important to you with whom you frequently interact believe and behave in ways that reinforce your beliefs and values, those beliefs and values are not so hard to maintain. If these "significant others" are indifferent or nonsupportive, on the other hand, your world view will be sustained only with great difficulty.

To elaborate this point is the burden of Paul Carnes's "Yoga Made Plausible," which offers a student's autobiographical view of involvements in a series of Berger's plausibility structures. Conversion and deconversion occur among changing scenarios of significant others. Carnes concludes by broaching the question that occurs to any critical student of this perspective: *Can* one transcend the influence of a network (or networks) of significant others and arrive at a world view that is "really mine"?

Notes

1. Emile Durkheim, *The Elementary Forms of the Religious Life* (New York: Free Press, 1947), p. 250.
2. Clifford Geertz, "Religion as a Cultural System," in *Anthropological Approaches to the Study of Religion*, ed. Michael Banton (London: Tavistock, 1966), p. 4.
3. J. Milton Yinger, "A Comparative Study of the Substructures of Religion," *Journal for the Scientific Study of Religion* 16 (March 1977): 76.
4. Ibid., p. 77.
5. These points are well presented by Roland Robertson, *The Sociological Interpretation of Religion* (New York: Schocken, 1970), p. 39.
6. A classic discussion of the religion-magic distinction is Bronislaw Malinowski, "The Art of Magic and the Power of Faith," in *Magic, Science, and Religion* (New York: Doubleday, 1955), pp. 69–90. A good, brief contemporary treatment is found in Thomas F. O'Dea and Janet O'Dea Aviad, *The Sociology of Religion* (Englewood Cliffs, N.J.: Prentice-Hall, 1983), pp. 7–10 and 117–23.
7. Sigmund Freud, *The Future of an Illusion*, rev. ed. (New York: Doubleday, 1964), p. 52.
8. Durkheim, *Elementary Forms*, p. 62.
9. This paragraph is based upon Thomas Luckmann, *The Invisible Religion* (New York: Macmillan, 1967), pp. 103–104.
10. Ibid., pp. 61–63.

R E A D I N G   1 . 1

Conclusion from *The Elementary Forms of the Religious Life*

Emile Durkheim

The theorists who have undertaken to explain religion in rational terms have generally seen in it before all else a system of ideas, corresponding to some determined object. This object has been conceived in a multitude of

Emile Durkheim (1858–1917) was one of the founding fathers of modern sociology.
Reprinted with permission of Macmillan Publishing Co., Inc. and George Allen & Unwin Ltd. from Emile Durkheim, *The Elementary Forms of the Religious Life*, translated by Joseph Ward Swain. New York: The Free Press, 1963.

ways: nature, the infinite, the unknowable, the ideal, etc.; but these differences matter but little. In any case, it was the conceptions and beliefs which were considered as the essential elements of religion. As for the rites, from this point of view they appear to be only an external translation, contingent and material, of these internal states which alone pass as having any intrinsic value. This conception is so commonly held that generally the disputes of which religion is the theme turn about the question whether it can conciliate itself with science or not, that is to say, whether or not there is a place beside our scientific knowledge for another form of thought which would be specifically religious.

But the believers, the men who lead the religious life and have a direct sensation of what it really is, object to this way of regarding it, saying that it does not correspond to their daily experience. In fact, they feel that the real function of religion is not to make us think, to enrich our knowledge, nor to add to the conceptions which we owe to science others of another origin and another character, but rather it is to make us act, to aid us to live. The believer who has communicated with his god is not merely a man who sees new truths of which the unbeliever is ignorant; he is a man who is *stronger*. He feels within him more force, either to endure the trials of existence, or to conquer them. It is as though he were raised above the miseries of the world, because he is raised above his condition as a mere man; he believes that he is saved from evil, under whatever form he may conceive this evil. The first article in every creed is the belief in salvation by faith. But it is hard to see how a mere idea could have this efficacy. An idea is in reality only a part of ourselves; then how could it confer upon us powers superior to those which we have of our own nature? Howsoever rich it might be in affective virtues, it could add nothing to our natural vitality; for it could only release the motive powers which are within us, neither creating them nor increasing them. From the mere fact that we consider an object worthy of being loved and sought after, it does not follow that we feel ourselves stronger afterwards; it is also necessary that this object set free energies superior to these which we ordinarily have at our command and also that we have some means of making these enter into us and unite themselves to our interior lives. Now for that, it is not enough that we think of them; it is also

indispensable that we place ourselves within their sphere of action, and that we set ourselves where we may best feel their influence; in a word, it is necessary that we act, and that we repeat the acts thus necessary every time we feel the need of renewing their effects. From this point of view, it is readily seen how that group of regularly repeated acts which form the cult get their importance. In fact, whoever has really practised a religion knows very well that it is the cult which gives rise to these impressions of joy, of interior peace, of serenity, of enthusiasm which are, for the believer, an experimental proof of his beliefs. The cult is not simply a system of signs by which the faith is outwardly translated; it is a collection of the means by which this is created and recreated periodically. Whether it consists in material acts or mental operations, it is always this which is efficacious.

Our entire study rests upon this postulate that the unanimous sentiment of the believers of all times cannot be purely illusory. Together with a recent apologist of the faith[1] we admit that these religious beliefs rest upon a specific experience whose demonstrative value is, in one sense, not one bit inferior to that of scientific experiments, though different from them. We, too, think that "a tree is known by its fruits,"[2] and that fertility is the best proof of what the roots are worth. But from the fact that a "religious experience," if we choose to call it this, does exist and that it has a certain foundation—and, by the way, is there any experience which has none?—it does not follow that the reality which is its foundation conforms objectively to the idea which believers have of it. The very fact that the fashion in which it has been conceived has varied infinitely in different times is enough to prove that none of these conceptions express it adequately. If a scientist states it as an axiom that the sensations of heat and light which we feel correspond to some objective cause, he does not conclude that this is what it appears to the senses to be. Likewise, even if the impressions which the faithful feel are not imaginary, still they are in no way privileged intuitions; there is no reason for believing that they inform us better upon the nature of their object than do ordinary sensations upon the nature of bodies and their properties. In order to discover what this object consists of, we must submit them to an examination and elaboration analogous to that which has substituted for the sensuous idea of the world another which is scientific and conceptual.

This is precisely what we have tried to do, and we have seen that this reality, which mythologies have represented under so many different forms, but which is the universal and eternal objective cause of these sensations *sui generis* out of which religious experience is made, is society. We have shown what moral forces it develops and how it awakens this sentiment of a refuge, of a shield and of a guardian support which attaches the believer to his cult. It is that which raises him outside himself; it is even that which made him. For that which makes a man is the totality of the intellectual property which constitutes civilization, and civilization is the work of society. Thus is explained the preponderating role of the cult in all religions, whichever they may be. This is because society cannot make its influence felt unless it is in action, and it is not in action unless the individuals who compose it are assembled together and act in common. It is by common action that it takes consciousness of itself and realizes its position; it is before all else an active cooperation. The collective ideas and sentiments are even possible only owing to these exterior movements which symbolize them. . . . Then it is action which dominates the religious life, because of the mere fact that it is society which is its source.

In addition to all the reasons which have been given to justify this conception, a final one may be added here, which is the result of our whole work. As we have progressed, we have established the fact that the fundamental categories of thought, and consequently of science, are of religious origin. We have seen that the same is true for magic and consequently for the different processes which have issued from it. On the other hand, it has long been known that up until a relatively advanced moment of evolution, moral and legal rules have been indistinguishable from ritual prescriptions. In summing up, then, it may be said that nearly all the great social institutions have been born in religion. Now in order that these principal aspects of the collective life may have commenced by being only varied aspects of the religious life, it is obviously necessary that the religious life be the eminent form and, as it were, the concentrated expression of the whole collective life. If religion has given birth to all that is essential in society, it is because the idea of society is the soul of religion. . . .

. . . our definition of the sacred is that it is something added to and above the real: now the ideal answers to this same definition; we cannot explain one without explaining the other. In fact, we have seen that if collective life awakens religious thought on reaching a certain degree of intensity, it is because it brings about a state of effervescence which changes the conditions of psychic activity. Vital energies are overexcited, passions more active, sensations stronger; there are even some which are produced only at this moment. A man does not recognize himself; he feels himself transformed and consequently he transforms the environment which surrounds him. In order to account for the very particular impressions which he receives, he attributes to the things with which he is in most direct contact properties which they have not, exceptional powers and virtues which the objects of everyday experience do not possess. In a word, above the real world where his profane life passes he has placed another which, in one sense, does not exist except in thought, but to which he attributes a higher sort of dignity than to the first. Thus, from a double point of view it is an ideal world. . . .

... the collective ideal which religion expresses is far from being due to a vague innate power of the individual, but it is rather at the school of collective life that the individual has learned to idealize. It is in assimilating the ideals elaborated by society that he has become capable of conceiving the ideal. It is society which, by leading him within its sphere of action, has made him acquire the need of raising himself above the world of experience and has at the same time furnished him with the means of conceiving another. For society has constructed this new world in constructing itself, since it is society which this expresses. Thus both with the individual and in the group, the faculty of idealizing has nothing mysterious about it. It is not a sort of luxury which a man could get along without, but a condition of his very existence. He could not be a social being, that is to say, he could not be a man, if he had not acquired it.

Notes

1. William James, *The Varieties of Religious Experience.*
2. Quoted by James, *op. cit.*, p. 20.

R E A D I N G   1 . 2

Religion as a Cultural System

Clifford Geertz

There are at least three points where chaos—a tumult of events which lack not just interpretations but *interpretability*—threatens to break in upon man: at the limits of his analytic capacities, at the limits of his powers of endurance, and at the limits of his moral insight. Bafflement, suffering, and a sense of intractable ethical paradox are all, if they become intense enough or are sustained long enough, radical challenges to the proposition that life is comprehensible and that we can, by taking thought, orient ourselves effectively within it—challenges with which any religion, however "primitive," which hopes to persist must attempt somehow to cope.

Of the three issues, it is the first which has been least investigated by modern social anthropologists (though Evans-Pritchard's

Clifford Geertz is a member of the faculty of Social Sciences at the Institute for Advanced Study, Princeton University.

Reprinted with permission from Michael Banton, ed., *Anthropological Approaches to the Study of Religion.* © 1966 Tavistock Publications, Ltd., London.

(1937) classic discussion of why granaries fall on some Azande and not on others is a notable exception). Even to consider people's religious beliefs as attempts to bring anomalous events or experiences—death, dreams, mental fugues, volcanic eruptions, or marital infidelity—within the circle of the at least potentially explicable seems to smack of Tyloreanism or worse. But it does appear to be a fact that at least some men—in all probability, most men—are unable to leave unclarified problems of analysis merely unclarified, just to look at the stranger features of the world's landscape in dumb astonishment or bland apathy without trying to develop, however fantastic, inconsistent, or simpleminded, some notions as to how such features might be reconciled with the more ordinary deliverances of experience. Any chronic failure of one's explanatory apparatus, the complex of received culture patterns (common sense, science, philosophical speculation, myth) one has for mapping the empirical world, to explain things which cry out for explanation tends to lead to a deep disquiet—a tendency rather more widespread and a disquiet rather deeper than we have sometimes supposed since the pseudoscience view of religious belief was, quite rightfully, deposed. After all, even that high priest of heroic atheism, Lord Russell, once remarked that although the problem of the existence of God had never bothered him, the ambiguity of certain mathematical axioms had threatened to unhinge his mind. And Einstein's profound dissatisfaction with quantum mechanics was based on a—surely religious—inability to believe that, as he put it, God plays dice with the universe.

But this quest for lucidity and the rush of metaphysical anxiety that occurs when empirical phenomena threaten to remain intransigently opaque is found on much humbler intellectual levels. Certainly, I was struck in my own work, much more than I had at all expected to be, by the degree to which my more animistically inclined informants behaved like true Tyloreans. They seemed to be constantly using their beliefs to "explain" phenomena, or, more accurately, to convince themselves that the phenomena were explainable within the accepted scheme of things, for they commonly had only a minimal attachment to the particular soul possession, emotional disequilibrium, taboo infringement, or bewitchment hypothesis they advanced and were all too ready to abandon it for some other, in the same genre, which struck them as more plausible given the facts of the case. What they were *not* ready to do was abandon it for no other hypothesis at all; to leave events to themselves.

And what is more, they adopted this nervous cognitive stance with respect to phenomena which had no immediate practical bearing on their own lives, or for that matter on anyone's. When a peculiarly shaped, rather large toadstool grew up in a carpenter's house in the short space of a few days (or, some said, a few hours), people came from miles around to see it, and everyone had

some sort of explanation—some animist, some animatist, some not quite either—for it. . . . Toadstools play about the same role in Javanese life as they do in ours and in the ordinary course of things Javanese have about as much interest in them as we do. It was just that this one was "odd," "strange," "uncanny"—*aneh*. And the odd, strange, and uncanny simply must be accounted for—or, again, the conviction that it *could be accounted* for sustained. One does not shrug off a toadstool which grows five times as fast as a toadstool has any right to grow. In the broadest sense the "strange" toadstool did have implications, and critical ones, for those who heard about it. It threatened their most general ability to understand the world, raised the uncomfortable question of whether the beliefs which they held about nature were workable, the standards of truth they used valid. . . .

As a religious problem, the problem of suffering is, paradoxically, not how to avoid suffering but how to suffer, how to make of physical pain, personal loss, worldly defeat, or the helpless contemplation of others' agony something bearable, supportable—something, as we say, sufferable. . . . Where the more intellective aspects of what Weber called the Problem of Meaning are a matter of affirming the ultimate explicability of experience, the more effective aspects are a matter of affirming its ultimate sufferableness. As religion on one side anchors the power of our symbolic resources for formulating analytic ideas in an authoritative conception of the overall shape of reality, so on another side it anchors the power of our, also symbolic, resources for expressing emotions—moods, sentiments, passions, affection, feelings—in a similar conception of its pervasive tenor, its inherent tone and temper. For those able to embrace them, and for so long as they are able to embrace them, religious symbols provide a cosmic guarantee not only for their ability to comprehend the world, but also, comprehending it, to give a precision to their feeling, a definition to their emotions which enables them, morosely or joyfully, grimly or cavalierly, to endure it.

Consider in this light the well-known Navaho curing rites usually referred to as "sings" (Kluckhohn and Leighton, 1946; Reichard, 1950). A sing—the Navaho have about sixty different ones for different purposes, but virtually all of them are dedicated to removing some sort of physical or mental illness—is a kind of religious psychodrama in which there are three main actors: the "singer" or curer, the patient, and, as a kind of antiphonal chorus, the patient's family and friends. The structure of all the sings, the drama's plot, is quite similar. There are three main acts: a purification of the patient and audience; a statement, by means of repetitive chants and ritual manipulations, of the wish to restore well-being ("harmony") in the patient; an identification of the patient with the Holy People and his consequent "cure." The purification rites involved forced sweating, induced vomiting, etc., to expel the sickness from the patient physically. The chants, which are numberless, consist mainly of simple optative phrases ("may the patient be well," "I am getting better all over," etc.). And, finally, the identification of the patient with the Holy People, and thus with cosmic order generally, is accomplished through the agency of a sand painting depicting the Holy People in one or another appropriate mythic setting. The singer places the patient on the painting, touching the feet, hands, knees, shoulders, breast, back, and head of the divine figures and then the corresponding parts of the patient, performing thus what is essentially a communion rite between the patient and the Holy People, a bodily identification of the human and the divine (Reichard, 1950). This is the climax of the sing: the whole curing process may be likened, Reichard says, to a spiritual osmosis in which the illness in man and the power of the deity penetrate the ceremonial membrane in both directions, the former being neutral-

ized by the latter. Sickness seeps out in the sweat, vomit, and other purification rites; health seeps in as the Navaho patient touches, through the medium of the singer, the sacred sand painting. Clearly, the symbolism of the sing focuses upon the problem of human suffering and attempts to cope with it by placing it in a meaningful context, providing a mode of action through which it can be expressed, being expressed, understood, and being understood, endured. The sustaining effect of the sing (and since the commonest disease is tuberculosis, it can in most cases be only sustaining) rests ultimately on its ability to give the stricken person a vocabulary in terms of which to grasp the nature of his distress and relate it to the wider world. Like a calvary, a recitation of Buddha's emergence from his father's palace or a performance of *Oedipus Tyrannos* in other religious traditions, a sing is mainly concerned with the presentation of a specific and concrete image of truly human, and so endurable, suffering powerful enough to resist the challenge of emotional meaninglessness raised by the existence of intense and unremovable brute pain.

The problem of suffering passes easily into the problem of evil, for if suffering is severe enough it usually, though not always, seems morally undeserved as well, at least to the sufferer. But they are not, however, exactly the same thing—a fact I think Weber, too influenced by the biases of a monotheistic tradition in which, as the various aspects of human experience must be conceived to proceed from a single, voluntaristic source, man's pain reflects directly on God's goodness, did not fully recognize in his generalization of the dilemmas of Christian theodicy Eastward. For where the problem of suffering is concerned with threats to our ability to put our "un-disciplined squads of emotion" into some sort of soldierly order, the problem of evil is concerned with threats to our ability to make sound moral judgments. What is involved in the problem of evil is not the adequacy of our symbolic resources to govern our affective life, but the adequacy of those resources to provide a workable set of ethical criteria, normative guides to govern our action. The vexation here is the gap between things as they are and as they ought to be if our conceptions of right and wrong make sense, the gap between what we deem various individuals deserve and what we see that they get—a phenomenon summed up in that profound quatrain:

The rain falls on the just
And on the unjust fella;
But mainly upon the just,
Because the unjust has the just's umbrella.

Or if this seems too flippant an expression of an issue that, in somewhat different form, animates the Book of Job and the *Baghavad Gita*, the following classical Javanese poem, known, sung, and repeatedly quoted in Java by virtually everyone over the age of six, puts the point—the discrepancy between moral prescriptions and material rewards, the seeming inconsistency of "is" and "ought"— rather more elegantly:

We have lived to see a time without order
In which everyone is confused in his mind.
One cannot bear to join in the madness,
But if he does not do so
He will not share in the spoils,
And will starve as a result.
Yes, God; wrong is wrong:
Happy are those who forget,
Happier yet those who remember and have deep insight. . . .

Thus the problem of evil, or perhaps one should say the problem *about* evil, is in essence the same sort of problem of or about bafflement and the problem of or about suffering. The strange opacity of certain empirical events, the dumb senselessness of intense or inexorable pain, and the enigmatic unaccountability of gross iniquity all raise the uncomfortable suspicion that perhaps the world, and hence man's life in the world, has no genuine order at all—no empirical regularity, no emotional form, no moral coher-

ence. And the religious response to this suspicion is in each case the same: the formulation, by means of symbols, of an image of such a genuine order of the world which will account for, and even celebrate, the perceived ambiguities, puzzles, and paradoxes in human experience. The effort is not to deny the undeniable—that there are unexplained events, that life hurts, or that rain falls upon the just—but to deny that there are inexplicable events, that life is unendurable, and that justice is a mirage. The principles which constitute the moral order may indeed often elude men, as Lienhardt puts it, in the same way as fully satisfactory explanations of anomalous events or effective forms for the expression of feeling often elude them. What is important, to a religious man at least, is that this elusiveness be accounted for, that it be not the result of the fact that there are no such principles, explanations, or forms, that life is absurd and the attempt to make moral, intellectual or emotional sense out of experience is bootless. The Dinka can admit, in fact insist upon, the moral ambiguities and contradictions of life as they live it because these ambiguities and contradictions are seen not as ultimate, but as the "rational," "natural," "logical" (one may choose one's own adjective here, for none of them is truly adequate) outcome of the moral structure of reality which the myth of the withdrawn "Divinity" depicts, or as Lienhardt says, "images." . . .

If we place the religious perspective against the background of three of the other major perspectives in terms of which men construe the world—the commonsensical, the scientific, and the aesthetic—its special character emerges more sharply. What distinguishes common sense as a mode of "seeing" is, as Schutz (1962) has pointed out, a simple acceptance of the world, its objects, and its processes as being just what they seem to be— what is sometimes called naive realism—and the pragmatic motive, the wish to act upon that world so as to bend it to one's practical purposes, to master it, or so far as that proves impossible, to adjust to it. The world of everyday life, itself, of course, a cultural product, for it is framed in terms of the symbolic conceptions of "stubborn fact" handed down from generation to generation, is the established scene and given object of our actions. Like Mt. Everest it is just there and the thing to do with it, if one feels the need to do anything with it at all, is to climb it. In the scientific perspective it is precisely this givenness which disappears (Schutz, 1962). Deliberate doubt and systematic inquiry, the suspension of the pragmatic motive in favor of disinterested observation, the attempt to analyze the world in terms of formal concepts whose relationship to the informal conceptions of common sense become increasingly problematic—these are the hallmarks of the attempt to grasp the world scientifically. And as for the aesthetic perspective, which under the rubric of "the aesthetic attitude" has been perhaps most exquisitely examined, it involves a different sort of suspension of naive realism and practical interest, in that instead of questioning the credentials of everyday experience, that experience is merely ignored in favor of an eager dwelling upon appearances, an engrossment in surfaces, an absorption in things, as we say, "in themselves": "The function of artistic illusion is not 'make-believe' . . . but the very opposite, disengagement from belief—the contemplation of sensory qualities without their usual meanings of 'here's that chair,' 'That's my telephone,' . . . etc. The knowledge that what is before us has no practical significance in the world is what enables us to give attention to its appearance as such" (Langer, 1957, p. 49). And like the commonsensical and the scientific (or the historical, the philosophical, and the artistic), this perspective, this "way of seeing" is not the product of some mysterious Cartesian chemistry, but is induced, mediated, and in fact created by means of symbols. It is the artist's skill which can produce those curious quasiobjects—po-

ems, dramas, sculptures, symphonies—which, dissociating themselves from the solid world of common sense, take on the special sort of eloquence only sheer appearances can achieve.

The religious perspective differs from the commonsensical in that, as already pointed out, it moves beyond the realities of everyday life to wider ones which correct and complete them, and its defining concern is not action upon those wider realities but acceptance of them, faith in them. It differs from the scientific perspective in that it questions the realities of everyday life not out of an institutionalized skepticism which dissolves the world's givenness into a swirl of probabilistic hypotheses, but in terms of what it takes to be wider, nonhypothetical truths. Rather than detachment, its watchword is commitment; rather than analysis, encounter. And it differs from art in that instead of effecting a disengagement from the whole question of factuality, deliberately manufacturing an air of semblance and illusion, it deepens the concern with fact and seeks to create an aura of utter actuality. It is this sense of the "really real" upon which the religious perspective rests and which the symbolic activities of religion as a cultural system are devoted to producing, intensifying, and, so far as possible, rendering inviolable by the discordant revelations of secular experience. It is, again, the imbuing of a certain specific complex of symbols—of the metaphysic they formulate and the style of life they recommend—with a persuasive authority which, from an analytic point of view, is the essence of religious action.

Which brings us, at length, to ritual. For it is in ritual—i.e., consecrated behavior—that this conviction that religious conceptions are veridical and that religious directives are sound is somehow generated. It is in some sort of ceremonial form—even if that form be hardly more than the recitation of a myth, the consultation of an oracle, or the decoration of a grave—that the moods and motivations which sacred symbols induce in men and the general conceptions of the order of existence which they formulate for men meet and reinforce one another. In a ritual, the world as lived and the world as imagined, fused under the agency of a single set of symbolic forms, turn out to be the same world. . . . Whatever role divine intervention may or may not play in the creation of faith—and it is not the business of the scientist to pronounce upon such matters one way or the other—it is, primarily at least, out of the context of concrete acts of religious observance that religious conviction emerges on the human plane.

However, though any religious ritual, no matter how apparently automatic or conventional (if it is truly automatic or merely conventional it is not religious), involves this symbolic fusion of ethos and world-view, it is mainly certain more elaborate and usually more public ones, ones in which a broad range of moods and motivations on the one hand and of metaphysical conceptions on the other are caught up, which shape the spiritual consciousness of a people. . . .

Whenever Madrasi Brahmans (and non-Brahmans, too, for that matter) wished to exhibit to me some feature of Hinduism, they always referred to, or invited me to see, a particular rite or ceremony in the life cycle, in a temple festival, or in the general sphere of religious and cultural performances. Reflecting on this in the course of my interviews and observations I found that the more abstract generalizations about Hinduism (my own as well as those I heard) could generally be checked, directly or indirectly, against these observable performances (Singer, 1958).

For an anthropologist, the importance of religion lies in its capacity to serve, for an individual or for a group, as a source of general, yet distinctive conceptions of the world, the self, and the relations between them, on the one hand—its model *of* aspect—and of rooted, no less distinctive "mental" dispositions—its model *for* aspect—on the other.

From these cultural functions flow, in turn, its social and psychological ones.

Religious concepts spread beyond their specifically metaphysical contexts to provide a framework of general ideas in terms of which a wide range of experience—intellectual, emotional, moral—can be given meaningful form. The Christian sees the Nazi movement against the background of The Fall which, though it does not, in a causal sense, explain it, places it in a moral, a cognitive, even an affective sense. An Azande sees the collapse of a granary upon a friend or relative against the background of a concrete and rather special notion of witchcraft and thus avoids the philosophical dilemmas as well as the psychological stress of indeterminism. A Javanese finds in the borrowed and reworked concept of *rasa* ("sense-taste feeling-meaning") a means by which to "see" choreographic, gustatory, emotional, and political phenomena in a new light. A synopsis of cosmic order, a set of religious beliefs, is also a gloss upon the mundane world of social relationships and psychological events. It renders them graspable.

But more than gloss, such beliefs are also a template. They do not merely interpret social and psychological processes in cosmic terms—in which case they would be philosophical, not religious—but they shape them. In the doctrine of original sin is embedded also a recommended attitude toward life, a recurring mood, and a persisting set of motivations. The Azande learns from witchcraft conceptions not just to understand apparent "accidents" as not accidents at all, but to react to these spurious accidents with hatred for the agent who caused them and to proceed against him with appropriate resolution. *Rasa*, in addition to being a concept of truth, beauty, and goodness, is also a preferred mode of experiencing, a kind of affectless detachment, a variety of bland aloofness, an unshakeable calm. The moods and motivations a religious orientation produces cast a derivative, lunar light over the solid features of a people's secular life.

References

Evans-Pritchard, E. E. 1937. *Witchcraft, Oracles and Magic among the Azande.* Oxford: Clarendon Press.

Kluckhohn, C. 1953. "Universal Categories of Culture." In *Anthropology Today,* edited by A. L. Kroeber, 507–23. Chicago: University of Chicago Press.

Kluckhohn, C., and Leighton, D. 1946. *The Navaho.* Cambridge, Mass.: Harvard University Press.

Langer, S. 1957. *Feeling and Form.* New York: Scribner's.

Lienhardt, G. 1961. *Divinity and Experience.* Oxford: Clarendon Press.

Reichard, G. 1950. *Navaho Religion.* 2 vols. New York: Pantheon.

Schutz, A. 1962. *The Problem of Social Reality.* Vol. 1 of *Collected Papers.* The Hague: Martinus Nijhoff.

Singer, M. 1958. "The Great Tradition in a Metropolitan Center: Madras." In *Traditional India,* edited by M. Singer, 140–82. Philadelphia: American Folklore Society.

R E A D I N G   1 . 3

The Problem of Definition in Religion

Melford E. Spiro

Most functional definitions of religion are essentially a subclass of real definitions in which functional variables (the promotion of solidarity, and the like) are stipulated as the essential nature of religion. But whether the essential nature consists of a qualitative variable (such as "the sacred") or a functional variable (such as social solidarity), it is virtually impossible to set any substantive boundary to religion and, thus, to distinguish it from other sociocultural phenomena. Social solidarity, anxiety reduction, confidence in unpredictable situations, and the like, are functions which may be served by any or all cultural phenomena—Communism and Catholicism, monotheism and monogamy, images and imperialism—and unless religion is defined substantively, it would be impossible to delineate its boundaries. Indeed, even when its substantive boundaries are limited, some functional definitions impute to religion some of the functions of a total sociocultural system. . . .

Melford E. Spiro is a member of the Department of Anthropology at the University of California at San Diego.

In sum, any comparative study of religion requires, as an operation antecedent to inquiry, an ostensive or substantive definition that stipulates unambiguously those phenomenal variables which are designated by the term. This ostensive definition will, at the same time, be a nominal definition in that some of its designata will, to other scholars, appear to be arbitrary. This, then, does not remove "religion" from the arena of definitional controversy; but it does remove it from the context of fruitless controversy over what religion "really is" to the context of the formulation of empirically testable hypotheses which, in anthropology, means hypotheses susceptible to cross-cultural testing.

But this criterion of cross-cultural applicability does not entail, as I have argued above, universality. Since "religion" is a term with historically rooted meanings, a definition must satisfy not only the criterion of cross-cultural applicability but also the criterion of intracultural intuitivity; at the least, it should not be counterintuitive. For me, therefore, any definition of "religion" which does not include, as a key variable, the belief in superhuman—I won't muddy the metaphysical waters with "supernatural"—beings who have power to help or harm man is counterintuitive. Indeed, if anthropological consensus were to exclude such beliefs from the set of variables which is necessarily designated by "religion," an explanation for these beliefs would surely continue to elicit our research energies.

Even if it were the case that Theravada Buddhism postulates no such beings, I find it strange indeed, given their all but universal distribution at every level of cultural development, that Durkheim—on the basis of this one case—should have excluded such beliefs from a definition of religion, and stranger still that others should have followed his lead. But this anomaly aside, is it the case that Buddhism contains no belief in superhuman beings? (Let us, for the sake of brevity, refer to these beings as "gods.") It is true, of course, that Buddhism contains no belief in a creator god; but creation is but one possible attribute of godhood, one which—I suspect—looms not too large in the minds of believers. If gods are important for their believers because—as I would insist is the case—they possess power greater than man's, including the power to assist man in, or prevent him from, attaining mundane and/or supermundane goals, even Theravada Buddhism—Mahayana is clearly not at issue here—most certainly contains such beliefs. With respect to supermundane goals, the Buddha is certainly a superhuman being. Unlike ordinary humans, he himself acquired the power to attain Enlightenment and, hence Buddhahood. Moreover, he showed others the means for its attainment. Without his teachings, natural man could not, unassisted, have discovered the way to Enlightenment and to final Release.

The soteriological attributes of the Buddha are, to be sure, different from those of the Judaeo-Christian-Islamic God. Whereas the latter is living, the former is dead; whereas the latter is engaged in a continuous and active process of salvation, the former had engaged in only one active ministry of salvation. But—with the exception of Calvinism—the soteriological consequences are the same. For the Buddhist and the Western religionist alike the Way to salvation was revealed by a superhuman being, and salvation can be attained only if one follows this revealed Way. The fact that in one case compliance with the Way leads directly to the ultimate goal because of the very nature of the world; and, in the other case, compliance leads to the goal only after divine intercession, should not obscure the basic similarity: in both cases man is dependent for his salvation upon the revelation of a superhuman being. (Indeed, there is reason to believe . . . that Buddhist worship is not merely an expression of reverence and homage to the One who has revealed the Way, but is also a petition for His saving intercession.)

But superhuman beings generally have the power to assist (or hinder) man's attempts to attain mundane as well as supermundane goals, and when it is asserted that Buddhism postulates no such beings, we must ask to which Buddhism this assertion has reference. Even the Buddhism of the Pali canon does not deny the existence of a wide range of superhuman beings who intervene, for good and for ill, in human affairs; it merely denies that they can influence one's salvation. More important, in contemporary Theravada countries, the Buddha himself—or, according to more sophisticated believers, his power—is believed to protect people from harm. Thus Burmese peasants recite Buddhist spells and perform rites before certain Buddha images which have the power to protect them from harm, to cure snake bites, and the like. And Buddhist monks chant passages from Scripture in the presence of the congregation which, it is believed, can bring a wide variety of worldly benefits.

There are, to be sure, atheistic Buddhist philosophies—as there are atheistic Hindu philosophies—but it is certainly a strange spectacle when anthropologists, of all people, confuse the teachings of a philosophical school with the beliefs and behavior of a religious community. And if—on some strange methodological grounds—the teachings of the philosophical schools, rather than the beliefs and behavior of the people, were to be designated as the normative religion of a society, then the numerous gods and demons to be found in the Pali canon—and in the world-view of most Theravadists, including the monastic virtuosos—find more parallels in other societies than the beliefs held by the numerically small philosophical schools.

Finally—and what is perhaps even more important from an anthropological point of view—the Pali canon is only one source for the world-view of Buddhist societies. Indeed, I know of no society in which Buddhism represents the exclusive belief system of a people. On the contrary, it is always to be found together with another system with which it maintains an important division of labor. Whereas Buddhism (restricting this term, now, to Canonical Buddhism) is concerned with supermundane goals—rebirth in a better human existence, in a celestial abode of gods, or final Release—the other system is concerned with worldly goals: the growing of crops, protection from illness, guarding of the village, etc., which are the domain of numerous superhuman beings. These are the *nats* of Burma, the *phi* of Laos and Thailand, the *neak ta* of Cambodia, etc. Although the Burmese, for example, distinguish sharply between Buddhism and *nat* worship, and although it is undoubtedly true—as most scholars argue—that these non-Buddhist belief systems represent the pre-Buddhist religions of these Theravada societies, the important consideration for our present discussion is that these beliefs, despite the long history of Buddhism in these countries, persist with undiminished strength, continuing to inform the world-view of these Buddhist societies and to stimulate important and extensive ritual activity. Hence, even if Theravada Buddhism were absolutely atheistic, it cannot be denied that Theravada Buddhists adhere to another belief system which is theistic to

its core; and if it were to be argued that atheistic Buddhism—by some other criteria—is a religion and that, therefore, the belief in superhuman beings is not a necessary characteristic of "religion," it would still be the case that the belief in superhuman beings and in their power to aid or harm man is a central feature in the belief systems of all traditional societies.

But Theravada Asia provides only one example of the tenacity of such beliefs. Confucianist China provides what is, perhaps, a better example. If Theravada Buddhism is somewhat ambiguous concerning the existence and behavior of superhuman beings, Confucianism is much less ambiguous. Although the latter does not explicitly deny the existence of such beings, it certainly ignores their role in human affairs. It is more than interesting to note, therefore, that when Mahayana Buddhism was introduced into China, it was precisely its gods (including the Bodhisatvas), demons, heavens, and hells that, according to many scholars, accounted for its dramatic conquest of China.

To summarize, I would argue that the belief in superhuman beings and in their power to assist or to harm man approaches universal distribution, and this belief—I would insist—is the core variable which ought to be designated by any definition of religion. . . . This raises a final unwarranted conclusion, viz. that religion uniquely refers to the "sacred," while secular concerns are necessarily "profane." Thus, if "sacred" refers to objects and beliefs of ultimate concern, and "profane" to those of ordinary concern, religious and secular beliefs alike may have reference either to sacred or to profane phenomena. For the members of Kiryat Yedidim, an Israeli *kibbutz*, the triumph of the proletariat, following social revolution, and the ultimate classless society in which universal brotherhood, based on loving kindness, will replace parochial brotherhood, based on competitive hostility, constitutes their sacred belief system. But, by definition, it is not a religious belief system, since it has no reference to—indeed, it denies the existence of—superhuman beings.

Similarly, if communism, or baseball, or the stockmarket are of ultimate concern to some society, or to one of its constituent social groups, they are, by definition, sacred. But beliefs concerning communism, baseball, or the stockmarket are not, by definition, religious beliefs, because they have no reference to superhuman beings. They may, of course, serve many of the functions served by religious beliefs; and they are, therefore, members of the same functional class. Since, however, they are substantively dissimilar, it would be as misleading to designate them by the same term as it would be to designate music and sex by the same term because they both provide sensual pleasure. (Modern American society presents an excellent example of the competition of sports, patriotism, sex, and God for the title, perhaps not exclusively, of "the sacred." Indeed, if the dictum of Miss Jane Russell is taken seriously—God, she informs us, is a 'livin' doll'—I would guess that, whichever wins, God is bound to lose.)

SELECTION 1.A

On Commitment

Walter Kaufmann

Some who love Big Brother claim that, deep down, everybody loves Big Brother; only some of us fail to realize it. To be more precise: some modern theologians argue that everybody is committed, whether he knows it or not. Some put the point this way: the question is merely who our gods are, for everybody has some gods. Others claim that all men have some ultimate concern or something that is holy to them, and the question is only whether the object of this concern is really ultimate or rather idolatrous. Some admit that most men have many ultimate concerns and are really "polytheists"; others insist that true ultimacy involves monotheism, and that as long as we are dealing with many concerns none can be really ultimate.

All these ways of speaking are metaphorical, evocative, and exceedingly unclear. Not only frivolous people lack any ultimate concern and are in an important sense uncommitted but the same is true of millions of very serious college students who wonder what they should do with themselves after graduation. There is nothing to which they greatly desire to give themselves, nothing that matters deeply to them. They are not shallow; they are not playboys; they enjoyed many of their courses and appreciate the opportunity to discuss their problems with sympathetic professors. They do not say: nothing matters to me. What they do say is: no one or two things matter more to me than anything else. These young men and women constitute the uncommitted generation; and it seems better to recognize this difference than to gloss it over by claiming that everybody has his own ultimate concern.

In any case, what is an "ultimate concern"? What is mine? What is my "God"—if these theologians are right and everybody ultimately has his "God"? I am not noncom-

The late Walter Kaufmann was Stuart Professor of Philosophy at Princeton University.
From *The Faith of a Heretic* by Walter Kaufmann. Copyright ©1961 by Walter Kaufmann. Reprinted by permission of Hazel D. Kaufmann.

mittal, not adrift, not hard put to find some project to devote myself to. I feel no inclination to pose as a cynic, saying: nothing is holy to *me*. But what, specifically, *is* holy to me?

The fashionable assumption that what is holy to a man is what he is ultimately concerned with is extremely dubious. When we say that something is holy to a person, we often mean that he won't stand for any humorous remarks about it, that the object is taboo for him in some sense. But such a taboo does not necessarily indicate any ultimate concern, perhaps only an underdeveloped sense of humor.

The dedications of at least some of my books, including this one, point to deep concerns, but hardly to "gods" or to any one "ultimate" concern. Some sense of responsibility to the six million Jews killed in my lifetime, especially to some whom I loved and who loved me, and to millions of others, Jew and Gentile, killed in our time and in past centuries, is certainly among my deepest feelings. Still, that is hardly my ultimate concern. Neither is this book, though I am deeply involved in that. Nor is it at all plausible to say that these are symbols for something more ultimate.

Perhaps I come closest to discovering my ultimate concerns when I ask what I consider the cardinal virtues. . . . But here, too, it is exceedingly difficult to know just what virtues one considers most important. And if one selects several, does that make one a polytheist?

The point at stake here is not autobiographical. I merely want to bring out how unhelpful and misleading many fashionable statements about commitment are. And in-stead of confining myself to semantic considerations, I have tried to take these statements as seriously as possible, seeing what they might mean if one applied them to oneself.

Much of the talk in this vein that one hears from theologians can hardly be taken seriously. It is said that man must have a god, or that man always worships either God or an idol, and that man cannot find true existence in the worship of an idol. One asks oneself whether Shakespeare, Goethe, or Van Gogh worshiped God or—hateful thought—unlike our theologians, never did find "true existence." Surely, some great artists are believers, and some are not; there is no party line among great artists in this matter; and it is futile to argue who did, and who did not, achieve "true existence."

One question, however, is worth pressing. Who really has a single ultimate concern? If that phrase has any definite meaning, it would seem to imply a willingness to sacrifice all other concerns to one's sole ultimate concern. Having only one ultimate concern might well be the recipe for fanaticism. It is the mark of a humane person that he has several ultimate concerns that check and balance each other.

To have many commitments might seem to be the formula of an arid and scattered life, spread thin, lacking depth; but it is hard to generalize about that. Goethe had a staggering number of commitments—and a singularly rich and fruitful life, with no lack of passion or profundity. But one can safely generalize that those who, spurning more than one concern, insist on a single commitment either abandon humanity for fanaticism or, more often, engage in loose talk.

S E L E C T I O N   1 . B

Sun Dance: Sacrifice–Renewal–Identity

Joseph Epes Brown

It is a recurrent pilgrimage, and it is made with propriety, a certain sense of formality. I understand a little more of it each time. I see a little more deeply into the meaning of formality, the formality of meaning. It is a religious experience by and large, natural and appropriate. It is an expression of the spirit.

—N. Scott Momaday, "To the Singing, to the Drum"
Natural History, February, 1975.

A people's vision that speaks of Life, of sacrificial means for the recurrent renewal of life, and of suffering for identity with the source of life, is a vision that can neither be destroyed, denied nor ignored, even though such has been attempted.

Today as in the past, the annual "Sun Dance" ceremonies of the Plains Indians of North America give to these peoples, as indeed to all peoples, a message through example: affirming the power of suffering in sacrifice, revealing in rich detail the mystery of the sacred in its operations, in all life, and throughout all creation. It is here implied that where there is no longer affirmation nor means for sacrifice, for "making sacred," where man loses the sense of Center, the very energy of the world will run out. Such traditions affirm for those who listen (and just as inevitably for those who do not) that where the sacred in the world and in life comes to be held as irrelevant illusion, where evasion of sacrifice in pursuit of some seeming "good life" becomes a goal in itself, then, in the empty and concomitant ugliness of such a life and such a man-manipulated world, that

Joseph Epes Brown is a member of the Department of Religious Studies at the University of Montana.
From *Parabola* 3 (May 1978): 12–15. Reprinted with permission of the author.

ordering cycle of Sacrifice will and must be accomplished by Nature Herself so that there may be renewal again in the world.

In accordance with the mood and perspective of this statement, ethnographic description of the particulars of a Lakota, Arapaho, Gros Ventre, Blackfeet, Cree, Cheyenne, or Crow/Shoshone Sun Dance is neither appropriate nor necessary. For they share a single language of sacred act and vision, expressed in rich and varied dialects, and a composite statement is suggested to convey the essential elements common to them all.

Already in the cold darkness of winter's night there are preparations in the Plains for spring's advent and that celebration variously called "Dance for World and Life Renewal," "Dance Watching the Sun," or "The Thirst Dance." Sponsors come forward, advance vows are made by prospective participants, sacred materials gathered, songs of power are learned, transmitted again from elder to younger, and members of those guiding Societies meet and prepare for the "moon of grass growing," spring's time when the power of the sun will return to renew the life of the earth, to bring new strength, goodness and joy to all of life's beings. It is the one annual occasion when bands or clans, or even several allied nations, may come together to celebrate in solemnity and joy a sacred event, the beginning of a new cycle of life, to insure that the energy of this world and life will be renewed so that the cycle may continue. For three or four days of life-shaping formal rites and ceremonies, and in the additional camp days of preparation and endings, individual and group will better know the power of suffering in sacrifice, yet also, in joyful celebration of life and life's season, a little of the mysteries of this life, thus also of the mysteries of death.

Out of timbers brought from the mountains, to construct the circular ceremonial lodge, the lodge of "new birth," "new life," the "thirst lodge," is to reenact the creation of world and cosmos. In horizontal orientations, the lodge doorway situated at the East is the place whence flows life in light; from the South comes growth in youth; from the West comes ripeness, full fruit, the middle age of man; and in the North is completion, old age leading to death which again leads to new life. At the center of the lodge the most sacred sacramental cottonwood tree—rooted in the womb of earth as mother and stretching up and out to the heavens—is axis of the world and male generative principle. Into and out from this central point and axis of the lodge flow the powers of the six directions; when man in awful ceremony is actually tied to this Tree of the Center by the flesh of his body, or when women make offerings of pieces cut from their arms, sacrifice through suffering is accomplished that the world and all beings may live, that life be renewed, that man may become who he is.

The qualitatively defined powers of the directions, the effective actualization of sacrifice, cannot be operative so long as man retains impurity. So it is that participants initially purify themselves in the little universe of the round sweat lodge where forces generously released from the rocks of earth, from air, fire and water, cleanse man and give new life. Indeed, in the days and nights of ritual and ceremony which follow, means are used to maintain participants in a state of purity, through sacrificial concentration on Sun or Center, or through the purifying agency of smokes from tobacco, from burning sweet grass and other wild grasses, from sweet sage and cedar.

Special persons are chosen for specific ritual functions; they become what they personify: "Earth Maker," "Lodge Maker," and the venerable sacred woman of purity who is the earth herself in all her powers and with all her blessings. Without the presence of this most sacred woman there can be no Sun Dance, for the duality of cosmic forces, the complementarity of male and female, are essential to the creative act, are central to realization of totality. To better translate cosmic realities and process into immediate visible and effective experience, on the bodies of participants are painted with prayer and earth-colors the forms of sun, moon, stars, hail, lightning, the varied elements of nature.

At certain times special altars are constructed upon the earth with simple means but of profound import: a place on the earth is cleared and made sacred, directions of the world are delineated always in reference to Center; man's relationship to the cosmos is established, his true "path of life" defined. Ceremonial pipes, themselves portable altars, are ever present with these earth altars. The pipe or straight pipe-stem is associated with the central sacred tree, as both are axes, both trace the Way, both express the male generative principle, and both speak of sacrifice.

Dancers wear and use whistles made of the wing-bone of the eagle to which eagle plumes are attached. In recreating the cry of eagle to the powerful rhythm of song, dance, and drum, the Eagle is present in voice and being, man's vital breath is united with the essence of sun and life. Through such ritual use of sacred form man becomes Eagle, and the eagle in his plumes is the Sun. So it happens at each morning's greeting of the new sun, dancers face the East holding their eagle plumes towards the sun's first rays, bathing the plumes in the new light of life, then placing the plumes in movements of purification to the head and to all parts of the upper body, dancing the while to the rhythm of heroic song. Dignified movements of dance facing Sun or Tree are sustained in the suffering of thirst day and night through the beat of the drum, the heart and life of the world, now one with man's own heart and life. The strength of such identity of rhythm, it has often been said, carries on within man's be-ing many months after such celebrations are completed.

Through rich and varied means specific forms of life are celebrated, honored, within the lodge. Living decorated trees may be planted, moisture bearing cat-tails are offered by friends and relatives for the dancers' bed, or chokecherry bushes are planted in con-junction with sacred rites and altars. High in the fork of the sacred tree there is an offering nest for Thunderbird; some form or aspect of the bison is hung upon the tree, and an eagle, or rawhide effigy of man himself. Small chil-dren may even sometimes fashion and bring into the lodge little clay animals two by two: elk, deer, rabbits, kitfox, dogs, otter, even grasshoppers. Thus present within the lodge is that which grows from the earth, those who live in the waters, those who walk on the earth, and those who fly above the earth. The powers of all things and all beings are present here in this holy place.

The Sun Dance, thus, is not a celebration by man for man; it is an honoring of all life and the source of all life, that life may go on, that the circle be a cycle, that all the world and man may continue on the path of the cycle of giving, receiving, bearing, being born in suffering, growing, becoming, giving back to earth that which has been given, and so finally to be born again. So it is told that only in sacrifice is sacredness accomplished; only in sacrifice is identity possible and found. It is only through the suffering in sac-rifice that finally freedom is known and laughter in Joy returns to the world.

here am I behold me
I am the sun
behold me
> —Lakota Sun-Rise
> Greeting Song

READING 1.4

Plausibility Structures

Peter Berger

One of the fundamental propositions of the sociology of knowledge is that the plausibil-ity, in the sense of what people actually find credible, of views of reality depends upon the social support these receive. Put more simply, we obtain our notions about the world origi-nally from other human beings, and these no-tions continue to be plausible to us in a very large measure because others continue to af-

Sociologist Peter Berger is University Professor at Boston University.
Excerpts from *A Rumor of Angels* by Peter L. Berger. Copyright © 1969 by Peter L. Berger. Re-printed by permission of Doubleday & Company, Inc.

firm them. There are some exceptions to this—notions that derive directly and instan-taneously from our own sense experience—but even these can be integrated into mean-ingful views of reality only by virtue of social processes. It is, of course, possible to go against the social consensus that surrounds us, but there are powerful pressures (which manifest themselves as psychological pres-sures within our own consciousness) to con-form to the views and beliefs of our fellow men. It is in conversation, in the broadest sense of the word, that we build up and keep going our view of the world. It follows that this view will depend upon the continuity and consistency of such conversation, and that it will change as we change conversation partners.

We all exist within a variety of social networks or conversational fabrics, which are related in often complex and sometimes contradictory ways with our various conceptions of the universe. When we get to the more sophisticated of these conceptions, there are likely to be organized practices designed to still doubts and prevent lapses of conviction. These practices are called therapies. There are also likely to be more or less systematized explanations, justifications, and theories in support of the conceptions in question. These sociologists have called legitimations. . . .

Thus each conception of the world of whatever character or content can be analyzed in terms of its plausibility structure, because it is only as the individual remains within this structure that the conception of the world in question will remain plausible to him. The strength of this plausibility, ranging from unquestioned certitude through firm probability to mere opinion, will be directly dependent upon the strength of the supporting structure. This dynamics pertains irrespective of whether, by some outside observer's criteria of validity, the notions thus made plausible are true or false. The dynamics most definitely pertains to any religious affirmations about the world because these affirmations are, by their very nature, incapable of being supported by our own sense experience and therefore heavily dependent upon social support.

Each plausibility structure can be further analyzed in terms of its constituent elements—the specific human beings that "inhabit" it, the conversational network by which these "inhabitants" keep the reality in question going, the therapeutic practices and rituals, and the legitimations that go with them. For example, the maintenance of the

Catholic faith in the consciousness of the individual requires that he maintain his relationship to the plausibility structure of Catholicism. This is, above all, a community of Catholics in his social milieu who continually support this faith. It will be useful if those who are of the greatest emotional significance to the individual (the ones whom George Herbert Mead called significant others) belong to this supportive community—it does not matter much if, say, the individual's dentist is a non-Catholic, but his wife and his closest personal friends had better be. Within this supportive community there will then be an ongoing conversation that, explicitly and implicitly, keeps a Catholic world going. Explicitly, there is affirmation, confirmation, reiteration of Catholic notions about reality. But there is also an implicit Catholicism in such a community. After all, in everyday life it is just as important that some things can silently be taken for granted as that some things are reaffirmed in so many words. Indeed, the most fundamental assumptions about the world are commonly affirmed by implication—they are so "obvious" that there is no need to put them into words. Our individual, then, operates within what may be called a specifically Catholic conversational apparatus, which, in innumerable ways, each day confirms the Catholic world that he coinhabits with his significant others. . . . The details of all this vary in different circumstances, especially as between a situation in which the plausibility structure is more or less coextensive with the individual's overall social experience (that is, where Catholics constitute the majority) and a situation in which the plausibility structure exists as a deviant enclave within the individual's larger society (that is, where Catholics are a cognitive minority). But the essential point is that the plausibility of Catholicism hinges upon the availability of these social processes.

Yoga Made Plausible: A Personal Account

Paul Carnes

Berger's thesis about plausibility structure to me was very interesting and thought-provoking. If we think about what we regard as real, we can easily see that much of it is dependent on some kind of social support. If a particular social base disappears, then rather than go out on our own and find our own unique new reality, we are very likely (and in Berger's view we must) find another social base that will define the world for us and involve us in a new community of believers.

On many points from my own experience, I would agree with Berger. On some I would not. I use some examples from my own past that I think in many respects demonstrate Berger's plausibility structure in action.

For a while a few years ago I was deeply into the drug culture. My attachment to it was strong, for I was just recovering from disillusionment with the radical social protest thing. By this time I was seeing revolution as just a violent ego trip. But getting back to drugs, I began to want to find explanations for the spheres of reality I was experiencing during drug trips. When I came to the university, I was still trying to figure out this reality and find some group that would help me do this. Then one day I looked out my window to see a class sitting on the field in front of the dorm. I went down to see what it was about. It turned out to be a class in yoga. It looked like an interesting trip so I tried it.

As I got more into the yoga philosophy and Eastern doctrines I found they seemed to ex-

plain much. They explained not only drug-induced consciousness, but life as a whole. Pain and suffering, death, work, everything was given a place in a larger system. My disillusionment with politics was confirmed as correct since the physical world was essentially an illusion. Now I had an excuse for nonaction. The law of karma and other Indian doctrine took away my guilt about dropping out.

Looking back on it, I can see how I was steadily encouraged to become more and more yogic. It seemed so gradual. First I began attending classes regularly. Here we did exercises and got a steady dose of yogic philosophy. They work it well. While you are in a mellow frame of mind (candles lit, incense burning, darkness, and you're relaxed from the exercises and eating some fruit), the leader raps to you. You suddenly realize that you are thinking like he is, but you don't know exactly why.

For the really dedicated there are classes other days, too. But for these you have to go down to the Ashram (the place where the leader lives along with other real devotees). This greatly aids them in converting you. The Ashram is isolated. Gradually you come earlier and leave later until eventually you are spending a lot more time there. Then you occasionally eat with them. If you stay with it as I did, you eventually move into the Ashram to live. Once you do this and are fully into the fold, the plausibility structures become very visible and ever present. Rituals keep you with the group. Everyone has to get up at the same time—4:30 a.m. Then all take a cold shower, exercise for an hour, then chant for an additional hour. Then everyone eats together. Unless you have an outside job or classes to attend, you work with the others

Paul N. Carnes, Jr., graduated from the University of New Mexico in 1972.
Reprinted with permission.

around the Ashram. They even give the work a special name—Karma Yoga—so that you feel somehow more holy for having done it. After lunch, more work or perhaps reading. All the books, of course, are "religious," which tends to reinforce you in your beliefs and keep doubts at bay. Evening classes are again filled with ritual. Finally, periodic discussions during the day with members and with the leader help to increase your faith that what you are doing is ultimately the best thing—the true path.

The whole attempt, then, is to structure your days in such a way that you can have no free time in which to do something "wrong." You are presented with a routine that, if followed, is guaranteed to lead you to liberation (no questions about it; just ask the leader; just read this book, etc.). All over the building are pictures of holy men, yogis from India, saints. Nothing mundane is present. You're in the world of the sacred—completely.

Periodically feasts and celebrations are held either at the Ashram or in the mountains. At these reaffirmations of the group, outsiders may be invited. This helps members in that they can feel "superior" ("I'm glad I'm not like that"), and can enhance their sense of belonging by helping others see through the veil of maya, or illusion, and place themselves on the path to enlightenment. When newcomers attend classes, the same pattern can be seen. You talk only of the good points of being a yogi: good food, feel high all the time, living your life for God. Neglected are the bummers—getting up early, cold shower, hard work, no meat or drugs.

Eventually, you are given a chance to lead some of the classes. This is a definite sign that you have arrived and tends to cement you more tightly into the group.

Everything will be fine—but only if you can maintain the game. But with me, doubts began to creep in. The thing that probably started me on the road to deconversion was old friends. I had not totally isolated myself (as would have been ideal). I went out with old friends to the mountains, to parties. This brings on a crisis. They're all doing one thing and you for some reason can't. You refuse to get stoned; they ask why. You give the established reasons. O.K. Inside, though, you'd really like to but it would bring down everything you believe in (your plausibility structure is pretty vulnerable). All you can do is hope that when you become higher (a new level of consciousness) you won't feel any desire to partake of such amusements.

As Berger puts it, the supportive therapies go to work when the leader finds out you have doubts. He tells you how remaining on the path would guarantee you freedom from the cycle of rebirth. You don't want to blow it, so you go on your way determined to suffer inconvenience now so that you'll be free from dying and being reborn. A fellow devotee got bummed out when she was continuously asked to do the dishes. When she complained, the leader told her "do it for God." This was the classic answer. Since God was everything, how could you refuse? The leader was closer to God than you were, anyway.

But my friends finally got to me. The clincher came when one of them said to me casually, "That's great if you really dig it, but I'd rather get high, sleep till noon, and eat steak." I got this flash which said, so would I. I suddenly realized I had a choice in how I lived so I moved out the next day and returned to the "normal world." From then on, I tried to construct my own individual reality. I tried to take whatever I felt to be truth wherever I found it. I began to find no one plausibility structure satisfactory. Each plausibility structure seems to put you in a game and every game is limited. To step out of the game (all games) is hard. I guess Berger would say it's impossible. But I think you have to try to hit some middle ground between letting the group make your world, and being a total loner.

A D D I T I O N A L R E A D I N G S

Articles

Bibby, Reginald W. "Religion and Modernity: The Canadian Case." *Journal for the Scientific Study of Religion* 18 (1979): 1–17. An example of research based on Yinger's approach: A significant proportion of Canadians believe "ultimate questions" to be unanswerable.

Machalek, Richard, and Martin, Michael. " 'Invisible' Religions: Some Preliminary Evidence." *Journal for the Scientific Study of Religion* 15 (1976): 311–21. Adaptation of Yinger's research on "ultimate questions" to an American community.

Parsons, Talcott. "The Theoretical Development of the Sociology of Religion." *Journal of the History of Ideas* 5 (1944): 176–90. Functionalism traced in the works of Pareto, Malinowski, Durkheim, and Weber.

Segal, Robert A. "The Myth-Ritualist Theory of Religion." *Journal for the Scientific Study of Religion* 19 (1980): 173–85. Myth and ritual are centrally important in modern as well as primitive religion.

Stark, Rodney, and Bainbridge, William Sims. "Of Churches, Sects, and Cults: Preliminary Concepts for a Theory of Religious Movements." *Journal for the Scientific Study of Religion* 18 (1979): 117–33. Proposes an exclusivist definition of religion together with an argument for the essential role of "compensators" or rewards based on supernatural grounds.

Books

Demerath III, N. J., and Hammond, Phillip E. *Religion in Social Context.* New York: Random House, 1969. Good introduction to the development of sociology of religion through its classic authors.

Yinger, J. Milton. *The Scientific Study of Religion.* New York: Macmillan, 1970. A lucid and detailed presentation of the functionalist approach. Conflict theory is stated by contrast, though in less detail.

Cross-cultural References

Beck, Peggy V., and Walters, A. L. *The Sacred: Ways of Knowledge, Sources of Life.* Tsaile, Ariz.: Navajo Community College Press. Thorough description with personal accounts of the sacred ways of America's largest Indian tribe, the Navajo.

Campbell, Colin. *Toward a Sociology of Irreligion.* London: Macmillan, 1971. Case studies of secularist, humanist, and rationalist movements, particularly in Great Britain, together with a critique of the functionalist perspective.

Geertz, Clifford. *The Religion of Java.* New York: Free Press, 1960. Detailed anthropological study examining patterns of integration and conflict in a complex culture.

Shinn, Larry D. *Two Sacred Worlds: Experience and Structure in the World's Religions.* Nashville: Abingdon, 1977. Development of sacred myths and rituals in Hebrew and Buddhist traditions.

CHAPTER | 2

Religion as Integrating Force

Chapter 1 looked at religion as provider of a symbolic interpretive framework. Religious belief and ritual offer ways of coming to terms with the stark realities of bafflement, death and suffering, and moral dilemma. But the functionalist perspective also sees religion as binding its adherents to the "sacred cosmos" through festival and joyful ceremony. Religion, then, truly creates a sacred world and sustains it through ritual celebration, which in turn acts to enhance a sense of oneness with members of our community or society.

Enhancing group solidarity stems, of course, from Emile Durkheim's discussion of religion's tendency to sacralize the norms and values of the larger society. A *particular* expression of this function is the power of religion to reintegrate or "bring back together" members of a group in the face of events that threaten to disrupt or even tear apart the fabric of community. Death is, of course, the most disruptive of these events.

Bronislaw Malinowski, in a reading from his *Magic, Science, and Religion*, shows how funeral rites "give body and form to the saving beliefs" of immortality, thus helping survivors both to break the bonds that have held them to the departed loved one, and to re-form themselves in the face of shattered morale and "shaken solidarity." The life-affirming aspects of the culture are restated; the continuity of the group and its traditions are assured even in the disintegrating experience of death.

But religion's power is also apparent in celebration. At major turning points in the life-cycle, religious rites solemnly link an event to the larger or "cosmic" sacred world. Jewish bar and bas mitzvah and Christian baptism come to mind. In Selection 2.A,

Eugene S. Geissler reflects on the wedding of his daughter. The intertwining of sacred and secular stands out. Bread and wine are offered at the mass; afterwards wines and cheese, breads and cookies are served beyond the receiving line. The joining together of husband and wife stirs memories of the sacredness of mother and father's *own* marriage (a linking to tradition) and consciousness of "walking with God in the cool of the evening." Marriage is stamped with the sacred; links with the cosmos are reaffirmed.

Robert Bellah's widely discussed essay "Civil Religion in America" points to a series of interrelated religious themes visible throughout American history, themes that are integrative on the *societal* level (as opposed to the individual or smaller group level illustrated in the previous two readings). These themes may be couched in the familiar phrases of the Judeo-Christian tradition, but together they constitute a kind of national faith distinct from the religion of churches and synagogues. They may be employed to buttress the status quo and affirm the order of things as they are. But they may also be used *prophetically*, that is, as a vehicle of protest against accepted values and present policies of the dominant society. Thus the American Revolution was viewed as an exodus from Europe and the beginning of "a new Israel." The Civil War and Lincoln's death added themes of death, sacrifice, and rebirth (a kind of prophetic calling to national rededication). The presidency of John F. Kennedy brought with it "the problem of responsible action in a revolutionary world," an opposition to tyranny, poverty, disease, and war wherever they are found.

Bellah's essay has seemed to some a potentially dangerous and historically inaccurate glorification of the nation-state. In a later commentary, however, Bellah responded:

I think it should be clear from the text that I conceive the central tradition of the American civil religion not as a form of national self-worship but as the subordination of the nation to ethical principles that transcend it and in terms of which it should be judged. I am convinced that every nation and every people come to some form of religious self-understanding whether the critics like it or not. Rather than simply denounce what seems in any case inevitable, it seems more responsible to seek within the civil religious tradition for those critical principles which undercut the ever-present danger of national self-idolization.[1]

But how may these "critical principles" of civil religion be maintained? By whom? Seven years after the publication of his essay on civil religion, Bellah wrote in *The Broken Covenant* of the dominance in America of technical reason, of the ideal of success, and of "unresponsive bureaucracies."[2] He called on the nation to conceive a new vision of national purpose, of liberty, of freedom. In a yet later essay, he deplored the rhetoric of the 1976 bicentennial celebrations, finding little to stem tendencies toward "luxury, dependence, and ignorance" and "a concern only for the private, a willingness to be governed by those who promise to take care of us even without our knowledgeable consent."[3]

Following the appearance of Bellah's essay and the discussion it stimulated, sociologists with an empirical bent were quick to "field test" Bellah's propositions. In "Who is Civil Religious?" Christenson and Wimberley ask if civil religion themes are truly shared by a large majority of Americans. They found indeed that some central themes *are* shared by considerable percentages of their respondents. But they raise an important question: Is it not possible for these themes, just because they *are* widely, perhaps uncritically, shared to be used by political candidates, officeholders, preachers, and patriots to legitimate policies that may actually be self-serving and supportive of particular constituencies rather than of the common good? Recognizing this possibility reminds us that it *is* important to identify civil religious themes as ideologies so that we may "anticipate rather than recall" their manipulation in these ways.

Richard K. Fenn's remarks, from *Toward a Theory of Secularization*, bring us to a major critique of the entire civil religion thesis. Rejecting the perspective associated with the tradition of Durkheim, Fenn asks whether there *is* a "cultural whole" to which civil religion refers. Answering in the negative, Fenn then calls into question the "reality" of civil religion; that is, whether it is anything more than a "cultural fiction" used by particular spokespersons who represent not society as a whole but their own particular, often conflicting interest groups and ideals. Fenn's own larger theory of secularization disallows for the reality of an overarching society that is more than the simple sum of its parts, a position that undercuts the linkage of civil religious symbols to society as a whole.

Notes

1. Robert N. Bellah, "Civil Religion in America," in *Beyond Belief: Essays on Religion in a Post-Traditional World* (New York: Harper & Row, 1970), p. 168.

2. Robert N. Bellah, *The Broken Covenant: American Civil Religion in a Time of Trial* (New York: Seabury, 1975), p. 155.

3. Robert N. Bellah, "Religion and Legitimation in the American Republic," in *In Gods We Trust*, ed. Thomas Robbins and Dick Anthony (New Brunswick: Transaction, 1981), p. 47.

R E A D I N G   2 . 1

Death and the Reintegration of the Group

Bronislaw Malinowski

Of all sources of religion, the supreme and final crisis of life—death—is of the greatest importance. Death is the gateway to the other world in more than the literal sense. According to most theories of early religion, a great deal, if not all, of religious inspiration has been derived from it—and in this, orthodox views are on the whole correct. Man has to live his life in the shadow of death, and he who clings to life and enjoys its fullness must dread the menace of its end. And he who is faced by death turns to the promise of life. Death and its denial—Immortality—have always formed, as they form today, the most poignant theme of man's forebodings. The extreme complexity of man's emotional reactions to life finds necessarily its counterpart in his attitude to death. Only what in life has been spread over a long space and manifested in a succession of experiences and events is here at its end condensed into one crisis which provokes a violent and complex outburst of religious manifestations.

Even among the most primitive peoples, the attitude towards death is infinitely more complex and, I may add, more akin to our own, than is usually assumed. It is often stated by anthropologists that the dominant feeling of the survivors is that of horror at the corpse and of fear of the ghost. This twin attitude is even made by no less an authority than Wilhelm Wundt the very nucleus of all religious belief and practice. Yet this assertion is only a half-truth, which means no truth at all. The emotions are extremely complex and even contradictory; the dominant elements, love of the dead and loathing of the corpse, passionate attachment to the personality still lingering about the body and a shattering fear of the gruesome thing that has been left over, these two elements seem to mingle and play into each other. This is reflected in the spontaneous behavior and in the ritual proceedings at death. In the tending of the corpse, in the modes of its disposal, in the post-funerary and commemorative ceremonies, the nearest relatives, the mother mourning for her son, the widow for her husband, the child for the parent, always show some horror and fear mingled with pious love, but never do the negative elements appear alone or even dominant.

The mortuary proceedings show a striking similarity throughout the world. As death approaches, the nearest relatives in any case, sometimes the whole community, forgather by the dying man, and dying, the most private act which a man can perform, is transformed into a public, tribal event. As a rule, a certain differentiation takes place at once, some of the relatives watching near the corpse, others making preparations for the pending end and its consequences, others again performing perhaps some religious acts at a sacred spot. Thus in certain parts of Melanesia the real kinsmen must keep at a distance and only relatives by marriage perform the mortuary services, while in some tribes of Australia the reverse order is observed.

As soon as death has occurred, the body is washed, anointed and adorned, sometimes the bodily apertures are filled, the arms and legs tied together. Then it is exposed to the view of all, and the most important phase, the immediate mourning begins. Those who have witnessed death and its sequel among

Bronislaw Malinowski (1884–1942) was one of the founders of modern anthropology.

Reprinted from Bronislaw Malinowski, "Magic, Science, and Religion," in *Science, Religion, and Reality*, edited by Joseph Needham (London: SPCK, 1925), with permission of the publisher.

savages and who can compare these events with their counterpart among other uncivilized peoples must be struck by the fundamental similarity of the proceedings. There is always a more or less conventionalized and dramatized outburst of grief and wailing in sorrow, which often passes among savages into bodily lacerations and the tearing of hair. This is always done in a public display and is associated with visible signs of mourning, such as black or white daubs on the body, shaven or disheveled hair, strange or torn garments.

The immediate mourning goes on round the corpse. This, far from being shunned or dreaded, is usually the center of pious attention. Often there are ritual forms of fondling or attestations of reverence. The body is sometimes kept on the knees of seated persons, stroked and embraced. At the same time these acts are usually considered both dangerous and repugnant, duties to be fulfilled at some cost to the performer. After a time the corpse has to be disposed of. Inhumation with an open or closed grave; exposure in caves or on platforms, in hollow trees or on the ground in some wild desert place; burning or setting adrift in canoes—these are the usual forms of disposal.

This brings us to perhaps the most important point, the two-fold contradictory tendency, on the one hand to preserve the body, to keep its form intact, or to retain parts of it; on the other hand the desire to be done with it, to put it out of the way, to annihilate it completely. Mummification and burning are the two extreme expressions of this two-fold tendency. It is impossible to regard mummification or burning or any intermediate form as determined by mere accident of belief, as a historical feature of some culture or other which has gained its universality by the mechanism of spread and contact only. For in these customs is clearly expressed the fundamental attitude of mind of the surviving relative, friend or lover, the longing for all that remains of the dead person and the

disgust and fear of the dreadful transformation wrought by death.

One extreme and interesting variety in which this double-edged attitude is expressed in a gruesome manner is sarcocannibalism, a custom of partaking in piety of the flesh of the dead person. It is done with extreme repugnance and dread and usually followed by a violent vomiting fit. At the same time it is felt to be a supreme act of reverence, love, and devotion. In fact it is considered such a sacred duty that among the Melanesians of New Guinea, where I have studied and witnessed it, it is still performed in secret, although severely penalized by the white Government. The smearing of the body with the fat of the dead, prevalent in Australia and Papuasia is, perhaps, but a variety of this custom.

In all such rites, there is a desire to maintain the tie and the parallel tendency to break the bond. Thus the funerary rites are considered as unclean and soiling, the contact with the corpse as defiling and dangerous, and the performers have to wash, cleanse their body, remove all traces of contact, and perform ritual lustrations. Yet the mortuary ritual compels man to overcome the repugnance, to conquer his fears, to make piety and attachment triumphant, and with it the belief in a future life, in the survival of the spirit.

And here we touch on one of the most important functions of religious cult. In the foregoing analysis I have laid stress on the direct emotional forces created by contact with death and with the corpse, for they primarily and most powerfully determine the behavior of the survivors. But connected with these emotions and born out of them, there is the idea of the spirit, the belief in the new life into which the departed has entered. And here we return to the problem of animism with which we began our survey of primitive religious facts. What is the substance of a spirit, and what is the psychological origin of this belief?

The savage is intensely afraid of death, probably as the result of some deep-seated instincts common to man and animals. He does not want to realize it as an end, he cannot face the idea of complete cessation, of annihilation. The idea of spirit and spiritual existence is near at hand, furnished by such experiences as are discovered and described by Tylor. Grasping at it, man reaches the comforting belief in spiritual continuity and in the life after death. Yet this belief does not remain unchallenged in the complex, double-edged play of hope and fear which sets in always in the face of death. To the comforting voice of hope, to the intense desire of immortality, to the difficulty, in one's own case, almost the impossibility, of facing annihilation there are opposed powerful and terrible forebodings. The testimony of the senses, the gruesome decomposition of the corpse, the visible disappearance of the personality—certain apparently instinctive suggestions of fear and horror seem to threaten man at all stages of culture with some idea of annihilation, with some hidden fears and forebodings. And here into this play of emotional forces, into this supreme dilemma of life and final death, religion steps in, selecting the positive creed, the comforting view, the culturally valuable belief in immortality, in the spirit independent of the body, and in the continuance of life after death. In the various ceremonies at death, in commemoration and communion with the departed, and worship of ancestral ghosts, religion gives body and form to the saving beliefs.

Thus the belief in immortality is the result of a deep emotional revelation, standardized by religion, rather than a primitive philosophic doctrine. Man's conviction of continued life is one of the supreme gifts of religion, which judges and selects the better of the two alternatives suggested by self-preservation— the hope of continued life and the fear of annihilation. The belief in spirits is the result of the belief in immortality. The substance of which the spirits are made is the full-blooded passion and desire for life, rather than the shadowy stuff which haunts his dreams and illusions. Religion saves man from a surrender to death and destruction, and in doing this it merely makes use of the observations of dreams, shadows, and visions. The real nucleus of animism lies in the deepest emotional fact of human nature, the desire for life.

Thus the rites of mourning, the ritual behavior immediately after death, can be taken as pattern of the religious act, while the belief in immortality, in the continuity of life and in the nether world, can be taken as the prototype of an act of faith. Here, as in the religious ceremonies previously described, we find self-contained acts, the aim of which is achieved in their very performance. The ritual despair, the obsequies, the acts of mourning, express the emotion of the bereaved and the loss of the whole group. They endorse and they duplicate the natural feelings of the survivors, they create a social event out of a natural fact. Yet, though in the acts of mourning, in the mimic despair of wailing, in the treatment of the corpse and in its disposal, nothing ulterior is achieved, these acts fulfill an important function and possess a considerable value for primitive culture.

What is this function? The imitation ceremonies we have found fulfill theirs in sacralizing tradition; the food cults, sacrament and sacrifice bring man into communion with providence, with the beneficent forces of plenty; totemism standardizes man's practical, useful attitude of selective interest towards his surroundings. If the view here taken of the biological function of religion is true, some such similar role must also be played by the whole mortuary ritual.

The death of a man or woman in a primitive group, consisting of a limited number of individuals, is an event of no mean importance. The nearest relatives and friends are disturbed to the depth of their emotional life. A small community bereft of a member, especially if he be important, is severely mutilated. The whole event breaks the normal course of life and shakes the moral foundations of society. The strong tendency on which we have insisted in the above description: to give way to fear and horror, to abandon the corpse, to run away from the village, to destroy all the belongings of the dead one—all these impulses exist, and if given way to would be extremely dangerous, disintegrating the group, destroying the material foundations of primitive culture. Death in a primitive society is, therefore, much more than the removal of a member. By setting in motion one part of the deep forces of the instinct of self-preservation, it threatens the very cohesion and solidarity of the group, and upon this depends the organization of that society, its tradition, and finally the whole culture. For if primitive man yielded always to the disintegrating impulses of his reaction to death, the continuity of tradition and the existence of material civilization would be made impossible.

We have seen already how religion, by sacralizing and thus standardizing the other set of impulses, bestows on man the gift of mental integrity. Exactly the same function it fulfills also with regard to the whole group. The ceremonial of death which ties the survivors to the body and rivets them to the place of death, the beliefs in the existence of the spirit, in its beneficent influences or malevolent intentions, in the duties of a series of commemorative or sacrificial ceremonies—in all this, religion counteracts the centrifugal forces of fear, dismay, demoralization, and provides the most powerful means of reintegration of the group's shaken solidarity and of the reestablishment of its morale.

In short, religion here assures the victory of tradition and culture over the mere negative response of thwarted instinct.

SELECTION 2.A

There Was a Wedding

Eugene S. Geissler

There was a wedding, first of all, in the garden of Paradise. It was the crowning point of creation. Through six long "days" God had worked up to it, prepared for it, taken great pains with it. Finally, he gave man and woman to each other and human love was born. God saw what he had done was *very* good, and he rejoiced within himself at what he had wrought. He blessed the man and woman and rested from his labors . . .

I have always thought that weddings should come off more simply than they do,

Eugene S. Geissler is an editorial consultant and free-lance writer living in Granger, Indiana.
Reprinted from Eugene S. Geissler, *There is a Season* (Notre Dame: University of Notre Dame Press, 1969), with permission of the author.

and here were these two young people, Mary and John, age twenty and twenty-two, quite ready and satisfied to have a "simple liturgical wedding." But a simple wedding is not easy to pull off. For one thing, a wedding besides being a liturgical affair is immediately also a social affair. It is not only a sacrament, but also a celebration. It is an event that calls for rejoicing with friends as well as an exchange of vows in the presence of the Church and the community.

. . . Then there was another wedding, many years later, during the "eighth day of creation," in Cana of Galilee. The mother of Jesus was there, and Jesus also was invited, together with his disciples, to the wedding. Again there was rejoicing and again there was a blessing. Jesus, anticipating marriage with his own bride, renewed married love with a miracle. Henceforth there would always be sufficient "wine" for the Christian celebration of married love . . .

So there you are. From time immemorial there has been this religious and this social side to a wedding, and whatever else may be nonessential, the service and the feasting are not. The first real question was how to combine the service and the feast in the simplest way possible without losing any of the good things that make a wedding a happy and holy event, a worshiping and a rejoicing time. With this as our yardstick we got heads together with the young couple and our neighbors and discovered a surprising unanimity concerning what would go and what would stay. The burden of the big dinner would have to go, we said; rice, flowers, featured attendants, the wedding march, cameras and popping flash bulbs in church would have to go. Hymns and songs, wine and friends, would have to stay.

. . . And then there is always a third wedding, when there is a wedding, and that is the wedding of this couple. Every wedding is always three weddings, and that is why a wedding is always a big thing . . .

Our basic decision was that the service and the feast would be one thing, and that the feast would follow immediately upon the service, that the liturgy would anticipate the social celebration immediately following it. We called this "the integrity of the celebration." For both aspects of this celebration we counted heavily on the help and presence of friends, neighbors, and members of the parish. What's a celebration anyhow—liturgical and/or social—without a community of people? We petitioned for an evening wedding Mass after dinner, and we would go from the nuptial Mass upstairs to the hall downstairs in the spirit of a liturgical-social celebration linked together as one.

. . . No wonder a wedding is such a grand affair. It is grand in its meaning and grand in

its context, with a history back to the very beginnings of human life. It really cannot be overdone except that it can become buried in its own embellishments . . .

The bride wore a chapel veil and a red and white suit made by her mother, which she will no doubt wear again and again. Instead of flowers, the bride carried a special lighted candle decorated in sign and symbol which she will no doubt light again on special occasions long after the flowers would be gone. Instead of featured attendants, along with the staid and studied wedding march (the father never did give the bride away), the two families, the parents, the two official witnesses and the bride and groom joined the priest in the entrance procession to the altar, while the congregation sang Psalm 93: "Cry Out With Joy to the Lord!" This psalm has a long history, since Old Testament times, as a processional hymn. Only the bride and groom entered the sanctuary with the priest, the official witnesses staying in the pews with the families. The groom took the candle from the bride and put it on the Easter candlestick so that it might shine before all that were in the house.

. . . Every wedding is unique, and every wedding is a public sign of something new that has never been before. But in marriage this uniqueness is not something that isolates or withdraws, that hides or is hidden. The uniqueness exposes, proclaims, draws the light, diffuses its own gift—like a candle. Because every man is different, he is called upon to do his own thing. Because two differences are joined in marriage, uniqueness is enriched and multiplied, and the possibilities are those of the greatest adventure known to man . . .

The marriage ceremony, now in English, needed only to be enunciated clearly by the priest, which it was, to be impressive and appreciated. The many blessings are their own sermon now that they can be understood by the people.

At the Offertory the two official witnesses

brought up the gifts of bread and wine. The bride and groom accepted them at the sanctuary and brought them to the priest. The congregation sang: "O Love That Nothing Can Efface."

The great Amen after the Canon really was the great Amen. If it is really to be the great Amen, it has to be sung several times over. It just cannot be the great Amen said or sung just once.

At Communion the wedding couple partook of the same bread and drank wine out of the same cup. The congregation sang: "God Is Love."

For the processional after Mass everybody sang "Now Thank We All Our God"; there are special verses for weddings.

. . . The wedding couple is at the dawn, not only of a new thing and a new day, but also at the dawn of original creation and its renewal. Everything is theirs for the having. No wonder that we rejoice. No wonder that we sing. No wonder that we wonder what the new day, the new dawn, the new creation and the new renewal will bring . . .

Downstairs, wines and cheeses, breads and cookies were available on tables immediately beyond the receiving line.

We had as much as possible discouraged gifts—though not too successfully as it turned out. What we wanted instead was the people themselves to rejoice with us, and if they wanted to bring something, a contribution of wine or cheese, bread or cookies, was welcome. For once, people said, they felt like part of the wedding.

The wedding cake was extraordinary, provided by a friend of the family and a friend of Mary's. So the celebration downstairs worked up to that with a special drink for all and a toast by the father of the bride. He toasted all friends present, he toasted the newly married couple on the threshold of so great an adventure as the founding of a family, and he toasted God and the groom's parents for having provided so fine a son.

. . . We stand beside each other, my wife and I, at this wedding of our daughter, recalling our own, interpreting every possibility in terms of the success and failure of our own: the warm light of fresh morning, the fierce noonday heat of long commitment, and the foretaste now and then of walking in the garden with God in the cool of the evening . . .

Because the weather featured one of the worst snowstorms of the century, only half the guests were able to make it. It is hard to postpone a wedding.

. . . This marriage is theirs now and we are hardly more than spectators. Do they look at us as we look at them? Will they remember us as we remember them? Will they draw strength from us, understanding, when they need it? Will they go beyond us in love? What they see in us is something that came later: a fire subdued, a candle burning low, a quiet passion of little signs that do not impress the young. We were overwhelmingly in love on our wedding day. Maybe they are too and maybe their love will be sufficient for them, as ours has been for us . . .

It was a good wedding as I remember it, all things working together for good: hymns and psalms, vows and blessings, Mass and Communion; best wishes and wine; songs, talk and laughter—and the beginning of a new Christian family. A lot like other weddings, only a little different.

. . . We didn't know, and they don't know, what it all means to marry and to be married. In fact, the weddings in which we are most involved are also those in which we are most preoccupied with externals. This is always distracting. It comes clear only later what it means, really means, to be married to this man and to this woman, or for the daughter to be married to this son. But this I do know: God saw what *he* had done and it was *very* good.

READING 2.2

Civil Religion in America

Robert N. Bellah

While some have argued that Christianity is the national faith, and others that church and synagogue celebrate only the generalized religion of "the American Way of Life," few have realized that there actually exists alongside of and rather clearly differentiated from the churches an elaborate and well-institutionalized civil religion in America. This article argues not only that there is such a thing, but also that this religion—or perhaps better, this religious dimension—has its own seriousness and integrity and requires the same care in understanding that any other religion does.[1]

The Kennedy Inaugural

Kennedy's inaugural address of 20 January 1961 serves as an example and a clue with which to introduce this complex subject. That address began:

We observe today not a victory of party but a celebration of freedom—symbolizing an end as well as a beginning—signifying renewal as well as change. For I have sworn before you and Almighty God the same solemn oath our forebears prescribed nearly a century and three quarters ago.

The world is very different now. For man holds in his mortal hands the power to abolish all forms of human poverty and to abolish all forms of human life. And yet the same revolutionary beliefs for which our forebears fought are still at issue around the globe—the belief that the rights of man come not from the generosity of the state but from the hand of God.

Robert N. Bellah is Ford Professor of Sociology and Comparative Studies at the University of California, Berkeley.
Reprinted with permission of *Daedalus*, Journal of the American Academy of Arts and Sciences, Winter, 1967, Cambridge, Massachusetts.

And it concluded:

Finally, whether you are citizens of America or of the world, ask of us the same high standards of strength and sacrifice that we shall ask of you. With a good conscience our only sure reward, with history the final judge of our deeds, let us go forth to lead the land we love, asking His blessing and His help, but knowing here on earth God's work must truly be our own.

These are the three places in this brief address in which Kennedy mentioned the name of God. If we could understand why he mentioned God, the way in which he did it, and what he meant to say in those three references, we would understand much about American civil religion. But this is not a simple or obvious task, and American students of religion would probably differ widely in their interpretation of these passages.

Let us consider first the placing of the three references. They occur in the two opening paragraphs and in the closing paragraph, thus providing a sort of frame for the more concrete remarks that form the middle part of the speech. Looking beyond this particular speech, we would find that similar references to God are almost invariably to be found in the pronouncements of American presidents on solemn occasions, though usually not in the working messages that the president sends to Congress on various concrete issues. How, then, are we to interpret this placing of references to God?

It might be argued that the passages quoted reveal the essentially irrelevant role of religion in the very secular society that is America. The placing of the references in this speech as well as in public life generally indicates that religion has "only a ceremonial significance"; it gets only a sentimental nod which serves largely to placate the more unenlightened members of the community, before a discussion of the really serious business with which religion has nothing whatever to do. A cynical observer might even say that an American president has to mention God or risk losing votes. A semblance of piety is merely one of the unwritten qualifications for the office, a bit more traditional than but not essentially different from the present-day requirement of a pleasing television personality.

But we know enough about the function of ceremonial and ritual in various societies to make us suspicious of dismissing something as unimportant because it is "only a ritual." What people say on solemn occasions need not be taken at face value, but it is often indicative of deep-seated values and commitments that are not made explicit in the course of everyday life. Following this line of argument, it is worth considering whether the very special placing of the references to God in Kennedy's address may not reveal something rather important and serious about religion in American life.

It might be countered that the very way in which Kennedy made his references reveals the essentially vestigial place of religion today. He did not refer to any religion in particular. He did not refer to Jesus Christ, or to Moses, or to the Christian church; certainly he did not refer to the Catholic Church. In fact, his only reference was to the concept of God, a word which almost all Americans can accept but which means so many different things to so many different people that it is almost an empty sign. Is this not just another indication that in America religion is considered vaguely to be a good thing, but that people care so little about it that it has lost any content whatever? Isn't Eisenhower reported to have said, "Our government makes no sense unless it is founded in a deeply felt religious faith—and I don't care what it is,"[2] and isn't that a complete negation of any real religion?

These questions are worth pursuing because they raise the issue of how civil religion relates to the political society, on the one hand, and to private religious organization, on the other. President Kennedy was a Christian, more specifically a Catholic Christian. Thus, his general references to God do not mean that he lacked a specific religious commitment. But why, then, did he not include some remark to the effect that Christ is the Lord of the world or some indication of respect for the Catholic Church? He did not because these are matters of his own private religious belief and of his relation to his own particular church; they are not matters relevant in any direct way to the conduct of his public office. Others with different religious views and commitments to different churches or denominations are equally qualified participants in the political process. The principle of separation of church and state guarantees the freedom of religious belief and association, but at the same time clearly segregates the religious sphere, which is considered to be essentially private, from the political one.

Considering the separation of church and state, how is a president justified in using the word *God* at all? The answer is that the separation of church and state has not denied the political realm a religious dimension. Although matters of personal religious belief, worship, and association are considered to be strictly private affairs, there are, at the same time, certain common elements of religious orientation that the great majority of Americans share. These have played a crucial role in the development of American institutions and still provide a religious dimension for the whole fabric of American life, including the political sphere. This public religious dimension is expressed in a set of beliefs, symbols, and rituals that I am calling the American civil religion. The inauguration of a president is an important ceremonial event in this religion. It reaffirms, among other things, the religious legitimation of the highest political authori

Let us look more closely at what Kennedy

actually said. First he said, "I have sworn before you and Almighty God the same solemn oath our forebears prescribed nearly a century and three quarters ago." The oath is the oath of office, including the acceptance of the obligation to uphold the Constitution. He swears it before the people (you) and God. Beyond the Constitution, then, the president's obligation extends not only to the people but to God. In American political theory, sovereignty rests, of course, with the people, but implicitly, and often explicitly, the ultimate sovereignty has been attributed to God. This is the meaning of the motto, "In God we trust," as well as the inclusion of the phrase "under God" in the pledge to the flag. What difference does it make that sovereignty belongs to God? Though the will of the people as expressed in majority vote is carefully institutionalized as the operative source of political authority, it is deprived of an ultimate significance. The will of the people is not itself the criterion of right and wrong. There is a higher criterion in terms of which this will can be judged; it is possible that the people may be wrong. The president's obligation extends to the higher criterion.

When Kennedy says that "the rights of man come not from the generosity of the state but from the hand of God," he is stressing this point again. It does not matter whether the state is the expression of the will of an autocratic monarch or of the "people"; the rights of man are more basic than any political structure and provide a point of revolutionary leverage from which any state structure may be radically altered. That is the basis for his reassertion of the revolutionary significance of America.

But the religious dimension in political life as recognized by Kennedy not only provides a grounding for the rights of man which makes any form of political absolutism illegitimate, it also provides a transcendent goal for the political process. This is implied in his final words that "here on earth God's work must truly be our own." What he

means here is, I think, more clearly spelled out in a previous paragraph, the wording of which, incidentally, has a distinctly Biblical ring:

Now the trumpet summons us again—not as a call to bear arms, though arms we need—not as a call to battle, though embattled we are—but a call to bear the burden of a long twilight struggle, year in and year out, "rejoicing in hope, patient in tribulation"—a struggle against the common enemies of man: tyranny, poverty, disease and war itself.

The whole address can be understood as only the most recent statement of a theme that lies very deep in the American tradition, namely the obligation, both collective and individual, to carry out God's will on earth. This was the motivating spirit of those who founded America, and it has been present in every generation since. Just below the surface throughout Kennedy's inaugural address, it becomes explicit in the closing statement that God's work must be our own. That this very activist and non-contemplative conception of the fundamental religious obligation, which has been historically associated with the Protestant position, should be enunciated so clearly in the first major statement of the first Catholic president seems to underline how deeply established it is in the American outlook. Let us now consider the form and history of the civil religious tradition in which Kennedy was speaking.

The Idea of Civil Religion

The phrase *civil religion* is, of course, Rousseau's. In Chapter 8, Book 4, of *The Social Contract*, he outlines the simple dogmas of the civil religion: the existence of God, the life to come, the reward of virtue and the punishment of vice, and the exclusion of religious intolerance. All other religious opinions are outside the cognizance of the state and may be freely held by citizens. While the phrase *civil religion* was not used, to the best of my knowledge, by the founding fathers, and I am certainly not arguing for the particular influence of Rousseau, it is clear that similar ideas, as part of the cultural climate of the late eighteenth century, were to be found among the Americans. For example, Franklin writes in his autobiography:

I never was without some religious principles. I never doubted, for instance, the existence of the Deity; that he made the world and govern'd it by his Providence; that the most acceptable service of God was the doing of good to men; that our souls are immortal; and that all crime will be punished, and virtue rewarded either here or hereafter. These I esteemed the essentials of every religion; and, being to be found in all the religions we had in our country, I respected them all, tho' with different degrees of respect, as I found them more or less mix'd with other articles, which, without any tendency to inspire, promote or confirm morality, serv'd principally to divide us, and make us unfriendly to one another.

It is easy to dispose of this sort of position as essentially utilitarian in relation to religion. In Washington's Farewell Address (though the words may be Hamilton's) the utilitarian aspect is quite explicit:

Of all the dispositions and habits which lead to political prosperity, Religion and Morality are indispensable supports. In vain would that man claim the tribute of Patriotism, who should labour to subvert these great Pillars of human happiness, these firmest props of the duties of men and citizens. The mere politician, equally with the pious man ought to respect and cherish them. A volume could not trace all their connections with private and public felicity. Let it simply be asked where is the security for property, for reputation, for life, if the sense of religious obligation *desert* the oaths, which are the instruments of investigation in Courts of Justice? And let us with caution indulge the supposition, that morality can be maintained without religion. Whatever may be conceded to the influence of refined education on minds of peculiar structure, reason and experience both forbid us to expect that National morality can prevail in exclusion of religious principle.

But there is every reason to believe that religion, particularly the idea of God, played a constitutive role in the thought of the early American statesmen.

Kennedy's inaugural pointed to the religious aspect of the Declaration of Independence, and it might be well to look at that document a bit more closely. There are four references to God. The first speaks of the "Laws of Nature and Nature's God" which entitle any people to be independent. The second is the famous statement that all men "are endowed by their Creator with certain inalienable Rights." Here Jefferson is locating the fundamental legitimacy of the new nation in a conception of "higher law" that is itself based on both classical natural law and Biblical religion. The third is an appeal to "the Supreme Judge of the world for the rectitude of our intentions," and the last indicates "a firm reliance on the protection of divine Providence." In these last two references, a Biblical God of history who stands in judgment over the world is indicated.

The intimate relation of these religious notions with the self-conception of the new republic is indicated by the frequency of their appearance in early official documents. For example, we find in Washington's first inaugural address of 30 April 1789:

It would be peculiarly improper to omit in this first official act my fervent supplications to that Almighty Being who rules over the universe, who presides in the councils of nations, and whose providential aids can supply every defect, that His benediction may consecrate to the liberties and happiness of the people of the United States a Government instituted by themselves for these essential purposes, and may enable every instrument employed in its administration to execute with success the functions allotted to his charge.

No people can be bound to acknowledge and adore the Invisible Hand which conducts the affairs of man more than those of the United States. Every step by which we have advanced to the character of an independent nation seems to have been distinguished by some token of providential agency. . . .

The propitious smiles of Heaven can never be expected on a nation that disregards the eternal rules of order and right which Heaven itself has ordained. . . . The preservation of the sacred fire of liberty and the destiny of the republican model of government are justly considered, perhaps, as *deeply*, as *finally*, staked on the experiment intrusted to the hands of the American people.

Nor did these religious sentiments remain merely the personal expresssion of the president. At the request of both Houses of Congress, Washington proclaimed on October 3 of that same first year as president that November 26 should be "a day of public thanksgiving and prayer," the first Thanksgiving Day under the Constitution.

The words and acts of the founding fathers, especially the first few presidents, shaped the form and tone of the civil religion as it has been maintained ever since. Though much is selectively derived from Christianity, this religion is clearly not itself Christianity. For one thing, neither Washington nor Adams nor Jefferson mentions Christ in his inaugural address; nor do any of the subsequent presidents, although not one of them fails to mention God.[3] The God of the civil religion is not only rather "unitarian," he is also on the austere side, much more related to order, law, and right than to salvation and love. Even though he is somewhat deist in cast, he is by no means simply a watchmaker God. He is actively interested and involved in history, with a special concern for America. Here the analogy has much less to do with natural law than with ancient Israel; the equation of America with Israel in the idea of the "American Israel" is not infrequent.[4] What was implicit in the words of Washington already quoted becomes explicit in Jefferson's second inaugural when he said: "I shall need, too, the favor of that Being in whose hands we are, who led our fathers, as Israel of old, from their native land and planted them in a

country flowing with all the necessaries and comforts of life." Europe is Egypt; America, the promised land. God has led his people to establish a new sort of social order that shall be a light unto all the nations.[5]

This theme, too, has been a continuous one in the civil religion. We have already alluded to it in the case of the Kennedy inaugural. We find it again in President Johnson's inaugural address:

They came here—the exile and the stranger, brave but frightened—to find a place where a man could be his own man. They made a covenant with this land. Conceived in justice, written in liberty, bound in union, it was meant one day to inspire the hopes of all mankind; and it binds us still. If we keep its terms, we shall flourish.

What we have, then, from the earliest years of the republic is a collection of beliefs, symbols, and rituals with respect to sacred things and institutionalized in a collectivity. This religion—there seems no other word for it— while not antithetical to and indeed sharing much in common with Christianity, was neither sectarian nor in any specific sense Christian. At a time when the society was overwhelmingly Christian, it seems unlikely that this lack of Christian reference was meant to spare the feelings of the tiny non-Christian minority. Rather, the civil religion expressed what those who set the precedents felt was appropriate under the circumstances. It reflected their private as well as public views. Nor was the civil religion simply "religion in general." While generality was undoubtedly seen as a virtue by some, as in the quotation from Franklin above, the civil religion was specific enough when it came to the topic of America. Precisely because of this specificity, the civil religion was saved from empty formalism and served as a genuine vehicle of national religious self-understanding.

But the civil religion was not, in the minds of Franklin, Washington, Jefferson, or other leaders, with the exception of a few radicals like Tom Paine, ever felt to be a substitute for

Christianity. There was an implicit but quite clear division of function between the civil religion and Christianity. Under the doctrine of religious liberty, an exceptionally wide sphere of personal piety and voluntary social action was left to the churches. But the churches were neither to control the state nor to be controlled by it. The national magistrate, whatever his private religious views, operates under the rubrics of the civil religion as long as he is in his official capacity, as we have already seen in the case of Kennedy. This accommodation was undoubtedly the product of a particular historical moment and of a cultural background dominated by Protestantism of several varieties and by the Enlightenment, but it has survived despite subsequent changes in the cultural and religious climate.

Civil War and Civil Religion

Until the Civil War, the American civil religion focused above all on the event of the Revolution, which was seen as the final act of the Exodus from the old lands across the waters. The Declaration of Independence and the Constitution were the sacred scriptures and Washington the divinely appointed Moses who led his people out of the hands of tyranny. The Civil War, which Sidney Mead calls "the center of American history,"[6] was the second great event that involved the national self-understanding so deeply as to require expression in the civil religion. In 1835, Tocqueville wrote that the American republic had never really been tried, that victory in the Revolutionary War was more the result of British preoccupation elsewhere and the presence of a powerful ally than of any great military success of the Americans. But in 1861 the time of testing had indeed come. Not only did the Civil War have the tragic intensity of fratricidal strife, but it was one of the bloodiest wars of the nineteenth century;

the loss of life was far greater than any previously suffered by Americans.

The Civil War raised the deepest questions of national meaning. The man who not only formulated but in his own person embodied its meaning for Americans was Abraham Lincoln. For him the issue was not in the first instance slavery but "whether that nation, or any nation so conceived, and so dedicated, can long endure." He had said in Independence Hall in Philadelphia on 22 February 1861:

All the political sentiments I entertain have been drawn, so far as I have been able to draw them, from the sentiments which originated in and were given to the world from this Hall. I have never had a feeling, politically, that did not spring from the sentiments embodied in the Declaration of Independence.[7]

The phrases of Jefferson constantly echo in Lincoln's speeches. His task was, first of all, to save the Union—not for America alone but for the meaning of America to the whole world so unforgettably etched in the last phrase of the Gettysburg Address.

But inevitably the issue of slavery as the deeper cause of the conflict had to be faced. In the second inaugural, Lincoln related slavery and the war in an ultimate perspective:

If we shall suppose that American slavery is one of those offenses which, in the providence of God, must needs come, but which, having continued through His appointed time, He now wills to remove, and that He gives to both North and South this terrible war as the woe due to those by whom the offense came, shall we discern therein any departure from those divine attributes which the believers in a living God always ascribe to Him? Fondly do we hope, fervently do we pray, that this mighty scourge of war may speedily pass away. Yet, if God wills that it continue until all the wealth piled by the bondsman's two hundred and fifty years of unrequited toil shall be sunk, and until every drop of blood drawn with the lash shall be paid by another drawn with the sword, as was said three thousand years ago, so still it must be said "the judgements of the Lord are true and righteous altogether."

But he closes on a note if not of redemption then of reconciliation—"With malice toward none, with charity for all. . . ."

With the Civil War, a new theme of death, sacrifice, and rebirth enters the civil religion. It is symbolized in the life and death of Lincoln. Nowhere is it stated more vividly than in the Gettysburg Address, itself part of the Lincolnian "New Testament" among the civil scriptures. Robert Lowell has recently pointed out the "insistent use of birth images" in this speech explicitly devoted to "these honored dead": "brought forth," "conceived," "created," "a new birth of freedom." He goes on to say:

The Gettysburg Address is a symbolic and sacramental act. Its verbal quality is resonance combined with a logical, matter of fact, prosaic brevity. . . . In his words, Lincoln symbolically died, just as the Union soldiers really died—and as he himself was soon really to die. By his words, he gave the field of battle a symbolic significance that it had lacked. For us and our country, he left Jefferson's ideals of freedom and equality joined to the Christian sacrificial act of death and rebirth. I believe this is a meaning that goes beyond sect or religion and beyond peace and war, and is now part of our lives as a challenge, obstacle and hope.[8]

Lowell is certainly right in pointing out the Christian quality of the symbolism here, but he is also right in quickly disavowing any sectarian implication. The earlier symbolism of the civil religion had been Hebraic without being in any specific sense Jewish. The Gettysburg symbolism (". . . those who here gave their lives, that that nation might live") is Christian without having anything to do with the Christian church.

The symbolic equation of Lincoln with Jesus was made relatively early. Herndon, who had been Lincoln's law partner, wrote:

For fifty years God rolled Abraham Lincoln through his fiery furnace. He did it to try Abra-

ham and to purify him for his purposes. This made Mr. Lincoln humble, tender, forebearing, sympathetic to suffering, kind, sensitive, tolerant; broadening, deepening and widening his whole nature; making him the noblest and loveliest character since Jesus Christ. . . . I believe that Lincoln was God's chosen one.[9]

With the Christian archetype in the background, Lincoln, "our martyred president," was linked to the war dead, those who "gave the last full measure of devotion." The theme of sacrifice was indelibly written into the civil religion.

The new symbolism soon found both physical and ritualistic expression. The great number of the war dead required the establishment of a number of national cemeteries. Of these, the Gettysburg National Cemetery, which Lincoln's famous address served to dedicate, has been overshadowed only by the Arlington National Cemetery. Begun somewhat vindictively on the Lee estate across the river from Washington, partly with the end that the Lee family could never reclaim it,[10] it has subsequently become the most hallowed monument of the civil religion. Not only was a section set aside for the Confederate dead, but it has received the dead of each succeeding American war. It is the site of the one important new symbol to come out of World War I, the Tomb of the Unknown Soldier; more recently it has become the site of the tomb of another martyred president and its symbolic eternal flame.

Memorial Day, which grew out of the Civil War, gave ritual expression to the themes we have been discussing. As Lloyd Warner has so brilliantly analyzed it, the Memorial Day observance, especially in the towns and smaller cities of America, is a major event for the whole community involving a rededication to the martyred dead, to the spirit of sacrifice, and to the American vision.[11] Just as Thanksgiving Day, which incidentally was securely institutionalized as an annual national holiday only under the presidency of Lincoln, serves to integrate the family into the civil religion, so Memorial Day has acted to integrate the local community into the national cult. Together with the less overtly religious Fourth of July and the more minor celebrations of Veterans Day and the birthdays of Washington and Lincoln, these two holidays provide an annual ritual calendar for the civil religion. The public-school system serves as a particularly important context for the cultic celebration of the civil rituals.

In reifying and giving a name to something that, though pervasive enough when you look at it, has gone on only semiconsciously, there is risk of severely distorting the data. But the reification and the naming have already begun. The religious critics of "religion in general," or of the "religion of the 'American Way of Life,' " or of "American Shinto" have really been talking about the civil religion. As usual in religious polemic, they take as criteria the best in their own religious tradition and as typical the worst in the tradition of the civil religion. Against these critics, I would argue that the civil religion at its best is a genuine apprehension of universal and transcendent religious reality as seen in or, one could almost say, as revealed through the experience of the American people. Like all religions, it has suffered various deformations and demonic distortions. At its best, it has neither been so general that it has lacked incisive relevance to the American scene nor so particular that it has placed American society above universal human values. I am not at all convinced that the leaders of the churches have consistently represented a higher level of religious insight than the spokesmen of the civil religion. Reinhold Niebuhr has this to say of Lincoln, who never joined a church and who certainly represents civil religion at its best:

An analysis of the religion of Abraham Lincoln in the context of the traditional religion of his time and place and of its polemical use on the slavery issue, which corrupted religious life in the days before and during the Civil War, must lead to the conclusion that Lincoln's religious convictions were superior in depth and purity to those, not only of the political leaders of his day, but of the religious leaders of the era.[12]

Perhaps the real animus of the religious critics has been not so much against the civil religion in itself but against its pervasive and dominating influence within the sphere of church religion. As S. M. Lipset has recently shown, American religion at least since the early nineteenth century has been predominantly activist, moralistic, and social rather than contemplative, theological, of innerly spiritual.[13] Tocqueville spoke of American church religion as "a political institution which powerfully contributes to the maintenance of a democratic republic among the Americans"[14] by supplying a strong moral consensus amidst continuous political change. Henry Bargy in 1902 spoke of American church religion as "la poésie du civisme."[15]

It is certainly true that the relation between religion and politics in America has been singularly smooth. This is in large part due to the dominant tradition. As Tocqueville wrote:

The greatest part of British America was peopled by men who, after having shaken off the authority of the Pope, acknowledged no other religious supremacy: they brought with them into the New World a form of Christianity which I cannot better describe than by styling it a democratic and republican religion.[16]

The churches opposed neither the Revolution nor the establishment of democratic institutions. Even when some of them opposed the full institutionalization of religious liberty, they accepted the final outcome with good grace and without nostalgia for an *ancien régime*. The American civil religion was never anticlerical or militantly secular. On the contrary, it borrowed selectively from the religious tradition in such a way that the average American saw no conflict between the two. In this way, the civil religion was able to build up without any bitter struggle with the church powerful symbols of national solidarity and to mobilize deep levels of personal motivation for the attainment of national goals.

Such an achievement is by no means to be taken for granted. It would seem that the problem of a civil religion is quite general in modern societies and that the way it is solved or not solved will have repercussions in many spheres. One needs only to think of France to see how differently things can go. The French Revolution was anticlerical to the core and attempted to set up an anti-Christian civil religion. Throughout modern French history, the chasm between traditional Catholic symbols and the symbolism of 1789 has been immense.

American civil religion is still very much alive. [In 1963] we participated in a vivid re-enactment of the sacrifice theme in connection with the funeral of our assassinated president. The American Israel theme is clearly behind both Kennedy's New Frontier and Johnson's Great Society. Let me give just one recent illustration of how the civil religion serves to mobilize support for the attainment of national goals. On 15 March 1965 President Johnson went before Congress to ask for a strong voting-rights bill. Early in the speech he said:

Rarely are we met with the challenge, not to our growth or abundance, or our welfare or our security—but rather to the values and the purposes and the meaning of our beloved nation.

The issue of equal rights for American Negroes is such an issue. And should we defeat every enemy, and should we double our wealth and conquer the stars and still be unequal to this issue, then we will have failed as a people and as a nation.

For with a country as with a person, "What is a man profited, if he shall gain the whole world, and lose his own soul?"

And in conclusion he said:

Above the pyramid on the great seal of the United States it says in Latin, "God has favored our undertaking."

God will not favor everything that we do. It is rather our duty to divine his will. I cannot help but believe that He truly understands and that He really favors the undertaking that we begin here tonight.[17]

The civil religion has not always been invoked in favor of worthy causes. On the domestic scene, an American-Legion type of ideology that fuses God, country, and flag has been used to attack nonconformist and liberal ideas and groups of all kinds. Still, it has been difficult to use the words of Jefferson and Lincoln to support special interests and undermine personal freedom. The defenders of slavery before the Civil War came to reject the thinking of the Declaration of Independence. Some of the most consistent of them turned against not only Jeffersonian democracy but Reformation religion; they dreamed of a South dominated by medieval chivalry and divine-right monarchy.[18] For all the overt religiosity of the radical right today, their relation to the civil religious consensus is tenuous, as when the John Birch Society attacks the central American symbol of Democracy itself.

With respect to America's role in the world, the dangers of distortion are greater and the built-in safeguards of the tradition weaker. The theme of the American Israel was used, almost from the beginning, as a justification for the shameful treatment of the Indians so characteristic of our history. It can be overtly or implicitly linked to the idea of manifest destiny which has been used to legitimate several adventures in imperialism since the early nineteenth century. Never has the danger been greater than today. The issue is not so much one of imperial expansion, of which we are accused, as of the tendency to assimilate all governments or parties in the world which support our immediate policies or call upon our help by invoking the notion of free institutions and democratic values. Those nations that are for the moment "on our side" become "the free world." A repressive and unstable military dictatorship in South Viet-Nam becomes "the free people of South Viet-

Nam and their government." It is then part of the role of America as the New Jerusalem and "the last best hope on earth" to defend such governments with treasure and eventually with blood. When our soldiers are actually dying, it becomes possible to consecrate the struggle further by invoking the great theme of sacrifice. For the majority of the American people who are unable to judge whether the people in South Viet-Nam (or wherever) are "free like us," such arguments are convincing. Fortunately President Johnson has been less ready to assert that "God has favored our undertaking" in the case of Viet-Nam than with respect to civil rights. But others are not so hesitant. The civil religion has exercised long-term pressure for the humane solution of our greatest domestic problem, the treatment of the Negro American. It remains to be seen how relevant it can become for our role in the world at large, and whether we can effectually stand for "the revolutionary beliefs for which our forebears fought," in John F. Kennedy's words.

The civil religion is obviously involved in the most pressing moral and political issues of the day. But it is also caught in another kind of crisis, theoretical and theological, of which it is at the moment largely unaware. "God" has clearly been a central symbol in the civil religion from the beginning and remains so today. This symbol is just as central to the civil religion as it is to Judaism or Christianity. In the late eighteenth century this posed no problem; even Tom Paine, contrary to his detractors, was not an atheist. From left to right and regardless of church or sect, all could accept the idea of God. But today, as even *Time* has recognized, the meaning of the word *God* is by no means so clear or so obvious. There is no formal creed in the civil religion. We have had a Catholic president; it is conceivable that we could have a Jewish one. But could we have an agnostic president? Could a man with conscientious scruples about using the word *God* the way Kennedy and Johnson have used it be elected chief magistrate of our country? If the whole God symbolism requires reformulation, there will be obvious consequences for the civil religion, consequences perhaps of liberal alienation and of fundamentalist ossification that have not so far been prominent in this realm. The civil religion has been a point of articulation between the profoundest commitments of the Western religious and philosophical tradition and the common beliefs of ordinary Americans. It is not too soon to consider how the deepening theological crisis may affect the future of this articulation.

The Third Time of Trial

In conclusion it may be worthwhile to relate the civil religion to the most serious situation that we as Americans now face, what I call the third time of trial. The first time of trial had to do with the question of independence, whether we should or could run our own affairs in our own way. The second time of trial was over the issue of slavery, which in turn was only the most salient aspect of the more general problem of the full institutionalization of democracy within our country. This second problem we are still far from solving though we have some notable successes to our credit. But we have been overtaken by a third great problem which has led to a third great crisis, in the midst of which we stand. This is the problem of responsible action in a revolutionary world, a world seeking to attain many of the things, material and spiritual, that we have already attained. Americans have, from the beginning, been aware of the responsibility and the significance our republican experiment has for the whole world. The first internal political polarization in the new nation had to do with our attitude toward the French Revolution. But we were small and weak then, and "foreign entanglements" seemed to threaten our very survival. During the last century, our relevance for the world was not forgotten, but our role was seen as purely exemplary. Our democratic republic rebuked tyranny by merely existing. Just after World War I we were on the brink of taking a different role in the world, but once again we turned our back.

Since World War II the old pattern has become impossible. Every president since Roosevelt has been groping toward a new pattern of action in the world, one that would be consonant with our power and our responsibilities. For Truman and for the period dominated by John Foster Dulles that pattern was seen to be the great Manichaean confrontation of East and West, the confrontation of democracy and "the false philosophy of Communism" that provided the structure of Truman's inaugural address. But with the last years of Eisenhower and with the successive two presidents, the pattern began to shift. The great problems came to be seen as caused not solely by the evil intent of any one group of men, but as stemming from much more complex and multiple sources. For Kennedy, it was not so much a struggle against particular men as against "the common enemies of man: tyranny, poverty, disease and war itself."

But in the midst of this trend toward a less primitive conception of ourselves and our world, we have somehow, without anyone really intending it, stumbled into a military confrontation where we have come to feel that our honor is at stake. We have in a moment of uncertainty been tempted to rely on our overwhelming physical power rather than on our intelligence, and we have, in part, succumbed to this temptation. Bewildered and unnerved when our terrible power fails to bring immediate success, we are at the edge of a chasm the depth of which no man knows.

I cannot help but think of Robinson Jeffers, whose poetry seems more apt now than when it was written, when he said:

Unhappy country, what wings you have! . . .
Weep (it is frequent in human affairs), weep for
    the terrible magnificence of the means,

The ridiculous incompetence of the reasons, the
    bloody and shabby
Pathos of the result.

But as so often before in similar times, we have a man of prophetic stature, without the bitterness or misanthropy of Jeffers, who, as Lincoln before him, calls this nation to its judgment:

When a nation is very powerful but lacking in self-confidence, it is likely to behave in a manner that is dangerous both to itself and to others.

Gradually but unmistakably, America is succumbing to that arrogance of power which has afflicted, weakened and in some cases destroyed great nations in the past.

If the war goes on and expands, if that fatal process continues to accelerate until America becomes what it is not now and never has been, a seeker after unlimited power and empire, then Vietnam will have had a mighty and tragic fallout indeed.

I do not believe that will happen. I am very apprehensive but I still remain hopeful, and even confident, that America, with its humane and democratic traditions, will find the wisdom to match its power.[19]

Without an awareness that our nation stands under higher judgment, the tradition of the civil religion would be dangerous indeed. Fortunately, the prophetic voices have never been lacking. Our present situation brings to mind the Mexican-American war that Lincoln, among so many others, opposed. The spirit of civil disobedience that is alive today in the civil rights movement and the opposition to the Viet-Nam war was already clearly outlined by Henry David Thoreau when he wrote, "If the law is of such a nature that it requires you to be an agent of injustice to another, then I say, break the law." Thoreau's words, "I would remind my countrymen that they are men first, and Americans at a late and convenient hour,"[20] provide an essential standard for any adequate thought and action in our third time of trial. As Americans, we have been well favored in the world, but it is as men that we will be judged.

Out of the first and second times of trial have come, as we have seen, the major symbols of the American civil religion. There seems little doubt that a successful negotiation of this third time of trial—the attainment of some kind of viable and coherent world order—would precipitate a major new set of symbolic forms. So far the flickering flame of the United Nations burns too low to be the focus of a cult, but the emergence of a genuine transnational sovereignty would certainly change this. It would necessitate the incorporation of vital international symbolism into our civil religion, or, perhaps a better way of putting it, it would result in American civil religion becoming simply one part of a new civil religion of the world. It is useless to speculate on the form such a civil religion might take, though it obviously would draw on religious traditions beyond the sphere of Biblical religion alone. Fortunately, since the American civil religion is not the worship of the American nation but an understanding of the American experience in the light of ultimate and universal reality, the reorganization entailed by such a new situation need not disrupt the American civil religion's continuity. A world civil religion could be accepted as a fulfillment and not a denial of American civil religion. Indeed, such an outcome has been the eschatological hope of American civil religion from the beginning. To deny such an outcome would be to deny the meaning of America itself.

Behind the civil religion at every point lie Biblical archetypes: Exodus, Chosen People, Promised Land, New Jerusalem, Sacrificial Death and Rebirth. But it is also genuinely American and genuinely new. It has its own prophets and its own martyrs, its own sacred events and sacred places, its own solemn rituals and symbols. It is concerned that America be a society as perfectly in accord with the will of God as men can make it, and a light to all the nations.

It has often been used and is being used today as a cloak for petty interests and ugly passions. It is in need—as is any living faith—of continual reformation, of being measured by universal standards. But it is not evident that it is incapable of growth and new insight.

It does not make any decision for us. It does not remove us from moral ambiguity, from being, in Lincoln's fine phrase, an "almost chosen people." But it is a heritage of moral and religious experience from which we still have much to learn as we formulate the decisions that lie ahead.

Notes

1. Why something so obvious should have escaped serious analytical attention is in itself an interesting problem. Part of the reason is probably the controversial nature of the subject. From the earliest years of the nineteenth century, conservative religious and political groups have argued that Christianity is, in fact, the national religion. Some of them have from time to time and as recently as the 1950's proposed constitutional amendments that would explicitly recognize the sovereignty of Christ. In defending the doctrine of separation of church and state, opponents of such groups have denied that the national polity has, intrinsically, anything to do with religion at all. The moderates on this issue have insisted that the American state has taken a permissive and indeed supportive attitude toward religious groups (tax exemption, et cetera), thus favoring religion but still missing the positive institutionalization with which I am concerned. But part of the reason this issue has been left in obscurity is certainly due to the peculiarly Western concept of "religion" as denoting a single type of collectivity of which an individual can be a member of one and only one at a time. The Durkheimian notion that every group has a religious dimension, which would be seen as obvious in southern or eastern Asia, is foreign to us. This obscures the recognition of such dimensions in our society.

2. Quoted in Will Herberg, *Protestant-Catholic-Jew* (New York, 1955), p. 97.

3. God is mentioned or referred to in all inaugural addresses but Washington's second, which is a very brief (two paragraphs) and perfunctory acknowledgment. It is not without interest that the actual word *God* does not appear until Monroe's second inaugural,

5 March 1821. In his first inaugural, Washington refers to God as "that Almighty Being who rules the universe," "Great Author of every public and private good," "Invisible Hand," and "benign Parent of the Human Race." John Adams refers to God as "Providence," "Being who is supreme over all," "Patron of Order," "Foundation of Justice," and "Protector in all ages of the world of virtuous liberty." Jefferson speaks of "that Infinite Power which rules the destinies of the universe," and "that Being in whose hands we are." Madison speaks of "that Almighty Being whose power regulates the destiny of nations," and "Heaven." Monroe uses "Providence" and "the Almighty" in his first inaugural and finally "Almighty God" in his second. See *Inaugural Addresses of the Presidents of the United States from George Washington 1789 to Harry S Truman 1949.* 82nd Congress, 2d Session, House Document No. 540, 1952.

4. For example, Abiel Abbot, pastor of the First Church in Haverhill, Massachusetts, delivered a Thanksgiving sermon in 1799, *Traits of Resemblance in the People of the United States of America to Ancient Israel,* in which he said, "It has been often remarked that the people of the United States come nearer to a parallel with Ancient Israel, than any other nation upon the globe. Hence 'Our American Israel' is a term frequently used; and common consent allows it apt and proper." Cited in Hans Kohn, *The Idea of Nationalism* (New York, 1961), p. 665.

5. That the Mosaic analogy was present in the minds of leaders at the very moment of the birth of the republic is indicated in the designs proposed by Franklin and Jefferson for a seal of the United States of America. Together with Adams, they formed a committee of three delegated by the Continental Congress on July 4, 1776, to draw up the new device. "Franklin proposed as the device Moses lifting up his wand and dividing the Red Sea while Pharoah was overwhelmed by its waters, with the motto 'Rebellion to tyrants is obedience to God.' Jefferson proposed the children of Israel in the wilderness 'led by a cloud by day and a pillar of fire by night.'" Anson Phelps Stokes, *Church and State in the United States,* Vol. 1 (New York, 1950), pp. 467–468.

6. Sidney Mead, *The Lively Experiment* (New York, 1963), p. 12.

7. Quoted by Arthur Lehman Goodhart in Allan Nevins (ed.), *Lincoln and the Gettysburg Address* (Urbana, Ill., 1961), p. 39.

8. Ibid., "On the Gettysburg Address," pp. 88–89.

9. Quoted in Sherwood Eddy, *The Kingdom of God and the American Dream* (New York, 1941), p. 162.

10. Karl Decker and Angus McSween, *Historic Arlington* (Washington, D.C., 1892), pp. 60–67.

11. How extensive the activity associated with Memorial Day can be is indicated by Warner: "The sacred symbolic behavior of Memorial Day, in which scores of the town's organizations are involved, is ordinarily divided into four periods. During the year separate rituals are held by many of the associations for their dead, and many of these activities are connected with later Memorial Day events. In the second phase, preparations are made during the last three or four weeks for the ceremony itself, and some of the associations perform public rituals. The third phase consists of scores of rituals held in all the cemeteries, churches, and halls of the associations. These rituals consist of speeches and highly ritualized behavior. They last for two days and are climaxed by the fourth and last phase, in which all the separate celebrants gather in the center of the business district on the afternoon of Memorial Day. The separate organizations, with their members in uniform or with fitting insignia, march through the town, visit the shrines and monuments of the hero dead, and, finally enter the cemetery. Here dozens of ceremonies are held, most of them highly symbolic and formalized." During these various ceremonies Lincoln is continually referred to and the Gettysburg Address recited many times. W. Lloyd Warner, *American Life* (Chicago, 1962), pp. 8–9.

12. Reinhold Niebuhr, "The Religion of Abraham Lincoln," in Nevins (ed.), *op. cit.,* p. 72. William J. Wolfe of the Episcopal Theological School in Cambridge, Massachusetts, has written: "Lincoln is one of the greatest theologians of America—not in the technical meaning of producing a system of doctrine, certainly not as the defender of some one denomination, but in the sense of seeing the hand of God intimately in the affairs of nations. Just so the prophets of Israel criticized the events of their day from the perspective of the God who is concerned for history and who reveals His will within it. Lincoln now stands among God's latter-day prophets." *The Religion of Abraham Lincoln* (New York, 1963), p. 24.

13. Seymour Martin Lipset, "Religion and American Values," Chapter 4, *The First New Nation* (New York, 1964).

14. Alexis de Tocqueville, *Democracy in America,* Vol. 1 (New York, 1954), p. 310.

15. Henry Bargy, *La Religion dans la Société aux Etats-Unis* (Paris, 1902), p. 31.

16. Tocqueville, *op. cit.,* p. 311. Later he says, "In the United States even the religion of most of the citizens is republican, since it submits the truths of the other world to private judgment, as in politics the care of their temporal interests is abandoned to the good sense of the people. Thus every man is allowed freely to take the road which he thinks will lead him to heaven, just as the law permits every citizen to have the right of choosing his own government" (p. 436).

17. U.S., *Congressional Record*, House, 15 March 1965, pp. 4924, 4926.

18. See Louis Hartz, "The Feudal Dream of the South," Part 4, *The Liberal Tradition in America* (New York, 1955).

19. Speech of Senator J. William Fulbright of 28 April 1968, as reported in *The New York Times*, 29 April 1968.

20. Quoted in Yehoshua Arieli, *Individualism and Nationalism in American Ideology* (Cambridge, Mass., 1964), p. 274.

R E A D I N G   2 . 3

Who Is Civil Religious?

James A. Christenson and Ronald C. Wimberley

Civil religion in America is "an understanding of the American experience in the light of ultimate and universal reality" (Bellah, 1967:18). It is differentiated from what some (Herberg, 1955; Warner, 1962; Yinger, 1961) have labeled "common religion" in that it is not a reduction of Christian principles to bare essentials nor a synthesis of religious pluralism in America. Likewise, it is not the politicization of religion. Civil religion draws upon civil events such as the 4th of July, documents such as the U.S. Constitution, personages such as Jefferson and Lincoln, and common religious beliefs such as the belief in God. Some basic tenets of civil religion are the belief that the United States is God's chosen nation; the perception of Divine sanctions and inherent morality in civil laws; and the ascription of sacred connotations to such secular symbols as flags, presidential inaugurations, and national holidays (Bellah, 1967:6–14; Cherry, 1970; Stauffer, 1973; Bennett, 1975). Recent research documents the empirically separate existence of civil religion from such religious dimensions as belief, experience, and behavior (Wimberley *et al.*, 1976; Wimberley, 1976). Civil religious beliefs have been found among most Christian denominations (Christenson and Wimberley, 1976).

Bennett (1975:81–82) argues that one should expect to find a generalized set of civil religious beliefs which would allow untrained believers to proclaim faith in the American system. If civil religion does serve as a point of convergence for "the great majority of Americans," as suggested by Bellah (1967:3;1970), the existence of civil religion in various social, economic, and demographic segments of society has not been explored. The present aim is to fill this void in the empirical literature and to discuss the implications of civil religious ideology as a potent social lever for manipulation.

James A. Christenson is Professor of Sociology at the University of Kentucky.

Ronald C. Wimberley is Professor of Sociology at North Carolina State University.

Work on this paper was partially supported by the University of Kentucky Agricultural Experiment Station and is published as journal article 76-14-121 with approval of the Director. Earlier support and data collection took place while the senior author was at North Carolina State University. This paper was presented at the Southern Sociological Society's 1977 meetings.

Reprinted from *Sociological Analysis* 39 (Spring 1978), with permission of the publisher.

Procedures

Data were gathered during 1975 through a statewide survey in North Carolina. Mail questionnaires were sent to 5,082 heads of household proportionally drawn from telephone listings. Approximately 86 percent of the households in North Carolina had telephone service. Because of deaths, physical incapacity, or inability to locate certain respondents either by mail or telephone, 578 were deleted. Of the remaining 4,504 potential respondents, 3,054 returned usable questionnaires for a response rate of 68 percent.

Four items were adapted from previous studies on indicators of civil religion.[1] Each item represented a five-point scale with a score of one indicating strongly disagree and a score of five indicating strongly agree. Evidence of convergent and discriminant validity for these indicators was established by means of an oblique, promax rotation of a principle axis factoring and a cluster analysis (Wimberley and Christenson, 1976). Summed item scores provided a composite civil religion measure ranging from a low of 4, showing strong disagreement with civil religious beliefs, to a high of 20 showing strong agreement with civil religion.

The analysis relies on descriptive statistics, including subcategory means, measures of association, and standardized regression coefficients. For sake of brevity, the presented statistics will summarize more than a dozen tables and scattergram plots.

Descriptive Classifications

If civil religious adherence is broadly based, as suggested by Bellah (1967; 1970), then such adherence should extend across religious, political, and social categories. If, on the other hand, civil religious adherence is tied to a group with particular characteristics—for instance, white, middle class females—then the assertions of Bellah may be questioned. Thus, the following descriptive analysis explores the breadth of civil religious adherence across a wide range of political, religious, and social categories.

Taken by itself, the total distribution of these civil religion scores centers around a median of 14.0, a mean of 13.8, and a standard deviation of 3.0.[2] Less than 20 percent of the sample members fall below a score of 12, the midpoint of the civil religion measure. Most respondents are fairly homogeneous in their civil religious adherence.

Religion

As indicated by Table 1(A), religious conservatives are more civil religious than the liberals. Yet, even among liberals, 60 percent score higher than the midpoint of the civil religious index. Similar results occur for civil religion and church attendance; the score gradually rises with frequency of attendance. Given that religiously conservative churchgoers are conventionally regarded as "more religious," these persons emerge as somewhat more civil religious as well.

Politics

Although the mean scores for all political affiliations in Table 1(B) are quite similar, Democrats outrank Republicans while independents appear less civil religious than people in either major party. As was the case for religious outlooks, political conservatives are more inclined toward civil religion. In terms of political behavior, voting in the 1974 off-year election has no relation to civil religion for, despite the large sample size, the difference between voters and nonvoters is statistically insignificant. In essence, then, conservatives and Democrats have higher civil religious leanings but this seems unrelated to whether one votes.

Social Aspects

Levels of family income, educational attainment, occupation, sex, and age show some within group variations on civil religion. This is summarized in Table 1(C). Social aggregates found to be particularly civil religious are the poor, the least educated, the unemployed, the retired, the elderly, and the few reporting as American Indians. Whites and nonwhites reveal no appreciable differences. The size of community in which one lives uncovers minor disparities in civil reli-

Table 1 *Descriptive Classification of Support for Civil Religion*

	Mean[1]	N	Gamma[2]	Eta
A. Religious				
Beliefs (self-identification)			−.252	.215
Conservative	14.4	1013		
Middle-of-road	13.7	928		
Liberal	12.3	500		
Church Attendance			.179	.188
Once a week or more	14.3	1043		
About 2 or 3 times a month	14.1	521		
About once a month	14.0	218		
Several times a year	13.3	467		
Not at all	12.3	351		
C. Social				
Annual Family Income			−.168	.177
Less than $3,000	14.6	201		
$3,000 to 5,999	14.7	267		
$6,000 to 9,999	14.0	519		
$10,000 to 14,999	14.0	669		
$15,000 to 24,999	13.1	649		
$25,000 or more	13.0	262		
Education			−.310	.336
Some grade school or less	14.8	193		
Completed grade school	15.0	167		
Some high school	14.8	386		
Completed high school	14.3	707		
Some college	13.7	529		
Completed college	12.6	308		
Some graduate work	12.1	150		
A graduate degree	11.4	206		
Occupation			—	.285
Unemployed	16.2	22		
Retired	14.8	289		
Laborers (including farm)	14.5	105		
Operators	14.5	256		
Service workers	14.5	83		
Crafts and foremen	14.5	381		
Farm owners and managers	14.3	124		
Sales	13.7	131		
Military	13.7	72		
Managers, proprietors	13.6	469		
Clerical	13.2	141		
Clergy	12.7	32		
College students	12.4	26		
Officials	12.2	11		
Professionals	12.1	381		

1. Despite the usually small fluctuations among those means, the largeness of the
sample contributes statistical significance in ANOV and T tests. All differences except for voting and
race are significant at the .001 level.

2. Gamma and Eta reflect the association of each classificatory variable with five categories of the civil religion index scores. Gammas are omitted when civil religion is related to nominal
attributes.

	Mean[1]	N	Gamma[2]	Eta
B. Political				
Party			—	.107
Democrat	14.0	1462		
Republican	13.8	558		
Independent	13.2	565		
Political Beliefs (self-identification)			−.143	.131
Conservative	14.2	1074		
Middle of the road	13.8	1163		
Liberal	12.6	337		
Vote in 1974 Election			−.006	.004
No	13.8	709		
Yes	13.8	1952		
Race			—	.054
American Indian	14.8	18		
Black	13.9	237		
White	13.8	2432		
Sex			—	.067
Female	14.2	585		
Male	13.7	2070		
Age			.146	.157
Less than 30	13.0	520		
30 to 39	13.7	568		
40 to 49	13.7	544		
50 to 59	14.0	523		
60 to 69	14.4	365		
70 or more	15.0	176		
Community Size			−.163	.178
On a farm	14.5	342		
In or near a small town	14.1	390		
In or near a town (2,500 to 9,999)	14.2	536		
In or near a small city (10,000 to 49,999)	13.7	658		
In or near a large city (50,000 to 199,999)	12.8	453		
In a metropolitan area (200,000 or more)	13.0	189		

gion scores. The more rural tend to rank higher than their urban counterparts. The only respondents falling below the halfway mark of the index are those having graduate degrees beyond college. Also less favorable to civil religious items are respondents with careers as professionals, officials, or ministers. Although the active religious clientele are generally the most civil religious, the clergy seem relatively indifferent about it. Overall, however, the findings lend support to Bellah's (1967:1970) assertion that civil religion rests in the masses.

A Multivariate Summary

Possible effects on civil religion from certain classification variables are analyzed separately by use of multiple regression.[3] Table 2 presents the resulting standardized partial regression coefficients. Inter-item correlations are also provided for visual inspection of the degree of interrelationship among the independent variables. With the exception of the education-income and political-religious beliefs, all correlations are .30 or less. Of the variables examined, civil religious ideology is most enhanced by low education and active, conservative religion. This corresponds with the earlier descriptive analysis. Although some of the other variables display nonzero effects on civil religion, these are quite trivial. Family income, for example, has no predictive ability. Combined, the multiple correlation for the exogenous variables only explains 18.4 percent of the civil religious variation. This modest amount of explained variance is in keeping with the conceptual positions that civil religion is not determined by the configuration of particular religious, political, or social categories but tends to cross over social and cultural identities.

Interaction Effects

To explore possible interactions among the independent variables, three-way analysis of variance is conducted with the major explanatory variables which were prominent in Table 2: religious beliefs, church attendance, and education.[4] The results are summarized in Table 3. Again, it is the bivariate links between each of the independent variables and civil religion which are significant; their main effects claim the high F values. No interaction is found between church attendance and education. Nor is there a three-way interaction.

Slight interactions between religious belief and education and between religious belief and church attendance do exist. Inspection of subcategory means, which are not reported here, indicated that a few well educated, religious conservatives and some poorly educated, religious liberals are highly civil religious. This is shown in the statistically significant, although weak, interaction between religious beliefs and education. A similar effect is apparent for religious belief and church attendance. Some conservative non-attenders and some liberal attenders have high civil religion scores. But while both of these interactions are significant in this large sample, their effects are small in comparison to the main effects.

Implications

While civil religion shows some variation with education, religious behavior, religious beliefs, and a few other things, the dominant finding is that a fair amount of civil religious consensus is found across most social segments.[5] This is evidenced by the clustering around a few civil religious scores, slight differences among subcategory means of descriptive variables, and the low percentage of variance explained by the combined impact of ten predictors. Only those in potential positions of power—professionals, ministers, and officials—appear to be neutral in civil religion.

While this analysis suggests that civil religion may receive broad support, questions should be raised as to whether it is an effec-

Table 2 Correlation Coefficients (R) and Standardized Partial Regression Coefficients (Beta) of Religious, Political, and Social Variables with Civil Religion Scale

Characteristics		X^1	X^2	X^3	X^4	X^5	X^6	X^7	X^8	X^9	X^{10}	Beta
Religious												
Conservative to liberal identity	X^1											−.13
None to frequent church attendance	X^2	−.23										.16
Political												
Conservative to liberal identity	X^3	.49	−.08									−.05
Party (Republican-Democrat)[1]	X^4	.04	−.01	.16								−.04
Social												
Education (low to high)	X^5	.20	−.30	.06	−.00							−.28
Income (low to high)	X^6	.07	−.25	−.05	−.07	.47						−.02
Race (nonwhite—white)	X^7	−.02	.00	−.13	−.20	.13	.20					.06
Sex (male—female)	X^8	.01	.07	.09	.08	−.09	−.30	−.18				.04
Age (young to old)	X^9	−.15	.12	−.13	.10	.30	−.24	.01	.05			.00
Community size (small to large)	X^{10}	.13	−.10	.08	−.01	.30	.25	.00	.02	−.12		−.05
Civil Religion index	X^{11}	−.25	.21	−.16	.03	−.33	−.17	.00	.07	.16	−.18	(dependent) $R^2 = .18$

1. Independents were omitted for this relationship in order to use a dummy variable of the two major parties.

Table 3 Three-way Analysis of Variance of Report Levels of Civil Religion and Test for Interaction Effects for Religious Beliefs, Church Attendance, and Education

Source	Sum of Squares	Degrees Freedom	Mean Square	F	Significance of F
Main Effects					
Religious beliefs (A)	597.2	2	298.6	39.6	.001
Church attendance (B)	508.0	2	254.0	33.7	.001
Education (C)	1,779.3	3	593.1	78.6	.001
Interactions					
AB interaction	230.6	4	57.7	7.6	.001
AC interaction	223.3	6	36.2	4.9	.001
BC interaction	55.0	6	9.2	1.2	.295
ABC interaction	78.7	12	6.6	0.8	.999
Residual	17,534.0	2,324	7.5		
Total	22,024.3	2,359	9.3		

tive ideology in America. Bell (1960:370) considers ideology as "the conversion of ideas into social levers." Examples include the divine right of kings, free market entrepreneurism, and egalitarian rights. Such ideologies may serve as integrative principles, unifying forces, and guidelines for action in ambiguous situations.

Although Bell may have seen an end to grand-scale ideologies as dominant forces in history, civil religion, nevertheless, seems to fit the parameters of an ideology. It purports to explain the development of American society, to direct choices about the legitimacy of society, and to provide a unifying element in American celebrations and crises. In response to the "end of ideology school," Stauffer (1973) similarly makes a case that civil religion as an ideology deserves study by sociologists and other students of religion.

Bennett (1975:95) suggests that while "civil religion may facilitate (political) system stability," it may also "lead to reduced critical thinking about public affairs on the part of the citizenry." This becomes a tradeoff. He (1975:84) summarizes that, on the basis of related political and religious beliefs, citizens tend to find the *status quo* acceptable and morally grounded. This links with trust in political leadership.

Stauffer (1973:419) cautions that citizens who feel issues to be overly complex may resort to their leaders for decisions which, in turn, allows the possibility that leaders may feel free to act on the basis of self interests. As a source of information and guidance in a democratic society, elected leaders have legitimate access to civil religious symbols and the structures to use them (Bennet, 1975:88–95). Bennett (1975:95) concludes that "manipulation of the referents of the civil religion can make the processes of identifying issues, developing policy, and mobilizing support, one-way affairs with leaders exercising the initiative which is normally prescribed for their constituencies."

While any ideology may be politically use-ful, many candidates and leaders seem capable of using civil religion as a lever for electoral support. Bellah (1967;1970) notes civil religion in actions by Jefferson, Lincoln, and Roosevelt. More recent presidents also have displayed this appeal. According to one study, former President Nixon drew strength from many civil religious citizens (Bourg, 1976:144–145).

Whereas an ideology may serve the high, universal ideals of a culture on one hand, it also may be used for particularistic, self-serving ends. The practical importance of identifying and documenting any ideology is to anticipate rather than to recall its manipulation. Since diverse peoples may adhere to civil religion, this ideology would seem to have some degree of political value. Perhaps this awareness may help squelch its abuse for personal political power. The widespread support for civil religion among the masses suggests the importance of these considerations in future research.

Notes

1. The items were: "America is God's chosen nation today"; "To me, the flag of the United States is sacred"; "Human rights come from God and not merely from laws"; and "If government does not support religion, government cannot uphold morality" (Wimberley, 1976:343).

2. Operationally a score of 14 represents agreement with at least two of the four items or strong agreement on at least one.

3. Since occupation is an attribute having more than two nominal categories, it is removed from the regressions. Voting or not voting in 1974 is also excluded due to its lack of relationship with civil religion in the Table 1 statistics. This nonrelationship was reconfirmed in a separate regression run.

4. To assure sufficient N's for each cell in the two and three way analysis of variance, the eight categories of education were collapsed to four: grade school, high school, college and graduate work. The five church attendance categories were collapsed to three: once a week or more, once a month or more, seldom or nonattendance.

5. It should be remembered that, while large and reasonably representative, this sample covers one state. For other places, the extent of any civil religious

differences in descriptive subcategories, bivariate relations, and regressions are unknown. While there may be similarities in other places, comparable data on other states or regions are lacking.

References

Bell, Daniel. 1960. The End of Ideology. Glencoe, Illinois: Free Press.

Bellah, Robert N. 1967. "Civil religion in America." *Daedalus* 96:1–21. 1970. Beyond Belief. New York: Harper and Row.

Bennett, Lance W. 1975. "Political sanctification: The civil religion and American politics." *Social Science Information* 14:79–106.

Bourg, Carroll J. 1976. "A symposium on civil religion." *Sociological Analysis* 37:141–149.

Cherry, Conrad. 1970. "American sacred ceremonies." Pp. 303–316 in P. E. Hammond and B. Johnson (eds.), American Mosaic. New York: Random House.

Christenson, James A. and Ronald C. Wimberley. 1976. "Civil religion and church religions." Paper presented at the annual meeting of the Association for the Sociology of Religion.

Herberg, Will. 1955. Protestant-Catholic-Jew. Garden City, New York: Doubleday.

Stauffer, Robert E. 1973. "Civil religion, technocracy, and the private sphere: Further comments on cultural interpretation in advanced societies." *Journal for the Scientific Study of Religion* 12:415–425.

Warner, Lloyd. 1962. American Life: Dream or Reality. Chicago: University of Chicago Press.

Wimberley, Ronald C. 1976. "Testing the civil religion hypothesis." *Sociological Analysis* 37, 4:341–352.

Wimberley, Ronald C. and James A. Christenson. 1976. "Civil religion and church and state." Paper presented at the annual meeting of the Society for the Scientific Study of Religion.

Wimberley, Ronald C., Donald A. Clelland, Thomas C. Hood and C. M. Lipsey. 1976. "The civil religious dimension: Is it there?" *Social Forces* 54:890–900.

Yinger, J. Milton. 1961. Sociology Looks at Religion. New York: Macmillan.

R E A D I N G   2 . 4

Secularization and the "Civil Religion"

Richard K. Fenn

The question of whether to take particular events seriously, e.g., a President's use of religious language in stating his view of the nation's identity and purpose, raises the more difficult question of whether there is a cultural whole from which this speech derives and to which it legitimately refers. That cultural whole, if it exists, is clearly more than certain symbols with an autonomous existence. The culture must exist elsewhere in individual consciousness, Constitutional law, institutional statements of purpose, educational policy, and so on. But to establish the existence of such a cultural whole inevitably requires a leap beyond the data, which in themselves are merely parts, fragments, and details of a larger picture whose existence can only be inferred, not demonstrated. That leap, I have argued, is made by the metaphoric reference to an American "society" and by theories of a "civil religion."

If one assumes, for instance, that that whole "society" exists or that there is a civil religion in America, particular details or incidents, e.g. religious symbols on national currency or at national memorial ceremonies, are more likely to appear to be authentic expressions of that universe of meaning. The burden of proof then rests upon those who claim that such speech is inauthentic: i.e., that it claims to represent a whole but actually expresses the private and partial interests of the speaker. . . . just such a burden is often assumed by groups whose interests and values are in conflict with other groups

Richard K. Fenn is Professor of Sociology at the University of Maine, Orono.

Reprinted from Richard K. Fenn, *Toward a Theory of Secularization.* SSSR Monograph Series, No. 1, with permission of the Society for the Scientific Study of Religion and the author.

which legitimate their actions by references to a majoritarian viewpoint. A prime example would be the attack by Black Muslims on the synthesis between Protestant Christianity and the individualistic ethos in American society which justifies making the individual responsible for the ills of poverty and discrimination. According to that view, poverty is due to sin rather than to unjust social processes and institutions. The Black Muslims have therefore seriously challenged the assumptions which have given the appearance of legitimacy to American institutions and practices. Dawson's (1958:204) point is well taken that groups and individuals which are alienated "from the dominant culture and the religion that is associated with it . . . inevitably undermine the existing synthesis of religion and culture and tend, often unconsciously and unintentionally, towards the secularization of culture."

Thus, the use of religious symbols in a secularizing society generates as well as allays questions about the nature of the whole. If there were an overarching national religion to which large numbers, even a majority of the nation, subscribed, such questions might not be raised. One would understand the politician's oath or blessing as an individual expression of widely shared religious commitments. But such is not the case in America. One historian notes, for instance, that Lincoln's use of religious themes in his addresses, however sincere he may have been, is largely idiosyncratic: not, in other words, sufficient evidence around which to base an argument that a "civil religion" integrates American society (Wilson 1974). An English sociologist observes that in the later stages of secularization, the use of religious symbols by a national politician simply indicates a difference in personal style or the canny political manipulation of religious images for political gain (B. Wilson 1976). Still another political analyst, writing of the use of Marxist themes by *Soviet* politicians, fails to take symbols seriously; Brezinski's comments would apply as well to the use of religious themes by American political institutions and leaders. Speaking of the political use of Marxist terms in contemporary Russia, he (1970:153) states:

This is a manifestation common to all doctrines in their intellectual decline. As practice increasingly deviates from prescription, symbolism and rhetoric gain in importance.

Religious symbols are taken seriously when they clearly and authoritatively rest upon or refer to a larger whole. Catholicism, for instance, claims that its truth rests upon and refers to what is true for all men, at all times and in all places. Attempts to debunk the Church's ideology therefore point to the particular religious, political, or social interests served by statements or policies of the Church. In the same way, when a political leader uses religious symbols, as in the case of Lincoln, the symbols enter the speaker's claim to be taken seriously: to be speaking for the societal whole. Lincoln claimed that he was speaking for the Union as a whole rather than as a fragmented set of warring factions. When a sociologist takes Lincoln seriously, moreover, it is not only because he believes Lincoln to be sincere; many might agree on that point. But in the case of Robert Bellah (1975:52), it is because the sociologist believes that Lincoln is speaking the religious language of the American nation; that he is articulating the symbols of belief and value which state the nation's underlying purpose and identity. When a social historian enters a debunking comment, therefore, it is one which says that Lincoln, however sincere, is speaking not for a collectivity such as the nation but for an elite, a region, or merely for himself. In the process of secularization,

therefore, doubt about religious symbols is stimulated by doubt concerning the whole which underlies or is represented by certain religious symbols. *The "civil religion" is more likely to be seen as a cultural fiction to the extent that the nation itself seems to be merely an arena for the conflicting and cooperative activities of the classes, ethnic groups, large corporations, and various organizations which pursue their ideals and their material interests under rules enunciated and enforced by the state.*

The awareness of a social whole then lends credence to religious symbols that express that underlying unity, and they in turn lend authority to those who use the religious symbols. Conversely, religious symbols, when used authoritatively, may also supply a sense of unity and wholeness to a particular society. A civil religion is precisely such an authoritative metaphor for the nation's underlying values and commitments. It is a metaphor because it speaks of a social system in terms that are appropriate only to the individual, terms of sacrifice and fidelity, birth and death. Whenever it is said that an organization or society "wills," "decides," "acts," "intends," "believes," or "hopes," such a metaphor is in progress. For instance, the terms appropriate to defining popular religious beliefs and actions are extended to the nation and become a metaphor frequently used on solemn national occasions and in political campaigns, i.e., a "civil religion." While there are Constitutional guarantees against giving the metaphor the force of state action, the Supreme Court has on occasion legitimated its decisions by reference to the "Christian" or "religious" convictions of the American people (Burkholder 1974:27–50).

Such official use of religious symbols, however, encourages opposition and resistance. In considering the "fourth" step in the secularization process, I will note how state action of this sort may be opposed by religious sects with deviant viewpoints or by individuals and groups engaged in a non-religious defense of basic rights. The presence of these contradictions raises questions about the cultural whole allegedly constituted by the nation, just as the political use of the religious symbols raises questions about the seriousness or authenticity of the speaker's commitments. But so long as the nation is spoken of as adhering to a national faith which is expressed in many of the dominant themes and symbols of the Judeo-Christian tradition, the metaphor reinforces the conviction that the nation is a whole which is more than the sum of its parts and which transcends whatever contradictions among the parts may exist. The conflict between a secular state and religious sects may be masked or transcended therefore, in a religious culture imputed to the nation as a willing and believing whole.

Secularization is therefore a process that undermines certain traditional bases of social authority. From the first work of Weber and Durkheim, sociological theory has clearly understood that secularization develops chronic conflict and uncertainty in modern societies regarding the sources of legitimate authority. If, as Weber indicates, secularization dissolves traditional cultural wholes, religious symbols invoking those lost unities will be little more than "ersatz": inauthentic substitutes for lost relationships. Durkheim's "mythic" solution . . . is to make axiomatic what secularization makes problematical: the underlying cultural unity which legitimates the authority of the society as a whole. But a dynamic theory of secularization necessarily allows for the dissolution of any hypothetical cultural unity in order to account for widespread uncertainty regarding the grounds and limitations of secular political and social authority. We have already considered several contemporary social theorists who argue persuasively against the notion that modern social systems depend on underlying or "latent" cultural uniformities; and there are some who are beginning to suggest that even the notion of a social system comprising a single structure of complex and interdependent social relationships imposes more integration than the facts of modern social life will warrant. Under these conditions it is logical to speak of secularization as leading eventually toward the "death of society." . . .

References

Robert N. Bellah, *The Broken Covenant* (New York: Seabury Press, 1975).

Zbigniew Brezinski, *Between Two Ages: America's Role in the Technetronic Era* (New York: Viking Press, 1970).

John Burkholder, "The Law Knows No Heresy," in *Religious Movements in Contemporary America*, edited by Mark Leone and Irving Zaretsky (Princeton: Princeton University Press, 1974), pp. 27–50.

Christopher Dawson, *Religion and the Rise of Western Culture* (Garden City: Doubleday, 1958).

Bryan Wilson, *The Noble Savage* (Berkeley: University of California Press, 1976).

John Wilson, "The Status of 'Civil Religion' in America," in *American Civil Religion*, edited by Russell E. Richey and Donald G. Jones (New York: Harper & Row, 1974).

A D D I T I O N A L   R E A D I N G S

Articles

Coleman, John A. "Civil Religion." *Sociological Analysis* 31 (1970):67–77. American civil religion is differentiated from political and religious institutions. Such is not the case, the author maintains, in civil religious patterns in other countries. A very suggestive article.

Hoge, Dean R. "Theological Views of America among Protestants." *Sociological Analysis* 37(1976):127–39. This entire issue is devoted to civil religion with comments on Robert N. Bellah's work.

Robbins, Thomas; Anthony, Dick; Doucas, Madeline; and Curtis, Thomas. "The Last Civil Religion: Reverend Moon and the Unification Church." *Sociological Analysis* 37(1976):111–12.
Smidt, Corwin. "Civil Religious Orientations among Elementary School Children." *Sociological Analysis* 41(1980):25–40. Orientations toward civil religion are learned early and held by a large proportion of elementary school children.

Books

Bellah, Robert N., and Hammond, Phillip E., eds. *Varieties of Civil Religion.* San Francisco: Harper & Row, 1980. Bellah's thinking on civil religion has developed since his original essay, as his contributions here show. The editors also contribute pieces on civil religion in other countries as well as comment on the relationship of the new religions in America to civil religion.
Gehrig, Gail. *American Civil Religion: An Assessment.* Monograph Series, no. 3. Storrs, Conn: Society for the Scientific Study of Religion, 1981. An excellent bibliographical essay with the author's own concluding assessment of the future of American civil religion.
Richey, Russell E., and Jones, Donald G., eds. *American Civil Religion.* New York: Harper & Row, 1974. Classic essays by Sidney E. Mead, Will Herberg, and W. Lloyd Warner, among others, make this a useful set of readings.
Warner, William Lloyd. *The Family of God: A Symbolic Study of Christian Life in America.* New Haven: Yale University Press, 1961. The integrative role of family and religious symbols and their intertwining in American culture.

Cross-cultural References

The Gehrig volume listed above has a section on cross-cultural civil religious themes; likewise the Bellah and Hammond volume also contains essays dealing with other countries' civil religions.
McDowell, Jennifer. "Soviet Civil Ceremonies." *Journal for the Scientific Study of Religion* 13 (1974):265–79. Public and private ceremonies are examined in the context of state-sponsored rituals versus the older religious rituals they are designed to replace.
Markoff, John, and Regan, Daniel. "The Rise and Fall of Civil Religion: Comparative Perspectives." *Sociological Analysis* 42 (1981):333–52. The authors maintain that modern civil religions fail in their integrative task in certain circumstances. They examine postrevolutionary France, Malaysia, and other national expressions of civil religion.
Regan, Daniel. "Islam, Intellectuals and Civil Religion in Malaysia." *Sociological Analysis* 37 (1976):95–110.

Two

Religious Organization

3

Mainstream Protestantism

"The trouble with organized religion is. . . . " However one may finish that sentence, it is certainly not meant to be complimentary, telling us that the mere fact of organization stifles religion's true spirit. But churches *are* organizations and could not continue or survive for long unless they were. It adds to our understanding of churches to look at them as organizations, sharing problems and dilemmas with other such human groupings. Social scientists suggest we look at organizations not just as "charts" of positions and authority lines but more dynamically, as "open systems" receiving "inputs" from their environments and selecting certain of these for processing into "outputs." Some outputs are then converted back into resources (such as capital goods), which help renew the original inputs. This approach helps explain how a system may—or may not—remain stable over time, for organizations have varying success (or luck?) in coping with their outside and inside settings. *Four* factors are usually identified in open-systems theory:[1]

1. *The environment.* Churches almost always experience some tension with their environments. In fact tension is a major concept in the view of some contemporary sociologists toward sectarian groups (see Chapter 4). But all religious groups—churches, denominations, sects, cults—must face the problem of legitimating themselves with the larger society and, in particular, with the state (note the struggles of the Unification Church or "Moonies" in recent years). All must deal with cultural changes in the larger society that affect how their members view the world (the "moral permissiveness" of our day). And all must deal with competitors for membership. Churches moving to the suburbs find themselves facing different sets of issues than their counterparts remaining in the inner

city. Continuity and stability depend on how these issues are resolved or at least managed over time.

2. *Resources.*   We are dealing with ideas, people, and materials. What does an organization stand for and stand by? Churches have theologies and belief systems. They attempt to inculcate these in the hearts and minds of their congregations. But not all ideas and ideals "go over." Conflict can arise over liberal versus conservative doctrines and their interpretations. If conflict is severe enough and cannot be resolved, groups may split off from the "mother church" and form their own band of faithful followers. "People" can be translated into person-resources. How bring new members in? From where recruit clergy if their number is diminishing? Should women be ordained or be in the ministry at all? What kinds of role conflicts do clergy experience? Material support usually refers to the collection plate, and numerous factors can affect how much is put into it: Are clergy taking unpopular stands on certain issues? Are services appealing to the congregation or to particular segments of it, say, teenagers? Structure enters here, too (see paragraph 4 below): Is income dependent solely on local membership giving, or do higher-level (regional, national) agencies also contribute, and if so, what percentage?

3. *Processes.*   Efficient buying and selling of goods and services is the hallmark of any well-run store or shop. Churches' "business" is the transforming of people's ideas, outlooks, and moral behavior. But *how* this is done—and how well—varies widely. *Teaching*, then, is a central communicative process in churches. But variation is to be expected. The more conservative churches or synagogues may hold their clergy accountable for teaching as a central function. The more liberal or "less strict" churches may expect expressive roles like counseling and emotional support. Recruitment and retention of new members are key processes, of course. In fact, all the processes mentioned can be viewed as *control* techniques or strategies, aimed at maximizing predictability and reducing uncertainties in these areas as much as possible.

4. *Structure.*   Words like specialization, centralization, authority, and standardization are central here. To what extent is the church's mission divided into specialized tasks? If it is divided into many, a central administrative structure usually emerges to coordinate the various activities and missions. Policies enacted reflect the structure of governance. Consider the churches involved in the civil rights movement of the 1960s and early 1970s: Congregationally controlled churches were often much less free to take stands than churches controlled by regional and national policy-making bodies. Similarly the structural location of clergy may favor or muffle radical tendencies: Some denominations "segregate" their "radical" clergy in posts such as university chaplaincies, where they can advocate change without upsetting middle-of-the-road parishioners.

"Instrumental rationality" appears as a tendency, particularly in larger churches and synagogues. The phrase refers to the "packaging" of "sacred experiences" in standardized forms such as sacramental rituals, catechisms, syllabi in seminaries, and fixed ordination procedures. The problem is that the *forms* can become sacralized and their meaning or spirit dampened, even lost. Possibilities of adaptation are foreshortened. Centralizing of power can make decisions easier but runs the risk of leaving in its wake conservatism, even apathy in the rank and file; or it can stir resentment over usurpation of power. None of these developments—specialization, centralization, standardization, and so on—are evils in themselves. Whether they inhibit or forward the work of church or temple depends upon how they are utilized and controlled with a view toward the church's fundamental mission (or missions).

The readings in this chapter deal with the more organizationally complex American and Canadian denominations. Structure and process, though usually not labeled as such, are central concerns in these readings. Canadian sociologist Harold Fallding looks at these larger denominations in both countries, first on the macro level of social structure. Canadian and American mainline churches have played differing roles in the formation of their respective national states, due mainly to the contrasting structures of governance in the two countries. Civil religion as a theme, adapted to the distinct character of the two nations, comes round again. These differences have also had a bearing on religious liberty in the two countries. Fallding's excellent discussion of the different outcomes of the struggle for liberty—mainly to prevent a formerly privileged denomination from becoming "established" (state-sponsored and protected) at the expense of others—helps explain why, in most Canadian provinces, taxpayers may designate education taxes for support of church schools. The struggle for similar arrangements (tuition vouchers, for example) continues today in the United States with the outcome seriously in doubt.

The remainder of Fallding's article illustrates how the larger churches in both countries pursued their goals as reflected in social teachings, pastoral ministry, and doctrinal statements. Four periods of history are sketched. Open-systems concepts are plainly visible though not explicitly mentioned. Resources and environments are also emphasized. City churches in both countries found themselves in the bewildering environment of rapid industrialization during the nineteenth century. They saw its consequences: "great social injustice, inequality, suffering, and want." The big denominations adapted, in somewhat different ways, to these challenges at the time and through the subsequent historical periods singled out. In our own day, the charismatic movement and relativistic morality are challenges currently confronting the churches. Not least important, in Fallding's view, is that mainline Protestantism, in wanting to influence the public life of the nation, has unwittingly opened the door for sectarian groups—since in order to *influence* the larger society, "religious initiative" must be unimpeded—and impeded it will be should any one church be favored by secular powers that be.

"Why Conservative Churches Are Still Growing" makes clear that some churches are growing today while others are losing membership or just breaking even. Why? Dean M. Kelley, a researcher for the National Council of Churches, had earlier identified the so-called "liberal churches," such as the United Presbyterian, United Methodist, and Episcopalian, as those losing members; while the Southern Baptists, Mormons, Jehovah's Witnesses, Seventh-Day Adventists, and others were gaining in numbers.[2] Kelley maintained that the latter churches provided meaning by insistently preaching the gospel and by not forsaking this "comforting function" to emphasize the prophetic or social-change oriented stance characterizing the mainline churches now losing members. In this update of his main theme, Kelley relies on a survey of laity and clergy in both the United States and Canada to elaborate further: It's not that the laity do not wish their clergy to engage in or preach social action; it's just that they don't want them doing these things *to the exclusion of* pastoral and comfort-bringing activities. Moreover, it is not the *content* of doctrine preached that makes one "meaning system" more convincing to a congregation than another. The key element is the quality of seriousness or "strictness," translated into "it will cost you to belong to this congregation." The "ecumenical" or large, mainline churches do not seem to approach their congregations in this way. Kelley says that people fall away from them because they don't see them as "very serious, and therefore not very convincing." Again we see an excellent example of basic open-systems concepts. Boundary structures clearly defined and doctrine firmly preached seem necessary to retain members in a voluntary association of believers when there is little else to coerce them to remain.

Kelley alludes in his conclusion to the United Presbyterian study on which the next reading is based. Perry and Hoge attempt to test one of Kelley's hypotheses, that "conservative theology and avoidance of social action are conducive to growth." The Presbyterian congregations studied do not seem to bear this out. No significant relationships occur between demands upon members, conservative theology, and evangelism on the one hand; and growth or stagnation on the other. So other environmental factors, external or internal, must be at work. Kelley notes these results in his concluding remarks but states that membership standards are only *one* criterion of strictness (Perry and Hoge do not ask, for example, how strict respondents' churches are about financial contributions and activities required, and it is not within their purpose to do so). This reading provides a fine example of how survey methods are utilized by sociologists of religion. It also emphasizes the importance of empirical evidence in assessing the strength or weakness of seemingly plausible explanations.

Theodore Caplow relies on recent and intriguing research (part of a 50-years-later follow-up of a classic community study) on Middletown, U.S.A. (actually Muncie, Indiana). He reviews the evidence for secularization, a term more fully discussed in the Concluding Postscript. Its use here reflects a common understanding: the extent to which individuals can "look upon the world and their own lives without the benefit of religious interpretation," as Peter Berger defines it in the Caplow selection. Religion as practiced by Muncie's church members, Protestant and Catholic, has changed very little; it is still very much a part of the cultural fabric. We see in this reading a continuation of the main theme of Chapter 2, religion as integrating force. What will be its future? Caplow's concluding sentence is indicative. The future will probably find the town's religion very much like past and present, "archaic, fragmented, and wonderfully untroubled." Chapters 7 and 8 will portray religious institutions in a much different role.

Notes

1. This chapter introduction is based largely on James Beckford, *Religious Organization: A Trend Report and Bibliography* (The Hague: Mouton, 1975). Adapted with permission of the author and the International Sociological Association.
2. Dean M. Kelley, *Why Conservative Churches Are Growing* (New York: Harper & Row, 1972), pp. 17–35.

READING 3.1

Mainline Protestantism in Canada and the United States of America: An Overview

Harold Fallding

When we attend to both likenesses and differences in comparing American and Canadian Protestantism, a striking fact emerges. It seems to be more in the impact made by Protestantism on the society that differences appear. When we look at the way Protestantism goes about pursuing its own goals, we find that much the same thing is done in the two countries. This supplies interesting evidence of the way a cultural system can override national divisions. Yet it is difficult to speak with any confidence about sameness or difference in many of the matters this paper will touch on, simply because of the unevenness in the data available. Where there is no indication in the literature of any difference in a particular matter, one is prone to assume the two countries alike. Yet it may simply indi-

Harold Fallding is Professor of Sociology at the University of Waterloo, Ontario.

Reprinted from *The Canadian Journal of Sociology* 3 (Spring 1978) with permission.

cate a lack of documentation. Let us, in any case, divide the analysis into two parts. First, Protestantism's impact on society will be examined, and in two aspects: (1) its role in nation making, and (2) the measures it has taken to secure religious liberty. Then its internal life will be examined by considering the adaptations it has made in three major areas: (1) social teachings, (2) evangelistic and pastoral ministry, and (3) doctrinal instruction.

Protestantism's Impact on the Society

The supreme requirement for keeping comparative research from nonsense is for things to be compared to the instances of the same thing. Giant United States with its distinct civilization and world leadership scarcely seems the same thing as modest Canada. Yet they are both independent, sovereign nations, and it is as such that they become candidates for comparison. At the same time, much of the difference in the religion of the two nations is the only to be expected result of their difference in scale. For, to the nearest million, America's population stood at 203 million in 1970, Canada's at 22 million in 1971. Not that mere numbers of people make such a difference, but what they can accomplish together does. Its numbers have allowed the United States an elaboration of life and culture that makes it recognizably its own civilization, but I doubt that this could be claimed for Canada. It is to this difference that we can attribute, for instance, the lower level of theological productivity in Canada. For Canada has no Reinhold Niebuhrs or Paul Tillichs to offer us. Rather, the religious leaders Canada celebrates, men like Laval, Strachan, Ryerson, Aberhart, Coady and Vanier, have been men of action devising forms of organization to implement received ideas. To this difference of scale we can also attribute, at least in part, the greater proliferation of new religious movements in the United States and the greater sectarian diversity.

1. Protestantism's Role in Nation Making

The two nations' different ideas of national mission have, however, had the same determining importance as scale. For, from the first, but especially from the time of the revolutionary war, the United States has been dedicated to distinctive nationhood, and it came in time to include world leadership under that mission. This has made it essentially innovating culturally. Canada, by contrast, is essentially a colonial development— although I mean colonial in the best sense: the extension, missionizing sense of taking a metropolitan culture to some new place. I do not believe Canada has ever found reason to repudiate this colonial character, even though it repudiated dependent colonial status. Canada remains a traditional society dedicated to consolidating in North America the British and French cultural traditions and, to a lesser extent, some other European traditions as well. The "diversity" on which Canadians sometimes pride themselves—the "mosaic"—is a diversity of that sort. This Canadian attachment to whence-we-came rather than where-we're-going is epitomized in the official philosophy of multiculturalism in contrast to the melting-pot philosophy that eventually came to the fore in the United States. The chronically resurgent, though at times tongue-in-cheek Quebec nationalism, is simply the kind of outcome that must be expected from that Canadian philosophy.

Canada struggled zealously for political independence from the parent authority, but this was a matter of achieving independence in the copy. The more faithful the copy they could make in North America of British and French institutions, the greater was the proof that Canadians could manage on their own. The more faithful this copy, likewise, the greater resistance they would offer to conquest by or absorption into the American political system. And that also is a concern that Canadians developed quite early. Saying this is not denying that adaptations were made to suit the vastly different conditions. It is merely to underline the fact that the Canadian idea was to live off a cultural inheritance.

But not only did the United States set distinctive nationhood before it, a religious component was integral with that self-conception. There is a sense in which it could be said that the nation was founded for religion's sake and even for Protestantism's sake. For the settlers were seeking religious freedom, and yet not only that. They also sought to establish an economy and polity, a science, technology and learning that would give expression to their Protestant belief. That they succeeded in taking leadership in these spheres and maintaining it is sufficiently evidenced, I think, in the research of people like the Beards (1934; 1939; 1957), Handlin (1952; 1954), Merton (1957:574–606), Baltzell (1966) and Lenski (1963). This religiously motivated public participation generated its own religious expression, and it became sufficiently autonomous for Bellah (1970: Chapter 9) to consider it a religious system in its own right now—he calls it "civil religion." This civil religion expressed the conviction that in public and cultural affairs men and women are pursuing the will of God. Because of that, Bellah claims, this civil religion is more distinctively Protestant than it is distinctively Christian even. He considers that John Kennedy, the first Catholic president, continued to give faithful expression to it, as is evident in his inaugural address. Bellah states:

That this very activist and noncontemplative conception of the fundamental religious obligation, which has been historically associated with the Protestant position, should be enunciated so clearly in the first major statement of the first Catholic president seems to underline how deeply established it is in the American outlook (Bellah, 1970: p. 172).

Canada's own variety of civil religion is different from this. It consists in the religious legitimation of sovereignty, a practice which it has inherited from Britain. The American civil religion sanctifies the future to be built whereas the Canadian civil religion upholds the authority established. The American civil religion is practiced apart from the churches, not in opposition to them, but as a kind of religious supplement. The civil religion of Canada is sponsored by the churches, but mainly today by the Anglican, Presbyterian and United, which churches perpetuate the nationality loyalty of the formerly established church in Britain. It is mainly a matter of supporting government and offering prayers for its success in securing order and justice. Since the ruling monarch is charged with defending the Christian faith and made head of the Church of England, the nation thus declares itself officially Christian and under Christ. Yet it is important to note that it is through coronation by a Protestant church that this subordination of political to religious authority is effected. It could not be said of Canada's civil religion, then, that its distinctiveness is more Protestant than Christian. But it could be said that Canada is made officially Christian through machinery set up in the Protestant church to give effect to the Protestant norm of the church-state relationship.

But Protestantism made more than this formal contribution to nationhood. The Anglican, Presbyterian and Methodist churches probably contributed as much to the consolidation of national unity in Canada as any other force operating immediately before and after confederation. Because their memberships reached into all sections of society and all regions of the country they had an interest in securing that unity, as Gwynne-Timothy (1968) has pointed out. Futhermore, as he also shows, the Anglicans' and Methodists' political concerns were translated fairly directly into the formation and policies of the Conservative and Liberal parties respectively. In these ways, then, more obliquely perhaps than in the United States, Protestantism offered its contribution to nation making. It seems it also assisted by offering the leadership for Canada's industrial development. At least it is the prevalent view that this was so, and in Quebec especially (Porter, 1965:91–98). If greater wealth allows greater social influence, Protestants may also have had greater influence because of this. Census tract data on median incomes in five widely separated Canadian cities showed higher incomes to be associated with Protestantism (Porter, 1965:98–103). Thus we have evidence in Canada just as in the United States of Protestants' public leadership, stemming from their activist understanding of religion. For it is, for them, not a thing apart, and must include economic, political and cultural expression.

I take it that the special point of observations like those of Herberg (1960) and Lenski (1963) is to show that religious traditions created communities *within* a society. To be Protestant, Catholic or Jew is to be socialized to a distinct subculture of a distinct community, and this will determine a great many traits, some of which seem to have little to do with religion directly. Thus they see the United States made a plural society now on the basis of religion overwhelmingly. This base has quite eclipsed ethnicity in generating cohesion and identity. Yet no society can exist at all simply as a plurality of communities standing as separate pillars. If there *is* a society we will find an integrating structure where community members come out of their enclaves and meet, and this is supplied by the economy and polity. It seems that entry into this public domain may be easier for one religious group than another because of the very nature of the religion it practices. I find it hard to set aside the conventional wisdom that sees Protestantism to have had an advantage here in propelling its people into public leadership. The recent disparagement of the WASP in North America must have something in it of the mixture of resentment and envy that we always heap on successful leaders.

2. The Measures Taken to Secure Religious Liberty

The innovating orientation of the United States is further evident in the way Protestantism went about securing religious liberty, thereby opening a door to sectarianism. The people were freed to experiment with a variety of religious movements that are quite distinctively American in character—even though they might prove to be exportable in the long run. Mormonism, Christian Science, Seventh Day Adventism, Disciples of Christ, Assemblies of God, Jehovah's Witnesses, and the American variety of Baptists—these are truly indigenous. Yet America's great religious diversity is mainly due to the welcome its religious freedom sounded to sects arising elsewhere—and not only to sects, for traditionalists like Catholics and Jews also responded. Elmer Clark (1965) counted over 400 sects in the United States a quarter of a century ago. The 1976 *Yearbook of American and Canadian Churches* (Jacquet, 1976) gives membership counts for 223 distinct religious bodies in the United States, as against only sixty-three in Canada. Yet we do have to get this in perspective. Most of the current American church membership is concentrated in a smaller number of these denominations, Westhues' (1976c: Table 1) table showing 87 percent of it to fall in 21 of them. Canada seems to have been just as willing as the United States to admit sects from elsewhere, although it cannot claim responsibility for starting a great many. But in Canada the church membership is even more concentrated than in the States, Westhues' (1976c: Table II) table on this showing 87 percent of it to fall within three denominations.

In both countries the Roman Catholics are the largest single body. In Canada they make between 40 and 50 percent of all churched people, in the United States between 30 and 40 percent. They are only outnumbered if the non-Roman Catholics are aggregated. As Figures 1 and 2 show, the very composition of

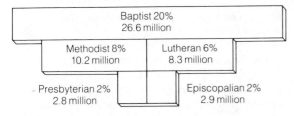

Figure 1. Scale diagram of the composition of mainline Protestantism in the United States (N = 131.2 million).

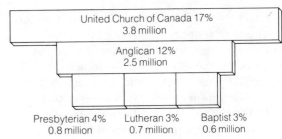

Figure 2. Scale diagram of the composition of mainline Protestantism in Canada. (Membership numbers are rounded to the nearest hundred thousand, percentages to the nearest one percent. The percentage figure (and box volumes) are rough ways of comparing the distribution of adherence to a core of religious denominations in the two countries. They are, however, calculated on different bases. Those for the U.S.A. in Fig. 1 are percentages of the total of all church memberships reported in the *1975 Yearbook of American and Canadian Churches*. Those for Canada in Fig. 2 are percentages of the religious affiliations reported to the 1971 Census of Canada.)

mainline Protestantism is quite different for the two countries. In Canada it means the United Church predominantly and then the Anglican church, with the Presbyterians, various Lutherans and various Baptists supplying a rather trailing tail. In the United States mainline Protestantism means the various Baptists overwhelmingly. (Twenty-four separate Baptist bodies contribute to the Baptist membership totalled from the *Yearbook.*) Then come the Methodists and various Lutherans, each of whom are less than half as numerous as the Baptists; and a trailing tail is supplied by the Presbyterians and Episcopalians. This means that American mainline Protestantism has a much greater admixture of the radical reformation. Or, to say it in another way, Canadian Protestantism is more directly derived from Roman Catholicism.

To me it seems significant that the important Protestant initiative in Canada took a different direction from sect formation—virtually an opposite one. I refer to the amalgamation in one United Church of Canada of Methodists, Presbyterians, Congregationalists, and Evangelical United Brethren, and the serious contemplation over thirty years of a merger between this United Church and the Anglican Church, as well as the more recent plan to incorporate the Churches of Christ in the union. I call this significant because the pursuit of union, as opposed to sectarian schism, can itself be viewed as a distillation of tradition. More essential than any of its distinctive expressions was Protestantism it-

self, and this movement represented a reaching back to a kind of Protestantism in general. To effect a union is to make a radical change, of course, and it is therefore not surprising that the initiative for this reorganization came from the more liberal and radical members of the churches concerned. But it was essentially an organizational change, and at the deeper cultural level it scarcely represented innovation. The very trite and conventional rehash of Protestant doctrine in the Articles of Union bears this out.

Protestantism's championship of religious liberty caused its less advantaged sections to oppose church establishment. This crusade had to be waged internal to Protestantism on occasion, since Protestant churches have themselves enjoyed establishment. In both Canada and the United States the anti-establishment movement won successes, but it is interesting to compare the different reasons for this and the different means taken and results achieved. Discussion of this question always suffers from the imprecision in the very notion of establishment, of course. To me it seems most usefully employed when it means that one or more religious organizations receive privileges from the state that are not enjoyed by the other religious organizations. Essentially then it refers to a monopoly, but it can be a monopoly in very diverse things.

In the United States, of course, the struggle was raised to the constitutional level, this being the culmination of persistent protests against Anglican privilege, coming mainly from Congregationalists, Presbyterians and Baptists (Hudson, 1973:83–105). Yet Congregationalists in the New England colonies swung the balance so successfully that their own privileges also generated resistance. The First, Fifth and Fourteenth Amendments of the Constitution were therefore designed to legally prescribe where religion shall stand in relation to the state. Each citizen has freedom to worship as he may choose and religious organizations are autonomous and equal with one another before the law. The constitution thus implements a principle of separation rather than one of mutually exclusive jurisdictions for church and state. Church and state shall be separately organized expressions of community solidarity, each finding its separate legitimation in the kind of public support it is able to win. It would, however, be rather unsociological to think the constitutional provisions created the religious freedom and toleration for which the United States has become known. Those provisions were expressions of a larger constellation of forces already at work. Moberg (1962) has summarized the observations of a number of authors on this matter. He states:

American religious freedom and toleration are the products of numerous historical factors. Among these factors are the large number and wide variety of competitive sects in the colonies with no established church common to all, the relative indifference to religious interests in the late 18th century because of the distractions of the tremendous opportunities of the expanding economic and social system, Locke's theory that

religion is a purely personal matter, the dominance of Protestantism with its tradition of toleration based upon its emphasis on direct access of the believer to Divine truth through the Bible, the identification of religious freedom with the larger struggle for liberty, the need for settlers which encouraged acceptance of immigrants with various faiths, the looseness of contacts with parental churches in Europe, and even the very small number of Catholics and Jews in America at the time of the Revolution. Frontier revivals emphasized inner spiritual experience and the equality of all in the sight of God, thus accelerating acceptance of "left-wing" Protestantism, which stressed religion as a way of life rather than a creed and upheld individualistic political doctrines that supported church-state separation. Out of such influences has come the "great tradition of the American churches," the voluntary principle of church support which is a corollary of constitutional separation of church and state. (Moberg, 1962: 369–70)

In Canada, things were resolved differently, although similar background factors favoring a greater freedom of thought and practice have also been noted. We will see that Canada's resolution of the issue was more *ad hoc* and piecemeal. It seems more in keeping with the traditional British way of proceeding, whereas the American action was a doctrinaire, ideological clean sweep. Yet that action, like most actions of its kind, scarcely swept as clean as was hoped. Privileges for the Roman Catholic church in Maryland and Louisiana were not easily removed; and other local privileges persisted.

It was in Ontario—then Upper Canada— that the character of Canada's dominant Protestantism was forged, and it was there that the question of church establishment was decisively resolved. Anglicanism had come into Canada enjoying the establishment it had enjoyed in England, yet this was continuously eroded. It was established in Nova Scotia, but freedom of religion and worship were legally secured for other Protestants at the same time. Because of the hostile relations between Britain and France, the French-Acadian Catholics were penalized and prohibited from owning land up till such time as the French threat abated in 1783. On the other hand, the Quebec Act of 1774 established the Roman Catholic church among the French Canadians of Quebec, whose Catholic parish is recognized in law, and in that *fait accompli* Canadian Protestantism has virtually acquiesced.

The established status accorded to Anglicanism in Nova Scotia was extended through the maritime provinces and into Lower and Upper Canada. But in Upper Canada it was resisted and defeated. It was mainly the Methodists there who opposed it, and the fact that the Anglicans comprised only a sixth to a fifth of the population partly explains their defeat. The main privileges that provoked resistance were the Anglicans' control of education and the lands set aside to endow the established church known as the Clergy Reserves (Walsh, 1968:173–6, 195–8). There were two distinct groups of Methodists in Upper Canada. They derived from Britain and the United States respectively, the latter being much the more numerous and influential—and they were under suspicion of disloyalty to the Crown. But it was they who sponsored the successful movement to abolish establishment for the Anglicans, whereas the British Methodists were inclined to defer to Anglican establishment as their brethren respectfully did in the home country.

Probably the most interesting outcome in Canada of all the inter-church jostling to exclude one another from privilege is the arrangement reached in five of the provinces for financing church schools. The situation in Quebec, Ontario, Newfoundland, Alberta, and Saskatchewan comes near to establishment for the Roman Catholic church, since it is only that church that makes provision for separate education on a large scale. While Christian Reformed, Seventh Day Adventist, Mennonite, and other non-Roman Catholics exploit these same arrangements, their numbers are very few by comparison. Since, under the arrangement, property holders *must* pay education taxes to the local authority but *may choose* to designate it for the support of church schools, you have in effect a public collection of money for the support of non-public schools. In the other provinces, excepting for British Columbia, other arrangements have also involved a degree of public support (Weir, 1934; Sissons, 1959; Clark, L., 1968; Westhues, 1976a; 1976b). In this form of establishment for the Roman Catholics Canadian Protestants seem also to have acquiesced. Thus the net result of Protestantism's crusade against establishment in Canada has been to deny it to any of its own branches but to leave the Roman Catholics in a generally favored position in Quebec, and in a favored position regarding education in most other provinces as well. So it seems those Protestants might not have been as *sharp* in their public dealings as they were *forward!*

The Internal Life of Protestantism

One of the best ways in which the character of a social institution is revealed is in the adaptations it makes to fluctuating demands in pursuing its goals. So I am making it a method to take note of any salient adaptations. As the reader will recall, adaptations in the following areas are the ones to be examined: (1) social teachings, (2) evangelistic and pastoral ministry, and (3) doctrinal instruction. I shall try to identify the phase of historical development in which each adaptation was manifested.

However, in thus venturing to name historic phases I would want to make clear how I see periodization to operate. To speak of a later phase means to recognize the introduction of some important new influence. But this does not necessarily mean that forces operating previously are extinguished. In a later phase the activity in a society can simply be

Figure 3   *Adaptations in Four Periods in the Internal Life of Protestantism*

Period		Adaptation
Settlement	*Social teaching*	Classical Protestant ethic or life-calling and social responsibility.
	Ministry	Revivalism.
	Doctrine	Classical Reformation teaching.
1865 Industrial expansion	*Social teaching*	Social gospel.
	Ministry	Professional ministry attempted. Missionary expansion. Ecumenicalism launched.
	Doctrine	Liberal theology ("modernism").
1915 Eclipsed national isolation	*Social teaching*	Compromise ethic.
	Ministry	Highly professionalized ministry achieved, with paralysis of the laity. Further missionary expansion. Further ecumenicalism.
	Doctrine	Counter-attack of fundamentalism and neo-orthodoxy.
1960 Secularization	*Social teaching*	Situationalism.
	Ministry	Innovation, spontaneity, charismatics. Repudiation of officialdom and professionalism. Grass roots ecumenicalism.
	Doctrine	Reconstruction theology.

more layered, since earlier practices may continue side by side with the newer ones. I would not think the detection of such survivals invalidates the claim that a new phase has been entered.

Figure 3 summarizes the adaptations noted in the following discussion and shows how I name the periods in which they occur. The indentation of the verticals is intended to diagram the layered character of the periodization.

1. Social Teachings

Protestant social teachings seem to have continued in the tradition of the original reformers and the puritans till around the time of the American Civil War—shall we say 1865. (The corresponding and almost coinciding turning point for Canada is Confederation, which occurred in 1867.) These tradi-

tional teachings encompassed the stress on a life-calling and social responsibility in general that led to the economic, political, and cultural initiative already noted. What change there was, was perhaps a certain vulgarization, in that the populace made the ideals its own and expected egalitarianism in their implementation (Elgee, 1964). The era was the one marked by great frontier activity, and may therefore be called the era of settlement.

After the Civil War a new ingredient was added to Protestant social teachings by the social gospel movement, a movement that peaked in the decade before World War I (Hopkins, 1940). The phase of social development then in train was really the great industrial expansion, and the social gospel movement partook of the evolutionary optimism inherent in that. It expressed a belief that social institutions can be what we choose to make them, and that Christian initiative must therefore be consciously applied there. In particular, since industrialism was entailing great social injustice, inequality, suffering, and want, the economy should be controlled to serve human welfare. Rauschenbusch (1907), the New York City German Baptist pastor, asked for an economy guided by mutual service and cooperation rather than competition in profit-making. His vision of a Kingdom of God established by such means made a kind of Christian alternative to revolutionary socialism. But the detailed blueprints varied from one advocate to another. A small group of self-styled Christian socialists did convene in Boston in 1889, under the leadership of W.P.D. Bliss, yet it seems that the social gospel in the United States did not radically challenge the capitalist system but asked mainly for planning within it. It was in Canada that the more collectivist note was struck.

This same social gospel movement spread through Canada and also peaked there before World War I (Crysdale, 1961; 1976; Allen, 1971; 1975). Yet its long-lasting outcomes were two delayed reverberations. During the depression years of the thirties William Aberhart's Baptist fundamentalism in Alberta drew inspiration from the social gospel and it led him to establish right-wing Social Credit (Irving, 1959; Schultz, 1959; Mann, 1962; Walsh, 1968:317–24; Boudreau, 1975). About the same time in Saskatchewan the Baptist minister Tommy Douglas, similarly inspired by the social gospel, led the Cooperative Commonwealth Federation to conspicuous success (Tyre, 1962; Shackleton, 1975). This was a socialist movement that was to be the precursor of the New Democratic Party.

The great general change of mood that followed the eclipse of the pre-war optimism brought a new emphasis in Protestant social teaching. It was epitomized, I would guess, in the writings of Reinhold Niebuhr (1932; 1943; 1945). Two world wars, a devastating economic depression, Nazism—such developments were stinging reminders of the persistence of sin, and it seemed that a realistic social teaching would be one that did not expect too much in view of that. Rather, it should make the Christian task one of limiting or containing social evils, this to be done by practice in the art of choosing the least evil of all the alternatives present. On such a basis Christians' participation in war, for example, was believed to be justifiable. We may call this the compromise ethic. I have the impression that it was very widely adopted, and probably more wholeheartedly in the United States than in Canada. It accustomed people to living by compromises and with a muddied conscience and clouded discernment. It is possible, as a result, that they were unnecessarily compromised often and too willingly gave themselves to avoidable evil in the belief that by doing so they were avoiding still more. I would suspect that it contributed to a general deterioration in moral discrimination in North America for which Watergate was nothing more than a barometric reading.

The phase of social development marked by this compromise social teaching might be taken to extend from around 1915 to the end of the 1950s—and perhaps we could characterize this as the era of eclipsed isolation. For both the economic and military upheavals of that era showed that the nations of the world are locked in interdependence and cannot hope to build society alone and apart. The compromise ethic at least showed an awareness that the task before the Christians was, for that reason, more complex and long-range than the preceding generation had thought.

With the 1960s something else again hit us, and we are still somewhat dazed by it. What is this phase of social development? How shall we name it? It is marked by a number of distinctive features, but it is hard to capture the essence of them all. It is the era of everybody's bid for power—student power, black power, women's power, gay power. The era of instant protest and instant remedies expected. The era of draft dodging and war resisting. The era of do your own thing. The era of mind your own business—for a sphere of private decisions and judgments is jealously enclosed. The era of everything made new—the new math, the new morality, the new theology. The era of revolutions declared accomplished—the sex revolution, the fitness revolution, the Quebec revolution, Vatican II and the *aggiornamento*. The era of affluence—or at least it was that at first and it is affluence, I would guess, that helped to get it launched. And, notwithstanding the desperate reassertion of the suffocating individual, it is the era of encroaching bureaucracy. Both assured wealth and bureaucratic omniprovidence have lifted people's feet off the ground and made them feel floated. Although its champions might not admit it, as an observer I would add that it is the era of acute unhappiness. This is partly the result of the expectation of instant satisfactions, whereas in fact gratifications only come to us as the products of cooperation over time. We live more happily if we are socialized to expect the delay and find satisfaction in the striving. The unhappiness also results from living too exclusively in one's personal time and place, from severing the wider loyalties that lift us out of ourselves. As a result, for all its urgency and activism, it is the era of inconsequentiality. For the gains made arrive out of any context that would make them meaningful. At times I indulge my fantasy in a surrealist scene of this time in which we live. It consists of an unwed couple who stand all day at the door receiving a stream of packages from Simpsons-Sears' and Eatons' vans and her Majesty's mailman. The packages arrive every minute on the instant, as ordered, and are taken through the wall via the doorway to be stacked in the yard beyond—for there is no house there.

What ethic has Protestantism proposed for this time of empty, impassioned restlessness? The ethic of situationalism. It is abroad in Canada and the United States alike, but more self-consciously so in the United States. This ethic concedes that there is truth in the great sense of relativism that underlies all the contemporary rearranging. What was right for another time and place is not necessarily right for now. What is right for another person is not necessarily right for me. What was right for me last time is not necessarily right for me this time. It all depends on the situation. Perhaps this current ethic is short on naming the general principles that are to be applied, however differently, to all situations. Perhaps it is also too much infected by the sickness it is supposed to help. For its atomizing of personal biography and human history into a series of situations neglects the distinctively religious vision of all situations cohering in a total situation in which, above all, the religions say, we must strive to locate ourselves. Possibly "secularization" is the correct word by which to characterize this era, using the term in the sociological sense of the fragmentation that results from rational differentiation during the interlude before the elements have been drawn into a coherence again. It is the direct outcome of the galloping specialization that catapults people into an endless variety of situations and of the mounting knowledge and communication that make them aware of the extreme relativity of the one they are in. Each one, being in his or her own special place, is impelled to defend his or her own cause—which is what accounts for the new individualism. Yet from their deep recesses individuals signal their willingness to come out if permitted to do so by participatory democracy.

2. Evangelistic and Pastoral Ministry

Now let us turn our attention to the evangelistic and pastoral ministry of the Protestant churches. Have there been distinctive adaptations here in any of the four periods we have now demarcated? The obvious one, of course, is the revivalism of the first period. The American Great Awakening of the eighteenth century, Moberg claims, "fixed the pattern of frontier religion" (Moberg, 1962:440). S.D. Clark (1965:90–172) notes that an evangelistic Methodism, expressed in love-feasts and camp meetings, became the dominant religious force in Upper Canada in the early part of the nineteenth century. These developments might be explained by the needs peculiar to an uprooted, largely frontier population. When conventional moral supports have been stripped away, there is a need for intensified social solidarity, spiritual experience, and moral strictness. American church membership records indicate that large numbers of people did indeed join the Protestant churches in the revival years of the eighteenth and nineteenth centuries (Moberg, 1962:441).

The memory of revivalism has continued with many Protestants, sometimes like a nostalgic sense of authentic religion that ought to be restored. The United Church that I attend in Waterloo, for instance, is far removed in its staidness from revival enthusiasm. Yet it has become standard practice to include a revival hymn in one of the three or four normally sung at a service, as if to affirm that element of the tradition. American churches between them have jointly sponsored a cycle of revival campaigns. In New York City, for instance, there was the Finney campaign in 1832, the Moody campaign in 1876, the Billy Sunday campaign in 1917, and the Billy Graham campaign in 1957. You will note that these recur at roughly forty-year intervals. In part they seem to be born of desperation over the organized churches' impediments to outreach, in part as a welcome means of rejuvenating the churches' own life. Does the forty-year interval indicate an unconscious wish to have every generation exposed at least once to this means of renewal? The greater scale and wealth of the United States means that evangelistic teams have been organized on a larger scale there. Yet these are itinerant, of course, and travel to Canada and other countries. Canada, however, has its own smaller scale

counterparts, such as the Leighton Ford and Marney Patterson teams.

The industrializing and eclipsed isolation periods were marked by attempts to consolidate an ever more qualified and professionalized ministry. Advocated and attempted in the industrializing period, a high degree of it was achieved in the period that followed. Enthusiasm gave way to formalism as charisma was routinized. This went to such an extreme toward the end that Protestant ministers were often bothered by dilemmas over the allocation of their time between very diverse demands (Blizzard, 1956; Campbell and Pettigrew, 1959; Cumming and Harrington, 1963; Hadden, 1969:211–221). Frequently they felt they were being distracted from their essential task—rather in the way that university professors can feel distracted from theirs. For a clergyman had to be a preacher, educator, administrator, group leader, counselor, organization man, prophet and priest—and there seemed to be no limit to the training that could be taken advantage of for doing any one aspect better.

This professionalization of the ministry has tended to confine the work of spiritual ministry to the appointed pastor, even though this is not directly in line with much Protestant theology. Baptists have never defined the pastor as uniquely able to minister to spiritual needs, all believers being called to do this for one another. Methodists from the beginning recognized lay preachers and leaders. Presbyterians considered the church elders to be the spiritual heads of the church, the preaching elder being only one among them. But professionalized ministry has *de facto* excluded the laity more and more from spiritual leadership. They become roustabouts to whom practical tasks are assigned if enough can be found for them; tasks like looking after the finances, singing in the choir, organizing the social evening or teaching in Sunday school. This is where the elders of the United Church of Canada now stand, for instance. Yet the eldership of that church was directly taken over from the Presbyterian conception. As a result of these developments the laity of mainline Protestantism is paralyzed, and this is one of the most arresting features of the state of North American religion in recent times in my opinion. Many of the laity are frustrated, feeling they are made of sterner stuff and called to greater things; the remainder, socialized to things as they are, feel that what they have is all they are entitled to expect, and their interest flags.

Routinizations of charisma other than professionalized ministry followed the eighteenth century revivalism. A zeal for missions was born from this same revivalism. Yet the eighteenth century was almost over before British and North American Protestants were committed to missions and organized for them. Congregational, Baptist and Methodist Episcopal missions were formed in the United States in the early decades of the nineteenth century. Efforts of the kind then gathered such momentum throughout the nineteenth century—there, in Canada and other places as well—that Latourette (1937-45: Vols. 4–6) was able to call it the great century of Christian expansion. But it was an expansion that continued till the middle of the twentieth century. Thus missionary extension coincided with industrial expansion at home and the breakdown of national isolation. Of this latter it was virtually a progenitor, of course.

So also was ecumenicalism—and it was partly missions that made it so. The word "ecumenical" did not take on its current usage till after the World Missionary Conference in Edinburgh in 1910. But the ecumenical movement was well away in the nineteenth century with its interdenominational and international missions, its Sunday school movement, tract societies and American Bible Society, with the formation of the world's Y.M.C.A. in 1878 and the World's Student Christian Federation in 1895. It is interesting that the ecumenical movement has always been as much an international development as an interdenominational one, and a

large part of its support is inspired by that. Its formal organizations crystallized more in Europe than North America, but its two official organs are represented in both Canada and the United States, these being the World Council of Churches and the International Missionary Council. These are bodies that foster cooperation and study in a variety of areas. But there are also separate national bodies. There is a Canadian Council of Churches. And the National Council of the Churches of Christ in the United States comprises twenty-three Protestant and seven Eastern denominations, which have between them a total membership of over 40 million.

In some ways, the organizational ecumenicalism to which this movement succumbed is a dreary, doctrinaire thing, and it has to be distinguished from the more spontaneous grassroots growth of inter-church cooperation. We noticed how Canada witnessed an exceptional development of the latter in the formation of its United Church. But it would be a mistake to ignore the fact that the United States has had its own expressions of grassroots ecumenicalism, the tendency toward sectarian division notwithstanding. Many mergers have occurred there. Lutherans particularly have evinced a tendency to unite again amongst themselves after previously dividing. A number of other denominations are the result of mergers; for example, the Congregationalist Christian Churches, the Evangelical and Reformed Church, the Methodist Church, the Evangelical United Brethren Church, the United Presbyterian Church in the United States, and the United Church of Christ.

Our fourth period—the secularization period—is marked by innovation in ministry. It is probably not true to say that "anything goes"—but almost anything does. Countless novelties have been tried in worship and outreach and preaching and teaching to communicate meaningfully with a population getting ever more submerged in meaninglessness. So rapid is the transformation evident in this time that adopting almost any traditional posture in almost any sphere of life can seem stultified. Church people, like everyone else, have declined to stand on ceremony or insist on conventions when letting them go has restored realism. In a general way, a greater spontaneity has been sought in worship, and it has brought a revival of charismatic expressions in some places. The ordination of women has been accepted. There is also a by-passing of church officialdom and professionalism to some extent, in that lay people are once again prepared to act more on their own initiative and authority. They have, for instance, given direct support to independent publishers, new missions and innovating service groups like World Vision and Bread for the World. Informal house meetings seem to have become commoner, and as often as not have crossed denominational barriers. Thus we have seen mainline Protestants who would have stood apart from it formerly, engaging in nondenominational action with the greatest of relish. This grass-roots ecumenicalism has sometimes involved Roman Catholics, a development facilitated, of course, by the Roman Catholics' new look at Protestantism.

3. Doctrinal Instruction

We have finally to consider the doctrinal instruction of the Protestants, asking whether there is anything distinctive in this in the four periods and the two nations. The really important time to pinpoint here is the entry into the churches of liberal theology, or what is often simply called "modernism." Up until that point in time Reformation or classical Protestant doctrine had continued to prevail. In one respect indeed, there had been a departure from the true originals, from Luther and Calvin; but it concerned the validating of Prostestant belief rather than its content. For the teachers at Princeton Theological Seminary followed the post-Reformation writers Melanchthon, Beza and Turretin, rather than Luther and Calvin, in saying that the Bible's authority meant its literal inerrancy. This view was reinforced by the adoption of the philosophy of Scottish realism at Princeton.

What developed, seemingly as a new thing, in liberal theology had its roots in the enlightened view that Biblical sources must be critically sifted, and that one should try to piece together a doctrine of the nature of Christ by giving greatest weight to the documents that seemed to have the greatest historical validity. Strauss' *Life of Jesus* in 1835 (Strauss, 1860) and Renan's *Life of Jesus* in 1863 (Renan, 1962) were the precursors of an eventual ferment of thought of the same kind, and it occurred during what we have identified as the period of industrial expansion. It accompanied the adoption of the evolutionary perspective of that era as well as the more general perspectives of science. It was in 1898 that the Churchmen's Union was formed in England, having for its aim the advancement of liberal religious thought. Thus the liberal theology era coincides largely with the era of the social gospel ethic and, along with that, it peaked just before the First World War.

From then on the liberal theology was worn down, both by the resistance presented by the fundamentalist movement and from within avant-garde theology itself. The controversy between fundamentalism and modernism reached its height in the 1920s (Carder, 1950; Cole, 1931; Dozois, 1963; Furniss, 1954; Walsh, 1968: 317–24). Many of the sects outside mainline Protestantism supplied the fundamentalist resistance, but much came from within it. This fundamentalism was essentially an expression of populist culture: its leadership came from the less professionalized pastors and training centers and was concentrated in rural areas. It did, however, draw a measure of scholarly support from the Princeton teaching. Its otherworldliness was a protest against the same materialism and popularity-ism that the Hippies protested against forty years later. It is usually characterized as "literalism," and it amounted to an attempt to reinstate a more literal acceptance of Biblical teaching. The tendency in avant-garde theology worked in the same direction, even though it opposed what it identified as extreme fundamentalism. For, what eventually became known as "form criticism" (Koch, 1969) showed that it was futile to seek some pure picture of Jesus apart from the way he appears in the gospels, and that he must be accepted as already "interpreted" through the various forms of thought and expression the writers employed. This return to the Bible, from both left and right as you might say, ushered in the phase in Protestant theology that can be called neo-orthodox. Theology was once again both more Biblical and more in the Protestant tradition. It was less optimistic about man than liberal theology, recognizing once again the widely ramifying effects of sin and the need of grace. This is the theology that characterized the era of eclipsed isolation and it thus coincides with the compromise ethic of that time. German in origin, its impact was most vividly felt in North America in the twenties and thirties. H.W. Schneider (1967) describes its coming in this way:

Systematic lamentations, imported from Germany during the twenties and thirties, descended on America like the voice of doom. After Spengler came Karl Barth, then Emil Brunner, then Karl Jaspers, and Paul Tillich; meanwhile, lamentations in another key were coming from the disciples and translations of Kierkegaard. A new vocabulary, a strange philosophy of history, a sophisticated use of the "Word of God," a trumpeting of transcendent judgment overwhelmed not only the spirit of American complacency but also the voices of American idealism. Thus the atmosphere became charged overnight with apocalyptic judgment (Schneider, 1967:134–5).

A decisive transcending of this kind of doctrine came with the sixties. The new theology was marked by the same relativism as marked the new morality. Dietrich Bonhoeffer's (1954; 1955; 1966; Woelfel, 1970) advo-

cacy of a "religionless" or "secular" Christianity came into its own. Harvey Cox (1965) found the "secular city" where we dwell the fitting scene for its implementation. So secular and religionless had this Christianity to be that some announced that God was "dead." These various startling expressions were clumsy and terribly misleading. I think they were wanting to say that earlier formulations of faith lose their validity with the passage of time—that all things human pass, even human images of the changeless. Not that the living God was dead but that our images of God had faded beyond recognition. These images must be continually reconstituted on the platform to which we have come at the time. Hence the great demand for honesty, as in John Robinson's *Honest to God* (1963). Hence also the great stress on originating activity as a characteristic of God. This is exemplified in the adoption of Whitehead's (1927; 1960) process philosophy and the process theology based on it (Griffin, 1973), in the adoption of Teilhard de Chardin's (1959; 1964) evolutionary vision, and in the adoption of Tillich's (1951–63; 1960) God of the depths from Whom our own actions spring. This is a muted theology that seems embarrassed even to refer to God. Yet I think it is not an embarrassment over God but over language. It arises from the feeling that language is so situation-bound that referring to God in any language save the one the moment breeds is a stultification. Possibly the best name to give it is "reconstruction theology." It is not a denial of the old, old story but an attempt to ensure that its telling will be as new in this crazy time as in any before.

Critical Conclusion

All the transformations we have followed in the second part of this paper were evident in both Canada and the United States. Possibly there was a lag, in that these transformations had their first North American realization in the United States. It seems significant that we have no ready instance of the diffusion going the other way. Possibly their more exaggerated expressions were located in the United States too. Possibly the swings and clashes between them were more violent there also. Yet here I am aware of generalizing on insufficient evidence. One should take time to track down, if possible, the precise truth in that impression.

But what, in conclusion, are we to make of this chameleon Protestantism, this creature that changes with every changing time? We have seen evidence enough that mainline Protestantism is indeed adaptive. At least on the face of it, it seems that both the smaller sects on the one side and the Roman Catholic church on the other, may be more resistant to changing with the times—although this too is only an impression, and one that closer inspection could belie. But if it is true, then the variation in this regard must be one of the most interesting features of North American religion, and one deserving more careful attention.

Some would say that Protestantism is too adaptive, too vacillating to be an authentic Christian expression even. It is, of course, less vacillating than this schematic treatment might suggest, simply because of the persistence through the later periods of the earlier patterns. But this is nevertheless an important critical question, or functional question if you prefer to put it that way—for functional and critical sociology are the same thing to me. (Of course, nothing can be *over*-adaptive in any technical use of the term. To say so is to speak colloquially, implying that it is adaptive at the expense of stability. So the question really ought to be phrased in that way.) Does mainline Protestantism lack the kind of stabilizing that would keep it witnessing to an unchanging truth through changing times? Or is it, alternatively, endowed with the flexibility that allows it to keep that truth relevant by highlighting different elements in it according to the need of the day? Certainly, the way in which Protestantism later repudiates some of its own earlier expressions looks like an admission of error. On the other hand, the fact that the repudiation occurs may indicate the persistence of a constant criterion of truth.

This is altogether too large a question to settle in so sketchy a paper as this. But I would hold it before you as the important critical—or functional—question to be asked. My own inclination is to say that mainline Protestantism is not adaptive at the expense of stability. As I view it, the dynamism of modern culture is to some extent Protestantism's own creation, and Protestantism has then continually to minister to people at the avant-garde positions into which it has propelled them. The propensity for adaptations we noted in the second part of the paper is all one with the Protestant nation making, sectarianism and disestablishment that we noted in the first. All along, Protestantism has wanted a spontaneous religion that is expressed in everyday and public life and the culture of the mind, a religion that is not a thing apart. This is why it has made the creation of nations, amongst other things, a religious mission. Since for that nation making religious initiative must be unimpeded, Protestantism opens the opportunity for sectarianism. Since religious initiative *will* be impeded if any religious organization is advantaged, Protestantism opposes establishment.

A similar evaluation can be made of the wide fluctuations in church life over time—from revivalism to professionalized ministry, for instance, from liberal to neo-orthodox theology, from the social gospel to the compromise ethic, etc. In these developments Protestantism shows itself emboldened to be experimental in religious culture, just as it is experimental in the scientific, technological, economic, and political spheres. In the experimental approach, often, one does not know how far to go till he has gone too far. Some self-correction is involved. Protestantism is apparently unabashed by this fallibility in religion if, through allowing it, it can come closer to where people are. Fallibility in religion is only to be expected, it seems to assume since, as it also assumes, infallibility belongs to God alone.

References

Allen, Richard
1971   The Social Passion. Toronto: University of Toronto Press.
Allen, Richard, ed.
1975   The Social Gospel in Canada. Ottawa: National Museums of Canada.
Baltzell, E. Digby
1966   The Protestant Establishment, Aristocracy and Caste in America. New York: Vintage Books.
Beard, Charles A. and Mary R.
1934   The Rise of American Civilization. Revised one volume college edition. New York: Macmillan.
1939   America in Midpassage. New York: Macmillan.
1957   A Study of the Idea of Civilization in the United States. New York: Macmillan.
Bellah, Robert N.
1970   Beyond Belief, Essays on Religion in a Post-Traditional World. New York: Harper & Row.
Blizzard, Samuel W.
1956   "The minister's dilemma." Christian Century 73:508–10.
Bonhoeffer, Dietrich
1954   Letters and Papers from Prison, edited by Eberhard Bethge, translated by Reginald H. Fuller, revised by Frank Clarke and others. New York: Harper & Row.
1955   Ethics, edited by Eberhard Bethge, translated by Neville Horton Smith. New York: Macmillan.
1966   The Cost of Discipleship. Revised and unabridged edition containing material not previously translated. London: S.C.M. Press.
Boudreau, Joseph A., ed.
1975   Alberta, Aberhart, and Social Credit. Toronto: Holt, Rinehart & Winston of Canada.
Campbell, Ernest Q. and Thomas F. Pettigrew
1959   "Racial and moral crisis: the role of Little Rock ministers." American Journal of Sociology 64:509–16.
Carder, W.C.
1950   "Controversy in the Baptist convention." Thesis, McMaster University.

Clark, Elmer T.
1965   The Small Sects in America. Revised edition. New York: Abingdon Press.
Clark, L.
1968   The Manitoba School Question. Toronto: Copp Clark.
Clark, S.D.
1965   Church and Sect in Canada. Toronto: University of Toronto Press.
Cole, Stewart G.
1931   The History of Fundamentalism. New York: Richard R. Smith.
Cox, Harvey E.
1965   The Secular City. London: S.C.M. Press.
Crysdale, Stewart
1961   The Industrial Struggle and Protestant Ethics in Canada. Toronto: Ryerson Press.
1976   "The sociology of the social gospel: quest for a modern ideology." In Religion in Canadian Society, edited by Stewart Crysdale and Les Wheatcroft, pp. 423–433. Toronto: Macmillan.
Cumming, Elaine and Charles Harrington
1963   "Clergyman as counselor." American Journal of Sociology 69:234–43.
Dozois, John D.E.
1963   "Dr. T.T. Shields (1873–1955), in the stream of Fundamentalism." B.D. Thesis. McMaster University.
Elgee, William H.
1964   The Social Teachings of the Canadian Churches: Protestant, the Early Period, before 1850. Toronto: Ryerson Press.
Furniss, Norman F.
1954   The Fundamentalist Controversy (1918–1931). New Haven: Yale University Press.
Griffin, David R.
1973   A Process Christology. Philadelphia: Westminster Press.
Gwynne-Timothy, John
1968   "The evolution of Protestant nationalism." In One Church, Two Nations? edited by Philip LeBlanc and Arnold Edinborough, pp. 20–53. Don Mills, Ontario: Longmans Canada.
Hadden, Jeffrey
1969   The Gathering Storm in the Churches. New York: Doubleday & Co.
Handlin, Oscar
1952   The Uprooted: The Epic Story of the Great Migrations that made the American People. Boston: Little, Brown.
1954   The American People in the Twentieth Century. Cambridge, Mass.: Harvard University Press.
Herberg, Will
1960   Protestant-Catholic-Jew: An Essay in Ameri-

can Religious Sociology. New York: Doubleday.

Hopkins, Charles H.
1940 The Rise of the Social Gospel in American Protestantism, 1865–1915. New Haven: Yale University Press.

Hudson,Winthrop S.
1973 Religion in America. An Historical Account of the Development of American Religious Life. 2nd edition. New York: Charles Scribner's Sons.

Irving, John A.
1959 The Social Credit Movement in Alberta. Toronto: University of Toronto Press.

Jacquet, C.H., ed.
1976 Yearbook of American and Canadian Churches. Nashville: Abingdon.

Koch, Claus
1969 The Growth of the Biblical Tradition: The Form-Critical Method. Translated from the 2nd German edition by S.M. Cupitt. New York: Scribner.

Latourette, Kenneth Scott
1937–45 A History of the Expansion of Christianity. New York: Harper & Bros.

Lenski, Gerhard
1963 The Religious Factor: A Sociological Study of Religion's Impact on Politics, Economics, and Family Life. Revised edition. New York: Anchor Books, Doubleday & Co.

Mann, W.E.
1962 Sect, Cult and Church in Alberta. Toronto: University of Toronto Press.

Merton, Robert K.
1957 Social Theory and Social Structure. Revised and enlarged edition. Glencoe, Illinois: Free Press.

Moberg, David O.
1962 The Church as a Social Institution. Englewood Cliffs, N.J.: Prentice-Hall.

Niebuhr, Reinhold
1932 Moral Man and Immoral Society. New York: Scribner's Sons.
1943 The Nature and Destiny of Man. 2 vols. New York: Scribner's Sons.
1945 The Children of Light and the Children of Darkness. London: Nisbet.

Porter, John
1965 The Vertical Mosaic: An Analysis of Social Class and Power in Canada. Toronto: University of Toronto Press.

Rauschenbusch, Walter
1907 Christianity and the Social Crisis. New York: Macmillan.

Renan, Ernest
1962 Vie de Jésus. Calmann-Lévy [1863].

Robinson, John A.T.
1963 Honest to God. London: S.C.M. Press.

Schneider, Herbert Wallace
1967 Religion in 20th Century America. Cambridge, Mass.: Harvard University Press.

Schultz, Harold J.
1959 "William Aberhart and the Social Credit Party: a political biography." Department of History Ph.D. thesis: Duke University.

Shackleton, Doris French
1975 Tommy Douglas. Toronto: McClelland and Stewart.

Sissons, C.B.
1959 Church and State in Canadian Education. Toronto: Ryerson Press.

Strauss, David Friedrich
1860 The Life of Jesus Critically Examined. Translation from the fourth German Edition by Marian Evans. 2 vols. New York: Calvin Blanchard [1835].

Teilhard de Chardin, Pierre
1959 The Phenomenon of Man. With an introduction by Julian Huxley. Translation by Bernard Wall. New York: Harper.
1964 Le Milieu Divin. An Essay on the Interior Life. London: Collins.

Tillich, Paul
1951–63 Systematic Theology. 3 vols. Chicago: University of Chicago Press.
1960 Love, Power and Justice: Ontological Analyses and Ethical Applications. New York: Oxford University Press.

Tyre, Robert
1962 Douglas in Saskatchewan, the Story of a Socialist Experiment. Vancouver: Mitchell Press.

Walsh, H.H.
1968 The Christian Church in Canada. Toronto: Ryerson Press.

Weir, G.M.
1934 The Separate School Question in Canada. Toronto: Ryerson Press.

Westhues, Kenneth
1976a "The adaptation of the Roman Catholic church to Canadian society." In Religion in Canadian Society, edited by Stewart Crysdale and Les Wheatcroft. pp. 290–306. Toronto: Macmillan.
1976b "Public versus sectarian legitimation: the separate schools of the Catholic church." Canadian Review of Sociology and Anthropology 13 (May): 137–53.
1976c "Religious organization in Canada and the United States." International Journal of Comparative Sociology 17:206–25.

Whitehead, Alfred North
  1927 Religion in the Making. Cambridge: Cambridge University Press.
  1960 Process and Reality, an Essay in Cosmology. New York: Macmillan.

Woelfel, James W.
  1970 Bonhoeffer's Theology: Classical and Revolutionary. Nashville: Abingdon Press.

Why Conservative Churches Are Still Growing

Dean M. Kelley

For at least a century the dominant national religious bodies in the United States have been increasing in membership with the nation's increase in population, coasting up the population escalator with the momentum of procreation. Then, in the mid-1960's, they reversed the trend, turned around, and descended the "up" escalator, which was still ascending at a rate of 1.4% per year—not an easy thing to do.

At the same time, a number of other religious bodies continued to increase at a rate not inferior to the population increase but significantly greater, suggesting not just the momentum of procreation but the impetus of significant attractiveness. These bodies appear to represent a different category from the first group, not only in respect to membership trends but in other respects as well, which are not easy to characterize in one word, but which form a pattern easily recognizable to those familiar with the religious scene in America. Perhaps the least pejorative label would be "nonecumenical."

For better or worse, one of the first to call

Dean M. Kelley, a United Methodist minister, is Director for Civil and Religious Liberty, National Council of Churches.

Revised from a paper presented at the annual meeting of the Society for the Scientific Study of Religion, 1976.

Reprinted from *Journal for the Scientific Study of Religion* 17(1978): 165–72, with permission.

attention to this curious and highly interesting contrast in membership trends—at least in hard-cover publications—was the book *Why Conservative Churches Are Growing,* which excited a certain amount of controversy, if not actual scandal, among those who thought such things were better off unannounced. Since then, and perhaps due in part to the aforesaid book, the statistical phenomenon referred to has become a matter of a rather general awareness, penetrating even the austere pages of the *Scientific American.*[1]

During the intervening four years, the membership trends have continued much as they had been characterized in that volume, with three possible exceptions, which were heralded by Ted Fiske on the front page of the N.Y. *Times* with the headline "Conservative Churches have *Stopped* Growing!" The churches referred to, of course, were the Presbyterian Church in the U.S., the Lutheran Church–Missouri Synod, and the Christian Reformed Church, which were reported in that year to have shown membership losses for the first time. (The former two were undergoing incipient schisms, and the pre-1972 curves of all three suggested that their growth was slowing and about to peak.)

No such decline, however, marks the rapidly growing churches, whose rate was significantly greater than the population increase; the Southern Baptist Convention, the

Church of Jesus Christ of Latter-day Saints, Jehovah's Witnesses, Seventh-Day Adventists, Church of the Nazarene, Salvation Army, etc. They continue to expand at rates that pose a marked contrast to the "mainline" or ecumenical churches.

The data from 1975, reported to the *Yearbook of American and Canadian Churches* for the 1977 edition, show a continuation of present growth trends. (There is an error in the reporting of the Mormon Church in the 1976 Yearbook: its membership in that year was 2,267,866 rather than the reported 2,683,573, making a curve more consistent with the latest figure, 2,336,715.[2]) These reported figures for 1975 will be reflected in the updated graphs which appear in the paperback edition of *Why Conservative Churches Are Growing*.

Though many people—and even some social scientists and scholars of religion—are not aware of the curious contrasts in membership trends that occurred during the past decade, no one has come up with a satisfactory explanation of (1) why it happened to these particular religious bodies and (2) why it happened at this particular time in history.

I would like to think that I offered a persuasive, or at least provocative, answer to the first question: that the denominations which grow are, by and large, those which do a better job at the essential function of religion, which I characterized as "making life meaningful in ultimate terms" (a characterization I believe was used by C. Wright Mills in his lectures at Columbia University in 1950, though I cannot find it in my notes, and Phil Hammond could not place its origin when I wrote him to ask about it twenty years later; it was a rather endemic concept around the Sociology Department at that time).

I am less satisfied with my answer to the second question, since the qualities I suggested accounted for the religious ineffectuality of the declining denominations had been present for some time before the decline set in. This discrepancy would require some kind of protractive mechanism to prolong the period of growth—or at least of relative stasis—after the effective discharge of the religious function had deteriorated.

I suggested that membership growth in the ecumenical churches continued for some time as a result of the secular trend of "religiosity,"and that that trend ended, or severely declined, in the early 1960's, either as a result of the general and increasing distrust of received institutions of all kinds, or as a result of the disillusionment of Roman Catholics with their Church, which relaxed many of its historic demands at Vatican Council II, and when this firm "anchor" church gave way, many less rigorous churches lost credibility as well. If the church which was thought to be most serious about its business suddenly abandoned its insistence on auricular confession, abstaining from meat on Fridays, nonrecognition of other religious bodies, and veneration of a whole array of saints, then why should anyone continue to be awed by its mandates, let alone those of churches which were seen to be less serious to begin with?

It is with this quality of "seriousness" that the book has mostly to do. The title has been a source of much misunderstanding. It is not really about "conservative" churches (whatever *they* are) or church growth, as such. In a way, the two opening chapters on church membership rates serve the same purpose as the 2 × 4 with which the farmer struck his mule in order to "get his attention." They pose the question of which churches are really to be taken seriously—those which have enjoyed traditional esteem while looking down their noses at the "sects" in the store fronts and Kingdom Halls *or* those which are drawing new members while the former are not. They point out the embarrassing contrast between the two sets of churches with the object of getting the formerly rather self-satisfied ecumenical churches to engage in some rudimentary self-evaluation which had previously not seemed necessary.

The editors at Harper & Row chose the title of the book to speak to people who hadn't yet read it.[3] If the title were to sum up the book, it would be something more like "Why Strict Churches Are Strong"—whether "liberal" or "conservative"—whether growing in members at the time or not. That is the basic message of the book, which—I hope—will remain, regardless of what happens to denominational membership trends, since it is not dependent upon them.

For some time I have been wishing that someone would come along to do for religion what Freud did for sex: to show that it has its own elemental drives, dynamics, and necessities, and is not to be "explained" in terms of other (e.g., economic, demographic, or political) factors, at least not entirely. I still hope someone will do so. Some of the explanations of current trends in church membership do not measure up to this hope.

To attribute decline in Presbyterian or Methodist or Episcopalian membership to the increase in family camping or other weekend attractions, or to "backdoor" losses of members losing interest, is not to explain much. Why do P, E, or M members go camping or golfing instead of to church, but Southern Baptists and Adventists apparently are able to resist this temptation? If Mormons and Jehovah's Witnesses have some way of minimizing defections, is that not another indication of their vigorousness as effective religious bodies? The declining birthrate may have hit Episcopalians harder than the Church of the Nazarene or the Assemblies of God, but is that the kind of "explanation" with which we should be content?

Have we no more to learn from this fascinating conundrum [than] that there is class differentiation among denominations? (How, then, to account for the rapid growth of the Evangelical Covenant Church, which is comprised mainly of managerial and professional people? "Because they're mostly Swedish." That is to substitute one "extraneous" explanation for another. What is it about the *reli-gious* qualities of the Evangelical Covenant Church that make it a magnet while the Episcopal Church seems to be opposite?)

I do not mean to suggest that class or ethnic or age or sex factors do not play a part, but do they exhaust the variance? Or is it that we simply do not yet know how to identify and quantify the *religious* factors? I suspect that studies of religion based on the techniques of public-opinion polling will probably not yield information of much greater value than public-opinion polls do. What profound insights into religious behavior do we gain by learning that 48.6% of respondents *say* they believe that the Son is of the *same* substance as the Father, 36.3% *say* they believe that the Son is of *like* substance to the Father, and 15.1% are undecided? What difference does it make? Back in the days when wars were fought over the iota of difference between *homo-ousion* and *homoi-ousion*, it may have mattered. But today it costs nothing to *say* one or the other—or actually to *believe* it.

The most revealing data that religious behavior (or any other behavior) is not to be found in respondents' assertions of assent to intellectual propositions formulated by the interviewer but in action that *costs* something in money (which is a relatively cheap level of cost), time, effort, anguish, involvement, or sacrifice. It simply *costs* more to be an Adventist than an Episcopalian, not just proportionately but absolutely and not just in money but in the much costlier materials of human life! (But then, that's easily understandable, since Episcopalians are richer, and it is well known that the wealthier the membership of a denomination, the lower the level of per capita contributions.)

One of the most cogent criticisms of *Why Conservative Churches Are Growing* is that which contends that a particular class-linked mode of religious behavior has been taken as the norm and all others subordinated to it (i.e., the religious style of lower-class sect-members). The implication of the critic is that this is an unfair comparison; that Episcopalians are just as religious as Adventists, albeit they show it in a different and less demonstrative way. In the eyes of God, that may be true, since only He knows the inner devotion of the heart. But to any outward observer, there is no comparison. In the double tithe, the time spent, the efforts made, the witnessing overtures to non-members, the constant preoccupation with the faith, the average Adventist so far outshines the average Episcopalian that they are not even in the same category of magnitude. If this is indeed the case, it suggests that religious behavior is actually more intensive (and extensive) among lower-class people (or at least among religious groups attracting such people), and that is a significant datum in itself.

A less cogent criticism is directed toward making Church membership statistics so central to the book's thesis, as though numbers were the main objective and criterion of the kingdom. This is an understandable misperception of the book, but still a misperception. Membership trends are seen as a crude but informative index of the vitality of a church (or other institution), particularly in a free-market competition among exclusivist rival faith-groups. The church-growth people have seized upon it as a resource, but in my view as well as R. Hudnut's, *church growth is not the point*. It is a *by-product* of a church that is vigorously meeting people's religious needs.

To other critics, that notion of what churches should be doing is even more deplorable. Somehow to them it smacks of pandering for the church to be concerned about meeting people's religious needs. They seem to view such a process as akin to "stroking" souls with mystical introspection, turning them inward, away from each other and the world's needs. They see the church's needing to choose between two mutually exclusive alternatives, in the words of the title of a recent work by Glock and Stark, "To Comfort *or* to Challenge" (emphasis mine).

The Churches are tempted to settle for

"comforting" people when they should be "challenging" them—a thankless task at best. And, according to this school of thought—reflected in works by Glock, . . . Hadden, Quinley, and McFaul—it was the ecumenical churches' recent efforts to "challenge" their members to engage in social action that precipitated the departure of disgruntled members who wanted to be comforted rather than challenged. Or worse, they dominated the local churches and drove out the prophetic young preachers and those who sympathized with them, refusing to contribute to the support of church programs that emphasized social action.

The supposition that church members want to be comforted rather than challenged and that they will withhold support or drive out the minister or leave the church if they are challenged rather than comforted is a gross calumny upon the laity, perpetrated in large part by the clergy (with the help of some social-science researchers who have relied on interviews with a sample composed almost entirely of clergy and drawn almost entirely from Northern California, i.e., Quinley).

A more reliable understanding is gained from the North American Interchurch Study, which reports interviews with over 3500 church people, laity *and* clergy, in the U.S. and Canada. It offers a much more charitable, and credible, view of what lay people expect of the church, and indicates a serious misunderstanding of their expectations by the clergy.

The clergy seem to believe that the laity does not want them to engage in social action, but they will go ahead and do so anyway, even into martyrdom, because it is their Christian duty! But that is not what the laity thinks at all. They said in interviews that a social witness is an essential part of the church's mission, and that they would consider it improper to withhold contributions just because they happened to disagree with the views of church leaders on such issues. Their dissatisfaction with the church was at another point, best indicated by the rank-order of the respondents' expectations of the local church (Cornell & Johnson, 1972, p. 80).

With surprising unanimity among clergy and laity—at least in the top choices—the following preferences were expressed:

A
1. winning others to Christ
2. provide worship for members
3. provide religious instruction
4. provide ministerial services
5. provide for sacraments

B
6. help the needy
7. support overseas missions
8. serve as social conscience to the community
9. provide fellowship activities
10. maintain facilities for congregation
11. support denomination
12. support minority groups
13. influence legislation
14. build low-cost housing

If one were to divide this series into two sections (which the researchers did not), with the first five items in group A and the remaining in group B, then one might characterize group A as the activities by which ultimate meaning is promulgated, inculcated, and nurtured; group B as the activities by which it is embodied, exercised, and practiced—once it has been acquired. The lay respondents did not *reject* the B activities, indeed felt they were *necessary*—perhaps more on the national or regional level than the local—but placed them in a position of *secondary* urgency. They did not *object* to the clergy giving attention to such things; *what they objected to was the clergy's doing them in preference to, to the exclusion of, almost as a substitute for, the A group.*

That is another way of putting the thesis of *Why Conservative Churches Are Growing.* Ecumenical churches are losing members, not because they are engaging in the B group of activities, but because they are muffing the A group. Non-ecumenical churches are flourish-

ing because they are effective at the A group. (It might be charged that they are weak on the B group, but that is not necessarily true; they must have a different way of doing the B group—opposing drinking, smoking, gambling, pornography, etc.—which may not be congenial to "liberal" social-gospel leaders, but is no less effective in fulfilling the religious function. In fact, it is possible that the religious function could be fulfilled fairly well without any B activities at all. It would be Christian heresy, but still an effective religious organization: the Jehovah's Witnesses are a case in point.)

The purpose of the church is not, and should not be, to "comfort" or to "challenge," "to meet people's religious needs" or "to explain the ultimate meaning of life," but to "preach the Gospel" and "win others to Christ." If it does that effectively, it will both comfort and challenge, it will meet people's religious needs by making life meaningful in ultimate terms, and—sooner or later—it will attract new members as well as retaining present members: it will grow.

In four years of giving talks around the country, reading reviews and correspondence, I have not encountered much disagreement with the first main point of the book: that the basic business of religion is to explain the ultimate meaning of life. The second main point has not been as fortunate: that the quality which makes one system of ultimate meaning more convincing is not its content but its seriousness/costliness/strictness. That is an ungracious notion that falls discordantly upon the debonair, modern "liberal" churchperson, producing such prodigies of Humpty-Dumptyism as the Unitarian who declared that, "we are very strict about permitting individual diversity!"—thus substituting for the object of strictness its functional opposite.

"Strictness" is usually caricatured as invariably authoritarian, harsh, punitive, irrational, etc. We are all captives of our historical experience, and it is a pity that almost the only experiences of strictness in Western culture have been marked by heresy trials, inquisitions, excommunications, autos-da-fé, persecutions, crusades, and pogroms; and that the only content about which it is thought possible to be strict is some kind of fundamentalism.

That need not be the case. The Anabaptists, being poor, could not afford the luxury of priests or preachers to tell them what to do, so they had to figure it out for themselves in a way that was the very essence of democracy. The difference between their mode and the modern church-meeting is that, once they reached a consensus, it was binding on all members. There's the rub! We resist the notion of "bindingness" in church affairs, and as a result they are seen—by members and outsiders—as not very serious, and therefore not very convincing.

Could not a modern congregation sit down together and search the Scriptures and ask themselves: What is it we are prepared—in obedience to God—to be serious about—if anything? What are we prepared—in obedience to God—to die for—if anything? If nothing, then the air would be cleared, and they would realize that theirs was not really a church but a clubhouse-with-a-steeple, and they could quit pretending to be a religion and everyone would be much relieved, including God, who could then turn her/his attention to more serious devotees. It should not require any very profound insight to suspect that people interested in religious help would be more drawn to a congregation or a denomination that was trying to be serious about its task than to one that was merely playing at it.

If ecumenical churches feel that they are as serious about what they believe as fundamentalists are, then it behooves them to find appropriate ways to exercise and communicate that seriousness. Why should the devil have all the good tunes?

One form of strictness mentioned in the book is rigorous membership standards. A couple of indications have caused me to wonder whether that is as central as I had supposed: the United Presbyterian study, which found no correlation between strictness of membership standards and gain or loss of members, and a report on a dozen fast-growing "body-life" churches in the Southwest, which make no special emphasis on membership standards at all. The church "membership" consists of whoever was in attendance at the booming services last Sunday.

In preparing the paperback edition of *Why Conservative Churches Are Growing*, I have been asked if I would make any changes. Essentially, I would not. I am unrepentant and unreconstructed. The curves are continuing much as they were, except for a slight flattening at the lower end of some downward arcs (becoming ogival, going from convex to concave, perhaps "bottoming out?" Let us hope so).

There are a few minor changes to be made: (a) the bibulous statistics on page 63 will be corrected: In 1950, over eleven million gallons of gin were consumed in England rather than eleven billion. (2) The hypotheses in the book are offered for testing. The sentence reading "Most of these can be verified empirically but have not been, for lack of time, resources, and facilities." The sentence seems to have offended Jeffrey Hadden dreadfully (Hadden, *Gideon's Gang*, 1974). What the sentence should say is: "Most of these can be tested but have not been." Rather than arrogantly asserting truth without proof, I invited testing, as should have been readily apparent from the last sentence of the same paragraph: "The risk of being wrong I gladly take, and if these hypotheses are disproved, no one will be more relieved than I." Despite all the howls of outrage and screams of annoyance, I am not aware that anyone has clearly disproved any of them, including the one on membership standards, which is, at worst, only under suspicion. (3) I shall try to leave out the graph of Roman Catholic church membership. It is not an accurate index of conditions in that church, which does not remove members from its rolls for any reasons except the most severe. A much more responsive measure might be attendance at Mass (off 10 million since 1963, according to Msgr. George Kelly). (4) There are also new and broader resurgences on the evangelical or non-ecumenical front, as outlined in *Newsweek* magazine, 25 October 1976, and other sources, that might be cited to substantiate the continuing invigoration of that end of the religious spectrum.

Just as there are many ways to articulate and inculcate ultimate meaning, so there are many ways in which seriousness can be expressed and evoked. Rather than exhausting the subject or saying the last word on it, I have hoped to stimulate others to explore it further, to compare the effectiveness of various modes of the meaning-enterprise, to develop and assess new and better ways of being serious about it. This seems to me a wide-open field for religious research.

Notes

1. See Nelkin (1976) where a graph appears at p. 36 comparing the membership trends of twelve national denominations, but on a scale which does not do justice to the contrasts of the past decade. The data of the chart are not referred to in the text.

2. Letter of Archivist to Editor. *Yearbook of Ameri-can and Canadian Churches*, 1977. Constante H. Jacquet, Jr. (Ed.). Nashville, Tenn., Abingdon.

3. With some success the book has brought in some $20,000 in royalties to the National Council of Churches, mostly from Southern Baptists, Missouri Synod Lutherans, and other non-ecumenical purchasers who would not normally contribute to the NCC—a fitting irony. The NCC paid my salary during a 3-month sabbatical as well as typing and photocopying costs, when it was not yet apparent whether the book would sell—or even whether there would be one.

References

Cornell, George and Douglas Johnson
  1972   Punctured Preconceptions. New York, Friendship Press.
Glock, Charles Y.
  1967   To Comfort or to Challenge. Berkeley: University of California Press.
Hadden, Jeffrey K.
  1969   The Gathering Storm in the Churches. Garden City, N.Y.: Doubleday.
  1974   Gideon's Gang. Philadelphia: United Church Press.
Hudnut, Robert K.
  1975   Church Growth Is Not the Point. New York: Harper & Row.
Kelly, George
  1976   Religious News Service 10 (11): 11.
McFaul, Thomas R.
  1974   " 'Strictness' and church membership." Christian Century 3:281–284.
Nelkin, Dorothy
  1976   "The science-textbook controversies." Scientific American 234 (33): 36.
Quinley, Harold E.
  1974   The Prophetic Clergy. New York: Wiley.

READING   3.2

Faith Priorities of Pastor and Laity as a Factor in the Growth or Decline of Presbyterian Congregations

Everett L. Perry and Dean R. Hoge

In the last 10 or 15 years, as many mainline denominations have been losing members, a vigorous debate has raged as to why. What factors have caused the declines? Many church leaders and observers have pointed to one factor or another.

Analysts of denominational trends have needed to make some distinctions when discussing factors. One distinction is between national factors (common to the entire denomination) and local factors (specific to one congregation). Both of these, in turn, can be usefully divided into contextual (external to the church) and institutional (internal to the church). The result is a fourfold categorization of factors—national contextual, national institutional, local contextual, and local institutional. Hoge and Roozen (1979) use this categorization in their review of existing research.

Growth or decline of congregations is the result of all four sets of factors. A major task of researchers is to weigh the relative importance of each of the four on local congregations. Hoge and Roozen have reviewed several attempts to do this, and they have concluded that, on the local level, contextual factors are relatively more important than

institutional factors. They estimate that 50 to 70 percent of the explanatory power of local factors is in contextual factors, and 30 to 50 percent is in institutional factors (1979:326). Other experts dispute this, saying that local institutional factors are more important (e.g., Kelley, 1979). The impact of national factors on local congregations has been more difficult to measure.

A second major task of researchers is to test the many hypotheses set forth by recent writers as to *which* contextual factors or *which* institutional factors are important, on both the national and local levels. To do this has been difficult due to lack of data. Testing such hypotheses on the national level requires data on social trends impacting the various denominations and also data on institutional changes at the denominational (i.e., national) level. Testing such hypotheses on the local level requires data—drawn from a sample of growing or declining congregations—in which a large number of contextual and institutional factors are measured.

The present paper reports on a test of hypotheses about specific local institutional factors affecting a large number of United Presbyterian congregations. It is limited to the local level and does not inspect national factors—for which another research approach is required. (On attempts to study national factors, see Hoge, 1979.) This paper is not able to assess the relative importance of local contextual versus institutional factors for United Presbyterian congregations, nor is it able to inspect a range of local contextual factors (such as change in socioeconomic

Everett L. Perry is Church Strategy Consultant, United Presbyterian Church.

Dean R. Hoge is Professor of Sociology at the Catholic University of America in Washington, D.C.

Financial support was provided by the Hartford Seminary Foundation and by the United Presbyterian Church. We would like to thank Mary Jeanne Verdieck for assistance.

Reprinted from *Review of Religious Research* 22 (March 1981) with permission of the Religious Research Association and the authors.

level or racial composition of the immediate neighborhood). Rather, it analyzes newly available data bearing on three local institutional factors discussed by prominent writers as explanations for congregational growth or decline.

The study of local institutional factors in any one denomination is directly relevant for other denominations also, since the factors are very similar from denomination to denomination in mainline Protestantism. Thus, our analysis, though limited to one denomination, has broad application.

Local Institutional Factors Causing Congregational Growth or Decline

The study of local institutional factors for understanding congregational growth or decline has much less of a history than the study of local contextual factors. Already in the 1930s, H. Paul Douglass demonstrated in study after study that "like community, like church" (see Douglass and Brunner, 1935; Schaller, 1965). Communities having an influx of middle-class white families were repeatedly found to have growth in their Protestant congregations. Researchers agree that local contextual factors undoubtedly have strong explanatory power, but so do local institutional factors.

Many local institutional factors have been discussed recently—theological tendency, effectiveness of leadership, program emphases, congregational harmony, small groups within the congregation, and so on. In a review of research, Hoge and Roozen conclude that the most important are overall satisfaction of laity with church worship and program, and congregational harmony and cooperation (1979:324). More research on specific factors is needed.

The present study assesses three local institutional factors being currently discussed in many quarters—the theological tendencies of pastors or laity, the amount of priority given to evangelism and membership growth, and

the compatibility between pastors and laity. We discuss each in turn.

(1) Theological tendencies of pastors or laity were given prominence in the book, *Why Conservative Churches Are Growing*, by Dean Kelley (1977). Although the word "conservative" is in the book's title, Kelley did not stress it nearly so much as his concept "strictness." He argued that congregations having the characteristics of strictness would grow, while others would not. Strictness includes the theological belief that one's own church has the Truth and that all others are in error, an intolerance of personal reinterpretations of religious truth by members of the church body, and an avoidance of cooperation with other religious bodies that might give rise to relativism in religious beliefs (1977:79–82). Strict churches grow because only in them do people find meaning and personal expansiveness. The theological tendencies of strict churches tend to be those of theologically conservative bodies in present-day Protestantism (see Hoge, 1979:192), so Kelley's arguments would also include the prediction that conservative theology would be associated with church growth.

(2) A priority on evangelism and membership growth has been repeatedly emphasized by writers in the Church Growth Movement. For example, Wagner (1976) has stressed that congregational growth can occur only when the pastor and people want to grow and consciously set out to do so (also see McGavran and Arn, 1977; Shannon, 1977). In Wagner's words, "The indispensable condition for a growing church is that it wants to grow" (1976:47). Otherwise, a congregation will be so preoccupied with its own life and program that it fails to work at reaching out to others.

Wagner also states that the social action emphases of many denominations in the 1960s accelerated membership decline in them, since social action received undue energy and attention, thus displacing evangelism as their main concern. Wagner sees social action as a distraction that can only harm church growth. Kelley makes a similar argument about social action, and he adds the further point that social action causes tension and alienation of members in religious groups whose members have low levels of commitment (such as mainline Protestantism today); hence social action can be expected to cause membership decline (Kelley, 1977:140).

(3) Compatibility of pastor and laity in any congregation has been stressed in recent discussions, mostly with regard to conflict management. In 1969 Jeffrey Hadden's book *The Gathering Storm in the Churches* described a widening gap between ministers and laypersons in Protestantism; it predicted that clergy-lay tensions would be a problem in years ahead. All observers agree that congregational tensions hinder membership growth and that clergy-lay tensions are especially damaging. Thus, incompatibility of pastor and laity in any congregation would be a major cause of membership decline.

These three factors have been prominent in the recent heated debates about church trends and their meaning for church policy. The debates have obvious theological implications: for example, church leaders supporting social action have generally argued that social action does not contribute to congregational decline.

Research on Presbyterian Congregations

In 1971 a study done by the Division of Evangelism, United Presbyterian Church, looked at 19 fastest-growing congregations and assessed some of the factors outlined above. The researchers found that the fastest-growing Presbyterian congregations were in the middle of the theological road, relative to other Presbyterian congregations, and that there was no relationship between the amount of social action involvement and congregational growth.

In 1974 the denomination named a special Committee on Membership Trends to investigate the decline. It carried out an extensive empirical study of 617 congregations in which many possible factors for growth or decline were tested. Of the 617, about one-third were fast-growing, one-third were fast-declining, and one-third were in the middle ground. The committee carried out initial analysis of the data (United Presbyterian Committee, 1976), and later Roof and his colleagues made further analysis to estimate the weighting of multiple factors (Roof, et al., 1979).

The Committee correlated congregational growth or decline with theological views of laity in the 617 congregations and found no clear pattern. They concluded that Kelley's theories about strictness and conservatism did not apply within the denomination: "We cannot conclude that the more conservative the approach or stance in the life of a congregation, the more likely it is to grow" (1976:51).

Roof and his colleagues tested the importance of social action involvement for growth or decline. They concluded that, contrary to Kelley's expectation, growing congregations are "a little more involved in social action" than the declining ones. When *types* of social action were distinguished, Roof et al. found that social service or providing aid to needy persons had a slight positive relationship with congregational growth, while action aimed at changing society had a slight negative relationship with growth (p. 213). This finding is consistent with the argument that social action entailing criticism of the social status quo can alienate members and prevent growth.

Roof et al. looked into the importance that laity put on congregational growth. Contrary to expectations, they found that laity in *declining* congregations were more concerned about congregational growth than those in growing churches. Taken alone, *concern* for growth is apparently not a very predictive factor.

Roof et al. had no measures of compatibility of pastors and laity. In general, the Presbyterian Committee and Roof et al. were limited by a lack of data from the pastors of the congregations. But questionnaire responses from the pastors have recently become available. The new data permit more extensive hypothesis-testing.

Four hypotheses are tested here.

H1:   Congregations whose pastors or laity are theologically strict and conservative tend to grow faster than others.

H2:   Congregations whose pastors or laity place high priority on evangelism tend to grow faster than others.

H3:   Congregations who perceive that their pastor, or the congregation as a whole, is strict, conservative, and evangelistically oriented tend to grow faster than others.

H4:   Congregations in which pastor and laity agree on their faith priorities are more likely to grow than are those in which pastor and laity disagree.

The first two hypotheses are studied by looking at self-reports by pastors and laity on a series of items about faith, theological views, and evangelism; the third, by looking at the ratings made by lay respondents about their pastors or their congregations as a whole; and the fourth, by computing a score of pastor-lay difference in each congregation.

Data

The Presbyterian Committee listed all 8,700 United Presbyterian congregations from the fastest-growing to the fastest-declining during 1968 to 1974. This period was one of serious membership decline (15.7 percent). A random sample of 350 congregations, stratified by size, was taken from the top, middle, and bottom segments of the listing.

All of the congregations chosen from the top of the list had grown at least 5 percent during the six years, all from the bottom of the list had lost at least 30 percent, and all from the middle range had lost between 0 and 20 percent during this period.

Two kinds of questionnaires were sent to each congregation. One, covering congregational characteristics, was to be filled out by the pastor or secretary. The second was to be filled out by five to 12 selected individuals per congregation, depending on size, including the pastor or pastors, a member of the session (ruling lay board), a trustee, a church school administrator or teacher, a choir director or member, a women's group leader, a men's group leader, a youth group leader, and other members typical of the congregation.

Of the initial sample, 79 percent of the congregations agreed to participate. Of these, 77 percent returned the congregational characteristics questionnaire, but only 54 percent of the questionnaires to lay individuals were returned (N = 617 congregations; N = 3994 lay individuals).

For testing our hypotheses we studied all the congregations in which (a) individual questionnaires had been returned by the sole or senior pastor and at least three lay persons, and (b) the present pastor had been in that congregation for at least two years. We assumed that after two years the pastor and people would be acquainted, and the pastor's influence would begin to be felt in congregational growth or decline. Two hundred four congregations met these criteria (54 of the most-declining sample, 73 of the "typical" sample, and 77 of the most-growing sample). The N for our study was 204 pastors and 1,327 laypersons.

Using the congregation as the unit of analysis, we aggregated each set of lay responses by computing the mean score for each variable. All variables in the present analysis have interval-level measurement.

Measures

For the measurement of congregational growth or decline we divided the 1968–1974 membership change by the 1968 membership figure. This produced the proportion of change; the mean was −.059.

For measures of faith priorities we used three indices plus 10 separate items. One of the questions asked, "*For you*, which three of the following are the most important aspects of your faith?" and then listed nine possible responses. From these we created three indices and used two items separately. The index scores were the mean of the item scores.[1] (1) A *Personal Guidance Index* was created from three responses: "Personal salvation in Christ," "Personal guidance in daily decisions," and "The sense of purpose, strength and security it gives." Each was scored 1 if checked, 0 if not. (2) An *Evangelistic Index* was created from two responses: "Talking about my faith with others to bring them to Christ" and "Bringing new members into the Church to share my faith." Each was scored 1 if checked, 0 if not. (3) A *Work of the Holy Spirit Index* was created from two responses: "The work of the Holy Spirit in the Church" and "The work of the Holy Spirit in the world." Each was scored 1 if checked, 0 if not.

Two individual responses were analyzed separately. They are (4) "Ministering to the needs of others," which we called the *Needs of Others Item*, and (5) "Changing society in the name of the Lord," which we called the *Changing Society Item*. In preliminary analyses we created an index from the two but found that the index score blurred the difference between the two items, one of which stresses social change while the other is limited to service to individuals.

Similar questions were asked of the pastor to report his perception of the congregation as a whole, and of the laity to report their perception of the pastor and of the congregation as a whole.

Six additional items stated theological views that serve as measures of strictness and conservatism. All six had five responses: "strongly agree," "agree," "disagree," and "strongly disagree," scored from 4 to 1, plus "no opinion," which was scored as missing data.[2] The items are shown in Table 1, items 6 through 11. Items 6, 8, 9, and 10 state positions of individualism and relativism; hence, they are scored in reverse throughout our analysis, so that "strongly disagree" has a score of 4, and "strongly agree" a score of 1.

Two items asked about the importance of evangelism. One asked "To what extent do you believe it is important for people to share their Christian beliefs with others?" The responses ranged from "very important" to "not at all important" and were scored from 4 to 1. A fifth response, "no opinion," was scored as missing data. Another asked "To what extent do you feel increasing the number of members would be good for your congregation?" The responses ranged from "to a very great extent" to "not at all," scored from 5 to 1. "No opinion" was scored as missing data. These two items are shown at the bottom of Table 1.

The items on strictness, conservatism, and evangelism (items 6 through 13 in Table 1) were asked of the pastors and the lay respondents, but no one was asked to rate the views of anyone besides himself or herself.

The Presbyterian data included local contextual factors, and in the analysis by Roof et al. they were found to be strong determinants of congregational growth or decline. Here our interest in local contextual factors is limited to their role as controls. We used three measures of neighborhood characteristics found by Roof et al. to influence congregational growth greatly, and we partialled out their influence when testing our hypotheses about local institutional factors. The three are: (1) "Has the school population of the area within ½ mile of your church building been changing over the past five years?" The responses were "no," "yes, increasing," and "yes, de-

Table 1 *Correlations of Self-Reported Faith Priorities of Pastors and Laity with Growth of Congregations*[a]

	Pastors	Laity (Aggregated)
Important Aspects of Your Own Faith		
(1) Personal Guidance Index	.18[b]	.16[b]
(2) Evangelistic Index	−.04	−.05
(3) Work of the Holy Spirit Index	−.05	.00
(4) Needs of Others Item	.02	−.12
(5) Changing Society Item	−.18[b]	−.13[b]
Indicators of Strictness and Conservatism		
(6) "To what extent do you agree with the statement that 'no one has the right to impose his beliefs on others'?" Strongly disagree.	.07	.17[b]
(7) "The Bible is the only infallible rule for faith and practice." Strongly agree.	.00	.14[b]
(8) "An individual should arrive at his own religious beliefs quite independent of the church." Strongly disagree.	−.03	.06
(9) "When you get right down to it, all the different churches are saying the same thing but they use different words." Strongly disagree.	−.07	.04
(10) "It is not as important to worry about life after death as about what we can do in this life." Strongly disagree.	.06	.15[b]
(11) "The primary purpose of this life is to prepare for the next life." Strongly agree.	.09	.07
Indicators of Priority of Evangelism		
(12) "To what extent do you believe it is important for people to share their Christian beliefs with others?" Very important.	−.05	.00
(13) "To what extent do you feel increasing the number of members would be good for your congregation?" Great extent.	−.03	−.39[b]

[a]N = 204. Partial correlations, controlling three contextual factors.
[b]Significant at .05 by one-tailed test.

creasing," scored 2, 3, and 1. (2) "Has the neighborhood within ½ mile of your church building changed in economic level in the past five years?" The responses were "increasing," "decreasing," and "no change," scored 3, 1, and 2. (3) "What is the approximate age of the homes within ½ mile of your church building?" The responses ranged from "under 5 years" to "60 years and over," and they were scored at the midpoint of each age interval to produce maximally exact data. These three variables were controlled in all hypothesis-testing.

Findings

We used correlations and partial correlations in the analysis. To check on the possibility that we might have overlooked important curvilinear relationships between the variables, we computed breakdowns of all the laity data (aggregated) relating to the congregational growth or decline. We divided each of the theological measures into eight levels, then plotted the mean congregational growth

Table 2 *Correlations of Laity Ratings of Faith of Pastors and Faith of the Congregation as a Whole, with Growth of Congregations*[a]

	Pastor's Faith Rated by Laity (Aggregated)	Faith of Congregation as a Whole Rated by Laity (Aggregated)
(1) Personal Guidance Index	.01	−.06
(2) Evangelistic Index	.13[b]	.14[b]
(3) Work of the Holy Spirit Index	−.09	−.09
(4) Needs of Others Item	.16[b]	−.04
(5) Changing Society Item	−.29[b]	.12[b]

[a]$N = 204$. Partial correlations, controlling three contextual factors.
[b]Significant at .05 by one-tailed test.

or decline rate for each level. There were no significant curvilinear relationships.

We review the hypotheses seriatum.

H1: Congregations whose pastors or laity are theologically strict and conservative tend to grow faster than others. Slight support for this hypothesis is found in Table 1. (In our exposition we regard all correlations weaker than ±.15 as too weak to be noteworthy and limit attention to stronger relationships.) Congregations whose pastors and laity are high on the Personal Guidance Index (Index 1 in Table 1) are slightly more likely to be growing than the others. Also, congregations whose laity disagree that "no one has the right to impose his beliefs on others" (that is, laity who support some ecclesiastical authority) and who stress the importance of thinking about life after death (items 6 and 10 in the table) are slightly more likely to be growing than the others. The correlations are all weak, including those on several theological items that appear to bear on strictness and conservatism. We conclude that the hypothesis is supported, but, because of the low correlations, it is of marginal importance as an explanation of congregational growth or decline.

H2: Congregations whose pastors or laity place high priority on evangelism tend to grow faster than others. Three measures in Table 1 test this hypothesis—the Evangelistic Index and items 12 and 13. The hypothesis is un-

supported. A noteworthy relationship occurred with item 13, which asks if increasing the number of members would be good for one's congregation. The laity in *declining* congregations tended to say "to a great extent," contrary to the hypothesis. Members of growing churches do not feel urgency about gaining new members, while those in declining churches do. To our surprise, pastors of growing churches and of declining churches made very similar responses to the item, again providing no support for the hypothesis.

H3: Congregations who perceive that their pastor, or the congregation as a whole, is strict, conservative, and evangelistically oriented tend to grow faster than others. This hypothesis is similar to the first two, except that it concerns perceptions by the laity rather than self-reports by pastors and lay respondents. The findings are shown in Table 2. Ratings of the pastor are more related to congregational growth or decline than are ratings of the congregation as a whole. Most important are items 4 and 5, regarding the pastor's perceived emphasis on social service and social action. Congregations in which the pastors are perceived as giving high priority to social service tend slightly to be growing more than others. Congregations in which the pastors are perceived as giving high priority to social action tend to be declining more than others. Here is evidence that social action critical of the social status quo tends to inhibit congrega-

Table 3   *Absolute Differences between Self-Report and Rating of the Other, by Pastors and by Laity, Correlated with Congregational Growth*[a]

	Absolute Differences between Pastor's Report of Own Faith and His Rating of the Congregation as a Whole	Absolute Differences between Lay Persons' Reports of Their Own Faith (Aggregated) and Their Rating of Their Pastor's Faith
(1) Personal Guidance Index	−.14[b]	.09
(2) Evangelistic Index	.04	.09
(3) Work of the Holy Spirit Index	.07	−.07
(4) Needs of Others Item	.01	.06
(5) Changing Society Item	−.13[b]	−.21[b]

[a]N = 204. Partial correlations, controlling three contextual factors.
[b]Significant at .05 by one-tailed test.

tional growth. Perceptions of the pastor's priorities in this respect are more important than perceptions of the congregation as a whole and also more important than the pastor's self-reported views.

It seems important that lay perceptions of pastors are more consequential than pastors' own self-reports. The laypersons may be misperceiving the pastors' views, or possibly the pastors are understressing their social action stances in their self-reports. In any event, we may infer that interpersonal tensions within congregations are behind some of these differences in perceptions. Apparently, the interpersonal differences regarding social action are very important in the growth or decline of some congregations. This is consistent with Kelley's argument that social action can be detrimental in low-commitment congregations if it runs counter to strongly held views of lay people (Kelley, 1977:140).

H4: Congregations in which pastor and laity agree on their faith priorities are more likely to grow than are those in which pastor and laity disagree. The findings are shown in Table 3. Of the ten tests of the hypothesis in the table, only one is strong enough to be noteworthy. It is that differences between pastor's and congregation's stress on social action to change society are associated with congrega-

tional decline. No other perceived pastor-lay differences as seen by either the pastors or by the lay respondents were associated with congregational growth or decline.[3]

We also computed pastor-lay differences using the self-reported views of each. None of the 10 correlations (equivalent to those in Table 3) were as strong as ±.15, so we conclude that no patterns exist. (The data are not shown here.) Again we see that perceptions of pastor-lay relationships are more consequential for church growth or decline than differences in views measured by the self-reports of each.

Conclusions

Most of the relationships scrutinized in this study turned out to be weak. We can say, as a general summary, that faith priorities and theological views of pastors and laity are not important determinants of congregational growth or decline in Presbyterian congregations. We did find two weak associations worth noting. First, an emphasis on faith as personal guidance and strength is found among pastors and laity slightly more in growing congregations than in declining congregations. Second, pastors who emphasize changing society as important to their faith, and whose laity see it as important in the pastor's faith, are found disproportionately often in declining congregations. The relationship between laity perceptions of the pastor's faith and congregational trends is somewhat stronger than the relationship between the pastor's own self-report and congregational trends. These findings provide no support for the notion that conservative congregations grow faster than others, but they provide mild support for the hypothesis that emphasis on social action among pastors is associated with membership loss.

Compatibility of pastors and laity was generally unimportant for understanding congregational growth or decline, with one exception: lay persons who described their pastors' concern about social action as quite different from their own concern tended to be in declining churches.

In general, the aspects of faith and theology studied here are no more than weak determinants of growth or decline in Presbyterian congregations. This conclusion is consistent with past research. Apparently the arguments about strictness, conservative theology, and evangelism made by Kelley and the Church Growth Movement writers are unimportant. Only their arguments about social action have a bit of relevance for understanding Presbyterian congregations.

Are the theories about strictness, conservative theology, and evangelism wrong, or are they simply not applicable to Presbyterians? Kelley, in commenting on the similar findings of the Roof et al. analysis, argued that the United Presbyterian Church is too lukewarm and too homogeneous to provide an adequate test of his theories. He said that a test across the full spectrum of Protestantism would, by contrast, prove the force of his views (1979:341). This is a crucial theoretical point. We are inclined to believe that Kelley overstresses the homogeneity of Presbyterian congregations and that enough difference in strictness, conservatism, and evangelism emphasis is present for at least a preliminary test of his theories.

But if Kelley is right about the Presbyterian congregations, then his theories are irrelevant for the denomination. Presbyterian congregations, in fact, vary widely in whether they are growing or declining; if they are too homogeneous in Kelley's terms for his theory to apply, then something else entirely is causing the growth or decline.

Regardless of this theoretical question, something else *is* causing congregational growth or decline in the United Presbyterian Church. Theological tendencies, priority given to evangelism, desire for growth, and compatibility of pastor and laity are *not* important causes. This conclusion is important for de-emphasizing the discussion of these particular local institutional factors. It says nothing about the role of other local institutional factors or the estimated explanatory power of all local institutional factors combined. Such questions lie beyond the present paper.

Notes

1. Because the items in the indices come from a composite question with responses in a fixed-sum format, the intercorrelations tend to be negative and Cronbach's alpha is meaningless. When the laity were asked to rate the pastor and the congregation as a whole, and when the pastor was asked to rate the congregation as a whole, an additional item was available in the questionnaire: "The work of the Holy Spirit in (his or her own life/their own lives)." This item was added to the Work of the Holy Spirit Index at those points, but not when a difference score was computed.

2. There was little missing data. In the laity responses, which were aggregated by congregation, there were no missing data at all. In the pastor responses missing data were impossible to measure in the composite item about important aspects of faith, but on the other items the missing data (including the choice of "no opinion" responses) were low, averaging only 1.7 percent.

3. On the Personal Guidance Index the median of the pastors' self-reports is 1.13 and the pastors' reports on the congregations is 1.66 on a scale of 0–3. On the Changing Society Item the median of the pastors' self-reports is 0.19 on a scale of 0–1. The median of the pastors' reports on the congregations as a whole

is 0.03. The median of the laity's self-reports is 0.10. The median of the laity's reports on the pastor is 0.14.

References

Douglass, Harlan Paul, and Edmund DeS. Brunner
  1935 The Protestant Church as a Social Institution. New York: Russell and Russell (reprinted, 1972).
Hadden, Jeffrey K.
  1969 The Gathering Storm in the Churches. Garden City, N.Y.: Doubleday.
Hoge, Dean R.
  1979 "A test of theories of denominational growth and decline." Pp. 179–97 in D. Hoge and D. Roozen (eds.), Understanding Church Growth and Decline, 1950–1978. New York: Pilgrim Press.
Hoge, Dean R., and David A. Roozen
  1979 "Some sociological conclusions about church trends." Pp. 315–33 in D. Hoge and D. Roozen (eds.), Understanding Church Growth and Decline, 1950–1978. New York: Pilgrim Press.
Kelley, Dean M.
  1977 Why Conservative Churches are Growing. 2nd ed. New York: Harper & Row.
  1979 "Is religion a dependent variable?" Pp. 334–43 in D. Hoge and D. Roozen (eds.), Understanding Church Growth and Decline, 1950–1978. New York: Pilgrim Press.

McGavran, Donald A., and Winfield C. Arn
  1977 Ten Steps for Church Growth. New York: Harper & Row.
Roof, Wade Clark, Dean R. Hoge, John E. Dyble, and C. Kirk Hadaway
  1979 "Factors producing growth or decline in United Presbyterian congregations." Pp. 198–223 in D. Hoge and D. Roozen (eds.), Understanding Church Growth and Decline, 1950–1978. New York: Pilgrim Press.
Schaller, Lyle E.
  1965 Planning for Protestantism in Urban America. New York: Abingdon.
Shannon, Foster H.
  1977 The Growth Crisis in the American Church: A Presbyterian Case Study. South Pasadena, California: William Carey Library.
United Presbyterian Church, Committee on Membership Trends
  1976 Membership Trends in the United Presbyterian Church in the U.S.A. New York: United Presbyterian Church.
United Presbyterian Church, Division of Evangelism
  1971 "A study of some growing churches in the United Presbyterian Church, U.S.A." Unpublished paper, multilithed. New York: United Presbyterian Church.
Wagner, C. Peter
  1976 Your Church Can Grow. Glendale, California: Regal Books.

S E L E C T I O N   3 . B

Looking for Secularization in Middletown

Theodore Caplow

I want to tell you this evening about one aspect of the Middletown III project, the comprehensive study of social change in Muncie that Howard Bahr, Bruce Chadwick, and I began in 1976. We called it Middletown III to

Theodore Caplow is Commonwealth Professor of Sociology at the University of Virginia.
An address given at the fifth annual meeting for the general membership of the Friends of the Alexander M. Bracken Library, April 27, 1982, at Ball State University, Muncie, Indiana. Reprinted with permission of the Friends of the Alexander M. Bracken Library and the author.

underscore its relationship to the classic studies conducted here many years ago by Robert and Helen Lynd, Middletown I in 1924–25 and Middletown II in 1935.

Middletown I was much more than a description of Muncie in 1924. It was a grandly designed study of social change in the six major sectors of community life: work, family, education, leisure, religion, and government. The Lynds were the first sociologists to grasp the necessity of studying social change as a movement from one precise point in time to another. To provide a base period for the 1924–25 study, they did a retrospective survey of Muncie in 1890, using diaries, letters, newspapers, official records, and what would now be called oral history interviews.

The scientific study of social change is intrinsically difficult because it requires us to compare the present—about which we know too much to see the forest for the trees—with the past—about which we remember too little to see either the trees or the forest clearly. The temptation is nearly irresistible to trim the facts of the past to match our present visions of progress or decay, and when the visions change, the facts must change with them. The extraordinary difficulty of understanding social change, if we start with the present and allow it to shape our image of the past, does not discourage journalists, politicians, preachers, and scholars from doing it that way. They find all sorts of encouraging trends when progress is in style and nothing but symptoms of malaise when degeneration is in fashion.

The collective memory is particularly fallible about the hopes, fears, and dreams of the past. Were factory workers in Muncie more worried about unemployment in 1924 than they are in 1982? Were high school students more obedient to their parents? Were religious beliefs assailed by fewer doubts? The answers to such questions that can be obtained by talking to elderly people who were around in 1924 were interesting but unreliable. Their memories cannot be entirely trusted because the temptation to mythologize is personal as well as collective. What parent describes to his children the treatment he received from his own parents without some mythologizing? An even more serious limitation of any attempt to reconstruct the past from the recollections of survivors is that most of them did not have the motives or the means to make careful observations of the world around them back in the base period. The partial reconstruction of the mental world of the past from documentary sources is sometimes feasible if the right documents can be found, and in their reconstruction of the cultural climate of Muncie in 1890, the Lynds leaned heavily on a few good diaries together with newspapers, sermons, and even fiction. But no reconstruction of the past comes close to the value of an eyewitness account by scientific observers who were on the scene at the right time gathering information on the topics that interest us now.

Replication—the repetition of a study after a lapse of time—is just as essential in the social sciences as in the physical sciences. The Lynds introduced replication into the arsenal of sociology when they went back to Middletown in 1935 to collect data about the six sectors of its culture to compare with the data they had collected under the same rubrics ten years before. Their report of the Middletown II project, called *Middletown in Transition* (1937), is the best available account of the effects of the Great Depression on American life. Although the Lynds warned against the incautious application of the Middletown findings to the entire United States, they *were* obviously applicable to some extent. "Despite some local and sectional peculiarities," wrote the *New York Times* reviewer of that book, "Middletown is a country in miniature, almost the world in miniature."

Like the Lynds, those of us involved in Middletown III are interested in Muncie less for its own sake than for the light it can shed on the larger society. None of us had any personal ties to this hospitable community when we first came here, but it drew us irresistibly because of the opportunity it offers to compare our contemporary observations point by point with the rich and meticulous data of Middletown I and Middletown II—better descriptions of the world of our grandfathers than are available for any other place in the country, perhaps in the world. With the addition of the copious data of Middletown III and of the related Black Middletown study conducted by my colleagues Rutledge Dennis and Vivian Gordon and with the reexamination of old censuses by Sandy Bracken and by the Bureau of the Census under a Middletown III contract, not to mention the graphic resources of Dwight Hoover's systematic collection of historic photographs, Muncie's position as America's specimen community appears unassailable—more is known about it than about any other.

Between 1977 and 1981, we conducted fourteen separate surveys as part of the Middletown III project: nine by written questionnaire, five by personal interview. The information I will use this evening is drawn principally from the 1977 housewives survey, which closely copied a 1924 interview survey conducted by the Lynds; the 1977 survey of the entire high school population, which closely copied the Lynds' 1924 survey of the same population; our 1978 surveys of the religious attitudes and practices of the general population and of the clergy; a 1979 interview survey about how people celebrated Christmas in 1978; and a small interview survey of local ministers in 1981.

Survey data are not as colorful and deeply textured as information obtained by direct observation, but on balance they are more reliable and those of us who have made extensive use of sample surveys in the study of social change could not be persuaded to dispense with them in favor of any other method. The survey method is particularly suited to the study of religious beliefs and practices nowadays when most adults construe their own beliefs and practices as voluntary and are happy to talk about them.

In the Middletown I study, more attention was given to religion than to the other five sectors of the culture. Indeed, the Lynds came here in 1924 to study the crisis of the Protestant churches at the grass-roots level. (Every generation perceives a crisis in the churches.) The expansion of that original assignment into a study of the entire community occurred during the field work as the Lynds became interested in the connections

between religion and the other sectors, but the religious sector retained its primacy in the Middletown I study. It received only cursory attention in the Middletown II study.

Robert Lynd was trained to be a Presbyterian minister, but he had already turned away from organized religion when he began to observe Muncie's churches in 1924, according to one of his closest friends who was still living here when we arrived. Like many other sociologists of his time, he viewed social evolution as an inevitable progression from social forms based on custom to social forms based on rational planning. According to this view, drawn from nineteenth-century extensions of Darwin's theory of the origin of species to the origin of social institutions, modern religion was supposed to be a vestige of a more primitive stage of society and was expected to disappear. This gradual but inevitable disappearance was called secularization, and that term recurs continually in the Lynds' discussion of the tendencies they saw in Muncie's churches and homes in the 1920s.

They thought of secularization as an irreversible process starting somewhere in the past and proceeding irresistibly into the future. As a concomitant of modernization, it would affect the more modernized elements of a population first. Thus, the theory of secularization implied that city people would abandon religion sooner than country people, the business class before the working class, men before women, the young before the old. The Lynds thought they had found this pattern in Muncie in the 1920s. It was at least unmistakable that women were somewhat more religious than men, and old people more than young people. They thought they saw more religious fervor in working-class churches and less religious zeal in the country than in the city. But appearances can be deceptive, even to scientific observers; and looking back, we think they may have been mistaken. By their own account, business-class families in 1924 reported much more church attendance than working-class families. The Lynds had no data at all on religious observance in rural areas and could only guess at it. Although women were more religious than men in the 1920s—as they still are today—it is not at all obvious that women are less modernized than men, and while the elderly are more devout than the young, that difference is more plausibly attributed to their increasing concern with mortality. The Lynds themselves were uncomfortably aware of a number of facts that did not square with the notion of secularization, for example, the increase in the relative number of churches and the disappearance of organized atheism in Muncie between 1890 and 1924.

Even today, many serious students of religion take secularization as much for granted as did the Lynds. Peter Berger, well known both as theologian and sociologist, writes: "By secularization we mean the process by which sectors of society and culture are removed from the domination of religious institutions and symbols. . . . As there is a secularization of society and culture, so there is a secularization of consciousness. Put simply, this means that the modern west has produced an increasing number of individuals who look upon the world and their own lives without the benefit of religious interpretation." Because secularization involves the soft facts of changing consciousness as well as the hard facts of changing social arrangements, it is a difficult trend to prove or disprove objectively. But the extraordinarily complete inventory of religious attitudes and practices in Muncie that the Lynds made in 1924 allows us to determine, with reasonable objectivity, whether there had been such a trend in this community in the past two generations.

We can do this by describing the effects that secularization would necessarily produce and then comparing the information about religion gathered for Middletown III with the information gathered for Middletown I to see whether those effects did actually occur between 1924 and the present.

If secularization had been underway in this community since 1924, it should have all or most of the following consequences:

1. a decline in the number of churches per capita;
2. a decline in the proportion of the population who regularly attend religious services;
3. a decline in the proportion of weddings and funerals held under religious auspices;
4. a decline in religious endogamy, that is the tendency to marry within a religious denomination;
5. a decline in the enrollment of religious schools;
6. a declining proportion of the labor force engaged in church occupations;
7. a decline in the average proportion of family income contributed to the support of religion;
8. the dwindling of new sects, and of new movements in existing churches;
9. increasing attention to secular topics in sermons and liturgy;
10. a decline in the more emotional forms of religious observance;
11. a decline in private religious devotions.

Here in Muncie we have reasonably accurate information about each of the foregoing indicators for two points in time more than fifty years apart.

The most fundamental indicator of religion—church attendance—shows a significant rise since 1924. Concomitantly, the differences in church attendance between men and women and between white-collar and blue-collar people have been diminished.

It may be argued of course that church attendance has little or nothing to do with religious conviction, but there is no evidence at all to support that position. Every serious study that has touched the subject has found a close relationship between church attendance and other forms of religious participation.

Alternatively, it might be contended that the subjective meaning of church attendance has changed over time so that, for example, while the fact of attending church formerly implied a deep religious commitment, it no longer does so. But there is no evidence for that proposition either.

In any case, the trend of church attendance does not stand alone. Of the eleven indicators we examined for evidence of secularization, only one—a slight rise in the proportion of interdenominational marriages—was in the expected direction. All the other trends run the opposite way. The number of churches per capita nearly doubled from 1924 to 1977. The proportion of marriages performed by clergymen increased from 63 percent in 1924 to 79 percent in 1979; the proportion of funerals at which clergymen officiated has not been discovered for 1924, but it was 99 percent in 1979. The proportion of the labor force engaged in religious occupations increased significantly, and the proportion of family income contributed to churches by working-class families (we do not have complete figures for business-class families) increased from 1.6 percent in 1924 to 3.3 percent in 1978. There was an unmistakable movement toward the more emotional forms of religious participation and a great proliferation of new sects. As to new movements in existing churches, the charismatic movement alone loomed larger in the 1970s than any new movement in the 1920s, and the number of revivals has increased faster than the population since 1924, although they do not last as long as they used to.

Of 102 sermons we sampled at random in Muncie churches in 1978, only two dealt with secular issues, and those not closely.

The majority of contemporary church members say that they pray privately, think about heaven often, experience God as a personal presence, believe in the fundamental tenets of Christianity, and judge their own

conduct by religious standards. Nearly half of the people who do not belong to any church report a fairly high level of religious commitment. Taken as a whole, the evidence seems to indicate more sacralization than secularization.

Of course, we cannot assume that the trend of religion here is the same as the trend everywhere else. Muncie's denominational distribution does not quite match that of the United States as a whole; it has too many Methodists and too few Catholics to be quite representative. Some of the religious figures who create a stir elsewhere in the country are lacking here: worker priests, women rabbis, Indian gurus, the tycoons of television preaching.

Yet it would be grossly inaccurate to think of Muncie as a museum of old-time religion. Pious as this community is, recent national surveys tell us that it is rather less pious than the country as a whole. When we compared our 1977–78 survey of religious belief and practice here with a nearly concurrent national survey of religious belief and practice by the Gallup Poll, we found that 16 percent of the Muncie sample reported "no religious preference" compared to 8 percent of the national sample, and only 32 percent of the Muncie sample reported weekly church attendance compared to 41 percent of the national sample. Although these differences are not overwhelming, they are statistically significant and all in the same direction. Whence we infer that if there has not recently been much secularization in Muncie, we are not likely to find much of it in the rest of the country.

We are not the first students of religion to raise doubts about the inevitability of secularization. Andrew Greeley did so a decade ago in an admirable book called *Unsecular Man* (1972) in which he showed that there was then no statistical evidence of the decline of religion in the United States and that, considered in absolute terms, the level of religious observance and practice in this country was extraordinarily high. Here in Muncie, where the evidence is much more comprehensive, we can see that the conventional forms of Christian piety—prayer, fasting, alms-giving, meditation—are all flourishing. What was supposed to be an age of skepticism has turned out instead to be an age of faith, closer perhaps to medieval Europe than to modern Europe in its spiritual climate.

For the country as a whole, we cannot completely dismiss the possibility that the persistence of traditional religion has not prevented some secularization of consciousness, but it is quite certain that the religious consciousness of Middletown has not changed greatly since the 1920s. The words and phrases that people use now to describe their inner religious experiences are so close to the language of their grandparents that we cannot tell them apart. The continuum of faith that the Lynds discovered in 1924 is still intact: at one extreme are people who put their total trust in themselves, at the other those who trust in God alone, in the middle those who divide their commitments between God and their families. But there are more people now at the religious end of this continuum.

With respect to the doctrinal differences that ostensibly account for the existence of so many Protestant denominations—disagreement about episcopal authority, free will and predestination, the efficacy of sacraments, infant or adult baptism, original sin, and the terms of salvation—we cannot find a flicker of interest among laymen, who for the most part are unaware of the beliefs they are supposed to hold on these contentious points. And although the clergy are aware of the finer points of theology, they are totally disinclined to argue them with the spokesmen of other denominations. The same harmonious spirit that suppresses theological arguments before they begin inhibits censure of other people's behavior. There is plenty of preaching against sinners in general in Muncie's churches—profligates, gamblers, irresponsible parents—but very little against individual

sinners. Hester Prynne would be welcomed at a church supper nowadays; after a little discreet whispering, they would treat her with special kindness.

The new tolerance is the most striking change that has taken place in Muncie's religion during the past half century. Indeed, it represents a departure from the mainstream of Christian history. Not only do Protestants speak well of each other's churches and benignly of Catholics, they abstain from condemnation of the heathen and think that children should be taught about Buddhism in the public schools. There is no longer any preaching against the Pope at revival meetings; there are few diatribes against the Jews in Easter sermons; the anti-Americanism displayed by Moslem fundamentalists in the Iran crisis aroused no anti-Moslem sentiment to speak of. The wrath of the godly is now reserved for such secular targets as abortionists, pornographers, and bureaucrats. Although Muncie's churches now support more foreign missionary activity than they did in 1924, the missionary purpose is now the relief of poverty and injustice rather than the displacement of alien religions. Religion in general is nearly as well thought of today as religion in particular.

The continued vitality of traditional religion in America is something of a puzzle because religion has recently been declining in other advanced industrial nations, and the hypothesis that modernization leads inevitably to secularization would be moderately plausible were it not for the American case. If the trends of the past two decades were to continue, organized religion would eventually become a negligible force in Germany and Britain, for example, but there would be no real change in the situation in this country.

The methods available to sociology for peering into the future are not very powerful and, to speak candidly, they do not work very well even in the hands of the masters of our discipline. Until quite recently, the usual basis of social prediction was some version of evolutionary theory—"the advance from the simple to the complex, through a process of successive differentiation"—as Herbert Spencer put it in 1857, but that hardly seems to apply. When it comes to the statistical prediction of the future of religion in Muncie, the most reliable device we have, the extrapolation of existing long-term trends, is not very helpful because past trends have been so inconclusive. The general level of religious practice is somewhat higher than it was half a century ago, but the level of religious belief appears to be about the same, and the leading elements of belief are almost unchanged. Organizationally, the Protestant churches have grown a little stronger and the Catholic church a little weaker. There is much more tolerance between churches and a form of ecumenical goodwill that was formerly lacking, but no more cooperation than

before toward common goals. The denominations of Middletown are perhaps more significant as sources of personal identity today than they used to be, but the difference is small and counterbalanced by a modest increase in interfaith marriages. The Rev. Rip van Winkle, Methodist minister, awaking in Muncie after a sixty-year sleep, would hardly know he had been away.

It is conceivable that major changes may occur in this community's religion—a widespread loss of faith, a wave of denominational mergers, some new messianic movement—but it is unlikely that such changes will occur without a prior transformation of our national society. Until that happens, Middletown's future religion will probably continue to resemble Middletown's past and present religion—archaic, fragmented, and wonderfully untroubled.

ADDITIONAL READINGS

Articles

The entire Winter 1982 issue of *Daedalus: Journal of the American Academy of Arts and Sciences* is devoted to religion in America. Articles by Martin Marty, W. Clark Roof, and Thomas Robbins and Dick Anthony are pertinent to this chapter. For a summary of the latter two articles, see Concluding Postscript of this volume.

Bahr, Howard M. "Shifts in the Denominational Demography of Middletown, 1924–1977." *Journal for the Scientific Study of Religion* 21 (1982): 99–114. Organized religion is alive and stable in this restudy of Middletown, U.S.A., with some evidence of intergenerational switching and some convergence of Catholics and Protestants in terms of background factors.

Bouma, Gary. "Keeping the Faithful: Patterns of Membership Retention in the Christian Reformed Church." *Sociological Analysis* 41 (1980):259–64. With Dean Kelley's thesis in mind, the author asks how one "strict" church succeeds in retaining its members.

Roof, W. Clark, and Hadaway, Christopher Kirk. "Denominational Switching in the Seventies: Going Beyond Glock and Stark." *Journal for the Scientific Study of Religion* 18 (1979):363–79. Switchers tend to move not from "conservative" to "liberal" denominations, as earlier postulated by Glock and Stark. A more complex pattern emerged in the 1970s. Increasing numbers of people have shifted to "none."

Swatos, William H., Jr. "Beyond Denominationalism? Community and

Culture in American Religion." *Journal for the Scientific Study of Religion* 20 (1981):217–27. How explain the rise of "nondenominational churches" at the expense of established churches? Local ties stressed by the former help retain members, while traditional denominations lose appeal by overidentification with remote church bureaucracies operating at a distance from local control and interests.

Books

Hoge, Dean R. *Division in the Protestant House.* Philadelphia: Westminster, 1976. Evangelical and liberal divisions within the United Presbyterian Church are examined with a view to discerning the conditions for church unity.

Lenski, Gerhard. *The Religious Factor.* New York: Doubleday, 1963. Classic study of the effects on socioeconomic status and achievement of membership in, and degree of commitment to, Catholicism and Protestantism.

Leone, Mark P. *Roots of Modern Mormonism.* Cambridge: Harvard University Press, 1979. Though one can argue whether Mormonism is a large sect or a bona fide denomination, there is little question that its organization is highly centralized. Leone's study shows how Mormon symbolism has developed to help maintain a religious minority in a culture not always receptive to it.

Marty, Martin E. ed. *Where the Spirit Leads: American Denominations Today.* Atlanta: John Knox, 1980. Major "families" or denominations are described in terms of current issues and trends. Excellent for comparative study.

Roof, Wade Clark. *Community and Commitment.* New York: Elsevier, 1978. Contrasts Episcopalian church members with "local" vs. those with "cosmopolitan" orientations. Degree of localism is an intervening variable when one looks at the effects of various demographic and personal factors on measures of religiosity. Commitment to the congregation is more a function of local belonging than of orthodoxy of belief.

Scherer, Ross P. *American Denominational Organization: A Sociological View.* Pasadena, Calif.: William Carey Library, 1980. Denominations are viewed from an open-systems perspective focusing on their environments as well as on their own organizational dynamics. Catholicism and Judaism in the United States are also represented in this collection.

4

Sectarian Religious Groups

The church-sect distinction has generated more discussion and more print than perhaps any conceptual framework in the sociology of religion. As "ideal-types" in the tradition of Max Weber, church and sect possess polar characteristics. These are well summed up by sociologists Demerath and Hammond:

The ideal-typical "church" and "sect" differ in both internal and external characteristics. Externally the church seeks to make its peace with the secular society surrounding it, whereas the sect is either aloof or hostile. Internally, the church has many of the earmarks of a bureaucracy with professionalized leadership, high valuation of ritual, and an impersonal evangelizing strategy that welcomes persons wherever and whatever they may be. The sect, on the other hand, is more of an amateurish social movement with lay, charismatic leadership, an emphasis upon perfervid spontaneity, and a sense of religious exclusiveness as reflected in high membership standards.[1]

The distinction has also been used to devise ways of looking at the *process* by which religious groups grow and evolve. In this light, new religious movements begin as cults and proceed to succeeding stages of sect, denomination, and finally church, each stage reflecting more accommodation to, and "being comfortable with," the larger secular society.

A sectlike group, however, may retain many or most of its characteristics over time, even in the face of growing membership. Adaptation to the larger society is by no means inevitable. In fact, as Stark and Bainbridge point out, some sects—such as the Amish and Mennonites, the snake handlers, those Mormon groups still advocating polygamy, and some "urgently millenarian" assemblies (such as Jehovah's Witnesses) —stay in a state of high tension with the larger society. High-tension groups may "encapsulate" themselves, allowing little contact with outsiders and therefore rarely recruiting from the larger society.

To differentiate between church and sect as conceptual "ideal-types" is the burden of the classical literature on the topic. The brief initial reading from H. Richard Niebuhr's *The Social Sources of Denominationalism* is a classic statement of the typology begun by Max Weber and elaborated by his disciple Ernst Troeltsch at the beginning of this century. "Institutional church" and "associational sect" are highlighted in contrast. The church has accommodated to the larger society; the sect maintains its distinctiveness and opposition, recruiting from the lower socioeconomic ranks. But let one generation pass and another arise that is financially better off and more socially accepted, and the sect begins to break down its former isolation. Moreover, "the discipline of work and expenditure" characteristic of sect members results in greater member affluence, with doctrinal and ethical compromises inevitably following. Soon after come an official, theologically educated clergy and a formalized creed, moving the sect further along toward the church end of the continuum.

Contemporary researchers William Sims Bainbridge and Rodney Stark have written extensively on sects, focusing centrally on the concept of *tension* between sect members and the "outside world." In their words,

Tension is equivalent to subcultural deviance and consists of three interacting components: 1) *difference* between the group and its environment in terms of beliefs, norms, and behavior; 2) *antagonism* arising from both sides noticing these differences; 3) *separation* in terms of social relations between the group and outsiders.

Bainbridge and Stark attempt through survey research to *measure* degree of tension. High tension is manifested in strong opinions, "different" behavior, and in social relations that cut members off from alignment and contact with the larger society. On a continuum of tension, for example, the Protestant Episcopal Church and the United Church of Christ would exhibit very low tension (or high accommodation) with their environment. The American Lutheran Church would show moderate tension, Southern Baptists moderately high tension, and Pentecostal churches and Jehovah's Witnesses very high tension. The authors call on survey research to measure the other side of the equation as well: To what extent do members of the larger society (as shown in a California survey) accept or reject persons belonging to various churches, in terms of "feeling friendly and at ease" with them? The difference-antagonism-separation theme is thus empirically illustrated. Formulation of research methods by which to measure tension is important, not least because similar research can reveal whether the second (and later) generations of sect members continue to retain sectlike characteristics; or whether, instead, they show accommodative tendencies, making their peace with the surrounding environment.

Developing church-sect typologies has not been the only concern of social scientists of religion. The function of the sect as "compensator" for low socioeconomic status is frequently affirmed. John B. Holt in 1940 suggested how holiness and pentecostal churches provided a supportive community for rural-to-urban migrants in the American South then experiencing the stresses of resettlement. These churches reiterated older, traditional modes of behavior. They provided a cushion, that is, "stable and secure social status in the midst of a feeling of isolation, social and economic insecurity."[3] In 1942 Liston Pope published his classic *Millhands and Preachers*, a study of the role of community churches in a setting of social upheaval occasioned by a major strike in the textile mills of Gastonia, North Carolina. The compensatory thesis has probably never been better stated:

The sects substitute religious status for social status, a fact which may help to account for their emphasis on varying degrees of Grace. . . . the newer sects divide their members, and people in general, into several religious classifications: saved, sanctified, baptized with the Holy Ghost, baptized with water, recipient of the first, second, or third blessing, and the like. What matters, then, if a Methodist has more money but has never been baptized with the Holy Ghost? As over against segregation from the community, the newer sects affirm separation from the world; in the face of exclusion on educational, economic, and religious grounds, they affirm exclusion from their own fellowship of those who engage in mixed bathing, dancing, card playing, bobbing the hair, gambling, baseball, county fairs, drinking, and using tobacco. Because they have no jewelry to wear, they make refusal to wear jewelry, including wedding rings, a religious requirement. They transmute poverty into a symptom of Grace. Having no money, they redeem their economic status by rigid tithing of the small income they do possess, and thus far surpass members of churches of any other type or denomination in per capita contribution, despite the fact that they stand at the bottom of the economic scale.[4]

Two decades later, sociologist Benton Johnson went several steps further. While admitting that members may *join* holiness groups for compensatory reasons, Johnson called attention to Liston Pope's observation that t   nill owners in Gastonia supported several sectarian churches because they believed churchgoers to be steady, reliable workers free of vices that would hinder their productivity. Johnson's own interviews with ten holiness ministers revealed that the latter, when presented with "two conflicting, generalized orientations toward life" —one more cautious and less achievement oriented, the other stressing mastery of one's life to achieve goals by striving for them—almost unanimously chose the second. "We ought to aim high, like the man said. If you had a call to the grocery business, then you ought to be ambitious for the glory of God, to be successful for Christ's sake."[5] Here convergence with dominant American success values is obvious. It calls into question any easy assumption of withdrawal or otherworldliness as a necessary and sole outcome of sectarian socialization.

"Themes of Power and Control in a Pentecostal Assembly," by John Wilson and Harvey K. Clow, represents a continuation of this kind of research. They too reject a merely compensatory view of pentecostalism. Focusing on the particular religious experiences of holiness church members, they see an important congruence between these experiences and the particular social circumstances of the members. If we grant the authors' premise, which is linked to a long, theoretical tradition ranging from Emile Durkheim to contemporary scholars like Mary Douglas, "bodily symbols are ways in which we speak about social relations." Speaking in tongues and spirit possession symbolize power to members concerned with "gaining victory over the flesh." But the devotees arrive at this power, so to speak, by giving themselves over to a ritually controlled experienced of *dis*order as they dance ecstatically "in the Spirit." The person self-dramatizes that much of life is not under one's control. By allowing "disorder" to enter one's life in this ritualized fashion, the person experiences that disorder can be followed by, or transformed into, order if only one takes advantage of the divine power available in the Pentecostal service. But, if poverty robs one of self-control and middle-class status would eliminate this situation, suppose middle-class status is not a realistic prospect? While, as the authors admit, a compensatory explanation is plausible here, it is insufficient. Loss of control is a positive value and is sought; the bodily release and reaffirmation that one *is* leading the good life already dramatize that one's social reality *is* "O.K.," despite the unattainability of a better material and social life.

"The Sect" is taken from the 1965–1975 restudy of Gastonia, North Carolina. Earle, Knudsen, and Shriver's study is no less thorough and enlightening than Pope's *Millhands and Preachers*. This short selection from *Spindles and Spires* returns us, in a sense, to Niebuhr's opening description of sects as children of "an outcast minority." Here is fervent testimony, immediate physical experience of being filled by "the Spirit," "providing for them a sense of community, participation, and euphoria not present in the more formal services." Despite conditions of oppression, however, this group shows no readiness to look at—much less take action against—the larger institutions responsible for their poverty and worldly powerlessness. It is business as usual in Gastonia, North Carolina.

Notes

1. J. Demerath III and Phillip E. Hammond, *Religion in Social Context* (New York: Random House, 1969), p. 157.
2. Rodney Stark and William S. Bainbridge, "American-Born Sects: Initial Findings," *Journal for the Scientific Study of Religion* 20 (1981): 138–39.
3. John B. Holt, "Holiness Religion: Cultural Shock and Social Reorganization," in J. Milton Yinger, *Religion, Society and the Individual* (New York: Macmillan, 1957), pp. 463–70.
4. Liston Pope, *Millhands and Preachers* (New Haven, Conn: Yale University Press, 1942), pp. 137–38.
5. Benton Johnson, "Do Holiness Sects Socialize in Dominant Values?" in *Religion, Culture, and Society*, ed. Louis Schneider (New York: John Wiley, 1964) p. 507.

R E A D I N G   4 . 1

The Ethical Failure of the Divided Church

H. Richard Niebuhr

One element in the social sources of theological differentiation deserves especial attention. Max Weber and Ernst Troeltsch have demonstrated how important are the differences in the sociological structure of religious groups in the determination of their doctrine. The primary distinction to be made here is that between the church and the sect, of which the former is a natural social group akin to the family or the nation while the latter is a voluntary association. The difference has been well described as lying primarily in the fact that members are born into the church while they must join the sect. Churches are inclusive institutions, frequently are national in scope, and emphasize the universalism of the gospel; while sects are exclusive in character, appeal to the individualistic element in Christianity, and emphasize its ethical demands. Membership in a church is socially obligatory, the necessary consequence of

birth into a family or nation, and no special requirements condition its privileges; the sect, on the other hand, is likely to demand some definite type of religious experience as a prerequisite of membership.

These differences in structure have their corollaries in differences in ethics and doctrine. The institutional church naturally attaches a high importance to the means of grace which it administers, to the system of doctrine which it has formulated, and to the official administration of sacraments and teaching by an official clergy; for it is an educational institution which must seek to train its youthful members to conformity in thought and practice and so fit them for the exercise of rights they have inherited. The associational sect, on the other hand, attaches primary importance to the religious experience of its members prior to their fellowship with the group, to the priesthood of all believers, to the sacraments as symbols of fellowship and pledges of allegiance. It frequently rejects an official clergy, preferring to trust for guidance to lay inspiration rather than to theological or liturgical expertness.

H. Richard Niebuhr (1894–1962) was Sterling Professor of Theology and Christian Ethics at Yale University.
Reprinted from H. Richard Niebuhr, *The Social Sources of Denominationalism* (New York: Henry Holt, 1929), by permission of Florence M. Niebuhr.

The church as an inclusive social group is closely allied with national, economic, and cultural interests; by the very nature of its constitution it is committed to the accommodation of its ethics to the ethics of civilization; it must represent the morality of the respectable majority, not of the heroic minority. The sect, however, is always a minority group, whose separatist and semi-ascetic attitude toward "the world" is reenforced by the loyalty which persecution nurtures. It holds with tenacity to its interpretation of Christian ethics and prefers isolation to compromise. At times it refuses participation in the government, at times rejects war, at times seek to sever as much as possible the bonds which tie it to the common life of industry and culture. So the sociological structure, while resting in part on a conception of Christianity, reacts upon that conception and reenforces or modifies it. On the other hand the adoption of one or the other type of constitution is itself largely due to the social condition of those who form the sect or compose the church. In Protestant history the sect has ever been the child of an outcast minority, taking its rise in the religious revolts of the poor, of those who were without effective representation in church or state and who formed their conventicles of dissent in the only way open to them, on the democratic, associational pattern. The sociological character of sectarianism, however, is almost always modified in the course of time by the natural processes of birth and death, and on this change in structure changes in doctrine and ethics inevitably follow. By its very nature the sectarian type of organization is valid only for one generation. The children born to the voluntary members of the first generation begin to make the sect a church long before they have arrived at the years of discretion. For with their coming the sect must take on the character of an educational and disciplinary institution, with the purpose of bringing the new generation into conformity with ideals and customs which have be-

come traditional. Rarely does a second generation hold the convictions it has inherited with a fervor equal to that of its fathers, who fashioned these convictions in the heat of conflict and at the risk of martyrdom. As generation succeeds generation, the isolation of the community from the world becomes more difficult. Furthermore, wealth frequently increases when the sect subjects itself to the discipline of asceticism in work and expenditure; with the increase of wealth the possibilities for culture also become more numerous and involvement in the economic life of the nation as a whole can less easily be limited. Compromise begins and the ethics of the sect approach the churchly type of morals. As with the ethics, so with the doctrine, so also with the administration of religion. An official clergy, theologically educated and schooled in the refinements of ritual, takes the place of lay leadership; easily imparted creeds are substituted for the difficult enthusiasms of the pioneers; children are born into the group and infant baptism or dedication becomes once more a means of grace. So the sect becomes a church.

Religious history amply illustrates the process. An outstanding example is the "Half-Way Covenant" of the New England churches, which provided for the baptism of the children of second-generation, unconverted parents who had "owned the covenant" and submitted to the discipline of the church without being able to attain full membership because of their lack of the experience of salvation. The rise of "birth-right membership" in the Society of Friends shows the same process at work while the histories of Mennonites, Baptists, and Methodists offer further illustrations. Doctrines and practice change with the mutations of social structure, not vice versa; the ideological interpretation of such changes quite misses the point.

The evils of denominationalism do not lie, however, in this differentiation of churches and sects. On the contrary, the rise of new sects to champion the uncompromising ethics of Jesus and "to preach the gospel to the poor" has again and again been the effective means of recalling Christendom to its mission. This phase of denominational history must be regarded as helpful, despite the break in unity which it brings about. The evil of denominationalism lies in the conditions which make the rise of sects desirable and

necessary: in the failure of the churches to transcend the social conditions which fashion them into caste-organizations, to sublimate their loyalties to standards and institutions only remotely relevant if not contrary to the Christian ideal, to resist the temptation of making their own self-preservation and extension the primary object of their endeavor.

R E A D I N G   4 . 2

Sectarian Tension

William Sims Bainbridge and Rodney Stark

We are engaged in an effort to construct an integrated set of deductive theories of major religious phenomena. In a recent paper (Stark and Bainbridge, 1979) we developed concepts necessary for a theory of religious movements. There we demonstrated why the long tradition of church-sect typologies failed to provide concepts useful for theorizing. Each of these typological schemes in the literature is constructed of a mass of loosely correlated features that result in a proliferation of mixed types which cannot be ordered. With no basis for ordering groups as more churchlike or more sectlike, it is impossible to develop or test theories which attempt, for example, to account for the transformation of sects into churches. Many other social scientists also have pointed to the serious inadequacies in church-sect conceptualizations (Gustafson, 1967; Goode, 1967; Eister, 1967; Dittes, 1971; Knudsen *et al.*, 1978).

We found no need, however, to develop our own conceptualizations of church and sect.

William Sims Bainbridge is Associate Professor of Sociology at Harvard University.

Rodney Stark is Professor of Sociology at the University of Washington, Seattle.

Reprinted from *Review of Religious Research* 22 (December 1980) with permission of the Religious Research Association and the authors.

Instead, we found that Benton Johnson (1963) had provided the needed conceptual clarity. By identifying a single axis of variation along which religious organizations may easily be ranked, Johnson achieved what is, in our judgment, the most important advance in this area since Niebuhr first proposed a church-sect theory in 1929. We are at a loss to know why others have continued to pursue obviously unsuitable typologies since Johnson's work appeared.

Johnson identified *tension with the surrounding sociocultural environment* as the *single* defining criterion of the church-sect dimension. Sects are in a state of high tension with their environment; churches are in a state of low tension, or even no tension at all. By excluding the multitude of loose correlates from the definitions of churches and sects, Johnson's conceptualization frees these other features for inclusion in theories about the origins and transformations of churches and sects. For example, since sects are no longer defined as having a converted rather than a socialized membership (and therefore no longer confront us with the need for mixed types when we observe sects such as the Amish with wholly socialized memberships), it now becomes possible to seek propositions about why and how the arrival of a generation of socialized members transforms religious movements. And, indeed, since discovering such propositions is our primary concern, we gladly adopted Johnson's definition for use in our theories.

Nevertheless, since we are concerned to produce theories that are easily testable, the question arises whether the notion of "tension" is specific enough to be operationalized. When this question was first raised by reviewers of a paper in which we used Johnson's tension axis of sectarianism, we were satisfied to point out some obvious and dramatic symptoms of tension. That is, we suggested that public disputes in which sects attacked more worldly institutions or in which society inflicted punishment on sects demonstrated a way to identify high degrees of tension.

Thus, for example, the annihilation of a sect by fire and the sword would be a sure indicator of extreme tension. Less violent conflict would also count, such as the recent court battle between the Amish and the State of Wisconsin over compulsory secondary education (Keim, 1975). Even in our tolerant society, acts of violence and repression against sects are common enough to serve as indicators in the most extreme cases. For example, members of many high-tension religious groups have recently suffered kidnapping and "deprogramming," including such groups as the Moonies, the Hare Krishnas, the Love Family, the Children of God, and the New Testament Missionary Fellowship (Patrick and Dulack, 1976).

Upon further reflection, however, we recognized that this was not a wholly satisfactory way to measure tension. To operationalize our theories it must be possible to rank groups along *all* degrees of the tension axis, not just at its end points. More continuous and sensitive measures are necessary.

We then noted that Johnson himself (1963:543) had suggested that a church-sect scale developed by Russell Dynes (1955)

might serve. Dynes had in fact come rather close to defining the church-sect dimension in terms of tension with the sociocultural environment:

The construct of the Church has generally signified a type of religious organization which accepts the social order and integrates existing cultural definitions into its religious ideology. The Sect, as a contrasting type, rejects integration with the social order and develops a separate subculture, stressing rather rigid behavioral requirements for its members. (Dynes, 1955:555)

However, Dynes's scale is not adequate. He did not follow his own definitions when he constructed it, but instead fell back on a list of putative correlates of the sect proposed by Liston Pope (1942). Thus Dynes created a scale rooted in the same tradition of typologies we seek to avoid. His scale is extremely culture-bound (consider the item "a congregation should encourage the minister during his sermon by saying *amen*" (Dynes, 1955: 556). This agree-disagree battery seeks to determine individuals' commitment to the particular trappings of *some* sects, primarily those of the rural South. Such a measure will not do what we need. Indeed, our concern is not to identify the religious preferences of *individuals*, but to find a way to characterize *groups* in terms of their degree of tension. For it is the origins and changes of groups that our theory about churches and sects seeks to explain.

Therefore, in this paper, we have turned aside from our theoretical pursuits in order to demonstrate the adequacy of the concept of tension. First, we discuss and specify the concept more fully. Then we examine data on several ways in which tension can be measured. Our first assessment of these data is to see whether they successfully differentiate among religious groups. The second is to see if they order groups in a way consistent with our qualitative sense of which groups are more and less sectlike. Finally, we assess whether these several different ways of measuring tension are consistent—do they rank the same groups in the same order. If we can demonstrate that the answer in each case is yes, then we can return to our theorizing with confidence that Johnson has provided us with an efficient and measurable way to define church and sect.

The Sample

All the tables reported in this paper are based on a sample of church members in four counties of Northern California who were sent a lengthy questionnaire. Complete details of the sample and research instrument are given in Glock and Stark (1966). The tables reported here are based on responses from 2326 members of 16 different Protestant denominations and from 545 Catholics. We present the Catholic data primarily for comparison with the higher-tension Protestant groups and will discuss the pattern of Catholic responses only briefly at the end of this paper. Previous publications intuitively ranked the Protestant groups from the most churchlike to the most sectlike (Glock and Stark, 1965; 1966; Stark and Glock, 1968), and we have followed the same ranking here. In all past usage a number of small denominations were collapsed into a single category and identified as "sects": the Church of God, the Church of Christ, Nazarenes, Assemblies of God, Seventh-Day Adventists, the Gospel Lighthouse, and the Foursquare Gospel Church. Here we have decomposed this generic category into its constituent denominations.[1] Two of these groups, the Gospel Lighthouse and the Foursquare Gospel Church, did not provide a large enough number of respondents for stable statistical results. They have been excluded from the analysis except for computations based on the total "sects" category or on "total Protestants."

Since even 15 denominations produce very large tables, we have collapsed some Protes-

tant denominations into "low tension" and "medium tension" groups. The "low tension" category includes Congregationalists, Methodists, Episcopalians, and members of the Disciples of Christ. The "medium tension" category consists of the Presbyterian, American Lutheran, and American Baptist denominations. Because Missouri Synod Lutherans and Southern Baptists stand at the borderline of sectarianism, we report data for these two "sectlike denominations" separately. The collapsing was done after careful examination of the data showed there was very little variation among the denominations making up the low- or the medium-tension categories. Economy is gained and no pertinent information is lost thereby.

The Concept of Tension

In his classic paper, Johnson only once uses the term *tension:* "a sect tends to be in a state of tension with its surroundings" (1963:544). In his primary definitions he speaks instead of sects rejecting their social environments. We, however, based our concepts on tension rather than on rejection, because rejection blurs a relationship that is a two-way street. The sect not only rejects society—it, in turn, is rejected by society. This two-way relationship is best captured by the inclusive concept of tension, as Johnson once says and often implies.

Tension with the sociocultural environment is equivalent to *subcultural deviance*, marked by *difference*, *antagonism*, and *separation*. The sect and the society disagree over proper beliefs, norms, and behavior. They judge each other harshly, each asserting its superiority over the other. The dispute is reflected in the social relations of sect members. Rejected by and rejecting the larger society, sects draw together in relatively closed and cohesive groups. In the case of extreme tension, sects will be socially encapsulated, and the members will have relatively little intimate contact with nonmembers (Cf. Wallis, 1977).

It might be objected that defining subcultural deviance in terms of difference, antagonism, and separation is to introduce yet another unideal collection of disparate variables that defies unambiguous measurement and confident use. But this triad of terms really describes a single concept, and the three are worth distinguishing primarily because they allow us to arrange the indicators of subcultural deviance in a meaningful pattern, thereby rendering them more intelligible and easier to survey. Traditional definitions of deviant behavior describe it not only as different from the standard set by dominant groups in the society, but also as punishable, drawing disapproval and negative sanctions of at least some level of severity. A deviant subculture provides a competing standard, setting deviant norms and thus asserting antagonism toward those of the larger society. Social relations across the border of a deviant subculture are strained, and therefore there is a strong tendency for a social cleavage to form, as people avoid painful disputes, separating the subculture from the surrounding community. Seen the other way around, without some degree of social separation, the subculture will find it difficult to sustain deviant norms and counteract the pressures to conform communicated through social relations with outsiders. In our future theoretical work, we will explore these issues more deeply. For now it is enough to explain that *deviant subculture* is a unitary concept, although we find it convenient to group its indicators under three headings.

There are two common standards against which we can measure deviance. First, we can follow a purely statistical approach, defining deviance as any significant departure from the average for the population as a whole. Second, we can emphasize the importance of power and influence, defining deviance as any behavior or characteristic that is scorned and punished by powerful elites in

society. The problem with the first approach is that it may define an elite as deviant, even when the elite has the power to enforce its standards on others. To a great extent elites represent the society with which the sects are in tension. For our purposes the proper standard is a combination of the two approaches, an informed analysis that is interested in both the population average and in the norms set by elites.

In many of our tables, the low- and medium-tension denominations are in fact very close to the average for Protestants as a whole. In other cases, the low tension group is somewhat far from the average, although the high tension groups tend to be farther from the average in the opposite direction. Perhaps both ends of the distribution represent tension with the social environment? But this conclusion, following the purely statistical model of deviance, is unwarranted. Ours is a relatively secular society in which the otherworldliness of high-tension sects does not harmonize with the assumptions built into economic, political, and nonreligious cultural institutions. Many studies have shown that the denominations we label "low tension" are in fact most favorably placed in the class structure. This is true for the respondents in our study, as several analyses showed. For example, only 13 percent of members of the low-tension denominations identified themselves as working-class, while fully 40 percent of the sect members applied this label to themselves. Forty percent in the low-tension group had completed college, compared with 17 percent of sect members. Fifty-five percent of those in the low-tension denominations held high-status jobs: professional, technical, and similar workers, or proprietors, managers, and officials. Half this proportion of sect members, 27 percent, said they held such high-status jobs. The low-tension end of the spectrum is anchored closest to the centers of societal power. This fact allows us to identify these denominations conclusively as the low-tension groups even when they depart somewhat from the average for the population as a whole. In a theocratic society, low tension might mean intense involvement in religion (of a certain kind), but in our secularized nation low tension means low levels of commitment to traditional religion.

Deviant Norms, Beliefs, and Behavior

Johnson (1963:544) drew the connection between tension and deviance, saying "religions enforcing norms on their adherents that are sharply distinct from norms common in secular quarters should be classed as relatively sectarian." At the other extreme, "bodies permitting their members to participate freely in all phases of secular life should probably . . . be classified as churches." We cannot specify *a priori* precisely which norms will be subjects of disagreement between high-tension groups and the rest of society, because sects will reflect the culture and the history of the particular societies in which they emerge. But in general we would expect that issues of personal morality will be the most common areas of dispute. If we wanted to identify sects in a society of which we had no previous knowledge, we would have to do a preliminary survey to identify norms concerning personal behavior that were foci of heated debate in religious circles. After that we could survey different religious groups to see which professed extreme minority views on these matters.

The survey data in hand primarily concern behavior *permitted* by secular society but *forbidden* by some religious groups. But we know that some kinds of behavior are prohibited by the larger society but encouraged by these groups. For example, several high-tension American sects encourage speaking in tongues, while such behavior would be considered psychopathological in a secular setting. Norms of mental health do differ significantly from one religious group to another,

with fundamentalist groups showing the greatest disagreement with the standards of psychiatrists (Larson, 1964; 1968). A few sects encourage ritual poison drinking and serpent handling, despite laws against these practices (La Barre, 1969). Several cults use hallucinogenic drugs despite their secular prohibition, including the Native American Church, the Rastafarians (Furst, 1972), and the Love Family, which initiated members through drug-induced revelations. We have data on some relatively mild forms of religious behavior required by the sects, but the clearest starting point is to look at behavior *prohibited* by the sects.

Table 1 shows that members of sects and higher-tension denominations do disagree with the majority on a number of moral issues. Members of sects are more likely than others to feel that morals in this country "are pretty bad and getting worse." The most extreme differences in this table are in attitudes toward dancing and the moderate use of alcohol. The overwhelming majority of members of low-tension denominations tolerate such behavior, while the majority of sect members reject it. These huge differences demonstrate strikingly that the sects do reject normative standards that are accepted by the society at large, while churches accept these standards. But differences need not be this large before they are significant. Obviously, a number of factors other than religious concerns may influence individual opinions. For example, gambling may be opposed on purely practical and economic grounds. The majority in every Protestant group disapproves of gambling, but the proportion is 20 to 30 percentage points higher in the sects than in the total Protestant population. *As groups*, the sects reject gambling more strongly than do the low-tension denominations, even if a majority in all Protestant groups are opposed to this behavior.

Table 2 shows that high-tension groups hold a number of deviant beliefs, opinions that are distinctly different from secular stan-

Table 1   *Deviant Norms*

| | Percent of Each Group Giving the Indicated Response | | | | | | | | | | |
| | Denominations | | Sectlike | | Sects | | | | | | |
	Low Tension (1032)	Medium Tension (844)	Mo. Luth. (116)	S. Bapt. (79)	C. of God (44)	C. of Christ (37)	Nazarene (75)	Assem. of God (44)	Seventh Day Ad. (35)	Total Prot. (2326)	Total Cath. (545)
The respondent feels that morals in this country "are pretty bad and getting worse."	41	47	53	71	66	73	71	84	83	48	43
The respondent disapproves of dancing.	1	9	28	77	77	95	96	91	100	18	1
The respondent disapproves of gambling.	62	67	81	96	89	100	92	98	97	69	27
The respondent approves of censorship of movies and books.	31	36	49	65	57	57	73	82	66	39	72
The respondent disapproves "highly" of someone who drinks moderately.	4	6	2	38	43	57	57	57	60	11	1
The respondent feels that drinking liquor would definitely prevent salvation.	3	3	1	15	30	38	39	30	46	7	2
The respondent is "rather concerned with trying to live as sinless a life as possible."	55	67	76	90	86	92	91	91	94	65	76
The respondent believes what we do in this life will determine our fate in the hereafter.	31	45	53	89	82	84	95	93	94	46	71

dards, even if two of these opinions are accepted by more than half of our sample of respondents. Low-tension denominations do not reject Darwin's theory, nor are they convinced by stories about the devil, biblical miracles, or the Second Coming. Medium-tension denominations tend to accept the historical reality of biblical miracles, including the story that Jesus walked on water, but these two beliefs describe a distant past that need not have much relevance for participation in contemporary secular society. Beyond their utility as indicators of disagreement, the five beliefs listed in Table 2 also represent tension because they indicate dissatisfaction with the world as it can be perceived by the human senses, studied by science, and analyzed by reason. Taken together, they indicate rejection of the world as it seems, or at least the feeling that the material world is not rich

enough unless supplemented by the supernatural. All people probably desire more than life can actually give them, but in Table 2 we see that this dissatisfaction is probably much greater for the sects than for the low-tension denominations.

One of the disadvantages of survey research is that we must usually accept at face value whatever our respondents tell us. Sometimes attitudes and opinions are very poor reflections of social reality and fail to predict behavior (Schuman and Johnson, 1976). Even self-report behavioral items may provide more direct evidence. Table 3 lists five such measures and has very much the same pattern of results as Table 1 and Table 2. Of course, the first one, frequent prayer, is not inherently deviant. Over two-thirds of our church-member respondents pray often or daily. But the sects are 25 percentage points above the low-

Table 2 *Deviant Beliefs*

| | Percent of Each Group Giving the Indicated Response | | | | | | | | | | |
| | Denominations | | Sectlike | | Sects | | | | | | |
	Low Ten-sion (1032)	Medium Ten-sion (844)	Mo. Luth. (116)	S. Bapt. (79)	C. of God (44)	C. of Christ (37)	Naza-rene (75)	Assem. of God (144)	Sev-enth Day Ad. (35)	Total Prot. (2326)	Total Cath. (545)
Darwin's theory of evolution could not possibly be true.	11	29	64	72	57	78	80	91	94	30	28
It is completely true that the Devil actually exists.	14	38	77	92	73	87	91	96	97	37	66
Biblical miracles actually happened just as the Bible says they did.	39	61	89	92	84	97	88	96	91	57	74
It is completely true that Jesus walked on water.	28	55	83	99	84	97	93	96	100	50	71
Definitely, Jesus will actually return to the earth some day.	22	48	75	94	73	78	93	100	100	44	47

tension denominations. High-tension groups have a somewhat higher norm for prayer, but much higher norms for saying grace, reading the Bible at home regularly, listening to religious programs, and spending evenings in church. Thus, high-tension denominations not only reject some important secular norms and hold deviant opinions, but also set unusual standards for positive religious behavior.

Sectarian Rejection of Society

High tension means not only *difference* from secular society, but also *antagonism* toward it. Table 4 lists four items that bear on *particularism*, "the belief that only one's own religion is legitimate" (Glock and Stark, 1966:20). The first two items give special honor to Christians, saying that heaven and salvation are reserved for true believers in Jesus Christ. High-tension groups within the Christian tradition are especially likely to agree with these two items. The pattern of responses to the statement that Hindu religion would prevent salvation is not the simple reflection of the two previous items as logic

would require it to be. It may be that rejection of Hindu religion by sect members is not stronger, because Hindus are not part of the surrounding American sociocultural environment. The last item in Table 4, tithing, shows that the sects, unlike any of the lower-tension groups, demand sacrifice for the sake of the sect, a personal investment on the part of members that indicates that they value the sect highly. Taken together, the items in Table 4 show that members of high-tension groups place very high value on their own groups.

Table 5 describes the social struggle that goes on at the border of high-tension religious groups. Members of the sects frequently attempt to convert others to their faith and, at the same time, are concerned about defending their religious group against outside influences. In part, conversion attempts may be public dramatizations of particularistic pride, but they are also based on hostility toward outsiders. Unless outsiders can be converted to the sect, sect members will have difficulty carrying on close relationships with them. Conversion appeals typically claim that the converting group is better than any other, and that the secular world is quite

Table 3 *Deviant Behavior*

	Denominations		Sectlike		Sects						
	Low Ten-sion (1032)	Medium Ten-sion (844)	Mo. Luth. (116)	S. Bapt. (79)	C. of God (44)	C. of Christ (37)	Naza-rene (75)	Assem. of God (44)	Sev-enth Day Ad. (35)	Total Prot. (2326)	Total Cath. (545)
	Percent of Each Group Giving the Indicated Response										
The respondent prays "quite often" or "regularly once a day or more."	63	71	80	87	89	92	85	91	91	70	76
Grace is said at all meals in the respondent's home.	16	25	41	53	66	65	69	80	77	28	22
The respondent reads the Bible at home regularly.	12	24	21	63	48	49	59	57	69	23	5
The respondent regularly listens to or watches religious services on radio or television.	7	10	13	28	18	22	33	34	40	12	6
In an average week, the respondent spends two or more evenings in church.	6	10	8	52	61	70	56	70	23	15	5

bad. Members of high-tension groups are more likely to distrust nonbelievers and to feel their community needs to be defended against non-Christian missionaries. For these people, the perimeter of their sect is a battle-front; the conversion struggle is a fight for acceptance from other persons, yet rejection of society as a whole. Interestingly, the Sev-enth-Day Adventist respondents are not espe-cially worried about Hindus (Table 4) or about other non-Christians (Table 5). This un-usual tolerance in a sect is probably the re-sult of this group's experience of persecution in overseas missionary work, which resulted in dedication to norms of toleration for self-defense if for no other reason.

Table 4 *Particularism*

	Denominations		Sectlike		Sects						
	Low Ten-sion (1032)	Medium Ten-sion (844)	Mo. Luth. (116)	S. Bapt. (79)	C. of God (44)	C. of Christ (37)	Naza-rene (75)	Assem. of God (44)	Sev-enth Day Ad. (35)	Total Prot. (2326)	Total Cath. (545)
	Percent of Each Group Giving the Indicated Response										
Only those who believe in Jesus Christ can go to heaven.	13	39	80	92	59	89	81	89	77	36	12
Belief in Jesus Christ as Savior is absolutely necessary for salvation.	47	71	97	97	96	97	93	100	94	65	51
Being of the Hindu religion would definitely prevent salvation.	4	15	40	32	32	60	35	41	17	14	2
Tithing is absolutely necessary for salvation.	8	12	7	18	52	43	45	39	69	14	10

Table 5 Conversion and Defense

| | Percent of Each Group Giving the Indicated Responses | | | | | | | | | | |
| | Denominations | | Sectlike | | Sects | | | | | | |
	Low Tension (1032)	Medium Tension (844)	Mo. Luth. (116)	S. Bapt. (79)	C. of God (44)	C. of Christ (37)	Nazarene (75)	Assem. of God (44)	Seventh Day Ad. (35)	Total Prot. (2326)	Total Cath. (545)
Once or more the respondent has tried to convert someone to his or her religious faith.	38	50	63	89	86	84	83	86	83	50	40
Often the respondent has tried to convert someone to his or her religious faith.	5	8	10	32	32	32	27	36	34	10	5
The respondent sometimes prays to ask God to bring someone else to Christian faith and belief.	26	38	48	87	84	95	85	86	89	40	37
The respondent is "very interested" in knowing the religious affiliation of people he or she meets.	12	16	19	44	34	49	32	39	34	18	9
The respondent feels "we should not allow missionaries from non-Christian religions to spread their teachings in a Christian community."	17	27	35	41	36	41	41	55	23	25	23
The respondent says, "I tend to distrust a person who does not believe in Jesus."	19	27	34	53	46	51	47	55	33	27	22

Table 6 Social Encapsulation

| | Percent of Each Group Giving the Indicated Responses | | | | | | | | | | |
| | Denominations | | Sectlike | | Sects | | | | | | |
	Low Tension (1032)	Medium Tension (844)	Mo. Luth. (116)	S. Bapt. (79)	of God (44)	C. of Christ (37)	Nazarene (75)	Assem. of God (44)	Seventh Day Ad. (35)	Total Prot. (2326)	Total Cath. (545)
Respondent disapproves of religious mixed marriages.	31	39	70	80	55	68	85	86	94	43	65
Respondent feels marrying a non-Christian would "possibly" or "definitely" prevent salvation.	9	16	22	20	46	51	68	73	57	18	27
Respondent says, "I fit in very well with my church congregation."	22	23	25	42	48	47	53	66	54	27	23
Half or more of the people the respondent associates with are members of his or her congregation.	29	37	36	51	77	59	72	75	69	38	47
Three or more of the respondent's five closest friends are members of his or her congregation.	22	25	26	49	61	65	65	66	83	29	36

High tension with the societal environment is not merely a matter of strong opinions and deviant behavior. It is also manifested in patterns of social relations. In extreme cases, high-tension groups separate completely from the social life of the larger society and retreat into geographical isolation. Such extreme separation is not just an antique phenomenon affecting Hutterites, Amish, and Mormons. Even in the twentieth century, some high-tension groups have fled their societies of origin, wandered in the wilderness, and sought completely new sociocultural environments (Zablocki, 1971; Bainbridge, 1978). Table 6 shows six indicators of less complete separation.

The first two items show that sects are most likely to disapprove of marriages with members of other religious groups. In tension with the social environment, their relations with outsiders are strained. Conversely, relations with other insiders are favored. Members of sects are more than twice as likely to say they "fit in very well" with their church congregation than are members of low-tension denominations. The sect member's friends are much more likely to be fellow members of the same group. Social separation from outsiders and closer relations with other insiders are implied by each other. Together, they constitute *encapsulation* of the sect, isolation of each high-tension subculture as a distinct, closed social world.

In a sociometric study of Protestant ministers, Balswick and Faulkner (1970:310) found that sectarian ministers were bound together in a "fairly tightly knit clique" in comparison to ministers of low-tension denominations who had "the most loosely structured interrelationships." This finding suggests that not only the members, but also the clergy of high-tension religious groups tend to be socially encapsulated. Further evidence for this observation is reported in a recent survey study of 1559 Protestant clergymen by Harold E. Quinley (1974). Unfortunately, the sample did not include ministers of small, radical sects, but there were 131 Missouri Lu-

therans and 167 Southern Baptists, and 42 percent of the total described themselves as Fundamentalist or Conservative. Quinley combined responses to several questionnaire items to produce a five-point index of religious orientation from "most modernist" to "most traditionalist." The 320 "most traditionalist" clergymen expressed views that place them at the high-tension end of the distribution. For example, they believed that "Jesus walked on water" and that "the Devil actually exists." The questionnaire also asked how frequently they visited informally with other ministers, either of their own denomination or of other denominations. Visits with fellow ministers of their own denomination did not vary significantly by religious orientation. Such visits were made less than once a month by 22 percent of the "most modernist" clergy and by 21 percent of the "most traditionalist." But there was a great difference in visits with clergy of other denominations. While only 28 percent of the "most modernist" clergy made such visits less than once a month, fully 52 percent of the high-tension ministers made interdenominational visits this seldom (Quinley, 1974:249).

Societal Rejection of Sects

We have shown that tension can be measured as rejection of the sociocultural environment by religious groups that have deviant norms, that struggle in conversion and defense, and that are somewhat socially encapsulated. It remains to be shown that the other side of tension, rejection by the larger society, can be measured and gives the same general results. The California survey included a few social distance items which allow us to compare public acceptance of seven religious groups. A recent Gallup poll also included social distance measures that bear on this point.

Table 7 summarizes social distance data from the California survey. The original ques-

Table 7   *Social Distance*

| | Percent of Each Group Giving the Indicated Responses | | | | | | | | | | |
| | Denominations | | Sectlike | | Sects | | | | | | |
	Low Tension (1032)	Medium Tension (844)	Mo. Luth. (116)	S. Bapt. (79)	C. of God (44)	C. of Christ (37)	Nazarene (75)	Assem. of God (44)	Seventh Day Ad. (35)	Total Prot. (2326)	Total Cath. (545)
Would feel friendly and at ease with a Methodist.	82	86	83	82	87	70	80	82	86	84	57
Would feel friendly and at ease with an Episcopalian.	84	80	82	62	80	60	60	71	77	80	65
Would feel friendly and at ease with a Roman Catholic.	73	72	78	58	68	49	48	52	71	70	78
Would feel friendly and at ease with a Jew.	72	69	75	49	71	70	52	68	77	69	63
Would feel friendly and at ease with a Jehovah's Witness.	29	32	26	27	25	49	13	18	46	29	27
Would feel friendly and at ease with an Atheist.	29	23	19	16	23	30	7	16	11	24	23
Would feel friendly and at ease with a Spiritualist.	26	22	22	18	16	43	9	5	3	23	25

tion actually listed 27 different categories of person, including such varied stimuli as "A German," "An Alcoholic," "A Conservative," "A Liberal," and "A Teetotaler." The respondent was asked to give his immediate reaction if he met someone about whom he knew nothing but the indicated label. In Table 7 we give the percentage of each group that "would feel friendly and at ease" with each stimulus person. The most important data are the two columns for "total Protestant" and "total Catholic." These figures suggest how much each stimulus group is accepted or rejected by church members as a whole. The majority of all respondents say they would probably feel friendly and at ease with a Methodist, an Epsicopalian, a Roman Catholic, or a Jew. That is, these church members find little problem with established conventional faith, even if this means a non-Christian faith. However, the Jehovah's Witnesses, the only sect among the stimuli, receives a *much* lower level of acceptance. Except for two fellow sects that show some warmth toward the Jehovah's Witnesses, there is rejection across the board. Atheists and Spirtual-

ists receive even greater rejection, primarily because the higher-tension denominations are less likely to accept them than is the low-tension group. Spirtualists are the nearest thing to *cult* members included in the questionnaire in any way. Elsewhere we have explained that cults, like sects, are in high tension with the sociocultural environment; cults can be distinguished from sects by the fact that their culture is exotic or novel (Stark and Bainbridge, 1979).

Comparable data were collected by a 1977 Gallup Poll of a national sample of about 1500 adults. Respondents were asked to indicate on a ten-point scale how much they liked or disliked each of 15 religious groups and three religious leaders. Because the respondents included people who were not church members, and because many may have felt inhibited from expressing a negative judgment of other citizens, we do not expect the levels of rejection to be very high. The number who failed to express any opinion at all varied from stimulus to stimulus, so we have removed them from our re-analysis, calculating the percentage of those holding a definite opinion who disliked the given group or leader. Only 6 percent disliked "Protestants," and the main Protestant denominations (Methodists, Lutherans, Presbyterians, Baptists, and Episcopalians) received low rejection scores, ranging from 4 to 8 percent.

Higher scores indicate some measure of rejection by the dominant groups in society. Catholics were disliked by 11 percent of the respondents, while between 12 and 15 percent rejected the following higher-tension groups: Southern Baptists, Eastern Orthodox, Evangelicals, Jews, and Quakers. Unitarians are disliked by 21 percent,[2] Mormons by 25 percent, and Seventh-Day Adventists by fully 27 percent. It is interesting that Pope Paul VI received the same score, 11 percent, as did Catholics, the religious group he led. Billy Graham got an intermediate score of 15 percent, about the same as Evangelicals at 14 percent. Sun Myung Moon, the leader of the deviant Korean cult familiarly called the Moonies (The Unification Church) got an extremely unfavorable rating—93 percent of those familiar with him dislike him. This shows that his cult is in extremely high tension with the sociocultural environment.

The Gallup data also permitted us to look at how several of the groups judged themselves. Between 47 and 60 percent of members in major Protestant denominations and the Catholic Church gave their own group a most highly favorable rating. Among the Mormons, relatively rejected by other respondents, fully 91 percent gave their own group the top score. As Gordon W. Russell (1975) has reported, Mormon respondents tend to see themselves as "the Chosen People." This reflects the pattern we have already found: high-tension groups are rejected by outsiders but evaluate themselves highly.

Although the main focus of our analysis has been comparison of low-tension and high-tension Protestant groups, attention should also be called to differences between the total Protestant and Catholic groups. Johnson suggests that "it is wise to classify Catholicism [in America] as somewhat more sectarian than most of the major Protestant bodies" (1963: 545–546). Certainly, when it was a weak religious minority in a predominantly Protestant country, as was the case decades ago, Catholicism experienced palpable tension with the sociocultural environment. For a variety of reasons, that tension has diminished over the years, but discrimination against members of the Catholic faith still exists in some sectors of important societal institutions (Greeley, 1977a; 1977b). The picture given by our tables is much simpler for the Protestant sects than for the Catholics. Often, the Catholic average is almost identical with the Protestant average. At other times, the Catholics are in the same direction from that average as are the Protestant sects, while occasionally the Catholics are on the side away from the sects. This pattern is not consistent with a simple description of Catholicism as a high-tension group. Rather, it reminds us that Protestantism and Catholicism are distinctly different traditions of religious culture. The best measures of Catholic tension in our data set are found in Table 6 and Table 7, where we see evidence of some social encapsulation and social distance separating Catholics and Protestants. Other tables were designed to measure the tension of sects within the Protestant tradition. We do not have the data to distinguish higher- and lower-tension groups within the Catholic tradition, nor to complete a definitive analysis of the relationship between American Catholicism and the sociocultural environment.

Conclusion

With Benton Johnson we have conceptualized the church-sect dimension in terms of *tension with the surrounding sociocultural environment*. This concept is equivalent to broad subcultural deviance marked by: (1) *difference* from the standards set by the majority or by powerful members of society; (2) *antagonism* between the sect and society manifested in mutual rejection; and (3) *separation* in social relations leading to the relative encapsulation of the sect. These are *not* to be considered as three different axes of tension or as three dimensions of sectarianism. Each is an integral aspect of tension. One might think of these as the three moving parts by which tension is created and sustained. And, like a set of moving parts, they are conceptually distinguishable for purposes of measurement, but it would be folly to disassemble the set.

The data we have examined justify use of tension as the ordering principle of the church-sect axis. Groups we intuitively regard as more churchlike or more sectlike displayed marked quantitative differences on the many different items we examined and did so in a very consistent way. Nevertheless, this paper is best regarded as no more than a successful reconnaissance. We have made do with items written for other purposes. Clearly, it would be possible to construct much more sensitive and appropriate measures of tension and thereby gain much greater precision in ranking various religious groups. Indeed, it would be desirable to consider measures based on policies, procedures, and structures of religious organizations as such, in addition to measures created by aggregating individual-level data. Some promising work along those lines has already been accomplished by Michael Welch (1977).

Whatever improvements in measurement that can be achieved, the important point, in our opinion, is established by our results. Theoretical use of the concept of tension is warranted: *tension can be measured*. This is extremely important, for no significant theories concerning the origins and transformations of religious movements can be tested *unless* it is possible to rank order religious groups in an unambiguous way. For example, it is impossible to test the hypothesis that the arrival of an adult generation of socialized members tends to transform sects *if* we cannot be sure that particular religious groups

are (or are not) less sectlike at time two than at time one. This is a very old hypothesis. That it has not yet been tested is indicative of the impediment created by the multidimensional typological schemes that produced primarily unorderable mixed types. Tension opens the door to testing this and all the many other things we think we know about the church-sect process. And, clearly, it is time we got on with the job. Fifty years have now passed since H. Richard Niebuhr first made it evident that a church-sect theory was desirable and likely to be possible.

Notes

1. We have not attempted to order groups within the sect category in terms of impressionistic judgments of which are more or less sectlike. Given the results we present in this paper, and especially if items were designed for the specific purpose of measuring aspects of tension, it would be a simple matter to generate relative tension scores for any given set of religious bodies.

2. It is clear that so far as Americans are concerned Unitarians are regarded as deviant in terms of irreligiousness. It is worth noting that Unitarians do not belong to the National Council of Churches, since the full name of that organization is National Council of Churches of Christ, thus excluding Unitarians for rejection of the divinity of Jesus. Thus a low-tension religious identity in America today is not to be irreligious, but to claim membership in a denomination that is well accommodated to the world. That is, President Dwight Eisenhower probably spoke for the majority when he stressed the importance of "a deeply felt religious faith—and I don't care what it is." But, of course, Eisenhower did not care what it was under the assumption that "it" would not be something "far out." And Americans approve of any religion—Protestant, Catholic, Jewish—so long as it is a "normal" faith—one well adapted to its sociocultural environment. Perhaps a very accurate way to determine how people really feel about various religions is to get their honest feelings about having their children convert to various groups.

References

Bainbridge, William Sims
   1978 Satan's Power, Berkeley: University of California Press.

Balswick, Jack O., and Gary L. Faulkner
  1970 "Identification of ministerial cliques: A socio-metric approach." Journal for the Scientific Study of Religion 9:303–310.
Dittes, James E.
  1971 "Typing the typologies: Some parallels in the career of church-sect and extrinsic-intrinsic." Journal for the Scientific Study of Religion 10:375–383.
Dynes, Russell R.
  1955 "Church-sect typology and socio-economic status." American Sociological Review 20:555–560.
  1957 "The consequences of sectarianism for social participation." Social Forces 35:331–334.
Eister, Alan W.
  1967 "Toward a radical critique of church-sect typologizing." Journal for the Scientific Study of Religion 6:85–90.
Furst, Peter T. (ed.)
  1972 Flesh of the God: The Ritual Use of Hallucinogens. New York: Praeger.
Glock, Charles Y., and Rodney Stark
  1965 Religion and Society in Tension. Chicago: Rand McNally.
  1966 Christian Beliefs and Anti-Semitism. New York: Harper and Row.
Goode, Erich
  1967 "Some critical observations on the church-sect dimension." Journal for the Scientific Study of Religion 6:69–77.
Greeley, Andrew M.
  1977a The American Catholic: A Social Portrait. New York: Basic Books.
  1977b An Ugly Little Secret: Anti-Catholicism in North America. Kansas City: Sheed Andrews and McMeel.
Gustafson, Paul
  1967 "UO-US-PS-PO: A restatement of Troeltsch's church-sect typology." Journal for the Scientific Study of Religion 6:64–68.
Johnson, Benton
  1963 "On church and sect." American Sociological Review 28:539–549.
Keim, Albert N. (ed.)
  1975 Compulsory Education and the Amish. Boston: Beacon Press.
Knudsen, Dean D., John R. Earle, and Donald W. Shriver, Jr.
  1978 "The conception of sectarian religion: An ef-fort at clarification." Review of Religious Research 20:44–60.
La Barre, Weston
  1969 They Shall Take up Serpents. New York: Schocken.
Larson, Richard F.
  1964 "Clerical and psychiatric conceptions of the clergyman's role in the therapeutic setting." Social Problems 11:419–428.
  1968 "The clergyman's role in the therapeutic process: Disagreement between clergymen and psychiatrists." Psychiatry 31: 250–263.
Patrick, Ted, and Tom Dulack
  1976 Let Our Children Go! New York: Ballantine.
Pope, Liston
  1942 Millhands and Preachers. New Haven: Yale University Press.
Quinley, Harold E.
  1974 The Prophetic Clergy. New York: Wiley-Interscience.
Russell, Gordon W.
  1975 "The view of religions from religious and non-religious perspectives." Journal for the Scientific Study of Religion 14:129–138.
Schuman, Howard, and Michael P. Johnson
  1976 "Attitudes and behavior." In Inkeles, Alex, James Coleman, and Neil Smelser (eds.), Annual Review of Sociology, Volume 2. Palo Alto Annual Reviews.
Stark, Rodney, and Charles Y. Glock
  1968 American Piety: The Nature of Religious Commitment. Berkeley: University of California Press.
Stark, Rodney, and William Sims Bainbridge
  1979 "Of churches, sects, and cults: Preliminary concepts for a theory of religious movements." Journal for the Scientific Study of Religion, 18:117–131.
Wallis, Roy
  1977 The Road to Total Freedom: A Sociological Analysis of Scientology. New York: Columbia University Press.
Welch, Michael R.
  1977 "Analyzing religious sects: An empirical examination of Wilson's sect typology," Journal for the Scientific Study of Religion 16:125–139.
Zablocki, Benjamin
  1971 The Joyful Community. Baltimore: Penguin.

R E A D I N G   4 . 3

Themes of Power and Control in a Pentecostal Assembly

John Wilson and Harvey K. Clow

It is customary to account for the appeal of Pentecostalism by ascribing compensatory functions to the sect (Calley, 1965; Schwartz, 1970; O'Dea and Poblete, 1970; Wilson, 1961). This kind of theory assumes that religion transvalues experience, usually by offering compensation in the hereafter for the pains of the present resulting from deprivation, marginality, insecurity, anomie and so on. While it is probably true that many Pentecostals do have instrumental motives, there can be no doubt that this compensation theory is inadequate as an interpretation of Pentecostalism. First, it is one-sided in its method of working backward from meanings imputed to sect participation to predisposing conditions. This means that religious symbols are treated as merely the secondary result of the social order, as purely expressive. Second, it fails to show how beliefs influence the perception of social processes, how symbols function as codes of social control. Third, it fails to acknowledge the grounding of the religious experience in pre-existing networks of family and occupational roles.

Durkheim (1965) encouraged us to see religious symbols as a means of comprehending and making intelligible social relationships. Religion does not offer a magical means of escaping from social circumstances but replicates them. We should expect to find congruence between religious symbols and our sense of social structure.

John Wilson is Professor of Sociology at Duke University.

Harvey K. Clow is a free-lance writer residing in Durham, North Carolina.

Reprinted from *Journal for the Scientific Study of Religion*, 1981, 20(3):241–250, with permission.

Although most sociological treatments of Pentecostalism highlight speaking in tongues and Spirit possession, it is rare that their symbolism is taken seriously. In this paper, we seek to do precisely that, basing our analysis on the theory that bodily symbols are very commonly used to replicate the social situation. Bodily symbols are ways in which we speak about social relations. It is commonly acknowledged that social relations constrain the way in which the physical body is perceived. It is equally true that the physical experience of the body, always modified by the social categories through which it is known, sustains a particular view of society. Accordingly, "we would always expect some concordance between social and bodily experiences of control" (Douglas, 1970: 68). The symbolism of the body plays an enormously important role in Pentecostalism. The most powerful of these symbols concern glossolalia and Spirit possession, with its accompanying trance states, but body symbolism plays a vital role as well in the Pentecostal system of ethics, where the contrast between good and evil is expressed in the duality of spirit and flesh, and where sickness and health are associated with evil and good social relations. In this paper, we will argue that Pentecostal ritual and symbolism say a lot about the everyday social relations of its devotees. We argue for the replication theory, not by postulating some predisposing conditions, but by ethnographic observation of Pentecostal ritual and detailed analysis of Pentecostals' sense of social structure. We will attempt to show that the theme of self-control is paramount in this Pentecostal assembly and that Pentecostal ritual speaks directly to this theme.

Methods

It was not our intention to study a new religious sect. After visiting a number of Pentecostal churches, a research site was chosen, mainly because it was an established, all-white congregation, showing a fairly even mix of sex and age categories. The junior author spent two and a half years observing this assembly, attending approximately 50 Sunday Schools, 100 worship services, 75 Sunday evening services, 40 Wednesday evening services and 20 Saturday evening services. In addition, five gospel singings, four revivals, and three weddings were attended. The observer participated in singing and praying and contributed offerings but made no attempt to disguise his research interests.

Additional data on family and work life were gathered by means of approximately 50 lengthy interviews with nine informants. Initially, these interviews were focused around religious issues to ensure not only a common language of discourse but also a thorough understanding of Pentecostal ritual. With the benefit of this insight and rapport with informants, subsequent interviews dealt with issues of family life and work orientation. These interview data are subject to the criticism of representativeness common to all such data, but informal conversations with other members of the assembly add to our confidence that the views expressed were typical of this group.

The Church

The church observed is part of the Holiness movement which began around the turn of the century, largely as an offshoot of Methodism (Ahlstrom, 1972: 816). By the first decade of the century, two tendencies had appeared within this movement: a moderate "Holiness" tendency exemplified by the Church of the Nazarene, and the extreme "Pentecostal" tendency exemplified by the Assemblies of God. The principal difference between them lay in their interpretation of the sanctification of "Spirit Baptism" experience. For Holiness believers, this experience was marked by "boisterous praying, great bodily exercises, or vociferous and constant shouting," while for the Pentecostals it was by "some supernatural sign—a vision, a dream, speaking in tongues" (Nichol, 1966: 6). The Pentecostal movement subsequently divided several times, mainly over points of doctrine. For example, "three-stage" as opposed to "two-stage" baptism groups formed; and trinitarians opposed unitarians. The latter, "Jesus Only" supporters, are convinced that only if one is baptized in "the name of Jesus" (instead of in the name "of the Father, Son, and Holy Ghost") is baptism in accordance with Scripture (Nichol, 1966:116).

The church under study, a "Jesus Only" church, was founded in 1931. It is part of an association of Pentecostal assemblies, now numbering seven, spread across two southern states. These assemblies have little contact with each other. The church has a membership of about 50. It is all-white and evenly divided between the sexes. Although older people are over-represented, there are enough people in their 20s who regularly attend worship services to impart a sense of youth and vitality to the group. Most members describe themselves as working class. Most of the men and many of the women work in manual and largely unskilled jobs in textile and tobacco mills and warehouses. A few are self-employed in a small way (a painter, a mechanic) and some have clerical jobs (typist, insurance clerk). The members of the group are not poor and seem to have steady work histories (the "stable" working class described by Schwartz), but they see themselves as standing beneath the middle class.

Beliefs

At the heart of the Pentecostal religious experience lie ideas about spiritual power—how it is acquired, what it can do, how it is recognized, and the manner in which it is retained. The Pentecostal neophyte is taught that Jesus will free him from sin and that His power (in the form of the Holy Ghost) will enter and dwell within him if he repents. Repentance is not merely the renunciation of sin, however. One must "yield to Jesus"; the "world" must be abandoned and a "life of Jesus" begun. The "flesh" will no longer govern if the individual will follow the lead of the "spirit" within.

This opposition between flesh and spirit parallels that drawn by Durkheim (1965: 297) between soul and body:

The soul has always been considered a sacred thing; on this ground it is opposed to the body which is, in itself, profane . . . it inspires those sentiments which are everywhere reserved for that which is divine . . . and we may say that, in a certain sense, there is divinity within us. For society, this unique source of all that is sacred, does not limit itself to moving us from without and affecting us for the moment; it establishes itself within us in a durable manner.

The soul symbolizes the presence of society within, and stands in opposition to, the individual body; so too, for Pentecostals, the Holy Spirit symbolizes the voice of conscience (society), and the flesh symbolizes egoistic desires.

Pentecostals teach that human beings are weak without the power of the Holy Spirit. Weakness leads to and is manifested by sin. In the group we observed, the three most frequently mentioned sins were drinking (alcoholic beverages), smoking (cigarettes) and "other things" (fornication). "Flesh" is sin in its individual manifestations; "the world" is sin in its collective manifestations (i.e., social practices, laws, customs); "the Spirit" is an internal, supernatural power which, if strong in the believer, will preclude his sinning in either of these aspects.

The practice most frequently condemned in the group is "drinking." Consumption of alcohol is seen as the root cause of many other evils, principally because it leads to loss of self-control. One informant described its insidious effects:

A man will not run off with other women or gamble until he begins to drink. If he drinks he'll end up running around on his wife, spending money on booze, not food, and treating his family badly. Drinking causes him to do something he wouldn't have done. When I used to drink I'd argue and get into fights. Next morning I'd realize I shouldn't have done it—and I wouldn't have if I hadn't drank.

Although smoking is a lesser evil than drink, it is a threat because a man cannot control his need for it—and it is only a small step from smoking to drinking and to other temptations of the flesh.

Judging by their conception of repentance and sin, then, Pentecostals see life as precarious and uncertain, an enterprise demanding unceasing vigilance and care. At no time do Pentecostals cease to feel that "backsliding" is a possibility, that self-control might slip and the flesh predominate.

Ritual

The chief aim of Pentecostal ritual is receiving and retaining possession of the Holy Spirit. Initiation rituals "call down" the Spirit (culminating in water baptism), and confirmatory rituals (e.g., speaking in tongues, "dancing in the Spirit") supply periodic opportunities to reaffirm Spiritual power. For example, during the ceremony of "laying on of hands," when sinners are called forward to the altar to repent of their sins, or when healing takes place, members join hands so that the Spirit might descend from God through the group leaders to the rest of the group. Members speak of a "powerful force" filling their bodies at this time. One informant spoke of sometimes having no feeling at all in his body, a numbing sensation, while at other times his body felt as if it were on fire.

Spiritual progress in this group is identical to that reported by Kroll-Smith (1980: 17) on the basis of his observations of a similar assembly. Individual progress is marked by a movement from a transcendent Christ who calls to sanctification to an immanent Christ who dwells within: "the spirit will come to reside in her, giving her a power which transcendent encounters can only approximate."

During rituals in which the gifts of the Spirit are manifested, members also speak about their experiences in terms of having their bodies taken over by a superior force. One says, "I feel like I'm floating"; another says, "It's a burning sensation, like heat." The laying on of hands is a process of "yielding":

The first time hands were laid on me I was 'drunk in the Holy Ghost.' I felt blessed. I felt peaceful, but as though I had no control over myself. I fell back on the floor. I remember falling but not hitting the floor.

Pentecostals say they know that Jesus is real when they feel the *power* of the Holy Ghost. Being "in the Spirit" is described by means of spatial metaphors ("close to God"), and metaphors of liberation ("a door flung open") but above all by metaphors of power ("the Spirit took over").

Pentecostal worship thus focuses upon and is designed to emphasize feeling rather than thought or contemplation. Its dominant symbols are those which have to do with states of dissociation between body and mind. For the Pentecostal, God is not so much seen as heard—and not so much heard as felt. It is a religion of "inner feeling" which is made manifest in bodily states. By learning the rhetoric of sin and repentance, by undergoing

water baptism and by speaking in tongues, the Pentecostal confronts the possibility of loss of self—and finds self located within a cosmological scheme in which abandonment of control is part of the redemptive process.

In summary, the Pentecostal idea of supernatural power is as follows:

(1) It is envisaged as taking the form of a spirit which is present in the believer's soul;

(2) this spirit comes from and is identified with "Jesus" (believers speak of having Jesus within them);

(3) this spirit is acquired initially by repenting of one's sins and by being baptized in water and Spirit;

(4) most believers acquire the Spirit through the "laying on of hands" by leaders of the group, who have, in turn, been "touched" by Jesus;

(5) the power of the Spirit shows itself as abandonment of control (dancing in the Spirit) and "leadings," or guides to future conduct;

(6) the power of the Spirit slips away or "leaks" so that it must be continually "refilled" in worship services;

(7) to be refilled in the Spirit, one must be leading a "good Christian life."

These ideas are very much focused on the individual and his ability to retain control over the self. The group is merely the expedient whereby this condition is achieved.

Although Pentecostalism is a highly individualistic religion, its meaning and function cannot be understood unless the role of the group is appreciated. The group serves to validate the individual's experiences—and does so in such a way as to link feelings experienced within the worship services to the everyday, profane experiences of the believer. This is achieved in the following manner.

There are no objective forms of behavior which would enable the outside observer unmistakably to identify Spirit possession. Pentecostals might tremble, weep, whistle, snap their hands, jump about, dance, speak in tongues, "run the aisles," and even lapse into unconsciousness. It is the "good" Christians in the group whose judgment validates these displays. These validators are known to live exemplary lives and have achieved leadership status on that basis. There is little doubt that they use the context of daily life to make their judgment about the authenticity of displays during the worship service.

Among this group of Pentecostals, there was a collective awareness of whether each member was leading a good Christian life. This determined how each member's behavior was judged. As one informant put it: "not all hollerin' and jumping around is in the Spirit." Thus, although all members must at one time or another display the gifts of the Spirit, only a few are permitted to display them regularly. The behavior of these "good" Christians is usually the focus of the service, providing an example for others who follow suit and in so doing validate the "good Christian" display; behavior *not* validated by the "good" Christians is treated as private display. The group thus has a status hierarchy measured in terms of ethical, everyday criteria like integrity, respectability, and steadfastness and symbolized in terms of spiritual displays. An orderly life (an outward display) thus reflects the controlling power of the Spirit (on the inside).

All this is consonant with the general Pentecostal ideas about ethics. Pentecostals lay down few ethical commands, unlike groups such as the Seventh Day Adventists, whose members know and obey a comprehensive and detailed set of ethical directives (Schwartz, 1970: 172). For Pentecostals, there is no morally sanctioned way to work, to consume, or to perform family obligations. The precarious and uncertain nature of the life free of sin is a much stronger theme in Pentecostalism than in sects which have collective, rigidly codified and precisely detailed plans for living. Rather than having laws of God

which must be obeyed (actually, a much more self-assured belief), the Pentecostal is continually confronted with the necessity of individual choice where the means for choosing are never absolutely known and the choice never permanent. The ritual brings the believer face-to-face with that which he is taught to fear most—loss of self-direction—and interprets this danger in a benign manner.

Work

Pentecostals view themselves as members of the working or lower middle class. They do not spontaneously identify themselves in terms of class at all, but when prompted will, without much hesitation, assign themselves to these categories. Their self-perception is largely corroborated by the kinds of work they actually do: textile mill operative, lumber mill foreman, car salesman, painter, electrician, telephone operator, domestic servant, and so on.

Pentecostals consider work as a necessary means of obtaining a living, as an arena in which to display their distinctive Christian qualities in witness, and as an opportunity to proselytize among their fellow workers. However, work itself is not a central life interest to them. In common with most other working class people, Pentecostals do not see themselves engaged in careers but as holding down a job or doing a certain kind of work. Unlike the subjects of Schwartz's research, they do not conceptualize their work-life as a "status trajectory." The textile mill operative has occupied the same job for the last 20 years; another person has held the same clerical job for 21 years, the electrician for 11 years.

Pentecostals endorse the meritocratic view of American society, but they do not see themselves as fully sharing in this system. This is reflected in their attitude toward their children. They believe that a good education is necessary today to secure a good job and they would like their children to have better jobs than they have themselves, but at the same time they express fears that today's educational system (especially college) is a secular system which will weaken the faith of their children. They appear not to push their children to stay in school.

Pentecostals stress the virtues of steady, hard work, but in no sense do they conceive of this in Horatio Alger terms. They see hard work as a way of *avoiding* unemployment, poverty, and general disrespect rather than as a way of getting to the top. Work seems to them as much a place for *sliding* as a place for climbing. They couple this commitment to hard work with a strong sense of obligation both to employers and (where appropriate) to customers or clients. Thus, one informant says:

A man shouldn't want more than he is earning. He shouldn't sit down and do nothing when the boss isn't working. A Christian should do his job to the best of his ability; there's no excuse for him not doing his job. If it's worth doing, it's worth doing right.

This sense of obligation to the boss is coupled with a ready acceptance of job hierarchies and work discipline. Another informant says:

There are natural boss men and workers. If you are not a boss man you should be content to have someone else over you.

Another informant associates lack of obedience to backsliding in general:

So much of your alcohol, marijuana, LSD, and mental illness is caused by people wanting to work in their own way, not realizing they are under submission to the foreman, and he is to someone else. I believe in discipline and as you go up the ladder you should let the light shine so people will respect you for the position you hold. You must be self-disciplined.

Several of the Pentecostals in this group were in business on their own in a small way—as salesmen, tow-truck operators, craftsmen,

and so on. Here the worth of work was measured by honesty and fair-dealing. Many had chosen self-employment to escape as far as possible the cash nexus and clearly sought to downplay this aspect of their work. For this group, fair-dealing meant not taking advantage of the client/customer.

A man who charges [an outrageous price] will also lie, and do anything to take you in. If a man is a Christian he will be straight with you in what he says and charges for his work. A person living right is going to talk right.

Pentecostals frequently contrast their sense of obligation and scrupulousness toward employers and customers with its absence in others. Their ideal seems to be a system of reciprocity in which the cash nexus is only a secondary consideration.

Hard work is, for Pentecostals, not only a duty owed to God (and one's employer or client), but also an example to be set for others, a form of everyday witnessing by people who are not otherwise active evangelists. Honesty at work means more than being truthful. It means integrity—and the connotations of wholeness, soundness, and uprightness are intended. Consideration means personal care, even love, for one's fellow workers. It is explicitly counterposed to the uncaring and impersonal economic system in which most of them are forced to live. Thus, Pentecostals will proudly tell of their charging customers only what they are able to pay.

The quality which undergirds all those just described, that which is seen above all else to mark off the good worker from the bad, is self-discipline and self-control. Whatever our work, they say, we "must learn to discipline our conversation, actions, appearance, our dealings with others, even our attitudes." Self-control is the foundation of other virtues such as honesty, humility and patience.

Self-control is necessary for every job, especially those you don't like. The Spirit helps Spirit-filled Christians to have self-control on those jobs they don't want to do. The Spirit gives us the strength to resist the urge not to work. After prayer I feel stronger and I can do the job.

When Pentecostals speak of self-control they frequently mention the use of alcohol, which is then linked to other undesirable behavior like absenteeism, tardiness, laziness, or being an unfaithful husband or wife. These sins indicate above all else lack of self-discipline.

The strong self-discipline by means of which Pentecostals give meaning and coherence to their work suffuses their whole lives and emerges as a prominent theme in all their attempts to convey what being a Pentecostal means. The good Christian is one who will show self-discipline in the face of temptation. As one informant put it:

You must get the flesh into subjection to the Spirit. You can't be a good Christian without self-discipline.

The idea of self-control means *both* control over the self and the control which the Holy Spirit exercises over the true believer. Control of the self is thus a value in itself, regardless of what it might lead to, a value which can only be realized, however, through possession by the Holy Spirit. The believer has to lay himself open to a stronger power in order to have power over himself. Conversely, the believer proves to himself his "infilling" by the Spirit by the success he has with self-discipline. The Holy Ghost stands in opposition to the "flesh" or the "world." The "flesh" is not sinful in itself but must always be kept under control, for it may become "excited" by the "things of the world" and commit sin. Thus a man may look upon a beautiful woman without sinning, but unless he has the Holy Ghost to help him overcome his desires, he will succumb to the flesh and lust for her.

The Spirit also shows itself in the everyday life of the Pentecostal through "leadings" which teach, guide, and instruct the believer by bringing to mind a scriptural passage, by pointing out one of a number of options, or

by assigning supernatural significance to everyday occurrence. If a believer has "his mind on Jesus," then he will receive a "leading" which he interprets both as a directive and as an indication of the power of the Spirit. He knows he has power because he has received the leading, and this knowledge in itself gives him strength to carry out the leading. But more than this, the believer exercises self-discipline when he follows the leading: the Spirit may lead, but the individual must exercise his own will if he is to follow.

Discussion

Why should Pentecostal services be marked above all by rituals in which people lose total control of themselves? We would like to argue that the worship service in part articulates the Pentecostal's concern with how much he is really in control of his own thoughts, desires, and feelings. Behind this anxiety lies the Pentecostal's perception that modern life demands constant watchfulness and care. Abandonment of control in ritual is a "safe" way of thinking about the possibility of lack of control which Pentecostals articulate in their everyday world. Ritual in no way compensates for this lack of control; rather, it reconceptualizes it and gives the believer a new way of dealing with it in his daily life.

Sennett and Cobb (1972: 23) have pointed out that the major threat to working class people is a fall into a poverty level which robs them of self-control. They seek above all else to retain the means to deal with the world in a controlled way. Sennett and Cobb assume, however, that ascent into the middle class is the only way this can be achieved. Pentecostalism suggests that it is possible to "handle" this threat in a different way. Although Pentecostals speak of "gaining victory over the flesh," their religious life is actually a series of encounters with disorder and its successful overcoming. A person who "dances in the Spirit" is expressing the possibility that his social life (like his body now) is not in his control. He is also being told that, by harnessing the Spirit through self-discipline, disorder can come to mean something else. Ritual does not offer a means of escape but a representation, in metaphors of bodily control, of how life is actually lived. Social experience, expressed first in ritual, is thus interpreted again in the light of ritual.

Mary Douglas (1970) has argued that there will be a consonance between social relationships and religious symbolism. The body is a particularly important symbolic resource. Bodily "dissociation" (trance, "dancing in the Spirit," speaking in tongues) replicates a social experience which is similarly "loosely structured." Douglas suggests that trance states will be more commonly found where social controls are weak. Interviews with Pentecostals reveal not absence of social control so much as anxiety about maintaining control. Accordingly, Pentecostals do not simply abandon themselves in their worship services. Instead, there is *controlled disorder:* rituals in which the idea of total loss of self-control is introduced and dealt with.

Conclusion

The spiritual power which Pentecostalism offers can clearly be interpreted in an instrumentalist way, as something the believer will receive or be able to use to further profane ends in the world of work, family, and social life in general. The "leadings" which the Spirit provides are valuable resources for the believer to employ to protect and enhance his status. As such, Pentecostalism is open to interpretation in terms of compensation for deprivation. There are other meanings in Pentecostal ideas about power, however, and these do not fit so easily into the deprivation thesis. Spiritual power is manifested in bodily dissociation, which means a loss of

control on the part of the believer. Furthermore, this loss of control is positively valued. It is sought, welcomed, and its regular manifestation reserved for leaders of the group. While bodily dissociation clearly provides emotional release, it also provides a way of handling the fact that there are a great many aspects of the everyday life over which people in the working class have little control. The ritual does not provide a magical means of acquiring this control but a way of expressing and dramatizing that social reality in a meaningful and satisfying way. The symbols *replicate* reality; they are an expression of the tension which, after all, composes social life. In the ritual symbolism of Pentecostalism, people can recognize what is difficult to admit openly and yet what is patently clear to all and sundry, that the ideal is not attainable.

References

Ahlstrom, Sydney
1972   A Religious History of the American People. New Haven: Yale University Press.
Calley, Malcolm
1965   God's People. London: Oxford University Press.
Douglas, Mary
1970   Natural Symbols. New York: Pantheon Books.
Durkheim, Emile
1965   The Elementary Forms of the Religious Life. New York: The Free Press.
Kroll-Smith, J. Stephen
1980   "Testimony as performance: The relationship of an expressive event to the belief system of a holiness sect." Journal for the Scientific Study of Religion 19:16–25.
Nichol, John
1966   Pentecostalism. New York: Harper and Row.
O'Dea, Thomas and Renato Poblete
1970   "Anomie and the 'quest for community': The formation of sects among the Puerto Ricans of New York." Pp. 180–198 in Thomas O' Dea (ed.), Sociology and the Study of Religion. New York: Basic Books.
Schwartz, Gary
1970   Sect Ideologies and Social Status. Chicago: University of Chicago Press.

Sennett, Richard and Jonathan Cobb
  1972   The Hidden Injuries of Class. New York: Knopf.

Wilson, Bryan
  1961   Sects and Society. London: Heinemann.

S E L E C T I O N   4 . A

The Sect

John R. Earle, Dean D. Knudsen, and Donald W. Shriver, Jr.

Sectarian groups have been a prominent part of Gastonia's religious life since its earliest days. Mill churches, regardless of denomination, were frequently sectarian in character, and sect-type groups have continued to emerge especially among the poor and socially marginal of the city.

Geographically, sect groups have been centered in or near old mill villages, in inexpensive housing. Participants in sectarian services are predominantly local residents who attend because of the proximity of the church building to their homes. Most sectarian groups are dominated by mill workers or unskilled workers in mill-related industries. The building is often of concrete block construction, though some meet in old churches that have been abandoned or sold by groups with newer facilities. The building includes an auditorium, perhaps with washrooms for men and women, but no educational facilities. Services are frequent, long, and led by any one of several people. The preacher has an elementary school education and may have taken some correspondence courses from a Bible institute. He remains with the group as long as he feels that he is being supported by

the people, or until he receives a "call" to another work. There is little formal organization and no public accounting of the meager finances of the group. Contributions are often small, forcing the preacher to obtain employment in secular work in order to support himself and his family.

A visitor to a sectarian service climbs three wooden or cinderblock steps to enter a small, bare room which has old, unmatched pews seating 150 people. On one Thursday night in the middle of a week-long revival, about 60 people—including 10 children—are present at the time the service is scheduled to begin. Drums, a guitar, a piano, and an electronic organ are being played, the songs having pronounced rhythms which involve the audience almost involuntarily in clapping of hands, tapping of feet, or movement of the body. The mood of those in attendance is informal. A dozen teenagers sit together and talk, while the older people move freely about the room to talk to others.

A crudely constructed pulpit and a speaker's pew are on the platform at the front. Hanging on the wall to the right of the pulpit is a bulletin board announcing:

John R. Earle is Professor of Sociology at Wake Forest University.

Dean D. Knudsen is Associate Professor of Sociology at Purdue University.

Donald W. Shriver, Jr. is President of Union Theological Seminary in New York City.

Reprinted from John R. Earle, Dean D. Knudsen, and Donald W. Shriver, Jr., *Spindles and Spires* (Atlanta: John Knox Press, 1976), with permission.

Offering Today	14.38
Attendance Today	74
Attendance Last Sunday	61
Offering Last Sunday	14.36
Monthly Offering	74.35

Opposite on the left is a sign with large letters,

JESUS SAVES.
WHERE WILL YOU SPEND ETERNITY,
HEAVEN OR HELL?

The preacher and his two associates move to the platform from the audience where they have been talking and shaking hands, and the service begins. After announcing the song, one of the men moves about, all the time singing into the microphone which he holds close to his face. The beat of the music is pronounced, and the people present respond with a rhythmic clapping. A prayer follows, accompanied by shouts of "Hallelujah," "Praise God," "Yes, Jesus," "Glory," and is followed by another hymn, and then another, again with rhythmic participation by the audience. The mood of emotional excitement builds; and a young woman, about thirty-five, begins to moan and utter "hallelujah." Several persons move into the aisles, arms waving in the air, eyes closed, heads jerking. A man skips around the room, while several women stagger into walls and pews as if intoxicated, in an apparent state of ecstasy.

Songs follow in quick succession, each a seeming jumble of noise and confusion. As a prayer is begun, the people kneel and pray aloud, each oblivious to the words of the pastor, whose voice only occasionally can be heard above those of the congregation. During the rising and waning of the prayers, one little girl puts her fingers to her ears. Four or five teenagers join in. Suddenly, the prayer stops. Those present rise as if by signal and take seats in the pews. Testimonies follow, with people exhorted to "tell about what Jesus has done." Brother Charles tells of his hospitalization for tests, ending with the statement that the doctors "spent all this time and they scratched their heads and can't find anything for certain—but Jesus is certain and I'll rely on him." Others offer testimonies that are barely audible above the frequent shouts of "Amen," "Praise God," "Thank you, Jesus." Another song, a prayer, and the Scripture reading follow, punctuated by shouts of

the audience. Yet another song is sung while an offering is being taken, following an appeal for enough money to take care of a special need known by the pastor. The contributions are counted, and another appeal is made for additional funds while the song continues through innumerable verses and choruses, finally ending with shouts of "Glory," "Hallelujah," "Praise God."

The sermon begins with the preacher describing the "foolishness of most people in the world" and their careless disdain of the "fact that Jesus died for them, to deliver them from hell." Certain themes appear repeatedly in his sermon: "salvation," "punishment of the evil in these last days," "the danger of giving in to the world," "God will see you through," "open your heart to Jesus." The faithful of God are pictured as being free from the bonds of religious doctrine and tradition, and willing to "let God go" by shouting, clapping, dancing, and singing.

An emotional pitch is reached at the end of the sermon. The preacher exhorts all who have not been saved to come forward. Though almost drowned out by the singing and clapping, his fervor increases, and before the hymn is over tears are streaming down his cheeks as he pleads: "I've done all I can now. I've told you. When your time to die comes, don't say that I didn't tell you. Don't say I didn't tell you. Don't say I didn't do what I could."

One young man steps out of a back pew and comes down the aisle to the altar and kneels. Soon he is followed by a few more young people, one girl about eight years old and others ranging up to eighteen, though most are about fifteen. As they come forward, the preacher continues his exhortation. They gather around the altar and various adults come to "back them up" in their struggles. Amid weeping, moaning, and praying, those who have come are prayed over and "prayed through." Until well past 11:00 P.M., the shouting continues.

The sect meeting is a dramatic contrast to

the uptown church service. The object of the sectarian meeting is not to communicate a message, but rather to induce a religious experience. The attender is to experience the euphoria of "feeling at liberty" and "being free," without regard to church form or structure or traditions. On the one hand, the activities of many sectarian groups appear faintly contrived, a form of "patterned spontaneity," in which the people respond to cues and appeals in a consistent way. On the other, the sect offers a religious outlet for those who seek an experience, providing for them a sense of community, participation, and euphoria not present in the more formal services. Despite this communality of spirit there is no evidence to suggest that these groups represent a challenge to the established order. They are poorly organized; they lack resources; and their understanding of social reality is privatistic, nearly synonymous to that of their uptown counterparts. . . .

ADDITIONAL READINGS

Articles

Apel, William D. "The Lost World of Billy Graham." *Review of Religious Research* 20 (1979): 138–49. Historical and theological roots of Graham's preaching in the setting of his vocation as an evangelist.

Dearman, Marion. "Christ and Conformity: A Study of Pentecostal Values." *Journal for the Scientific Study of Religion* 13 (1974): 437–53. Sociologist Benton Johnson had asked in earlier research if holiness religions socialize their adherents into dominant cultural values. The author validates Johnson's insights, finding support among Pentecostals for achievement, external conformity, nationalism, and patriotism.

Harrison, Michael I., and Maniha, John K. "Dynamics of Dissenting Movements within Established Organizations." *Journal for the Scientific Study of Religion* 17 (1978): 207–24. Why do some dissenting movements remain within their "parent organizations" while others separate into sectarian bodies? Case studies of neo-Pentecostal movements yield types of movement-organization relationships.

McGaw, Douglas B. "Meaning and Belonging in a Charismatic Congregation: An Investigation into Sources of Neo-Pentecostal Success." *Review of Religious Research* 21 (1980): 284–301. An excellent study of ways in which the two functions of *meaning* and *belonging* are enhanced, thus strengthening members' commitment to the congregation.

Warner, R. Stephen. "Theoretical Barriers to the Understanding of Evangelical Christianity." *Sociological Analysis* 40 (1979): 1–9. Sociologists too easily assume evangelicalism to be the religion of the disinherited and marginal and that it will therefore succumb to cultural advance. Considered passé, evangelicalism fails to be studied as is "mainline religion."

Books

Anderson, Robert Mapes. *Vision of the Disinherited: The Making of American Pentecostalism.* New York: Oxford University Press, 1979.

An excellent history of the Pentecostal and holiness tradition in the United States.

Beckford, James. *The Trumpet of Prophecy: A Sociological Study of the Jehovah's Witnesses.* New York: Halsted-Wiley, 1975. A case study of a rapidly growing sectarian body.

Hadden, Jeffrey K., Swann, Charles E. *Prime-Time Preachers: The Rising Power of Televangelism.* Cambridge, Mass.: Addison-Wesley, 1981. The influence of leading television evangelists is examined along with their sources of funding and potential social and political power.

Hunter, James Davison. *American Evangelicalism: Conservative Religion and the Quandary of Modernity.* New Brunswick, N.J.: Rutgers University Press, 1983. Probably the best study to date of the emerging political initiative by evangelical Christians who feel threatened by the apparent loss of traditional moral definitions in American culture.

Pope, Liston. *Millhands and Preachers: A Study of Gastonia.* New Haven: Yale University Press, 1942. A classic account of the role of sectarian churches in the social order of a mill town in North Carolina.

Schwartz, Gary. *Sect Ideologies and Social Status.* Chicago: University of Chicago Press, 1970. Sects differ in their ideological responses to the world and generate different sets of attitudes in their members.

Cross-cultural References

Glazier, Stephen D. *Perspectives on Pentecostalism: Case Studies from the Carribean and Latin America.* Washington, D.C.: University Press of America, 1980. Views one of the area's fastest growing religious movements. Puerto Rico is included among the studies.

Kowalewski, David, and Greil, Arthur L. "Religious Sectarianism and the Soviet State: The Dynamics of Believer Protest and Regime Response." *Review of Religious Research* 24 (1983): 245–60. Soviet reactions toward sectarian group protest demonstrations are contrasted with those toward nonsectarian church groups.

5

American Catholicism: A Church in Crisis

"The church of immigrants"—thus have historians frequently described Roman Catholicism in the United States. Just as importantly, "the end of the immigrant era" characterizes the church following the end of World War II. Both eras must be understood in order to grasp the vast changes, even upheavals, currently being experienced by Roman Catholicism—a theme amply suggested in the titles of the readings for this chapter.

Roman Catholics made up scarcely 1 percent of the population at the time of the signing of the Constitution; and though Catholics suffered under a number of social and legal restrictions, they were regarded as loyal Americans and patriots. All this began to change with the inpouring of Irish and, later, German Catholic immigrants in the 1820s. Nativism and its political expression in the antiforeigner, anti-Catholic Know-Nothing party labeled Catholics as unwanted visitors loyal principally to a foreign power, the papacy. Catholics in New York and Philadelphia were attacked by mobs, convents were burned, priests tarred and feathered. In the period of great immigration following the Civil War, when literally millions of Catholics from southern and eastern Europe arrived, anti-Catholicism again arose, crystallizing in the American Protective Association in the late 1880s and the Ku Klux Klan in the years immediately preceding and following World War I.

Roman Catholic leaders, particularly bishops, reacted to this atmosphere in one of two ways. The "Americanizers" among them (a minority) emphasized American freedom and democracy as a climate in which Roman Catholicism could flourish. Catholicism should therefore adapt to American organizational styles, including more democratic governance of parishes and dioceses. These bishops, along with many others less liberal, were quick to endorse the nascent American trade union movement in the face of Vatican pressures to condemn the new movement as inimical to the faith of Catholic workingmen.

But the predominant view was defensive. Catholics were to be protected from a hostile Protestantism; they were to be warned against cooperating with non-Catholics in political and social ventures. Andrew Greeley has spelled out the consequences of this attitude in terms of church policies adopted and maintained well into this century:

Separate school systems, separate charitable organizations, strong social controls, anti-intellectualism, fear of close contact with Protestants, belligerent defense of one's own rights, suspicion of attempts at intercreedal activity, strong loyalty to Rome, vigorous emphasis on sexual morality, and close alliance with international Catholicism—these were the characteristics of immigrant Catholicism. The Church was a garrison at war, and there was precious little room for individual freedom, much less dissent within the garrison, or communication with the enemy on the other side of the garrison walls. The parish Church and its vast array of social and religious activities became the bulwark of Catholicism in the United States. Its pastor was the unquestioned lord spiritual of the neighborhood, and, together with the precinct captain, also the lord temporal. . . . the necessity of presenting a united front to the nativist world outside was questioned by very few Catholics.[1]

In a sense, the fears of the hierarchy were partially unjustified, for the very virulence of nativist hatreds fused ethnicity and Catholicism together in the immigrants' consciousness and fostered their self-definitions as Irish Catholic, Italian Catholic, Polish Catholic, German Catholic, Mexican Catholic, and so on. Though large numbers left the church, the vast majority remained and exhibited loyalty in the most unmistakable way possible: unprecedented financial support of their parish church, school, convent, rectory, and charitable institutions in parish and diocese.

The end of World War II saw the beginning of Roman Catholic advance in the educational and occupational worlds of American society.[2] These assimilative trends, resulting in a new breed of younger clergy and laity, would probably have resulted in challenges to the "old style" of authoritarian governance and religious training even without the dramatic occurrence of the Second Vatican Council.

That the Second Vatican Council, extending from 1962 through 1965, touched off changes in the Catholic Church is probably the understatement of the past twenty years. Much has been written about these changes and their consequences. In attempting to make the Catholic Church more "relevant" to the modern world—as opposed to its prior stance of viewing the world as dangerous, threatening, and subversive of Catholic values—Pope John XXIII and the worldwide assembly of Catholic bishops in Rome enacted doctrinal and liturgical changes that had far-reaching effects. The church was described as the "People of God," a concept elaborated in a chapter *before* the treatment of the church as hierarchy in the council's *Dogmatic Constitution on the Church.* Liturgy, including the mass spoken in the languages of the people rather than in Latin, was to be culturally adapted. Freedom of conscience was the subject of a council document. These changes were intended to bring the church closer to the people and to increase participation by the laity in the church's worship services. A new openness toward non-Catholics was also part of the council's intent, to encourage ecumenical conversation or dialogue. After a few years of what seemed an unproblematic transition to a "new style" of Catholicism, John XXIII's successor, Pope Paul VI, issued the encyclical document *Humanae Vitae* in June 1968. It reaffirmed the church's traditional condemnation of artificial means of birth control. The reaction in the United States and Canada involved not only a continuance on the part of the laity to disregard this teaching (as subsequent survey research indicated) but dissent on the part of some Catholic theologians. Many Catholic priests told inquirers to "follow their own conscience." American bishops stood solidly behind the pope; Canadian bishops also expressed compliance but cited the principle of freedom of conscience. The aftermath of this event, then, made clear that the church's authority structure no longer carried the same "clout" as in centuries past. Catholics felt freer to act in "deviant" ways without fearing the social or ecclesiastical consequences that had previously inhibited such behavior.[3]

The readings selected for this chapter discuss these important changes and their consequences in considerable detail. In "Restructuring Catholicism," Jesuit sociologist Father Joseph Fichter uses the occasion of a symposium on the work of the late Thomas O'Dea to reflect on themes of adaptation and renewal. He sees a certain individualism as an unfortunate consequence of the changes discussed and the switch from what he calls "monophasic loyalty" to "polyphasic consensus." Older unities have been broken and newer ones are developing. Strains and dilemmas are pervasive. What will eventually emerge from changes "occurring at the bottom of the structure" remains to be seen. One very real possibility is a divided church, as priests' senates and bishops' conferences take stands on controversial issues, such as nuclear disarmament and Third World issues of poverty and human rights. Furthermore, stricter requirements for receiving baptism and for getting married in the church will require reeducation of a laity used to centuries-old practices.[4]

"Catholic Education in Three Cultures" illustrates the changes previously discussed in terms of survey research. The authors ask whether Catholic education affects the beliefs and practices of young American and Canadian Catholics in the 18-to-29-year age bracket. In a chapter previous to the one from which this reading is taken, the authors indicated that most young Catholics in both countries remain identified as Catholics; and that 41 percent of American Catholics, 37 percent of Canadian English-speaking Catholics, and 31 percent of French-speaking Catholics of this younger group attend mass at least two or three times a month. Very few attend the sacrament of confession. But they report feeling close to God and "pray quite often." But the research does not report all good news for those concerned with the maintenance of Catholic orthodoxy:

On the negative side, young Catholics from all three groups seem to have rejected the Church as teacher. The majority accepts only a few doctrinal and social principles—the existence of life after death, the immorality of homosexuality and of abortion on demand. On most doctrinal and moral questions only a minority of young people take the Church's position. The Church's standing as a moral (as opposed to doctrinal) teacher has been particularly eroded. The Church's position on birth control is rejected by more than 90 percent of the Catholic youth of all three cultures. Likewise the position on divorce is rejected by 85 percent or more of young Catholics from the three cultures. Eighty percent or more of the young adults reject the wrongfulness of premarital sex.[5]

But what about those who have attended Catholic schools? Are they any different? The answer is a complicated "yes." Catholic schools have an effect stronger than that of Catholic family or spouse; when young Catholics go through a "life-cycle crisis" in their mid-twenties, they are more likely to return to Catholic life if they have attended Catholic schools. Attending Catholic schools integrates the young person into the Catholic community and institutions such as parish organizations. These findings, as the authors point out, have policy implications at a time when Catholic schools are a severe expense to the Catholic community.

Finally, Sister Elaine M. Prevallet suggests that the apparent breakup of a long, authoritative tradition need not bring personal chaos. She restates changes cited by previous authors but interprets them as a welcome challenge to appropriate personally the meaning of one's faith, because external guidelines are no longer reliable. Her essay demonstrates the symbolic vitality of long-established religious traditions; for in the process of encountering and dealing with vast cultural and historical changes, these traditions exhibit considerable flexibility in the interpretation of doctrine and ethics. Such flexibility results in expanded meaning of these symbols. This expansion then permits the kind of gradual, at times painful reappropriation illustrated in this personal reflection.

Notes

1. Andrew M. Greeley, *The Denominational Society* (Glenview, Ill.: Scott, Foresman, 1972), pp. 189–90.
2. These changes are well documented by Andrew Greeley, *The American Catholic: A Social Portrait* (New York: Basic Books, 1977), chap. 3.
3. The consequences of the decision concerning birth control are discussed in Greeley, *The American Catholic*, chap. 7.
4. For an excellent discussion of these changes see David K. O'Rourke, "Revolution and Alienation in the American Church," *Commonweal*, 11 February 1983, pp. 76–79.
5. Joan L. Fee, Andrew M. Greeley, William C. McCready, and Teresa A. Sullivan, *Young Catholics* (New York: Sadlier, 1981), p. 19.

R E A D I N G   5 . 1

Restructuring Catholicism

Joseph Fichter

Far-reaching decisions for change emerged from the Second Vatican Council. Our topic here is limited to some considerations of the manner in which Roman Catholicism has tried to preserve its identity while attempting to modernize itself during the years since the close of the Council in December, 1965. In other words, we are bypassing all the multiple relationships that the Council established with the so-called non-Catholic world, with other ecclesial communities, Christian and non-Christian, and concentrating only on internal modernization. How has Catholicism itself changed internally to implement the decisions of the Council?

The difference between decisions to change and the implementation of those decisions seems to be endemic to all plans and projects of reformation. What O'Dea says of the bishops is probably applicable to all people who are involved responsibly in grand plans of reform. "It is doubtful that many bishops at Rome understood the scope of the transfor-

Joseph H. Fichter, S.J. is Professor Emeritus of Sociology at Loyola University of New Orleans.
Reprinted from *Sociological Analysis* 38 (Summer 1977), with permission.

mation they were initiating." They knew the continuity of the traditions, but many of them also seemed unaware that there were important elements of discontinuity. "Once removed from the press of conciliar demands and the stimulus of world attention, back in the familiar provincial atmosphere of their own dioceses, most bishops sought to apply brakes." Switching his metaphor, O'Dea added that "life is a fountain, not a kitchen tap, and the movement for reform and renewal just cannot be turned off" (1968:xiii).

Adaptation and Renewal

It is perhaps an oversimplification to say that some Catholics, including bishops who were committed to implement the conciliar documents, are living in the past, while the rest of us are living in the present. The so-called new era of human history is one in which organized religion, and all the people adhering to it, are attempting to live their lives in a meaningful way. While there are some attempts to escape this new age—as in the case of small separatist communes and sects—and there are attempts to combat this new age—as in the case of revolutionaries and some theologians of liberation—the great majority of religionists are trying to find an accommodation with contemporary civilization.

We are restricting our analysis to Catholicism itself, and to the people who are willing to accept and promote change within the Church, and here we find a significant contrast between the effort to reform the system and the effort to reform the people. John McEleney, one of the commentators on Vatican II, made the clear distinction between structural adaptation and personal renewal. He remarks that adaptation "is concerned with changes that are necessary on behalf of external contemporary needs and the outward circumstances of our times, whereas the term renewal refers to interior renovation of the spirit by which the very essence of religious life . . . should be lived ever more profoundly" (Abbott, 1966:464).

He leaves no doubt that he gives priority to personal reform over structural adaptation. He claims that "only from this deepened spiritual insight and life of the religious calling may we expect authentic renewal and adaptation of the religious institutes to the peculiar necessities of the Church in our modern world" (Abbott, 1966:465). He is commenting on the conciliar decree, *Perfectae Caritatis*, which is directed at religious orders and congregations, but he finds a broader support for this generalization in the document itself which tells us: "the fact must be honestly faced that even the most desirable changes made on behalf of contemporary needs will fail of their purpose unless a renewal of spirit gives life to them" (Abbott, 1966:469).

Granting primacy to personal and spiritual conversion should not obscure the fact that the Council also proposed to shift the Church structure from a monophasic to a polyphasic system. Power and authority, responsibility and decision-making, were to be distributed throughout the Church. It is uncertain whether the bishop delegates really understood that this is what they were doing when they hammered out the document on the Church, *Lumen Gentium*.[1] Perhaps this became clear only later when Cardinal Suenens perceptively declared that the "central idea" of the Council was the principle of shared responsibility (Suenens, 1968:4). Hans Küng was fully aware of this when he called it an "epochal structure transformation," that is, the decision to transform the pre-conciliar authoritarian structure into an "ecclesial community" (Küng, 1968:4).

Obviously, this was not meant to be reorganization as an end in itself, nor was it meant to be a profane substitute for basic personal spirituality. The content of structural adaptation was more than a mere shift in the power system, in the lines of communication, in the development of communal participation. It was to be an analysis and reformation in the belief system, in ethical and moral norms, in the whole matter of liturgies and devotions. All of these elements were to be restudied, reinterpreted and modernized. This is what is meant by the so-called structural approach to the new Church, and it was intended to have an impact for change in the personal lives of Christians.

While it is reasonable to expect that these contrasting efforts should be coordinated, that personal renewal and structural adaptation should proceed simultaneously, the fact is that these approaches have suffered a differential emphasis. It is almost as though they have been divorced from each other and that the *aggiornamento* had to follow one or the other of the divorced parties, but not both. Roughly one may say that just after the Council closed, the emphasis appeared to be on the need for restructuring the Church. The principles of collegiality and subsidiarity were to be made effective at all levels of the system, the bishops sharing with the Pope, the priests with the bishops, the laity with the priests.

As the years passed, however, there grew a kind of disaffection, even disenchantment, with this innovative structural concept.[2] The original expectations have diminished, and the enthusiasm has waned, because the promised adaptation has not occurred, or because where it was attempted the pace of change was extremely slow. I have elsewhere called this a "failure of nerve" in the top management of the Church (Fichter, 1974:84). The triennial Synod of Bishops was introduced as a mechanism of co-responsibility, but it has been rendered practically inoperative by the tight control of Pope Paul VI. The Dutch Catechism, approved by Cardinal Alfrink in 1966, triggered a fully traditional papal statement on the Christian creed. The findings of the papal commission on demographic problems were repudiated and replaced by the completely conservative encyclical, *Humanae Vitae*. A more recent document from Rome dashed any prospect of sacerdotal ordination of women in the Catholic Church.

These and similar barricades to modernization not only slowed down structural adaptation; they demonstrated that the authoritarian monophasic system continues in force at the Vatican. Many of the progressives in the Church became discouraged; most of the voices of structural reform have fallen silent.[3] In their place new voices began to be heard. Attention was called to the need for personal sanctity, for spiritual conversion, for internal reform of moral attitudes and behavior. The central notion here is that nothing matters so much as a rebirth of spirituality in the hearts of people. A good society is made by good people; the Church will flourish to the extent that its members turn their hearts and minds to God.

Renewal was to replace adaptation. The most spectacular manifestation of this proposition is in the continuing growth of the Pentecostal movement, not only in the Catholic Church, but simultaneously in the main-line Protestant Churches that had previously left this religious modality to the splinter groups and smaller religious sects.[4] The significance

of this development is exemplified by Cardinal Suenens, the earlier chief architect of structural adaptation, who has now become one of the leading hierarchical spokesmen for inner Charismatic renewal (Suenens, 1975).

Abstract Individualism

It would be a mistake to suggest that structural reform is profane and secular, while personal reform is sacred and religious, but this is the impression one gains from those who insist that spiritual regeneration is the one and only way. On the other hand, the experience of personal conversion, of the born-again Christian, cannot be shrugged off as insignificant and inconsequential. It is deeply embedded in the traditions of all world religions. Spectacular conversions, revelations and visions, are commonly recorded in the lives of the great founders of religious movements. From them flow important consequences. In these instances, like that of Francis of Assisi and Ignatius Loyola, there resulted organizations and institutions that involved large numbers of people who had a collective impact on their contemporary culture.

There is a sense, however, in which the emergent success of these conversion experiences, involving large numbers of organized followers, is open to simplistic and delusive interpretations when applied only to the individual convert. From the point of view of social regeneration, of system transformation, and of the reform of so-called sinful social structures, this individualistic approach is relatively inconsequential. For many people, however, it is an appealing notion which assumes that there is a simple way to change the world: the ultimate responsibility for *aggiornamento* rests with each individual.

This fallacy of individualism has pervaded western thought since the time of Hobbes and Locke, and seems to have a special hold on many contemporary Americans. Suddenly we become aware of ecology and the waste of material resources. Lyndon Johnson wandered the corridors of the White House, turning off the lights. Middle-class families feel heroic in deciding on one meatless day a week. To conserve fuel you drive your car under fifty-five miles an hour. The campaign to recycle paper and beer cans gets a great deal of publicity. There is almost a spiritual fervor about these individual efforts of self control and moderation. Yet they do not begin to touch the wastefulness and irrationality of the entire American system of production, advertising, distribution and consumption.

Locating the basic problem, and the ultimate solution, in the individual betrays an ignorance of the operative counter-influence of structures and institutions.[5] And this is probably nowhere so evident and persuasive as it is in the sphere of religion. Criticism of this individual approach and solution does not mean that personal repentance and conversion are stupid or useless. One may say that social responsibility is everybody's responsibility and that restructuring the social order somehow *begins* when people take cognizance of its needs. On the other hand, one may more safely contend the converse: that a reformed social order affects the behavior of individuals to the point of compliance, if not to inner conviction and conversion.

The important point to realize is that the insistence on personal transformation as the *only* way, "the way," to improve the society, or the Church, or the family tends to undermine the collective effort at reform. The tendency to denounce the sordid secular system, to renounce all organized effort to redeem that society, has its parallels throughout the history of Christianity. There are enough research studies to show that many contemporary Christians opt for the comfortable pew, insist that religion must give them consolation with no insistence on social reform.[6] This negative attitude toward the "outside" world is matched by an unwillingness to see any need for structural reform within the organized Church.

Analogous to the concept of personal conversion, which is attributed to the grace of God, or the work of the Spirit, is the concept of consciousness-raising, which is not necessarily attributed to divine intervention or inspiration.[7] To raise one's consciousness involves both a cognitive and an affective conversion. The first is a solid knowledge of the empirical situation of human needs, a comprehension of the amount and enormity of our social problems. The second is an attitude of compassion for the people who are in need, who are suffering in the midst of these social iniquities. The person who is both knowledgeable and compassionate in this regard is in a state of social awareness.

If one goes no further than consciousness-raising, or social awareness, one is still at the level of the individualistic approach to a better society. In the case of the Church, or in other forms of collectivities, or in the total society, the requirement for reformation is that this social awareness be translated into social action and movement.[8] Perhaps there are many saintly souls who possess an acute social awareness, but we are still unconvinced that human effort should be expended in doing something about the situation. The most confirmed individualists among them may insist that such effort is useless and unneeded. If we pray with utter trust in God, He will intervene to feed the poor, stop warfare, eliminate crime, reduce greed, remove all injustices from the world.

There is a kind of fatalism, if not a phoney religiosity, involved in this assumption that if God wants us to have a better world He will somehow bring it about. This line of reasoning continues with the belief that the Holy Spirit is always with the Church; God will bring about the reforms needed in the ecclesiastical system; He will provide the necessary guidance for the hierarchical bureaucracy.[9] This description is not meant to be a caricature. It is the oft-repeated conviction of the most zealous proponents of personal regeneration and spiritual salvation.

Demythologizing the Church

The traditions of Christianity are replete with myths and allegories, with attempts to use human language to define or describe divine mysteries. When O'Dea proposes to show how Vatican II began the demythologizing of the Catholic Church he meant that the delegates were trying to speak in a more contemporary and appropriate fashion. It is questionable, however, that the Council succeeded in the effort to change the language and the concept of the Church from a juridical, vertical, hierarchical structure into the pilgrim People of God, the community of the faithful. Indeed, the images and biblical metaphors persist: the Church is a sheepfold, a vineyard, the temple of the Holy Spirit, the spouse of the Lamb.[10] Avery Dulles wrestled with this problem of language, but was constrained to use the same mythological language in discussing models of the Church, among them the Church as mystical communion, as sacrament and as herald. He suggests that the "societal model" of the Church was in "peaceful possession" for over three hundred years, but was displaced successively by several other models: the Mystical body, the People of God, Sacrament and Servant (Dulles, 1974:28). It should be clear that these are the images, the myths, made popular in the writings of theologians. O'Dea suggests the need to distinguish between analogical and experiential statements about religion (1968:166–168).

Sociologists take cognizance of such symbolic descriptions and their meanings, but escape their ambiguities by looking at the empirical data on an organized religion. Whether one calls this the "societal model" as Dulles does, or complains that this is an incomplete model of the Church, as all biblical scholars do, the fact is that there are large numbers of people "doing" religion together and identifying themselves as Roman Catholics. These are the people sociologists are looking at when they study structures, functions, roles and relations.[11] The religious system does not exist in a vacuum, and there are both analogies to, and interaction with, other social systems: political, educational, occupational and others.

It is also a fact that an organized religion can be culture-bound. The Catholic Church is imbedded in Western history; it was institutionalized in European culture. The desire to universalize Catholicism was interpreted as an effort to Europeanize the foreign peoples to whom the missionaries went. There was an official unwillingness to concede that Catholicism could take on a variety of cultural forms. The missionaries who tried to adapt the Christian religion to the Chinese, or Japanese, or Indian culture found themselves in real trouble with Rome. The Oath against the Chinese rites is the most famous of the prohibitions against enculturation.[12]

The lessons of anthropology were learned reluctantly and with difficulty, and only recently, by the Vatican.[13] Native clergy were seldom appointed to positions of ecclesiastical responsibility, and it was not till modern times that native black Africans were elevated to the episcopacy. If Christianity is potentially a universal religion, it ought to find root in any and all of the myriad of cultures of the world. Indeed the social scientist can make a case for this argument in the fact that Irish Catholicism differs from that of Italy; Spanish Catholicism differs from that of Germany. The manner in which religion is practiced by the people varies from one culture to another; but these examples still tend to fall within the wide ambit of European culture.

As the Catholic Church continues to struggle with this problem of de-Europeanization, it is simultaneously faced with the problem of adaptation to modern culture. To demythologize the Church is not only a matter of vocabulary. It means also the recognition that we are now in a new stage of humanity; contemporary culture is different from that of the past. Here again, as in the case of non-European acculturation, there has been both delay and resistance. The condemnation of the modernists by Pius X in 1907 was a setback to the confrontation that is now urgently upon us.[14]

There is a further element that enormously complicates this attempt to adapt Catholicism to modern culture. This is the fact that, unlike the many foreign cultures to which European Christianity is asked to adapt itself, and which often tend to represent a fairly integrated and identifiable system, contemporary Western civilization tends to be in disarray. O'Dea (1968:157) remarks that there has been a "bitter and prolonged conflict" between two perspectives on the world: on the one hand, transcendence, substance and ontology: on the other hand, immanence, process and history.

These two perspectives constitute a dilemma, but apparently not a dilemma in which a choice must be made. Somehow we have to live with both transcendence and immanence, with both the sacred and the profane although the emphasis on one perspective over the other may lead us either to the concept of personal regeneration or to the concept of structural transformation. Nevertheless, as O'Dea says, this dilemma amounts to a "basic conflict" built into the structure of religious institutions (1968:159).

At two levels the delegates to Vatican II indicated a recognition of the need for modernization. The first looked backward with "the critical reappraisal of the institutionalism and other-worldly emphasis inherited from the past." The second looks forward to the "new stress of the Church as a community of men in Christ and on man's worldly vocation" (O'Dea, 1968:160). The appraisal of the past and the hopes of the future lead to a genuine appreciation for the abilities of human beings. One of the most significant statements of the Pastoral Constitution (*Gaudium et Spes*) is that "modern man is on the road to a more thorough development of his own personality, and to a growing discovery and vindication of his own rights" (Abbott, 1966:240).

O'Dea's statement that "the Roman Catholic Church bears the future of Christianity as a whole" (1968:176) goes far beyond anything I am attempting to discuss in this paper. How Catholicism relates to the destiny of Christianity as a whole, or how Catholicism adapts to the modern scientific, materialistic culture, is certainly a significant theme for further study. At the moment, however, let us restrict our attention to the manner in which the organization of the Church is trying to adapt itself to the modern concept of social organization and structure.

The Polyphasic Church

People who are calling for a return to Christian origins, to the simple communal life style of the early Church, are nostalgic for an organized religion that was loosely structured; had no cardinals, no Holy Office, no Vatican bureaucracy. They want a restoration of the kinds of personal relations that exhibit love and concern, and that seemed to have distinguished the Christians from the pagans. Essentially too, they are asking for a restructuring of the Church to a system in which the social distance is lessened between the administrators and the rank-and-file faithful.[15]

In one of his pre-conciliar writings O'Dea discussed the "dilemma of administrative order" which occurs when a religious body becomes routinized, organized and bureaucratized. He makes the sociological observation that "structures which emerge in one set of conditions and in response to one set of problems may turn out later to be unwieldy instruments for handling new problems under new conditions. Functional precedents established in handling earlier problems can become dysfunctional in later situations, and even become formidable obstacles blocking any forthright action" (O'Dea, 1966:93).[16]

The Church of Constantine was not the Church of Peter and Paul. The Church at the time of the Great Western Schism was not the Church of the Council of Trent. This is not to say that the manner in which the Church adapted itself to the changing circumstances at these different historical periods was rational and ideal. We know that there is always mutual influence: religion influences culture and is also influenced by culture. We may well say, for example, that in the Roman Catholic Church the medieval adaptation of its structural arrangements was appropriate to medieval socio-cultural conditions. The Church's imitation of the royal tradition in the political sphere was what people were accustomed to, and probably preferred.

The historical and sociological problem is that this form of ecclesiastical organization tended to be frozen by the decisions of the Council of Trent. This monophasic structure means that power, authority and decision-making were centralized at the Vatican. The general procedure was that directives came down from Rome to the diocese, from the bishops to the priests, from the pastors to the people (Fichter, 1974:57–72). It should be noted that this was not originally peculiar to the Church. This system of management had long been accepted in all phases of life, civil government, private business, university education, as well as in religion.

The Reformation was a challenge to this exclusive and central form of church government, and the counter-reformation at the Council of Trent did not relax the structural rigidity. Indeed, in the Catholic Church, the monophasic system seemed to "prove out" by the subsequent experience of the splintering of Protestantism. Those who stayed with the Pope stayed with the Catholic Church. All others are schismatics, if not heretics. Within the Roman Church the principle of loyalty and obedience to the top central authority was the basis of Christian solidarity and brotherhood.

Catholic apologists pointed to the prolif-eration of Protestantism into numerous churches, denominations and sects as proof of the vitality of the monophasic principle. What now seems odd is that this principle continued to be applied to Catholicism while everything else was changing. Western civilization was in flux. People fought and died for a polyphasic system, for the right to freedom and self-determination, for decentralized and representative forms of organization. This concept was gradually introduced not only in the political structure, but also in business and industry, into higher education and the professions, and even into the kinship system.

The crucial structural test of Vatican II was the question whether, and to what extent, this traditional centralized system could give way to a multi-faceted system of government. The realizations came clear in the Council that the traditional ecclesiastical system was not a *given*, which was immutable and to which people had to conform. The Church was now seen as a man-made structure, the result of many human decisions over many centuries. The notion that the Church could be remade in a modern fashion, also as the result of human effort, underlines the proposition that the Church exists to serve the people (Dulles, 1974:83–96).

The switch from monophasic loyalty to polyphasic consensus was not expected to be a brief and easy transition. No one realistically expected that the new pattern could be suddenly substituted for the old one. The crucial fact is that the transition is moving at a snail's pace even though the Council fathers recognized that in the world at large men are beginning to see things "in their changeable and evolutionary aspects." There is an ever-increasing number of "men and women who are conscious that they themselves are the artisans and the authors of the culture of their community." There has occurred then "the birth of a new humanism, one in which man is defined first of all by his responsibility toward his brothers and toward history" (Abbott, 1966:261).

The People's Church

This seems to be the sticking point for the disgruntled and disillusioned Catholics who are still waiting for basic structural adaptation in the Catholic Church. In the new pluralistic system there was to be consensus—without destroying the loyalty of the faithful to the head of the Church—and it was to become a substantial basis of organizational solidarity. The official hierarchical attempts to implement this process were made grudgingly and cautiously. They have been clumsy and largely unsuccessful.

There is still a widely held thesis, especially in the hierarchical churches and perhaps more especially among American Catholics, that change must be instituted at the top of the structure. The direction of the church comes from Rome and from bishops who preserve the *magisterium* and who know what is best for all the faithful. This thesis has long been challenged, of course, by the congregational types of churches, even though we know that the large "free churches" are highly structured with an upper locus of decision-making (Harrison, 1959).

What seems to be happening now is that more and more Catholics are simply disregarding the official pronouncements of the church hierarchy. They are not in revolt. They are not openly disrespectful of the prelates, but they are simply no longer impressed by the need of attending to directives and prohibitions. Nowhere is this more evident than in the matter of contraception, both in belief and practice. At the level of the clergy one sees this in the decline of the daily recitation of the breviary, or more noticeably in the beards and long hair and nonclerical apparel of priests. Catholic women continue to push for equality within the Church, even for ordination in spite of Pope Paul's declaration that this cannot be.

O'Dea would have called this a situation of crisis and strain and dilemma, and it may well be interpreted in that fashion. It may be seen also as symbolic of the modernity of which he spoke so often. The church is being modernized in spite of itself. It appears that the changes are occurring at the bottom of the structure, that customs and attitudes are developing among people who are true believers and consider themselves faithful children of the Church. This is not a matter of a popular referendum, but it is an example of the "signs of the times" which the ecclesiastical authorities can not forever ignore.

The highly publicized convention in Detroit, the "Call to Action" which involved Catholic laity from all over the country, may be the beginning of recognition of folk religion. It provided an upward channel of communication through which the voice of the people was heard. For large numbers of Catholics this apparatus seemed cumbersome, and many are waiting to see whether "anything happens" as a result of these meetings. Meanwhile American Catholicism is experiencing adaptation at the grass roots. The most significant aspect of this change is the switch of emphasis in the basis of moral and religious guidance. Dependence on legislation from above has largely switched to dependence on the conscience of the people.

Notes

1. The third chapter, articles 18–29, attempts a fresh pastoral interpretation of the episcopate (Abbott, 1966:37–56).

2. "At this time, ten years after the Council, when a certain shift to the right has come to characterize political life, the Catholic Church on the whole seems to have lost interest in the renewal" (Baum, 1975:177).

3. The failure of reform appears to be a desirable thing in the opinion of James Hitchcock. "The hierarchy tends to equate Catholicism with the well being of the structure, the radicals tend to blame the structure for all the Church's ills" (Hitchcock, 1971:180).

4. For a sociological study of Catholic Pentecostalism see Joseph H. Fichter (1975).

5. "To reduce the Christian message to a truth about personal salvation is to suppress a basic dimen-

sion of this message and to transform it into an ideology sanctioning individualism" (Baum, 1975:197).

6. One of the "reasons" why the conservative churches are growing is that they are attending to spirituality and not to social reform. The question is well balanced in David Moberg, *The Great Reversal: Evangelism versus Social Concern* (1972).

7. It has been almost a slogan of the Women's Liberation Movement to raise the consciousness of discrimination, and "conscientization" is a common term in the Latin American theology of Liberation (Gutierrez, 1973:91–116).

8. The concept of social sin, especially of "sinful social structures," seems difficult to comprehend for individualists and personalists. See Patrick Kerans, 1974.

9. Pope Paul VI issued an encyclical on *Evangelization* in December, 1975, in which he made no mention of the need for social reform. This omission seems odd in the light of the statement for "Justice in the World," given by the Third Synod of Bishops, 1971: "Action on behalf of justice and participation in the transformation of the world fully appears to us as a constitutive dimension of the preaching of the gospel."

10. The first chapter of *Lumen Gentium*, articles 1–8, speaks of the Church as a "mystery" which indicates that as a divine reality it "cannot be fully captured by human thought or language" (Abbott, 1966:14).

11. Alexander Schmemann goes so far as to say that "as long as we debate institutions and structures and not the mystery of the Church in her depths, we are by-passing the real issue" (Suenens, 1975:19).

12. Malcolm Hay (1956:190–192) reprints the decree of the Sacred Congregation of Propaganda of December 8, 1939, which finally rescinded the oath on Chinese rites.

13. In *Gandium et Spes*, article 58, we read that the church "is not bound exclusively and indissolubly to any race or nation, not to any particular way of life or any customary pattern of living, ancient or recent" (Abbott, 1966:261).

14. The encyclical *Lamentabili Sane*, July 3, 1907, contained the Syllabus of modernist errors, and *Pascendi Dominici Gregis*, September 8, 1907, roundly condemned the modernists.

15. The *Gemeinschaft* of the religious sect has held

a fascination for sociologists as well as for Catholics who dream of remodeling the contemporary church according to the early Christian community described in the Acts of the Apostles.

16. This is a reflection of his earlier article, "Five Dilemmas in the Institutionalization of Religion" (1961: 30–39).

References

Abbott, Walter (ed.) 1966. The Documents of Vatican II. New York: New York Association Press.

Baum, Gregory. 1975. Religion and Alienation. Paramus: Paulist Press.

Dulles, Avery. 1974. Models of the Church. Garden City: Doubleday.

Fichter, Joseph. 1974. Organization Man in the Church. Cambridge: Schenkman.

———. 1975. The Catholic Cult of the Paraclete. New York: Sheed and Ward.

Gutierrez, Gustavo. 1973. A Theology of Liberation. Maryknoll: Orbis.

Harrison, Paul M. 1959. Authority and Power in the Free Church Tradition. Carbondale: Southern Illinois University Press.

Hay, Malcolm. 1956. Failure in the Far East. London: Spearman.

Hitchcock, James. 1971. The Decline and Fall of Radical Catholicism. New York: Herder and Herder.

Kerans, Patrick. 1974. Sinful Social Structures. Paramus: Paulist Press.

Küng, Hans. 1968. Truthfulness: The Future of the Church. New York: Sheed and Ward.

Moberg, David. 1972. The Great Reversal: Evangelism versus Social Concern. Philadelphia: J. B. Lippincott.

O'Dea, Thomas F. 1961. "Five Dilemmas in the Institutionalization of Religion." *Journal for the Scientific Study of Religion* 1:32–39.

———. 1966. The Sociology of Religion. Englewood Cliffs, N.J.: Prentice-Hall.

———. 1968. The Catholic Crisis. Boston: Beacon Press.

Suenens, Leon-Joseph. 1968. Coresponsibility in the Church. New York: Herder and Herder.

———. 1975. *A New Pentecost?* New York: Seabury.

R E A D I N G   5 . 2

Catholic Education in Three Cultures

Joan L. Fee, Andrew M. Greeley, William C. McCready, and Teresa Sullivan

Attendance at Catholic schools continues in the late 1970s to have the same moderate and statistically significant impact on the behavior of young Catholic adults, as has been found in our earlier studies. More than eight years of Catholic schooling does not produce a statistically significant impact on attitudes toward birth control, living together, and frequency of prayer. Neither did Catholic education produce such an impact in the analysis reported on the education of Catholic Americans based on 1974 data (Table 1). Nor is there a significant difference between those who had more than eight years of Catholic schooling. However, on all the other tested variables—Mass attendance, communion reception, belief in life after death, activity in parish organizations, thought of religious vocation, Catholic periodical reading and TV watching, participation in home liturgy and study groups, and opposition to abortion—Catholic schools do have a statistically significant effect.

How impressive is the magnitude of that effect? The question is no more easy to answer now than it was in either our 1965 or 1975 reports. Those who attended Catholic schools are twice as likely to receive commu-

Joan L. Fee is Manager of Marketing for SPSS, Inc.

Andrew M. Greeley is Professor of Sociology at the University of Arizona and Senior Study Director of the National Opinion Research Center at the University of Chicago.

William C. McCready is Director of the Center for the Study of American Pluralism at the National Opinion Research Center and Associate Professor of Sociology at the University of Chicago.

Teresa A. Sullivan is Associate Professor of Sociology at the University of Texas at Austin and Training Director at the Population Research Center.

Reprinted from Joan L. Fee, Andrew M. Greeley, William C. McCready, and Teresa Sullivan, *Young Catholics in the United States and Canada* (New York: Sadlier, 1981), with permission.

nion almost every week, to belong to parish organizations, to think of religious vocations, and to attend home liturgies. Indeed, only 12 percent of them have considered a vocation, but that is twice as many as the 6 percent who have not had more than eight years of Catholic schooling; and only 10 percent have attended a home liturgy, but that is still twice as high as the 5 percent of those who have not had more than eight years of Catholic schooling. Are these differences large or small? Almost 70 percent of those who have had more than eight years of Catholic school do not go to communion almost every week. In that respect, clearly, Catholic schools have failed. Furthermore, a little more than a quarter of those who have attended Catholic schools are uncertain about life after death (less than 10 percent say they do not believe in life after death, the others report they do not know for certain). If the goal is 100 percent commitment to human survival, then Catholic schools have failed. If the goal is notably and significantly to improve the likelihood of believing in life after death, then Catholic schools have succeeded.

In the propaganda for Catholic schools many years ago, it often seemed to be said that Catholic schools would turn out almost without exception exemplary Catholics. The critics of Catholic schools, taking that "argument" as a norm, have never ceased to point out enthusiastically the schools simply do not achieve such a goal. The defenders of Catholic schools who accept such a statement of the question have been embarrassed and defensive.

Any serious reading of the educational impact literature would reveal that schools should not reasonably be expected to undo the work of home, family, peer group, neigh-

Table 1   *The Results of Catholic Schooling* (Percent)

	More than Eight Years	Eight Years or Less
Mass attendance (almost weekly)	43*	32
Communion (almost weekly)	32*	17
Pray (at least several times a week)	57	53
Believe in life after death	72*	60
Member of parish organization	13*	5
Thought of vocation	12*	6
Read a Catholic periodical	37*	25
Watch Catholic TV	21	8
Attended home liturgy	10*	5*
Participated in study group	17*	11
Opposed abortion (if no more children wanted)	64*	54
Living together sinful	23	20
Birth control sinful	4	6

*Significant at .05 level or better.

borhood, social class, and ethnic culture. Though schools can make a difference under some circumstances, the boundless American faith in the power of formal education has never been sustained either by empirical evidence or by everyday impression.

Where does this leave us on the subject of the effectiveness of Catholic schools? They do not produce graduates who are universally exemplary Catholics. They do have some effect. How much effect? Far more effect in terms of statistical size than is used to justify racial integration. Is the effect worth the cost? One would think, given the difficulty of affecting human religious behavior at all, that the effect is worth the cost until an alternate system, technique, or method can be devised that does as well.

This interpretation is basically the same one that was originally presented in the *Education of Catholic Americans* [1966] and appeared in *Catholic Schools in a Declining Church* [1976]. Catholic schools do have a limited effect, a not unimpressive effect as educational impact effects go. It does not seem reasonable to give up on them unless one has an alternative system which will produce the same effect at less cost.

There are striking similarities and some interesting differences in the effectiveness of Catholic schools in the United States and in French and English Canada (Table 2). Indeed, the correlation coefficient for the United States and for English Canada between number of years of Catholic education and adult religious attitudes and behaviors, for instance, is frequently identical. In English Canada, Catholic schools produce a stronger impact on belief in life after death; in the United States a greater likelihood of thinking seriously of a religious vocation, of being active in a parish organization, of being opposed to mercy killing and abortion, of describing self as one who is close to the Church, and of marrying a Catholic spouse. On the whole, as measured by the summary "Catholicity" scale (measuring communion reception, belief in life after death, consideration of religious vocation, membership in a parish organization), Catholic schools have a somewhat higher impact in the United States than they do in English Canada.

In French Canada, however, the picture is rather different. Catholic schools do have a significant impact on the reception of communion and belief in life after death, and, also, a stronger impact than in the United States on the sense of closeness to the Church, and a stronger impact than in English Canada on a prolife position. But, gen-

Table 2 *Correlations with Number of Years of Catholic Education in the United States and Canada* (Coefficient=Pearson's r)

	USA	English Canada	French Canada
Mass	.10*	.10	.03
Communion	.16*	.17*	.10*
Prayer	.05	.05	.03
Life after death	.12*	.18*	.11*
Vocation	.16*	.08	.06
Parish activity	.15*	.05	.03
Close to church	.09*	.06	.14*
Pro life	.13*	.02	.10*
Permissiveness	.06	.08	.04
Catholic marriage	.13*	.00	.04
"Catholicity" scale	.25*	.19*	.02

*Significant at .05 or better.

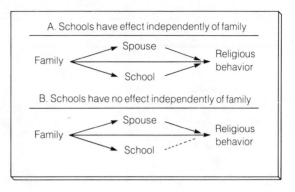

Figure 1. Two models of the effects of Catholic education

erally, the correlation coefficients are lower in French Canada than they are in English Canada or in the United States—suggesting that, perhaps, in a mostly Catholic culture (in the same sense that other religious denominations are a very small minority) such as French Canada, cultural forces may be far more important in affecting things like religious vocations, parish activity, and Sunday church attendance than the number of years of Catholic school the person has attended. It also may be that in a situation where virtually all primary education and much secondary education is carried on under Catholic auspices, the schools will have somewhat less effect than in a pluralistic society where there is more freedom of choice. However, the authors of the present report do not propose to be specialists on this phenomenon in Canada and must leave further examination of these data and more sophisticated and subtle interpretations to Canadian scholars.

The Effect of Catholic Schools: Real or Imagined?

In the previous NORC report [Greeley et al., 1976], the possibility that it might well be Catholic families, either of origin or procreation, which produce the apparent effectiveness of Catholic schools, was considered. Perhaps those who come from religious families are more likely to go to Catholic schools and hence, will appear more Catholic in adult life—but will the real reason be their family and not their school? Perhaps, also, those from devoutly Catholic families will marry devout spouses and the spouse will contribute to the level of Catholicity. Could it be that what appears to be the Catholic school effect is, in fact, an effect of the family in which one is reared and the family which one is formed?

Figure 1 presents two alternative models to test this possibility. The first one, while conceding that the family affects the choice of the spouse as well as religious behavior, and also has an effect on whether one goes to Catholic schools, does not account entirely for the impact of Catholic schools. The second model, with a dotted line between school and religious behavior, says that when the effect of the family of origin and the spouse are taken into account there will be no Catholic school impact, at least not one that is statistically significant or worth noticing substantively.

The appropriate regression equations were written to enable us to choose between the two models for both the United States and

Table 3 *Standardized Correlations with "Catholicity" Scale Testing Models in Figure 1* (beta)

	Unmarried Respondents	Married Respondents
Family religiousness	.11	.14
Religiousness of spouse		.21
Family spirit "joyful"	.13	.13
Catholic education	.19	.17
(Religious images)	.26	.19
English Canada		
Family	.38	
Schools	.16	
French Canada		
(Communion reception the dependent variable)		
Family	.14	
Schools	.21	

Canada. The religiousness of the family of origin (measured by whether the family was religiously mixed and dogmatically Catholic and by how often the parents went to Mass and received communion) and the religiousness of spouse (measured by the respondent's description of his or her spouse's religiousness) and the religious "joyfulness" of the respondent's parents . . . were included in the equation. (A high score on the image scale indicates that the respondent is likely to think of Jesus and Mary as "warm" and of God as a "lover" and of heaven as "paradise of pleasure and delight." This scale correlates powerfully with religious devotion, marital satisfaction, sexual fulfillment in marriage, rejection of sexual permissiveness, and social commitment.) All of these factors do, indeed, make their own independent contribution to a person's position on the Catholicity scale (Table 3). However, the impact of Catholic schools is not diminished greatly by taking these other factors into account, and for unmarried respondents is second only to the religious "images" in its effectiveness in producing "Catholicity." There is no connection between the number of years of Catholic schooling and warm religious images, suggesting a major opportunity for improvement

in the Catholic educational enterprise. For married respondents, the religiousness of the spouse has somewhat more impact than does Catholic education, but it is still a strong correlate of religious behavior. For the third time, then, NORC research has demonstrated that the effectiveness of Catholic schools is not a function of the religiousness of the family from which a person comes or of the family which the person has formed. Catholic schools have their own statistically significant independent effect, which as educational impact effects go is important enough.

Furthermore, the same phenomenon can also be reported in Canada. Indeed, in French Canada, once the religiousness of the family is taken into account, the correlation between the years of attendance at Catholic school and the increased reception of communion suggests that the presence in French-Canadian Catholic education of a considerable number of young people from less devout families depresses the measured impact of Catholic school attendance. This raises the interesting possibility that the rather lower correlations for French Canada noted in Table 3 are the result of the fact that in French Canada there is not nearly so much self-selection on the basis of family religiousness and the enrollment of young people in Catholic schools.

Catholic Schools and Identification with the Church

What is the secret of the "modest" or "moderate" or "important" effect of Catholic education on the behavior of young Catholic adults? Readers may choose their own words depending on their criteria for educational success—though we would remind them that in most educational research, betas of .15 and .20 are taken very seriously indeed. How can the effectiveness of Catholic schools be explained? Is it the result of specific religious instruction, of different techniques used, or the various courses taught? Is it the integration of religion with other parts of the curriculum, or, perhaps, the integration of the educational experience with the liturgical life of the parish or school?

Our assumption at the beginning of the present project was that, however important any of these factors might be, the primary effectiveness of Catholic schooling was based on cultural and social structural factors. Those who attended Catholic schools, we suspected, would have a closer sense of affiliation to the Church simply because they had spent more time on Church property and would more likely have more experience with religious personnel, over and above the influences of their families, either of origin or procreation. We argued it is precisely this sense of "closeness" to the Church which would be the primary intervening variable between Catholic schooling and religious behavior in adult life. Figure 2 presents a schematic model describing this expectation.

It will be recalled that there was a modest statistically significant correlation between Catholic education and self-description as being "close to the Church" (on a five-point scale describing a number of concentric circles from the center to the periphery of the Church). Even though the size of this correlation was small, it still seemed to us that it would be a decisive factor.

To test our expectation we used residual

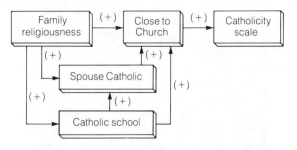

Figure 2. Model to test explanation of effect of Catholic school being attributable to a greater sense of closeness to (or nonalienation from) the Church

analysis to reduce the difference between two groups by taking into account various intervening factors. In Table 4 we apply the model presented in Figure 2 to the twenty-two percentage points difference in those high on the Catholicity scale between respondents who had more than eight years of Catholic education and those who had less than eight years, or no Catholic education. One by one prior variables are introduced into the residual model—in this case, the religious background of one's family of origin and the religious identity of one's spouse. About a third of the difference between those who have had more Catholic education and those who have had less can be accounted for by familial factors, but *all* of the rest of the difference is accounted for by the fact that those who have gone to Catholic schools feel that they are closer to the Church. It must be remembered that this feeling of "closeness" is over and

Table 4 *Table Test of Model in Figure 2*

	Eight Years	Less
Difference in "Catholicity" between those who have more than eight years of Catholic education and those with less	57%	35% = 22%
		Proportion Explained
Family background	5 points	.23
Spouse Catholic	7 points	.32
Closeness to Church	10 points	1.00

above whatever closeness to the Church might be accounted for by either spouse or family of origin. It is "pure" Catholic school effect.

The secret of the schools, if it may be called that, is that they integrate young people more closely into the Catholic institutional community. However, not all those who go to Catholic schools are close to the Church. But, it is the greater "closeness" of some of those who go to Catholic schools which "explains" virtually all of the religious effectiveness of Catholic education. The point for Catholic policy makers is clear: If you can find another institution that can have the same effectiveness in integrating young people into the Catholic community and Catholic institutions, you do not need Catholic schools. Unless and until we find such a technique, then the continuing decline of the proportion of Catholic population in Catholic schools will inevitably lead to a *diminished* level of Catholic commitment in years ahead.

Catholic Schools and Life Cycle

. . . . we [have previously] identified, described, and explained a "mini–life cycle" which affects many young Catholics in their 20s. Religious practice declines sharply in the early and middle 20s and then rebounds, though not quite so sharply, at the end of the 20s. Does attendance at Catholic schools facilitate that rebound, impede it, or have any effect at all?

First of all (Table 5), the relationship between the number of years at Catholic schools and the Catholicity scale is higher the more mature a person is. The correlation is .37 for the age cohort 29 and 30 years old. The greatest impact of the Catholic school in other words, is precisely at that time in life when young people are beginning to return to regular religious practice. A quite powerful payoff for Catholic schooling seems to take place at that time.

Table 5   *Impact of Catholic Schools and CCD* (Coefficient = Pearson's r)

	Catholic Schools	CCD
Mass	.10*	.08*
Communion	.16*	.06
Prayer	.05	.01
Life after death	.12*	.01
Parish organizations	.15*	.00
Vocation	.16*	.04
Pro life	.13*	.01
Permissiveness	−.06	+.07
"Catholicity" scale	.25*	.02
Closeness to Church	.09*	−.03

*Significant at .05 or better.

The age cohort effect of Catholic schools can be demonstrated also by percentage differences. In Table 6, for example, the rise in the proportion high on the Catholicity scale is confined almost entirely to those who have had more than eight years of Catholic schooling. For this group, between the middle and late 20s there is an increase in 15 percentage points in the proportion high on the Catholicity scale, whereas for those who had eight years or less of Catholic schools, the increase is only 3 percentage points. In the regular (nearly every week) reception of communion, those who have had eight or more years of Catholic school declined from 49 to 20 percent between the early and middle 20s, and then rebounded to 32 percent, whereas those who do not attend Catholic schools more than eight years declined from 29 percent to 11 percent, and then only increased 2 percentage points in the final years of their 20s. Finally, the Mass attendance of those who have gone to Catholic schools goes up 17 percentage points, while those who had less Catholic education only increases 3 percentage points. The religious revival of the late 20s is almost exclusively concentrated in that proportion of the young Catholic population which has had substantial amount of time in Catholic schools.

For ecclesiastical policy makers this is an extremely important point to reflect upon: If

Table 6 *Evaluation of CCD and Catholic Education*

	Catholic Schools	CCD
Teaching Quality Excellent or Very Good (Percentages)		
Grammar	42	28
High school	45	21
Classes Somewhat or Very "Informal" (Percentages)		
High school	31	58
Involved in "Some or More" Activities outside the Classroom (Percentages)		
High school	32	18
Simple Correlations between Quality and Methods of Teaching and "Catholicity Scale"		
Informality	.27	.02
Activities	.30	.04
Years	.25	.02

you are going to get young people back at the end of their 20s, then you better have provided them with an opportunity for more than eight years of Catholic education. The explanatory model for the effectiveness of Catholic schools presented in Figure 2 also operates when it is limited to the oldest age cohort in the sample—those at the end of the decade of their 20s. Those who have attended Catholic schools are more likely to return to the Church because they have more religious spouses and because their feelings of closeness to the Church are increasing (Table 7). Maturity and marriage seem to intensify that

identification with the Catholic community and with Catholic institutions, which Catholic schools have inculcated.

Finally, does Catholic school attendance incline a young person to choose not merely a spouse who is a Catholic, but also one who is more likely to be a devout Catholic and therefore more likely to activate and reactivate a respondent to religious devotion? The question is hard to answer because it is difficult to separate spouses' influence on respondents from respondents' influence on spouses. Yet, if one considers the three-variable model presented in Figure 3, one can see that it is possible to make a tentative test. We know that Catholic education affects the communion reception of our respondents. We also know there is a relationship between Catholic education, between the respondent's own communion reception, and the spouse's communion reception. Logically, there ought not to be a direct correlation (the line at the top of the triangle) between the number of years a respondent went to Catholic schools and the communion of her or his spouse. How, after all, could a husband's Catholic education affect a wife's communion reception, except, say, through the example of the husband's communion reception?

If there is a statistically significant standardized correlation (beta) on the direct path between Catholic education and spouse's

Table 7 *Catholic Behavior by Catholic Schools and CCD* (Percent)

Behavior	Average	10 or More Years in Catholic Schools	10 or More Years in CCD
Mass (2 or 3 times a month or more)	24	49	45
Communion (2 or 3 times a month or more)	21	34	21
Pray (several times a week)	53	65	55
Pope infallible	24	34	20
Seriously considered vocation	6	13	2
Birth control wrong	5	5	3

Conclusion: So duration of CCD attendance does not improve relative impact compared to Catholic schools.

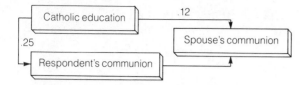

Figure 3. Spouse's communion reception and own Catholic education, holding constant respondent's communion reception

communion reception, then there is at least some evidence the spouse was more devout to begin with and was in part chosen precisely because of his or her devotion. Indeed, the beta coefficient on the top line of the triangle is statistically significant at .12. Thus, it would appear that those who attended Catholic schools do choose somewhat more devout spouses than those who did not attend Catholic schools. Succinctly, the more Catholic schooling one has, the more likely that person will choose a devout spouse.

This phenomenon, however, seems to be limited to women. If the model in Figure 3 is run separately for both sexes, the coefficient on the top line deteriorates to zero for men, and for women rises to .17. The longer a young woman has attended a Catholic school, the more likely she is to seek and find a husband whose religious devotion will reinforce her own.

Summary

In our 1976 report [Greeley et al.], we argued that the Catholic schools seemed even more important to the Church in times of transition than they did in times of stability. (In 1966 a study [Greeley and Rossi] had been undertaken before most of the effects of the Second Vatican Council were experienced by the Church.) The present study, limited to Catholics who have matured since the Second Vatican Council, confirms and reinforces this conclusion, both for the United States and for Canada. The answer to Mrs. Ryan's [1964] fa-

mous question, "Are Catholic Schools the Answer?" as the research evidence shows, seems to be that they may not be the absolute answer, but they are the best answer that exists and they are getting to be a more important answer with the passage of time. Catholic schools seem to be especially important at the decisive religious (and as we have demonstrated in *The Young Catholic Family* [1980]) and marital turning point that takes place at the end of the decade of the 20s. The tables that are presented . . . should make somber reading for those ecclesiastical administrators who have been reluctant to build Catholic schools and who have stood by taking little action as the proportion of Catholics attending such schools has declined. It is possible, of course, that those who had less Catholic education may return to religious practice at a later stage in their lives. They certainly do not do so, however, by the end of their 20s.

The first NORC report (*The Education of Catholic Americans*, 1966) demonstrated that Catholic schools had an effect independent of the families' religious background. The second report [*Catholic Schools in a Declining Church*, 1976] demonstrated that this effect was more important in the post-conciliar Church than previously thought, and was especially strong for young people. In this report we have added two critical new bits of information:

1. The Catholic schools are especially important for young people at the religious turning point at the end of the third decade of their lives.
2. The schools exercise their effectiveness primarily through an integrating effect: tying people into the Catholic community and Catholic institutions.

Other research carried on in such disparate countries as Australia and Peru, and our own preliminary investigation of Canada, parallels the NORC findings (1966) on the *Education of Catholic Americans*. The problem posed by

Peter H. Rossi (to whom this report is dedicated in the year of his presidency of the American Sociological Association) twenty years ago has basically been solved: How much impact on adult Catholics do Catholic schools have and by what dynamics are such influences produced?

The fact that Catholic school enrollment continues to decline, almost entirely because of the failure of Church leaders to build new schools (Greeley, McCready, McCourt, 1976), in the light of these continued research findings must be considered a telling example of the failure to use research as an important

component in the process of ecclesiastical decision-making.

References

Andrew M. Greeley, *The Young Catholic Family* (Chicago: Thomas More Press, 1980).
Andrew M. Greeley, William C. McCready, and Kathleen McCourt, *Catholic Schools in a Declining Church* (Kansas City: Sheed and Ward, 1976).
Andrew M. Greeley, and Peter Rossi, *The Education of Catholic Americans* (Chicago: Aldine Publishing, 1966).
Mary Perkins Ryan, *Are Parochial Schools the Answer?* (New York: Harper & Row, 1964).

S E L E C T I O N   5 . A

The Experience of Being a Roman Catholic in a Time of Change

Sister Elaine M. Prevallet, S.L.

In this attempt to reflect upon "the experience of being a Roman Catholic in a time of change," I shall try to do two things: first, I shall try to stay in touch with my own experience, and second, I shall try to relate broader theological issues to that experience. At the outset, I should probably say that my experience is not exactly typical—if indeed there be any such thing as typical. It is conditioned by my profession as a teacher of theology in a college which has very rapidly changed from a rather conservative Catholic college for women to an independent co-ed institution with a religiously heterogeneous student population—with the revision and re-

Sister Elaine M. Prevallet, formerly professor of Religious Studies at Loretto Heights College in Denver, is currently director of Knobs Haven Retreat Center in Nerinx, Kentucky.
Originally presented at a regional meeting of the American Academy of Religion, Denver, Colorado, April, 1972. Revised and published with the author's permission.

vamping of my own teaching approach and a refocusing of questions demanded by the changed context here. My profession, in any case, demands that I stay in touch with students' questions and perceptions, and hence effectively ensures that my own thinking be consistently challenged and changing. Secondly, my experience is conditioned by the fact that I am a sister, and some groups of sisters have been among the most aggressive and progressive in making the changes we felt were necessary to bring our Christian dedication into the twentieth century. This has been especially challenging for me, because it necessitated a rather thorough rethinking of the tradition of spirituality in which I was reared, a consistent attempt to separate the peripheral and nonessential from the core of my commitment, the accidental trappings from the substance. What went on for me in that context is perhaps a miniature of what is and has been going on in the whole Church—an attempt to distinguish the essential from the peripheral. Yet my experience may be different from that of many other Roman Catholics in that my thinking and rethinking was done within and for a community of intelligent and dedicated persons, whose challenge hopefully kept and keeps me from too timid settlements with any given status quo.

My position, then, is only more or less similar to that of other persons within the Roman Catholic community. But precisely here we can note a significant change in the picture—and in the experience—of Roman Catholicism: a shift from a very stable, well-ordered group who all knew and professed the same faith in the same words—the Catholic monolith—to groups of persons who have found or are finding communities of support and are coming to find their own faith and take their own stand. We have, all of us, I imagine, felt ourselves shaken, our security threatened, our faith called into question. As one might expect, there are different ways of reacting. Some will become impatient with the slowness of change, decide the Church is antiquated and hopeless, and drop out. Some will sever affiliation but for the opposite reason: the Church has changed so fast and so radically as to be unrecognizable as the Church one knew and loved, so radically changed that one feels no identification with it, is disillusioned and disappointed by it—and so drops out. It could, no doubt, be called an identity crisis. It is no longer so easy to know what it means to be a Roman Catholic or so easy to say what a Roman Catholic believes or holds on various issues.[1] One is thrown much more upon one's own resources, and one is turned more personally toward others who share one's faith. From that standpoint, an identity crisis can be a valuable prelude to a new level of self-consciousness, commitment, and genuine community, as opposed to a mere collectivity. One has to search to find one's own home ground.

Perhaps one can speak with some accuracy of a relativistic perspective as having had great impact upon Catholic consciousness.[2] Contemporary historical consciousness is one factor in the kind of de-absolutizing we have undergone; the experience of plurality is another. Ecumenical awareness is surely part of this perspective. We have had, in the last decade, to admit that the Spirit of God is not bound by the structure of the Roman Catholic or even of the Christian churches; we have had to admit that Protestants—and even Jews, Buddhists and Moslems—may turn up in heaven, not in spite of but because of their religious beliefs and practice. Experientially this has meant a modification of many absolutist attitudes among Roman Catholics: from thinking we knew it all, no doubt with some arrogance, to greater humility before the truth; from believing that everyone had to believe and say it our way to an attitude of openness to one's Christian or non-Christian neighbor as a possible source of insight into truth; from thinking that once we had mastered the Baltimore catechism we "knew our faith" to what Gordon Allport calls an "heuristic approach" to faith,[3] allowing for growth, change, provisionalness, doubt, discovery.

Equally in the area of morality—focused in the birth-control controversy but helped along by changes such as that in the law of Friday abstinence and the possibility of fulfilling one's obligation by going to Mass on Saturday instead of Sunday—there is less trust of ecclesiastical laws as absolutes. It may sound preposterous to equate the issues of birth control or abortion with the issues of whether or not one eats meat on Friday and goes to Church on Sunday, but in point of fact, deviation from the Church's stance on all those issues were taught to us as mortal sins, equally absolute in deserving damnation. It was, of course, a naive and unnuanced moral sensitivity, yet the change has spawned distrust and even cynicism. If a thing could be a mortal sin deserving of hell one day and nothing at all the next, simply by ecclesiastical fiat, then how trusting can we be of any ecclesiastical laws or moral pronouncements at all? And again, there are varieties of responses. Some persons learn to think through their moral positions and arrive at a more carefully nuanced and personally appropriated moral sense, and some retire into positions of negativism. Experientially the former has meant bearing the responsibility for much more serious thought and information gathering, making many more decisions, and, of course, living with many more unanswered questions.

Another powerful influence within Roman Catholicism is the movement to relate the Church to the public and political life of the times. Since Second Vatican's document "On the Church in the Modern World," the impetus toward a social-gospel interpretation of Christianity has gained strength and vitality, urging active involvement in the shaping of society, protest against unjust social structures and policies, and critique of the status quo. A critical stance had long been represented in American Catholicism by Dorothy Day and the Catholic Worker movement, which has given consistent and powerful witness both to pacifism and to concern for the poor. In the 60s there were Catholics protesting both racism and the Vietnam war. That impulse continues now in more institutional form as American bishops, both individually and collectively, speak out about the immorality of nuclear armaments. But the challenge to take a position on issues of social justice complicates the relationships of American Catholics to each other and to the hierarchy.[4] Many have found the hierarchy unduly slow in forming its conscience on urgent matters. Many, on the other hand, resent actions, especially by clergy, which signal the Church's intrusion into the life of the world. Once again, the identity of Roman Catholics has been diversified, this time by social conscience.

The women's movement presents still another issue. Many women find their position simply unconscionable: in a church dominated by an all-male hierarchy, excluded from ordination, oppressed by the sexist perspective and language in Scripture, in Church prayers and pronouncements. Because they are systemically excluded, women have no recourse; they either put up with it, or they leave the Church. In this case, an increasing number of persons are experiencing frustration and anger from oppression within the Church itself.

All of this points up a fundamental change in Roman Catholic attitudes toward authority. That is, of course, part of the larger picture of a changing world and society. It has been noted that in a stable society, a rigid hierarchical system is adequate, because its task is simply to provide instructions on how to behave in a framework in which the major outlines of conduct are already agreed upon by all. But in a society of rapid social change, it seems clear that a hierarchy will have to assume a different style and role.[5] In 1972 there appeared a declaration signed by thirty-four well-known Roman Catholic theologians from different countries, which spoke of the Church as suffering from a crisis of leadership and confidence.[6] It suggested that the crisis "is largely due to the ecclesiastical system which in its development has remained behind the times and still exemplifies monarchial absolutism: pope and bishops remain for all practical purposes the exclusive rulers in the church, combining the legislative, executive and judicial powers in one hand." The style of leadership that has characterized the Roman Catholic Church seems out of joint in a society that is undergoing such rapid social change as ours, and in which participation and intelligent assent must be the keynote of advance. There is an obvious dilemma: there are those in the Church who look to an answer-giving kind of leader.[7] These people are disappointed, for if Rome or the bishops give some answers, they do not give nearly enough to allay these people's fears. For others, they give too many and give them in areas where their silence would be better appreciated. In short, the leadership can't win. The solid structure of the Roman Catholic institution has experienced some cracks.

But the theologians' statement also evidences a vigor and health which persist in Roman Catholicism. They call first for a return to the gospel of Jesus Christ, and give some practical guidelines to help overcome what they identify as a situation of stagnation and resignation: Do not remain silent; do something yourself; act together; seek provisional solutions; and finally, don't give up.

It is good to hear these voices speaking of courage and hope. The task—reform of both society and the Church—seems so massive as to be paralyzing. And so if one must speak of the experience of being a Roman Catholic in a time of change, one necessarily speaks of confusion and uncertainty, unsettledness and doubt, disillusion and frustration. But one can also speak of personal conviction and commitment, challenge and inner growth, courage and hope. All of these are our individual and collective experience. Our theologians say, "Why should we continue to hope? . . . There is hope because we believe that the power of the Gospel of Jesus Christ shows itself time and again as more powerful than all our human failures and foolishness in the church, stronger than all our discouragement." That is where we are. It is a time when this story, relayed by Thomas Merton from his contact with the Buddhists, has a lot of meaning for us:

This friend of Merton's had to leave Tibet or be killed when the Chinese Communists took

over all the Tibetan monasteries. The Lama was isolated in the mountains, living in a peasant's house and wondering what to do next. He sent a message to a nearby abbot friend of his saying, "What do we do?" The abbot sent back a strange message: "From now on, brother, everybody stands on his own feet." Merton comments on this message, "We can no longer rely on being supported by structures which may be destroyed at any moment by a political power or political force. You cannot rely on structures. The time for relying on structures has disappeared. They are good, and they should help us, and we should do the best we can with them. But they may be taken away, and if everything is taken away, what do you do next? From now on, brother, everybody stands on his own feet."[8]

Notes

1. For instance, in "On So-called 'Partial Identification' with the Church," Heinz Schlette strongly challenges the model of "total identification" with the Church that used to characterize Roman Catholic thought and ideal. In Johannes Metz, ed., *Perspectives of a Political Ecclesiology*, *Concilium* series, vol. 66 (New York: Herder & Herder, 1971), pp. 35–49.

2. James Kelly, "The New Roman Church: A Modest Proposal," *Commonweal*, 3 December 1971, pp. 222–26.

3. Gordon Allport, *The Individual and His Religion* (New York: Macmillan, 1950), p. 81.

4. Daniel Berrigan discusses his relation to the Catholic radical tradition as well as his relation to the Roman Catholic establishment in Berrigan and Coles, *The Geography of Faith*, pp. 124–32.

5. D. Hay, "The Natural Selection of Hierarchies," *New Blackfriars* 51 (1970), p. 140.

6. Reprinted in *The National Catholic Reporter*, 31 March 1972, pp. 8, 17.

7. Terminology used by Andrew M. Greeley, "Sociology and Church Structure," in T. Urresti, ed., *Structures of the Church*, *Concilium* series, vol. 58 (New York: Herder & Herder, 1970), pp. 27–28.

8. James V. Douglass, *Resistance and Contemplation* (New York: Doubleday, 1972), p. 55.

A D D I T I O N A L   R E A D I N G S

Articles

Dann, Graham M. S. "Religious Belonging in a Changing Catholic Church." *Sociological Analysis* 37 (1976): 283–97. Post-Vatican II

Catholicism is best understood as an organization allowing various modes of belonging rather than as a monolithic bureaucracy according to Max Weber.

Dixon, Robert C., and Hoge, Dean R. "Models and Priorities of the Catholic Church as Held by Suburban Laity." *Review of Religious Research* 20 (1979): 150–67. Catholic laity in three suburban Virginia parishes are asked to rate twenty-one church priority statements. Personal and family concerns rate highest. This study is also valuable for statements of five different models of the Catholic church.

Greeley, Andrew M. "American Catholics Going their Own Way." *New York Times Magazine,* 10 October 1982. An informal and colorful portrayal of American Catholics who practice their faith on their own terms as traditional church "boundaries" have grown vague.

———. "Selective Catholicism: How They Get Away with It." *America,* 30 April 1983. The author's research on religious imagery is correlated with young Catholics' dissent from certain Catholic teachings and their degree of religious practice. The conclusion is that "the selective Catholics are going to be with us for a long time."

Westhues, Kenneth. "Stars and Stripes, the Maple Leaf, and the Papal Coat of Arms." *Canadian Journal of Sociology* 2 (1978): 245–61. A macro-scale analysis of differences in the Catholic churches of the United States and Canada, considering contrasts in the structure and history of the two societies—a rich, provocative treatment.

Books

Ebaugh, Helen Rose Fuchs. *Out of the Cloister: A Study of Organizational Dilemmas.* Austin: University of Texas Press, 1977. Rates of change and membership retention and loss in religious orders of women. On the same topic, see San Giovanni below.

Fichter, Joseph H. *The Catholic Cult of the Paraclete.* New York: Sheed and Ward, 1975. Catholic pentecostals have also been studied by McGuire (see below).

Greeley, Andrew M. *The American Catholic: A Social Portrait.* New York: Basic Books, 1977.

———. *Crisis in the Church: A Study of Religion in America.* Chicago: Thomas More, 1979.

———, McCready, William C., and McCourt, Kathleen. *Catholic Schools in a Declining Church.* Kansas City: Sheed and Ward, 1976. The books of Andrew Greeley are probably the best-known sociological analyses of American and, more recently, Canadian Catholicism. Greeley also writes with colleagues associated with the National Opinion Research Center.

McGuire, Meredith B. *Pentecostal Catholics: Power, Charisma, and Order in a Religious Movement.* Philadelphia: Temple University Press, 1982.

McSweeney, William. *Roman Catholicism: The Search for Relevance.* New York: St. Martin's, 1980. An excellent historical analysis of events leading to the Second Vatican Council in the early 1960s and a thoughtful reflection on the subsequent state of the church following the Council.

San Giovanni, Lucinda. *Ex-Nuns: A Study of Emergent Role Passage.* Norwood, N.J.: Ablex, 1978.

Stewart, James H. *American Catholic Leadership. A Decade of Turmoil, 1966–1976: A Sociological Analysis of the National Federation of Priests' Councils.* The Hague: Mouton, 1978. An organizational study of priests' councils struggling with new relationships to bishops and with issues ranging from celibacy to promoting justice and peace issues and fiscal responsibility.

Cross-cultural References

Levine, Daniel H., ed. *Churches and Politics in Latin America.* Beverly Hills: Sage, 1980. Essays focusing on changing patterns of church involvement in various Latin American countries, with some emphasis on "progressive" or social-change oriented Catholicism based on liberation theology.

Lewins, Frank W. *The Myth of the Universal Church.* Canberra: Australian National University, 1978. European Catholics emigrating to Australia form the setting for an analysis of church policy on the Roman, Australian episcopal, and local parish levels. Organizational conflict and integration is a key sociological theme.

Vaillancourt, Jean-Guy. *Papal Power: A Study of Vatican Control over Lay Catholic Elites.* Berkeley: University of California Press, 1980. Develops models of authority and control in analyzing Vatican-laity relations as exemplified in the Third World Congress of the Lay Apostolate held in Rome, 1967.

6

American Judaism

Exiled first by the Babylonians in 586 B.C. and again by the Romans in A.D. 70 after the failure of the Jewish revolt against Caesar's legions, Jews have a history unique among the world's peoples. For almost nineteen hundred years they lived in a situation of *diaspora* (being dispersed or scattered), moving throughout the Mediterranean basin, later into Europe, Africa, and even into Afghanistan, India, and China. As world empires crumbled, connections between the far-flung communities practically vanished. Jewish communities, then, have often had to cope by themselves with changing environments of non-Jewish cultures and have varied widely in how much they acculturated and assimilated to these surrounding worlds.

These worlds have, of course, frequently been hostile to Jewish communities in their midst. Least receptive have been so-called Christian countries. Christianity proved itself intolerant toward other major religions, suppressing them where this proved feasible (the Muslims were eventually expelled from Spain and Italy). But Jews were treated as an exception. They were to be tolerated in a subordinate state, for their eventual conversion would be a sign of the Second Coming of Christ. "The Church taught that the exile and submissive state of the Jews was a God-inflicted penalty for the Jewish repudiation of Christ and could thus be regarded as evidence for the truth of Christianity."[1] But popular beliefs of Christians went tragically further, labeling Jews as "Christ killers" and, beginning with the Crusades (eleventh to fourteenth centuries), taking revenge upon them as infidels and accusing them of being Satan's allies on earth. They were even suspected of ritually murdering Christian children and of bringing on the Black Death of the fourteenth century by poisoning water wells. Massacres of Jews, or pogroms, sometimes followed upon these accusations. At the same time, Jews were often welcomed by European rulers from the early Middle Ages through the eighteenth century as a class of merchants and financiers who could render valuable services to crown and kingdom. Although some Jews throughout Western history have converted to Christianity or simply forsaken their faith without conversion, the vast majority maintained their religious traditions and continue to do so today.

But the way those traditions have been expressed has undergone considerable variation over the centuries. Essential to keep in mind is that these variations have been, to a very large extent, responses to the larger social-cultural-religious environments in which Jews have found themselves. As long as Jews were consistently ghettoized, discriminated against, and at times exiled and killed, they understandably clung to their traditions embedded in Old Testament and Torah and kept them intact. Orthodoxy was both the sign of and nourishment for their identity as a distinctive people with a special destiny or covenant made with them by the Creator.

Structural and ideological changes in modern Europe, however, greatly affected the lives of Jews. As long as feudal institutions existed, as in much of eastern Europe and Russia until the mid-nineteenth century, Jews were legally, economically, and residentially segregated. But new situations offering new opportunities were developing in the industrializing cities of France, Germany, Holland, and England. Ideologically the values of the Enlightenment, emphasizing reason, scientific knowledge, and religious and ethnic tolerance, served to diminish prejudice among the more educated city dwellers. Religious pluralism became the accepted situation with the growth of Protestant churches in these countries. All of these developments, taken together, served to break down the isolation of Jews. Stephen Sharot nicely summarizes the picture as the nineteenth century began:

The attainment of full legal and political equality was a slow process in many European states, but the Jewish separation of the late medieval and early modern period was almost irreversibly demolished between 1791 and 1813. The central European Jews were subject to civil disqualifications and excluded from a number of occupations until late in the century, but they were no longer isolated in ghettos, excluded from the major towns, or limited to a few despised occupations. . . . In contrast to Russia, where there was a strong element of physical coercion in the movement of the Jews to the towns in the undeveloped pale of settlement, the expanding economies of central and western Europe provided new opportunities for Jewish skills, and the movement to urban areas was often followed by a high rate of economic mobility.[2]

These effects had little impact on the feudal agricultural and small-town Jewish settlements in Russia and eastern Europe; Jews there had little reason to distinguish between Judaism as religion, as culture, or as nationality. They continued to be a separate, discriminated-against, and visible minority. But Jews who had taken the path of acculturation and upward mobility and discovered more acceptance for themselves in western European cities made major changes in religious services in order to appear less "different" and "foreign" and to increase their acceptance by the Gentile majority. Reform Judaism began in Germany in the first decade of the last century and spread to other western European countries and to North America. A chief aspect of these changes was a concern for decorum in contrast to the loud prayer chanting, spontaneous body movements, and freedom to leave and enter during services, which characterize more Orthodox services. Gone, too, were references to God's chosen people, the Messiah's coming, and the return to Zion. Messianism was replaced by a doctrine stressing a coming period of peace and harmony when all peoples would be united in one set of beliefs. All of these changes accorded well with the flourishing of liberal Protestantism in both Germany and the United States during the latter part of the nineteenth century.

The picture becomes still more complex, however, as we turn to eastern Europe. It remained a bastion of Jewish Orthodoxy; the area was also deeply affected by socialist currents of thought. Those Jews regarding themselves as socialists—or anarchists—rejected religion as reactionary and counterprogressive. Radical Jews were among the large masses who migrated to the United States between 1880 and 1914 and were prominent in some socialist-inspired strikes and street demonstrations, particularly in New York and Chicago. The European scene, then, in the latter 1800s was a divided one: Eastern European and Russian Jews were mainly Orthodox with contrasting minority elements of socialist Jews; western Europe offered a milieu that enticed Jews toward accommodation and upward mobility, particularly in the large cities. Yet this situation by no means signified the abatement of anti-Semitism in western Europe. England was probably the least anti-Semitic environment, Germany the most anti-Semitic. Germans of the lower middle class trying to break into white collar jobs resented competition from Jews who were traditionally skilled in clerical occupations. "Supposed differences in 'blood' rather than differences in religion and culture, became the major legitimation for prejudice and discrimination."[3] Removal of legal and residential barriers, then, did not end anti-Semitism. In early twentieth-century Germany, Jews were not welcome in such institutions as the judiciary, the universities, and fraternal and professional associations.

In sum, pressures to acculturate were greatest in those countries where Jews had moved out of the ghetto isolation characteristic of Russia and Poland. These pressures were obvious and understandable in countries like England, where the stratification system was probably most open to Jewish upward mobility. But such pressures were also present in Germany, Austria, and Hungary, where the "social exclusion of Jews was often legitimized by religio-cultural particularism, and many Jews strove to overcome what they perceived as the major obstacle to social acceptance and honour."[4] Even reformed Jews were not considered "insiders," but most central European Jews continued to hope for eventual acceptance and integration as "complete" members of their respective nation-societies.

The United States. Jewish immigrants, at first almost entirely from Germany and later from Poland and Russia, were prominent among the millions of European settlers who came to America between the end of the Civil War and the beginning of World War I, the period known as "the Great Migration" to the United States. Numbering only fifteen thousand in 1840—a mixture of Spanish, Portuguese, Dutch, and German, many of whom were among the nation's earliest immigrants—Jews grew to a population numbering over two million by 1914.

By religious background, many immigrant families were by no means Orthodox. We have already noted that some Jews, influenced by the ideals of the Enlightenment and the structural factors previously cited, had undergone considerable emancipation from traditional Jewish observances. German rabbis in this country responded by developing Reform Judaism, which emphasized a liberal humanism and employed ritual practices reminiscent of American Protestantism. By the end of the nineteenth century, however, a reaction developed among Jews who were dissatisfied with this pattern and wished to return to a measure of Jewish tradition but not to strict Orthodoxy. Thus was born Conservative Judaism. Fidelity to Jewish law, literature, and language was a keynote, yet with a flexibility deemed appropriate to Jews adjusting to a new cultural setting.

The essence of the Conservative position, then, is liberalization. While Conservatism believes that liberalization is its own justification, it also holds that liberalization makes possible the promotion of observance. . . . In addition to liberalization, the Conservative platform has two additional planks. One is "innovation," the development of new observances or procedures which are required when there is a need to substitute for, modify, or extend the traditional *mitzvoth* (the commandments of the Jewish sacred system). The other is "beautification," the requirement that the *mitzvoth* be practiced in an esthetic a manner as possible—"the Jewish home beautiful." In sum, the Conservative position is that liberalization—in combination with innovation and beautification—will succeed in averting the evil decree of non-observance.[5]

Thus Conservative Jews, comprising the largest membership of the three traditions in America, have played a kind of moderate or compromising role between the Orthodox and Reform-minded Jews.

Like other immigrant groups, Jewish Americans witnessed a considerable dropping away from Jewish tradition among their second- and third-generation members. This did not necessarily entail a loss of Jewish identity,

for even if you ceased to think of yourself as Jewish, the larger society was still prepared to define you as a Jew unless you became formally a member of a gentile denomination, something which few Jews were willing to do. Secondly, the disaster of the Second World War to European Judaism produced a reaction in most American Jews that precluded any denial of their Jewishness.[6]

Post–World War II Judaism, then, saw perhaps a majority of American Jews experiencing a heightened sense of identity *as a people*—an identity further strengthened by the emergence of the State of Israel, particularly its striking victory over the Arabs in the 1967 Six-day War. Religious observance in terms of frequent synagogue attendance and regular observance of dietary customs, however, has not been characteristic of the average American Jew.

This does not indicate a diminished importance of the synagogue or temple. The first reading, by prominent Jewish sociologist Marshall Sklare, analyzes several functions of the contemporary synagogue. First, synagogue affiliation varies inversely with the size of the Jewish population. In communities where Jews number less than twenty-five thousand or so, affiliation tends to be well over 50 percent and ranges as high as 80 percent. In large metropolitan areas with sizable Jewish populations, affiliation is considerably diminished. Sklare attributes this pattern to differential pressures toward assimilation. In small communities, each person or family is usually asked to join, "forced into casting his ballot. A refusal to join means placing himself in the assimilationist camp." Such solicitation is much less likely in large Jewish communities; there is a consequent reduction of pressure to make a decision for "survival." Thus in large communities, such as New York, synagogue membership is considered unnecessary for identity as a Jew. Sklare also points to the educative function of the synagogue as a religious center. Even less committed Jews are induced to affiliate because of the desire to enroll their children in religious education classes as well as to attend services themselves on the High Holidays. Additional ties are effected by congregational sponsorship of clubs for high-school youngsters, young adults, young marrieds, and so on. Whether or not the synagogue stimulates more than social affiliation—whether it also serves to deepen Jewish religious faith in the consciousness of its membership—is a debatable issue discussed by Sklare. He feels that the congregational structure of American Judaism guarantees the freedom of dissatisfied Jewish groups to establish synagogues that embody the orientations they desire.

"American Jewish Denominations," by Bernard Lazerwitz and Michael Harrison, should be read with an awareness of the historical background sketched in this introduction. Orthodox, Conservative, and Reform "branches" of Judaism could, like Protestant denominations, be considered reflective of social and economic differences within the larger population—in this case Jewish Americans. Lazerwitz and Harrison make use of a national sample of the American Jewish population, taken in 1970–71, to investigate the social and economic characteristics "of individuals identifying and affiliating with each of the three major denominations [Orthodox, Conservative, and Reformed] and on the traits of the unaffiliated or unidentified." The results show that socioeconomic differences between the three denominations have diminished but not disappeared. Sharp differences do appear by generation, however. "The least Americanized are more attracted to Orthodoxy, while the most Americanized gravitate toward Reform or express no denominational preference. Conservative Judaism constitutes a middle ground." The Orthodox come out most clearly Jewish as defined by traditional beliefs, practices, and organizational involvements, with Reform and nonidentified adults the least committed in these respects. Yet Reform Jews are highly involved in Jewish organizations and are politically more liberal than Orthodox or Conservative, reflecting some effects of higher socioeconomic status. The unidentified are much more ready to marry outside the Jewish community and, as they see themselves may be only marginally Jewish. Thus while the traditional "social sources" (social and economic status) of Jewish denominationalism may be less important, "Americanization" (in terms of duration by generation in this country) imprints the denominational preferences of American Jews. The authors speculate that differences will remain but will be based mainly on "matters of belief and behavior," as persons less concerned with these matters drift away from *any* of the three major affiliations.

Marvell Ginsburg's "The Right of the Jewish Child to Be Jewish" humorously illustrates the plight of the Jewish child raised in a culture that challenges this ethnic identity and security at every turn. Massive assimilative pressures, buttressed by omnipresent mass media and advertising, go beyond those pressures toward upward mobility already discussed. How does one counter the attraction of Santa Claus and Friday night football games?

Notes

1. Stephen Sharot, *Judaism: A Sociology* (London: David & Charles, 1976), p. 25. This chapter introduction relies heavily on Sharot's treatment.

2. Ibid., pp. 65–66.

3. Ibid., p. 117.

4. Ibid., p. 129.

5. Marshall Sklare, *Conservative Judaism: An American Religious Movement* (New York: Schocken Books, 1972), p. 269.

6. Andrew M. Greeley, *The Denominational Society: A Sociological Approach to Religion in America* (Chicago: Scott, Foresman, 1972), pp. 198–99.

READING 6.1

The American Synagogue

Marshall Sklare

From the attendance statistics of New York City, Boston, and numerous other communities we might expect that the American synagogue is a struggling institution that is banished to the periphery of Jewish life and located predominantly in neighborhoods where the foreign-born reside. Nothing could be further from the truth. The American synagogue is a vital institution; it is by far the strongest agency in the entire Jewish community. Many hundreds of new synagogues—Reform, Conservative, and Orthodox—were built as a consequence of population movement after World War II. The process continues. As new Jewish neighborhoods and suburbs develop, new synagogues are established or old synagogues are transferred to new locations. Not only have synagogues been built in areas where Jewish life is intensive but sooner or later they are organized even in places that attract the more marginal Jewish families.[1] The number of synagogues, the value of their buildings, and their location in all areas where the Jewish population totals more than a handful of families all attest to the predominance of this institution in American Jewish life.[2]

We already know that only a minority of American Jews can bring themselves to patronize the synagogue with any degree of regularity in connection with its function as a house of prayer. Yet the continuing construction of new buildings, as well as the prosperity of established institutions suggests that the American synagogue must be more than

Marshall Sklare is on the faculty of American Jewish Studies, Department of Near Eastern and Judaic Studies, Brandeis University.
From Marshall Sklare, *America's Jews.* Copyright © 1971 by Marshall Sklare. Reprinted with the permission of Random House, Inc.

a house of prayer. To help us discover its real nature, we must first know what proportion of America's Jews are affiliated with a synagogue.

There are no reliable nationwide statistics on affiliation. The most notable aspect of synagogue affiliation is that it varies greatly with the size of the Jewish population. In small communities affiliation commonly reaches well over 80 percent, despite the high intermarriage rates characteristic of such communities. In Flint, Michigan, for example, where the Jewish population is under 3,000, a total of 87 percent of the Jews in the community are affiliated with a synagogue.[3] In communities of intermediate size (10,000 to 25,000 Jewish population), the level of affiliation is lower—commonly over 70 percent are synagogue members. Thus in Providence the figure is 77 percent, in Springfield it is 76 percent, in Rochester, N.Y., 71 percent, and in Camden it reaches the exceptionally high figure of 82 percent.[4] In large Jewish communities the rate of affiliation is much lower, commonly running at about 50 percent of the Jewish population. Thus in Detroit 49 percent are affiliated while in Boston the figure is 53 percent.[5] New York is *sui generis*—while no study is available observation suggests that the affiliation rate is measurably lower than it is in any other large city.

Unlike the observance of many *mitzvot*, which . . . tend to be concentrated in one segment of the population, synagogue membership is widely diffused. Irrespective of community size, membership is common in all segments of the population, with the following exceptions: it is somewhat more concentrated among the prosperous as well as among those with children between the ages of five and fifteen. Significantly, the rate of affiliation among the foreign-born is no higher than among the native-born. Even in the large cities where the rate of affiliation is so low, most nonmembers have belonged to a synagogue at one time or another. Former members include, for example, the widow who resigned after her husband's death and who now lives in reduced circumstances, or the prosperous family that dropped out after their children had a Bar Mitzvah or Confirmation. Furthermore, some of those who have never been affiliated will do so in the future. This is the case with many young marrieds who will join when they move from city apartments to suburban homes, or when they have children old enough to enroll in a Sunday or Hebrew School.

Whatever criticisms former members may have, and whatever the situation of those who have never affiliated, it is hard to find a principled opponent of the American synagogue.[6] Those who are outside of the synagogue are not firm opponents of the institution. Absence from the membership rolls does not generally represent a clear commitment to any rival institution. It does mean of course that the individual has been strongly influenced by the secularization process. But any critical observer would be quick to point out that most synagogue members have been vitally affected by the same process.

The lack of principled objection to the synagogue and the affiliation of diverse segments of the population must be added to our previous findings about wide differences in affiliation rate between smaller and larger communities. There is little to suggest that Jews in smaller communities are more sacred in their orientation than their metropolitan cousins. In fact a case can be made for precisely the opposite conclusion: that they are more secular in orientation, and much less traditional in their thinking. Why then do those who reside in smaller communities affiliate with greater frequency?

The smaller the community the clearer is the threat of assimilation and the clearer it is that the future of Jewish life rests upon the personal decision of each individual Jew. The decision to affiliate with a synagogue, then, means to vote yes to Jewish survival. And the smaller the community the more literal the voting metaphor: since every individual in the small community is asked to join, he is forced into casting his ballot. A refusal to join means placing himself in the assimilationist camp unless of course he has provided clear-cut evidence to the contrary by becoming intensely involved with some alternative Jewish agency. The larger the community the less chance of solicitation by significant others, the less pressure to make a decision for survival, and above all, the more remote the threat of assimilation.

Clearly in the largest communities, especially in New York, synagogue membership does not have high symbolic significance. Since many people lack the feeling that Jewish identity requires synagogue membership, nonaffiliation does not mean a vote for assimilation. Conversely, one's resignation from a synagogue is not interpreted as meaning disloyalty to the group. In the metropolis, then, the synagogue must appeal on the basis of its instrumental as well as symbolic functions. However, a substantial proportion of the population finds the synagogue unessential to its needs. These people have little interest in the classical functions of the synagogue—religious services and study by adult males of Jewish texts. Nonclassical functions that the synagogue has added also do not attract them. Their children may be too young or too old for Hebrew School or Sunday School. Furthermore they are not interested in the social activities provided by the synagogue, for they already are a part of a satisfying clique. Generally their group is entirely Jewish and dates back to friendships that were cemented in adolescence or early adulthood. Others are not attracted to the synagogue's social activities because they have a rich social life within their family circle. Finally in the largest communities a host of organizations and causes of a specifically Jewish nature are available outside of the orbit of the synagogue.

Whether situated in a large or small community the synagogue is focused upon Jewish survival. It need not have been so—conceivably the synagogue in America could have followed a different course and insisted that as a religious institution it was an end in itself rather than a means for Jewish survival. Such a stance would exclude those who were strongly secular in orientation, or at least require that they accept a subordinate position. But there is religious justification for the synagogue moving in the direction it has: in Judaism the preservation of the Jewish people as a group is an act of religious significance.

The American synagogue has accepted the secular Jew on his own terms; the institution has been more concerned with transforming him than with erecting barriers to his admission. In most congregations membership is open to all; no test of the applicant's religious attitudes or observance of *mitzvot* is required. While in many Reform or Conservative congregations an applicant for membership is generally sponsored by a member of the synagogue or by one of its officials, this is only for the purpose of screening those who have an objectionable moral reputation. The exceptions to the rule are certain Orthodox congregations that are interested in an applicant's observance of *mitzvot*. Such institutions prefer to restrict their roster to those whose behavior is in conformity with certain selected religious norms.

Since the typical American Jewish congregation is formed by local initiative rather than by the authority of a central body, every synagogue is free to determine its own program and ritual.[7] Furthermore, because the polity—the form of religious organization—among American Jews is congregational rather than episcopal, each synagogue is the equal of all others. Residents join together to hold religious services and to establish a school for their children. They raise the funds necessary to build an edifice and to hire a professional staff. The synagogue is organized in the form of a corporate body that holds periodic membership meetings at which the affairs of the institution are discussed and officers and board members elected. The board is responsible for determining the policies of the institution, although on strictly religious questions, as well as in certain other areas, the advice and consent of the rabbi is commonly solicited.

The prototype of the contemporary American synagogue is the "synagogue center." This is the synagogue that compromises with the culture while serving the need for Jewish identification. Recognizing the impact of acculturation this type of synagogue expands its program far beyond the traditional activities of prayer and study. It seeks encounter with the Jew on his own secular level and it strives to reculturate him. The content and procedures of religious services are adapted to give them greater appeal, with Reform synagogues, Conservative synagogues, and Orthodox synagogues each handling the problem of cultural adaptation in characteristic fashion. Although traditionally there is no sermon during the weekly Sabbath service, part of the process of adaptation involves the introduction of this feature. Thus the sermon has become a standard feature of the weekly service in Reform, Conservative, as well as in some Orthodox congregations. The sermon is employed as an instructional as well as a hortatory device.

All synagogues sponsor some kind of program of adult Jewish study, although its character, and the importance attached to it, varies greatly from congregation to congregation. With the exception of some Orthodox synagogues women are free to participate in the program. In many places the traditional textual approach to study has been modified or supplemented. New kinds of courses have been introduced. But Jewish learning for children rather than for adults constitutes the real focus of the congregation's educational efforts. With the exception of certain Orthodox synagogues all congregations sponsor a Jewish school. While the majority of those who attend are of elementary school age, most schools aim to retain their youngsters after the high point of the educational experience: Bar Mitzvah, Bat Mitzvah, or Confirmation.

For the less-committed the opportunity for Jewish education is a strong inducement to affiliate. In most newer neighborhoods of the city, and in the suburbs, the only available Jewish religious schools are those conducted under congregational auspices. Some congregations make membership mandatory for enrollment, while others adjust their tuition fees to provide a financial incentive for membership.

Another important motivation for affiliation is the desire of secular-minded Jews to attend religious services on the High Holidays. While daily services, Sabbath services, and festival services are open to all, the demand for seats on the High Holidays is so large that admission is commonly restricted to ticket holders. In some congregations tickets are distributed only to members while in other synagogues they are sold to the public, but at a higher price than that made to members. Since most High Holiday services today are conducted under the auspices of a synagogue, the institution is in a position to attract individuals who might not ordinarily be interested in an affiliation. The phenomenon of "mushroom synagogues"—opened during the High Holidays by private entrepreneurs—is on the wane and the phenomenon is rarely encountered in more prestigious neighborhoods. It has been replaced by the practice of established congregations that hold overflow services for the High Holidays, or of Reform congregations that conduct services on a double shift.

Most congregations sponsor a variety of clubs for high school youth, young adults, young marrieds, adult women, adult men, and the elderly. These organizations provide the synagogue member with another tie to the congregation. They are particularly crucial for individuals who are not strongly involved in the classical functions of prayer and study. Generally the organization composed of adult women (the "sisterhood") is the most vital of these clubs. Membership in the clubs is so widespread that in the intermediate size Jewish community they enroll far more members than any other Jewish organization. In Providence, for example, 53.2 percent of all men age fifty to fifty-nine are members of a synagogue-affiliated club, as are 55 percent of the women.[8] Recreational and associational opportunities are not limited to the synagogue affiliates, however. There are congregational socials and parties, dinner dances, specialized activity groups, and fund-raising drives. All strive to increase the interaction among members. In the New York area in particular many synagogues provide a variety of athletic facilities.[9]

The contemporary synagogue is a large institution by traditional standards. While older Jewish neighborhoods in the largest cities may contain a dozen or more small congregations in addition to two or three large ones, an average synagogue in a newer neighborhood of a metropolis or suburb will generally enroll over 500 families. Congregations of this size have many members who confine their participation to specialized activities, or who participate very irregularly. Given the large size of most congregations and the specialized, irregular, or even nonparticipation of members, the printed word becomes a vital part of congregational life. Thus most congregations publish a bulletin at regular intervals. The bulletin contains the time of services and the topic of the weekly sermon, the schedules of the clubs, information about adult education lectures and courses, and news of the school. Of equal if not greater significance are the personals columns of the bulletin. Births and deaths are announced, donors are listed, names of active workers are publicized, and significant milestones in lives of members and their families are featured, including birthdays, wedding anniversaries, graduations, and promotions.

While synagogues of the more traditional variety contrast sharply with the synagogue-center type of institution, it is the synagogue characteristic of modern Israel which places the contemporary American synagogue in boldest relief. The core of the program of the Israeli synagogue is the traditional activities of prayer and study. Worship activities are centered on the three daily services and the Sabbath service. Some men remain after the daily services, or come early, for the purpose of studying various sacred texts. They do this either by themselves, in pairs, or in groups. Most synagogues are small. Each has its official, its leaders, and its congregants. However, individuals think of themselves as praying at a particular synagogue rather than being affiliated with it in any formal sense. Most synagogues do not have a professional staff—rabbis are employed by a central authority rather than by a particular congregation. While attendance and participation at services and in the study circles ebbs and flows, and although at certain holidays worshippers appear who are absent at other occasions, the interaction of the group of men who pray and study together constitutes the foundation of the institution.

Unlike the United States, then, the synagogue in Israel offers little other than the classical functions of prayer and study of the sacred system by adult males. Unlike the United States, its existence and prosperity is not interpreted as a promise of Jewish survival at a time when the acculturation process is so advanced as to make survival difficult to assure. And unlike the United States, the Israeli synagogue is not perceived as an emblem of Jewish identity or as the guarantor of the Jewish future. Rather, the nationhood of Israel is viewed as assuring Jewish survival.

In essence, then, the synagogue in Israel has little symbolic significance; it exists as an end in itself rather than as a means to an end. Because it does not occupy the unique role that it does in the United States, the Israeli synagogue is a much weaker institution. It reaches a much smaller proportion of the population than its American counterpart.

Even if the American synagogue is generally a means to an end rather than an ultimate value, it is still a religious institution. As such it is subject to evaluation by a unique yardstick—the yardstick of spirituality. Critics of the synagogue, while conceding that it makes a valuable contribution to Jewish life, are prepared to argue that it is nonetheless more of a liability than an asset. Some maintain that the American synagogue protects the individual from the demands of the Jewish religion as much as it exposes him to them. In a scathing indictment of the American synagogue Rabbi Eugene Borowitz, a leading Reform thinker, has commented:

... the average synagogue member ... comes ... to join the synagogue because there are few if any socially acceptable alternatives to synagogue affiliation for one who wants to maintain his Jewish identity and wants his children to be Jewish, in some sense, after him. Though this is not the only motive or level of concern to be found within the synagogue today, the Jew who does not rise above such folk-feeling unquestionably and increasingly represents the synagogue's majority mood. More than that, however, it must be said that he also represents the synagogue's greatest threat. . . . His new-found affluence and his need for status within the community have made the big building with the small sanctuary, the lavish wedding with the short ceremony, and the fabulous Bar Mitzvah celebration with the minimal religious significance well-established patterns among American Jewish folkways. . . . What does it say of Jewish life in America when Reform Judaism appeals because it demands so little but confers so much status? when people blandly proclaim that they are nonobservant Orthodox Jews;

when Conservative Judaism makes a virtue of not defining the center so that it may avoid alienating those disaffected on either side.[10]

Borowitz believes that the synagogue should become a more sectarian institution, that it should be transformed to become an end rather than a means, and that it should relinquish its function of providing identity for the secular-minded, ethnically oriented Jew. Proponents concede that this policy will mean that many who presently belong will feel compelled to sever their affiliation (or, if not, have it severed for them), but their eventual assimilation is viewed as the price which must be paid for the survival of Judaism. Proponents hope that the loss of the masses will be compensated, at least in part, by the affiliation of those who—they claim—have remained outside or at the margin of congregational life because of an understandable distaste for the American synagogue. As Borowitz sees it:

Clarifying Jewish faith might bring many to the conclusion that they cannot honestly participate in Judaism and the synagogue. . . . No one wishes to lose Jews for Judaism, but the time has come when the synagogue must be saved for the religious Jew, when it must be prepared to let some Jews opt out so that those who remain in, or who come in, will not be diverted from their duty to God. As the religion of a perpetual minority, Judaism must always first be concerned with the saving remnant, and so long as the synagogue is overwhelmed by the indifferent and the apathetic who control it for their own nonreligious purposes, that remnant will continue to be deprived of its proper communal home.[11]

More ethnically oriented religionists have proposed less drastic remedies. One such idea is the *havurah*, a local group composed of individuals who belong to congregations but find such institutions to be so lax and undemanding that they require other avenues to express their Jewishness. It is claimed that banding together and forming a fellowship or *havurah* will protect and advance the spirit-

ual life of those individuals who are ready for a richer religious diet than the synagogue makes available:

The *havurah* is certainly *not* intended either to supplant the congregation or even to downgrade it. There is no doubt that the congregation serves many vital functions . . . [but its] insufficiency inheres . . . in the heterogeneous character of the constituency. And the main aspect of that insufficiency lies in the fact that belonging to congregations is often no more than an innocuous gesture. . . . Rabbis assume that the vast majority will attend only three times a year. Little—often nothing—is actually required besides the payment of dues. No commitment is asked; none is generally given.

Now, while this may appeal to the escapists and the irresponsible, it does not appeal to those who are looking for a place in which they can take their Judaism seriously in the company of likeminded Jews. Thus, *commitment* is the key to one of the essentials of *havurah*.[12]

The American synagogue is considerably more differentiated than its critics assume. Population size and density permitting, a variety of congregations are commonly established. Even when such congregations are similar in ideological preference they cater to different segments of the community. Such population segments are generally distinguishable by secular differences such as class position and level of general education but frequently they are also separated by differences relating to Jewishness: levels of acculturation, differing conceptions of spirituality, and contrasting degrees of observance of the *mitzvot*.

Lakeville, for example, is served by four Reform synagogues. All of the congregations are distinctive. One of them—the Samuel Hirsch Temple—is highly individual in its approach. In its conscious effort to break with the synagogue-center type, it has been called a synagogue for people who do not like to join synagogues. For a long time the congregation resisted constructing a synagogue building, because the leaders did not want to become involved in the type of activity that a building would entail. Furthermore, the Samuel Hirsch Temple in Lakeville has banned all clubs, and thus it does not have a sisterhood or men's club. The congregation has sought to confine its program to the traditional activities of worship and study, though these activities are of course conducted in a style that differs markedly from the traditional approach.[13]

Differences in the Reform group are paralleled and even accentuated among traditionalists. Far Rockaway, New York, for example, is a community that is as Orthodox in reputation as Lakeville is Reform. Beneath its seeming uniformity there is great diversity among the many small synagogues in the area, and considerable difference between the two largest institutions: the White Shool and Congregation Shaaray Tefila:

The White Shool has developed primarily as a synagogue for the young layman who was once a yeshiva bochur [student in a school for advanced Talmudical learning]. . . . It is unique as an American synagogue in that it numbers among its congregants about thirty-five ordained, non-practicing rabbis. The congregation has no chazan [cantor] but instead uses a battery of its own unusually gifted baaley-tefilah [prayer-leaders] who "work" in rotation. . . . [The rabbi] not only gives more classes . . . than the average rabbi, but he offers them on a generally much higher level. In some areas—such as Gemorah [Talmud]—he may give shiurim [classes] on the same subject to different groups at different levels . . . like the European Rav, the largest part of the rabbi's time is given over to learning Torah and preparing shiurim . . . while a relatively small portion is devoted to the social duties and obligations which take up ninety per cent of the average American rabbi's time.

Shaaray Tefila is tailored . . . to serve the total Jewish community rather than being primarily geared to the intensively Torah-educated Jew. Shaaray Tefila's decorous, dignified service, led by a capable chazan, gives the synagogue and its divine worship an air of sacred reverence and respect for the Almighty. Many White Shool'ers, however, whose own synagogue breathes an atmosphere of an informal camaraderie prevalent in a "second home," feel uncomfortable in the dignified atmosphere of Shaaray. . . . On the other hand, most Shaaray'ites would feel ill at ease in the White Shool, where a considerable amount of conversation goes on during the service. The White Shool, to them, is an "overgrown shtibel" [an intimate setting for prayer and religious study] and far too undecorous.[14]

As we noticed earlier those who wish to change the American synagogue are tempted to do so either by going outside of the synagogue or by somehow convincing established institutions of the error of their ways and seeing to it that they implement higher standards of spirituality. But another option is open to the elitists: they are free to establish their own synagogues. This option is afforded by the congregational structure of American Judaism, guaranteeing as it does the independence of the local synagogue. If this option is exercised the burden of proof will then be on the elitists for they will be compelled to demonstrate the superiority of their institutions over the standard American synagogue center. Since the individual Jew is able to exercise freedom of choice such new congregations will find themselves competitors in the open market of affiliation. The American Jew, then, is free to remain unaffiliated, to retain his present affiliation, or to establish a new institution that offers him a more congenial spiritual atmosphere.

Notes

1. Note the case of Park Forest, Ill. See Herbert J. Gans, "The Origin and Growth of a Jewish Community," in Marshall Sklare (ed.), *The Jews: Social Patterns of An American Group* (New York: Free Press, 1958).

2. So great is the stress on the building of synagogues that it has drawn the attention of students of art and architecture. See, for example, Avram Kampf, *Contemporary Synagogue Art: Developments in the United States 1945–1965* (New York: Union of American Hebrew Congregations, 1966).

3. Albert J. Mayer, *Flint Jewish Population Study:*

1967 (Processed, Flint, Mich.: Flint Jewish Community Council, 1969), p. 45.

4. See Sidney Goldstein, *A Population Survey of the Greater Springfield Jewish Community* (Springfield, Mass.: Springfield Jewish Community Council, 1968), p. 93.

5. Albert J. Mayer, *Jewish Population Study-Series II* (Detroit: Jewish Welfare Federation of Detroit, 1964–1966), p. 24; and Axelrod et al., op. cit., p. 136.

6. In Springfield where inquiry was made into reasons for nonaffiliation, the most frequent response was the cost of synagogue membership. Only about one out of ten went so far as to say their reason for nonaffiliation was a lack of interest.

7. In recent years the congregational unions such as the Union of American Hebrew Congregations (Reform), the United Synagogue (Conservative) and the Union of Orthodox Jewish Congregations of America (Orthodox) have taken greater initiative in forming new congregations.

The most notable exception to the freedom of the local congregation to determine its own affairs are synagogues affiliated with Young Israel (Orthodox). Title to the property of a Young Israel synagogue is vested in the national movement. The purpose of the arrangement is to prevent a congregation from insti-

tuting religious practices that violate Orthodox norms.

8. Sidney Goldstein, *The Greater Providence Jewish Community: A Population Survey* (Providence: General Jewish Committee of Providence, 1964), p. 141.

9. One important aspect of the synagogue center (very much emphasized in the writings of Mordecai M. Kaplan, for example) is the conception that nothing Jewish should be alien to the synagogue—that the synagogue should offer its facilities to all Jewish organizations that make a contribution to Jewish survival and that it should seek to facilitate the work of such organizations. But inasmuch as there are inherent strains in the relationship of the congregation to the community, this is more easily said than done.

10. Eugene B. Borowitz, *A New Jewish Theology in the Making* (Philadelphia: The Westminster Press, 1968), pp. 45–46.

11. Ibid., pp. 53–54.

12. Jacob Neusner and Ira Eisenstein, *The Havurah Idea* (New York: The Reconstructionist Press, n.d.).

13. Marshall Sklare and Joseph Greenblum, *Jewish Identity on the Suburban Frontier* (New York: Basic Books, 1967).

14. Michael Kaufman, "Far Rockaway–Torah-Suburb By-the-Sea," *Jewish Life* 27, no. 6 (August 1960), 25–28.

R E A D I N G   6 . 2

American Jewish Denominations: A Social and Religious Profile

Bernard Lazerwitz and Michael Harrison

Religious associations have historically been one of the most prominent forms of voluntary association in American society. In addition to differing along theological lines, religious groups have often mirrored important social divisions within the American population and, thereby, have formed focal points for the expression of the interests and sentiments of socially distinct subgroups. Within American

Bernard Lazerwitz and Michael Harrison are Professors of Sociology at Bar-Ilan University in Ramat-Gan, Israel.

Reprinted from *The American Sociological Review* 44 (1979) with permission of the American Sociological Association and the authors.

Protestantism this tendency toward differentiation achieved legitimation in the denominational principle (Mead, 1963; Parsons, 1960: 295). The character and functioning of American Protestant denominations has been the subject of a considerable body of research and commentary (e.g., Niebuhr, 1929; Anderson, 1970; Berger, 1969; Gaustad, 1962; Glock and Stark, 1965; Greeley, 1972; Laumann, 1969; Stark and Glock, 1968; Wilson, 1968a; 1968b).

On the other hand, less attention has been directed to the development of analogous denominational tendencies within smaller non-Protestant groups. Of particular interest is the development of a tripartite denominational structure within American Judaism. Several historical analyses trace the development of the American Jewish denominations (e.g., Sklare, 1972; Steinberg, 1965; Blau, 1969; 1976; Glazer, 1972; Liebman, 1965; 1973; Poll, 1969). In addition, surveys of individual metropolitan Jewish communities, such as those by Axelrod (1967), Dashefsky and Shapiro (1974), Goldstein and Goldscheider (1968), Lazerwitz (1973a), and Sklare and Greenblum (1967), provided some data on the characteristics of the members of these denominations. These local studies, however, typically suffer from sample designs that omit marginal members of the Jewish population, have limited sample sizes, and do not lend themselves to generalizations about American Jewry as a whole. Moreover, these local studies typically pay too little attention to individuals without any denominational preference or to those with denominational identifications who do not join synagogues. Large-scale sample surveys of the general American population cannot illuminate differences within American Jewry, since they include too few Jewish respondents.

In this report we analyze nationwide survey data on the American Jewish population which finally provide an authoritative basis for the development of generalizations about the ethnic, religious, and social characteristics of Jewish Americans who do and do not identify and affiliate with the major denominations. This first report presents these data in a form which permits comparisons with the available data on Protestant Americans. Subsequent reports from this study will examine the data's implications for some of the important theoretical questions about the sources and consequences of denominational differentiation. Even in the basic form in which they are presented here, these data make it clear that Jewish denominational involvement and differentiation are empirically more durable and important than they have previously been considered to be.

Methods

Sample Design

The National Jewish Population Survey (NJPS) was a national survey of the United States Jewish population conducted from the early spring of 1970 to the end of 1971 for the Council of Jewish Federations and Welfare Funds. The sample yielded 5,790 household interviews at a 79% response rate. For the purpose of this survey, Jews were defined as persons who reported themselves Jewish or, failing this, as a person who had at least one Jewish parent. The sample design had to take into account that American Jewry constitutes only a few percent of the total American population, that a sizable proportion do not live in neighborhoods with high concentrations of Jewish residents, and that many are not listed on readily available communal lists. The final design was a complex, multi-stage two-phase, disproportionately stratified, cluster sample. This design was guided by a variation of the city directory/block supplement sampling approach described in Lazerwitz (1968:314–20) and Kish (1965:352–8). Details on the sample, its response characteristics, and generalized sampling errors appear in Lazerwitz (1973b; 1974; 1978a). When a sampled household was found to contain a Jewish resident, basic information about the family was obtained and, via the Kish (1949) technique, one adult Jewish respondent was then selected from among all the Jewish adults in residence. (At this survey phase, there was additional subsampling within just the New York area.) Interviews with 4,305 adult Jewish respondents from this final sampling stage provide the national data reported here.

Variable Definition and Measurement

For reference, we summarize here the variables analyzed in this report:

(1) Jewish Denominational Identification and Synagogue Membership. Respondents were classified into four categories on the basis of their expressed denominational identifications. Individuals who did not identify with a denomination or said they were "just Jewish," were classified as having no denominational identification. In addition, respondents were asked whether they were members of a synagogue.

(2) Jewish Identification Indices. A set of items indicative of various aspects of religious and ethnic identification was used to create indices of the nine dimensions of Jewish identification described in Lazerwitz (1973a:205–10).[1] In brief these indices are:

Childhood home Jewish background—the Jewish aspects of respondents' childhood homes, covering items such as parental religious involvement, their Jewish organizational activities, and home holiday celebrations.
Jewish education—the type and amount received during childhood and adolescence.
Religious observance—respondents' present synagogue attendance, home religious observances of the Shabbat and the annual cycle of religious holidays, and observance of the dietary laws.
Pietism—observance of the more individualistic forms of religious expression such as private prayers and fasting.
Jewish ideology—extent to which being Jewish and retaining Jewish values are felt to be desirable and intrinsically worthwhile.
Ethnic community involvement—the extent to which a respondent's dating, courtship behavior, friends, family life, and social life have been confined to Jews.
Jewish organizational involvement—extent of membership, activity, and leadership in Jewish voluntary associations.

Jewish socialization of one's children—degree of respondent's past, present, and anticipated efforts to socialize his or her children into Jewish life.
Concern for world Jewry—attitudes toward Israel and degree of concern over the fate of Jews in difficult circumstances in the rest of the world.

(3) Secular Correlates of Jewish Identification. The NJPS data permitted the measurement of the following types of behavior and attitudes:

Membership and participation in general community voluntary associations—here summarized by an index which is a slightly modified version of the Chapin scale.
Political orientations—an index of attitudes to such issues as school busing and aid to welfare recipients. More liberal responses received higher index scores.
Religious background of spouse—information on the religious and denominational preference of the wives of male respondents when the couple first met.

(4) Socioeconomic Characteristics. This variable covered respondent's education, the occupation of the head of the household, and total family income for the year prior to the survey.

(5) Demographic Characteristics. This variable covered respondent's sex and age:

Generation in the United States—ranked as respondent foreign born; both parents foreign born; both parents born in the United States.[2]
Family-life cycle—respondents were grouped into ten categories ranging from unmarried respondents, through married couples with young or adolescent children, to couples whose children had left home, to elderly respondents living alone.

Analysis

Denominational Identification and Affiliation

The NJPS data indicate that most American Jewish adults continue to identify with one of the major Jewish denominations and to join their synagogues. Half of the respondents reported that they were presently members of a synagogue. This figure underestimates the degree of informal association with synagogues, since membership entails expenses which some individuals are unwilling, or unable, to sustain. Moreover, data to be presented below suggest that many older respondents with grown children, who do not currently belong to synagogues, were previously members. Similarly, some of the younger members may be expected to join a synagogue as they enter their childrearing years.

Overall, 86% of the respondents reported a denominational identification. Among synagogue members, 14% identified with Orthodoxy, 49% with Conservative Judaism, 34% with Reform Judaism, and 3% indicated no preference. Among those without a synagogue membership, 7% preferred Orthodoxy, 35% preferred Conservative Judaism, 33% preferred Reform, and 25% had no preference.

Given the importance of both synagogue membership and denominational identification, we may obtain a more precise picture of denominational patterns within American Jewry by combining our measures of these two key variables. The cross tabulation of the four-category denominational preference variable and the dichotomous membership variable yields an eight-fold typology of denominational orientations. However, the sample sizes of two of the eight subgroups are too small to justify their inclusion in statistical analyses. Respondents without a denominational identification rarely reported synagogue memberships. Moreover, there are only 174 residents who identify themselves as Orthodox Jews and who are not members of a synagogue. Therefore, in subsequent tables, we shall report on the six major combinations of denominational identification and affiliation.

Social Characteristics

Table 1 provides data on the demographic and socioeconomic characteristics of individuals identifying and affiliating with each of the three major denominations and on the traits of the unaffiliated or unidentified. As we shall show later, the ordering of the categories in the table is in terms of their emphasis on Jewish traditions. The Orthodox members represent the highly traditional pole of this dimension, while those without denominational preferences are at the opposite pole. Conservative Judaism is tradition-minded, but, in practice, more flexible in its demands on its members than Orthodoxy, while Reform Judaism is the least traditional of the three denominations.

The sex distributions of the members of most of the six subgroups are similar to that of the overall Jewish adult population. The prominent exception is that of members of Reform synagogues, two-thirds of whom are women. These synagogues would appear to have greater appeal for women because they deemphasize the traditional religious distinctions between the sexes and are thus closer to the current secular ideal of sexual equality.

Taken together, the data on the age, life cycle situation, and generation point to definite differences between the six categories. Over a third of the members of Orthodox synagogues are over sixty, and over half were born abroad. These first generation members include refugees from Nazism, as well as aged representatives of the eastern European mass immigration that came to an end in the early 1920s. The third generation is scarcely represented among the Orthodox. The Reform and Conservative denominations are distinctive in their high percentage of mar-

Table 1   *Demographic and Social Characteristics by Denominational Identification and Affiliation of Jewish Adults, NJPS, 1971*

| Characteristics | Total Adult Sample | Orthodox Member | Conservative | | Reform | | No |
			Member	Not Member	Member	Not Member	Identification
Sex—% Women	56%	57%	51%	54%	68%	56%	50%
Age							
20–39 years	30%	27%	27%	20%	24%	48%	37%
60 and over	27%	36%	24%	38%	24%	19%	29%
Family Status							
Married with children under 16 years in household	43%	30%	57%	29%	57%	38%	38%
Generations in U.S.							
Foreign-born	21%	52%	24%	27%	7%	11%	17%
Both parents U.S. born	20%	5%	16%	13%	25%	24%	37%
Socioeconomic Status							
College grads.	35%	23%	34%	18%	52%	40%	41%
Professional	33%	31%	30%	23%	39%	38%	38%
Owners and managers	29%	29%	44%	43%	20%	16%	17%
Family Income							
$20,000 or more	24%	16%	24%	12%	33%	28%	28%
n	4,305	399	1,160	616	841	548	475

ried synagogue members with children under 18. Studies of members of synagogues and liberal churches (e.g., Sklare and Greenblum, 1967; Nash, 1968) suggest that many of these individuals are drawn to religious affiliation because of their desire to provide their children with a basic religious identification. Despite these similarities between the Reform and Conservative groups, the affiliates of Reform include more third generation and less foreign-born individuals. Nonmembers who identify with Conservative Judaism are older than both Reform and Conservative members. Such people apparently include more tradition-minded individuals who are not currently active in synagogues. In contrast, those nonmembers who identify with Reform or those who have no denominational identities include a disproportionate number of younger, unmarried adults. Third generation Americans are especially prominent among those expressing no denominational identification.

The strong generational differences between the subgroups reflect the influence of the Americanization process. The least Americanized are more attracted to Orthodoxy, while the most Americanized gravitate toward Reform or express no denominational preference. Conservative Judaism constitutes a middle ground. Multivariate analysis of the relationships between the demographic and denominational variables shows that the sizable life cycle and generational differences between the denominational groups are stable, with controls for the other variables, while the sex and age differences are much smaller.[3]

Table 1 also provides data on the socioeconomic characteristics of the six subgroups. As the figures for the total sample indicate, American Jewry has become heavily middle- and upper-middle class. Sixty-two percent of the employed heads of households in the sample work as professionals, managers, or owners. Over a third of all

American Jewish adults are college graduates. As a result of the overwhelmingly middle-class character of the American Jewish population, socioeconomic differences between the denominations have become muted, although they have not disappeared. The full tables on educational attainments show that there is a clear gradient: the Orthodox have the lowest levels of formal education, followed by the Conservative nonmembers, the Conservative members, and Reform nonmembers. The Reform members are the most educated subgroup. Similarly, Reform Judaism is distinguished among the three denominations in its ability to attract professionals and the more wealthy segments of American Jewry. The nonidentified individuals and those nonmembers identifying with Reform Jewry are also highly educated and well-off. Only the Orthodox and those without denominational identities include sizable proportions of blue-collar members (16% and 18%, respectively).

In general, then, the demographic and socioeconomic characteristics of the six denominational subgroups correspond to what might have been predicted on the basis of a hypothesis that the denominations may be ordered on a continuum from the least Americanized Orthodox through the Conservatives to the highly Americanized Reform and nonidentified groups. Contrary to this general pattern, however, those without denominational preferences are a highly heterogeneous group, composed of a mixture of the high-status younger adults and the lower status old. The elderly nonidentified appear to be the carriers of the Jewish socialist and secularist tendencies which have all but disappeared from contemporary American Jewish life. Thus, the nonidentified group closely resembles those adults in the general American population who express no religious preference (see Lazerwitz, 1961:575–76).

At the beginning of the twentieth century, Orthodoxy was the dominant form of Judaism for those eastern European immigrants who had not rejected religion in favor of socialism and freethinking. Reform appealed to the minority of higher status Jews, many of whom were of German origin or descent. Conservative Judaism emerged as the denomination of the second generation descendants of eastern European Jewry. While the denominations today still reflect something of these historic divisions, the differences have been greatly reduced by the socioeconomic achievements of most American Jews and the high proportion of marriages between Jews of different national origins.

Jewish Identification

While socioeconomic differences between the denominations are apparently declining, there are still strong differences between the denominational groupings in their patterns of Jewish identification. Table 2 gives the percentage of each of the subgroups who received high scores on the indices of Jewish identification described above.[4] The table reveals a clear rank order among the groups; the Orthodox are the most highly identified, followed by Conservative members, Conservative nonmembers, Reform members, Reform nonmembers, while the nonidentified adults rank lowest. The ranking of the members of the denominations on the dimensions of religious behavior and piety corresponds to the differing emphasis given by the denominational leaders to traditional observance. The pattern, however, also occurs on most of the other dimensions, where official denominational differences are less clear-cut. Thus, the data show that the denominational groupings are, in effect, ranked on their members' degree of ethnic Jewish identification as well as their religious traditionalism. Multivariate analysis suggests that these patterns are the result of a combination of processes of self-selection and influence. Individuals appear to choose the kind of denominational affiliation that most closely resembles the style of Jewish identity they desire for themselves and for

Table 2   *Percent Having High Levels of Jewish Identification by Denominational Identification and Affiliation of Jewish Adults, NJPS, 1971*

		Denominational Groups					
Identity Indices	All Adult Sample	Orthodox Member	Conservative Member	Conservative Not Member	Reform Member	Reform Not Member	No Identification
J. background	36%	65%	38%	49%	29%	21%	17%
J. education	36%	70%	50%	35%	38%	14%	15%
Rel. behavior	33%	87%	59%	25%	26%	5%	3%
Pietism	42%	84%	64%	57%	25%	17%	8%
Ideology	36%	71%	52%	38%	36%	12%	11%
Ethnic comm. involvement	36%	71%	55%	37%	22%	17%	12%
J. organization	29%	63%	49%	16%	43%	5%	7%
J. socialization children	39%	56%	48%	49%	37%	21%	16%
World Jewry	29%	29%	38%	22%	34%	22%	25%

their children, and then appear to be influenced by this denominational context.

The most important deviations from the ranking in Table 2 are the high levels of involvement of Reform members in Jewish organizations and the low level of involvement in such organizations among Conservative nonmembers (who include a substantial proportion of older adults).

Table 3 provides illustrative items from four of the indices in order to help illuminate the factors leading to denominational differences and similarities. Keeping a kosher home is a form of religious behavior called for by both Orthodox and Conservative Judaism, but it is optional for Reform Jews. In addition, it is something of a folkway among

many first- and second-generation Jews, more of whom are identified with Conservative Judaism than with Reform. Frequent synagogue attendance is encouraged by all denominations and is a function of a variety of institutionalized influences as well as individual religious feelings. As a result, it varies between denominations and is more characteristic of members than of nonmembers. Membership in Jewish organizations is encouraged by all denominations and is similar among members of all three denominations, but it is less common among nonmembers. This pattern again reminds us that many Reform members are highly active in organized Jewish life despite their tendency to be lower than the members of other denominations in religious

Table 3   *Illustrative Identity Items by Denominational Identification and Affiliation of Jewish Adults, NJPS, 1971*

		Denominational Groups					
Identity Indices	All Adult Sample	Orthodox Member	Conservative Member	Conservative Not Member	Reform Member	Reform Not Member	No Identification
Kosher home	30%	87%	42%	40%	6%	6%	9%
Frequent syn. attendance	13%	51%	24%	3%	13%	2%	1%
Member 2 or more Jewish org.	24%	39%	40%	14%	41%	7%	5%
Visited Israel	16%	26%	18%	15%	20%	8%	13%

observance and background. Since the state of Israel has become a central, unifying symbol of the Jewish people, visiting Israel has become frequent among most subgroups. The less intensely identified and affiliated subgroups also have lower percentages of individuals who have visited Israel.

Secular Correlates of Jewish Identification

A few items in the NJPS permit the examination of the degree to which members of the denominational subgroups differ in attitudes and behavior reaching beyond the realm of Jewish institutions. The first two entries in Table 4 show a strong association between denominational identification and mate-selection patterns. The first entry shows that most couples had the same denominational identification when they originally met. Moreover, men with a denominational identification rarely met and married women with no identification. The second row of the table shows the percentage of husbands who reported that their wives were not Jewish when they originally met. Intermarriage percentages are equally low for Orthodox and Conservative men, are roughly double for men identifying with Reform, and jump to 17%

for those having no identification. These data make it clear that many of the Jewish men expressing no denominational preference are at the margins of the organized Jewish community.

The last two entries in Table 4 provide some indication of the attitudes and involvement of the respondents in the non-Jewish, general community. These data show that Reform members and nonmembers are more liberal politically than individuals associated with Orthodox and Conservative Judaism. Although this tendency partially reflects the higher socioeconomic status of the Reform Jews, multivariate analysis shows that it is not fully accounted for by this factor. Service to the general community and political liberalism are strong traditions within Reform Jewish life and historically have played an important part in the denomination's ideology. Despite their similarities to Reform, individuals lacking denominational identification are much less active in general community voluntary associations. In sum, the data show clearly that aspects of secular behavior and attitudes are strongly associated with denominational identification among American Jews.

Table 4 *Secular Correlates of Denominational Identification and Affiliation of Jewish Adults, NJPS, 1971*

Characteristics	All Adult Sample	Orthodox — All	Orthodox — Member Only	Conservative — All	Conservative — Member Only	Conservative — Not Member	Reform — All	Reform — Member Only	Reform — Not Member	No Identification
% men marry within denomination	56%	65%	—	67%	—	—	62%	—	—	55%
% men marry non-Jewish women	7%	3%	—	4%	—	—	9%	—	—	17%
% high gen. vol. assoc.	29%	—	19%	—	32%	10%	—	50%	37%	20%
% high political issues	37%	—	27%	—	29%	23%	—	49%	42%	59%

Conclusions

Our intention in this report has been to provide a basic profile of the social and religious characteristics of individuals affiliating and identifying with Jewish denominations or having no denominational identification. We have omitted the presentation of conventional significance tests because they would add little to the results. The consistency of the patterns shown here, the large sample size, and the persistence of the major differences between the denominations when controls are introduced in multivariate analyses (e.g., Lazerwitz, 1978b) were sufficient to convince us that the patterns reported are unlikely to have been due to chance variations.[5]

In concluding, we shall briefly review our findings on Jewish denominational patterns. Then we shall compare and contrast Jewish and Protestant denominational differentiation and make some observations on the durability of the denominational pattern within American society.

The Major Patterns

Are the classic "social sources" of Jewish denominationalism disappearing with the increasing Americanization of the American Jewish community? It has been found that the historic differences between the denominations in terms of socioeconomic factors have declined considerably. While differences of education, occupation, and income do still appear among the subgroups, such differences are small and may be expected to decline even further. However, generations in the United States, a clear reflection of Americanization, are still a substantial source of distinction among the groups.

Differences in religious behavior and belief are strong and appear to be stable. These differences are not accounted for by the social and demographic characteristics of those belonging to, or identifying with the various denominations. Rather, denominational identification and affiliation with a synagogue are strongly associated with variations in Jewish behavior and orientations. At one pole are the Orthodox Jews, a small but active minority within American Jewry, who retain the highest levels of traditional Jewish behavior and ingroup involvement. At the other extreme are Jews without any denominational identification who rarely affiliate with Jewish institutions and ignore most Jewish traditions. The Conservative and Reform Jews maintain a position between these two poles; the Conservatives are nearer to the Orthodox pattern and the Reform are closer to that of the unidentified.

Our data also show that within the Jewish community, where religious and ethnic orientations are deeply intertwined, denominational identification and affiliation do have important secular correlates. The NJPS provides evidence on marital patterns, political attitudes, and membership in general community organizations, while other possible correlates are as yet unexplored. The Orthodox are characterized by greater political conservatism and greater involvement in the Jewish community than in the general, non-Jewish, community. Reform and Conservative Jews more typically appear to combine lower levels of Jewish involvement with more political liberalism and active participation in the general community. Jews without a denominational identification are less active in both Jewish and non-Jewish associations. This pattern may reflect their preference for more individualistic, and unconventional, sources of satisfaction and belonging.

Comparisons with Protestantism

The evidence from NJPS supports the assertions of Glock and Stark (1965), Greeley (1972), and others that America continues to be a "denominational society." Within American Jewry, as within American Protestantism (Glock and Stark, 1965; Stark and Glock, 1968) congregants continue to be divided into religiously distinctive camps. In Judaism, the lines of ideological division and the denominational structure closely resemble those found in Protestantism. Among both Jews and Protestants there are clear divisions between an inactive sector, liberals, moderates, and conservatives. Moreover, in both religious groups the more conservative denominations are closer to a sectarian position in their social structure and ideology. These structural and ideological parallels have their counterpart in some noteworthy similarities at the level of individual behavior. The NJPS data, like the Lazerwitz (1973a) study of Protestants and Jews in Chicago, point to parallels between the levels of traditional religious behavior among Orthodox Jews and fundamentalist Protestants, among Conservative Jews and Protestants preferring Conservative denominations, among Reform Jews and liberal Protestants, and among those Jews and Protestants with no denominational preferences. The Chicago study also found similarities in the involvement of Reform Jews and liberal Protestants in general community organizations, and in their greater political liberalism. However, the actual levels of liberalism among all Jews, apart from the Orthodox, exceeded the Protestant levels.

Denominational identification and membership have strong associations with aspects of Jewish life that are above and beyond Jewish institutional boundaries. Can the same conclusion be drawn with respect to Protestant denominations? The search for such consequences of Protestant denominationalism has yielded little in the way of consistent results (Bouma, 1973; Rojek, 1973; Schuman, 1971; Winter, 1974). Perhaps the inability of researchers to find consistent and substantial secular consequences of involvement in Protestant denominations stems from their tendency to ignore differences between church

members and nonmembers and the frequent absence of data on those who consider themselves Protestants but have no denominational preference. On the other hand, given the intensity and resourcefulness with which the search has been pursued, it may well be that there are quite limited Protestant denominational consequences in the political and economic areas. In contrast, the dual status of American Jewry as a minority religious-ethnic group heightens the likelihood that differences in Jewish loyalty and belief will produce political and economic correlates. It seems more likely that there are direct effects of Protestant denominational orientations on values and behavior which are especially subject to individual discretion and less institutionally regulated, such as patterns of family life and use of leisure time.

The NJPS findings reinforce the position that socioeconomic status, ethnicity, and degree of urbanization or Americanization, now play, or soon will play, a less prominent role in sustaining denominational differences than in the past. While race and historical regional differences still contribute to Protestant denominationalism, the end of mass immigration, the urbanization of the United States, and the predominantly middle-class character of Protestant Americans (Anderson, 1970) and Jews indicate that the classic social sources of denominationalism are drying up. Instead, among both Jews and Protestants, religious and ethnic orientations are becoming increasingly independent of their original social correlates. Moreover, the tendency of increasing numbers of Jews and Protestants to eschew affiliation with organized religion may sharpen denominational differences rather than weakening them further. As the least committed drift away from religious affiliation, they will leave behind those for whom matters of belief and behavior have the most significance. Should these trends within the American Jewish and Protestant communities continue, we would anticipate the emergence of a denominationalism based more on variations of belief and religious style than on social and economic divisions.

Notes

1. Details on these indices are available from the authors. There have been some limited operational changes in the indices of these dimensions in response to changes in specific questions on the national survey in contrast to the earlier Chicago area survey used in Lazerwitz (1973a).

2. To save space, we dropped the one parent native/one parent foreign-born category.

3. Portions of this multivariate analysis appear in Lazerwitz (1978b).

4. The scores for the various indices were ranged from high to low. Then they were divided into three categories in which the number of interviews were as nearly equal as possible. The category with the highest average score is called high-level identity.

5. Some comment about significance testing is in order. First, this survey's complex, multistate, clustered sample data require special sampling error treatment which is presented in detail in Lazerwitz (1974). In general, the sample design effect (the blowup over simple random sampling) is 3.5. Anyone who wants to do significance testing with any of the percentages of this survey needs to multiply simple random sampling errors by 3.5 before plugging them into any significance testing equation.

References

Anderson, Charles
1970   White Protestant Americans—From National Origins to Religious Groups. Englewood Cliffs: Prentice-Hall.
Axelrod, Morris, Floyd Fowler, and Arnold Gurin
1967   A Community Survey for Long Range Planning: A Study of the Jewish Population of Greater Boston. Boston: Combined Jewish Philanthropies of Greater Boston.
Berger, Peter
1969   The Sacred Canopy, Garden City: Doubleday.
Blau, Joseph
1969   Modern Varieties of Judaism. New York: Columbia University Press.
1976   Judaism in America. Chicago: University of Chicago Press.
Bouma, Gary
1973   "Beyond Lenski: a critical review of recent 'Protestant Ethic' research." Journal for the Scientific Study of Religion 12: 141–56.

Dashefsky, Arnold, and Howard Shapiro
1974   Ethnic Identification Among American Jews. Lexington: Lexington Books.
Gaustad, Edwin
1962   Historical Atlas of American Religion. New York: Harper and Row.
Glazer, Nathan
1972   American Judaism. Chicago: University of Chicago Press.
Glock, Charles, and Rodney Stark
1965   Religion and Society in Tension. Chicago: Rand McNally.
Goldstein, Sidney, and Calvin Goldscheider
1968   Jewish Americans: Three Generations in a Jewish Community. Englewood Cliffs: Prentice-Hall.
Greeley, Andrew
1972   The Denominational Society. Glenview: Scott Foresman.
Kish, Leslie.
1949   "A procedure for objective respondent selection within the household." Journal of the American Statistical Association 44: 380–7.
1965   Survey Sampling. New York: Wiley.
Laumann, Edward
1969   "The social structure of religious and ethnoreligious groups in a metropolitan community." American Sociological Review 34: 182–95.
Lazerwitz, Bernard
1961   "A comparison of major United States religious groups." Journal of the American Statistical Association 56: 568–79.
1968   "Sampling theory and procedures." Pp. 278–328 in Hubert Blalock (ed.), Methodology in Social Research. New York: McGraw-Hill.
1973a   "Religious identification and its ethnic correlates: a multivariate model." Social Forces 52:204–20.
1973b   The Sample Design of the National Jewish Population Survey. New York: Council of Jewish Federations and Welfare Funds.
1974   Sampling Errors and Statistical Inference for the National Jewish Population Survey. New York: Council of Jewish Federations and Welfare Funds.
1978a   "An estimation of a rare population group: the United States Jewish population." Demography 15:389–94.
1978b   "An approach to the components and consequences of Jewish identification." Contemporary Jewry 4:3–8.
Liebman, Charles
1965   "Orthodoxy in American Jewish life." American Jewish Year Book 66:21–97.

1973   The Ambivalent American Jew: Politics, Religion, and Family in American Jewish Life. Philadelphia: Jewish Publication Society.

Mead, Sydney
1963   Lively Experiment: The Shaping of Christianity in America. New York: Harper and Row.

Nash, Dennison
1968   "A little child shall lead them: a statistical test of the hypothesis that children were the source of the 'religious revival'." Journal for the Scientific Study of Religion 7: 238–40.

Niebuhr, H. Richard
1929   The Social Sources of Denominationalism. New York: Holt.

Parsons, Talcott
1960   Structure and Process in Modern Societies. Glencoe: Free Press.

Poll, Solomon
1969   "The persistence of tradition: Orthodoxy in America." Pp. 118–49 in Peter Rose (ed.), The Ghetto and Beyond: Essays on Jewish Life in America. New York: Random House.

Rojek, Dean
1973   "The Protestant Ethic and political preference." Social Forces 52:168–77.

Schuman, Howard
1971   "The religious factor in Detroit: review, replication, and reanalysis." American Sociological Review 36:30–48.

Sklare, Marshall
1972   Conservative Judaism: An American Religious Movement. New York: Schocken.

Sklare, Marshall, and Joseph Greenblum
1967   Jewish Identity on the Suburban Frontier. New York: Basic Books.

Stark, Rodney, and Charles Glock
1968   American Piety: The Nature of Religious Commitment. Berkeley: University of California Press.

Steinberg, Stephen
1965   "Reform Judaism: the origin and evolution of a 'Church' movement." Journal for the Scientific Study of Religion 5: 117–29.

Winter, J. Alan
1974   "Quantitative studies of the applicability of the Weber thesis to post World War II U.S.A.: a call for redirected efforts." Review of Religious Research 16:47–58.

Wilson, Bryan
1968a "Religion and the churches in contemporary America." Pp. 73–110 in William McLaughlin and Robert Bellah (eds.), Religion in America. Boston: Beacon Press.
1968b "Religious organization." Pp. 428–37 in David Sills (ed.), International Encyclopedia of the Social Sciences, 13. New York: Macmillan.

S E L E C T I O N   6 . A

The Right of the Jewish Child to Be Jewish

Marvell Ginsburg

I want to share a problem of deep concern: "The right of the Jewish child to be Jewish." In thinking about how to begin to explore this problem distressing Jewish parents and

Marvell Ginsburg is Director of the Department of Early Childhood of the Board of Jewish Education of Metropolitan Chicago.
    Based on a presentation at the 75th Anniversary of the Religious Education Assocation. Nov. 21, 1978, in Chicago.
    Reprinted from *Religious Education* 74 (May–June, 1979), with permission.

educators today, I felt "in the beginning" might be the best place to start—our beginning, the Bible. Jewish ventures into bicultural living probably began when God, in the book of Genesis 12:1 said to Abraham whom we consider to be the father of the Jewish people, "Get thee out of thy country, and from thy kindred and from thy father's house, unto a land that I will show thee."

As we all know, Abraham, no youngster at age seventy-five, left Haran for the land of

Canaan with his wife, his nephew and household servants. Not only did they encounter the Canaanite people, but also the Perrizite people. Having encountered these new cultures, Abraham was to soon experience the Egyptian as well, for there was a famine in Canaan. Abraham had to quickly learn to communicate with various cultures and certainly with their leaders.

My intent is not to present a Bible lesson but rather illustrate that Jewish history is a four-thousand-year-old experience with biculturalism. While our ancient universal "mother tongue" was and continues to be Hebrew, beginning with the Bible, because of our history of persecution, captivity and continued uprooting, we have learned to quickly adapt to the cultural settings and languages in which we found ourselves. Not only have we preserved Hebrew, but over the centuries have had to learn Akkadian, Arabic, Aramaic, Persian, Greek, Spanish, French, German, Russian, English and many other languages. Now history is coming full cycle with modern Hebrew being spoken in Israel. Not only did we learn many tongues, but developed a variety of Jewish vernaculars based on those tongues. For example, during the Byzantine period we developed Gregos based on Greek. During our Golden Era in Spain, we developed Ladino. During one thousand years in eastern Europe we developed Yiddish. Each of these had its own rich literary and cultural treasures.

Myths and legends often reveal a great deal about the values of a culture. As we know, the Jewish people developed through Abraham, his son Isaac and his grandson Jacob. Jacob's son, Joseph, eventually became second in command to the Pharaoh of Egypt. Subsequently with the deaths of Jacob and that Pharaoh a new Pharaoh arose "who knew not Joseph" and enslaved those ancient Hebrews for about four hundred years.

It certainly could be expected that in four hundred years a minority "ethnic" group could easily become totally assimilated into the majority culture. Yet one of the legends of our tradition, in explaining the exodus from Egypt, tells us that the Jewish people were redeemed because "they preserved their own Hebrew language, their cultural observances, continued to give their children traditional Hebrew names and maintained their (ethnic) identity."

If an enslaved people could do that over a four hundred year period and a continually uprooted people for two thousand years, how did the free, American Jewish community get into the plight which is the basis for this discussion?

Normally parents are the first and most important teachers of their children. Along with general socialization of the child, they are also the transmitters of their particular culture with its integral value system.

Recently, a four-year-old child commented to his teacher in his Jewish nursery school, "My daddy doesn't know how to say the brahot (Hebrew blessings). He didn't go to my nursery school! But I'm teaching him!"

This incident serves to highlight some specific aspect of the problems facing Jewish educators today. It seems as though three and four year olds have to transmit to their elders. If we examine the generally agreed upon goals in the U.S. Government Title VII type programs we find the following: "improved self concept, socio-economic development, academic achievement and an appreciation for the many linguistic and cultural heritages in the United States."

The Jewish group in America over the last 75–100 years has largely achieved sound socio-economic development and academic achievement. Roughly 85 percent of Jewish high school graduates go on to college. (We are not including in this group the recent Jewish immigrants from Russia and South America.)

This generation of Jewish children is in the mainstream of American life. The problem lies in their lack of knowledge and experience with our own ancient cultural heritage and language, leading to a diminished sense of self-acceptance, pride and general wholesome emotional well-being.

In their great eagerness to become Americanized, the great wave of Jewish immigrants, who came to these shores in the nineteenth century, zealously pushed their children to learn English, the American way, and to become part of "the melting pot," even while they, themselves, sought out and lived in the warmth and support of "their own kind" in almost transplanted replicas of European enclaves on these shores.

Oscar Handlin, in his study of immigrants, found this to be a prevalent pattern among most immigrant groups. He tells us that in their eagerness to be American, most of the · first born generation tried to cast off all traces of their immigrant parents' backgrounds. As soon as they could, they moved out of the ethnic neighborhoods, seeking higher status, anonymous white, middle class "American" neighborhoods. Many changed their names, noses and ways of living.

They go themselves out from their fathers' houses with a vengeance speaking only English and casting off traditional observances. The second and third American born generations, feeling more secure as Americans, with English as their mother tongue, nonetheless had deep identity problems. Was there such a thing as an "American"? Wasn't America composed of a plurality of peoples? There was inner discomfort, a longing, a searching for one's unique roots.

For Jews, this discomfort becomes particularly acute at Christmas and Easter, which are totally outside Jewish tradition since Judaism does not accept the divinity of Christ but rather sees him as a wise man. Out of the mouths of babes, we say, we learn much. Here is an example of the young Jewish child's struggle to make sense out of his world. It happened, many years ago, when I taught in a Jewish nursery school. It was in the midst of all our preparations and teaching of Hanukkah. I noticed Freddy and Jer-

emy sitting under a table. Four year old Freddy was pretending to read a story to his younger friend. As I ambled by, what do I hear but "Twas the night before Christmas," etc. When Freddy reached the line, [I said] "Hey, Freddy, who is this St. Nick guy?" Freddy answered with great patience. "Don't you know, that's Santa Claus' Jewish name?" With the foregoing in mind, let us now take a look at the first goal of the aforementioned.

Title VII Goals: Improved Self-Concept

Miller and Hutt in their study "Value Interiorization and Personality Development" state "a type of value inconsistency which handicaps the child's attempts to synthesize a socially acceptable ego results from membership in a minority group which differs from the dominant group in ethnic, economic and historic prototypes."

Perhaps this need for ego synthesis contributed in part to the "Black Is Beautiful" campaign for consciousness raising of Black identity. This movement was probably of great service in enabling and encouraging other ethnic groups to search for their ethnic identity. In a research study on "Ethnicity and Mental Health," Joseph Giordano states, "The present reassertion of ethnicity in this country goes much deeper than political motives, convenience in organizing, or intergroup conflict and competition. It is a search for identity in a time of rapid worldwide change."

Erik Erikson, in his classic work on identity, has begun to develop a framework for understanding the link between the individual, his ethnic group, and society. He describes Freud's own deep sense of ethnic identification as consisting of ". . . many obscure emotional forces which were the more powerful the less they could be expressed in words; as well as a clear consciousness of inner identity, the safe privacy of an inner mental construction."

Freud conceived of ethnic identity as ". . . suggesting a deep commonality known only [to] those who share in it, and only expressible in works more mythical than conceptual."

Erikson himself links the individual to his group. Identity, he says, is "a process located in the core of the individual and yet also in the core of his common culture—a process which establishes, in fact, the identity of these two identities."

Dr. Alfred Messer, in his clinical work with immigrant families, suggests that the healthy adult needs some feeling of the historical continuity of his existence to establish a sense of identity.

Giordano views the psychological function of ethnicity as fulfilling that need, functioning to link the past with the future.

Ethnic identity, then, offers the individual, in Kurt Lewin's words, "a ground on which to stand."

The search for identity is a basic psychological need, and ethnicity is a powerful and subtle influence in determining its shape and form.

In the introduction to his section on "Reflections on the American Identity" in his classic work, *Childhood and Society*, Erikson focuses on the problem of ego identity and its anchoring in cultural identity. He states, ". . . (the mentally ill) patient of today suffers most under the problem of what he should believe in and who he should—or, indeed, might—be or become."

What to believe in and who he or she should become—this then, is the major problem facing the American Jewish youngster today. He or she, just as many other minority group children in America, faces many assaults on his or her inherent psychological need and human right to grow up naturally and happily as part of his/her own religious, cultural group. Yet when speaking of the culturally disadvantaged, I doubt whether most people would include Jewish children in that group. In a sense we Jews have "made it" in

America. But perhaps our "making it" may also be our unmaking.

The American experience is historically a unique one for the Jewish people. With the exception of modern Israel and brief periods of sovereignty mentioned in the Bible, it is the first time in our long history that we are *born* into a society with equal rights. We no longer need depend on the ruler of a given historical period to bestow or withdraw citizenry or rights according to his or her mood, economic or religious pressures, or other societal forces. However, the very freedom which has enabled us to advance on the socio-economic and educational ladders has also contributed to the attrition of our rich cultural past. We have the freedom to opt out. Unfortunately, too many are doing just that!

It is this battle for Jewish cultural religious survival which challenges both Jew and non-Jew alike. A weekend or nonexisting Jewish tradition is an impoverishment of mankind as well.

Many societal factors compound the problem. As in the general population, there is a continuing attrition of sound Jewish life. As we know, Judaism has always centered around a strong family unit as the basis for the good life. The Jewish divorce rate is growing and the Jewish birth rate declining precipitously. In fact we have the dubious honor of being the first ethnic group in this country to achieve below zero population growth—1.7. The intermarriage rate between Jew and non-Jew is increasing rapidly. While this may be part of the American democratic process, it does not strengthen Jewish survival. There has been a great deal of apathy on the part of many Jewish parents to give their children *any* kind of Jewish formal education or home Jewish experiences. Many of them did not have it themselves, so don't know how currently in the Chicago metropolitan area less than one third of all eligible Jewish school age children attend any kind of Jewish schooling. A kind of "laughter through tears" in-joke we tell among ourselves is about the parent who insists on a maximum Jewish education BUT in only one hour per week!

When we talk about societal forces undermining a particular cultural group we are probably getting into the arena of "right vs. right." The majority certainly has a right to its cultural expressions, value manifestations and celebrations. Yet it is some of these very same expressions, values and celebrations which contribute in some measure to the undermining of the minority group child's sense of completeness and psychological comfort. I recall my own children asking me when they were young, "Mommy, how come there aren't any Hanukkah decorations on the streets? Don't they know its Hanukkah?"

They, too, were caught up in the compelling beauty, warmth and glow of Christmas even though they were raised in a home rich with Jewish observance and received a very intensive Jewish education (in more than one hour a week!).

When our oldest daughter was ten, she "snuck" her two younger siblings out of the house one day to visit Santa Claus at our local shopping center, a few blocks away.

When they finally told us about it, apparently after a strong twinge of conscience, they said they just wanted to see what it was like to sit on Santa's lap and get Christmas candy. But they told him he couldn't bring them presents because they celebrated Hanukkah.

Then to make everything o.k. they hastened to reassure me, "But don't worry about a thing, mommy! We looked both ways before crossing the street and went on the green!"

Well, here we are today, looking both ways, inside and outside majority-minority needs for healthy cultural growth.

Thank God we live in a democracy which gives us a green light to go ahead with explorations on the other side of the street!

It may be that we won't find complete answers and satisfaction on the other side of the street. But we do have to cross over to find out.

Over the years various groups have either tried to get Christmas out of the public schools or Hanukkah into them. Neither approach really solved anything. There are some few schools which have "Holiday around the world" type themes in December.

My interest is not to focus on this issue alone. There are many things that happen in the on-going life of the Jewish child which are part of the "American way," that erode his Jewish self-image. It is not done maliciously but is an integral part of American schooling and life style. For example many school events and football games are on Friday nights and Saturdays, the Jewish Sabbath.

There is lack of awareness by public school administrators and teachers (and by many Jews) that the three biblically commanded pilgrimage festivals, Sukkot (Feast of Booths), Passover and Shavuot (the spring festival commemorating the group of the Ten Commandments), are Holy Days. Children of observant Jewish families are often made to feel ashamed of or are penalized for staying out of school to attend synagogue services on these holidays. Many teachers will not offer make up work or schedule tests on other days.

Some progress has been made in our society to upgrade and reinforce self esteem for children of a number of racial groups via representation pictorially in children's books, and on TV programs such as "Sesame Street." So far, this has not been done for the Jewish child.

As a matter of fact, there is only one Jewish children's TV program in the United States. That one program originates . . . in Chicago and is seen only locally. It is the Emmy award winning show "The Magic Door" produced by the Broadcasting Commission of the Chicago Board of Rabbis. Interestingly enough 80 percent of the viewers are non-Jewish!

I would not like to leave the impression that the Jewish educational community is sitting idly by wringing its hands. Far from it.

The Jewish educational community is laboring mightily to "raise positive Jewish consciousness" in the children and families we do reach. But there's a vast unaffiliated, untouched group out there bombarded by all the aforementioned forces militating against their being Jewish!

Yet, just as we have survived one historical catastrophe after another and place our faith in what the Bible calls the "saving remnant," we continue to work in hope.

In contrast to the decline in enrollment in most forms of Jewish schooling across the land, one type has increased in numbers and enrollment dramatically—the Jewish parochial day school. These schools, indeed, offer the most intensive, maximum, Jewish immersion into learning and living. Such children usually attend Hebrew language, Judaic value oriented summer camps and many also spend at least a summer in Israel in some type of work-study program. But we are only talking about 20 percent of those children who receive any kind of Jewish schooling.

There are other kinds of afternoon Hebrew programs and weekend religious schools which the Board of Jewish Education services. In addition we operate a High School

of Jewish Studies and two experimental early childhood centers. These centers are in newly developed areas where there are very few if any Jewish services. Here we reach out to young families and try to bring the richness of their tradition to them.

I do not have any world-shaking, definitive solutions for our problems. Certainly, one could suggest that writers of school text books, children's literature and TV programs now make a conscious effort to include Jewish children's life experiences, and that the public school system be sensitized to the rhythm of the Jewish calendar. "The right of the Jewish child to be Jewish" is an issue important to concerned, religious leaders. We are all involved in trying to raise the level of spiritual, moral, humane living leading to a "good" society. We all know that a strong individual not only leads a happier, more constructive life and is a better citizen but enriches his or her own culture and contributes to the mainstream of American life as well.

Perhaps the psalmist sums up what each of us separately and collectively need to help each other achieve: "Raise up the child in the way he should go and when he is old he will not depart from it."

ADDITIONAL READINGS

Articles

Berger, Alan L. "Hasidism and Moonism: Charisma in the Counterculture." *Sociological Analysis* 41 (1980):375–90. Comparative study of charismatic authority in two religious movements. Suggests modification of Weber's notion of the precariousness of charismatic leadership.

Himmelfarb, Harold S. "The Study of American Jewish Identification: How it is Defined, Measured, Obtained, Sustained and Lost." *Journal for the Scientific Study of Religion* 19 (1980): 48–60. Review of previous studies with summary of environmental influences on Jewish identity: generation, community, socioeconomic status, and events of Jewish history.

Lasker, Arnold A. "What Parents Want from the Jewish Education of Their Children." *Journal of Jewish Communal Service* 70 (1976): 393–403. Survey research of parents who send their children to Orthodox, Conservative, and Reform day schools. Parents vary, to some extent by religious tradition, in emphases on ritual observance, faith, and background of Jewish knowledge as expected outcomes of Jewish education.

Schoenfeld, Stuart. "The Jewish Religion in North America: Canadian and American Comparisons." *Canadian Journal of Sociology* 3 (1978): 209–31. Jewish identification and religious behavior in the differing national contexts of Canada and the United States. A comprehensive treatment.

Steinberg, Stephen. "Reform Judaism: The Origin and Evolution of a 'Church Movement'." *Journal for the Scientific Study of Religion* 5 (1965):117–29. Critical use of the church-sect continuum to study the rise of Reform Judaism in Europe and the United States.

Weinfeld, Morton. "The Jews of Quebec: Perceived Antisemitism, Segregation, and Emigration." *Jewish Journal of Sociology* 22 (1980):5–20. Quebec Jews perceive antisemitism less in daily experiences than in matters of public policy such as affirmative action and Middle East negotiations which can work at odds with Jewish interests.

Besides *Jewish Journal of Sociology, Jewish Social Studies* and *Commentary* frequently deal with religious themes in the Jewish community.

Books

Konvitz, Milton R. *Judaism and the American Idea.* Ithaca, N.Y.: Cornell University Press, 1978. A constitutional lawyer examines the Judaic roots of such key American concepts as democracy, the rule of law, inalienable rights, and equality of opportunity.

Martin, Bernard, ed. *Movements and Issues in American Judaism: An Analysis and Sourcebook of Developments Since 1945.* Westport, Conn.: Greenwood Press, 1978. This volume surveys articles of contemporary research on the American Jewish community; also includes a survey article on Canadian Judaism. Invaluable bibliographical source for further reading and research.

Neusner, Jacob. *American Judaism: Adventure in Modernity.* Englewood Cliffs, N.J.: Prentice-Hall, 1972. Excellent study of the diversity within the American Jewish community by one of its foremost scholars.

Quinley, Harold E., and Glock, Charles Y. *Anti-Semitism in America.* New York: Free Press, 1979. Summary of a major research project carried on between 1963 and 1975 and involving the publication of six books.

Cross-cultural Studies

A vast literature exists on Judaism in global and other national settings. An excellent overall historical-sociological analysis is Stephen Sharot, *Judaism: A Sociology* (London: David & Charles, 1976). The horror of the Nazi holocaust of European Jews is central to an understanding of contemporary Jewry. See Alvin H. Rosenfeld, *A Double Dying: Reflections on Holocaust Literature* (Bloomington: University of Indiana Press, 1976).

Three

Religion and
Social Conflict

7

Religious Institutions in Conflict

Chapter 1 discussed the functionalist view regarding religion's role in the social order. In that view, religion is said to uphold society's dominant norms and values by bringing support, consolation, and reconciliation in terms of individual and group needs. It gives a sacred character to a society's overarching conceptions of purpose and destiny, as in civil religious themes. Religious beliefs and worship, both official and popular expressions, can buttress the identity of particular groups within a society, as discussed in Chapter 6. Religion can give ceremonial reaffirmation to the various passages through the life-cycle, as in confirmations and bar mitzvahs, puberty rites and Mexican-American *quincinieras*, or coming-out celebrations as a girl reaches her fifteenth birthday. The following summary is apt:

Religion, then, in the view of functional theory, identifies the individual with his group, supports him in uncertainty, consoles him in disappointment, attaches him to society's goals, enhances his morale, and provides him with elements of identity. It acts to reinforce the unity and stability of society by supporting social control, enhancing established values and goals, and providing the means for overcoming guilt and alienation.[1]

As Randall Collins points out, however, "since religion symbolizes the major facts of society, it has always had to make room for social conflict in its system of symbols. Since societies are never totally unified, religion must always describe the existence of rival gods, heretics, evil spirits, or the devil. The symbolism of religion mirrors the social world."[2] But this social world is indeed rife with conflict of many kinds, not only those involving a cosmic struggle between the forces of good and evil. As scholars have tried to come to grips with the pervasiveness of conflicts and understand how conflict bears upon the social order, a rival theoretical framework has developed to challenge the familiar functionalist understandings.

In opposition to the tradition associated with Durkheim, conflict sociologists see every society as tending to change; change is as widespread, as characteristic, or more so, than stability. Fundamental to this perspective is the postulation of scarce resources in any society. Not only are everyday goods in short supply, but basic resources such as water, precious metals and fibers, foodstuffs, construction materials, fibers, and forms of energy are objects of struggle. Powerful groups in society control more of these resources and their distribution than other groups. Those with power to control resources assure a continuous supply for their own needs. They also create and support ideologies and mythical "canopies" to legitimate their claim to a monopoly of society's goods, including status symbols of prestige and dominance. As Max Weber pointed out, any human group attempts to legitimate whatever dominance it may achieve by establishing and cultivating a belief in its legitimacy.[3] Classes formed on the basis of wealth, honor, and power are the most salient features of any society in this perspective, which owes so much to Karl Marx (though non-Marxist conflict theories also exist[4]).

Religion can be a powerful basis for, or reflection of, important social cleavages in society. In Northern Ireland, identification as Protestant or Catholic is intertwined with divisions based on class and privilege, with Catholics sharing relatively little decision-making power. Religion readily becomes a master symbol of division; the underlying reality is still more complex.[5] Conflicts can occur *within* religious groups, as well; Shiite and Sunnite Moslems exhibit severe discord in the contemporary Middle East. Religious cleavages also characterize Israel, as Orthodox Jews object to such things as public buses on the Sabbath. Closer to home, conservative versus liberal Christians, even within a single denomination, find themselves opposed on sensitive policy issues like abortion and compulsory school prayer. Religious particularism, or the view that "our religion" has *the only* way to salvation or true enlightenment, can set group against group. Splitting off of "heretical" sects can generate bitter strife as the new devotees vaunt their "purer religion" over the "mother church," which they define as "selling out" to the world. Or the entire wider society is painted as the world, the flesh, and the home of the devil. Believers may select certain trends, movements, and practices as inimical not only to religion but to the nation as well (see Lorentzen, "Evangelical Life Style Concerns Expressed in Political Action" in this chapter). Important to remember is that such antagonism to "what is going on out there" may partially reflect quarrels with the larger society—too much government in our lives, taxes too high, too soft a stand against world communism—that apparently have little to do with religious themes.

Finally, of course, religion may give rise to prophetic outcries against injustices in society—the oppression of orphans and widows, in the words of the Old Testament prophets. Although the prophetic is often listed under functions of religion in standard treatments of functionalism, it seems more appropriate to place it under the heading of conflict.[6]

Having said all this and noting religion's long history of supporting the status quo, under what conditions can religion become a challenge to order? How can it act as a stimulus to change, even revolutionary change? Max Weber discussed the prophetic function of religion, of course, but we turn here to a useful contemporary treatment of the same theme. Four such aspects of religion may be singled out.[7]

1. *Religious doctrine.* Justice and love are core themes not only in the Judeo-Christian scriptures but in other religious traditions as well. Groups advocating change can draw upon them to galvanize their followers to action. Buddhist *karma* may legitimate a ruling caste but can also justify usurpation of power, since it accepts movement "upward" from one's position depending upon past conduct and accumulated merit. Divine Providence is a lens through which even oppression and slavery may be viewed as "for our good"; but the same Providence can summon believers to "take heed of the times" and take up arms against the tyrant. In parallel, "the *Bhagavad Gita* has been used to support the doctrines of the Bengali terrorists fighting British colonial rule in the early years of this century and Gandhi's doctrine of nonviolence."[8] Not all religious doctrines lend themselves to change, of course. The divine right of kings is a case in point. But most religious views of the social order are sufficiently ambiguous for use by supporters of social change insofar as themes of justice and concern for one's fellow human beings can be invoked.

2. *Organizational factors.* Not all world religions have the organizational framework we associate with Western churches. Hinduism lacks a formally organized hierarchy and clergy to exercise authority and speak for a body of lay people. Correspondingly it has rarely acted as a critic of society or government. Buddhism is another matter. Given a fairly well-structured ecclesiastical hierarchy, it can become a vehicle for political protest and advocacy of change, as in Vietnam during the war years. Best known for its worldwide organizational structure is the Roman Catholic church. Its bureaucratic "layerings" are also a communications network for transmitting teachings and policies. To the extent that it has or is thought to have influence over its followers, the Catholic church has been a power for governments to reckon with. Salient examples today are Northern Ireland and Central and South America. The Russian Orthodox church before the Bolshevik Revolution of 1917 and the Scandinavian Lutheran churches are also heavily bureaucratized

but have not been vehicles of protest. Tight organizational structure alone is not a sufficient condition for change advocacy.

3. *Leadership.* Religious movements for change, whether in the direction of return to a former status quo or toward a new vision to be implemented, frequently demand energetic leadership and prophetic inspiration. Millenarian movements often display this kind of charismatic leadership. "The millenarian prophet's ambitious and challenging vision of what the world ought to be increases the expectations and dissatisfactions which can lead to a revolutionary situation."[9] Not all conditions, of course, are favorable to the emergence of charismatic leadership. The dynamic vision of "how things ought to be" can come from *within* the existing organizational leadership. A contemporary example is the leadership within some American and Canadian churches that articulates a religiously based opposition to the nuclear arms race. If recruitment practices within the churches restrict the admittance of potential leaders by screening out persons considered as potential "boat-rockers," charismatic leaders may arise outside the institutional channels to articulate and symbolize a new vision of "what ought to be." Let us report that the *direction* indicated by change-advocating leaders, whether institutional or outsider-charismatic, can be either toward return to a past seen as cast aside, neglected, or even rejected; or toward embrace of a new conception—perhaps a utopian social order in which justice and love can reign (Jim Jones's early vision of the People's Temple) or the application of teachings to a new situation (such as "test-tube life" or nuclear war). In any case, whether return to a past or an advance in new directions are urged, leadership will attempt to legitimate its proposals in terms of the doctrinal resources of its tradition.

4. *Situational factors.* Occurring outside religious communities and institutions, situational factors such as sheer geographical proximity may be important in explaining why a religion spreads to a particular society or region. A factor such as fighting for survival can bring about alteration of doctrine; thus French Huguenots in the closing decades of the sixteenth century abandoned Calvin's teaching of nonresistance to civil authority. They felt they had to resist in order to survive in a military struggle with France's Catholic ruling elites. The militancy of normally quiescent Buddhist sects in Southeast Asia is partially a result of persecution by hostile governments.

Colonial rule is a nonreligious factor bearing on both successes and failures of native and "imported" religions. Native faiths have become inspirational sources of resistance to colonialism, helping unite peoples by creating an awareness of their distinctiveness. Western faiths have been pressured, currently experienced by African Christianity, to adopt long-held doctrines such as monogamous marriage to the plural marriage patterns of some societies. These situations cast religion into the role of stimulus for a growing nationalism and resurgence of older identities, unities, and a resistance to outside cultural influences. The Iranian Revolution of the late 1970s featured the Ayatollahs as symbols of resistance to corrupt and degrading Western life-styles and values that were proclaimed as inimical to a God-given traditional way of life. An inherent risk for religion in these circumstances, as history demonstrates, is its identification as the "state religion" of a successful revolutionary party. It then becomes vulnerable over time to being viewed as the ideological support of an established order that has grown corrupt, indolent, self-serving.

It is not easy to separate into neat categories the strictly political or technical issues on the one hand from issues that are religious or involve religious values on the other. As sociologist Carroll Bourg observes, at least *three* issues appear salient in society's debates about current major problems and our future direction as the twentieth century draws to a close. These three issues involve religious dimensions because they "touch upon basic beliefs about life versus death, feeding versus starvation, war versus peace, resources for families to take care of themselves versus penury and misery, the good of the earth for all versus benefits for the few."[10] These issues are (1) the debate over the buildup of nuclear power; (2) the search for new sources of energy in the context of trying to preserve our environment; and (3) the problem of adequate employment in a time when "those on the job must have considerably more than muscle power in the high technology and knowledge industries."[11] One might add to this list the perennial issue of human rights about which religions have always had something to say.

The readings in this chapter each have a distinct bearing on the religion/political power relationship. The opening excerpt from Karl Marx's "Anti-Church Movement—Demonstration in Hyde Park" illustrates Marx's conviction that religion is a social product created by human beings in interaction. Like other social or cultural products, it comes to be seen over time, through the process that Marx called "alienation" (following the philosopher Hegel), as a force external to mankind, one that stands over them and to which they must submit. Moreover, religion is basically a control mechanism for the upper classes. As Marx bitterly points out, religion helps justify their dominance and protect their privileges, in this case by legitimating the passage of certain laws. The status quo is affirmed and strengthened at the expense of the working classes. The legislative bill in question clearly discriminates against the men and families making their living in the factories while leaving the pleasures of the aristocracy in their carriages untouched.

"The Church in Opposition" by Canadian sociologist Kenneth Westhues contrasts, in a sense, with the stinging observations of the angry Marx. As the work of Guenter Lewy informs us, religion has played a revolutionary role, under certain circumstances, in history.[12] Westhues selects the religious body *as an organization* (not as religious individuals) for his unit of analysis. He further specifies the four aspects previously outlined (doctrine, organization, leadership, and situation) by asking which conditions may provoke a religious organization to take an oppositional posture—not defensively but "an offensive, aggressive stance." Westhues uses a resource-mobilization perspective to analyze a series of case studies of religiously inspired opposition. Reviewing familiar concepts of sociological analysis, he finds the church-sect typology of little usefulness in analyzing oppositional stance. Degree of orthodoxy fares little better nor does locus of control (is control vested in the local congregation or in a higher-up bureaucratic office?). Westhues finds it more fruitful to focus on the preferences of dominant groups or coalitions comprising the religious organization. Will their preferences and interests be served by change, whether the interests be long- or short-range? Any investigator, of course, must determine which interests are involved as well as the composition of the membership. If members feel the same way concerning the disputed issues, the church is more likely, of course, to take an oppositional stance. Finally a theological tradition containing at least some belief elements that are at variance with aspects of the social order being critiqued is significant.

Westhues's analysis bears careful reading because it warns us against the simplistic belief that one can "deduce the social role a religious body will play directly from its theological tradition." His analysis is eminently sociological in its careful discernment, with support from particular case studies ranging from Canada to Paraguay, of those combined factors that are likely to propel a church into conflict with policies of the larger society. These factors constitute resources that must be present and mobilized before "prophetic action" is predictable.

Louise J. Lorentzen next describes a case study of a 1978 race for a Democratic senatorial nomination, in which Christian evangelicals organized to elect a candidate known as a "Christian leader." Unlike Westhues's study, an already constituted organization is not the subject in this essay. A social movement perspective is useful here. Borrowing from Max Weber's distinction between social and economic orders, Lorentzen turns to "status politics," in which groups contend for superior prestige rather than for economic superiority as a means of attaining power. In present-day America, status enhancement can be translated for a group into the following question: How can our life-style be protected, defended, and perpetuated? The author clearly identifies issues about which evangelicals feel threatened by current American trends, issues including the role of women, the unity of the family, abortion, and prayer in public schools. These issues are folded into religious wrappings, so to speak, and in the process become potent symbols for rallying people who had previously stayed away from political activity. Although the evangelicals did not succeed in electing their man to the party ticket, 70 percent of those contacted said they would work again toward the election of a political representative. This reading provides a clear example of the previously discussed intertwining of religious and secular values into a "symbolic package" containing enough meaning to propel people into change-oriented collective action.

The pastoral letter by the National Conference of Catholic Bishops sets before us the prophetic stance of one of the largest Christian churches. As Joseph Fichter pointed out in Chapter 5, the Catholic church may be moving from a "monophasic" to a "polyphasic" consensus, but the hierarchy of bishops does not appear to be acting in a traditional and autocratic fashion. The bishops' efforts, paralleled in mainline Protestant churches that have taken firm stands on nuclear disarmament and other sensitive public issues, appear calculated to stir up thought and debate rather than to pronounce authoritatively. Stands against nuclear war and, perhaps, against certain aspects of modern economies, as illustrated in the 1983 statement of the Canadian bishops, "Ethical Reflections on the Economic Crisis," are nevertheless bound to evoke sharp reaction. Such stands mark rare instances in North American Catholic history when Catholic leadership took an oppositional stance toward a central facet of national policy. If ecumenical activity on such social and moral issues results, the churches could be powerful agents of moral critique in North American societies. They could also see their own ranks seriously divided on sensitive issues of policy. If the mainline churches can persuade the laity to back controversial stands of the church leadership, institutional religion could influence the direction of policy issues such as human rights and nuclear disarmament. The relevance of doctrine, in this case going back to the Second Vatican Council, is a factor to be taken seriously, as are the new organizational structures (such as the National Conference of Catholic Bishops) that help galvanize church leaders into taking "tough stances."

Notes

1. Thomas F. O'Dea and Janet O'Dea Aviad, *The Sociology of Religion* (Englewood Cliffs, N. J.: Prentice-Hall, 1983), p. 16.

2. Randall Collins, *Sociological Insight* (New York: Oxford University Press, 1982), p. 37.

3. Max Weber, *Economy and Society*, ed. Guenther Roth and Claus Wittich, vol. 1 (Berkeley: University of California Press, 1978), p. 213.

4. See the work of Gerhard Lenski, *Power and Privilege* (New York: McGraw-Hill, 1966).

5. See the excellent brief treatment of the Northern Ireland conflict in Mere-

dith McGuire, *Religion: The Social Context* (Belmont, Calif.: Wadsworth, 1981), pp. 166–79. This introduction is based partially on McGuire's approach to conflict.

6. O'Dea and Aviad, *Sociology of Religion*. See prophetic activity within the functionalist framework, not an uncommon view, though it may be tagged as situationally "dysfunctional." Cf. Chapter 1 of this volume.

7. Guenther Lewy, *Religion and Revolution* (New York: Oxford University Press, 1974). These factors are developed by Lewy in Part V, "Religion and Revolution: Theoretical Perspectives," on which the following discussion is based.

8. Ibid., p. 554.

9. Ibid., p. 573.

10. Carroll J. Bourg, "Politics and Religion," *Sociological Analysis* 41 (1980), p. 304.

11. Ibid.

12. Lewy, *Religion and Revolution*, Part V.

READING 7.1

Anti-Church Movement—Demonstration in Hyde Park

Karl Marx

London, June 25, 1855

It is an old and historically established maxim that obsolete social forces, nominally still in possession of all the attributes of power and continuing to vegetate long after the basis of their existence has rotted away, inasmuch as the heirs are quarrelling among themselves over the inheritance even before the obituary notice has been printed and the testament read—that these forces once more summon all their strength before their agony of death, pass from the defensive to the offensive, challenge instead of giving way, and seek to draw the most extreme conclusions from premises which have not only been put in question but already condemned. Such is today the English oligarchy. Such is the *Church*, its twin sister. Countless attempts at

reorganization have been made within the Established Church, both the High and the Low, attempts to come to an understanding with the Dissenters and thus to set up a compact force to oppose the profane mass of the nation. There has been a rapid succession of measures of religious coercion. The pious Earl of Shaftesbury, formerly known as Lord Ashley, bewailed the fact in the House of Lords that in England alone five millions had become wholly alienated not only from the Church but from Christianity altogether. *"Compelle intrare,"* replies the Established Church. It leaves it to Lord Ashley and similar dissenting sectarian and hysterical pietists to pull the chestnuts out of the fire for it.

The first measure of religious coercion was the Beer Bill, which shut down all places of public entertainment on Sundays, except between 6 and 10 p.m. This bill was smuggled through the House at the end of a sparsely attended sitting, after the pietists had bought

Karl Marx (1818–1883), well known for his critique of capitalism and its institutions, is the founder of modern communism.

Reprinted by permission of Schocken Books, Inc. from *Marx and Engels on Religion*. Introduction copyright © 1964 by Schocken Books, Inc.

the support of the big public-house owners of London by guaranteeing them that the license system would continue, that is, that big capital would retain its monopoly. Then came the Sunday Trading Bill, which has now passed its third reading in the Commons and separate clauses of which have just been discussed by commissions in both Houses. This new coercive measure too was ensured the vote of big capital, because only small shopkeepers keep open on Sunday and the proprietors of the big shops are quite willing to do away with the Sunday competition of the small fry by parliamentary means. In both cases there is a conspiracy of the Church with monopoly capital, but in both cases there are religious penal laws against the lower classes to set the consciences of the privileged classes at rest. The *Beer Bill* was as far from hitting the aristocratic clubs as the *Sunday Trading Bill* is from hitting the Sunday occupations of genteel society. The workers get their wages late on Saturday; they are the only ones for whom shops open on Sundays. They are the only ones compelled to make their purchases, small as they are, on Sundays. The new bill is therefore directed against them alone. In the eighteenth century the French aristocracy said: For us, Voltaire; for the people, the mass and the tithes. In the nineteenth century the English aristocracy says: For us, pious phrases; for the people, Christian practice. The classical saint of Christianity mortified *his* body for the salvation of the souls of the masses; the modern, educated saint mortifies *the bodies of the masses* for the salvation of his own soul.

This alliance of a dissipated, degenerating and pleasure-seeking aristocracy with a church propped up by the filthy profits calculated upon by the big brewers and monopolizing wholesalers was the occasion yesterday of a *mass demonstration* in Hyde Park, the like of which London has not seen since the death of George IV, "the first gentleman of Europe." We were spectators from beginning to end and do not think we are exaggerating

in saying that *the English Revolution began yesterday in Hyde Park*. The latest news from the Crimea acted as an effective ferment upon this *"unparliamentary," "extra-parliamentary"* and *"anti-parliamentary"* demonstration.

Lord *Robert Grosvenor*, who fathered the Sunday Trading Bill, when reproached on the score of this measure being directed solely against the poor and not against the rich classes, retorted that "the aristocracy was largely refraining from employing its servants and horses on Sundays." The last few days of the past week the following poster, put out *by the Chartists* and affixed to all the walls of London, announced in huge letters:

"New Sunday Bill prohibiting newspapers, shaving, smoking, eating and drinking and all kinds of recreation and nourishment, both corporal and spiritual, which the *poor people* still enjoy at the present time. *An open-air meeting* of artisans, workers and *'the lower orders'* generally of the capital will take place in Hyde Park on Sunday afternoon to see how religiously the aristocracy is observing the Sabbath and how anxious it is not to employ its servants and horses on that day, as Lord Robert Grosvenor said in his speech. The meeting is called for three o'clock on the right bank of the Serpentine" (a small river in Hyde Park), "on the side towards Kensington Gardens. Come and bring your wives and children in order that they may profit by the example their *'betters'* set them!"

It should be borne in mind, of course, that what *Longchamps*[1] means to the Parisians, the road along the Serpentine in Hyde Park means to English high society—the place where of an afternoon, particularly on Sunday, they parade their magnificent horses and carriages with all their trappings, followed by swarms of lackeys. It will be realized from the above placard that the struggle against clericalism assumes the same character in England as every other serious struggle there—the character of a *class struggle* waged by the poor against the rich, the people against the aristocracy, the "lower orders" against their "betters."

At three o'clock approximately 50,000 people had gathered at the spot announced on the right bank of the Serpentine in Hyde Park's immense meadows. Gradually the assembled multitude swelled to a total of at least 200,000 due to additions from the other bank. Milling groups of people could be seen shoved about from place to place. The police, who were present in force, were obviously endeavouring to deprive the organizers of the meeting of what Archimedes had asked for to move the earth, namely, a place to stand upon. Finally a rather large crowd made a firm stand and *Bligh* the Chartist constituted himself chairman on a small eminence in the midst of the throng. No sooner had he begun his harangue than Police Inspector Banks at the head of 40 truncheon-swinging constables explained to him that the Park was the private property of the *Crown* and that no meeting might be held in it. After some *pourparlers* in which Bligh sought to demonstrate to him that parks were public property and in which Banks rejoined he had strict orders to arrest him if he should insist on carrying out his intention, Bligh shouted amidst the bellowing of the masses surrounding him:

"Her Majesty's police declare that Hyde Park is private property of the Crown and that Her Majesty is unwilling to let her land be used by the people for their meetings. So let's move to Oxford Market."

With the ironical cry: "God save the Queen!" the throng broke up to journey to Oxford Market. But meanwhile, Finlen, a member of the Chartist executive, rushed to a tree some distance away followed by a crowd who in a twinkle formed so close and compact a circle around him that the police abandoned their attempt to get at him.

"Six days a week," he said, "we are treated like slaves and now Parliament wants to rob us of the bit of freedom we still have on the seventh. These oligarchs and capitalists allied with sanctimonious parsons wish to do *penance* by mortifying us instead of themselves for the unconscionable murder in the Crimea of the sons of the people."

We left this group to approach another where a speaker stretched out on the ground addressed his audience from this horizontal position. Suddenly shouts could be heard on all sides: "Let's go to the road, to the carriages!" The heaping of insults upon horse riders and occupants of carriages had meanwhile already begun. The constables, who constantly received reinforcements from the city, drove the promenading pedestrians off the carriage road. They thus helped to bring it about that either side of it was lined deep with people, from Apsley House up Rotten-Row along the Serpentine as far as Kensington Gardens—a distance of more than a quarter of an hour. The spectators consisted of about two-thirds workers and one-third members of the middle class, all with women and children. The procession of elegant ladies and gentlemen, "commoners and Lords," in their high coaches-and-four with liveried lackeys in front and behind, joined, to be sure, by a few mounted venerables slightly under the weather from the effects of wine, did not this time pass by in review but played the role of involuntary actors who were made to run the gauntlet. A babel of jeering, taunting, discordant ejaculations, in which no language is as rich as English, soon bore down upon them from both sides. As it was an improvised concert, instruments were lacking. The chorus therefore had only its own organs at its disposal and was compelled to confine itself to vocal music. And what a devil's concert it was: a cacophony of grunting, hissing, whistling, squeaking, snarling, growling, croaking, shrieking, groaning, rattling, howling, gnashing sounds! A music that could drive one mad and move a stone. To this must be added outbursts of genuine old-English humor peculiarly mixed with long-contained seething wrath. "Go to church!"

were the only articulate sounds that could be distinguished. One lady soothingly offered a prayer-book in orthodox binding from her carriage in her outstretched hand. "Give it to your horses to read!" came the thundering reply, echoing a thousand voices. . . .

Note

1. *Longchamps:* a hippodrome in the outskirts of Paris.—Ed.

R E A D I N G   7 . 2

The Church in Opposition

Kenneth Westhues

My purpose is to suggest under what conditions a religious body can be expected to assume a stance of opposition toward its milieu. By a stance of opposition is meant here the mobilization of such an organization's resources toward some basic structural change of the social order. Since this dependent variable has been subjected to very little systematic research in the past, the following points of clarification deserve to be made in preface.

First, the concern here is with the religious body as an organization, not on individuals identified with it. Western history offers numerous examples of ministers, priests and theologians who challenged the social and political orders confronting them. Indeed, the ministry appears to be both a haven and a breeding-ground of rebels. The rebellion of individuals, however, must be sharply distinguished from a rebellious stance on the part of the religious body. Neither can one assume that the same factors which explain social psychological orientations of clerics also explain the official policies of their denominations. Only the latter purpose is relevant in the present study.

Secondly, oppositional stance as here de-

fined does not embrace minor issues of mainly religious significance, like stores remaining open on Sunday or various kinds of "blue laws." It is limited to instances of conflict between church and social order in which the church seeks some major structural change, like a new form of government, a reorganization of housing, welfare, industry, banking or some other sector of the economy, a major shift in foreign policy, the widening or narrowing of rights on ethnic or racial bases, or other changes of comparable significance.

Thirdly, by an oppositional stance is meant something more than the general condemnation of the "world" evident to varying degrees in most religious bodies. The transcendental element present almost by definition in religious organizations implies at least some formal detachment from the existing order, but not necessarily a corresponding mobilization of resources toward changing it. Only when the resources available to the religious body are consciously and purposely directed toward major societal change will it be said to have assumed a stance of opposition.

A fourth clarification concerns religious bodies which resist persecution by the established authority in the society at large. In North America, Mormon, Hutterite, Mennonite, Doukhobour and other sects have at

Kenneth Westhues is Professor of Sociology at the University of Waterloo, Ontario.
Reprinted from *Sociological Analysis* 37 (Winter, 1976), with permission.

various times entered into conflict with secular authorities over governmental attempts to enforce compliance with civil law. In these cases, the religious body has indeed mobilized its resources against the existing order, but only to secure autonomy for itself as a social island, not for the sake of changing the wider society. The focus of this article is not on such defensive action on the part of a church or sect, but rather on cases of espousal of an offensive, aggressive social stance.

Fifth, conflict between the religious body and the societal status quo must be distinguished from conflict simply within the religious sector. If Moore (1963) is correct, many processes of change within the institution of religion, even those involving rancour and dissension, are not relevant to other institutions; conflict over the "death of God," "process theology," or other theological trends may be cases in point. Similarly, a religious body may undergo major upheavals in its internal structure without changing its stance toward the social and political realities confronting it. Such upheavals fall outside the scope of the present study.

Sixth, and finally, the issue of effectiveness must remain distinct from the issue of resource-mobilization itself. My concern here is limited to the latter. Among the resources typically available to a religious body, perhaps the most basic is the moral authority of the Sunday sermon and of official pronouncement. If the church controls schools, universities, newspapers, radio stations, political parties, labor unions, hospitals, or other organizations, these are resources potentially mobilizable toward dissident goals. Liquid assets, stocks, equipment (from buses to duplicating machines), buildings, expertise and property are other resources, which might be used to effect social and economic change. Obviously, the effectiveness of an oppositional stance is utterly dependent upon the extent of resource availability and upon the skill of resource utilization. This study limits

its concern, however, to the oppositional stance itself, leaving the effectiveness issue for separate analysis elsewhere.

It can be objected that oppositional stance has been defined here so narrowly that instances of its occurrence are quite rare. While to my knowledge no catalogue exists of such instances, it is safe to say that were one compiled, it would be a far more slender volume than a catalogue listing instances of support by religious bodies for the status quo. The role of religion in social change, however, will be more adequately ascertained by focusing on infrequent occasions of genuine dissidence than on some wider category embracing both genuine agitation for change and that which is more apparent than real.

The review in the following section of factors prompting religious bodies to assume an oppositional stance relies simply on a selection of documented instances which have been the subject of earlier research. Particular attention is paid to the following cases: (1) Baptist sects in Nova Scotia in the late 1700s (Clark, 1945, 1948), which organized resistance to British colonialism; (2) The Prophetic Bible Institute in Alberta in the 1930s (Clark, 1945; Mann, 1955), led by William Aberhardt, which evolved into the Social Credit Party; (3) Also in the 1930s, the cooperative movement for economic reform in the Catholic diocese of Antigonish, Nova Scotia (Coady, 1939; Laidlaw, 1971); (4) The support of the Quebec Catholic hierarchy for the Asbestos strike in 1949 (Garry, 1970; Dion, 1974); (5) Espousal by various churches of the cause of racial integration in the American South since World War II (Wood, 1970, 1972; Osborne, 1967; Lamanna and Coakley, 1969; Campbell and Pettigrew, 1959); and (6) The organized opposition of the Catholic Church in Paraguay to the Stroessner government since the late 1960s (Westhues, 1973, 1975). What these six cases have in common, though they occurred at widely divergent points in time and space, is that in each of them, a religious body mobilized its resources against the established order. The section below re-views six factors or conditions which might distinguish these and other cases from the more typical pattern of support for the exist-ing order by religious bodies.

Conditions Provoking an Oppositional Stance

1. Church versus Sect

Until now, the principal output of research on religious bodies has been a variety of ty-pologies, most of them derived from Tro-eltsch's (1931) distinction between church and sect. Some authors (Niebuhr, 1929; Wach, 1944; Becker, 1932; Gustafson, 1973; Stark, 1967) have added new types like *eccle-sia, universal church, cult* and *denomination,* while others (Johnson, 1957; Wilson, 1959; Pope, 1942; Gustafson, 1967; Goode, 1967) have attempted to systematize the variables differentiating various types; still other re-searchers (Dynes, 1955; Demerath, 1961) re-defined Troeltsch's typology to apply to indi-viduals instead of religious bodies. While some of these efforts at typologizing have little to do with social change, at least one (Johnson, 1963) distinguishes types of reli-gious organization on the basis of their orien-tation to the social environments in which they exist. Johnson defines the church as a religious group which accepts its environ-ment, a sect as one which rejects it.

If such a typology appears intuitively use-ful in the present context, a glance at the six cases listed above reveals its inadequacy. The Nova Scotia Baptist bodies and Aberhardt's movement would be regarded as sects by Johnson (as well as by most other authors), but neither he nor anyone else would con-sider Catholicism a sect in Quebec or Para-guay. Further, in Wilson's (1970) typology of sects, the reformist and revolutionary types account for but a minority of cases; those sects which fall into his "introversionist,"

"manipulationist," and "thaumaturgical" categories manifest little interest in doing battle with their social environments, even while they prefer to isolate themselves from the outside world. It appears obvious that the various typologies, even those most congenial to the present purpose, fail to distinguish re-ligious bodies which assume an oppositional stance from those which do not.

Although these typologies may be useful for other purposes, two reasons may be noted for their failure to predict rebellion by a reli-gious body against its host society. First is that the typologies concern general and en-during organizational postures, while rebel-lion may be specific to a particular time and issue. Throughout most of Paraguayan or Quebec history, for example, the Catholic Church has played a supportive "churchly" role; this fact has not, however, prevented this religious body from shifting to an aggres-sive oppositional stance in appropriate cir-cumstances. Secondly, these typologies have been defined, at least for present purposes, too much on the basis of the professed belief systems of religious bodies and too little on the basis of actual organizational behavior. Religious sects which condemn the world are more often a safety-valve, channeling discon-tent in other-worldly directions, than they are a vehicle for attempting social change. In-deed, some such sects appear to act as instru-ments for the integration of their members into mainstream society (Johnson, 1961).

2. Orthodoxy

As mentioned earlier, orthodoxy has been treated in some micro-level studies as an at-tribute of persons, and related to orientation to social change. Orthodoxy can also be re-garded as an attribute of a religious body, however, a characteristic of its organizational ideology. By content-analyzing official theo-logical pronouncements or by assessing the beliefs of its ministers and other religious functionaries, a given religious body can be ranked high or low in orthodox beliefs. Using the latter method, Stark and Foster (1970) ordered American Protestant denominations along this dimension. The United Church of Christ and the Methodist and Episcopal Churches scored low in orthodoxy, while the Missouri Lutheran and Southern Baptist Churches were placed at the opposite end of the continuum.

A necessary or sufficient relationship between orthodoxy and oppositional stance, however, is no more in evidence at the organizational level than at the individual level. The fundamentalism of Aberhardt's Prophetic Bible Institute and of the Baptist sects in Nova Scotia was linked with aggressive action for change. A positive relationship between orthodoxy and oppositional stance is also suggested by Winter's argument (1974) that "liberal" theology in recent American Protestantism suggests not resistance but accommodation to contemporary managerial capitalism.

On the other hand are cases which suggest a negative relationship between these two variables. White (1970) contrasts the critical thrust of Protestant neo-orthodoxy with the supportive thrust of contemporary Mormon neo-orthodoxy. The dissident posture of the Catholic Church in Paraguay and other Latin countries coincided with a certain liberalization of that church's belief structure. Wood (1970), in analyzing the racial policies of 28 white American denominations, found the fundamentalist ones significantly *less* likely to criticize a segregated society. In contrast to its youth activist predecessor, the fundamentalist "Jesus People Movement" (see Balswick, 1974) was notably disinterested in seeking to effect social change.

The contradictory evidence concerning orthodoxy and stance toward change among religious bodies is clearest, perhaps, in the contrast of black and white Protestant fundamentalist denominations in the American South (see Johnson, 1967:441). The former supported the civil rights movement, the latter opposed it or remained uninvolved. In this case and in others, degree of orthodoxy of a religious body's theology is probably best regarded as irrelevant to the stance it assumes toward its host society, except that in particular circumstances, some supra-empirical beliefs may be appropriated as symbols of a certain orientation to change.

3. Locus of Control

Most formulations of the church-sect typology implicitly suggest that the sectarian emphasis on lay authority and on attention to the popular concerns of the membership accounts for the greater likelihood among sects of criticism of the social order. Hierarchical control of churches, by contrast, which insulates the policy-makers from the concerns of the membership, is posited as one determinant of the supportive role they are expected to play. Some evidence supports this contention. The radicalism of Baptist sects in early Nova Scotia was undoubtedly due in great part to the articulation in the policy of these religious bodies of the feelings of the exploitation among their lay members. The same is true in the case of the dissidence of prairie sects during the depression, of black sects during the American civil rights movement, and of various millennial movements (see Lanternari, 1965; Burridge, 1969). In a survey of clergy in Ohio in the late 1960s, Blume (1970) found those from congregationally-organized bodies more involved in a campaign for open housing than those from hierarchically-organized bodies. Historically, moreover, there is no shortage of examples (like the Catholic Church during the *ancien regime* in France, the Orthodox Church in Czarist Russia, or the Anglican Church in modern Canada) of religious bodies under hierarchical control pledging firm allegiance to the established order.

Recent research, however, suggests that hierarchical control in some instances is positively related to the adoption of an oppositional stance. The Catholic Church challenged norms of racial segregation in the United

States by integrating its parochial schools well before the Supreme Court ruled to that effect for public schools (Lamanna and Coakley, 1969). Wood (1970) showed that hierarchically-controlled denominations were far more aggressive in combatting racial discrimination than were congregational denominations under lay authority, even controlling for degree of fundamentalism. Wood (1972) has even shown evidence that implementation of integrationist values was dependent on the extent to which the denominational leadership was free of the constraining voice of the membership. McNamara attributed the success of New Mexico Catholic priests involved in anti-poverty programs to the church's polity structure, "which traditionally is not open to response from the laity" and which "enabled the priest directors to proceed regardless of opposition from conservative lay Catholics" (1969:699). These studies in the United States, as well as the dissidence cited earlier of the Catholic Church in Paraguay, demonstrate not only that the hierarchically-controlled religious body can assume an oppositional stance, but also that such a stance is sometimes assumed precisely because the hierarchy is not constricted by the voice of the lay membership.

As in the case of the church-sect distinction and degree of orthodoxy, locus of control appears to be unrelated to adoption of a stance of opposition by a religious body. If congregational control appears positively related to such a stance in one sub-set of cases, it is negatively related in a different sample. The conclusion must be that other variables than these distinguish aggressively dissident religious bodies from those which support the *status quo.*

4. *The Preferences of Dominant Groups*

Cyert and March (1959), in their behavioral model for the study of organizations, portray the organization as a coalition of a variety of groups, each with its own particular preferences. In the structure of most religious

bodies, a number of such groups may be discerned, including the membership at large, the lay leadership, the clergy, the clerical executive (for example, an episcopacy), the chief executive officer (pope, patriarch, moderator), staff agencies (like a religious education directorate or publications office), and special auxiliary organizations (religious orders, missionary groups). Each of these groups can be expected to hold particular goals and preferences, congruent with its structural position. If a religious body is viewed as a coalition of such groups, an explanation of its stance toward societal change necessarily begins with an examination of the internal structure of power and an attempt to ascertain which are the dominant members of the coalition. It is plausible to expect *that when the preferences of dominant groups would be served by societal change, the religious body will be directed to assume an oppositional stance toward the status quo.*

The general term *preferences* is purposely used in this hypothesis. There is no need here to enter into the debate over primacy of values or interests in explaining orientation to change, even though this distinction has been used in relevant research (Neal, 1965; Stewart, 1973). Probably the importance of narrower and shorter-range interests has received too little emphasis in explaining the behavior of sub-units of religious bodies. . . .

One need not assume, however, that narrow, short-range and selfish interests necessarily explain all the preferences of sub-units of a religious body. Indeed, career religious insulated from conventional life may direct their religious body toward a rebellion which ultimately costs them their followers and even their lives, for the sake of values in which they believe. Similarly, church executives who are loyal to what they believe is an eternal organization may lead it in a dissident direction, incurring immense short-range costs in the hope of long-range benefits. It is reasonable to expect that the lay membership, by virtue of its less complete absorption by the religious body and its more immediate involvement in the society at large, is supportive of an oppositional stance only when this stance promises to further more proximate economic and social interests. It is not necessary here to specify to which particular rewards the various sub-units of a religious body are most responsive. It is enough to point out that these awards vary across sub-units, because of their divergent social locations, that the preferences of clergy, laity, episcopacy and other constituent groups seldom coincide, and that the preferences of the dominant constituent groups are the critical determinant of the adoption by a religious body of an oppositional stance.

The hypothesis offered above also suggests the importance of careful empirical analysis of the internal structure of power in religious bodies, and the pitfalls of relying on official definitions of that structure. Takayama (1975: 26), in his study of 29 American Protestant denominations, found "a pervasive lack of close correspondence between the traditional definitions of authority and the realities of organizational power and interests." In particular, he noted the powerful role played by specialized departments at the central office of all three types of denomination, the congregational, presbyterian and episcopal (Winter, 1968, observed a similar phenomenon). In his study of the Catholic Church in Brazil, Bruneau (1973) found that the organizational complexity (that is, the presence of many sub-units, each with a modicum of power and its own preferences) of some dioceses prevented change-oriented bishops formally in control from implementing an oppositional policy. Mutchler's (1971) studies in Colombia and Chile document the power of "staff experts" in a Catholic Church officially under pure hierarchical control. The utility of traditional distinctions between congregational and hierarchical religious bodies need not be denied in order to insist that actual structures of power are seldom quite that simple.

If it is true that the preferences of domi-

nant groups are the critical determinant of an oppositional stance, this hypothesis should resolve the apparent contradictions reported in preceding parts of this section. In a brief survey, at least, the evidence points in this direction. In the Baptist sects of Nova Scotia, the Prophetic Bible Institute of Alberta, and in the black denominations of the American South more recently, a basically congregational structure was associated with an oppositional stance because the membership felt aggrieved by the existing social order and saw these religious bodies as a vehicle for changing it. In Wood's (1970) study of white denominations in the South, congregational structure was associated with a supportive stance toward racial segregation because in this case the membership perceived nothing to be gained from integration. In general, it appears reasonable to attribute radical activism by sect-like religious bodies not to their congregational locus of power, but rather to the fact that their members tend to come from disadvantaged sectors of the society and use the sectarian structure of power for their own ends.

The same hypothesis explains instances in which religious bodies under basically hierarchical control choose to rebel by analysis of the rewards rebellion offers to the hierarchy. Westhues (1973) has attributed the dissidence of the Paraguayan Catholic Church to pressures being felt by its bishops; having seen in Cuba and elsewhere what it cost the church to have supported a conservative, traditional dictatorship, the Paraguayan bishops considered that the church would benefit in the long run from opting for modernization early and opposing the conservative Stroessner regime. A similar argument is relevant to the case of the Quebec hierarchy's support for the Asbestos strike in 1949. Dion (1974:214) has written that "the Church saw clearly that the very survival of the Catholic trade union movement was at stake in the conflict." The Quebec bishops could ill afford to throw the weight of church support behind Duplessis and an American mining company when that support might bear the cost of an irretrievable loss to the church of the loyalty of Quebec labor. The constraints of the situation thus made it wholly rational for the bishops to abandon Duplessis and to organize the massive campaign to send food and supplies to the workers in Asbestos.

It thus appears that by examining the internal structure of power in religious bodies and the preferences of the dominant subunits, contradictory findings concerning the relationship of oppositional stance to the church-sect typology, to degree of orthodoxy and to locus of power are tentatively resolved. It is likely that these latter variables are spurious predictors of rebellion by a religious body and that the key predictor is the rewards rebellion offers to those who are in power.

5. Composition of the Membership

Even if hierarchically organized, no religious body is completely immune from the power of its membership; in most modern societies, religious bodies must rely on donations of members for the bulk of their income. Hence an explanation of why a church or sect assumes a rebellious posture must look specifically to characteristics of the membership, even if it occupies a minor place in the formal organizational structure of power. In this connection, Gusfield's (1962) theory of social movements is relevant. He distinguishes two conditions; in the first, "linked pluralism," intermediate associations cut across class and status lines, while in the second, "superimposed segmentation," the boundaries of these associations coincide with those of class and various status-groupings. Gusfield argues that the first condition inhibits the mobilization of an association in a dissident direction, while the second enhances the prospect of such mobilization. Since a religious body is one form of intermediate association, Gusfield's work suggests an hypothesis *that the more homogeneous is its membership with respect to the issues of potential conflict with the established order, the more likely is it to assume an oppositional stance.*

Two particular pieces of research on the stance of American religious bodies toward change bear directly on this hypothesis. Glock and Ringer (1956), in a study of the Protestant Episcopal Church, compared the official policy of the church with the attitudes of parishioners on various issues. They found that on issues where parishioners were relatively homogeneous, the church either took a strong stand or equivocated, but in any case the episcopal hierarchy did not directly challenge the views of the membership in articulating an official policy. In the second study, Hougland et al. (1974) found that the Methodist Church "submerged" its change-oriented goal of complete abstinence from liquor as its membership became less homogeneous in support of that goal. Faced with divided sentiment among its members on the temperance issue, the church continued to pay lip service to the cause while steadily reducing the resources spent on its behalf.

Sectarian bodies tend to have homogeneous memberships almost by definition. One *joins* a sect as opposed to being born into it, and such joining has been shown to occur largely because the convert perceives similarities between himself and those already members (Lofland and Stark, 1965). One of the reasons for the statistically higher frequency of rebellion by sects than by churches is undoubtedly the greater homogeneity among the members of sects. Churches, which admit members more by birth and family tradition than by choice, are more likely to find a plurality of classes and status groups in their memberships.

Nonetheless, cases were cited initially of the Catholic Church espousing an oppositional stance in the diocese of Antigonish, in Quebec and Paraguay. It is worth noting that in all three cases, there was a relatively homogeneous and powerless Catholic population under the domination of forces identified with non-Catholic outsiders. In eastern Nova Scotia during the depression, major economic control lay in the hands of non-local companies, whether American, British, or Upper Canadian. In the strike at Asbestos, the American Johns-Manville Company was pitted against the Quebec Catholic workers. In modern Paraguay, an American-supported military dictatorship is portrayed as the exploiter of honest, rural Catholic peasants.

Further, in all three cases one finds that key clerical and hierarchical leaders were of local origin and thus could identify with the lay membership. Moses Coady, a diocesan priest and leader of the Antigonish movement, was born on Cape Breton; the Paraguayan bishop who has led the fight against the government was born in the rural interior. All three locales are notable for the fact that the bulk of the clergy have been born and educated in the local area. In these cases, at least, relative homogeneity of the Catholic population and strong local ties of the clergy seemed to contribute to the adoption by a usually supportive religious body of an oppositional stance against the established order.

6. Theological Tradition

A final variable for explaining oppositional stance concerns qualitative characteristics of the religious body's belief system. The existence of competing preferences among various sub-units does not imply that there is not also a shared commitment to certain distinctive goals and values. If there is variance *within* religious bodies in the ideas held by constituent groups, there is also variance *between* religious bodies in the goals, values, beliefs and world-view which they represent. Theological tradition, as the term is used here, is a specific application to religious bodies of the more general concept of organizational constitution, the basic normative structure which defines its limits and goals (Zald, 1970; White, 1972a). Unlike the concept of orthodoxy, theological tradition does

not concern the degree of certitude with which certain beliefs are embraced but instead attributes of those beliefs themselves. It is expected *that the more at variance with a given social order is the theological tradition of a religious body, the more likely is it to assume an oppositional stance.*

Theoretical support for this hypothesis is offered by Hinings and Foster (1973), who have attempted to apply the conceptual apparatus of organizational sociology to churches; they argue that the analysis of churches differs from that of other organizations since, in the former case, causal priority must be assigned to charter goals and theology. Empirical support is suggested by Hammond (1974:185), who found a clear positive relationship between revivalism and anti-slavery politics in Ohio in the early nineteenth century and showed convincing evidence that "in these circumstances, religious belief had a direct effect on political behavior, because doctrine prescribed that a particular political choice was required by a believer's religious obligations." Similarly, McNamara attributed the successful maintenance of change-oriented roles by social action priests in New Mexico to "general Catholic acceptance of their activities as not incompatible with a traditional function of the church, bettering the lot of the poor" (1969:700).

It would be a mistake to try to deduce the social role a religious body will play directly from its theological tradition. Christian churches in Western history have deduced enough contradictory policies from the Scriptures to demonstrate the futility of such an exercise. Nonetheless, the pro-capitalist theme in the Protestant tradition (Weber, 1930), long-standing distrust of capitalism in the Catholic tradition, or the racial doctrines of the Mormon tradition (White, 1972b) should facilitate adoption of an oppositional stance in societies based on opposing beliefs, provided such a stance is perceived as rewarding to those groups which control the religious body involved. It is no accident, for example, that in the theology of the Antigonish movement (see Coady, 1939), in the posture of the contemporary church in Paraguay, as well as in the "theology of liberation" espoused widely by the Catholic Church in South America, the traditional anti-capitalist orientation of this church appears as the basis for criticism of social and economic arrangements.

Conclusion

The preceding section has analyzed a variety of instances of opposition by religious bodies to the social orders confronting them, for the purpose of defining those conditions which prompt such opposition. This analysis suggests that there is no necessary relationship between oppositional stance and the church-sect typology, degree of orthodoxy, or locus of control. The single most critical condition for explaining such a stance, one applicable to all the instances considered, was the potential rewards it offered to the dominant-group or groups within the religious body, in light of their own preferences. In a probabilistic sense, the analysis also suggested that the more homogeneous is the membership with respect to the issues of rebellion and the more at variance with the existing social order is the religious body's theological tradition, the more likely is the adoption of an oppositional stance.

Three weaknesses of this project should be pointed out in conclusion. First is that, although a wide range of data and research reports has been considered here, the instances of rebellion reviewed by no means constitute a random sample of all such instances. The hypotheses which help explain this sample of cases are not necessarily applicable to another sample; further research on other instances of espousal of change by religious bodies can test these hypotheses further. Secondly, it has not been my intention to offer a complete model for explaining why churches and sects sometimes mobilize their resources in favor of change. While additional studies will undoubtedly add other variables to the three suggested here, the outline offered in this article should at least point the way to a more detailed theoretical framework in the future. Thirdly, by limiting the dependent variable to oppositional stance itself, no effort has been made to explain under what conditions such a stance results in the change desired. The issue of effectiveness remains as an important focus for future research.

Notwithstanding these inadequacies, this article has been intended to demonstrate the utility of studies of religion and social change at the intermediary level of the religious body. It is an empirical fact that churches and sects sometimes espouse the cause of change. The most basic purpose of this essay has been to offer such espousal as a phenomenon to be explained, one which cannot be adequately researched at the macro-level of the society or the micro-level of the individual.

References

Balswick, J. 1974. "The Jesus People Movement: a Sociological Analysis." Pp. 359–66 in P. H. McNamara (ed.), *Religion American Style.* New York: Harper.
Becker, H. 1961 (first published 1932). "Four Types of Religious Organization." Pp. 252–55 in A. Etzioni (ed.), *Complex Organizations.* New York: Holt.
Blume, N. 1970. "Clergyman and Social Action." *Sociology and Social Research* 54:237–48.
Bruneau, T. C. 1973. "Obstacles to Change in the Church: Lessons from Four Brazilian Dioceses." *Journal of Inter-American Studies* 15:395–414.
Burridge, K. O. L. 1969. New Heaven New Earth. Toronto: Copp Clark.
Campbell, E. Q. and T. F. Pettigrew. 1959. Christians in Racial Crisis. Washington: Public Affairs.
Clark, S. D. 1945. "The Religious Sect in Canadian Politics." *American Journal of Sociology* 51:207–16.
1948. Church and Sect in Canada. University of Toronto Press.
Coady, M. M. 1939. Masters of Their Own Destiny. New York: Harper.
Cyert, R. M. and J. G. March. 1959. "A Behavioral Theory of Organizational Objectives." Pp. 76–90 in

M. Haire (ed.), *Modern Organization Theory*. New York: Wiley.

Demerath, N. J. III. 1961. "Social Stratification and Church Involvement: the Church-Sect Distinction Applied to Individual Participation." *Review of Religious Research* 2:146–54.

Dion, G. 1974. "The Church and the Conflict in the Asbestos industry." Pp. 205–26 in P. E. Trudeau (ed.), *The Asbestos Strike*. Toronto: James Lewis and Samuel.

Dynes, R. R. 1955. "Church-Sect Typology and Socioeconomic Status." *American Sociological Review* 20:555–60.

Garry, G. 1970. "The Asbestos Strike and Social Change in Quebec." Pp. 252–61 in W. E. Mann (ed.), *Social and Cultural Change in Canada* I. Toronto: Copp Clark.

Glock, C. Y. and B. B. Ringer. 1956. "Church Policy and the Attitudes of Ministers and Parishioners on Social Issues." *American Sociological Review* 21:148–56.

Goode, E. 1967. "Some Critical Observations on the Church-Sect Dimension." *Journal for the Scientific Study of Religion* 6:69–77.

Gusfield, J. R. 1962. "Mass Society and Extremist Politics." *American Sociological Review* 27:19–30.

Gustafson, P. M. 1967. "UO-US-PS-PO: a Restatement of Troeltsch's Church-Sect Typology." *Journal for the Scientific Study of Religion* 6:64–68. 1973. "Exegesis on the Gospel According to St. Max." *Sociological Analysis* 34:12–25.

Hammond, J. L. 1974. "Revival Religion and Antislavery Politics." *American Sociological Review* 39:175–86.

Hinings, C. R. and B. D. Foster. 1973. "The Organization Structure of Churches: a Preliminary Model." *Sociology* 7:93–105.

Hougland, J. G., J. R. Wood and S. A. Mueller, 1974. "Organizational 'Goal Submergence': The Methodist Church and the Failure of the Temperance Movement." *Sociology and Social Research* 58:408–16.

Johnson, B. 1957. "A Critical Appraisal of the Church-Sect Typology." *American Sociological Review* 22:88–92. 1961. "Do Holiness Sects Socialize in Dominant Values? *Social Forces* 39:309–16. 1963. "On Church and Sect." *American Sociological Review* 28:539–49. 1967. "Theology and the Position of Pastors on Public Issues." *American Sociological Review* 32:433–42.

Laidlaw, A. F. 1971. The Man From Margaree. Toronto: McClelland, Stewart.

Lamanna, R. A. and J. J. Coakley. 1969. "The Catholic Church and the Negro." Pp. 147–94 in P. Gleason (ed.), *Contemporary Catholicism in the United States*. Notre Dame University Press.

Lanternari, V. 1965. The Religions of the Oppressed. New York: Mentor.

Lofland, J. and R. Stark. 1965. "Becoming a World-Saver: a Theory of Conversion to a Deviant Perspective." *American Sociological Review* 30:862–75.

Mann, W. E. 1955. Sect, Cult and Church in Alberta. University of Toronto Press.

McNamara, P. H. 1969. "Priests, Protests, and Poverty Intervention." *Social Science Quarterly* 50:695–702.

Moore, W. E. 1963. Social Change. Englewood Cliffs: Prentice-Hall.

Mutchler, D. E. 1971. The Church as a Political Factor in Latin America. New York: Praeger.

Neal, M. A. 1965. Values and Interests in Social Change. Englewood Cliffs: Prentice-Hall.

Niebuhr, H. R. 1929. The Social Sources of Denominationalism. New York: Henry Holt.

Osborne, W. A. 1967. The Segregated Covenant. New York: Herder. 1969. "The Church as a Social Organization." Pp. 33–50 in P. Gleason (ed.), *Contemporary Catholicism in the United States*. Notre Dame University.

Pope, L. 1942. Millhands and Preachers. New Haven: Yale.

Stark, R. and B. D. Foster. 1970. "In Defense of Orthodoxy: Note on the Validity of an Index." *Social Forces* 48:38–93.

Stark, W. 1967. The Sociology of Religion (Volume Two). London: Routledge.

Stewart, J. H. 1973. "Values, Interests, and Organizational Change: the National Federation of Priests' Councils." *Sociological Analysis* 34, 4:281–95.

Takayama, K. P. 1975. "Formal Polity and Change of Structure: Denominational Assemblies." *Sociological Analysis* 36, 1:17–28.

Troeltsch, E. 1931. The Social Teaching of the Christian Churches (volume two). New York: Macmillan.

Wach, J. 1944. Sociology of Religion. Chicago: University of Chicago Press.

Weber, M. 1930. The Protestant Ethic and the Spirit of Capitalism. New York: Scribner's.

Westhues, K. 1973. "The Established Church as an Agent of Change." *Sociological Analysis* 34, 2:106–23. 1975. "Curses versus Blows: Tactics in Church-State Conflict." *Sociological Analysis* 36, 1:1–16.

White, O. K. 1970. "The Transformation of Mormon Theology," *Dialogue* 5:9–24. 1972a. "Constituting Norms and the Formal Organization of American Churches." *Sociological Analysis* 33, 2:95–109. 1972b. "Mormonism's Anti-Black Policy and Prospects for Change." *Journal of Religious Thought* 29:39–60.

Wilson, B. R. 1959. "An Analysis of Sect Development." *American Sociological Review* 24:3–15. 1970. Religious Sects. New York: McGraw-Hill.

Winter, G. 1968. Religious Identity. New York: Macmillan.

Winter, J. A. 1974. "Elective Affinities Between Religious Beliefs and Ideologies of Management in Two Eras." *American Journal of Sociology* 79:1134–50.

Wood, J. R. 1970. "Authority and Controversial Policy: the Churches and Civil Rights." *American Sociological Review* 35:1057–69. 1972. "Personal Commitment and Organizational Constraint: Church Officials and Racial Integration." *Sociological Analysis* 33, 3:142–51.

Zald, M. N. 1970. Organizational Change: the Political Economy of the YMCA. University of Chicago Press.

R E A D I N G   7 . 3

Evangelical Life Style Concerns Expressed in Political Action

Louise J. Lorentzen

Introduction

During the past half century, the majority of evangelical Christians have remained theologically and socially conservative and, with few exceptions, politically uninvolved. Their traditional approach to alleviating social problems has been evangelism aimed at individual regeneration rather than political action aimed at structural change. Although appeals for involvement in the political process have come from highly visible evangelicals, seldom have they stirred a participant audience. Only in the past decade, some indications of activism have emerged among a small minority of evangelicals who affirm a more liberal theology and life style (Gerstner, 1975; Linder, 1975; Marsden, 1975; Moberg, 1972; Pierard, 1970; Quebedeaux, 1978).

In this context, the race for the 1978 Democratic nomination for a U.S. Senate seat from Virginia is of considerable interest. This race was marked by the unprecedented involvement of evangelical Christians in Virginia state politics. In all, eight aspirants contended for the support of 2,795 convention delegates chosen at local mass meetings throughout the state. One of these aspirants, an evangelical Christian, was a newcomer to state politics and the Democratic party who announced his candidacy for the nomination only eight weeks before the mass meetings. Yet, in that brief time, he was able to secure 330 convention delegates, placing him third in the bid for the nomination. This 12 percent of the total number of delegates fell far short of establishing this evangelical candidate as a viable contender for the nomination. However, the relative success of his campaign is noteworthy because of (1) the brevity of the campaign effort, (2) the unique appeal based on the candidate's character and reputation as a Christian leader rather than his position on specific political issues, (3) the open solicitation of support from the ranks of evangelical church groups, and (4) the unprecedented response from those of evangelical faith who were unschooled and inexperienced in political activism.

Initial indications suggested that evangelicals who participated in the campaign were quite conservative in their stance on issues of

Louise J. Lorentzen is Research Assistant at the School of Nursing, University of Virginia.

Reprinted from *Sociological Analysis* 41 (Summer, 1980), with permission.

Table 1 *Summary Results of Virginia Delegate Survey—Delegate Position on Issues of Life Style and Morality*

Issue	Favor (%)	Oppose (%)	Undecided (%)
Equal Rights Amendment			
Republicans	21	70	9
Democrats (excluding evangelical delegates)	66	24	10
Evangelical candidate delegates	4	90	6
Death Penalty for First Degree Murder			
Republicans	73	11	16
Democrats (excluding evangelical delegates)	38	45	17
Evangelical candidate delegates	55	18	27
Decriminalization of Marijuana			
Republicans	26	59	16
Democrats (excluding evangelical delegates)	54	30	16
Evangelical candidate delegates	7	87	6
Abortion Funding for Women on Welfare			
Republicans	35	54	11
Democrats (excluding evangelical delegates)	58	30	12
Evangelical candidate delegates	1	93	6
Affirmative Action Quotas			
Republicans	6	86	8
Democrats (excluding evangelical delegates)	27	55	19
Evangelical candidate delegates	13	70	16

Source: Abramowitz et al., 1978:14–15. This table has been amended from a more extensive table presented by Abramowitz, McGlennon, and Rapoport in an unpublished paper, "Summary Results of the Virginia Delegate Survey" (1978). Percentages are based on the numbers of respondents indicated above.

Note: Thus the response rate at the Democratic Convention was only 481 of the possible 2,795 delegates (17 percent), and at the Republican Convention, only 455 of the 7,800 delegates (6 percent). Though the biases inherent in this data collection procedure are obvious, the results do give some indication of the stance of the state-wide evangelical contingent.

life style and morality, more conservative than other Democrats and often more conservative than Republicans (see Table 1).[1] Conservatism in life style has generally been associated with conservative theology and a lack of involvement in political activism among evangelicals. This incongruity between the traditional stance of noninvolvement and the recent activism of seemingly conservative evangelicals prompted this case study. The objective of the research was to ascertain who, by theological conviction and life style characteristics, participated in this political action, how they were motivated, and what was the nature of their goals. This information would lead to an assessment of whether participation in this campaign was an anomaly or a bellwether of change in the orientation of evangelicals to politics.

Political Participation in a Theoretical Context

Because of the conservatism in belief and life style found among these evangelicals and the social bases of support developed by the candidate, the explanations for this unprecedented movement into politics are set within the framework of the theory of status politics. This approach is in contrast to most theories, which premise economic motivations for political movements. The theory of status politics has evolved from the distinction

Weber made between class and status group orientations.

According to Weber, there exist within a community a social order and an economic order, each possessing potential to influence the other. The economic order is defined by the participation of various groups (classes) in the distribution of material resources and the knowledge of their use. In contrast, groups defined by the distribution of prestige characterize the social order. Status is derived from the degree of prestige (termed variously social honor or social esteem) accorded by the community to the group based on some specific shared quality of that group. Such qualities, taken collectively, characterize a particular life style. A similar life style can be expected of all who belong or wish to belong to a group. Closure of the group is thus achieved, and the exclusiveness of membership is dependent on the ability to display the necessary qualifications for membership (Weber, 1946:187–91).

Though a group may be accorded prestige based on the possession of material resources, this is but one quality which characterizes a group; as such, material wealth need not be present in order for a group to achieve status (Weber, 1946:187). Prestige is accorded to a group in varying positive or negative degrees depending on the perceived worthiness or valuation of the elements which define the group—elements such as "values, beliefs, consumption habits, and the cultural items differentiating nonclass groups from each other" (Gusfield, 1963:18). A hierarchical arrangement of groups is based on the amount of prestige received. Placement in the hierarchy of status groups (like that of social classes) determines how members of a specific group will approach and be approached in social interaction, thus reflecting the relative power of the group.

In both the economic and the social order, power is defined as the probability of given individuals or groups "to realize their own will in a communal action even against the

resistance of others who are participating in the action" (Weber, 1946:180). Thus, power may be exerted by a group—either a class or a status group—to influence the distribution of material resources or the distribution of prestige, respectively.

Using Weber's definition of status and status group orientations, Richard Hofstadter and Seymour Martin Lipset were early contributors (during the 1950s) to the development of the theory of status politics in their explanations of support for the Progressive Movement, the Ku Klux Klan, and McCarthyism. Each of these groups was seen as attempting to affect the distribution of prestige, and thus of power. In 1963, Gusfield further developed this explanation of political conflict in his treatment of the American Temperance Movement in the volume, *Symbolic Crusade*. In his work, Gusfield pointed out the symbolic nature of specific conflicts aimed at restoring, maintaining, or enhancing the prestige of a particular life style.

More recent works, such as those of Zurcher et al. (1971) and Page and Clelland (1978), have amended the theory still further to explain political struggles over moral principles and the protection of life style. Respectively, these analyses dealt with a controversy over acceptable textbooks and a conflict over distribution of pornographic materials.

Change in perspective is apparent in the contemporary use of the theory of status politics. Emphasis is now placed on life style protection rather than on status enhancement. Because particular life styles are accorded varying degrees of prestige and the relative amount of prestige received determines a given group's status, it is apparent that status is indeed defined by society's valuation of a particular life style. Thus, Page and Clelland do not see status politics as "the attempt to defend against declining prestige but the attempt to defend a way of life" (Page and Clelland, 1978:266). They state, "style of life can be maintained or propagated only to the extent that its adherents exercise some control over the means of socialization and social intercourse" (Page and Clelland, 1978:267). This attempt to defend a way of life is readily apparent in the motivations of Progressives, Ku Klux Klanners, McCarthyites, Prohibitionists, and opponents of pornography.

The issues around which such groups rally in an attempt to protect a life style are often symbolic; that is, they are relatively narrow in scope but stand for a larger whole. This is not out of keeping with political conflicts in the economic sphere. Control of the influences that bear upon the maintenance of a life style is essential, yet an issue relatively narrow in scope may stand for and serve to reinforce a way of life—a system of belief. Conflicts come as a result of attempts by opposing groups "to build and sustain moral orders which provide basic meaning for human lives" (Page and Clelland, 1978:279). "Protestors are expressing a direct concern about the erosion of their control over their way of life" (265). Page and Clelland, thus, have replaced the term "status politics" with "the politics of life style concerns," a term more aptly descriptive of the expressed motivations for such movements (Page and Clelland, 1978:266–267).

Clarification of the concepts—status, prestige, and life style[2]—and their use in this context leads to an ease of application and a better understanding of non-economic political movements. In those earlier analyses that focused on status discontent as the motivating factor of such movements, it was necessary to document a perception of and threat to the status of a group as well as a motivation to enhance or preserve that status. In later analyses of such movements, focus on life style rather than on status facilitated the identification of motivations in empirical analyses. Participants in what have been called status movements perceive and verbalize their actions as a means of protecting their life style rather than their status. A primary concern with the preservation of a life style is appa-

rent in all the descriptions of non-economic political movements.

That a dominant life style is accorded greater prestige, and thus higher status, cannot be denied. That placement in the status hierarchy also influences the power of a given group is apparent. However, in the social realm, life style is the exogenous variable with prestige, status, and power dependent thereupon. To focus on status is theoretically to put the cart before the horse and expect locomotion.

Thus, life style concern is the *motivating factor*, and preservation and protection of a life style are the *goals* of non-economic political movements. As such, these goals are instrumental in nature. The *tactics* employed to reach the goal of life style protection may be either *instrumental*, oriented directly at protecting or defending a life style, or *symbolic*, representing the many instances and circumstances that call for action but are not directly connected to the goal.

The subject of the present research is a conservative group, previously inactive in politics, which recently entered the political arena. It was hypothesized that the motivation for such action was concern over the preservation of a life style and, further, that the goal of this action was life style protection. In this instance, merely to place a representative in political office is to employ a tactic which symbolically legitimates a way of life. Conversely, to expect such a representative purposely to effect legislation is to employ an instrumental tactic to bring about accomplishment of the goal—life style protection.

Sampling Procedure and Description of Respondents

Interviews were conducted with supporters of the evangelical candidate who attended two local mass meetings—one in a city and one in a county district in Virginia. One hundred and thirty-six registered voters who attended these meetings declared their support for the evangelical candidate; subsequently 13 were elected as delegates to the State Nominating Convention. In-depth, personal interviews with 12 of these 13 delegates yielded the qualitative data that is the basis of this research. In addition, telephone interviews were solicited with a 50 percent random sample (N=62) of individuals selected from among the remaining mass meeting attendees who declared their support for the evangelical candidate. Among these persons, 55 interviews were completed, an 89 percent response rate. These telephone interviews provided the quantitative data in support of the qualitative findings. For ease in future reporting, these two samples will be referred to as the "delegate sample" and the "mass sample." Significant differences between samples are explained to allow a qualitative analysis supported by the findings from the quantitative sample.

In age, education, income, socio-economic status,[3] marital status and number of children per family, no significant difference between the delegate and mass samples was found. There was, however, a significant difference in sex between the two samples. Ninety-two percent of the delegate sample was male, 8 percent female (N=12); 49 percent of the mass sample was male, 51 percent female (N=55). The predominance of males

as delegates supports the traditional view of the male leadership role which would be expected among conservative evangelicals (Quebedeaux, 1978:77–78).

One further difference in life style was found significant: the length of residence in one's neighborhood (see Table 2). Though the indication is that delegates were a more geographically mobile group, this has little bearing on this research. With these two exceptions—sex and length of residence—no differences between the samples on demographic or life style characteristics were found.

No significant difference in theological belief was found between the delegate sample and the mass sample; however, those in the delegate sample were more inclined to witness their faith for the purpose of converting others than were those in the mass sample. The leadership role in which delegates were cast is likely associated with the ability to influence others. This may explain the difference found.

A significant difference was found between the samples on an index of political knowledge. Individuals in the delegate sample tended to be more knowledgeable of those in political office; however, the experience of having been a delegate may have influenced this.

One further difference was found between

Table 2 *Sample Differences*

	Delegate Sample			Mass Sample			
	Mean	s.d.	N	Mean	s.d.	N	Difference
Age	34.6 yrs.	10.79	12	34.1 yrs.	11.22	55	t=.14, p=.89
Education	16.5 yrs.	3.00	12	15.3 yrs.	2.72	53	t=1.33, p=.23
Income	$20,333	162.56	12	$15,424	99.08	53	t=1.0, p=.33
Socioeconomic status	59	17.25	12	49	27.92	54	t=1.2, p=.12
Children per family	1.6	1.51	10	2.0	1.98	44	t=.67, p=.49
Length of neighborhood residence	1.6 yrs.	1.58	12	4.2 yrs.	4.18	55	t=−2.38, p=<.01
	% of Respondents			% of Respondents			
Sex	92% male			49% male			
	8% female	N=12		51% female	N=55		X^2=5.64, df=1, p=.02
Marital status	83% married			70% married			
	17% unmarried	N=12		30% unmarried	N=55		X^2=1.63, df=4, p=.80

the samples: they varied in reasons for attending the mass meeting. This difference is related to the process by which individuals became delegates. Those in the delegate sample were more likely to have had personal contact with the candidate, and this was their reason for attending the mass meeting.

Life Style Orientation

The common denominator among those who participated in the subject political action was their adherence to an evangelical faith—that is, they believe in the full authority of the Scriptures, the necessity of a conversion experience as a means to salvation, and the necessity of evangelism. This belief system provides for evangelicals an organization of life. In relating their experience before coming to evangelicalism, respondents described a search for spirituality and an ethical orientation to life which was fulfilled upon conversion to this faith. *Rebirth is a reorientation to life* guided by faith, as well as a means to salvation.

Unity among this group outweighed a diversity of affiliation and evangelical orientation. While some belonged to evangelical factions within denominational churches—Baptist, Episcopal, Mennonite, and Presbyterian—the vast majority, 82 percent (N=55), belonged to nondenominational bodies. Within the nondenominational bodies were charismatics as well as conservative evangelicals. The diversity in affiliation and orientation was not met with a well-defined separation of identity among these evangelicals. All those of an evangelical faith are identified as "believers." Friendships cut across denominational and nondenominational affiliations, and ties of association are maintained through religiously-oriented social contacts. These ties and a common evangelical faith contributed to a collective identity which superseded variation in affiliation and orientation and thus provided a common base for concerted political action.

Those from denominational groups accounted for the few instances of more liberal theological interpretation. Those from the nondenominational groups were conservative as indicated by a literal interpretation of the Bible and a creationist view of the origins of man. Given that the majority of these individuals were of a nondenominational affiliation, a conservative theological interpretation was most pervasive.

Conservatism in theological belief was accompanied, as expected, by an individualistic approach to social problems: 85 percent (N=55) of the respondents emphasized evangelism aimed at individual regeneration as a solution to social ills. This approach to social concern does not explain the movement into political action. However, since conversion to the evangelical faith brings a reorientation to life in the present, a conservative life style based on theological belief is affirmed. It becomes important to these individuals to maintain and protect their life style. The possibility to "live well as far as faith is concerned" provides a key to explaining political action on the part of theologically conservative evangelicals.

Solidarity and commitment to the evangelical faith and life style were maintained through the structure and frequency of social interaction among members of these evangelical groups. All respondents reported attending church services weekly, and in 35 percent (N=55) of the cases, two to three times a week. Sixty-one percent (N=55) of the respondents reported also meeting in smaller groups for Bible study and prayer meetings. One respondent aptly described how these smaller groups strengthen commitment. He stated that interaction

has to be in small groups because if you belong to anything big, . . . a lot is lost. . . . But in the smaller group—seven, eight, or ten people that meet all the time—it's a family. When someone is hurting, you can't deny that you know it. There's a commitment here to one another. This is the family structure, not the biological family, but a family . . . and the responsibilities of the family are there. Then, of course, we share to the larger family—[the congregation]. But if you don't belong to a very small family, you have no commitment.

The analogy to the family and the dependence and acceptance found therein was used frequently by evangelicals in describing the individuals and groups to which they are committed.

Sixty-five percent of the respondents also reported attending such religiously-oriented social groups as Christian Women's Club, Women Aglow, and Full Gospel Business Men's Fellowship. Eighty-three percent (N=55) reported that half or more of their social activities were church-related. A moderately high association (r_s=.37, p=.01, N=53) was found between the degree to which social activities were church-related and close friends were of the same faith—further evidence that such interaction enhanced the development of a close-knit group of persons of similar social and religious orientation.

The impact of social change in the secular culture of America was also an influence on these evangelicals and, in many instances, was a cause for deep concern. Such concern centered especially on the pervasiveness of liberal influences that come to bear on the family.

The ideal family was seen as a close-knit unit in which husband and wife assume traditional roles. As one respondent explained the basis of this relationship:

God has set up a God-ordained authority structure where God is the head of Christ, Christ is the head of man, and man is the head of woman. . . . The man is ordained by God to be the head of the home, of the household, of the family unit; and this is the system that works best for human society.

Variation in the interpretation of this "ideal" authority structure existed. However, the influence of this traditional model based on theological principles was apparent regard-

less of interpretation. Also, conservatism concerning the female role was more readily apparent within this group than it is among the population as a whole. Respondents were asked four questions from a national survey concerning the changing role of women (Anonymous, 1979). Though 53 percent (N=35) of these couples included an employed wife, these evangelicals were more likely than the population as a whole to see a wife's primary role as that of mother and homemaker. They were also more apt than the general population to perceive deleterious effects to children when the mother is employed. Though a move away from the traditional roles of wife as homemaker and husband as breadwinner may be seen even within this conservative group, such a trend is problematic to a group trying to maintain a traditional family structure based on scriptural principles.

Apprehension and even outrage were expressed at the influences that bear upon children. The family is not only a protective environment in which to rear children, but it is also the stage for socialization to the evangelical faith. Secular influences, at times, were seen as contrary to this process, especially those influences that are institutionalized in the public schools. As related by a respondent, this concern centered around

prohibiting the name of God to be mentioned in schools, prayers and Bible reading out of the schools. . . . requiring secular humanism to be taught in schools—that man is able to meet all his own needs, [is] self-sufficient. It exalts the man!

These evangelicals exhibited only a moderate affirmation of such secular activities as dancing, consumption of alcohol, and use of tobacco. They opposed gambling and the use of marijuana and were adamant in their stand against abortion. Indignation was expressed over the perceived implications and possible effects on the family of the Equal Rights Amendment.

The life style of these evangelicals was

centered on church and family and was seen as different from that of others. This difference, however, was seen as a key to the betterment of self and society. As one respondent related,

believers are going to have different behaviors—they are going to be different. I think that an example that the Lord used that we are the salt of the earth is certainly appropriate. I think as we live the believing life that we're going to have an influence on the country, as a preservative in terms of the moral climate and also as a flavoring in terms of just making the country still acceptable in terms of the Lord's sights.

The necessity of preserving the moral climate of America is, in effect, a means of preserving a life style, the evangelical life style. Much in the secular culture of America is at odds with the evangelical stance, especially the moral atmosphere and philosophies upon which it is based. In addition, many sociopolitical issues under consideration and many legislative actions were seen as symbolically supporting a more liberal life style. One respondent stated:

I feel as if the country is drifting away from the principles and stances that have in the past made it a strong country. I think that the Senate, especially the Senate, has gotten very liberal in their leanings and their philosophy.

This view was echoed by another:

there's a whole attitude in the country now that there is no right and wrong, that if it feels good, . . . then that's up to you. There's a breakdown of some sort of an ethic, and it's becoming a situation ethic type of thing. I think there needs to be a very strong Christian stance toward that type of attitude that I feel is pervading.

And yet a third respondent stated:

In evangelical Christianity, there is a strong, strong concern . . . for the state of the nation.

It is with this background that evangelical Christians approached the political arena in support of a candidate of like orientation.

Movement into Political Activism

The participants who actively supported the evangelical candidate were Republicans, Democrats, and independent voters, although a Republican influence was most pervasive. Forty-five percent (N=49) identified themselves as Republicans or reported a tendency to vote Republican. Twenty-nine percent reported Democratic orientations, and 26 percent identified themselves as completely independent. As one respondent explained,

basically [evangelical] Christians are conservative in terms of their political belief and would normally tend to favor a Republican candidate who would be labeled conservative.

This observation was further supported by self-identification: 38 percent (N=52) identified themselves as conservative, 31 percent as middle-of-the-road, and only 10 percent felt they were liberal or radical in their political orientations. The remaining 21 percent of the respondents stated they did not know how to classify themselves.

Delegates from across the state who supported the evangelical candidate displayed a similar pattern of conservatism in political orientation, especially on morally-laden political issues. They were often more conservative even than Republicans. Yet the evangelical candidate's supporters aligned themselves with the Democratic party though many had tended toward a Republican orientation on issues and in previous partisan identification. This suggests that their motive was more the means by which they might put an evangelical in office than their agreement with the stance of the party under whose banner their candidate ran.

These evangelicals had very little prior experience in active support of a political candidate. Furthermore, only 45 percent (N=55) reported "usually"[4] voting in national, state, and local elections during the past three years, as compared to 70 percent (N=2549) in a national sample (Verba and Nie, 1972). An anomaly in the evangelical group's pattern of low political participation is that 36 percent of this group reported contacting elected representatives about problems or issues of concern; this is almost three times the rate found in the national sample. The evangelicals' contacts related to morally-laden issues such as abortion, curricula and prayer in schools, and the Equal Rights Amendment. This, indeed, is an indication of concern that existed prior to the present political action and, in part, explains the ease with which this group was mobilized.

As indicated, this group of evangelicals exhibited conservatism in theological and social orientations. They saw themselves as apart from the mainstream of secular culture and exhibited considerable solidarity within their group. Concern was expressed over decline in moral standards and the consequent influences that bear on the evangelical life style. Though numerous attempts had been made to influence the stand of elected representatives, these evangelicals had not been active in support of candidates for elected office.

This background of conservatism, concern, and non-involvement was utilized in gaining their support. The candidate whom they supported not only possessed a faith and social orientation similar to theirs but also presented himself as a political novice with a calling to duty. He identified evangelicals' lack of involvement in politics as the reason they are unable to control the influences that are a source of their concern. He also educated them in the political process by which they might make their voices heard.

This appeal for active involvement was combined with a system of outreach to the evangelical community that utilized the existing structure of evangelical social contacts. Given that this is a close-knit group of similar orientation, few initial contacts were necessary to develop a considerable basis of support in a short period of time. The effectiveness of using this social network to de-

velop support can be seen in that 84 percent (N=55) of supporters at the mass meetings learned of the candidate through church and friends. Cassette tapes announcing the candidacy and the political process necessary for support were sent to church groups; however, these tapes and conventional media sources had much less effect.

This candidate's appeal for involvement was received by evangelicals trying to maintain a traditional, morally conservative life style—who express concern over governmental actions that legitimate and, through their symbolic connotation, give greater prestige to a more liberal element of American society. In a "symbolic crusade" aimed at preserving the life style to which they are committed, the tactic of these evangelicals was to place a representative of like orientation in a position of political prestige and power in order that he might bring recognition to their values. Fifty-nine percent (N=55) of those who supported this evangelical candidate hoped only that he would bring a "Christian influence" to bear; 27 percent anticipated that he might bring "integrity" and "a moral influence" to government. Only 10 percent voiced a desire for legislative action, and 4 percent for responsible government. In the possibility to bring a morally conservative "Christian influence" to government is the possibility to legitimate and protect the conservative evangelical life style.

Though the candidate did not win the nomination, the success of the movement was apparent to those who participated. In a short period of time evangelicals had rallied and effectively made an impact on the political sphere. And, while only 9 percent (N=55) had ever participated in such an action previously, 71 percent (N=55) stated they will again work for the election of a political representative. Their efforts now are aimed at educating evangelicals state-wide on how to continue involvement. The basis of political activism has been laid; a course of future participation appears probable. Thus, the success of this movement appears to be not an anomaly but a precursor to continued political involvement by evangelicals.

Conclusion

The 1978 race for a U.S. Senator from Virginia saw the onset of political activism among previously uninvolved, conservative evangelical Christians. The seeds of activism were sown during the past decades as the divergence in social orientation between this traditionally-oriented group and the more liberal secular culture became more apparent. A perceived decline in morals and the perception of legislative issues that symbolically support a more liberal element of American society have motivated evangelicals of various orientations—non-denominational as well as denominational, conservative as well as charismatic—to this concerted political activism. In a symbolic crusade aimed at preserving the life style to which they are committed, the tactic of these evangelicals was to place a representative of like orientation in a position of political prestige and power in order that he might bring a "Christian influence" and "high moral standards" to bear. In this was seen the possibility to preserve the moral climate of America and, in so doing, legitimate and protect the conservative evangelical life style.

Notes

1. The Virginia Delegate Survey was administered at both the Republican and Democratic Nominating Conventions by Professors Alan Abramowitz, John McGlennon and Ronald Rapoport of the College of William and Mary. Questionnaires were "distributed at the respective convention halls to each city and county delegation based on the number of convention votes which the delegation would cast (Abramowitz, et al., 1978:2–3). No attempt was made to follow up on unreturned questionnaires.

2. These concepts are well defined by Zurcher et al., 1971: " 'Social status' refers to the distribution of prestige among individuals and groups in a social

system. 'Prestige' means the approval, respect, admiration, or deference a person or group is able to command by virtue of his or its imputed qualities of performances. 'Style of life' refers to the system of values, customs, and habits distinctive to a . . . group."

3. A socioeconomic status score was computed using the Duncan Socioeconomic Status index (SEI) (Featherman, et al., 1975) based on Bureau of Census occupational codes. A family SEI score was computed using the respondent's SEI score if unmarried, the husband's score when married, and the wife's score when married with the husband unemployed. The possible range of these scores was 3 to 96.

4. That is, they voted 75 percent or more of the time, missing no more than one voting opportunity in the past three years.

References

Abramowitz, Alan, John McGlennon, and Ronald Rapoport. 1978. Summary results of Virginia delegate survey. Unpublished Paper.

Anonymous. 1979. "Opinion roundup—the modern woman: how far has she come?" *Public Opinion*, (January/February):35–40.

Featherman, David L., Michael Sabel and David Dickens. 1975. A manual for coding occupations and industries into detailed 1970 categories and a listing of 1970 basic Duncan socioeconomic and NORC prestige scores, working paper #75-1. Unpublished paper. University of Wisconsin.

Gerstner, John M. 1975. "The theological boundaries of evangelical faith." Pp. 21–37 in David F. Wells and John D. Woodbridge (eds.), *The Evangelicals*. Nashville, Tenn.: Abingdon Press.

Gusfield, Joseph R. 1963. Symbolic Crusade: Status Politics and the American Temperance Movement. Urbana: University of Illinois Press. 1963. "Pseudoconservative revolt revisited: a postscript (1962)." Pp. 97–103 in Daniel Bell (ed.), *The Radical Right: The New American Right Expanded and Updated*. Garden City, New York: Doubleday.

Linder, Robert D. 1975. "The resurgence of evangelical social concern (1925–75)." Pp. 189–210 in David F. Wells and John D. Woodbridge (eds.), *The Evangelicals*. Nashville, Tenn.: Abingdon Press.

Marsden, George M. 1975. "From fundamentalism to evangelicalism: a historical analysis." Pp. 122–42 in David F. Wells and John Woodbridge (eds.), *The Evangelicals*. Nashville, Tenn.: Abingdon Press.

Moberg, David O. 1972. The Great Reversal: Evangelism Versus Social Concern. Philadelphia: J. B. Lippincott Co.

Page, Ann L. and Donald A. Clelland. 1978. "The Kanawha County textbook controversy: a study of the politics of life style concern." *Social Forces*, 57:265–81.

Pierard, Richard B. 1970. The Unequal Yoke: Evangelical Christianity and Political Conservatism. Philadelphia: Lippincott.

Quebedeaux, Richard. 1978. The Worldly Evangelicals. New York: Harper & Row.

Verba, Sidney and Norman H. Nie. 1972. Participa-
tion in America: Political Democracy and Social Equality. New York: Harper & Row.

Weber, Max. 1946. From Max Weber: Essays in Sociology. (Eds. and Trans.) H. H. Gerth and C. Wright Mills. New York: Oxford.

Zurcher, Louis A., Jr., *et al.* 1971. "The anti-pornography campaign: a symbolic crusade." *Social Problems*, 19:217–38.

S E L E C T I O N   7 . A

From The Pastoral Letter on War and Peace

The Catholic Bishops of America

[This reading is not a summary of *The Pastoral Letter on War and Peace*. It is a brief excerpt intended to illustrate the engagement of religious teaching with current policy issues. The entire letter should be read to understand the full context in which the bishops address a very complex set of issues.]

"The whole human race faces a moment of supreme crisis in its advance toward maturity." Thus the Second Vatican Council opened its treatment of modern warfare.[1] Since the council, the dynamic of the nuclear arms race has intensified. Apprehension about nuclear war is almost tangible and visible today. As Pope John Paul II said in his message to the United Nations concerning disarmament: "Currently the fear and preoccupation of so many groups in various parts of the world reveal that people are more frightened about what would happen if irresponsible parties unleash some nuclear war."[2]

As bishops and pastors ministering in one of the major nuclear nations, we have encountered this terror in the minds and hearts of our people—indeed, we share it. We write this letter because we agree that the world is at a moment of crisis, the effects of which are

evident in people's lives. It is not our intent to play on fears, however, but to speak words of hope and encouragement in time of fear. Faith does not insulate us from the challenges of life; rather, it intensifies our desire to help solve them precisely in light of the good news which has come to us in the person of Jesus, the Lord of history. From the resources of our faith we wish to provide hope and strength to all who seek a world free of the nuclear threat. Hope sustains one's capacity to live with danger without being overwhelmed by it; hope is the will to struggle against obstacles even when they appear insuperable. Ultimately our hope rests in the God who gave us life, sustains the world by his power and has called us to revere the lives of every person and all peoples.

The crisis of which we speak arises from this fact: Nuclear war threatens the existence of our planet; this is a more menacing threat than any the world has known. It is neither tolerable nor necessary that human beings live under this threat. But removing it will require a major effort of intelligence, courage and faith. As Pope John Paul II said at Hiroshima: "From now on it is only through a conscious choice and through a deliberate policy that humanity can survive."[3]

As Americans, citizens of the nation which was first to produce atomic weapons, which has been the only one to use them and which today is one of the handful of nations capable of decisively influencing the course of the nuclear age, we have grave human, moral and political responsibilities to see that a "conscious choice" is made to save humanity.

This letter is therefore both an invitation and a challenge to Catholics in the United States to join with others in shaping the conscious choices and deliberate policies required in this "moment of supreme crisis.". . .

. . . In preparing this letter we have tried through a number of sources to determine as precisely as possible the factual character of U.S. deterrence strategy. Two questions have particularly concerned us: (1) the targeting doctrine and strategic plans for the use of the deterrent, particularly their impact on civilian casualties; and (2) the relationship of deterrence strategy and nuclear war-fighting capability to the likelihood that war will in fact be prevented.

Moral Principles and Policy Choices

Targeting doctrine raises significant moral questions because it is a significant determinant of what would occur if nuclear weapons were ever to be used. Although we acknowledge the need for deterrent, not all forms of deterrence are morally acceptable. There are moral limits to deterrence policy as well as to policy regarding use. Specifically, it is not morally acceptable to intend to kill the innocent as part of a strategy of deterring nuclear war. The question of whether U.S. policy involves an intention to strike civilian centers (directly targeting civilian populations) has been one of our factual concerns . . .

In our consultations, administration officials readily admitted that while they hoped any nuclear exchange could be kept limited, they were prepared to retaliate in a massive way if necessary. They also agreed that once

any substantial numbers of weapons were used, the civilian casualty levels would quickly become truly catastrophic and that even with attacks limited to "military" targets the number of deaths in a substantial exchange would be almost indistinguishable from what might occur if civilian centers had been deliberately and directly struck. These possibilities pose a different moral question and are to be judged by a different moral criterion: the principle of proportionality.

While any judgment of proportionality is always open to differing evaluations, there are actions which can be decisively judged to be disproportionate. A narrow adherence exclusively to the principle of noncombatant immunity as a criterion for policy is an inadequate moral posture for it ignores some evil and unacceptable consequences. Hence, we cannot be satisfied that the assertion of an intention not to strike civilians directly or even the most honest effort to implement that intention by itself constitutes a "moral policy" for the use of nuclear weapons.

The location of industrial or militarily significant economic targets within heavily populated areas or in those areas affected by radioactive fallout could well involve such massive civilian casualties that in our judgment such a strike would be deemed morally disproportionate, even though not intentionally indiscriminate.

The problem is not simply one of producing highly accurate weapons that might minimize civilian casualties in any single explosion, but one of the increasing likelihood of escalation at a level where many, even "discriminating," weapons would cumulatively kill very large numbers of civilians. Those civilian deaths would occur both immediately and from the long-term effects of social and economic devastation. . . .

These considerations of concrete elements of nuclear deterrence policy, made in light of John Paul II's evaluation, but applying it through our own prudential judgments, lead us to a strictly conditioned moral acceptance of nuclear deterrence. We cannot consider it adequate as a long-term basis for peace.

This strictly conditioned judgment yields *criteria* for morally assessing the elements of deterrence strategy. Clearly, these criteria demonstrate that we cannot approve of every weapons system, strategic doctrine or policy initiative advanced in the name of strengthening deterrence. On the contrary, these criteria require continual public scrutiny of what our government proposes to do with the deterrent.

On the basis of these criteria we wish now to make some specific evaluations:

1. If nuclear deterrence exists only to prevent the *use* of nuclear weapons by others, then proposals to go beyond this to planning for prolonged periods of repeated nuclear strikes and counterstrikes, or "prevailing" in nuclear war, are not acceptable. They encourage notions that nuclear war can be engaged in with tolerable human and moral consequences. Rather, we must continually say no to the idea of nuclear war.

2. If nuclear deterrence is our goal, "sufficiency" to deter is an adequate strategy; the quest for nuclear superiority must be rejected.

3. Nuclear deterrence should be used as a step on the way toward progressive disarma-

ment. Each proposed addition to our strategic system or change in strategic doctrine must be assessed precisely in light of whether it will render steps toward "progressive disarmament" more or less likely.

Notes

1. Vatican II, "The Pastoral Constitution on the Church in the Modern World" (hereafter: Pastoral Constitution), 77. Papal and conciliar texts will be referred to by title with paragraph number. Several collections of these texts exist although no single collection is comprehensive; see the following: *Peace and Disarmament: Documents of the World Council of Churches and the Roman Catholic Church*, (Geneva and Rome: 1982) (hereafter: Documents, with page number). J. Gremillion, *The Gospel of Peace and Justice: Catholic Social Teaching since Pope John*, (Maryknoll, N.Y.: 1976). D. J. O'Brien and T. A. Shannon, eds., *Renewing the Earth: Catholic Documents on Peace, Justice and Liberation*, (N.Y.: 1977). A. Flannery, OP, ed., *Vatican Council II: The Conciliar and Post Conciliar Documents*, (Collegeville, Minn.: 1975); W. Abbot, ed., *The Documents of Vatican II*, (N.Y.: 1966). Both the Flannery and Abbot translations of the pastoral constitution are used in this letter.

2. John Paul II, Message to the Second Special Session of the United Nations General Assembly Devoted to Disarmament, (June 1982), 7 (hereafter: Message U.N. Special Session 1982).

3. John Paul II, Address to Scientists and Scholars, 4; Origins, 10 (1981) p. 621.

ADDITIONAL READINGS

Articles

Davidson, James D.; Elly, Ronald; Hull, Thomas; and Nead, Donald. "Increasing Church Involvement in Social Concerns: A Model for Urban Ministries." *Review of Religious Research* 20 (1979): 291–314. Most church members develop their social orientations on the local level and not from national church offices or officials. A case study of a neighborhood development project shows under what conditions an urban ministry *can* be developed and what its structures and goals should be.

Johnson, Stephen D., and Tamney, Joseph B. "The Christian Right and the 1980 Presidential Election." *Journal for the Scientific Study of Religion* 21 (1982): 123–31. Residents of "Middletown" interviewed indicate that religion, particularly religious fundamentalism, did *not* play any significant role in the 1980 presidential election.

Lienesch, Michael. "Right-Wing Religion: Christian Conservatism as a Political Movement." *Political Science Quarterly* 97 (1982): 403–25. Various social movement theories are explored to explain the "New Christian Right" and its politics of protest.

Nelsen, Hart M., and Baxter, Sandra. "Ministers Speak on Watergate: Effects of Clergy Role during Political Crisis." *Review of Religious Research* 23 (1981): 150–66. Comparison of fundamentalist and conservative ministers with more liberal clergy on the likelihood of speaking out on Watergate and other issues of social morality.

Books

Campbell, Ernest Q., and Pettigrew, Thomas F. *Christians in Racial Crisis: A Study of Little Rock's Ministry.* Washington: Public Affairs Press, 1959. A classic study of the effects of cross-pressures from congregations and from official church policies and pronouncements upon the stance of ministers caught in racial turmoil.

Hadden, Jeffrey K. *The Gathering Storm in the Churches.* New York: Doubleday, 1969. Perhaps no better analysis exists of the dilemmas encountered by mainline churches and ministers in taking active roles in the 1960s struggle for civil rights.

Neal, Marie Augusta, S.N.D. deN. *A Socio-Theology of Letting Go: The Role of a First World Church Facing Third World Peoples.* New York: Paulist Press, 1977. A rich, prophetic volume challenging the churches to confront a civil religion that legitimates first-world dominance and privilege at the expense of perpetuating worldwide social injustice.

Quinley, Harold E. *The Prophetic Clergy: Social Activism among Protestant Ministers.* New York: John Wiley, 1974. Lay-clergy polarization over churches' social involvements is analyzed in detail, utilizing a 1968 survey of California ministers. Modernist and traditionalist clergy form a principal typology.

Cross-cultural References

Aho, James A. *Religious Mythology and the Art of War: Comparative Religious Symbolisms of Military Violence.* Westport, Conn.: Greenwood Press, 1981. Cultures of Mexico, India, China, Japan, Palestine, Islamic countries, as well as the Christian West, exhibit myths of war and military ethics to justify "holy wars." A provocative study with an excellent bibliography.

Esposito, John L., ed. *Islam and Development: Religion and Sociopolitical Change.* Syracuse: Syracuse University Press, 1980. Resurgent Islam is an increasingly prominent force for social change. These essays ranging from Nigeria to Pakistan are helpful in understanding rejection of Western models of progress.

Journal of International Affairs 36 (Fall/Winter, 1982/83), "Religion and Politics." Articles cover Iran, Central America, Northern Ireland, Brazil, South Africa, Indonesia, Poland, U.S. Middle East Policy, and Vatican policy in Eastern Europe.

Lewy, Guenter. *Religion and Revolution.* New York: Oxford University Press, 1974. An excellent series of essays detailing how various religious movements throughout history have contributed to social change, even violent revolution. The author's introduction and concluding theoretical perspectives enhance the usefulness of this volume.

Smith, Donald Eugene, ed. *South Asian Politics and Religion*. Princeton: Princeton University Press, 1966. Case studies of religion and politics throughout the various religious traditions of South Asia.

8

Religion according to Class, Race, and Sex

Two themes associated with one of sociology's founding fathers, Max Weber, are (1) how the Calvinist work ethic contributed to the development of Western capitalism, and (2) the kinds of religious expressions that are associated with different social classes. *The Protestant Ethic and the Spirit of Capitalism* states Weber's conviction that a particular interpretation of John Calvin's view of the Christian calling in this world became an incentive for profit making in a capitalist economy, or what Weber called the rational pursuit of wealth. For Weber, as for most of us, this relationship seemed strange. Hasn't any version of Christianity called for the *rejection* of worldly gain as dangerous to one's salvation? Aren't riches the pitfall in the journey to save one's soul? Staring Weber in the face, though, was the historical fact that the rising merchant classes had embraced Protestantism in England, Holland, and Germany. Indeed, these countries stood out as more economically progressive. They had industrialized faster than Italy, Spain, and Portugal, the so-called "Catholic countries" of southern Europe. Was there something about the Protestant faith, or some version of it, that helped further the capitalistic enterprise against all expectations that were rooted in the traditional Christian emphasis on the blessings of poverty? Weber acknowledged that none of the great reformers—Luther, Calvin, Knox—had thought of their teachings as incentives to capitalism. But Weber thought he saw in Calvin's doctrine of predestination an *implicit* incentive for accumulation of profit.

Weber reasoned that believers confronted with a teaching that some are damned and others are called to eternal bliss by God's choice, regardless of any foreseen merits or demerits on their part, were cast into a very troubled state of mind or conscience. How was one to be satisfied that one was indeed among the elect and not among the damned? No priest could help, since priestly intercession was rejected. No sacraments would avail, not even confession, for sacraments were not carriers of grace and relief of conscience, as in the Catholic world. Any possible solace lay in the duty to consider oneself as chosen and to reject as the devil's work any doubts about one's final destiny. To bolster one's faith and thus self-confidence, *work* was the answer—ceaseless devotion to one's occupation, considering it as a calling. To make his case, Weber turned to doctrine as expressed in preaching, particularly among England's Puritan divines. Richard Baxter and even John Wesley himself proclaimed the discipline of work as essential to prove oneself favored in the sight of God, of being among the elect. To have the *fruits* of such labor— that is, wealth accumulated through work—was to accept a gift of God. To be sure, one could not use wealth for enjoying worldly pleasures, to engage in vain displays of material goods or "status symbols," as we would call them today. But one could amass wealth and reinvest it, justifying one's ensuing wealth as the consequence of following one's calling. Weber laid particular emphasis on the systematic, planned pursuit of wealth that characterized the successful capitalist businessman. This *kind* of gainful pursuit was what distinguished Western-style capitalism from other varieties found in non-Western cultures.

Thus the term "Protestant ethic" has come to mean in our own day a devotion to the systematic, unrelenting pursuit of wealth through disciplined hard work. Modern research, following Weber's leads, has asked whether Catholics are as achievement oriented as Protestants. Such research has been particularly prominent in the United States with its large numbers of Protestant denominations. Do Catholics attain the same levels of success as Episcopalians, Methodists, and so on?

In the early 1950s, Gerhard Lenski examined results of the first Detroit area survey in his book *The Religious Factor*. He concluded that Catholics, particularly those with close ties to the Catholic community, were less likely to rise in the economic system (comparing son's occupation to father's) than Protestants. Catholics were more likely to be bound into the network of the extended family and to ascribe less importance to intellectual independence and "thinking for oneself." Less tied to tradition, Protestants—particularly at the upper middle-class level—seemed more prepared to "take on" the American success ethic and to be upwardly mobile in job and career.

More recent research has indicated a flattening out of differences between Catholics and Protestants as Catholics have risen from recent-immigrant status and proceeded to higher levels of education and income. Andrew Greeley's analysis, based upon national samples of Catholic and Protestant family incomes in the mid-

1970s, showed that "the income achievement of Catholics provides little support for a theory of Catholic lack of industry or ambition."[1] Catholic family income was $1,421 above the national average; in northern metropolitan areas, it was $1,211 above the average. Therefore, concluded Greeley, "the argument that Catholicism impedes financial success in the United States should be considered closed; it does not."[2] He also examined educational achievement:

Irish Catholics have the highest level of educational attainment of any Gentile white ethnic group—though they are only one-tenth of a year higher than the British Protestants. German Catholics are virtually at the national average . . . and the eastern and southern European Catholics trail off to various fractions of a year beneath the national average.[3]

Social Class and Religion. Social classes reflect an unequal distribution of wealth and therefore an unequal distribution of opportunity in a society. Weber added to this basic concept of class the idea of "status honor," in which certain groups in a society display "honorific" symbols such as special clothing, particular foods, or even permission to carry arms where other groups are denied this "privilege." Among the "goods" that particular social classes and status groups may possess are shared religious ideas and traditions.

Weber's distinctive contribution lay in his doctrine of "elective affinity." Different classes and groups have divergent material interests that can *give rise to* diverse kinds of religious beliefs. At the same time, groups may "reach out" toward, or *be attracted to,* particular belief systems or emphases within a tradition that reflect their own interests and that legitimate—or protest—their position in society. Such groups and classes can then become "carriers" of certain traditions and may become instrumental in spreading the teachings they value to other groups and people. Let us consider Weber's examples:

The life pattern of a warrior has very little affinity with the notion of a beneficent providence, or with the systematic ethical demands of a transcendental god. Concepts like sin, salvation, and religious humility have not only seemed remote from all elite political classes, particularly the warrior nobles, but have indeed appeared reprehensible to its sense of honor. . . . he does not require . . . anything beyond protection against evil magic or such ceremonial rites as are congruent with his caste, such as priestly prayers for victory or for a blissful death leading directly into the hero's heaven.[4]

Weber's insights were put to work in the writings of later researchers. Noting the functions of religion in Middletown, U.S.A., just after the Great Depression, Robert S. and Helen Merrell Lynd observed:

Thus, under the wrenching impact of a prolonged experience like the depression, religion may oscillate like the needle of a compass seeking the pole pull of people's greatest need for reassurance. Among *meagerly educated people* on the South Side, the needle may swing back to what they have been told since infancy is the unfailing Rock of Ages, and the gap between what the intellectual world may call "religion" and "reality" may increase with a popular huddling back to fundamentalism; while the many *business-folk* religion may be allowed to become less insistently dogmatic theologically . . . and its full weight may swing behind the moral condemnation of radicalism and the emotionally craved bolstering of the *status quo*.[5]

James West in his study of Plainville, U.S.A., noted the close alignment of class status with certain religious expressions:

A few people try to cross class lines through religion but none succeeds. Theoretically no obstacle keeps lower-class people out of the Christian Church, but "they wouldn't feel comfortable there." One upper-class widow had identified herself with the Holiness Church, whose great light and leader she was until her death in 1940. Members of her class criticized the affiliation, and she lost respect in their eyes, but her class status remained unchanged, though upper-class people tried to visit her on her deathbed at times when they would find her surrounded by the fewest of "them ignorant Holinists."[6]

In the early 1950s, William H. Whyte, Jr., studied the new suburban community of Park Forest, Illinois. He noted the ways in which churches adapted to the ethos of camaraderie and "doing things with and for other people," an ethos that was flattening out the social-class and denominational differences that previous community researchers had observed. Convinced that the new residents had little concern for traditional denominational differences, the recently arrived Protestant minister decided to found one "United Protestant Church."

He wanted a *useful* church, and to emphasize theological points, he felt, was to emphasize what is not of first importance at the price of provoking dissension. "We try not to offend anybody," he explains . . . "I think this is the basic need—the need to belong to a group. You find this fellowship in a church better than anywhere else. And it is contagious. In a community like Park Forest, when young people see how many other people are going to church regularly, they feel they ought to . . . We pick out the more useful parts of the doctrine to that end."[7]

Reviewing this research from the vantage point of the early 1970s, Rodney Stark concluded that the entire range of social-class/religiosity studies done in the United States, if focused on *church members*, demonstrated that

the upper classes show superior religious commitment on religious knowledge, public ritual and organizational participation. The lower classes excel on belief, religious experiences, personal devotionalism, and communal involvement.[8]

Such differences are predicted by theories of economic deprivation: the poor are religious in those respects in which religion serves as compensation for suffering and hardship. For the upper classes, belonging to church organizations and participating in rituals "has come to be defined as a manifestation of higher social status, which demonstrates that one is respectable, substantial, responsible, and proper."[9]

But Stark pointed to the importance of looking at national samples of the *general population*. Here lower-class persons are *less* religious than middle-class or high-status persons on practically all manifestations of religious commitment (the sample examined was of white non-Southerners). Taking the population as a whole, Stark concluded that poverty "operates mainly to shut persons off from religion rather than to drive them into faith as a means of compensation."[10]

As important as social class may be, however, denomination has powerful effects as well. Protestant church members differ widely on such matters as the existence of God, the divinity of Jesus, and the existence of life after death. These belief differences are related mainly to membership in liberal, moderate, or conservative Protestant church bodies; and these memberships *cut across all categories of social class*. Denominational upbringing and belonging, then, is critically important for religious beliefs. The view becomes somewhat more complicated, however, if one looks at *attendance*. Social-class effects *do* appear to be important *within* denominations. Among Baptists, according to mid-1970s survey data of the general population, upper- and middle-class members are more likely to attend regularly; among Methodists, Lutherans, and Presbyterians, working-class persons attend more regularly than upper middle-class or lower-class "belongers." In fact, upper-class Episcopalians and Presbyterians are among the lowest of *any* combination of class and denomination in regular attendance.[11]

Finally, is there any relationship between people who are occupationally and educationally "on the move up" and the denomination(s) with which they affiliate? Do most people, in other words, stay where they "religiously are" no matter what happens to their occupational or educational status? The answer is basically yes: About 75 percent remain where they are regardless of mobility up *or* down. One mid-1970s study indicated that only a combination of high degree of education *and* of occupational mobility resulted in some denominational switching, and then for just under half of those involved.[12]

In "The Religion of the Poor: Escape or Creative Force?" Harry G. Lefever thoughtfully reflects upon results of research on the poverty-religiosity relationship. Compensatory functions do appear, he indicates; but the religion of the poor also challenges the status structure by offering an "alternative of relative equality." Using anthropologist Victor Turner's dialectical model of community, which stresses emphasis on social hierarchy (structure) in alternating phases with expressions of nonstructured equality (communitas), Lefever suggests that the poor "serve as a constant reminder to the larger society of just how precarious and fabricated the hierarchical status system really is."

The role of religion in racial and ethnic group identity, and as a means of group protest against oppression, has received much attention from historians and social scientists. The function of Black churches in the antislavery struggles and in developing Black leadership that played a critical role in the civil rights struggle (and continues to do so) is the theme of "Out of the Cauldron of Struggle," by Vincent Harding. Tracing the history of Black liberation efforts, Harding stresses the offering of a new vision, of renewed possibilities for America, by Black Americans engaged in this struggle.

The subordination of women has been legitimated by major theological doctrines in both Christianity and Judaism. Both religions reflect a patriarchal society in which women were not only socially inferior but were defined as secondary and inferior members of the human species. Feminist attacks have frequently singled out religion for its reinforcement of sexual inequality. Rosemary Radford Ruether, who has written extensively on this subject, notes the thick layers of symbolism that function to reinforce subordination and make it seem a taken-for-granted social fact, the reversal of which is a major challenge to contemporary feminists. Ruether reminds us that feminists in religion are by no means agreed on how to redress the errors and distortions of centuries. Groups that she characterizes as evangelical feminists, liberationist feminists, and goddess movements entertain distinctive critiques and differ in their strategies for freeing women for participation that respects their dignity and self-expression. Her concluding remarks set the basic issue in stark relief: "What is clear is this: the patriarchal repression of women and women's experience has been so massive and prevalent that to begin to take women seriously will involve a profound and radical transformation of our religion."

Notes

1. Andrew M. Greeley, *The American Catholic: A Social Portrait* (New York: Basic Books, 1977), p. 57.
2. Ibid.
3. Ibid., p. 58.
4. Max Weber, *The Sociology of Religion* (Boston: Beacon Press, 1963), p. 85.
5. Robert S. Lynd and Helen Merrell Lynd, *Middletown in Transition: A Study in Cultural Conflicts* (New York: Harcourt Brace, 1937), p. 316.
6. James West, *Plainville, U.S.A.* (Westport, Conn.: Greenwood, 1971), p. 160.
7. William H. Whyte, Jr., *The Organization Man* (New York: Doubleday, 1957), pp. 406–7.

8. Rodney Stark, "The Economics of Piety: Religious Commitment and Social Class," in *Issues in Social Inequality*, ed. Gerald W. Thielbar and Saul D. Feldman (Boston: Little, Brown), pp. 494–95.

9. Ibid., p. 495.

10. Ibid., p. 500.

11. This paragraph is based on the excellent presentation by H. Paul Chalfant, Robert E. Beckley, and C. Eddie Palmer, *Religion in Contemporary Society* (Sherman Oaks, Calif.: Alfred, 1981), pp. 371–412.

12. Robert H. Lauer, "Occupational and Religious Mobility in a Small City," *Sociological Quarterly* 16 (1975), pp. 380–92.

R E A D I N G   8 . 1

The Religion of the Poor: Escape or Creative Force?

Harry G. Lefever

The question of the relationship of the religion of the poor to the development and maintenance of culture and social structure is a controversial one. Proponents on one side argue that the religion of the poor provides an escape from the deprivations of lower-class life (Niebuhr, 1929; Pope, 1942; Glock & Stark, 1965; Elinson, 1965), and that the religious behavior of the poor can be best characterized as disorganized (Holt, 1940; Poblete & O'Dea, 1960) and pathological (Cutten, 1927; Boisen, 1939a, 1939b; Alland, 1962; Kaplan, 1965).[1] Proponents on the other side argue that the religion of the poor is not so much disorganized as it is organized according to the values and norms of lower-class life in general, and that the religious poor make positive contributions to the development and maintenance of culture and the social order (Johnson, 1961; Gans, 1968; Valentine, 1968; Hannerz, 1969; Gerlach & Hine, 1970; Rainwater, 1970).

The controversy is misplaced because what is overlooked is that the relationship is a dy-

Harry G. Lefever is Professor of Sociology at Spelman College, Atlanta, Georgia.

Reprinted from *Journal for the Scientific Study of Religion*, 16 (1977): 225–36, with permission.

namic one, and in many respects paradoxical. The religion of the poor is *both* a reflection of the social order and a source of influence on the social order. On the one hand, it enables the poor to find some compensation for the material and social rewards they are denied now. On the other hand, it is a source of social influence, and makes a positive contribution to the development of personality, social structure, and culture.

The arguments that follow will attempt to do justice to both sides of the paradox. However, since the escapist interpretation has received more attention than the other side, this paper will focus on the unique social organizational features of the religion of the poor and on the positive contributions that the religious poor make to the structuring of personality, society, and culture.

Karl Marx is referred to often as the major proponent of the idea that religion functions as an escape for the poor. Marx said that religion is the "opium of the people," by which he meant that religion provides an illusory escape from the troubles of the real world. But even Marx recognized that religion can function as more than an escape, that at times religion is a form of protest against the conditions of oppression in a society.

Religious distress is at the same time the *expression* of real distress and the *protest* against real distress. Religion is the sigh of the oppressed creature, the heart of a heartless world, just as it is the spirit of an unspiritual situation. It is the opium of the people. (Marx & Engels, 1957: 42, emphasis theirs)

Marx, however, had very little to say about the protest function of religion. His writings dealt more with the way religion reflects the social order than with the way religion shapes the social order.

In contrast is the scholarship of Max Weber, who wrote extensively about the paradoxical nature of religion. Weber did not deny the partial truth of the escapist interpretation of religion, but he recognized that what is equally true is that religion makes a positive impact on the larger society. According to Weber, religion makes two major positive contributions to social structure and social change. First of all, he argued that there is a charismatic quality to religion, which endows the religious person (usually a leader) with an aura of "extraordinariness" (1947: 361). The consequence for the individual believer who experiences or comes into contact with charisma is that he is set relatively free from any specific environment where he finds himself at a particular time. Thus, religion functions as a breakthrough from the ordinary routine. Religion in this sense is innovative and change-producing, and tends to encourage the autonomy of religious faith from secular life.

Secondly, Weber recognized that religion has a positive and potent impact on the secular environment (1904–05). The religious believer who is serious about his commitment puts all of his activities, sacred and secular, under the control of religiously prescribed norms. As a consequence, when the religiously committed person participates in the secular realm his motivation for action is re-ligiously grounded. Whereas in the first instance religion tends to make for disengagement from the routine-ordering of society, in the second instance it tends to encourage re-engagement with it. Thus, the same religion can support both the process of deculturation (lifting the constraints from the culturally trapped individual) and the process of reso-cialization (integrating the individual into the larger social environment).[2]

If Weber was right (and I believe he was), then one should be able to understand the effect of the religion of the poor (or any social group) as more than merely an escape from reality. Without denying the possibility or evidence that religion may at times function as an escape, what follows is an attempt to develop a theoretical perspective that would make it possible to understand and explain the positive psychological and organizational features associated with the religion of the poor. The basic assumption is that the religion of the poor can be understood as more than a lack of social organization, or as being merely pathological, neurotic, or anomic in nature. The religious meaning systems that develop are more than rationalizations, more than neurotic responses, more than false-hoods and illusions, more than mere epiphenomena (Spiro, 1965: 100–113; Maslow, 1964: 44; Firth, 1959).

Religious data have a mode of being that is peculiar to themselves; *they exist on their own plane of reference*, in their particular universe. The fact that this universe is not the physical universe of immediate experience does not imply their non-reality. . . . A religious datum reveals its deeper meaning when it is considered on its plane of reference, and not when it is reduced to one of its secondary aspects or its contexts. (Eliade, 1961: 5f. Emphasis his)

Religious symbols arise and are transmitted as much from a realistic perception of the world as from a false or neurotic one and have the potential to create a convincing model of reality and a blueprint for social behavior (Geertz, 1966: 1–46).[3]

More specifically, it is argued in what follows that the religious patterns of the poor contribute in significant and positive ways to the process of identity formation and to the development and maintenance of cultural values and norms. The analysis of how this occurs will proceed from an examination of two different levels of social structure—first, the level of the immediate social environment of the poverty community, and second, the relationship between the poverty community and the larger social environment.[4]

The Religion of the Poor and the Immediate Social Environment

To the outsider looking in, the social patterns of the poverty community often appear to be disorganized. However, what appears to be social disorganization may be, in fact, a type of social organization different from that characteristic of the larger society (Whyte, 1943; Gans, 1962; Liebow, 1967; Hannerz, 1969; Rainwater, 1970). The restricted social networks and the expressive cultural style of the poor, viewed from the more immediate context, may be very functional forms of social organization. Social and cultural patterns are much more dynamic, and much more capable of forming structural alternatives than the middle-class bias of the outsider often allows.

An example from my observations of religious behavior within a low-income white neighborhood in Atlanta, Georgia (Lefever, 1971) will illustrate how what appears as social disorganization from the perspective of the larger society can be seen to have a clear structure of norms and role expectations when viewed from the perspective of the group.

The religious services observed were, for the most part, an improvised set of interactions, delicately woven together from the contributions of both the individual and the group. The typical service was both personal and corporate at the same time, with a taut tension established between the two. Beyond a doubt, the group context was important; much of the action that occurred in the services would not have taken place in private or in isolation. But in the final analysis, within the group context, it was the individual performance that really counted.

This individual-corporate dialectic was suddenly impressed upon me one Sunday evening as I was attending a service of about twenty assembled at one of the holiness churches. At the time when testimonies were called for, an old man, about seventy, stood up to testify. The others in the audience (mostly women) hardly turned to look at him. Instead they were whispering, and passing notes and papers between them. Once in a while a few nods of agreement were given, but the man was virtually ignored. The same thing happened when the minister was preaching. Twice a woman from the front row got up, walked to the piano, and put slips of paper into the prayer box. Others talked together and passed things back and forth.

The entire service was an alternating pattern of involvement and noninvolvement; of attentiveness and inattentiveness. And often the change from one side of the pattern to the other was very rapid. That is, those who seemed inattentive or bored one minute would be giving a lively testimony or speaking in tongues the next minute.

To my usual way of reacting to such situations, the inattentiveness of the audience seemed out of place, and, in fact, very rude. I expected people to turn their heads and at least pretend that they were listening to the person giving the testimony or to the preacher. To my way of looking at it, it would have been appropriate for the preacher to stop preaching until he had their attention. From the perspective of my middle-class expectations, the attentive-inattentive, involvement-noninvolvement sequence suggested disorganization and anarchy.

However, to describe the service as disorganized is to misunderstand the structure of the group. From their viewpoint it was not inattentiveness. They did not mind that several things were going on at the same time. It was expected that each individual should make his own contribution in the way that he himself chose. The ritual of public prayers was a good example of this, the way each individual prayed his prayer aloud at the same time. It was corporate—those praying gathered around the altar—but at the same time, it was individual, as each offered a separate prayer. This, in microcosm, was how the entire service was structured.

The significance of this paradox of a highly individualized type of religious expression within the context of the group is stated well by Bruce Rosenberg.

No doubt a great deal of the appeal of this kind of service is that it frees the minds of the audience from concern with what language, music, or story element is to come next, and so they are freer to involve themselves with the rhythm and the music and the emotion of the performance. Consequently, the audience is freer for active participation in the service, participation which is expressed in the cries of joy, in clapping, in dancing, or whatever. Both the knowledge of the performance and the freedom to participate in it thus allows the congregation member to participate in the service and the sermon individually while he is expressing that individuality publicly; through his own singing, his own shouting, and his own clapping, the church member is to a certain degree creating his own service. Not only is he, by his active participation in the service, influencing the preacher in several ways, but he is creating a personal religious experience, and expressing it while the rest of the congregation are creating theirs. (1970:105)

What goes on in the churches of the poor, then, is not disorganization so much as it is a particular kind of organization. It is a type of organization that has parallels to the jazz performance. Each person present is a potential player who takes his turn to improvise on the general theme of the meeting. Each performer adds his individual contribution at the time he picks up the cue. The improvisation could not take place apart from the group, but the group is secondary in importance to the individual. The congregation provides the context, but it is the quality of the individual contributions, from both preacher and audience, that makes the difference between an effective and ineffective service. A service with a group of religious virtuosos[5] can turn out to be a really lively time. Sometimes the substance of virtuosity is lacking, but the form is usually there.

An awareness of the dynamic and improvised nature of social organization in the poverty community also helps one to understand the processes of identity formation among the poor. Persons from all status levels in society develop their identities to some extent out of the matrix of primary relationships, associated especially with family and peer-group structures. But, persons in the middle and upper status levels, in addition to the primary relationships they have with family and peers, also develop an intricate network of secondary and tertiary relationships. For low-status persons, however, significant secondary and tertiary relationships are often lacking. Or, in many instances, the ties they do have with secondary institutions (e.g., employer, policeman, welfare worker, landlord) only remind them of how powerless and dependent they are. Therefore, in order to get a more favorable evaluation of who they are, they turn to their relatives, friends, and peers who are close at hand, and with whom they interact on a face-to-face basis. The consequence of this is that a heavy burden for identity formation is placed upon establishing meaningful primary relationships.

In the poverty community, there are different contexts available where significant primary relationships can be developed. The most common contexts are the home and the street. But equally available to those who choose it is the context of the church.

Whether one or several of these contexts is chosen, the nature of interaction among relatives, friends, and peers is similarly characterized. Whether in the home, on the street, or in church, within the poverty community the types of behavior that are encouraged and rewarded are those that are expressive and dramatic.

Rainwater (1970), in his study of the residents of the Pruitt-Igoe housing project in St. Louis, describes the expressive style of ghetto cultural life and indicates its importance for identity formation.

In the expressive life style instrumental orientations to living are consistently downgraded, recognized mainly in terms of the bare necessity of keeping the body and soul together from day to day, while self-expression is emphasized, elaborated, and held out as possessing intrinsic merit. (1970:378)

Associated with the expressive style is a particular type of personal identity which Rainwater elaborates with the aid of two metaphors—the stage and the marketplace. The metaphor of the stage suggests the idea of the "dramatic self," the basic component of which is the constant search to maintain social reciprocity by mutual entertainment of each other. The metaphor of the marketplace suggests the idea of "the self-as-currency," or the way selves are symbolically exchanged.

In their world, one learns that one has to "go for yourself," relying on the response of others to measure success. If one is successful in creating a dramatic self, a kind of security has been gained because that self can neither be taken away nor spent (at least in the short run). If one is successful in establishing relationships of symbolic reciprocity with others similarly seeking to maximize a dramatic self, then the self is constantly replenished. (1970:379)

In the poverty community, the public religious service provides an excellent setting for the poor to present themselves to each other. During the service, the self-identities of the members are enhanced as they symbolically exchange selves, and as they mutually entertain each other. The interactions that occur during the process of the service, for the most part, are not based on prescribed roles or on formal, predetermined statuses. Instead, interactions are determined largely by individualized expressive styles. In order for the exchange of selves and the entertainment of each other to be successful, each individual present needs to learn to express himself. The consequence of this is that the public religious service tends to be dramatic and demonstrative. In the context of the service, the religious participant learns that he has to "go for himself." He learns to present himself, and then to rely on the response of others to determine the meaning of his actions. The extent to which he is able to obtain a favorable response determines, to a large degree, the clarity with which his identity is established.

The Religion of the Poor and the Larger Social Environment

The focus on the norms that guide interaction in the more immediate environment of the poverty community is thus an important key to the understanding of the religious patterns of the poor. But the question of the relationship of the poor to the larger social environment still remains. And here, as is the case at the more immediate level, the relationship between religion and society is a dynamic one. On the one hand, religion is an adaptive mechanism that enables the poor and oppressed individuals and groups to find some spiritual compensation for the material and social benefits they are denied daily. They may not have much wealth, status, or power now, but they are redeemed in the eyes of their Lord and can look forward to an eternity in heaven. In other words, religion provides an alternative orientation that offers a more favorable self-judgment than that accorded them by the larger society.

But that is only one side of the relationship, the negative one. Unfortunately, it is the side that is most often emphasized by scholar and layman alike. There is, however, another possible way to understand the relationship. That is, the religion of the poor, rather than merely providing an escape to some "sweet bye and bye," can also be understood as contributing in positive ways to social structuring and to the culture-building process. Two such contributions will be suggested.

First of all, the religion of the poor offers a challenge to the hierarchical structure of the general status system. Over against the status-bound social order, where individuals are related to one another on the basis of "more" or "less," an alternative of relative equality is offered. As Gary Schwartz has pointed out, a major function of religious ritual is to create "an experience of moral equality between men that is unencumbered by status considerations" (1970:84).

Victor Turner (1969) has studied in depth the social consequences of the ritual process. His research focused on African societies, but what he found there can be applied to an analysis of the religious rituals of the poor in this country. In fact, he suggests that such an application is possible.

Turner's point of departure is the "liminal phase" of the rites of passage as identified by Arnold van Gennep (1960). Van Gennep had shown that all rites of passage are marked by three phases: separation, margin, and aggregation. During the first phase the individual or group is detached from some earlier fixed point in the social structure, or from some set of cultural conditions. In the second phase, the "liminal" (*limen*, threshold in Latin), the characteristics of the ritual subject are ambiguous. He has few or none of the attributes of the past or coming state. In the third phase, the passage is completed. The ritual subject finds himself once again in a relatively stable niche in the social structure, with clearly defined rights and obligations vis-a-vis others in the society (Turner, 1969:94f).

It is the second phase, the liminal period,

that is singled out by Turner for his analysis of the ritual process. The liminal phase is important because it is in the ambiguous condition of liminality that a major alternative to the hierarchical secular social structure is created. At this point of transition, there arises a system of relationships that Turner terms "communitas." Communitas stands juxtaposed over against normal social structure. Communitas breaks in through the interstices of structure, at the edges of structure, or beneath structure. It is thus usually associated in some way with marginality and inferiority (1969:

There are . . . two major "models" for human interrelatedness, juxtaposed and alternating. The first is of society as a structured, differentiated, and often hierarchical system of politico-legal-economic positions with many types of evaluation, separating men in terms of "more" or "less." The second, which emerges recognizable in the liminal period, is of society as an unstructured or rudimentarily structured and relatively undifferentiated *comitatus*, community, or even commission of equal individuals who submit together to the general authority of the ritual elders. (1969:96)

Communitas and structure are not polar opposites. Rather, they are related to each other in dialectical fashion. Both are basic components of the human experience. The opposites, as it were, constitute one another and are mutually indispensable.

Society . . . seems to be a process rather than a thing—a dialectical process with successive phases of structure and communitas. There would seem to be . . . a human "need" to participate in both modalities. Persons starved on one in their functional day-to-day activities seek it in ritual liminality. The structurally inferior aspire to symbolic structural superiority in ritual; the structurally superior aspire to symbolic communitas and undergo penance to achieve it. (1969:203)

To exaggerate one modality at the expense of the other results in negative consequences. To emphasize communitas without structure is sentimentality, and results in an incapability to maintain social and economic order over long periods of time (1969:203). On the other hand, to emphasize structure without communitas leads to despotism and overbureaucratization (1969:129).

In our society, the danger lies in the extreme of overbureaucratization. Highly differentiated roles and specialized division of labor, combined with technology and the computer, make communitas extremely difficult to attain. But some interstices of structure are left, and it is within these interstices that the significance of the religious rituals of the poor is to be found. From their position of weakness, the poor challenge the power of the strong. With their emphasis on status-equality, the divisions and the differentiations of the larger society are questioned. Their presence at the fringes of structure is a constant reminder of just how precarious and fabricated the hierarchical system of relationships really is. As the court jester in the royal court, the lowly of our society perform the role of poking fun at the pretensions of the mighty.

Turner, of course, applied his analysis to traditional societies. But as Harvey Cox (1969) points out, the Feast of Fools performed a similar function in medieval Europe. The Feast of Fools was an annual festival which was celebrated with much revelry and satire. The priests donned bawdy masks and sang silly ditties, while minor clerics painted their faces and strutted around in the robes of their superiors. In general, mockery was made of the stately rituals of the church and court. The importance of the festival from a sociological perspective is that "it exposed the arbitrary quality of social rank and enabled people to see that things need not always be as they are" (1969:5). By unmasking the pretense of the powerful, their power, somehow, seemed less irresistible (1969:5).

The effect of the religion of the poor in contemporary American society, then, to some extent parallels that of the rituals of liminality in traditional societies and the Feast of Fools in medieval society. Clearly, the effect of the religion of the poor on American society is not as great as was the impact of the tribal rituals of liminality and the Feast of Fools on their respective societies. But for those who will take note, a similarity in function can be seen to exist.

This leads to the second contribution of the religion of the poor to the general culture-building process. And that is that the poor tend to emphasize certain values, which are a basic part of human experience, but which are often ignored by those who hold dominant positions of wealth, power, and prestige.

It would be a mistake, of course, to romanticize the life of the poor. But hopefully without doing so, the point can be made that it is often the "inferior" or "marginal" groups of a society who at times are representative of universal human values. Turner (1969: 110), for example, reminds us that the good Samaritan in Jesus' parable, the Jewish fiddler in Chekhov's "Rothschild's Fiddle," the Negro slave Jim in Mark Twain's *Huckleberry Finn*, and Sonya, the prostitute in Dostoevsky's *Crime and Punishment*, were all "inferior" or "marginal" persons in the societies they were a part of, and yet, each represented a type of universal value. The same role is frequently played by "inferior" groups within a society, such as the Hebrews in the ancient Near East, the Irish in early medieval Christendom, the Swiss in modern Europe, and Blacks in America (Turner, 1969:109; Harding, 1969).[6]

The poor, because of the daily existential crises they face, have an understanding of tragedy and suffering that is frequently lacking from the sensibilities of the nonpoor. The poor, who are forced "to make do with string where rope is needed" (Miller, 1965:31), often have to face the consequences of having the string break. Hunger, unpaid bills, job layoffs, broken promises, insults and indignities from caretaker agencies, all are tightly woven in the daily fabric of the lives of the poor—and, of course, sickness and death. These latter two, although universal experiences, loom larger in importance for the poor than for others better off in the society. This is so because the poor, unlike the nonpoor, have to face them more directly and more immediately. There are fewer protective devices, such as insurance and preventive checkups, to shield them from the harshness of these experiences.

So, clearly, tragedy and suffering do have their impact upon the sensibilities of the poor. Their experiences of tragedy and suffering form a prism through which their view of the world is filtered. The possible consequence, of course, is that their view is distorted. As the light of their experiences passes through this prism it is deflected, and what they think they see is not really the way things are.

Thus, a world view based on tragedy and suffering can be illusionary and misleading. But equally illusionary and misleading is a world view that attempts to remove all elements of tragedy and suffering from human experience, such as some middle-class ideologies and some middle-class religions try to do. The high priest of the middle-class comforting cult is often referred to as Norman Vincent Peale (1952). The view of life that Peale and those of his theological ilk portray is one which is devoid of doubt, despair, temptation, and failure. All mystery and transcendence are removed from human experience, along with the sense of judgment and accountability. In their place, they offer a one-dimensional model of man, in which everything is sweetness and light.[7]

One illusion, of course, is no better than another. An extreme tragic sense of life is equally suspect along with a view of life from which all sense of pathos has been removed. Both do injustice to a view of man that incorporates both his grandeur and misery.

But since our concern at the moment is with the contributions that the religion of the poor makes to the larger culture, it can be said that the tragic sense of life that is associated with the poor is a needed corrective for the over-optimistic view of man that is so prevalent in the dominant culture. On this point, the religious poor join company with the small band of novelists, playwrights, and theologians who also recognize that human experience is suffused with tragedy and suffering.[8]

However, how does one reconcile the tragic view of life that is expressed by the religious poor with the fact that the religious services of the poor are also demonstrative and dramatic, that is, that humor and joy are a basic component of the worship experience? At first glance, this seems like a contradiction. Logically it would appear that life is either passively endured or it is actively celebrated. If endured, the appropriate ritualistic mood would be somberness; if celebrated, the appropriate mood would be joyfulness. And yet, the fact is that in the religious behavior of the poor, both somberness and joyfulness are inextricably combined.

What appears at first to be a contradiction is really a paradox. And that is, that the ability to celebrate with abandon is most often found among those people who are no strangers to pain and oppression. Real celebration is not a retreat from the realities of injustice and evil, but occurs most authentically where these negative realities are recognized and confronted, not where they are avoided (Cox, 1969:25). To realize this makes for a better understanding of the sharp contrast that exists between the undemonstrative character of much of middle-class religion in America and the demonstrative character of so much of lower-class religion. Adherents of middle-class religion find it difficult to develop religious expressions of worship in which they celebrate with real abandon because they are oblivious and immune to the depths of tragedy and suffering. In contrast, those who are forced daily to face the realities of poverty have developed forms of religious expression that are festive and dramatic precisely because they have known, at first hand, what it means to experience tragedy, suffering, injustice, and evil.

Conclusions

This paper has argued that the functions and characteristics of the religion of the poor are complex, multifaceted, and paradoxical. The religion of the poor functions as both an escape and a creative force, as both a palliative and as a positive source of cultural and social meaning. The religion of the poor from an outside perspective is disorganized, but when viewed from within is seen as a type of behavior that is organized according to its own set of values and norms.

Too often the paradoxical nature of the religion of the poor has been overlooked. Too many scholars have emphasized only the escapist, palliative, and disorganized side of the religious behavior of the poor. In an effort to correct a one-sided interpretation, this paper has focused on describing and analyzing the other side of the paradox, the way the religion of the poor is creative, socially organized, and positive in its psychological and social consequences.

More specifically, the argument of this paper was that the religion of the poor contributes in significant and positive ways to the processes of identity formation and to the development and maintenance of cultural values and norms. The public religious service within the poverty community forms a stage, upon which, in dramatic fashion, the identity-conferral and identity-seeking roles are dynamically played. Within the context of the service the members present themselves to each other, and their self-identities are enhanced as they symbolically exchange selves, and as they mutually entertain each other.

With regards to the larger social environment, two contributions of the religion of the poor were discussed. First of all, it was suggested that the religious patterns of the poor

offer a challenge to the hierarchical structure of the general status system. The religious poor, with their emphasis on status equality, serve as a constant reminder to the larger society of just how precarious and fabricated the hierarchical status system really is. And, secondly, the religious poor offer an understanding of tragedy and suffering that is frequently lacking from the sensibilities of the religious nonpoor. The tragic sense of life associated with the religion of the poor is a needed corrective for the over-optimistic, one-dimensional view of man shared by the dominant culture, a view from which most elements of tragedy and suffering have been removed. In contrast to the majority of middle-class ideologies and middle-class religions, the religious poor offer a model of man which incorporates aspects of both his grandeur and misery, and a view of human experience in which both somberness and joyfulness are inextricably combined.

Notes

1. For a review of the literature that is critical of the disorganization, maladjustment theories, see Hine (1969).
2. Several recent empirical studies support the Weberian thesis regarding the paradoxical nature of religion. See Johnson (1961), G. Marx (1967), Robbins (1969), and Lebra (1970).
3. Geertz makes a distinction between "religious models *of* reality" and "religious models *for* reality."
4. I am indebted to Elizabeth Bott (1957) for an understanding of the importance of the distinction between the immediate and larger social environment.
5. Max Weber used the concept of the religious virtuoso to discuss a particular type of religious leader. I am applying it here to the entire congregation, both preacher and audience. For Weber's discussion, see Weber (1904–05:162–163).
6. Robert Blauner points out that the soul orientation so basic to Black culture can be looked at "as a philosophy of life or world view that places tragedy, suffering, and forbearance in a more central position than does the dominant American ethos" (1970:357).
7. For critiques of the religious views of Americans from which the tragic sense of life is absent, see Marty (1959: ch. 2) and Herberg (1960: ch. XI).
8. For example, novelists William Faulkner and Thornton Wilder, playwright Ingmar Bergman, and

theologians Paul Tillich, Reinhold Niebuhr, and James Cone. On their view of suffering and tragedy as well as in their expressive life style discussed above, the religious poor also share many similarities with the contemporary middle-class charismatic groups and the counterculture movement of the sixties. To elaborate on these similarities is not possible within the confines of this paper.

References

Alland, Alexander, Jr.
1962 " 'Possession' in a revivalistic Negro church." Journal for the Scientific Study of Religion 1: 204–213.

Blauner, Robert
1970 "Black culture: Myth or reality?" In Norman Whitten and John Szwed (Eds.), Afro-American Anthropology, pp. 347–366. New York: Free Press.

Boisen, Anton T.
1939a "Economic distress and religious experience." Psychiatry 2:185–194.
1939b "Religion and hard times." Social Action 5: 8–35.

Bott, Elizabeth
1957 Family and Social Network. London: Tavistock Publications.

Cox, Harvey
1969 The Feast of Fools. Cambridge: Harvard University Press.

Cutten, George
1927 Speaking with Tongues. New Haven: Yale University Press.

Eliade, Mircea
1961 "History of religions and a new humanism." History of Religion 1:1–8.

Elinson, Howard
1965 "The implications of pentecostal religion for intellectualism, politics, and race relations." American Journal of Sociology 70:403–415.

Firth, Raymond
1959 "Problem and assumption in anthropological study of religion." Journal of the Royal Anthropological Institute 89:129–148.

Gans, Herbert
1962 The Urban Villagers. New York: The Free Press.
1968 "Culture and class in the study of poverty: An approach to antipoverty research." People and Plans, pp. 321–346. New York: Basic Books.

Geertz, Clifford
1966 "Religion as a cultural system." In Michael Banton (Ed.), Anthropological Approaches to the Study of Religion, pp. 1–46. New York: Frederick A. Praeger, Inc.

Gerlach, Luther, and Virginia Hine
1970 People, Power, Change. Indianapolis: Bobbs-Merrill.

Glock, Charles, and Rodney Stark
1965 "The origin and evolution of religious groups." Religion and Society in Tension, pp. 242–259. Chicago: Rand McNally.

Hannerz, Ulf
1969 Soulside. New York: Columbia University Press.

Harding, Vincent
1969 "The uses of the Afro-American past." In Donald R. Cutler (Ed.), The Religious Situation 1969, pp. 829–840. Boston: Beacon Press.

Herberg, Will
1960 Protestant-Catholic-Jew. New York: Doubleday.

Hine, Virginia H.
1969 "Pentecostal glossolalia: Toward a functional interpretation." Journal for the Scientific Study of Religion 8: 211–226.

Holt, John
1940 "Holiness religion, cultural shock, and social reorganization." American Sociological Review 5:740–747.

Johnson, Benton
1961 "Do holiness sects socialize in dominant values?" Social Forces 39:309–316.

Kaplan, Berton
1965 "The structure of adaptive sentiments in a lower class religious group in Appalachia." Journal of Social Issues 21:126–141.

Lebra, Takie S.
1970 "Religious conversion as a breakthrough for transculturation: A Japanese sect in Hawaii." Journal for the Scientific Study of Religion 9: 181–196.

Lefever, Harry G.
1971 Ghetto Religion: A Study of the Religious Structures and Styles of a Poor White Community in Atlanta, Georgia. Unpublished Ph.D. dissertation, Emory University.

Liebow, Elliot
1967 Tally's Corner. Boston: Little, Brown.

Marty, Martin
1959 The New Shape of American Religion. New York: Harper.

Marx, Gary
1967 "Religion: Opiate or inspiration of civil rights militancy among Negroes?" American Sociological Review 32:64–72.

Marx, Karl, and Friedrich Engels
1957 On Religion. New York: Schocken Books. 1964 reprint.

Maslow, Abraham H.
  1964 Religion, Values, and Peak-Experiences. Columbus: Ohio State University Press.

Miller, S. M.
  1965 "The American lower classes: A typological approach." In Arthur B. Shostak & William Gomberg (Eds.), New Perspectives on Poverty, pp. 22–39. Englewood Cliffs, N.J.: Prentice-Hall.

Niebuhr, H. Richard
  1929 The Social Sources of Denominationalism. New York: Holt, Rinehart & Winston.

Peale, Norman V.
  1952 The Power of Positive Thinking. Englewood Cliffs, N.J.: Prentice-Hall.

Poblete, Renato, and Thomas O'Dea
  1960 "Anomie and the quest for community: The formation of sects among the Puerto Ricans of New York." American Catholic Sociological Review 21:18–36.

Pope, Liston
  1942 Millhands and Preachers. New Haven: Yale University Press.

Rainwater, Lee
  1970 Behind Ghetto Walls. Chicago: Aldine.

Robbins, Thomas
  1969 "Eastern mysticism and resocialization of drug users: The Meher Baba cult." Journal for the Scientific Study of Religion 8:308–317.

Rosenberg, Bruce
  1970 The Art of the American Folk Preacher. New York: Oxford University Press.

Schwartz, Gary
  1970 Sect Ideologies and Social Status. Chicago: University of Chicago Press.

Spiro, Melford
  1965 "Religious systems as culturally constituted defense mechanisms." In Melford Spiro (Ed.), Context and Meaning in Cultural Anthropology, pp. 100–113. New York: Free Press.

Turner, Victor
  1969 The Ritual Process. Chicago: Aldine.

Valentine, Charles
  1968 Culture and Poverty. Chicago: University of Chicago Press.

Van Gennep, Arnold
  1960 The Rites of Passage. Chicago: University of Chicago Press.

Weber, Max
  1947 The Theory of Social and Economic Organization. New York: Oxford University Press.
  1904– The Protestant Ethic and the Spirit of Capi-
  05 talism. New York: Charles Scribner's Sons. 1958 reprint.

Whyte, William F.
  1943 Street Corner Society. Chicago: University of Chicago Press.

R E A D I N G   8 . 2

Out of the Cauldron of Struggle: Black Religion and the Search for a New America

Vincent Harding

Let us begin near the beginning. If we take the emergence of the recognizable, organized Afro-Christian fellowships which first arose during the Revolutionary War period whether in Savannah, Georgia, or in Petersburg, Virginia, or in Philadelphia, Pennsylva-

Vincent Harding is Chairman of the Institute of the Black World in Atlanta and a faculty member of Pendle Hill, a Quaker study center near Philadelphia.
Reprinted from *Soundings* 61, 3 (1978), with permission of *Soundings* and the author.

nia—then it should be clear that the birth of the Black churches was a move toward pluralism. Their very surging into existence was a challenge to the Europe-oriented nature of white Christianity. But these first attempts at organized Afro-Christian fellowships were not only a move for religious pluralism. Any close observer who looked at the struggle of Black churches for autonomy and independence would have recognized that this struggle of Black churches for existence was, indeed, part of the struggle of Black people for self-definition, on the one hand, and for a new freedom in society on the other. It is significant that the very beginnings of organized Black religion came during the tumult, chaos and ferment of the Revolutionary period in this country, for what we sought was even more profoundly revolutionary than what the white revolutionaries were seeking.

We were seeking a whole new order of things. We could not get it at the outset, but even our initial attempts to create those first Baptist and AME churches were real struggles. They did not come out of conference documents declaring that now this shall be. They were real, hard, physical struggles. In Philadelphia, for instance, Black people literally massed in the aisles of their meeting places so that white preachers could not get to the pulpits to take them over from Black preachers. When they organized in Savannah, Andrew Bryan and his followers in the Baptist church there suffered whippings, arrests and dispersion by the white authorities. Insisting on their right to create the first Black Baptist church in that area, they came back again and again to organize and to reorganize until the Black Baptists were established in Georgia.

Was it out of that struggle that one day a man named Martin Luther King, Jr. came? Yes, it was, and we need to understand the full significance of that struggle for a little Black Baptist church in Savannah, Georgia. Not simply religious pluralism, but political, cultural, social and economic challenge to the very nature of American society was being offered in those so-called religious struggles. As the antebellum period went on, the struggle of Black people continued. We know something, I think, about the role of Black religion in the fight against slavery. In the South that role was represented to us in most catastrophic ways through the names of people like Gabriel Prosser or Denmark Vesey or Nat Turner who came out of the heart of the Afro-Christian religion of their time. They

were the most obvious manifestations of the bringing together of Black religion and Black revolutionary struggle for freedom.

On another level, at the other end, there were always those quiet Blacks in the cabins and in the canebrakes who created the tradition of simply praying for freedom as a part of their struggle; if you look through the documents, it is amazing how often you will find Black people who were not simply caught praying for freedom, but who were whipped until they bled because they were praying for freedom. And they kept on praying for freedom until freedom was theirs. This, too, was part of the struggle, not simply the obvious outer battle, but the inner spiritual battle which is no less important and no less crucial to the struggle for a new pluralism and a new American society.

We probably know best that out of Black religion came the songs of judgment on American white religion—the songs that said you white folks are "jiving": "Everybody talking about heaven ain't goin' there. Heaven, heaven, gonna walk all over God's heaven." "You better mind, you better mind. You got to give an account of yourself at the Judgment. You better mind." Or the songs that carried it even further: "Go down Moses, Way down in Egyptland, Tell old Pharaoh to let my people go." And, of course, always the songs of hope, like the one that began in the fields: "I shall overcome; I shall overcome someday." Through their religion Black people were calling for another vision of America, calling for another understanding of American society.

In the North as well the Black churches and Black religious leaders were central to the anti-slavery struggle. They were there in the Vigilance committees, there when Black people came running out of the South in search of freedom. The Black churches, the Black ministers, the Black congregations were there to gather them in to give them food, to give them shelter, to send them on their way to Canada or to bring them into the community of work and worship. The Black church was there in the peculiarly Northern struggles against discrimination and segregation; and the names of men like Henry Highland Garnett, William Ray, David Walker and Jermain Loguen ought to be familiar to all of us, but I know they are not.

All of this, though, was part of the search out of the cauldron of struggle, out of the matrix of Black religion. All of this was part of the search to break the white monolith called America, to create and to bring into being a pluralistic society.

While Black people were struggling from the base of the institutions of their religion in America, Black religion in America was at the same moment also saying to Black people, "We must turn to Africa, we must look to Africa." They looked to Africa as part of a search for identity. They looked to Africa as part of their sense of mission under God's Providence. They looked to Africa as a way of being independent of white domination. And even though they were looking to Africa in the search for identity, in the search for mission, in the search for independence, what we realize—paradoxically at times—is that identity, a sense of mission, and a sense of independence are all necessary to become a real part of a pluralistic society. So even as they were looking to Africa, Black people were preparing themselves to participate as critical co-creators of a new American society here on these tortured grounds.

The coming of the Civil War smashed many of the plans that Black people had made to emigrate to Africa. Some people, like Martin Delany, were literally on the edges of the American continent ready to go back to their homeland when the war changed all of their plans. But the war was not only a smasher of plans; it also brought with it an appearance of the opening up of new opportunities for the creation of a new society. Indeed, one of the most fascinating bodies of literature of the period is composed of the sermons, speeches, and articles which present a Black

theodicy, and Afro-American reading of God's liberating purposes in the Civil War, interpretations which often plunged more deeply to the heart of the war's terrible illuminating darkness than the best intuitions of an Abraham Lincoln. From the outset, from the first rumors of war, there were voices and visions in the Black communities of North and South which declared—against the loud protestations and heavy wisdom of the Union's political and intellectual leaders—that *their* God, the God who had delivered Israel, was at work. Somehow, these Black men and women knew that *their* God would use the war as a consuming fire to destroy the institution of slavery. The Black churches and their spokesmen were the key repositories of this prophecy, the major trumpets of its message.

Such Black vision most often carried with it great Black hope for new beginnings in America. After the war was over, Black religion played a central role in organizing and inspiring Black people for their crucial role in the new Reconstruction experiment in the South. Blacks understood Reconstruction as an attempt, at least in the conquered Confederacy, to create a new pluralistic political order. Black people saw themselves working for a new society in the South. With the help of allies from North and South they tried to organize themselves to create this new society. Black preachers were consistently among the key political leaders of this move to create a new society in the South. Black churches were the organizing bases for the transformational struggle, for the struggle in which a once-enslaved Black people had to transform themselves as well as transform their society.

Often the spirit of Black religious revivalism filled the Reconstruction political campaigns so that people could not tell whether they were going to a political campaign or to a revival meeting. Very often they were going to both. There was the hum of Black religion on the edges of the constitutional conventions and in the new legislatures that came into being all across the South. As one reads the documents of those Black people, who met regularly to decide and declare what they wanted, you see them everywhere raising the issue of what we now call the common good. They lifted up the need for a society that would engage the gifts, the talents and the visions of all of its members. They asked for a society—and were willing to work for a society—which would benefit all of its people, where the strong would help the weak even if the weak could give no quid pro quo.

To a large degree it was their white allies who betrayed their vision and helped another American vision prevail—the vision of expansion over the Indians, of moving out into the Pacific; the vision of railroads and factories, of American capitalism. That other vision prevailed over the humane visions that were being put forward in the post-Civil War period by Black people when they spoke out of their best religious sense.

As a result, Black people had to endure the bitterness and the terror of the post-Reconstruction years. That was the period when the greatest task of all was the task of holding on to our humanity in the midst of a dehumanizing situation. That was the time when the greatest task was in many cases simply to hold on to our lives in the midst of the lynch mobs and the crowds who gathered to see us burned alive. That was the time when the greatest task was to hold on to the vision that our own best gifts would one day be used to help build a new society in America. We had to hold on to these things, this vision, this understanding, this sense of ourselves; we had to hold on to them through a horrible period in our lives, because we knew that if we lost these things then there was no hope for us, for our children, or for America. And in this period, the role of Black religion was absolutely central in holding us up lest we should fall.

Out of the structures of Black religion we created new institutions, new churches, lodges, benevolent societies, schools, coura-geously edited newspapers, many of them in the South. All of these fed into the critical role of maintaining the vision, maintaining the vision that there could be something else, maintaining the hope that there could be another America beyond the disfranchisement and terror, beyond the lynchings, beyond the burnings. All these contributed to the hope, the Black hope that could create such a testimony as "Nobody knows the troubles I've seen, Glory, Hallelujah!" What kind of a word is that? "Nobody knows the troubles I've seen, Glory, Hallelujah!"

In that hard time, the same time in which we were trying to maintain the vision for America, we were engaged again in the familiar dialectic of our experience. Churches were organizing for migration and for emigration: migration to the West, to Kansas, to Oklahoma, to California; emigration to Africa. Edward Blyden, Bishop Henry McNeil Turner, and many others were crossing all through the South, preaching to Black people the necessity for a new pride, a new sense of mission, a new responsibility for Africa. Out of this preaching of the 1880's, the 1890's and the turn of the century, many Black people in America did, indeed, go back to the African homeland; in a strange and resonant sense they had, in some cases, a crucial effect on the building of a new African freedom struggle at the beginning of the twentieth century.

But by the time of World War I, much of the more radical force and the radical hope of Black religion was operating outside of the Afro-Christian institutional setting. Men and women were raising new questions outside of the Black churches, raising questions to Black people in the churches and to white people in the churches about the relationship of Black people to white American Christianity and its basic assumptions. So we began to see phenomena like the Moorish Science Temple coming not out of study conferences but out of the back streets of Newark, New Jersey. In little meetings Black men declared,

"We are not coloreds; we are not niggers; we are Moors; we are the Moorish people, the tribe of the Moors revived here in America." They were certainly not Christians. Indeed, they became direct descendents of the Nation of Islam. One sees this spirit in the Garvey movement and in the ferment of the post-World War I Black America that helped to lift Garvey to a height that had not been known by Black leadership up to that time, though it was a height for which he was ultimately unprepared. Ferment came out of the Black community as through migration we created our new place in American industrial society. Garvey came into the midst of that great human movement. Out of the Garvey forces came the African Orthodox church, questioning anew the apparently monolithic nature of American society and of American Christianity.

In the period at the end of the twenties and the beginning of the Depression there came upon the scene Father Divine, another of that set of Messianic figures who stand outside of the traditional institutional expressions of Black religion. Yet Father Divine was for America the ultimate testimony to the plural nature of God. Here was one who came claiming that God, God himself, was a southern Black sharecropper—a fascinating starting point for a new American theology! And, of course, in this same period of ferment, we first saw in Detroit, Michigan, the intimations of the group called the Temple People who under the leadership of Elijah Muhammed later became the Nation of Islam, offering some intimations of its powerful, highly influential voice of judgment on white American Christianity. By the post-World War II period, this was a voice that no one could ignore, at least not in the Black community. And when that voice became one with the voice of Malcolm X, its power was at once deeply disturbing and increasingly attractive to many of us who were Black in America. Beyond the direct political implications of this development, what that voice

did, what Malcolm X did, what the Muslims did—which we so often do not notice—was to offer another non-white, non-western base for Black religious sensibility. So now it becomes more fully clear that what these movements represent—and there were many less well-known ones like them—what they tell us, is that Black religion anticipated much of the non-western religious revival in American society. This revival in many cases came out of the Black community before it was seen any place else. The search for a new religious pluralism in American society takes place, you see, not only through the churches, but through other forms of religious organization as well. It surged up out of the cauldron of Black struggle, became the expression of a people in search of a self-definition which would provide integrity and hope for their lives. All of these developments were part of the Black subversion of white religious, political and social domination of America.

By the early 1960's, that campaign of subversion had exploded into a massive assault in the courts and on the streets for the right of Black people to participate in all of the public institutions of the society—from the dirty bathrooms in filling stations to the floor of the U.S. Congress. I hope we understand that this struggle was, at least partly, a struggle to be seen, to be heard, to be dealt with. I trust we understand as well that unless men and women and children are seen and heard and dealt with directly as human beings there can be no true pluralistic relationship. It was we who by the beginning of the 1960's pressed this issue of confrontative pluralism into the heart of the American society. In the South our movement was a very special movement. It took on the combined fervor and hope of the earlier Reconstruction period. It embodied the mass attraction of the Garvey movement and it had much of the organizing and singing force of the left-wing labor struggles of the 1930's. We were at once in search of ourselves and in search of America.

Black religion was central to this pilgrimage campaign known as the Civil Rights or Freedom Movement—central to its fervor, central to its hope and central to its early organizing style. The Black churches all over the South were the organizing basis for that movement. The Black churches, taking their risks and paying their prices in burnings and bombings and in mortgages cut off, provided the meeting, praying and marching grounds for that movement. The religious symbolism of the Black community, the language of the Black religious community, at many times even the ineffable faith of the best of Black religion were endemic to that movement. That is why as early as 1957 Martin King could speak as if everybody understood what he meant when he said: "We are here to redeem the soul of America." That is why he could come proclaiming the need for loving white people, for structuring a just society, for creating a new loving community in America, for doing the will of God. And the extent to which America was and is deadly uncomfortable with that language may well be the measure of its dying. (And the extent to which men and women are now reinvestigating the realities behind such language is the extent to which we may dare to hope.)

Of course, the role of the preachers always leaped beyond language into action. King, Fred Shuttlesworth, C. T. Vivian, Jim Lawson, Kelly Miller Smith, Jim Bevel, Charles Sherrod, John Lewis, C. K. Steele, Ralph Abernathy and Wyatt T. Walker are only the beginning of a long list of the best known in the South. And Malcolm—yes, he too was a minister, remember—moved in his own way in the North. Behind the ministers and behind the language and behind the symbols, of course, were the critical masses of the Black people of the South. Because it was a search for hope, for new beginnings, it was a religious crusade in many, many ways, and in case we have forgotten, I want to remind you about the spirit in which so many people carried on. Let me read just one short section

of a reminiscence from John Lewis, who was one of the early leaders of SNCC and prior to that one of the early organizers in Nashville's exemplary student movement in 1959 and 1960. John is speaking in a magazine interview here and he shares something that will help us catch again the sense of what was going on and how deeply religious this movement was. He said,

Woolworth's was where the first violence occurred. A young student at Fisk, Maxine Walker, and an exchange student named Paul LePrad, were sitting at the counter at Woolworth's. This young white man came up and hit Paul and knocked him down and hit the young lady. Then all type of violence started. Pulling people, pushing people over the counter, throwing things, grinding out cigarettes on people, pouring ketchup in their hair, that type of thing. Then the cops moved in and started arresting [Black] people.

That was my first time, the first time for most of us, to be arrested. I just felt . . . that it was like being involved in a Holy Crusade. I really felt that what we were doing was so in keeping with the Christian faith. You know, we didn't welcome arrest. We didn't want to go to jail. But it became . . . a moving spirit. Something just sort of came over us and consumed us. And we started singing, "We Shall Overcome," and later, while we were in jail we started singing "Paul and Silas, bound in jail, had no money for their bail. . . ." It became a religious ceremony that took place in jail. I remember that very, very well, that first arrest.

Even after we were taken to jail, there was a spirit there, something you witness, I guess, during a Southern Baptist revival. People talk about being born again or their faith being renewed. I think our faith was renewed. Jail in a sense became the way toward conversion, was the act of baptism, was the process of baptism.[1]

The movement did not, of course, remain in that heady stage. As in every struggle of human beings, other stages were necessary, other stages were unavoidable. By 1966, under the immediate stimulation of some of the speeches of that audacious spirit of Black religion, Rev. Adam Clayton Powell, Jr., and under the television cameras of the nation, Stokeley Carmichael and Willie Ricks in Mississippi raised the cry of Black Power. No longer, "I love everybody," but "Black Power." (It took many people a long time to realize that those two slogans were not necessarily incompatible; and, indeed, those two must necessarily be joined together for any true pluralism in America.) Of great importance, too, was the fact that Black Power brought to the movement a much more fundamental—or at least more outspoken—political and economic critique of white American values, politics and foreign policy, especially focusing on the Vietnam War.

Out of this new vision, out of this Black Power stress, came a new understanding, a new possibility for a politically conscious Black theology to be done. And out of the Black theology, whatever we think of it, came a new challenge to white American Christianity. Out of Black theology came new questions about America's public religion and whom it includes. Out of Black Power and Black Studies and Black History came new questions about America's past, America's received, official culture—who it had included and who it had excluded, and what, therefore, it had meant.

By the late 1960's the powerful force of the Black movement, combined with the repressive forces of the American government which it brought out into the open, had helped to inspire and create other movements raising new questions and dealing with new values, new possibilities—new sexual values, new racial values, new political values, new economic and cultural values. The Black movement in America had, indeed, helped to create the opening toward which it had always been reaching: the possibility for a real American pluralism to come into being. The substance, the reality, was still very vague, but now the possibility was there more than ever before. The Black movement had created the stage for the possibility of a Second Coming of America.

What shall it be? What are the elements of its substance? How shall it be defined? Who shall define it, this New Coming of America? Will it come about, be brought, in any way that is humane? These, it seems to me, are the kinds of questions we ought to be exploring in departments of religious studies. That is why . . . we are all amateur Americans. We are all amateur Americans because America is an amateur situation. The tryouts are still going on. America is still an experiment that could go absolutely wrong.

Occupying a land mass which is continental in breadth and amazingly variegated in texture and geography, living in a country where the cries of the original, nearly annihilated natives and the enslaved Black immigrants may still range through the air, sharing a national body politic which is made up of all the peoples of the world, we are uncertain how to respond as the cities and countryside reverberate with apparently dissonant, irreconcilable calls from all the peoples for recognition of all their roots, all their grievances, all their interests and all their integrity. Located at such a place and in such a moment in history, we are now struggling for the definition, for the meaning of America, for our own age. Religious pluralism, of course, is only one element of that struggle. Much more important is the fact that a truly pluralistic and humane society must be undergirded and overarched by a common vision of the public good, and no vaguely articulated, or selfishly contrived pluralism may be used as an escape from that common sense of what we need as a community of people. For without that capacity to see ourselves ultimately as a community, without that common basis on which community must be built, we are in tremendous danger of disintegrating into hundreds of private, warring, special interests (who will not, for instance, pay taxes to support the well-being of the whole; who will, for instance—at astonishingly young ages—physically attack helpless, elderly citizens to grab the pittances of their social security and welfare money; who will, for instance, pour life-destroying industrial wastes into rivers, or produce essentially poisonous products for profits alone). "Where there is no vision, the people perish. . . ."

The older American visions, including the older public, civil religion, are now essentially in shambles. To a large degree, they ought to be, because they never included Black Americans nor a whole lot of other people here and elsewhere. But the fact remains that no new society is possible without new vision, without a controlling, defining vision, wielded by a directing social force in the society. What will be the content of the new vision for the new society? Who will be the members of the critical, transformative social force? These are the critical questions to which we must address ourselves. They present a massive arena for exploration and experimentation.

I do not claim to be the bearer of any answers now, but I can affirm one thing: if we are to have a truly humane and a truly pluralistic society, then committed Black people must play a central role in the creation of the new vision and in the ordering of the new society. Why do I say that? There are three or four reasons. The first reason why Black people must play a central role in the creation of the new American society is the experience and history that we have had with white racism in America. It has taught us that we simply cannot afford to put our future into anybody else's hands, whether John Brown or Abraham Lincoln or Jimmy Carter—once hopefully known as JC. That is one reason. We must be engaged as participants, as leaders.

Secondly, we have *earned* the right to be co-creators of the new America. We Black people, whether we know it or not, whether anybody else knows it or not, have earned the right and the legitimacy through our unbroken and creative struggle for freedom in this country, for a new kind of America.

Through our struggle we have shaped and been shaped by a religion—and a sense of community—which can be profoundly humanizing, for it has long been the religion of the oppressed. Our religion has caught up in itself all of the glory and the agony of the universal human condition; not the "universal" human that we usually talk about in the western world, but the *universal* human condition. Reaching out beyond itself, reaching out beyond its oppressors, reaching out beyond the religion of its oppressors, our religion has caught up all of the great human experiences of scattering, of defeat, of trial and tribulation, of hope and ecstasy. Black religion at its best overflows with hope in the humane possibilities of America. It has borne that hope in the possibilities of America, even in the face of inhumanity, chaos and death. Is that what Bellah calls "the faith of loss?" Or is Black religion involved in something still more mysterious, absurd and overwhelming? "Nobody knows the trouble I've seen, Glory! Glory, hallelujah!" Whether whites or others like it or not, whether we Black people like it or not, women and men who have come through, who have created such a spiritual crucible in the struggle for a humanizing freedom, have both earned the right and created the responsibility to participate centrally in the making of a new America, in the search for a new vision.

Thirdly, and others have said this in many other ways, we are America's best bridges to the non-white majority of the world. Our religion and philosophy with their easternness, their life-affirming, nature-joining components, our historic experience with oppression and suffering, our knowledge of white western technological ways: all of these qualify us to serve in the struggle to make America safe for a new relationship to the rest of the world. (And in a most imperfect but fascinating way, Andy Young is a portent of both the possibilities and the dangers of that coming role.)

Fourthly, we must be involved in the creation of the new vision and the new ordering of the new society just because of our style. Any humane living that is really new in America needs our magnificently audacious and creative style—and enough said about that.

Now none of this denies our own amateur status as Americans. In a sense, though, we Blacks are professional amateurs at the re-creation of America. Still we must also recognize the many dangers built into our current situation as Blacks in America. There are profound internal problems within the Black community. On the bottom levels of its developing class structure there are men, women and children with too large an experience of being victims, too heavy a mentality of being victims and not being able to do anything for themselves. At the bottom layers of our class structure there are too many people who have been excluded from the processes of disciplined work and productivity and who do not know how to participate in or build their own society. They will need a tremendous amount of reviving and revitalization. At all levels of the Black community we have had a massive exposure to the modern Americanization process, especially TV and movies and their great emphasis on selfishness, greed, and violence, and on the exploitation and debasement of ideas, institutions and human beings. And at the top, what we used to call "the classes" of the Black community, we have come to the point where we are frighteningly dependent for our livelihoods on the local and national governmental sectors in the society. We are coming to a point where we are in great danger of owing our total allegiance to America as it is, not as it could be. In reaction some of our best minds in the universities, in the public sector and in the churches are tending toward cynicism and privatism and despair at the loss of all that was best about our religion. And these are only some of the most obvious dangers that beset us.

Still, in the face of these dangers, following the great and maddening tradition of Black

religion, I dare to hope. I dare to hope that Black people will continue to provide leadership to the community of visionaries that I believe is persistently coming up out of America. I believe that we will continue to provide leadership to the company of seers, to the fellowship of hope which our movement has helped to create. I believe that Langston Hughes spoke a deep truth and saw a great vision when he wrote forty years ago:

O, let America be America again—
The land that never has been yet—
And yet must be—
The land where *every* man is free.
The land that's mine—
The Poor man's, Indian's, Negro's, ME—
Who made America,
Whose sweat and blood, whose faith and pain,
Whose hand at the foundry, whose plow in the rain,
Must bring back our mighty dream again.

O, yes,
I say it plain,
America never was America to me,
And yet I swear this oath—
America will be!
An ever-living seed.
Its dream
Lies deep in the heart of me.

We, the people, must redeem
Our land, the mines, the plants, the rivers,
The mountains and the endless plain—
All, all the stretch of these great green states—
And make America again![2]

This is a glorious amateurism, isn't it? In the cauldron of the struggle to recreate a pluralistic, humane America, these words are another way of expressing the genius of Black religion, another way of saying, "Nobody knows the troubles I've seen, Glory! Glory, hallelujah!"

Notes

1. Jim Sessions and Sue Thrasher, "A New Day Begun: Interview with John Lewis," *Southern Exposure,* IV, 3, 20.

2. "Let America Be America Again," copyright © 1938 by Langston Hughes; renewed 1965 by Langston Hughes. Reprinted by permission of Harold Ober Associates.

R E A D I N G   8 . 3

The Feminist Critique in Religious Studies

Rosemary Radford Ruether

Effects of Women's Exclusion on Theological Culture

The exclusion of women from leadership and theological education results in the elimination of women as shapers of the official theological culture. Women are confined to passive and secondary roles. Their experience is not incorporated into the official culture. Those who do manage to develop as religious thinkers are forgotten or have their stories told through male-defined standards of what women can be. In addition, the public theological culture is defined by men, not only in the absence of, but against women. Theology not only assumed male standards of normative humanity, but is filled with an ideological bias that defines women as secondary and inferior members of the human species.

Many examples of this overt bias against women in the theological tradition can be cited. There is the famous definition of woman by Thomas Aquinas as a "misbegotten male." Aquinas takes this definition of women from Aristotle's biology, which identifies the male sperm with the genetic form of the embryo. Women are regarded as contributing only the matter or "blood" that fleshes out the form of the embryo. Hence, the very existence of women must be explained as a biological accident that comes about through a deformation of the male seed by the female "matter," producing a defective human or woman who is defined as lacking normative human standing.

Rosemary Radford Ruether is Georgia Harkness Professor of Applied Theology at Garrett-Evangelical Theological Seminary in Evanston, Illinois.
Reprinted from *Soundings* 64 (Winter, 1981), with permission of *Soundings* and the author.

Women are regarded as deficient physically, lacking full moral self-control and capacity for rational activity. Because of this defective nature women cannot represent normative humanity. Only the male can exercise headship or leadership in society. Aquinas also deduces from this that the maleness of Christ is not merely a historical accident, but a necessity. In order to represent humanity Christ must be incarnated into normative humanity, the male. Only the male, in turn, can represent Christ in the priesthood.

This Thomistic view of women is still reflected in Roman Catholic canon law where it is decreed that women are "unfit matter" for ordination. If one were to ordain a woman it, quite literally, would not "take," any more than if one were to ordain a monkey or an ox. Some recent Episcopalian conservatives who declared that to ordain a woman [is] like ordaining a donkey are fully within this medieval scholastic tradition. Whether defined as inferior or simply as "different," theological and anthropological justifications of women's exclusion from religious learning and leadership can be found in every period of Jewish and Christian thought. Sometimes this exclusion of women is regarded as a matter of divine law, as in Old Testament legislation. Christian theologians tend to regard it as a reflection of "natural law," or the "order of nature," which, ultimately, also is a reflection of divine intent. Secondly, women's exclusion is regarded as an expression of woman's greater proneness to sin or corruption. Thus, as in the teaching of I Timothy, women are seen as "second in creation but first in sin" (I Timothy 2, 13–14).

The male bias of Jewish and Christian theology not only affects the teaching about woman's person, nature and role, but also generates a symbolic universe based on the patriarchal hierarchy of male over female. The subordination of woman to man is replicated in the symbolic universe in the imagery of divine-human relations. God is imaged as a great patriarch over against the earth or Creation, imaged in female terms. Likewise Christ is related to the Church as bridegroom to bride. Divine-human relations in the macrocosm are also reflected in the microcosm of the human being. Mind over body, reason over the passions, are also seen as images of the hierarchy of the "masculine" over the "feminine." Thus everywhere the Christian and Jew are surrounded by religious symbols that ratify male domination and female subordination as the normative way of understanding the world and God. This ratification of male domination runs through every period of the tradition, from Old to New Testament, Talmud, Church Fathers and canon law, Reformation Enlightenment and modern theology. It is not a marginal, but an integral part of what has been received as mainstream, normative traditions.

The Task of Feminism in Religious Studies

The task of women's studies in religious education is thus defined by this historical reality of female exclusion and male ideological bias in the tradition. The first task of feminist critique takes the form of documenting the fact of this male ideological bias itself and tracing its sociological roots. One thinks of works such as Mary Daly's first book, *The Church and the Second Sex* (Harper, 1968), or the book I edited, *Religion and Sexism: Images of Women in the Jewish and Christian Traditions* (Simon and Schuster, 1974). These works trace male bias against women from the Scriptures, Talmud and Church Fathers through medieval, Reformation and modern theologians. They intend to show that this bias is not marginal or accidental. It is not an expression of idiosyncratic, personal views

of a few writers, but runs through the whole tradition and shapes in conscious and unconscious ways the symbolic universe of Jewish and Christian theology.

The second agenda of feminist studies in religion aims at the discovery of an alternative history and tradition that supports the inclusion and personhood of women. At the present time, there are two very distinct types of alternative traditions that are being pursued by religious feminists. Within the Jewish and Christian theological academies the alternative tradition is being sought within Judaism and Christianity. However, many feminists have come to believe that no adequate alternative can be found within these religions. They wish to search for alternatives outside and against Judaism and Christianity. Some of these feminists are academically trained religious scholars who teach in religious studies or women's studies in colleges and universities and others are more self-trained writers that relate to the popular feminist spirituality movement, such as Starhawk (*The Spiral Dance*, Harper, 1979) and Z. Budapest (*The Holy Book of Women's Mysteries*, Susan B. Anthony Coven No. I, 1979).

This latter group draw their sources from anthropology and historical scholarship of matriarchal societies and ancient religions centered in the worship of the Mother Goddess rather than the patriarchal God of Semitic religions. They see the worship of the Mother Goddess as a woman's religion stemming from pre-patriarchal or matriarchal societies. This religion is believed to have been suppressed by militant patriarchal religions, but survived underground in secret, women-centered, nature religions persecuted by the dominant male religion. Medieval witchcraft is believed to have been such a female religion. Modern feminist witchcraft or "Wicca" sees itself as the heir to this persecuted goddess religion.

Writers of this emergent goddess religion draw from an anthropological scholarship of matriarchal origins that developed in the nineteenth century and which many scholars today regard as outdated and historically dubious. There has not yet been an opportunity for an adequate dialogue between these counter-cultural religious feminists and academic feminist scholarship. This is doubly difficult since goddess religion is not simply a matter of correct or incorrect scholarship, but of a rival faith stance. Most goddess religionists would feel that even if an adequate historical precedent for their faith cannot be found in the past, it should be created and they are creating it now.

The question of the relation of Jewish and Christian to post-Christian feminist religion will be discussed again later in this paper. For the moment, I will discuss some aspects of the search for an alternative tradition within Judaism and Christianity and its incorporation into theological education in seminaries and religious studies departments.

There now exists a fair body of well-documented studies in alternative traditions within Scripture and Jewish and Christian history. These studies show that male exclusion of women from leadership roles and theological reflection is not the whole story. There is much ambiguity and plurality in the traditions about women and the roles women have actually managed to play. For example, evidence is growing that women in first-century Judaism were not uniformly excluded from study in the synagogues. The rabbinic dicta against teaching women Torah thus begins to appear, not as a consensus of that period, but as one side of an argument—that eventually won—against the beginnings of inclusion of women in discipleship.

Similarly the teachings of I Timothy about women keeping silence appear, not as the uniform position of the New Testament Church, but as a second generation reaction against widespread participation of women in leadership, teaching and ministering in first-generation Christianity. Indeed the very fact that such vehement commandments

against women learning and teaching were found in the traditions should have been a clue to the existence of widespread practices to the contrary. Otherwise, the statements would have been unnecessary. But because the documents were used as Scripture or normative tradition, rather than historical documents, this was not realized.

The participation of women in early Christianity was not simply an accident of sociology, but a conscious expression of an alternative anthropology and soteriology. The equality of men and women in the image of God was seen as restored in Christ. The gifts of the prophetic spirit, poured out again at the Messianic coming, were understood, in fulfillment of the Messianic prediction of the prophet Joel, to have been given to the "maidservants" as well as the "menservants" of the Lord (Acts 2, 17–21). Baptism overcomes the sinful divisions among people and makes us one in the Christ: Jew and Greek, male and female, slave and free (Galatians 3, 28). Thus, the inclusion of women expressed an alternative theology in direct confrontation with the theology of patriarchal subordination of women. The New Testament now must be read, not as a consensus about women's place, but rather as a conflict and struggle over two alternative understandings of the gospel that suggested different views of male and female.

This alternative theology of equality, of women as equal in the image of God, as restored to equality in Christ and as commissioned to preach and minister by the Spirit, did not just disappear with the reassertion of patriarchal norms in I Timothy. It can be traced as surfacing again and again in different periods of Christian history. The strong role played by women in ascetic and monastic life in late antiquity and the early Middle Ages reflects a definite appropriation by women of a theology of equality in Christ that was understood as being applicable particularly to the monastic life. Celibacy was seen as abolishing sex-role differences and restoring men and women to their original equivalence in the image of God. As the male Church deserted this theology, female monastics continued to cling to it and understood their own vocation out of this theology. The history of female monasticism in the late Middle Ages and the Counter-Reformation is one of a gradual success of the male Church in suppressing this latent feminism of women's communities. It is perhaps then not accidental that women in renewed female religious orders in Roman Catholicism today have become militant feminists, to the consternation of the male hierarchy. . . .

Translation of Women's Studies in Religion into Educational Praxis

Obviously women cannot affect an educational system until they first secure their own access to it. It has taken approximately one hundred and twenty-five years for most schools of theological education to open their doors to women and then to include women in sufficient numbers for their concerns to begin to be recognized. Women began to enter theological schools of the Congregational tradition beginning with Oberlin in the 1840s and Methodist institutions in the 1870s. Only in the 1970s have some Roman Catholic and Jewish seminaries been open to women. Moreover, even liberal Protestant institutions did not experience any "critical mass" of female students until the 1970s.

Usually, access to theological education precedes winning the right to ordination. Winning the educational credentials for ordination then becomes a powerful wedge to winning the right of ordination itself. It is for that reason that there may be efforts to close Roman Catholic seminaries, at least those directly related to Rome, to women. Rumor has it (as of this writing) that a decree has been written but not yet promulgated in Rome forbidding women to attend pontifical semi-

naries (which would include all Jesuit seminaries, but not most diocesan and order seminaries). Women's tenure in professional schools of theology cannot be regarded as secure until they win the right to ordination. Only then can they develop a larger number of women students and attain the moral and organizational clout to begin to make demands for changes in the context of the curriculum.

Generally, demands for feminist studies begin with the organization of a caucus of women theological students. They then begin to demand women's studies in the curriculum and women faculty who can teach such courses. In many seminaries, particularly in U.S. liberal Protestant institutions, there has been some response to these demands: some women faculty have been hired, and some women's studies incorporated into the curriculum. It is at this point that we can recognize several stages of resistance to the implied challenge to the tradition.

One standard strategy of male faculty is to seek and retain one or two women on the faculty, but to give preference to women who are "traditional scholars," not feminists. This is fairly easy to do by the established rules of the guild, while, at the same time, appearing to be "objective." Feminist studies are nontraditional. They force one to use non-traditional methods and sources and to be something of a generalist. Their content is still in flux and experimentation. Rare is the person who can fulfill the expectations of both traditional scholarship and feminist scholarship equally well. So it is easy to attack such persons as "unscholarly," and to fail to tenure them in preference to those women who prefer to be "one of the boys." As of this writing there is an alarming erosion of feminist faculty talent in theological education through precisely this method. This has forced feminist scholars in theological education to band together in a new national organization, Feminist Theology and Ministry, in order to defend the employment of feminists in existing institutions of theological education.

Efforts are also underway to create new, alternative settings for women's studies in religion. For example, groups in the Boston-Washington corridor and in Chicago (largely, but not exclusively, Roman Catholic) are seriously considering the development of autonomous feminist theology schools for women, since the existing (especially Roman Catholic) institutions have proved so unfavorable to their interests.

In some other settings a decade-long struggle for women's studies in religion is beginning to bear fruit. For example, at the Harvard Divinity School, bastion of "traditional" education, a pilot program of graduate assistants in women's studies in various fields has continued for some eight years, for much of this time under constant threat of liquidation. However, a study of the program located one of its chief flaws in the lack of prestige and respect given to the women's studies teachers by the tenured faculty. As a result, a new level of funding has been developed to allow this program to be continued and eventually to be converted into a permanent research center for women in religion, with five full-time junior and senior faculty appointments. It remains to be seen whether this expanded "prestige" will not result in some of the same pressure to prefer traditional over feminist scholars.

In the development of feminist studies in the curriculum, most institutions move through several stages. The first stage is a grudging allowance of a generalist course on women's studies in religion that is taught outside the structure of the curriculum and usually by a person marginal to the faculty. The male faculty tend to feel little respect for the content of the course (about which they generally know nothing) or its instructor, and no commitment to its continuance as a regular part of the curriculum.

The second stage is when faculty begin to acquire women in one or more regular fields who are both respected as scholars and prepared to do women's studies. Women's studies courses can then be initiated that are located in the various regular disciplines of the curriculum, such as Biblical studies, Church history, theology, ethics, pastoral psychology, preaching and liturgy or Church administration. These courses, however, are taught as occasional electives. They attract only feminist students, mostly females and a few males. The rest of the student body is not influenced by them. Most of the faculty ignore them. The new material in them does not affect the foundational curriculum. In other words, women's studies in religion goes on as a marginal and duplicate curriculum. There is now a course in "systematic theology" and a second one on "feminist" theology. The foundational courses continue as before. Therefore, implicitly, they claim the patriarchal bias in theology as the "real" or "true" theology.

The third stage would come when feminist studies begin to affect the foundational curriculum itself. Here we might detect two more stages. The third stage would be when foundational curricula continue as usual, except for an occasional "ladies' day" when women's concerns are discussed. Thus, for example, one would teach twelve weeks of traditional male Church history, and then one week in which "great women" are considered. The fourth and optimum situation would be reached when feminist critique really penetrates the whole foundational curriculum and transforms the way in which all the topics are considered. Thus, it becomes impossible to deal with any topic of theological studies without being aware of sexist and nonsexist options in the tradition and bringing that out as an integral part of one's hermeneutic. Thus, for example, one would understand St. Paul as a man whose theology is caught up in ambivalent struggle between various alternatives: between an exclusivist and a universal faith, between an historical and an eschatological faith, and between a patriarchal and an integrative faith. The way he handled the third ambiguity, moreover, conditioned fundamentally the way he handled the first two ambiguities. Thus, one cannot understand Paul as a whole without incorporating the question of sexism into the context of his theology.

Generally we can say that most seminaries who have dealt with women's studies at all are somewhere between stage one and stage two, usually at stage one. A few have done an occasional "ladies' day" in the foundational curriculum. Few have even begun to imagine what it would mean to reach the optimum incorporation of feminism into the foundational curriculum, as a normal and normative part of the interpretive context of the whole. Moreover women's studies in religion has not yet matured to the point where it is able to offer a comprehensive reconstruction of methodology and tradition in various fields. For example, a genuine feminist reconstruction of systematic theology is yet to be written.

Even further down the road is the "retraining" of male faculty who are able to take such work into account. There are exceptions. Occasionally one finds that prodigy, a male professor who early recognized the value of the feminist critique and has been able, easily and gracefully, to incorporate it into his teaching with a minimum of defensiveness or breast-beating. In general, however, one would have to say that women's studies in theological education is still marginal and vulnerable. The conservative drift of the seminaries means that increasing numbers of women students themselves are non- or anti-feminist. Cadres of explicitly hostile white male students are emerging. Constant struggle is necessary to maintain momentum or even to prevent slipback. The recent publication of the book *Your Daughters Shall Prophesy* (Pilgrim Press, 1980), reflects on this ten-year struggle for feminist theological education in several major educational settings.

Alternative Views of Feminism and Religious Studies

Finally, we must say that feminists in religion are by no means united in what they understand to be the optimum feminist reconstruction of religion. We also have to reckon with the fact that religion is not simply an academic discipline. It is an integral part of popular culture. Concern with it has to do with *modus vivendi* of large numbers of people in many walks of life. It shapes mass institutions, the Church and the Synagogue, as well as alternative religious communities that emerge to fill people's need for life symbols. Thus, the interest in feminism and religion has an urgency, as well as a rancor, that is different from that in academic disciplines.

There are several different lines that are emerging both in academics and across the religious institutions and movements of popular culture today. One group, who could be identified as evangelical feminists, believe that the message of Scripture is fundamentally egalitarian. Scripture, especially the New Testament, proposes a new ideal of "mutual submission" of men and women to each other. This has been misread as the subjugation of women by the theological tradition. These feminists would help to clean up the sexism of Scripture by better exegesis. It would be incorrect to interpret these evangelical feminists as always limited by a pre-critical method of scriptural interpretation. Their limitations are often more pastoral than personal. They are concerned to address a certain constituency, the members of the evangelical churches from which they come, with the legitimacy of an egalitarian understanding of Biblical faith. They sometimes limit themselves to this kind of exegesis because they know it is the only way to reach that constituency.

A second view, which I would call the "liberationist" position, takes a more critical view of Scripture. People with this view believe there is a conflict between the prophetic, iconoclastic message of the prophetic tradition, with its attack on oppressive and self-serving religion, and the failure to apply this message to subjugated minorities in the patriarchal family, especially the women and slaves. The vision of redemption of the Biblical tradition transcends the inadequacies of past consciousness. It goes ahead of us, pointing toward a new and yet unrealized future of liberation whose dimensions are continually expanding as we become more sensitive to injustices which were overlooked in past cultures. Liberationists would use the prophetic tradition as the norm to critique the sexism of the religious tradition. Biblical sexism is not denied, but it loses its authority. It must be denounced as a failure to measure up to the full vision of human liberation of the prophetic and gospel messages.

A third group, we mentioned earlier, feel that women waste their time salvaging positive elements of these religious traditions. They take the spokesmen of patriarchal religion at their word when they say that Christ and God are literally and essentially male, and conclude that these religions have existed for no other purpose except to sanctify male domination. Women should quit the Church and the Synagogue and move to the feminist coven to celebrate the sacrality of women through recovery of the religion of the Goddess.

Although I myself am most sympathetic to the second view, I would regard all these positions as having elements of truth. All respond to real needs of different constituencies of women (and some men). It is unlikely that any of these views will predominate, but all will work as parallel trends in the ensuing decades to reshape the face of religion.

The evangelical feminists address themselves to an important group in American religion who frequently use Scripture to reinforce traditional patriarchal family models. Evangelical feminists wish to lift up ne-

glected traditions and to give Biblicist Christians a basis for addressing the question of equality. They will probably get the liberal wing of these churches to modify their languages and exegesis. The first creation story of women's and man's equal creation in the image of God will be stressed, rather than the second creation story of Eve from Adam's rib. Galatians 3, 28 will be stressed in Paul rather than Ephesians 5, and so forth. They might get some denominations to use inclusive language for the community and maybe even for God.

The liberationist wing would want Churches to take a much more active and prophetic role in critiquing the sexism of society, not only on such issues as abortion rights, gay rights and the ERA, but also on the links between sexism and economic injustice. They would press churches with a social gospel tradition into new questions about the adequacy of a patriarchal, capitalist, and consumerist economy to promote a viable human future.

The impact of the separatist goddess religions is more difficult to predict. Traditional Jews and Christians would view these movements as "paganism," if not "satanism." The Goddess movements are likely to respond in an equally defensive way and to direct their feelings against feminists who are still working within Churches and Synagogues. A lot depends on whether some mediating ground can be developed. On the one side, there would have to be a conscious rejection of the religious exclusivism of the Jewish and Christian traditions and a recognition of the appropriateness of experiencing the divine through female symbols and body images. The Goddess worshippers, in turn, might have to grow out of some of their defensiveness toward their Jewish and Christian sisters and start thinking about how we are to create a more comprehensive faith for our sons, as well as our daughters.

This is not to be construed as a call for such feminists to become (or return) to Judaism or Christianity, but rather a growth toward that kind of maturity that can recognize the legitimacy of religious quests in several kinds of contexts. As long as "goddess" feminists can only affirm their way by a reversed exclusivism and denial of the possibility of liberating elements in the Biblical tradition, they are still tied to the same exclusivist patterns of thought in an opposite form.

A creative dialogue between these two views could be very significant. Counter-cultural feminist spirituality could make important contributions to the enlargement of our religious symbols and experiences. We might be able to experience God gestating the world in Her womb, rather than just "making it" through a divine phallic fiat. We would rediscover the rhythms that tie us biologically with earth, fire, air and water which have been so neglected in our anti-natural spiritualities. We would explore the sacralities of the repressed parts of our psyches and our environmental experiences. Many worlds that have been negated by patriarchal religion might be reclaimed for the enlargement of our common life.

It is not clear what all this might mean. It might well be the beginning of a new religion as momentous in its break with the past as Christianity was with the religions of the Semites and the Greeks. But if it is truly to enlarge our present options, it must also integrate the best of the insights that we have developed through Judaism and Christianity, as these religions integrated some (not all) of the best insights of the Near Eastern and Greco-Roman worlds. What is clear is this: the patriarchal repression of women and women's experience has been so massive and prevalent that to begin to take women seriously will involve a profound and radical transformation of our religions.

ADDITIONAL READINGS

Articles

Bibby, Reginald, and Mauss, Armand L. "Skidders and their Servants: Variable Goals and Functions of the Kid Road Rescue Mission." *Journal for the Scientific Study of Religion* 13 (1974): 421–36. Divergences in the goals of clients, leaders, and lay supporters occur in a setting that provides meals and beds for down-and-out men.

Lefever, Harry G. "The Value Orientations of the Religious Poor." *Sociological Analysis* 43 (1982):219–30. Using Talcott Parsons's pattern variables, the author points out the individualistic and conversion-centered emphasis of a poor white community in the American South.

Neal, Marie Augusta, S.N.D. deN. "Women in Religious Symbolism and Organization." In *Religious Change and Continuity*, edited by Harry M. Johnson, pp. 218–50. San Francisco: Jossey-Bass, 1979. Sexism in symbol and in organization is under challenge, undermining the legitimation of men as dominant in both religious and secular spheres. An excellent, comprehensive essay with an extensive bibliography.

Nelsen, Hart M.; Madron, Thomas W.; and Yokley, Raytha L. "Black Religion's Promethean Motif: Orthodoxy and Militancy." *American Journal of Sociology* 81 (1975): 62–81. Is Black religion a spur to militant activism for social change or an opiate in the Marxist sense? The authors review a noted study by sociologist Gary Marx. They conclude that an orthodox orientation, as opposed to a sectarian one, is more related to militancy.

Roof, W. Clark. "Socioeconomic Differentials Among White Socioreligious Groups in the United States." *Social Forces* 58 (1979):280–89. White ethnic Catholic groups (Irish, German, English and Welsh, French, Slavic, Polish, Italian, and Spanish-speaking) have made significant social and economic gains, leaving only a small gap between Protestants and Catholics in overall socioeconomic status.

Books

Cone, James H. *A Black Theology of Liberation.* Philadelphia: J. B. Lippincott, 1970. A theological legitimation of Black activism for social change in America.

Coward, Harold, and Kawamura, Leslie, eds. *Religion and Ethnicity,* Waterloo, Ontario: Wilfrid Laurier Press, 1978. Canadian scholars examine the relationship between ethnicity and religion in the adjustment of various immigrant groups to Canadian society.

Daly, Mary. *The Church and the Second Sex.* New York: Harper & Row, 1975. Subordination of women in the Catholic church.

Nelsen, Hart M., and Nelsen, Anne Kusener. *Black Church in the Sixties.* Lexington: University Press of Kentucky, 1975. A historical review of major authors specializing in the Black church, followed by an analysis of Gallup Poll data through the 1950s and 1960s, plus the authors' own study.

Ruether, Rosemary R., ed. *Religion and Sexism: Images of Woman in Jewish and Christian Traditions.* New York: Simon & Schuster, 1974. An excellent, wide-ranging collection of essays on women's subordination in both Judaic and Christian history.

Simpson, George E. *Black Religions in the New World.* New York: Columbia University Press, 1978. An almost encyclopedic historical and comparative analysis of Black religions in North and South America, Great Britain, and the Caribbean.

Washington, Joseph H., Jr. *Black Religion.* Boston: Beacon Press, 1964.

————. *The Politics of God.* Boston: Beacon Press, 1969.

————. *Black Sects and Cults.* New York: Doubleday, 1972.

Cross-cultural References

Falk, Nancy A.; and Gross, Rita M., eds. *Unspoken Worlds: Women's Religious Lives in Non-Western Cultures.* San Francisco: Harper & Row, 1980. Cultures in Africa, India, Korea, Iran, Japan, and Bolivia are among those covered.

Four

New Religious Expression

9

The New Religions

The so-called "new religions" blossoming on the North American landscape of the 1970s and 1980s have probably generated more attention than any other topic in the sociology of religion. Front-page headlines and magazine cover stories have featured the Unification church of Sun Myung Moon, "Jesus Freaks," the Children of God, and, of course, the tragic mass suicide of hundreds ending the existence of Jonestown in the fall of 1978. Less spectacular but continuing to gain adherents are Eastern-inspired movements and groups such as Transcendental Meditation, Divine Light Mission, and Krishna Consciousness. If one defines religion inclusively (see Chapter 1), personal growth movements such as *est*, Silva Mind Control, Scientology, and Synanon also qualify as "new religions."

But religious life in the Northern Hemisphere has always been in a state of ferment. "New religions" are nothing new. The North American continent has given birth to "local" offspring such as Mormonism, Christian Science, Seventh Day Adventism, Scientology, and Jehovah's Witnesses, to mention a prominent few. The religious history of the Western world since the Protestant Reformation has exhibited pluralism, doctrinal relativism, and the undermining of fixed authority. True, many churches and religious movements have had to overcome fierce opposition and at times outright persecution; but the overall trend of recent centuries has clearly been toward live-and-let-live and the freedom to preach and organize new ways of believing, worshiping, and practicing.

The First Amendment to the U.S. Constitution forbids the establishment of any one religious tradition as "official" and has generated a climate of legal protection for religious expression. Furthermore, the various "great awakenings" or religious revival periods in

North America have produced a legacy of individualism favoring the emergence of new forms of religiosity.

But new traditions and ideas are insufficient to explain North American receptivity to religious change and pluralism. Great movements of people westward generated a situation in which "religious surveillance, coercion, and conformity were out of the question."[1] Individual and group religious impulses were able to emerge and take hold with little resistance in a "frontier" setting. Mormonism was born in a frontier setting and continues to flourish. But older religious traditions, too, were constantly revitalized, at times breaking off splinter groups that sought a "purer" or "more authentic" way of worshiping and proclaiming the gospel in contrast to the alleged laxity of middle-class churches.

Not that all new inspirations stemmed from the Christian tradition; Ralph Waldo Emerson spoke for a nineteenth-century romantic transcendentalism in which

the world is not the product of manifold power, but of one will, of one mind; and that one mind is everywhere active, in each ray of the star, in each wavelet of the pool; and whatever opposes that will is everywhere balked and baffled, because things are made so and not otherwise. . . . All things proceed out of the same spirit, and all things conspire with it.[2]

Out of his vision came a strong critique of tradition and praise for human self-reliance. The doctrines of Emanuel Swedenborg contributed to a nineteenth-century interest in spiritualism and to the emergence of health and food cults that continue to this day. Forms of Christian belief and worship incorporated some of these themes. New Thought, out of which came Christian Science, Religious Science, and today's Unity church, is a notable example.

Historian Sidney Ahlstrom has phrased the situation well:

Given the extraordinary pluralism and, more importantly, the unremitting fecundity of the American religious tradition, the general observation is warranted that the appearance of many new religious impulses during the 1960s and 1970s can best be seen as a continuation of a venerable tradition—not only because they continue to be formed but because they also maintain an explicit or implicit social critique.[3]

The critique in question has been more than a protest against materialism or worldliness. Robert N. Bellah maintains that the modern prominence of science, technology, and bureaucratic organization emphasizes a tradition of "utilitarian individualism" that downplays shared or community goals and values.[4] Instead it promotes the maximizing of individual interest and "technical reason" or of means that "work toward" the attainment of goals. These means can readily become ends in themselves. Individual freedom to pursue private goals thus not only supersedes concern for the common good, for the upbuilding of the community, but also for the pursuit of higher goals such as a more equitable distribution of resources and opportunities. Such "higher" themes, expressed in the written and spoken words that comprise our civil religious heritage, have formed a large part of our national life. But bringing those values into full "competitive" expression against the ethos of utilitarian individualism has required carrier groups or movements such as the post–World War II drive for civil rights begun by Martin Luther King, Jr., in the name of justice and Christian love.

The struggle for civil rights inevitably brought a critique of American political, social, and economic institutions that accused these institutions of perpetuating racism by their policies. But not just "America" was called into question—so too were the churches for not living up to their ideals. The established churches appeared in this light as too comfortable with the status quo and all too willing to support existing policies, including the Vietnam War in the mid-1960s. Churches and synagogues seemed oblivious of the prophetic tradition denouncing social injustice and the senseless slaughter of innocents. "Established religion," in other words, seemed almost hostile to concerns with human life and livable conditions, concerns expressed not only in the antiwar movement but also in proenvironmental groups.

Add to these themes the disillusion experienced by many activists with American political institutions—the national elections of 1968 and 1972 seemed to many a repudiation of what America "really stood for"—and the turning of many Americans to nontraditional religious groups becomes more understandable. Eastern themes became attractive: Worldly striving is an illusion; industrial society promotes unhappiness by holding out consumer striving for more and better goods; fighting the bureaucracies gets you nowhere; isn't it better to find ways of reconciling with the inevitable? Violence can best be counteracted by forming peaceful, harmonious communities that cultivate simple life-styles based on farming and handicrafts. Integration of the races *is* possible under religious "sacred canopies"—such as the ideal of Jim Jones in forming the People's Temple. The degradation of the drug culture can be overcome by joining religious groups promising a true "high," union with Jesus, or self-transcendence under the discipline of an Eastern guru. Bellah remarks:

To some extent the successor movements, especially the explicitly religious ones, have been survival units in a quite literal sense. They have provided a stable social setting and a coherent set of symbols for young people disoriented by the drug culture or disillusioned with radical politics.[5]

But new "survival units" do not spell the end of social criticism. While some expressions, such as the human potential movement or an Eastern-inspired group like Meher Baba may help devotees re-adapt to mainline American society, "sympathizers of the oriental religions tend to be as critical of American society as political radicals, far more critical than the norm."[6] Some Jesus movement groups such as the World Liberation Front see American society as headed for an apocalyptic disaster, as do millenarian groups whose long tradition views the present as a terribly bleak period preceding the "inbreak" of the kingdom and its time of judgment.

Social scientists are, of course, interested in the conditions under which new religions such as cults arise and in devising various classifications and typologies to further our understanding of these groups. As Allan W. Eister has noted, history shows that cults and cultic movements have flourished in times of marked change, particularly in the major "orientational" institutions of society. These institutions are represented in such persons as teachers, preachers, painters, editors, poets, novelists, dramatists, composers, and journalists. When a sense of dislocation and cultural discontinuity is reflected through these cultural "mirrors," persons may readily feel a sense of disorientation, of abandonment by the secure and familiar, thus becoming candidates for cultic groups that fill this meaning vacuum.[7] Stark, Bainbridge, and Doyle, noting that the American and Canadian Pacific coastal states and provinces have the lowest rates of church membership together with a high rate of new cult development, hold that "secularization, as evident in low church membership rates, is a self-limiting phenomenon that in turn prompts revival and/or the formation of new religions."[8] Failed meaning systems are replaced with new forms.

Sect and cult have been distinguished more precisely by contemporary sociologists. Stark and Bainbridge, as we have seen in Chapter 4, postulate that *both* sects and cults are "deviant" religious groupings; that is, they find themselves in, or bring themselves to, a *state of tension* with their surrounding social-cultural-political environments. The present order of things is regarded as threatening, dangerous, collapsing, or just plain evil. How, then, do sects *differ* from cults? Sects, as previously hinted, break off from a parent body in order to reaffirm the "old faith." Something has gone wrong; the old church has somehow grown unfaithful by compromising with the world. It is now time to go back to the neglected fundamentals, to be once again true to the original tradition now cleansed of harmful growths and errors.

Cults, on the other hand, are more innovative. Usually they do not claim ties with existing groups or traditions. The cult may be imported from another culture, such as Eastern-oriented modes of worship; or it may emerge as new *within* the culture, borrowing from existing elements but introducing a new "revelation" or insight (such as a flying saucer that will come down and "save" the faithful remnant). Over time, of course, a cult may become established, losing tension with its environment and eventually becoming a "church" within the society. Along the way, a cult may be subject to sectarian splitting off, as some members come to think it is losing its authenticity. In all cases, cults (and all religions) offer "compensators" to their members, rewards that are not immediately subject to clear, unambiguous evaluation. Heaven, of course, is an example; "personal fulfillment" or "control over evil influences in your life" are others. In any case, religious compensators contain some supernatural element in their makeup.[9]

In terms of the "generality" of compensators offered, Stark and Bainbridge suggest three types of cults: (1) *Audience cults* feature vague, weak compensators and are very loosely organized; members engage in a kind of "consumer activity." Devotees of astrology or of other doctrines or mystiques available through books, newspapers, magazines, or even radio and television are examples. Audiences may come together only rarely (as in conventions) or for brief periods, such as to hear a lecture. (2) *Client cults*, on the other hand, offer more specific compensators. They may purport to heal, to cure neurosis (psychoanalysis and dianetics), to "clear" the mind of obstacles to the unhampered pursuit of one's goals (Scientology, *est*), or to induce calm and serenity by their practice (Transcendental Meditation, yoga). (3) *Cult movements* offer a *system* of compensators purporting to provide a more "complete" meaning framework to their members, thus becoming more fully compensatory than either audience or client cults.[10] The Unification church or Krishna Consciousness are examples. Major commitments of time and money are frequently asked. Such movements engender opposition from their environments and are, by that fact, in a high state of tension with their surroundings. Ties with conventional institutions may be broken, setting off efforts by former friends and family members to "recapture" and "un-brainwash" the individual through deprogramming techniques.

Explaining *sects* and *cults*, then, remains two separate theoretical tasks. Sectarian theory asks why and under what conditions splitting off occurs from a parent religious body. Cultic theory asks why a given sociocultural setting is conducive to cult formation; and by what processes people form cults, how cults secure and socialize recruits (giving rise to sometimes elaborate theories of conversion), and what functions particular cultic groups seem to serve for their members. Further theoretical challenges include theories of development and transformation of sects and cults.

Our readings begin with a comprehensive survey of new religious groupings in Montreal, with some comparisons made with the Bay Area of San Francisco, site of another large-scale investigation of new religious membership. Using a broad definition of "new religious movements," Frederick Bird and Bill Reimer found that one-fifth of the adult population in the San Francisco Bay Area and one-third in Montreal had participated in at least one of the groups surveyed; yet the drop-out rate is also high, as only 8 percent of the total sample participated at any one time. The authors fully delineate the characteristics of the participants and distinguish four kinds of movements "in terms of the relationship between the participants and whatever the group itself considers to be the ultimate and revered source of power and well-being." Do participants, for example, seek to contact a supernatural source of power or find harmony with the cosmos or the ways of nature? Finally, remarkably few have been involved with countercultural groups such as those espousing Buddhist, Hindu or Moslem beliefs; or with derivatives thereof like Bahai's or some spiritualist groups. Most have sought out Western-type devotional groups or apprenticeship movements such as the personal growth kind—*est*, Arica, Silva Mind Control, and so on. The authors ask whether interest in these groups and movements correlates with cultural periods in which people feel that control over their destinies is diminishing.

From his book-length study of the Divine Light Mission, James V. Downton, Jr., speculates on the stages that one goes through in becoming a full-fledged member of that movement. His stage model of conversion is compared with the well-known version of John Lofland.

Counterposed to Downton's model is Robert W. Balch's "Looking Behind the Scenes in a Religious Cult." His study of a UFO cult provides him with a "backstage" view of the role playing that occurs among devotees. It is not beyond them to make "sidebets" on the outcome of the leaders' predictions and to reserve part of themselves for return to "normal life" in case the leaders' promises prove false. Conversion may not, in this case, be as total as Downton's reading would suggest.

"The Farm; and Role Expectations for Women" analyzes a "Jesus commune" of the 1970s with particular attention to the sex roles grounded in the group's scriptural interpretation. Although Christian sects differ widely, this one relies on clear-cut role assignments, in striking contrast to the permissive, egalitarian norms that characterize North American culture in recent years.

Steven M. Tipton's portrait of *est* reveals the elements that make this movement appealing to educated middle-class persons who, though socialized into expectations of a utopian social order stemming from the 1960s cultural changes, have been disappointed by realities of the adult world of bureaucratic constraints. *Est* gives them a "rule-egoism," which meets their need for self-fulfillment involving sensitivity to interpersonal relationships and reconciliation to the demands of a bureaucratic occupational order.

"The Tnevnoc Cult" is a tongue-in-cheek allegory of a mythical American nineteenth-century cult. The authors manage to work into their account most of the processes of recruitment, socialization and resocialization, legitimation with the larger society, and so on. It is also a cautionary tale. The severe repression of contemporary cults (or some of them) ignores history. The "Tnevnocs" were by no means as harmful as their contemporaries painted them. Given time, they accommodated to the larger society and eventually fitted into the familiar American pattern of religious pluralism.

Notes

1. Sydney E. Ahlstrom, "From Sinai to the Golden Gate: The Liberation of Religion in the Occident," in *Understanding the New Religions*, ed. Jacob Needleman and George Baker (New York: Seabury, 1978), p. 12.
2. Quoted in Sydney E. Ahlstrom, *A Religious History of the American People* (New Haven: Yale University Press, 1972), p. 601.
3. Ahlstrom, "From Sinai to the Golden Gate," p. 19.
4. Robert N. Bellah, *The Broken Covenant* (New York: Seabury, 1975); pp. 154–63.
5. Robert N. Bellah, "New Religious Consciousness and the Crisis in Modernity," in *Understanding the New Religions*, p. 342.
6. Ibid., p. 343.
7. Allan W. Eister, "An Outline of a Theory of Cults," *Journal for the Scientific Study of Religion* 11 (1972), pp. 321–26.
8. Rodney Stark, William Sims Bainbridge, and Daniel P. Doyle, "Cults of America: A Reconnaissance in Space and Time," *Sociological Analysis* 40 (1979), p. 359.
9. Rodney Stark and William Sims Bainbridge, "Towards a Theory of Religion: Religious Commitment," *Journal for the Scientific Study of Religion* 19 (1980), p. 123.
10. William Sims Bainbridge and Rodney Stark, "Cult Formation: Three Compatible Models," *Sociological Analysis* 40 (1979), p. 284.

READING 9.1

Participation Rates in New Religious and Para-Religious Movements

Frederick Bird and Bill Reimer

Since the middle of the 1960s a large number of New Religious and Para-Religious movements either have been established, or if already established, have greatly expanded their number of adherents. Many scholars have attempted to explain the significance of these movements by referring to them as a religious revival (McLoughlin, 1978), as examples of experimental religion (Wuthnow, 1978), as an expression of political disenchantment (Tipton, 1977), or as the emergence of a new humanism (Westley, 1978a, b; Bellah, 1976). In the present paper, we will analyze these movements and examine their significance by looking at the characteristic

Frederick Bird and Bill Reimer are respectively Associate Professors of Religion and Sociology at Concordia University, Montreal, Quebec.

Reprinted from *Journal for the Scientific Study of Religion*, 21 (1982), with permission.

rates with which people have participated in these movements. We will be raising and answering four questions: What percentage of the adult population have ever participated in these movements? What is the typical form of their participation? Are there significant characteristics of those who have participated? And are there any differences among participants in relation to the kinds of New Religious movements with which they have been affiliated?[1]

In brief, survey data collected in Montreal indicate that a surprisingly high proportion of the adult population have participated in New Religious and Para-Religious movements (somewhere between one-fifth and one-fourth of the population), but that most persons who do participate become involved only for a while and then drop out. While a core of persons have become committed members of these groups, the typical participant is a transitory affiliate. In relation to social and economic status, participants are more likely to be younger, unmarried, and middle class, but the differences here are not dramatic. More marked differences exist with regard to life style variables, where participants are much more likely to have gotten high on psychedelics, been involved with astrology, with the *I Ching*, etc. In relation to all these variables, participants in those movements herein labeled as counter-cultural devotional differ more decidedly from non-participants than did participants in other movements discussed here. Moreover, counter-cultural devotional participants were much more likely to have changed their religious identification and to have been involved in several of these groups. However, while participants in counter-cultural devotional groups more nearly correspond to the stereotyped public image of cult members, they represent only a very small proportion of persons who have become involved in New Religious and Para-Religious movements.

We collected data in Montreal in two surveys: one conducted in 1975 and another in 1980. The first survey was completed by 1607 adults who were in the process of registering for classes, mostly to be taken in the evening, at Concordia University. Since most of those registering were taking night classes, already held full time jobs, and were in the late twenties or thirties, this sample was clearly not typical of most undergraduate student bodies. Compared to the adult population of Montreal as a whole, this sample was much more likely to be anglophone, somewhat more likely to be single, more likely to hold middle class occupations, and to be younger in age. In spite of these limitations, the sample has considerable utility. The survey permitted us to question a large number of present and former participants in New Religious movements outside the context of their own groups and to compare their responses to a large number of persons who had never participated in these movements. It allowed us to compare participation rates between categories of people and to analyze characteristics of participants. The sample is less reliable as a gauge of the absolute level of participation in these movements. However, the survey does permit us to make educated estimates in this regard, both by comparing our data with those collected elsewhere and by taking into consideration the likely biases of the sample.

In 1980 the first survey was supplemented by a census of participation rates in nine selected movements as reported by the movements themselves. Here we recognize that self-reported membership statistics must be treated as estimates likely to be inflated. Given the absence of rigorous data with regard to participation rates in New Religious movements, these surveys provide an initial basis for examining the characteristic forms of this participation. They can also be compared with a similar survey conducted in the San Francisco Bay Area.

Overall Participation Rates

Considering the quite divergent views about New Religious movements, it is not at all clear what kinds of groups and associations ought to be included under this label. Some seem to associate these movements largely with Eastern religions, others insist upon including a wide variety of human potential groups, and many would include groups like Self-Realization Fellowship, Theosophists, Baha'is, and Spiritualists which have existed in North America for several generations. We have adopted a fairly broad definition (see Bird & Reimer, 1976; Bird, 1979): movements which, since the middle 1960s, have greatly expanded their numbers, exist apart from exclusive Christian and Jewish denominations, and use rites and symbols traditionally associated with religions even though many are quite secular by their own understanding.[2] We have, therefore, included within the rubric "New Religious and Para-Religious movements" groups like T'ai Chi and Transcendental Meditation, both of which use traditional religious imagery and techniques and both of which consider themselves to be generally secular in orientation. We have also included older groups like the Charismatics or Neo-pentecostals as well as the Spiritualists, because they have recently expanded their popular appeal, and they exist as supplements rather than competitors to the organized, denominational patterns of American religion. We have also included a number of new therapy movements, groups like EST, ARICA, Scientology, Psychosynthesis, and Silva Mind Control, because in symbolism and ritual they seek to give birth to a reservoir of sacred power within each person (cf. Westley, 1978a, 1978b).

Using this broad definition of New Religious and Para-Religious movements, we may observe that the overall rates of participation in these movements is surprisingly high,

nearly a third (see Table 1). In the San Francisco Bay Area survey, conducted in the early 1970s, 21% of the adult population had participated in a variety of groups identified by its questionnaire, but this questionnaire excluded from consideration a number of groups which we listed: Spiritualists, Other Eastern, Other Buddhists, Divine Light Mission, Other Therapy groups, and some Martial Arts like Aikido and T'ai Chi which have explicit religious aspects. Had these groups been in their survey form, it is reasonable to assume that the overall level of participation would have been higher, since the level of participation in these excluded groups has not been insignificant. In any event, the Montreal survey listed a wider range of groups. By oversampling a somewhat younger, better educated population, our survey no doubt also oversampled those persons more likely to participate in New Religious movements. If these biases were reduced, then we would expect a significant decline in the reported participation rates, probably down to 18% to 22% of the adult population. While these participation ratios may seem to be higher than expected, the significance of this fact cannot be judged without further examining both the characteristic forms of this participation and the kinds of groups that succeed in gaining the largest numbers of affiliates [see Table 2].

Patterns of Participation

The typical adherent of these New Religious and Para-Religious movements establishes a peripheral, transitory relationship to one of these groups and then drops out. These terms must be explained.

It is possible to distinguish two forms of participation. In one form, persons join an exclusive religious group which assumes they do not belong at the same time to other religious groups or at least that they commit a large proportion of their time, feelings, and

Table 1 *Rates of Participation in Various New Religious and Para-Religious Movements*

	Montreal Survey	Bay Area Survey*
A. Western Devotional		
Charismatics	1.9%	6.0%
Jesus groups	—	2.5%
Campus Crusade	—	2.9%
Other Western	3.1%	—
B. Counter-Cultural Devotional		
Spiritualists	3.1%	—
All Buddhist groups	2.3%	—
Zen Buddhists	—	2.6%
Baha'i	2.0%	—
Divine Light Mission	1.2%	—
All other Eastern	4.0%	—
Krishna Consciousness	—	1.6%
C. Apprenticeship/Discipleship Groups		
Yoga	12.3%	7.9%
Transcendental Meditation	6.7%	5.3%
Scientology	.8%	1.1%
EST	—	1.5%
Synanon	—	3.1%
Other therapy	4.9%	—
Martial Arts	6.0%	—
D. Total Rate of Participation	31.7%	21.0%
Sample N =	1607	1000

*As reported in Wuthnow, 1976 (pg. 275)

Table 2 *Types of Participation in a Selection of New Religions and Para-Religious Movements in Montreal (1980)**

	Numbers of Affiliates	Numbers of Members	
Krishna Consciousness	800	66	(Householders, Celibates)
Spiritual Healing church	200	36	(Regulars)
LeJourdain (Charismatic)	1,500	310	(Staff plus an estimate of those most directly involved)
National Research Institute for Self-Understanding (Palmistry)	3,950	50	(Staff, mediators, members)
International Meditation Institute	200	90	(Core, regulars)
Transcendental Meditation (those ever initiated)	14,725	275	(Instructors, Siddhis)
Integral Yoga Institute	300	56	(Pre-Monastics, monastics, close members)
Sivanada Yoga (on mailing list)	7,000	204	(Staff, regulars)
Sri Chinmoy followers	70	25	(Initiated)

*Participation data as reported by groups themselves.

identification. Such memberships become a major source of meaning, values, and norms for individuals involved. All New Religious movements have succeeded in winning such a commitment from the persons who assume leadership in these groups and/or who devote themselves in these groups with an intense religious fervor. Such "committed members" provide the core or central cadre for these movements. In some movements, like the Divine Light Mission, the Zen center, Nichiren Shoshu Sokagakkai, or the Unification Church, most members are so committed.

Other persons, however, may have a more peripheral or transitory form of affiliation. Perhaps they are students enrolled in a specific, time-limited class such as yoga, T'ai Chi, or Silva Mind Control; or they are clients who have at one time made use of a service such as palm reading or spiritual counseling; or they are initiates who have at one time been given instructions in personal, private practice of meditation; or they are persons who attended occasional festivals or retreats sponsored by such groups as Krishna Consciousness society or a Charismatic cadre; or they are curious and intrigued audiences witnessing a Spiritualist Medium. Such affiliates may even attend these classes, festivals, counseling sessions, or meetings on a regular but occasional sequence. These various New Religious and Para-Religious movements may thus exert influence on some persons' moral outlook, even though they have not committed themselves to these movements to the point of membership.

There are various examples of this pattern of loose affiliation. Thus, the local Krishna temple in Montreal includes 66 adult members, but some 250 people regularly attend their Sunday open houses. Most Yoga and therapy groups provide courses for hundreds of students, who take classes but never accept the invitation to become more closely involved. While some Charismatics belong to specific prayer groups, many simply attend periodic retreats, luncheon meetings, or occasional prayer services established by a core of committed members. Thousands of persons who have been initiated into Transcendental Meditation or have had their palms read by a Palmist/Astrologer make no attempts to pursue a closer connection with these groups. In the recent census of nine New Religious movements in Montreal, 95% of the 29,000 persons participating in nine groups surveyed would be classed as affiliates rather than members of these groups.

The drop out rate from New Religious and Para-Religious movements is extremely high. According to the Montreal Survey, 75.5% of all those who had ever participated in those movements were no longer participants.[3] Thus in Montreal, current participants represented only 8.4% of the total sample. When we examine the drop out rates for particular groups, several complex factors seem to be involved (see Table 3). A high drop out rate is anticipated by a number of yoga and therapy groups, which often view themselves as providing classes and not soliciting members. A high turnover rate is characteristic also of groups like the Baha'is and the Spiritualists, both of whom stage regular meetings for the public from which they expect to gain a few but not many new regular participants. High drop out rates are to be expected from groups like Divine Light, Scientology, Dharmadatu, and Nichiren Shoshu which make excessive demands on adherents. These high drop rates mean that the typical adherent has only a transitory relationship to these groups.[4] While the transient experience may be significant—for example, an involvement with a therapist may deeply affect a client—it is likely that the typical participant will be more influenced by the many factors unrelated to these movements.

Table 3   *Drop Out Rates for Various New Religious and Para-Religious Movements*

	Total Number of Persons in Sample Who Have Ever Participated	Total Number of Current Participants	Drop Out Rates
Transcendental Meditation	96	43	55.2%
Buddhist groups	37	13	64.9%
Martial Arts	96	32	66.3%
Other Western	49	16	67.3%
Charismatics	31	10	67.7%
Therapy groups	78	25	67.9%
Other Eastern	64	18	71.8%
Spiritualists	50	13	74.0%
Divine Light	20	5	75.0%
Yoga groups	196	46	76.5%
Baha'i	32	6	81.2%
Scientology	13	0	100.0%

Factors Related to Participation

1. SES Variables

In comparison to the adult population in general, participants in New Religious and Para-Religious movements are likely to be younger, single, female, and middle class. The differences are not marked and are dramatic only in particular groups. For example, participants were somewhat more likely to be younger in age but the variations here were not significant (see Table 4). The most dramatic differences seem to be between groups. According to the 1980 census of memberships, three groups—Transcendental Meditation, Krishna Consciousness Society and the International Meditation Institute—attracted 55% of their adherents from persons under 30, while six other groups attracted only about 26% of their adherents from the same age group (see Table 5). The latter groups—including Spiritualists, a Palmist, two yoga groups, a Charismatic group and Sri Chinmoy Followers—by their own report were more successful in attracting persons between the ages of thirty and fifty. It is not at all clear that New Religious and Para-Religious movements primarily or especially attract young persons. It is more likely the case that interest in these movements is related to an historic, generational shift in religious orientations, which initially in the late 1960s attracted young persons in greater proportions but which has subsequently attracted persons from all age groups. It is interesting that the most recent data, from 1980, indicate a somewhat higher participation rate for persons over 30 than the 1975 survey.

There is not a significant difference between participants and non-participants with regard to current occupational class. To be sure, some particular new religious movements, like some traditional denominations, have proven to be more successful in recruiting middle class or working class partici-

Table 4   *Age of Participants*

	Under 25	25 to 34	35 Plus	N
Present participants	38%	46%	15%	130
Former participants	45%	45%	10%	372
Non-participants	39%	45%	16%	1084

0 = .0477 (Wilcoxon's signed ranks test, coefficient of differentia)

Table 5 *Age of Participants in Selected Groups (as Reported by Groups Themselves)*

	N	Under 25	25–9	30–9	40–plus
Groups A: (Krishna Consciousness, Transcendental Meditation, International Meditation Institute)	15,170	25.1%	30.0%	29.1%	15.0%
Groups B: (Spiritual Healing Church, LeJourdain, Palmist, Integral Yoga Institute, Sivanada Yoga, Sri Chinmoy)	10,870	7.2%	18.7%	46.0%	38.9%

pants. For example, the Charismatics and the Spiritualists, by their own report, have a much larger proportion of working class participants than the yoga groups or Transcendental Meditation.

We know that some groups, like Krishna Consciousness and Divine Light, have been especially attractive to persons whose careers in education and employment are uneven and/or at a lower level than their parents.[5] One of the more intriguing findings in this regard is the fact that current male participants in these New Religious movements are much more likely to hold middle class occupational positions than either non-participants or former participants, and they are more likely also to be upwardly mobile. The difference between present and former participants is marked (see Table 6). It seems reasonable to conjecture that the success of current participants in their occupations is matched by their comparative success within the organization of these movements. It is possible that many have remained in these movements because the movements themselves rewarded them for their achievements in group sponsored activities.[6]

2. Life Style Variable

Compared to non-participants, present and former participants in New Religious and Para-Religious movements are significantly more likely to have experimented with astrology, divination, and psychedelic drugs.

Those persons who have had their charts cast by an astrologer or consulted the Chinese book of divination, the *I Ching*, are twice as likely to have been participants in these movements as persons who have never done so. Nearly a third of current adherents of these movements have had their astrological charts cast and gone through the ritual practice of seeking wisdom from the enigmatic wisdom of the *I Ching* (see Table 7). Involvement with these divination practices does signify an experimental attitude, as Wuthnow has argued (Wuthnow, 1978). We suspect that the relationship between involvement in New Religious movements and divination arts is even stronger. After all, the divination arts are sources of wisdom, originating from long, revered traditions that claim to be as reliable, if not more reliable, than the wisdom derived from the orthodoxies of science and rational philosophy. They provide an irrational, magical inspiration that often comes clothed in science-like expositions and craftsmenlike attention to details. They provide quite personal and private sources of guidance which are alternatives to those preferred by traditional denominational religions and moral systems. As in most New Religious movements, their wisdom is articulated in language that deviates from the ordinary language of common sense; wisdom is here gained through what amounts to a ritual-like experience rather than from discursive expositions (see Bird, 1978).

Table 6 *Occupational Status of Participants (Males, 25 Years Old or Older)*

	Percent with Higher Class Occupations*	Percent Whose Fathers Had Higher Class Occupations*	N
Current participants	90.5%	52.4%	21
Former participants	62.9%	66.7%	55
All participants (past and present)	71.1%	63.2%	76
Sample as a whole	67.0%	52.6%	297

*Higher class occupations: professional, technical, managerial, proprietors; Lower class occupations: clerical, sales, service, craftsmen, labor, other.

Table 7 *Use of Drugs and Divinization Arts*

	Percent Who Have Had Chart Cast by Astrologers	Percent Who Have Consulted I Ching	Percent High on Marijuana (3 Times Plus)	Percent High on LSD (3 Times Plus)
Present participants N 133	31.6% (42)	27.1% (36)	40.6% (54)	19.6% (25)
Past participants N 370	23.2% (86)	18.9% (70)	38.1% (141)	15.3% (57)
Non-participants N 1056	11.8% (125)	5.5% (58)	22.4% (238)	6.6% (70)
	$x^2 = 51.42$	$x^2 = 97.54$	$x^2 = 43.20$	$x^2 = 40.00$
	$P = .000$	$P = .000$	$P = .000$	$P = .000$

Persons who have become participants in New Religious movements are also twice as likely to have gotten high using marijuana or LSD three or more times (see Table 7). Thus, experimentation with drugs seems to be correlated with experimentation with religious movements and experimentation with divinization practices; participants in New Religious movements seem to evidence an experimental attitude at least with regard to these kinds of personal activities. However, what is common between participants in New Religious movements, users of psychedelics, and users of divinization arts is a specific kind of experimental attitude in which persons seek to have specific non-ordinary, self-reassuring experiences, often by faithfully adhering to ritual-like guide lines. After all, there are special cultic forms for dropping acid, just as for consulting the *I Ching*, for meditating, doing Zazen, Sufi dancing, receiving the Holy Spirit, or chanting.

Participation Rates in Different Kinds of Movements

New Religious and Para-Religious movements have assumed varied forms. For comparative purposes it is possible to distinguish four types of movements, in terms of the relationship between the participants and whatever the group itself considers to be the ultimate and revered source of power and well-being (see Bird, 1978: 1979). For some this sacred source is conceived as a self-transcending, omnipresent reality; a God, a spiritual realm, a sacred principle to which participants devote themselves. Such movements may appropriately be identified as devotional (see Smart, 1968) because of the central role of congregational practices of devotion. Such movements ordinarily seek members more than affiliates, and seek converts more than interested students.

Among such devotional groups, it is necessary to distinguish further between those which remain in accord with the prevailing religious beliefs of denominational religion—groups like the Charismatics, the Jesus groups, the Lubavitcher movement—and those which adopt antagonistic beliefs. The latter include movements adopting Buddhist, Hindu, or Moslem beliefs—Nichiren Shoshu or Shinran Buddhists, Divine Light or Krishna Consciousness, or Sufi groups—as well as groups with distinctive beliefs of their own at considerable variance from denominational beliefs—like the Baha'is or the Spiritualists. By making this distinction between western devotional and counter-cultural devotional groups, we can thereby distinguish movements which self-consciously reinforce and bolster prevailing beliefs of traditional denominations and other movements which directly challenge and counter these beliefs.

In a third kind of movement, the ultimate, revered source of personal power and well-being is conceived as existing in individualized form in the deepest recess of each person (see Westley, 1978b). These movements claim not one universal source to which all are directed but claim instead that sacred power exists in each person. People participate in these movements in order to gain the skills and knowledge necessary for them to learn this indwelling energy and intelligence. Like sorcerer's apprentices, they seek to gain mastery over these extraordinary powers by following the example of those more skilled in these arts. These movements are appropriately referred to as apprenticeship groups, since classlike settings for instruction are characteristic. Apprenticeshiplike relation-

ships are found in a wide variety of human growth groups and Para-Religious movements such as EST, ARICA, Silva Mind Control, and Psychosynthesis.

In a fourth kind of movement participants seek not so much to make contact with an extraordinary source of power and well-being as to harmonize their lives with the sacred ways of nature or the cosmos. What is necessary for such harmony is discipline. Participants seek to discipline their minds and bodies by practicing meditation in a variety of forms, from sitting motionless to movement in stylized forms. Discipline is learned by subjecting oneself as a disciple to one who has achieved self-mastery and harmony of mind and body. Yoga groups, T'ai Chi groups, Vedanta meditation groups, and Zen centers may all appropriately be referred to as discipleship movements because in all of them participants seek this kind of self harmony through disciplined forms of meditation (Smart, [1968]; Eliade, [1957]).

Discipleship and apprenticeship movements differ in several significant ways. Largely, apprenticeship groups utilize ideas and practices developed in North America or Europe from transcendentalism, occult traditions of wisdom, gnosticism, and transpersonal psychology. In contrast, discipleship groups are largely based on assumptions derived from religious traditions of Buddhism, Hinduism, and Taoism. However, both make the assumption that individuals may gradually enhance self-mastery by developing certain psychic skills. Both provide classes for large numbers of affiliate participants. In many cases, both envisage themselves as providing spiritual and psychic opportunities which are not competitive but supplementary to traditional denominational religion. For the purpose of analyzing these survey data, we have combined discipleship and apprenticeship movements.

When we examine the participation rates for various New Religious and Para-Religious movements, the most striking fact is that the overwhelming majority of participants have been involved either with western devotional groups or with discipleship/apprenticeship groups, not with counter-cultural devotional groups. Nearly nine of ten participants were involved in these former two groups, according to the Bay Area survey, and a slightly smaller figure in Montreal (see Tables 1, 2). (The somewhat smaller participation rates for these groups in Montreal reflects the fact that among the anglophone population of the city in 1975, various western devotional groups like the Charismatics, Jesus groups, and Campus crusade were not yet very developed.[7]) What is noteworthy is the low level of participation in the counter-cultural devotional movements, which have received the most public notoriety.

Participants in counter-cultural devotional movements differ from other participants and non-participants in several ways. Overall they seem to participate with greater excess. In relation to factors already analyzed, they are more likely to have consulted an astrologer or gotten high on psychedelic drugs repeatedly than participants in other movements. They are also more likely to have participated in a number of different New Religious and Para-Religious movements. Three-fifths of participants in these movements have been involved as well in at least one other New Religious movement, and two-fifths have been involved in three or more groups (see Table 8). More than other present participants, and especially more than past participants, current adherents of counter-cultural devotional groups correspond to the model of the religious shopper. Rather than simply dropping out, as most participants of New Religious and Para-Religious movements have done, adherents of counter-cultural devotional groups have sought out successive groups. Markedly more than the participants in any other New Religious movements, adherents of counter-cultural devotional movements have changed their religious identification. Most participants in New Religious and Para-Religious movements continue in the religious affiliation of their mothers (Table 8). In sharp contrast,

Table 8 *Comparison of Various New Religious and Para-Religious Movements*

	Counter-Cultural Devotional	Western Devotional	Apprenticeship/Discipleship	N
A. Participation* rates				
(1) Bay Area	12.1%	33.1%	54.8%	345
(2) Montreal	26.1%	10.4%	63.5%	748
B. Percent of participation in 3 or more movements	40.4%	25.0%	25.6%	
N =	203	80	465	
C. Percent of *current* participants who have adopted a religious identification different from mothers'.**	62.0%	27.0%	14.5% (except T.M.)	
			32.0% (Transcendental Meditation)	

*The number of participation exceeds the number of participants because some persons were members of several groups.

**This question was considered only for respondents whose mothers' religious affiliation was Protestant or Catholic.

three-fifths of the current members of counter-cultural devotional groups indicated that their religious identification differed from their mothers'.[8] It is reasonable to argue that involvement for many in these counter-cultural devotional groups has an intense religious significance.

The position of current participants in counter-cultural devotional groups is far from typical. The overwhelming majority of participants in New Religious movements do not change their religious identification, have not participated in any more than one such movement, and partcipate in these groups because of their practices, results, and/or the other people who are involved. The typical participant has not consulted the *I Ching* and has not been high on LSD. Although correlations exist with such factors, they are far from definitive. It is clear that persons from quite varied backgrounds enter these movements. Adherents of counter-cultural devotional groups, on the other hand, correspond more closely to the popular stereotype of so-called "cult followers." But these adherents are atypical of the much larger numbers of persons who have participated in New Religious movements generally.

Conclusions

This examination of participation rates in New Religious and Para-Religious movements leads to several general conclusions. While the participation rate in these movements, as defined herein, is comparatively high, the ratio of persons who continue to be adherents of these movements is exceedingly low. For most persons, participation is temporary and involves them only in the periphery of these groups. It is impossible to conclude that such an involvement is without much significance for the individual, of course, but it is possible to argue that this significance would be different were typical participants to become more involved.

With respect to age and social class, participants vary somewhat from the adult population in general. However, these differences do not seem to be marked enough to account for participation rates. Clearly younger and single persons can more easily make commitments to new organizations and activities, whether they involve evangelical religion or yoga groups.

As Wuthnow and McLoughlin have argued, the increasing interest in New Religious and Para-Religious movements represents an historical, generational shift in values and religious orientation (Wuthnow, 1978; McLoughlin, 1978). In assessing the significance of the increased participation in these non-orthodox forms of religion, it is necessary to recognize also an increase in traditional forms of evangelical and pentecostal religion, as well as a wide variety of human growth groups and popular therapies (Kelley, 1972; Bach, 1972). It is tempting to search for some general characteristics shared by these various movements, for example, their attention to feelings of personal well-being. The significance of this resurgent spirituality and therapeutic interest, however, probably lies in its variety rather than its commonality. What is evident is a new kind of pluralism, in which hosts of organizations, institutes, prayer groups, radio ministries, encounter groups, and meditation classes have emerged and exist alongside, often in tacit cooperation with traditional forms of denominational religion.

If one were to characterize this increasing interest in "new," "para," pentecostal, and evangelical religious movements in a single phrase, it might aptly be called "religion and the rise of magic." A broad, anthropological definition of magic would include such activities as divinization, non-medical healing, exorcising, communication with spirits, shamanistic practices to gain power, the cultivation of trancelike states, and the chanting of sacred names. These activities are widely evident in the resurgent spirituality of both new religious movements and many pentecostal groups as well as in the ritual-like use of psy-chedelics, and the fascination with astrology. If magic refers to sacred techniques for gaining power and well-being—and this is the way both Weber and Malinowski used the term—then there is much evidence for an increased interest in magical practices. (Of course, the term magic is not broad enough to cover many other activities of New Religious and Para-Religious movements; much of what takes place would more appropriately be described as mysticism.) Yet the phrase "Religion and the Rise of Magic" suggests a comparison between the period beginning in the mid-1960s and the period of the Enlightenment in Europe beginning in the late seventeenth century.

Keith Thomas examined this latter period in England in his study *Religion and the Decline of Magic* (1971). What was noticeable about this period both in England and France was the systematic way in which many traditional spiritual and magical practices lost their appeal (Despland, 1982). These practices, which had previously enjoyed the tolerance, if not support, of the churches, included divinization, non-medical healing, exorcising, communication with spirits, shamanistic practices, the cultivation of trancelike states, and the chanting of sacred names. For much of the period since the Enlightenment these "magical" practices have remained out of popular favor. However, these same kinds of practices, together with a renewed interest in mysticism, have recently gained considerable interest, as the high rates of participation in New Religious and Para-Religious movements make evident. Characteristically, as with traditional magical practices, persons establish transitory, affiliate relation with those sponsoring these activities. Typically, participation in these magical practices involves a particular kind of experimental attitude, in which one ventures one's luck by following ritual-like sacred forms.

Thomas' hypothesis about the reason for the decline of "magic" with the Enlighten-ment offers a plausible hypothesis for the increasing interest in New Religious and Para-Religious movements since the middle of the 1960s. He argues that the major factor which led to a disenchantment with magic—a disenchantment favored by the well-educated clergy—was not an increasing belief in science, nor was it a marked rise in the standard of living, both of which were to follow later. Rather, Thomas argues that magical practices of quite varied forms lost their enchantment as the population in general gained an increased confidence, born of their rationalized religious convictions, that they could shape their own lives, measurably affecting their own destinies. It is reasonable to argue, then, that the increasing attention to a wide variety of magic and mystical practices since the 1960s has arisen as a similar confidence has declined.

Notes

1. Research for this paper was made possible in part by several grants from the Quebec Ministry of Education. The authors would like to thank the following persons for helping to gather data cited herein: Susan Bernstein, Paul Schwartz, Elizabeth Sandul, Ann McManaman, and Shaarda Himes. We would also like to thank Frances Westley for a careful reading of this paper.

2. These movements correspond as a whole to what Sydney Ahlstrom has referred to as the emergence of "Harmonial Religion" in the late nineteenth and early twentieth centuries with their similar interest in health, the use of science, and mystical meditation. There are several noticeable differences: (1) unlike the previous Harmonial Religion, the contemporary New Religious movements have not typically formed distinct, exclusive denominations like the Christian Scientists, Unity, Science of Mind; (2) unlike Harmonial Religion, many contemporary New Religious and Para-Religious movements are derived from Buddhist, Hindu, Taoist, Moslem, or unorthodox Christian traditions.

3. These figures are almost exactly the same as that estimated by Buddhist groups with regard to their own drop out rates (Layman, 1978: 30).

4. The high drop rate from these New Religious and Para-Religious movements means that the actual number of persons who still consider themselves to be affiliates is probably less than half the number of

those reported by the group themselves. The movements report steady increase in the number of persons who have become involved. The total number of participants in nine groups surveyed was, by their own reports, twice as large in 1980 as in 1975. However, given the high rate of disaffiliation, we suspect that actual numbers of participants—whether as members or affiliates—have not grown measurably.

5. This statement is based on a random sample of core members undertaken in Montreal in 1974 and 1975.

6. These findings should be considered tentative because the sample as a whole seems to be over-weighted with persons of higher occupational class and because of the small number of cases (N = 21) who are males, over 25, and present participants of these groups.

7. The Charismatics have rapidly grown in numbers during the late 1970s in Montreal, especially among the francophone population.

8. The finding on Transcendental Meditation is interesting in this regard. In spite of the group's claim to be non-religious, a large number of the participants in our sample felt it necessary to list their religious affiliation as "other" or "several" rather than listing only the religious affiliation of their mothers.

References

Bach, Kurt
　1972　Beyond Words: The Story of Sensitivity Training and the Encounter Movement. Baltimore: Penguin Books.
Bellah, Robert
　1976　"New religious consciousness and the crisis in modernity." In Charles Y. Glock and Robert N. Bellah (Eds.), The New Religious Consciousness. Berkeley: University of California Press.
Bird, Frederick and William Reimer
　1976　"A sociological analysis of new religious and para-religious movements." In Stewart Cysdale and Les Wheatcroft (Eds.), Religion in Canadian Society. Toronto: Macmillan of Canada.
Bird, Frederick
　1978　"Ritual and charisma in new religious movements." In Jacob Needleman and George Baker (Eds.), Understanding the New Religions. New York: Seabury Books.
　1979　"The pursuit of innocence: New religious movements and moral accountability." Sociological Analysis 40: 4, 335–346.
Despland, Michel
　1982　"Norms and models in early modern France and England: A study in comparative religious ethics." Journal of Religious Ethics 10:68–102.
Eliade, Mircea
　1957　Yoga. Princeton: Princeton University Press.
Kelley, Dean
　1972　Why the Conservative Churches Are Growing? New York: Harper and Row.
Layman, Emma
　1978　Buddhism in America. Chicago: Nelson-Hall.
McLoughlin, William G.
　1978　Revivals, Awakenings and Reform. Chicago: University of Chicago Press.
Smart, Ninian
　1968　The Yogi and the Devotee. [Atlantic Highlands, N.J.: Humanities Press.]
Thomas, Keith
　1971　Religion and the Decline of Magic. London: Weidenfield and Nicholson.
Tipton, Steve
　1977　"Getting saved from the sixties." PhD Dissertation, Harvard University.
Westley, Frances
　1978a　"The cult of man: Durkheimian predictions and new religious movements." Sociological Analysis 39: 135–145.
　1978b　"The complex forms of the religious life: A Durkheimian view of the new religious movements." PhD Dissertation, McGill University.
Wuthnow, Robert
　1976a　The Consciousness Reformation. Berkeley: University of California Press.
　1976b　"The new religions in a social context." In Charles Y. Glock and Robert N. Bellah (Eds.), The New Religious Consciousness. Berkeley: The University of California Press.
　1978　Experimentation in American Religion. Berkeley: University of California Press.

READING 9.2

An Evolutionary Theory of Spiritual Conversion and Commitment: The Case of Divine Light Mission

James V. Downton, Jr.

Thoughts of conversion bring to mind sweeping changes of character, so profound in their impact that the idea of "rebirth" seems an apt description of its transformative power. When I began a study of the followers of Guru Maharaj Ji in 1972, I was interested in understanding how conversion and commitment were unique features of a broader spiritual evolution—a life of commitment to personal change and spiritual enlightenment. I was also curious to discover what modifications in the personal and social lives of followers would occur as a consequence of their conversions and their involvement in Divine Light Mission over time.

The study was based on intensive interviews with eighteen followers (or "premies" as they are called) plus follow-up interviews over five years' time. A lengthy questionnaire was also administered to premies in two other regions of the country, Hare Krishna followers in Denver, and a group of nonfollower students at the University of Colorado. An extensive treatment of the interview and questionnaire data can be found in my book on the movement—*Sacred Journeys: The Conversion of Young Americans to Divine Light Mission* (1979). Here, I want to lay out more completely than I did in the book the sequence of stages and specific steps premies took in the process of their spiritual evolution in order to clarify the theoretical structure of this incremental type of change.

James V. Downton, Jr. is Associate Professor of Sociology at the University of Colorado, Boulder.
Reprinted from *Journal for the Scientific Study of Religion* 19 (December 1980), with permission.

What I discovered from a detailed examination of the life histories of premies is that spiritual conversion and commitment are very gradual in their development. While conversion does appear to be a sudden change of awareness which can transform a person's identity and perception of reality, radical changes of personality are rare. Speaking of their conversions in 1972, premies tended to dramatize them, as new converts are prone to do, by emphasizing the profound nature of the changes they had experienced. One premie, for instance, characterized his conversion as the death of his "old self," so that, looking into his past, he felt as if he were examining someone else's life. Yet, after five years in the Mission, premies spoke of their conversions as having been evolutionary, not revolutionary, in their development.

The Mission: Origin, Beliefs, and Practices

Guru Maharaj Ji came to the United States in 1971 when he was 13 years old to give "Knowledge" to those who could show that they were sincerely interested. People were invited to "Knowledge" sessions, where Mahatmas were empowered to teach them four techniques of meditation. Each technique was intended to give the initiate a unique experience of the "Knowledge," which is a term used in the Mission to refer to the life force (or God). Eventually, over 50,000 predominantly white, middle-class youth received the Knowledge.

Premies believe that Guru Maharaj Ji (like

Christ, Buddha, and other great saints) is a living manifestation of the spirit and that he has come to bring peace to the world. They believe that the ego is the chief obstacle to peace and that surrender to Guru Maharaj Ji and to their inner spirit (God) is a necessary and vital step in the evolution of their consciousness and the salvation of mankind.

Meditation, satsang (which is discourse on the Knowledge), and service are salient spiritual practices in the Mission. These practices, as well as devotion to the guru, are thought to bring the premie into closer contact with the spirit. Thus, premies believe that the most promising way to make a fundamental change in themselves and to break out of the cycle of war, hatred, and violence in the world is to cultivate a deeper relationship to God through spiritual practice and surrender.

The Sequential Development of Spiritual Commitments

By carefully tracing both general stages and specific steps in the developing spiritual commitments of premies as a "value-added" process (Smelser, 1963), we understand why personal change proceeds by small increments rather than leaps and bounds, and how these young people reached the point of surrender to Guru Maharaj Ji. Their involvement in the Mission certainly could not have been predicted during the early period of their growing disillusionment with American society, for, even as hippies in the counterculture, other options were available to them. What we see is a funneling effect in the development of spiritual commitments similar to that described by Gerlach and Hine (1969), Hine (1970), and Lofland and Stark (1965), where options become progressively narrower the further along in the process the person moves. As Becker has said of commitment in general: "Each step tends to limit the alternatives available at the next step until the in-

dividual finds himself at a decision point with only one 'alternative' to choose from" (1961: 245).

The following stages and steps chart the development of the spiritual commitments of those premies who reported a dramatic personal change (conversion) as a consequence of their experience in the Knowledge session. This focus is taken in order to shed light on the dynamics of the conversion experience. (For an account of the cases where no "rebirth" experience was reported, see *Sacred Journeys* [1979]). The description of each stage is couched in fairly general terms so as to suggest its applicability to similar kinds of movements, while steps are specific to the premie experience and illustrative of the concrete elements which make up each stage.

Stage I: General Disillusionment with Conventional Values, Social Organization, and Solutions to Problems

This is a period of increasing disillusionment with the prevailing ideology, organization, and leadership of society, coupled with a growing fascination for unconventional lifestyles and solutions. Disenchantment with conventional society is rooted in the individual's negative experience with institutions, opportunities, and reward structures. In this sense, it might be viewed as little different from the process of defection from the church, which Mauss (1969) described as stemming from ideological, social, and emotional reactions to church dogma, organization, and practices.

Step 1: Discontent. Briefly, premie discontent stemmed, in large measure, from (1) their disenchantment with materialistic and competitive values, (2) their sense of alienation from others and the society at large, (3) their feelings of personal inadequacy, partly spawned by excessively demanding and unaccepting parents, and (4) their sense of aimlessness and meaningless as a result of their participation in the counterculture. These sources of discontent were not too different from those described by Nicholi (1974) in his study of seventeen college student converts to Christianity, among whom he found a widespread sense of social alienation, restlessness, and confusion about the meaning and direction of their lives.

Stage II: Deepening or Developing Faith in a Spiritual Solution to Problems

By itself, discontent is a poor predictor of spiritual conversion and commitment. For even people who oppose our society's competitive values and who experience feelings of alienation, aimlessness, and meaninglessness may not be available for a spiritual solution. That is, they may not be socially or psychologically free to take a spiritual direction. The following steps made premies freer to embrace a spiritual solution.

Step 2: Absence or Deterioration of Commitment to Conventional Religion and College. Premies had become disillusioned with the mainstream churches and dropped out in adolescence, freeing them to embark on a new spiritual direction. Similarly, dropping out of college as they did made them more available for involvement in the counterculture, which removed them from the influence of conventional career training and clothed them in a new ideology and life-style. More importantly, it introduced them to psychedelic drugs, which were eventually to create religious beliefs compatible with eastern spirituality.

Step 3: Spiritual Awakening Through Psychedelic Drugs. Psychedelic experiences changed the spiritual frames of reference for many of these young people. They testify to the fact that psychedelics revealed a powerful energy animating life which they came to see as spiritual in nature. This experience challenged their Judeo-Christian conception of God as a human form and made them more sympathetic to the eastern view of God as energy.

Later, they were attracted to eastern spiritual beliefs because such beliefs were generally compatible with their own. Thus, there was a continuity of beliefs, where personal ideologies held prior to joining were in general harmony with the movement's belief system. Other research has also found few drastic changes of belief among converts (Balch & Taylor, 1977; Lynch, 1977).

Step 4: Experimentation with Eastern Spiritual Practices. Premies who were spiritually awakened through their use of drugs soon began experimenting with meditation, chanting, and yoga as spiritual practices. Their positive experiences with those techniques deepened their disenchantment with drugs and counterculture life. Also, at this time, a new set of social norms was developing within the counterculture community, discouraging the use of drugs and putting a higher value on natural ways of "getting high," such as meditation. Already disillusioned with or "burnt out" on drugs, they welcomed the emergence of a new spiritual community within the counterculture.

Step 5: Development of Social Ties with Those in the Newly Emerging Spiritual Community. Where initially there had been social pay-offs for taking drugs, becoming active in the growing spiritual community eventually became, as one premie put it, "the hip thing to do." With their pattern of conformity changing in a spiritual direction, many were soon reading spiritual books and associating with spiritually inclined people. This turn toward spirituality was also encouraged by other factors: few countervailing group pressures discouraging their involvement in the new spiritual community; geographic distance from previous group pressures (especially parents); few opportunities which might have led to conventional careers; and, with no heavy career commitments, more time and energy for their newly developing spiritual interests.

Step 6: Increasing Interaction with "Spiritual People" and Decreasing Interaction with Those Who Were Critical of Their Spiritual Interests. This was the point at which social networks began to change, as premies moved to secure a better social balance for themselves. Deepening their spiritual interests, they spent less time with friends whose interests were not also changing or who opposed the course they were taking. Their attempt to escape from these conflicts freed them for fuller participation in the emerging spiritual group.

Step 7: Development of the Belief That the Spiritual Realm Holds the Key to the Resolution of One's Personal Problems and Society's Social Problems. Having abandoned hope that politics or counterculture tactics would transform our society and the world, recruits were ready to accept spirituality as the new answer. They had had sufficiently positive experiences with spiritual practices by then to feel some enthusiasm for the idea that their vision of the future might still be achieved by a sweeping spiritual revolution. This was the point at which their faith in change was rekindled.

Stage III: Growing Determination to Take a Spiritual Direction, Reflected in the Development of New Spiritual Ego-Ideal and Self-Image

Once a person has come to believe in a spiritual solution to personal and social problems, a change of self-image begins. Where, before, the individual may have perceived himself, for example, as a "hippie," atheist, or political revolutionary, there is a shift of perception or self-definition in a spiritual direction. As soon as this happens, a new phase of development begins, for possessing an image of oneself as a "spiritual person" increases availability for spiritual causes, practices, and groups.

Step 8: Strengthening of Spiritual Aspirations and Determination. Believing that a spiritual transformation is what they and the world needed, these young people developed a much stronger sense of will to move in a spiritual direction. This feeling of determination to take a spiritual course, which Starbuck (1914) also found in Christians before their conversion, is an extremely critical time, for the person is rearranging priorities and making decisions to focus resources of time, energy, etc., more narrowly in a spiritual direction.

Step 9: Creation of a Spiritual Ego-Ideal and Self-Image. Determined to move more deeply into matters of the spirit, these young people were soon defining themselves in spiritual terms. An image of themselves as "spiritual seekers" became the outward feature of a new ego-ideal, which included a set of goals and rules of conduct, giving them directions as to how they should change, what they should believe, and how they should behave as "spiritual people." In contrast to their hippie ideals, these new ideals were loftier, yet they were extensions of—not radical departures from—earlier goals.

Stage IV: Increasing Sense of Personal Futility Leading to Greater Psychological Receptivity to the Appeals of Unconventional Spiritual Leaders or Followers Who Make Bold Promises of Change

Grand ideals for oneself and the world naturally lead to feelings of personal inadequacy, based on the idea that the more idealistic a person's goals for change, the more incapable that person will feel in trying to reach them. A sense of personal futility, then, seems almost a natural outgrowth of excessive idealism.

Step 10: Ego Weakness Arising from the Increasing Discrepancy between Their New Spiritual Ego-Ideals and Their Capabilities. Aspiring toward rather lofty spiritual heights, these young people began to wonder whether they would be able to put into practice what they hoped to achieve. They found it difficult to discipline themselves and to love others without using drugs. The discrepancy between what they wanted to attain and what they could actually achieve was both great and sobering. In time, they began to feel as if they were incapable of making the change which their new ideals demanded of them, a source of ego weakness described by Cantril (1963) as a factor increasing a person's receptivity to mass movements.

Step 11: Increasing Feelings of Personal Futility. The more they tried to change on their own, the more hopeless these young people felt. Their wills seemed puny and inadequate as they faced the mysteries of the spiritual world and their goals for the future. At first, some hoped for enlightenment through personal effort, but they were disappointed by the almost imperceptible changes they seemed to be making on their own. Others turned to their spiritual friends for help, only to find them equally lost. Feeling incapable of changing themselves or understanding the spiritual mysteries they had discovered, many were ready to accept the belief that they needed a spiritual teacher to guide them.

Step 12: Beginning to Look for a Guru to Follow and a Spiritual Community to Join. Before they had heard about Guru Maharaj Ji and Divine Light Mission, many premies had already begun to search for a guru to follow and a spiritual community to join. Their sense of futility prepared them for surrender, while the fact that they had no firm social ties to a group made them available for mobilization to a community. Both of these factors made them more susceptible to recruitment.

Stage V: Contact and Increasing Attraction to an Unconventional Spiritual Movement as

a Result of Positive Interactions with Members and Ideological Compatibility with the Movement's Beliefs

These young people were well prepared to join a spiritual movement at this point, but why did they eventually join Divine Light Mission rather than one of the many other movements seeking recruits at that time? What attracts people to a movement is a combination of factors: how they become introduced to it, how personally rewarding their initial experiences are with members, how compatible the movement's beliefs are to their own, how they assess the movement's potential, and so forth.

Step 13: The Majority of These Young People Were Brought into Contact with the Mission Through Their Special Ties to Premies. Affinity for the premie community was partially a result of the trusting relationship they had developed with friends, relatives, and acquaintances who had already joined. Hearing so many positive comments about the Knowledge and Guru Maharaj Ji from people they trusted made them stop to wonder whether they themselves might not benefit from the Knowledge experience.

Step 14: Positive Interaction with Members and/or Guru. While social affinity did inspire interest, first impressions of premies and Guru Maharaj Ji were more important social factors increasing their attraction to the movement. All reported having positive experiences during their first contacts with members. (For two sides of the question regarding the role of social influences in the commitment process, see Heirich, 1977, who gives great emphasis to them in his Catholic Pentecostal research and Balch & Taylor, 1977, who argue that social influences had minimal impact on mobilization to a UFO cult.)

Step 15: Recognizing the Difference between Their Own Stage of Futility and the Apparent

Sense of Joy, Peace, and Commitment in the Behavior of Members. The more these young people associated with premies, the more convinced they became that they had something they wanted and needed. Some members in particular helped to kindle their interest, for they expressed beliefs and attitudes and behaved in ways which were in harmony with the spiritual ideals these eighteen people were trying to reach. By assuming that members had come closer to reaching the ideals they held for themselves, they could not help concluding that the Knowledge experience and devotion to Guru Maharaj Ji must be effective avenues toward a radical change. This made the movement all the more attractive to them.

Step 16: Assumption of the Ambivalent Status of "Aspirant-Outsider." In the new spiritual movements there is invariably a secret which is withheld, to be revealed only to those who seek initiation into the community of believers. Possession of the secret is what distinguishes insiders from outsiders, setting up a social gulf which can only be overcome through the decision to join and by adopting a social demeanor regarded by the community as appropriate for membership. Wanting access to this secret, the aspirant becomes sensitive to what is expected in order to make the transition from outsider to insider. Simmel (1964) discussed this social dynamic as one of the inherent features of secret societies.

Within Divine Light Mission, the Knowledge is the secret which sets up the social boundaries between insiders and outsiders. There was a point when many of these young people assumed the ambivalent position of "aspirant-outsider," when they had an affinity for the community but had not yet joined. No matter how emotionally drawn they felt to the movement or to the guru, the fact that they had not received the Knowledge kept them at a social distance.

Stage VI: Acceptance of the Problem-Solving Perspective of the Movement, Strengthening the Determination to Join

The participation of aspiring members in the activities of a movement before formal passage into membership prepares the way for the adoption of the movement's ideology. In a sense, they begin to think and act like members before they have been initiated.

Step 17: Initial Socialization into the Premie Community's Frame of Reference. Those who accepted the Mission's beliefs and were eager for community began to show signs of conformity quite early. As a prelude to surrender, they responded positively to the urging of Guru Maharaj Ji and premies to attend satsang and to do service in the ashrams. Increasing their contact with premies in this way, they became more familiar with the premie frame of reference. Thus, their transition into the social identity of "premie" or "devotee" was made gradually.

Step 18: Beginning to Espouse the Movement's Beliefs, to Participate in Its Rituals and to Employ Its Symbols. Having become more fully bonded to the premie community, although still separate from it by virtue of their ignorance of the Knowledge, most were soon articulating the movement's beliefs, participating in its rituals, and making its symbols visible to others in dress or by displaying pictures of the guru.

Step 19: Embracing the Problem-Solving Perspective of the Movement. During the time they were experimenting with the Mission's beliefs, rituals, and symbols a rising conviction was developing that the Knowledge and surrender to Guru Maharaj Ji were the answer they were seeking. The development of this belief effectively narrowed the options available to them, making their decision to receive the Knowledge inevitable.

Step 20: Increasing Determination to Join, Leading to the Decision to Join. The decision to receive the Knowledge and become a premie was made about this time, although a period of preparation normally followed. Developing the correct mental attitude was considered important. They were told they needed a strong desire for the Knowledge and a "child-like" heart, trusting and ready to be "filled up." They were warned not to have any expectations but just to be receptive to the Knowledge experience.

Stage VII: Initiation and Conversion: The Transformation of Awareness Resulting from a Shift in Identity from the Personality (Ego) to the Spirit (Life Force, or God)

It is widely known that initiation ceremonies bring the individual into a new relationship with the group. Access to the group's secrets, assumption of its collective identity, and acceptance of its rituals and symbols are aspects of the rite of passage into active participation as a full-fledged member. During this transition, the individual modifies a private world of beliefs, attitudes, and meanings in order to abide by the group's interpretation of reality.

When conversion includes such rites, it assumes a social character, shaped by group norms specifying what is appropriate behavior and what is an acceptable proof that the individual has adopted its view of reality. At times, a single act (such as speaking in tongues) may be regarded as a sign that the person has reached the point of decision to enter into a stronger spiritual relationship with the members of the community.

While conversion does have a social character and can be analyzed from that perspective, it may also be a transformative personal experience. For many premies, the Knowledge session struck deeply and made a permanent change in the way they perceived themselves and the world at large. During the Knowledge session, a sudden shift in their awareness led them to a new identity,

which became the basis for a gradual set of changes over the next several years. The following two steps are therefore critical aspects of the psychodynamics of conversion as a "rebirth" experience.

Step 21: Identification with Their Spiritual Essence. The sense of rebirth experienced during a conversion may result from a shift in identity, as the person quits identifying with the personality (ego) and begins to identify with the inner spirit. Most of these young people walked into the Knowledge session identifying with their egos; many left feeling they were spirit and believing that the ego was simply a product of social conditioning they need not take too seriously. This discovery put them in contact with what most came to call their "true self," or spiritual essence.

Step 22: Detachment from Their Personalities (Egos) as the Focus of Identity. Identification with the spirit during dramatic conversions leads to a sense of psychological detachment from the personality (ego), particularly its negative features. These changes create positive feelings bordering on the sublime, for the convert simultaneously identifies with the spirit, which is perceived as the source of peace and love, and relinquishes responsibility for the negative side of the personality, representing the evil and baser feelings. As a consequence, the individual's self-image becomes immediately more positive and the orientation to personal and social problems changes in an optimistic direction.

No longer identifying with their psychological problems, premies could relax and observe their personalities without being attached to what they felt and did. This sense of psychological distance from their problems had immediately positive results in most cases. For example, one premie, who had been so emotionally troubled before his conversion that he could not divulge his deeper problems to the psychiatrists he visited sporadically, found himself being amused by things he did and felt after receiving the Knowledge which had sent him into deep depressions earlier.

Perhaps this is one way a sudden change of perception and identity during conversion prepares the individual for an acceleration of development. It increases feelings of self-regard, self-confidence, and social union as a consequence of an identification with the spirit, while it reduces the sense of guilt for one's problems, negative feelings, and desires through the process of becoming emotionally detached from the ego. Therefore, emotional problems are not taken as seriously, which allows the energy normally channeled into worrying and depression to flow into more constructive thinking and activity. A process very similar to this is described by Clark (1977) in her delineation of the stages of transpersonal therapy, which she calls "identification" (taking responsibility for oneself), "disidentification" (disidentification from the ego and self-concept), and "self-transcendence" (concern with service to others and with the quality of life). These stages of development strongly resemble those I have described above as the critical psychodynamics of the conversion process; namely, identification with the spirit and detachment from the ego. It is in this context that we might wonder whether conversion and successful therapy are not in fact indicative of the same underlying process of development.

Stage VIII: Surrender to the Spirit (God) and to a Spiritual Leader, Characterized by Idealization of the Leader, Identification with Him, Conformity to His Initiatives, and Loss of the Capacity to Criticize Him (Features of the Role of "Devotee")

Surrender is the act of abandoning the individual will to authority. Feeling helpless, the convert seeks the intervention of a higher power. Surrender is a psychological state characterized by idealization of a leader, identification with him, conformity to his in-

itiatives, and the loss of the capacity to criticize him (factors I associated with the charismatic bond in an earlier work, 1973). (An alternative possibility is to investigate as well how individuals surrender to the group, Westley, 1977.)

Step 23: Surrender to the Inner Spirit (God) and to Guru Maharaj Ji. Premies came to believe that the way to enlightenment was to abandon egoistic concerns and to surrender to their inner spirit (God) and to Guru Maharaj Ji. As a method of change, surrender struck a comfortable balance between their need for order and predictability and their determination to reach enlightenment. By assuming the Guru Maharaj Ji was in complete control of everything (the result of their idealization of him as the Lord), premies achieved a sense of confidence about change and the future. Idealization also facilitated their identification with the guru, providing them with a model of behavior to emulate. Through identification, new values, beliefs, and attitudes could be internalized through the process of imitation. And the willingness to conform and not criticize their guru made premies more receptive to the course of change he advocated. They were secured at one level, but constantly encouraged to change at another. As Suzuki has shown in *The Training of the Zen Buddhist Monk* (1965), surrender as a method of learning and change is not intended to be too comfortable for the student. On the contrary, it is a challenge requiring a deep determination to change, a willingness to suffer, complete trust in the teacher, and perseverance in the face of difficulties. (For an excellent statement of the nature of the guru-devotee relationship, see Wach, 1962).

Step 24: Assumption of the Social Identity of "Devotee." There were two social identities these young people assumed after their initiation. "Premie" was the broadest, since it was synonymous with "member." Anyone who received the Knowledge and stayed in the Mission was considered a premie, whether they had actually surrendered or not. "Devotee" was a more commitment-laden identity a premie assumed during surrender. Its social requirements were more demanding, entailing the abandonment of autonomy to the spirit, obedience to Guru Maharaj Ji and selfless service.

Stage IX: Intensification of Commitment through Increasing Investments and Sacrifices, Greater Social Communion with Members, Reduction of Social Ties in the Outside World, and Mortification of the Ego

Once an individual has assumed a social identity which is tied directly to a movement, an enlargement of that person's commitment can be expected. For the assumption of such an identity is basically a decision to conform to the collectivity and to move more completely into its sphere of influence. Becoming active, the person comes into a new relationship with the social organization of the movement, which means coming under the influence of its commitment mechanisms. These mechanisms, ably described by Kanter (1968, 1972), are increasing investments and sacrifices, greater social communion with members and the reduction of social ties in the outside world, mortification (which leads to a new identity), and surrender. McGaw (1979) has taken a similar tack by identifying four processes affecting the intensity of commitment: 1) closure (primary group bonds with members), 2) strictness (the exclusiveness of those bonds to the community), 3) consensus (the community's and leadership's roles as reference groups), and 4) cohesion (belief consensus).

Step 25: Increasing Investments and Sacrifices for the Movement. Although several premies had begun to make investments and sacrifices for the movement prior to the Knowledge session, their initiation and the assumption of the "devotee" identity ushered in a new era of giving. For they were expected to dedicate their lives and resources to the movement. Not half-hearted effort, but total commitment was demanded from them. They were asked to give money, to distribute leaflets, to abstain from drugs, to rise early in the morning for meditation, and so on.

Mahatmas and the members of Guru Maharaj Ji's family, rather than the guru himself, were the strongest advocates of total sacrifice and dedication. But that is often the case in mass movements. It is normally the cadre of subleaders around the leader who are the major defenders of the leader's charisma and the most vehement spokesmen for the necessity of complete commitment. (See Gerth, 1940).

Step 26: Increasing Social Communion with Members and Decreasing Interaction with the Outside World. Social enclosure occurs when converts have become separated from people who oppose their spiritual direction and have become dependent on the movement for the satisfaction of needs. As these premies moved deeper into the Mission, they spent more and more time with premies, at satsang, while performing service, and, for many, while living in the ashrams. In fact, they found themselves wanting to associate primarily with other premies. They discounted the opposition of their parents as based on a lack of real understanding, and sometimes broke off friendships with nonpremies on the pretext of a conflict of interests. The extent of their social insulation over the last five years (although not very great) is revealed in the fact that close friendships and marriages were always with other premies. Even now, many are living communally with other premies in ashrams or loosely-structured cooperatives, called "premie houses."

Step 27: Mortification of the Ego. Mortification is the process by which the follower's ego is humbled. Through a series of degradation rites, such as prostrations and having to wait for the guru to arrive for a program (sometimes as much as two hours late), premies were constantly forced to observe the reactions of their ego. This is, we are told, one of the ways spiritual teachers from the east try to break down the dominance of the follower's ego in preparation for a thoroughgoing spiritual change. Through mortification practices, the follower's identity is slowly undermined, as are old beliefs and behavior, in order to make way for a new identity and pattern of behavior.

Stage X: Gradual Modification of Identity, Beliefs, and Behavior Through Commitment, which Secures the Individual's Adherence to the Movement's Norms and Practices and, Therefore, Insures the Accumulation of Experiences Considered by the Movement to Be Essential for a Thoroughgoing Change of Character and Outlook

Once within the movement, members begin slowly to change their identities, beliefs, and behaviors by conformity to group norms which offer a new vision of the world and by finding meaning in that view so that living achieves a deeper purpose; by identifying with a leader as an example of the new way of perceiving, knowing and being; by having their old identities uprooted through mortification; and by experiencing success with the new beliefs, attitudes, and behaviors in areas of life which had been dominated by confusion or failure. Simmonds' (1977) study of a Jesus movement group led him to conclude that no radical change of personality occurred for the participants either during or after their conversions. This finding is supported by my own conclusion that, while change does take place, it does so very gradually and over a long period of time. Simmonds' research is seriously limited by the fact that he was examining personal change only over a two and one-half month interval, a period much too short for assessing the extent of change (a fact he, himself, recognized).

The experiences of these premies since 1971 demonstrate how very gradually the personality changes, although perceptions may go through sudden alterations and can therefore create dramatic changes of a different order. What can be observed, especially among those who were the most emotionally disturbed before their conversions, is that personal problems developed earlier in life still persist, although they seem somewhat less severe and have a less profound influence on their behavior because premies no longer identify so strongly with their personalities. Now they seem more able to accept themselves and show signs of being able to cope more effectively with their own personal problems and the pressures of living in society. These are subtle, but nonetheless important, changes.

Stages in the Development of Unconventional Spiritual Commitments

While many specific steps premies took during their spiritual evolution are important for understanding the complexity and subtlety of change, only the stages will be mentioned here. Stated more generally, these stages provide a useful theoretical point of departure for comparing the growth of unconventional spiritual commitments in a variety of religious movements, keeping in mind that they are derived from a single movement and therefore may not be completely applicable to other movements.

Stage I: General disillusionment with conventional values, social organization, and solutions to problems.

Stage II: Deepening or developing faith in a spiritual solution to problems.

Stage III: Growing determination to take a spiritual direction, reflected in the development of a new spiritual ego-ideal and self-image.

Stage IV: Increasing sense of personal futility, leading to greater psychological receptivity to the appeals of unconventional spiritual leaders or followers who make bold promises of change.

Stage V: Contact and increasing attraction to an unconventional spiritual movement as a result of positive interactions with members and ideological compatibility with the movement's beliefs.

Stage VI: Acceptance of the problem-solving perspective of the movement, strengthening the determination to join.

Stage VII: Initiation and conversion: The transformation of awareness resulting from a shift in identity from the personality (ego) to the spirit (life force, or God).

Stage VIII: Surrender to the spirit (God) and to a spiritual leader, characterized by idealization of the leader, identification with him, conformity to his initiatives, and loss of the capacity to criticize him (features of the role of "devotee").

Stage IX: Intensification of commitment through increasing investments and sacrifices, greater social communion with members, reduction of social ties in the outside world, and mortification of the ego.

Stage X: Gradual modification of identity, beliefs, and behavior through commitment, which secures the individual's adherence to the movements' norms and practices and, therefore, insures the accumulation of experiences considered by the movement to be essential for a thoroughgoing change of character and outlook.

These ten stages agree in many respects with the theory of conversion by Lofland and Stark. Summarizing their findings from a study of a Pacific Coast religious cult, they concluded that, as a general rule, a convert to the cult would tend to:

1. Experience enduring acutely felt tensions
2. within a religious, problem-solving perspective
3. which leads to defining himself as a religious seeker;
4. encountering the cult at a turning point in his life;
5. wherein an affective bond to adherents is formed (or preexists)
6. where extra-cult attachments are low or neutralized;
7. and where, to become a "deployable agent" [a convert], exposure to intensive interaction is accomplished. (1965: 874)

There are a number of similarities between my formulation and theirs. Both begin with a notion of personal dissatisfaction, emphasize the importance of adopting a spiritual problem-solving perspective and self-image, regard positive feelings toward members as a salient feature of attraction, and acknowledge the importance of interaction within the movement as a factor increasing the likelihood an individual will join.

While Lofland and Stark's theory is compelling in many ways, there are stages in the spiritual evolution of premies which might help to refine and extend their theory. I will briefly mention some of the key ideas.

The state of personal futility adds a useful psychological component to the discussion of conversion. Based on the growing discrepancy between an individual's new spiritual ego-ideal and capabilities, futility sheds light on a possible motivation for the widespread tendency of religious converts to surrender to spiritual authorities. It also conforms to the psychological theory which claims that there is a collapse of the will prior to sudden conversions, a sense of personal futility which has become so great the person simply gives up. It is at that point, where the will ceases to function, that the conversion experience is thought to take place (see Starbuck, 1914; Christensen, 1965: 27–8).

Acceptance of the problem-solving perspective of the movement is another stage of the premie experience worth further exploration. This is an important phase of the conversion process because it focuses on the individual's rational evaluation of the movement. Here, the individual assesses the movement's orientation to change in terms of his or her private values, goals, and needs. The potential of the movement to satisfy personal hopes and collective goals is made and a self-conscious choice follows.

More attention also should be given to conversion as a developmental transition, as various psychologists have suggested (Starbuck, 1914; James, 1958; Allison, 1967, 1969; Levin & Zegans, 1974). There are a number of important and intriguing questions which need more careful examination and which I have discussed briefly above. What is the nature of the psychological changes or alterations of awareness which lead people to experience "rebirth"? How do those changes affect the convert's response to psychological problems and the world at large? How does conversion aid or impede personal growth? Is there an underlying process of change which can be found in the conversion process as well as in successful therapy?

A theory is not complete unless it goes beyond the point at which the individual joins a movement to the stages following initiation—namely, surrender (Stage VIII), the influence of organizational mechanisms which intensify commitments (Stage IX), and the personal changes which arise from commitment (Stage X). Surrender is a key issue bearing on the follower's changing relationship to the spirit and to a spiritual leader. Surrender, and the other mechanisms of commitment (investment and sacrifice, increasing social communion with members, termination of competing ties in the outside world, and mortification) not only account for the bonding of the individual to the community but help explain the pattern of uniformity among members. Finally, surrender and commitment induce changes in people; therefore they should be analyzed fully in terms of their positive and negative impact on personal identity, values, and behavior.

In an up-date of his earlier work with Stark, Lofland (1977) does move into the realm of the organizational mechanisms of commitment. There, he discusses the stages a person moves through on the way to membership and the organizational influences encountered at each point. The stages he describes are: 1) picking up (contact in a public place), 2) hooking (the process of bringing a prospective member into the movement's territory), 3) encapsulating (insulation of the prospective member within the movement community), 4) loving (persistent and numerous messages of love from the movement's members), and 5) committing (becoming gradually involved in patterns of participation within the movement, leading to heavier investments and sacrifices). While this formulation is interesting and important as a way of understanding the process by which a movement mobilizes new converts, Lofland fails to integrate these stages into his earlier theory (1965), so one is left wondering about their place in a more comprehensive theory of commitment. For, by themselves, these five stages are an inadequate rendering of the complexity of the larger process of commitment. A theory of conversion and commitment must not only take into account the influence of the movement's norms and mechanisms of commitment, but also the earlier stages and steps which prepared the individual or class of individuals to adopt the movement's view of reality and its recommended solutions for change. What I have tried to do here is delineate, in as much detail as my data allowed, the various stages and steps which seem to bear on the evolutionary nature of the entire process of change. By examining the life process of the convert, what we discover is that change is very gradual in nature, as individuals apparently shun excessive conflict and risks.

Even surrender and commitment, which insure conformity to new beliefs and behavior, are unlikely to produce sudden, drastic changes in converts. Looking at the gradual evolution of premies, I cannot help but agree with the conclusion of Marris in *Loss and Change* (1975). We assimilate new experiences, he says, by integrating them into an already reliable view of reality and by avoiding experiences which threaten to disrupt the sense we have made of the world. Therefore, he continues, change takes place gradually as the individual adds new elements to a reigning ideology, modifying what is perceived and known over such a long period of time that a sense of internal consistency is preserved. One premie captured the essence of this need for time when he said: "Looking back, nothing has ever pressured me to change. When the time was right, and I hesitated each time, I wasn't knocked down but was allowed to linger. When I was ready to stop eating meat or dealing drugs, I stopped. When I was ready for the next step, it came naturally" (Downton, 1979: 73).

References

Allison, Joel
  1967 "Adaptive regression and intense religious experiences." Journal of Nervous and Mental Disease 145: 452–63.
  1969 "Religious conversion: Regression and progression in an adolescent experience." Journal for the Scientific Study of Religion 8: 23–28.

Balch, Robert and David Taylor
  1977 "Seekers and saucers: The role of the cultic milieu in joining a UFO cult." American Behavioral Scientist 20: 839–60.
Becker, Howard S.
  1961 "The implications of research on occupational careers for a model of household decision-making." In Nelson Foote (Ed.), Household Decision-Making: Consumer Behavior. New York: New York University Press.
Cantril, Hadley
  1963 The Psychology of Social Movements. New York: John Wiley and Sons.
Christensen, Carl
  1965 "Religious conversion in adolescence." Pastoral Psychology 16: 17–28.
Clark, Frances
  1977 "Transpersonal perspectives in psychotherapy." Journal of Humanistic Psychology 17: 69–81.
Downton, James Jr.
  1973 Rebel Leadership: Commitment and Charisma in the Revolutionary Process. New York: The Free Press.
  1979 Sacred Journeys: The Conversion of Young Americans to Divine Light Mission. New York: Columbia University Press.
Gerlach, Luther and Virginia Hine
  1969 People, Power, Change. Indianapolis: Bobbs-Merrill.
Gerth, Hans
  1940 "The Nazi party: Its leadership and composition." American Journal of Sociology 45: 517–41.
Heirich, Max
  1977 "Change of heart: A test of some widely held theories of religious conversion." American Journal of Sociology 83: 653–80.
Hine, Virginia
  1970 "Bridge burners: Commitment and participation in a religious movement." Sociological Analysis 31: 61–66.
James, William
  1958 The Varieties of Religious Experience. New York: New American Library.
Kanter, Rosabeth Moss
  1968 "Commitment and social organization: A study of commitment mechanisms in utopian communities." American Sociological Review: 33: 499–517.
  1972 "Commitment and the internal organization of millennial movements." American Behavioral Scientist 16: 219–43.
Levin, Theodore and Leonard Zegans
  1974 "Adolescent identity crisis and religious conversion: Implications for psychotherapy."

The British Journal of Medical Psychology 47: 73–82.

Lofland, John and Rodney Stark
1965 "Becoming a world-saver: A theory of conversion to a deviant perspective." American Sociological Review 30: 862–75.

Lofland, John
1977 "Becoming a world-saver" revisited. American Behavioral Scientist 20: 805–18.

Lynch, Frederick
1977 "Toward a theory of conversion and commitment to the occult." American Behavioral Scientist 20: 887–908.

Marris, Peter
1975 Loss and Change. Garden City, N.Y.: Doubleday.

Mauss, Armand
1969 "Dimensions of religious defection." Review of Religious Research 10: 128–35.

McGaw, Douglas
1979 "Commitment and religious community: A comparison of a charismatic and a mainline congregation." Journal for the Scientific Study of Religion 18: 146–63.

Nicholi II, Armand
1974 "A new dimension of the youth culture." American Journal of Psychiatry 131: 396–401.

Simmel, Georg
1964 The Sociology of Georg Simmel (Kurt H. Wolff, trans.). New York: The Free Press.

Simmonds, Robert
1977 "Conversion or addiction: Consequences of joining a Jesus movement group." American Behavioral Scientist 20: 909–24.

Smelser, Neil
1963 Theory of Collective Behavior. New York: The Free Press.

Starbuck, Edwin
1914 The Psychology of Religion: An Empirical Study of the Growth of Religious Consciousness. London: The Walter Scott Publishing Co.

Suzuki, D. T.
1965 The Training of the Zen Buddhist Monk. New York: University Books.

Wach, Joachim
1962 "Master and disciple: Two religio-sociological studies." The Journal of Religion XLII: 1–21.

Westley, Frances
1977 "Searching for surrender: A Catholic charismatic renewal group's attempt to become glossolalic." American Behavioral Scientist 20: 925–40.

SELECTION 9.A

Looking behind the Scenes in a Religious Cult: Implications for the Study of Conversion

Robert W. Balch

Introduction

Joining a religious cult can bring about sudden and dramatic changes in behavior. One

Robert Balch is Professor of Sociology at the University of Montana.

An earlier version of this paper was presented at the meetings of the Association for the Sociology of Religion, Boston, 1979. The author thanks Harry Bredemeier, Susan Gal, Seward Hiltner, and Michael Moffatt for useful comments and criticisms. Reprinted from *Sociological Analysis* 41 (Summer, 1980), with permission.

common explanation for this is "brainwashing," as if these curious behavioral changes are caused by radical shifts in personality. It is not necessary to postulate fundamental changes in personality or values, beliefs and attitudes to account for the behavioral changes of those who join religious cults. Research on a millennial UFO cult has convinced me that role theory provides a simpler and more satisfactory explanation.

The group gained public attention in late

1975 when Walter Cronkite reported the sudden disappearance of more than twenty Oregonians after they listened to a mysterious couple known as "the Two," who called themselves Bo and Peep, claiming to be the two witnesses prophesied in Revelation 11. This couple (a man and woman in their mid-forties) expected to be martyred "within weeks," rise from the dead, perform miracles, and be "beamed up" to UFOs that would carry them off to an androgenous heaven known as the "Next Evolutionary Kingdom." They referred to their approaching martyrdom as "the Demonstration" because their death and resurrection would demonstrate the truth of their "Message" to the world.

In order to accompany them on their journey into space, Bo and Peep's followers had to give up all their worldly attachments, including friends, family, job, and material possessions. By overcoming all ties to the "human level," a biological transformation of their bodies would be completed when they boarded the UFOs. Bo and Peep called this transformation "Human Individual Metamorphosis," or in the cult's everyday language, "the Process." Once they reached the Next Kingdom, each member's body and soul would be permanently welded together in a single indestructible unit. Only by achieving membership in the "next Level" could their followers free themselves from the endless cycle of death and reincarnation.

After a brief highly publicized flurry of public meetings around the country, Bo and Peep recruited almost 200 followers, ranging in age from 14 to 75, with most in their early twenties. They tended to be single, highly mobile, and either unemployed or weakly committed to their work, including a few older men and women who left large families, good jobs, and expensive homes. Most members had at least a year of college, were self-defined spiritual seekers before joining, and most had dabbled in a wide variety of religious and self-help groups before deciding to follow the Two.

Data Collection

In 1975 I joined the UFO cult as a covert participant-observer,[1] and remained for seven weeks to observe and participate in almost every aspect of daily life in the cult, including the recruitment and socialization of new members. After leaving the group, 36 members who had dropped out were interviewed.[2] The interviews explored their activities as members, the reasons why they became disillusioned, and their reflections on the entire cult experience.

Since hidden observation is a questionable research strategy, it is worth noting that this paper probably would not have been written without it. Most of the findings that led me to question the popular view of religious conversion first emerged when "back-stage" posing as a member. Although initial observations were conducted without the knowledge of either the Two or their followers, the nature of the study was explained to everyone interviewed. Informants were not only very cooperative, but many indicated their belief that hidden observation was the only strategy that could effectively penetrate the social barriers that insulated members of the cult from the outside world.

Acting like a Believer

Acting like a believer meant conforming to a set of expectations specified by the Two—in other words, playing a role, which every member was expected to play. Status distinctions in the UFO cult were both informal and uncommon. The Two once appointed "group spokesmen" to coordinate family activities, and informally there was an inner circle that enjoyed privileged access to Bo and Peep. But the same behavior was expected of everyone.

The Two were fond of telling their audiences at public meetings that "there are no rules here," expressing the conviction that no one could complete his overcoming unless he willingly devoted all his energy to the Process. Rules implied coercion. But Bo and Peep provided a fairly specific list of "guidelines" for members who were determined to make it off the planet, and most members followed them closely.

When a seeker joined the UFO cult he was expected to give up all his "attachments" to the human level. Most obvious were friends, relatives and material possessions, but long hair, health food diets and even favorite expressions might also be considered attachments. Bo and Peep used the phrase "walking out the door of your life" to describe the process. Because the Two also expected their followers to lock the door behind them, they discouraged any contact with outsiders after joining. Many parents never heard from their children again. Others received post cards and letters intended to reassure them, but the messages usually had the opposite effect. Most of them were brief, impersonal and full of strange religious jargon. To the parents these letters seemed completely out of character. One mother in Oregon captured the feeling of parents generally when she said, "It's not like him. He's never done anything like this before."

Because members were expected to devote all their energy to the Process, any activity that detracted from this effort was considered an "energy-drain" that should be avoided. Some of the most prominent were sexual behavior, drug use, singing, and "socializing," which included idle talk about the past and burdening others with one's doubts.

The energy that normally would have been spent on mundane human activities was supposed to be devoted to "getting in tune" with "the Fathers" at the Next Level who would guide members through the remaining experiences they needed to overcome their humanness. Although Bo and Peep didn't prescribe a uniform method for getting in tune,[3] anyone familiar with the group could easily

recognize members who were "tuning in." They would be sitting quietly with eyes closed, for several hours a day, far away from other members of the group.

The member's role can't be understood without taking a look at the partnership. Like a miniature encounter group, the partnership (usually composed of man and woman) was designed to produce a heightened sense of self-awareness by developing "friction," a term referring to the normal antagonisms that were an inevitable part of the relationship. Although sexual contact was forbidden, partners were expected to be together 24 hours a day, never apart for more than 15 or 20 minutes, and then only for necessities like using the toilet or taking a shower.

Playing the role also required learning a special vocabulary that reflected Bo and Peep's unique cosmology. For example, if a member complained that his vehicle was a test for him, he would be referring to car trouble, but if he talked about exchanging his vehicle at the Next Level, he would be looking forward to the indestructible body he would receive after leaving the Earth. If he said, "It came to me . . ." or "I had a hit," he would be about to explain a message he received from one of the Fathers, but if he prefaced his remarks with, "it may be a spirit, but . . ." he would probably be venturing an opinion that others might think was "too human." Ordinary topics like work, money, love and television were eliminated. Instead they discussed spirit bombardment, the metamorphic process, heavenly gardens and graduation time. Language behavior on the "trip" had such a stereotypical quality that one disillusioned member, in a moment of rare objectivity, complained that whenever he asked a question he got a "tape recorded message" in reply.

Members also learned to dramatize their interpretations of events by using metaphorical speech. Consider the process of getting messages from the Next Level. Bo and Peep's followers learned to interpret hunches and random thoughts as messages from the Fathers. However, the word "message" is misleading because it implies unambiguous verbal communication. Once I overheard a member explaining his contact with the Father. "He speaks to me as clearly as I am speaking to you now," he said. However, he later admitted to me that "I don't actually hear his words, but the language is so clear that I might as well." On another occasion a 19-year-old woman claimed she could see a "glow" around people on the Process. While I do not dispute the possibility of human auras, I was either glowing like the others despite my disbelief, or her expression is an example of metaphysical speech. Another member once insisted he saw "energy lines" connecting me with members of the Next Level.

The member's role performance stood out most clearly during public meetings to recruit new followers. It was here that the UFO people most often resembled the popular stereotype of glassy-eyed cult members spouting mindless religious jargon. When presenting the Message, the group spokesmen often would stare blankly at the audience while parroting the standard script for dealing with the public.

Question: What is it like in heaven? Answer: That's like one dog asking another what it is like to be human.

Question: How do I know this isn't a con game? Answer: If our message speaks to you, you will feel it in your heart.

Question: How do you survive? Answer: The Father provides.

The blank expressions so often seen at these meetings reflected the members' determined efforts to protect themselves from spirit bombardment by tuning in to the Next Level.

A casual observer who happened across a campground full of Bo and Peep's followers would have seen pairs of individuals camped in separate sites preparing meals, reading the Bible or sitting quietly by themselves as if they were meditating. Compared with other campers he would have noticed little interaction except during the morning and evening when members would gather around the campfire. Discussion during these campfire meetings was quiet and orderly although punctuated by occasional laughter. A conspicuous absence of games, music, smoking and drinking would be noted. In fact, rangers consistently described the UFO people as model campers—clean, quiet and well-behaved. Overhearing members talking among themselves, an observer would undoubtedly have been struck by the uniformity of their speech, and might conclude that Bo and Peep had reduced their followers to "robots." So powerful was the leveling force of the member's role that even some informants had this feeling when they first arrived in camp. One of Bo and Peep's first recruits put it this way: "I was looking around thinking, 'My God, this is like zombie land.' They were in a totally different place. It was very weird."

It is important to realize that new recruits willingly adopted this role as soon as they arrived in camp. For example, my partner spent her first evening going from one campsite to the next quizzing old members about the rules she would have to follow on the Process. She was very concerned about doing everything right. Sometimes dramatic behavioral changes occurred even before indoctrination began. The day I joined, nine other new recruits showed up, but I could not distinguish them from the old members because they had already adopted Bo and Peep's stereotyped religious jargon. Once the jargon was learned it was easy to pick out new recruits because they misused the vocabulary and did not know all the rules yet. However, to outsiders these subtleties were obscured.

Appearances Can Be Deceiving

Full acceptance of Bo and Peep's Message usually came after intense involvement with other members of the cult.[4] Very few recruits accepted all of the Message at first. While they recognized many truths in the Message, they were usually skeptical about parts of it. Surprisingly, given the publicity about UFOs, when our informants were asked to identify the least plausible part of the Message, most said they had trouble believing they would really go to heaven in spaceships.

Although many parts of the belief system sounded far-fetched, most followers were self-defined spiritual seekers who were actively exploring new ideas and seeking out new experiences that would accelerate their spiritual growth. In the cultic milieu that produced the UFO cult anything is possible—reincarnation, auras, ascended masters, psychic communication with planets and even UFOs that take human beings to other levels of existence. In this environment seekers learn to be incredibly tolerant of a wide range of religious and pseudo-scientific beliefs. Because they believe so fully in the infinite possibilities of the universe, they often regard skeptical rationalism as an unhealthy obstacle to growth (Balch and Taylor, 1977).

Many informants reported they cultivated a cautious but openminded outlook at first:

I just went with a totally open mind. If they say, "I'm from another planet," I say OK, fine. I don't know that yet, but you can go ahead and believe what you want. I'm gonna find out.

Reservations often surfaced when new recruits first arrived in camp. Many were not prepared for what they found there. Consider the case of a conservative well-dressed man of 58 who left his wife and home to join in Colorado:

I'll have to admit that the feelings that crossed my mind at that time were, "My God, we have wiped out our lives, we have burned all bridges behind us." I mean, here we are at the mercy of a bunch of flakes who have nothing to lose, just goofing around. You know, dumb kids, goofy weedheads.

Like many others he decided to remain in the group for a while despite his second thoughts because, as he put it, he had burned too many bridges when he joined (Gerlach and Hine, 1970:99–158).

By the time they arrived in camp new members had committed themselves to the "trip" in several ways. They had announced their decision to friends and relatives and many of them even had their names printed in newspapers. They gave away virtually everything they owned and drove huge distances in a short time to reach their first campground. All these actions tended to commit them to the UFO cult (Becker, 1960; Festinger, 1956; Gerlach and Hine 1970), even when their commitment was not supported by complete conviction.

Earlier I said that full acceptance came only after intense involvement in the cult's day-to-day activities. While this is true, the term "full acceptance" is misleading because even the old-timers vacillated between what one of them called "murkiness and light." Belief in Bo and Peep's Message was always tenuous.

There were times when I felt growth, and then I would tell myself when I was down that I was probably kidding myself. I felt really bad because I wasn't growing, and then I would recall things that I read saying that was when the greatest growth took place—when you can't tell when things are happening. It was very up and down.

The up and down quality of conviction was one of the most distinctive features of membership careers in the UFO unit. Once my partner confessed that she never felt in tune with the Next Level.

When I try to tune in all I do is think about tuning in. I tune in and think about tuning in, and think about thinking about tuning in, but nothing ever happens. . . . I don't feel like I'm getting through.

However—and here is the important point—she continued to go through the motions of tuning in. During our family meetings she talked about her "hits" and "flashes" as if she had a clear connection with members of the Next Level, keeping her doubts to herself because Bo and Peep's guidelines discouraged open questioning. Other followers were shocked when she dropped out because she always appeared to be "in tune."

One of the original Oregon recruits told me, "The thing is, I had those doubts, but the other side of me would say, 'But you've got to have faith,' and then I would stuff it down." Because of their self-imposed restraints on communication, members often managed to hide their disillusionment, even from their partners. Of course, when members did reveal their doubts it was usually to their partners. In extreme cases their behavior became a hollow performance masking confusion and disbelief. One informant summed up the situation this way:

They were just going through the motions and using the right vocabulary, which concealed the fact that inside they were very mixed up.

During my field work many examples of the gap between belief and behavior became apparent. For instance, the day before one of our largest public meetings the couple who had been chosen to present the Message left camp to spend the day "getting in tune with the Father," but actually went to a Robert Redford movie. After the meeting the same couple was in charge of the "buffer camp" where new recruits were to be introduced. One later confessed that by then she no longer believed in Bo and Peep. Yet she faithfully carried out her responsibilities because she didn't think she had the right to turn others against the Two. Her partner, an ex-piano tuner, was widely regarded as one of the most "tuned in" people on the Process, but he carried an expensive set of piano tools in the trunk of his car so he could go to work again in case the Demonstration didn't happen. My point is that their overt behavior was misleading. They *looked* tuned in, *appeared* committed, but were simply playing a

role that concealed their real feelings, even from other members of the cult.

Continued role performance in the face of disillusionment constituted a side-bet (Becker, 1960) that allowed members to keep their options open while trying to come to terms with their doubts. By continuing to play the role, if only half-heartedly, they did not preclude the possibility of returning to the fold in the event of some unexpected development that might convince them that Bo and Peep were right all along. Many members, who still belong to the group, experienced periods of tremendous demoralization, but each time refused to burn their bridges by deviating too far from the path prescribed by the Two. Indeed, the member who used the expression "murkiness and light" to describe his constant vacillation stayed with the group for over a year after this remark was recorded.

Conclusion

This research convinced me that much of the current writing about conversion is misleading because writers don't know enough about the routine features of everyday life in cults. The private reality of life in a religious cult usually remains hidden beneath a public facade of religious fanaticism.

Social scientists have known for a long time that behavior is not always consistent with values, attitudes, and beliefs. By now this observation is common sense, but it has often not been applied in the study of religious cults. Underlying much of the current thinking about conversion is the assumption that the puzzling behavior of cult members is caused by sweeping personality changes.[5] The terms commonly used to explain conversion in cults betray this assumption. Brainwashing, thought reform, and coercive persuasion are all terms that focus attention on psychological change as if minds must be altered to change behavior.

I am proposing another point of view based on role theory in sociology. The first step in conversion to cults is learning to *act* like a convert by outwardly conforming to a narrowly prescribed set of role expectations. Genuine conviction develops later beneath a facade of total commitment, and it fluctuates widely during the course of the typical member's career. Many cult members never become true believers, but their questioning may be effectively hidden from everyone but their closest associates.

We all know the stereotype of the cult member: glassy eyes, plastic smile, mindless religious jargon. The picture may be oversimplified, but plenty of members fit that description. The UFO cult is a good example. When members presented their message to potential recruits they would stare blankly at the audience while parroting the standard script for dealing with the public.

Erving Goffman's (1959) dramaturgic model of social behavior is a useful way of conceptualizing these discrepancies. Goffman distinguishes between front-stage and back-stage behavior. Cult members are "on stage" when they deal with outsiders. In their efforts to impress the public with a united front they suppress the doubts, questions, and inner turmoil that might reveal as many doubting Thomases as there are true believers. In the case of the UFO cult, members would deliberately adopt an expressionless public facade to ward off bombardment by evil spirits. Once back in the safety of their own camps, they would start acting like real people again—joking, laughing, arguing, and worrying about their uncertain future. Even in camp their overt behavior could be deceiving. Members, and here I include myself in that category, were often misled by the continued role performance of those who were disillusioned. Like outsiders, we inferred conviction from their behavior without really knowing how they felt.

The lesson is simple: Don't be deceived by appearances. I believe that social scientists need to adopt the model of investigative reporting to discover what cult members say and do when they are not "on-stage" in front of the public or, if possible, even their peers. Only when we can penetrate the wall of secrecy that normally separates researchers from their subject matter will we begin to understand the nature of the psychological and behavioral changes that occur when someone joins a religious cult.

These observations have important implications for the study of conversion. When people join a religious cult they first change their behavior by adopting a new role. The changes may be sweeping and dramatic, but they are not necessarily supported by conviction. The boundless faith of the true believer usually develops only after lengthy involvement in the cult's day-to-day activities (Bromley and Shupe, 1979; Lofland and Stark, 1965). Some members go for months without ever resolving their doubts, yet they may still appear fully committed because outwardly they are acting the way they are expected to act.

Notes

1. During the early part of the study I worked closely with David Taylor who was then a graduate student in sociology at the University of Montana.

2. The sample is large considering how much detective work it took to locate ex-members. Bo and Peep's followers were not only highly mobile to begin with, but they came from almost every state and changed their names when they joined. Even as a participant-observer it was hard to learn much about the members because they were not supposed to talk about their previous identities. To make matters worse, they dropped out at unknown locations all over the country.

3. The process of getting in tune is described in Balch and Taylor, 1978.

4. For more complete discussion of the forces leading to full acceptance see Balch, 1979a and 1979b, and Balch and Taylor, 1978.

5. See Conway and Siegelman (1978) for a recent example.

References

Balch, Robert W. 1979a. "A role model of behavioral and psychological change during membership careers in religious cults." University of Montana, Missoula. Mimeo.
1979b. "Two models of conversion and commitment in a UFO cult." Paper presented at the annual meeting of the *Pacific Sociological Association.* Anaheim, California.

Balch, Robert W. and David Taylor. 1977. "Seekers and saucers: the role of the cultic milieu in joining a UFO cult." *American Behavioral Scientist* 20:839–860.
1978. "On getting in tune: some reflections on the process of making supernatural contact." Paper presented at the annual meeting of the *Pacific Sociological Association.* Spokane, Washington.

Becker, Howard S. 1960. "Notes on the concept of commitment." *American Journal of Sociology* 66:32–40.

Bromley, David G. and Anson D. Shupe, Jr. 1979. "Just a few years seems like a lifetime: a role theory approach to participation in religious movements." Pp. 159–85 in L. Kriesberg (ed.), *Research in Social Movements, Conflict and Change.* Greenwich: JAI Press.

Conway, Flow and Jim Siegelman. 1978. Snapping: America's Epidemic of Sudden Personality Change. Philadelphia: Lippincott.

Festinger, Leon. 1956. When Prophecy Fails. New York: Harper.

Gerlach, Luther P. and Virginia H. Hine. 1970. People, Power, Change: Movements of Social Transformation. Indianapolis: Bobbs-Merrill.

Goffman, Erving. 1959. The Presentation of Self in Everyday Life. New York: Doubleday.

Lofland, John and Rodney Stark. 1965. "Becoming a world-saver: a theory of conversion to a deviant perspective." *American Sociological Review* 30:865–875.

SELECTION 9.B

The Farm; and Role Expectations for Women

James T. Richardson, Mary W. Stewart, and Robert B. Simmonds

The Farm was nestled in a valley in the rich agricultural area of America's Northwest. It was about an hour's drive from a large Northwestern city, set in an area of productive farm land, surrounded by orchards of trees heavy with peaches and apples, and fields of berries. After driving over winding hilly roads, the rough cabins and meeting hall of the settlement could be seen from the crest of a hill.

Five long cabins were located on the edge of the small settlement. The dining hall,

James T. Richardson is Professor of Sociology at the University of Nevada, Reno.
Mary W. Stewart is Associate Professor of Sociology at the University of Missouri, Kansas City.
Robert B. Simmonds is Associate Professor of Sociology at the State University of New York, Cortland.

which was also a meeting hall, was in the center. A large grassy area between the cabins provided space for games and fellowship, and a sloping hill, ending in a natural amphitheater, was a comfortable and peaceful spot for large prayer gatherings, singing, and group fellowship. A farm house on a hill above the "labor camp" served as the residence for The Farm pastor, his wife, and several members who were year-round residents of The Farm, including other married couples. The cabins provided sleeping room for brothers and sisters who came from CCO's other houses for the summer to pick berries and other fruit, and to "get closer to the Lord." [CCO stands for Christ Communal Organization, a pseudonym given by the authors to the group under study.] The cabins were furnished sparingly, each having several bunk beds and shelves for clothes and the few personal belongings members brought with them. Two shower rooms were located between the men's and the women's cabins, and outhouses built by the brothers were nearby.

The settlement was shaded by fruit trees and evergreens. The large quiet trees provided isolated spots for small groups to engage in fellowship or for individuals to pray in solitude. A small earthen and wood structure built for the purpose of prayer assured isolation and privacy for those young Christians who needed its special solace.

During the week, the day began for most brothers and sisters at about 4:30 A.M. Before dawn, the "wake-up steward" came to each cabin to wake its sleeping residents. He tapped on the window of the sisters' cabins, entered the brothers' cabins and woke them with a Scripture reading. The brothers and sisters responded with "God bless you brother" or "praise the Lord" and their day began. For several hours, a few sisters had been preparing a simple but hearty breakfast for the young Christians. Breakfast was served in the dining hall in two shifts, at 5:00 A.M. and at 5:30 A.M. during the week. Group prayers were said and sung before each meal, with the brothers and sisters holding hands in a circle, asking the Lord to bless their food, and praying for his help with the day's work. The brothers and sisters stood in line to be served a breakfast of hot cereal, pancakes, or eggs and biscuits. Nothing was left on the plates—the simplest meal was considered a blessing.[1] By 6:30, the old yellow school bus, used to take the brothers (and some sisters) to the fields, was loaded. A few brothers remained at The Farm to do chores and repairs; most sisters remained behind to wash clothes, clean, and prepare the noon meal. Upon arrival in the fields, prayers were shared, and the workers teamed up to begin the day's work.

As a rule, members picked the fruit and berries on land owned or leased by CCO, but when workers could be spared, teams were hired out to other growers in the area. These young Christians were hard and steady workers, "working for the Lord," and were in great demand by other growers.[2] As the members worked, they shared stories of their path to conversion and sang spirituals. Picking berries was hard, hot work, as pickers literally crawled or "duck-walked" down the rows, pushing a container (called a flat) along the row with them. Most members of our research team did some picking and can testify to its rigor. We can also testify to the powerful dedication and fervor of the work crews, and the strange and moving experience of hearing a large work crew break out spontaneously into a song of praise while engaged in such an arduous task.

Sometimes a deacon would walk up and down the berry rows reading from the Bible. Sounds of "praise the Lord," "God bless You brother," and "thank you Jesus" often interrupted the readings. The noon meal was very simple and sparse, usually consisting of peanut butter sandwiches (with fresh strawberries) and water. During the half-hour meal break, Bible study by individuals was commonplace, and a prayer preceded the return to the fields. After lunch, the brothers and sisters returned to the fields and worked until mid or late afternoon.

Upon returning to the settlement, brothers and sisters had an hour or more of free time before dinner. This time was usually used for cleaning up, tending to individual ministries, fellowship, or prayer. The first horn for dinner sounded about 5:00 P.M., with another at 5:30. Prayers were said or sung, and individual members contributed their own prayers—asking Jesus to bless newcomers, to help a brother or sister with his or her trial, or thanking God for a productive day (or asking his help so that certain researchers would "see the light"). During the second major research visit to The Farm, spirituals were sung inside the dining hall and members were then led in prayer by one of the pastors before eating. Brothers and sisters mingled at meal time, talking quietly of the day's activities or plans for tomorrow. Conversation seldom centered on events or concerns "of the world."

After supper, there was generally about an hour between the meal and the evening prayer and Bible study meeting. During the evening prayer meeting, the entire body gathered on the grassy slope (or in the dining hall if weather was bad) to listen to Bible readings and Scriptural interpretations given by The Farm pastor or visiting CCO pastors, and sometimes to enjoy the commune's singing group doing Scriptural religious songs set to rock music, and to sing and pray together as a group. Announcements were made and organizational business was taken care of. The evening prayer meeting might last until 11:00 P.M. or later, by which time most residents were more than ready for rest. Some lingered in small groups and discussed the Bible, some remained to pray, and some talked over their trials with a fellow Christian. By midnight the camp was quiet, and only the light in the communal kitchen remained on, indicating that a sister was already preparing breakfast for the next morning.

During the summer of 1971, Sundays on The Farm were not usually work days, unless picking of a crop could not be postponed. On Sundays, breakfast was served later, and if possible, a favorite food was prepared. A more elaborate, hot meal was shared in mid-afternoon. Usually on the weekend, one evening (or perhaps afternoon) would be spent evangelizing in nearby towns. The residents would load into any available vehicle and go "witnessing." Great rejoicing would ensue if some new converts returned to The Farm with the members. During the second summer visit, Mondays were taken as the day of rest because pastors from throughout the state had a staff meeting at The Land on that day. On rest days, members did only the necessary chores and spent most of the day praying or engaging in fellowship. The men might play games, such as frisbee or softball, but

for the most part, members talked in quiet groups of three and four, wrote letters, read the Bible, and rested.

Since The Land has replaced The Farm in many of its functions and reflects the increasing differentiation and complexity of the group, a consideration of life at The Land will add to our discussion of the organization and changes it has undergone. . . .

Role Expectations for Women

Women may fill several major roles—those of "sister," wife, and mother. They also occupy other role positions in the occupational (steward) and organizational (formal authority) structures of CCO, although the decision-making positions available to women are limited to deaconess or patroness, both of which carry limited authority extending only to other sisters and limited primarily to household maintenance tasks. Women leaders are selected by the male leadership. The exclusion of women from leadership positions is characteristic of many early and contemporary communal movements, such as the Bruderhof discussed by Zablocki (1971), the Hutterites . . . and others (Nordhoff, 1966). Scriptural justifications cited by group leaders for the exclusion of women from authority are several, including I Timothy 2:11–12. "Let a woman learn in silence with all submissiveness. I permit no woman to teach or to have authority over men; she is to keep silent."

In the occupational or steward structure, certain positions are expressly provided for women, although these is some fluidity defining these roles. During our first visit to The Farm (in 1971), sisters were responsible for preparing meals, cleaning the cabins and the dining hall, washing and mending clothes, caring for children, and gardening. Sisters also worked in the fields and orchards during planting and harvest times. By 1973 at The Land, men had assumed primary responsibilities for cooking and were now called chefs, rather than cooks, and more women were involved in agricultural activities. There was, for example, a team of sisters who planted trees, a team of sisters who thinned and picked apples, and sisters who were directly involved with maintaining the goat dairy. Sisters were also an important part of the proselytizing efforts of the group. Work in which sisters engage, however, is usually defined as "women's work" and is as much a part of being a Christian wife and mother as it is of being an unmarried sister. When women work in areas dominated by men, it is made clear that they are not nearly as efficient or productive. For example, we were told that males on tree-planting teams averaged about a thousand trees a day, whereas women planting trees averaged less than four hundred. A leader pointed out that if a male could not average eight hundred trees a day by the third day of planting, he would usually be dismissed by his employer.

Although the roles of sisters and brothers have changed some during the period of study, women living with their husbands in separate quarters usually engage only in traditional female activities. Women are responsible for child care, cooking and serving meals, cleaning, and sewing. Some such activities are done in groups, such as groups of women having a sewing group to make clothes. Brothers and sisters share responsibility for work in the gardens.

Females in any position are expected to be submissive; as sisters they are to be submissive to males in the commune; before marriage they are to bow to the wishes of their fiancés, and as wives they are to be submissive to their husbands (unless said male directs them to "sin"). Just as God is the head of man and man the head of woman, woman is the head of her children, according to the CCO philosophy. A woman is given primary responsibility for raising their children, but her authority is implicitly granted by her husband. The behavioral expectation of submissiveness is perhaps the dominant expecta-

tion for all role positions filled by females in this religious communal organization. Other expectations, similarly, are consistent with the dominant one for females, no matter which of the available roles they may fill. In any role position, the female is expected to be nonaggressive, nurturing, self-effacing, and to engage in what is traditionally considered women's work.

Within CCO, there exists a clear pattern of definite, distinct "places" or positions to be filled by sisters. However, most male and female members assert that women are not inferior to men, although they are seen as "weaker vessels" and "in subservience to men just as men are in subservience to God." Sixty-six percent of the members interviewed during our first visit to The Farm said that men and women were equal, while 31 percent said women were not equal to men. Members seemed to see no contradiction between their statements that men and women were equal and the fact that women were not allowed to hold the same positions of authority or to have the same responsibilities as men. Members explained that all Christians are "equal in the eyes of the Lord," but that he has established unique places for males and females, and the place of the female is in subjection to the male. "And Adam said, This is now bone of my bones, and flesh of my flesh. She shall be called woman because she was taken out of man" (Genesis 2:23).

Women are viewed as being weaker vessels than men, more emotional, nurturant and docile, but to a degree, they are simultaneously viewed as sensuous beings and as temptresses. Their bodies may cause men to have fleshly desires, so women must dress and conduct themselves in a manner which will not arouse males and which will not show vanity or pride. Women are given the responsibility of avoiding sexually charged situations and must take care not to "stumble" (sexually arouse) the brothers. During our visits of 1972 to The Farm, a sister was publicly chastised after inadvertently exposing a breast while working in the fields, thus "stumbling" a brother (who complained to a pastor). Women are placed in the position of agreeing that their bodies can cause sin, because such ideas are a part of the basic belief structure of the group. Men are absolved of much responsibility for sexual encounters or stimulation, since, according to CCO beliefs, it is their God-given nature to become automatically aroused at the sight of certain parts of the female body, or by any other indication, however implicit, of sexual availability.

As indicated, there have been some changes in the women's place in CCO during our several years of association with them. During our first visit, women were not only expected to be subservient to men, they were expected to be rather servile. They dressed in very nondescript, formless clothes, waited on males, and queued at the end of the food line. At that time, less than 20 percent of the members at The Farm were women. By the time of our second visit to The Farm a year later, we noted some changes in the expectations placed on women *and* an increase in the number of women in the group—up to about 35 percent were female. In the interim between our visits, CCO leaders had met to discuss the place of women and perhaps as a result of dissatisfaction among women with their "place," had come to the conclusion that, although women were "weaker vessels" and were not, according to Scripture, to supervise men, neither were they to be accorded the status of servants. CCO leaders felt that they needed to bring the behavior of group members "into line with the Scriptures." Hence, we noted some changes in interaction between the males and females and changes in the definition of a woman's place. No longer were brothers altogether free from household chores; for example, men were expected to volunteer to work in the kitchen, and more women were allowed to work in the fields. We view these changes as indications of organization attempts to gain more

female members and to retain the sisters already in the commune, even though such attempts were always couched in Scriptural terms. Plainly the group would have problems in maintaining itself if too few females became members to furnish wives for all the males. Thus, in this age of more liberal ideas concerning sex roles, the move toward liberalization of the female role can be viewed, we think, as an action in support of group maintenance. Also, as Kanter (1973, p. 300) points out, the very act of living communally "may potentially reduce the differentiation between men and women," as such a life-style makes status distinctions harder to maintain.

By 1973, other changes in sex roles had occurred. More women are now included on missionary teams, and women no longer wait in line to eat after all the men have been served. Dress norms had also liberalized some, with at least one female at The Land seen wearing cutoffs (shorts). During our 1974 visit, we noted the behavioral changes mentioned above as well as other changes in appearance of the sisters. Although they still avoid tight-fitting, revealing clothes, most sisters wore jeans and blouses, their long hair was usually loose, sometimes in braids, some wore earrings, rings, and bracelets. Their appearance was similar to that of many of their more hippie-oriented peers in colleges and high schools. One leader reported that, as of 1977, the dress code for females had changed even more. He said, "You may be amazed to learn that we allow tasteful bikinis and other 'tempting' attire. As a matter of fact, we are generally disgusted with dress codes, formal and informal, and feel it is a part of the clothesline gospel Christianity that we earnestly reject as hypocritical."

Leaders now state that the proportions of males and females are closer to equal than ever before. Because of our lack of access to organization membership records (they claim that very few records are kept, and this seems to be true), the proportion of females must be estimated. There do appear to be more females than previously, with females probably comprising about 40 percent of the total membership. In 1974 a new class for the Lamb's School had about 35 percent females, and this level has been maintained and even raised since then.

More changes could occur related to the role of women in CCO, especially given the authority of the leaders to revise their interpretations of Scripture to justify needs and behavioral expectations. So far, however, CCO leaders have steadfastly refused to allow any women to hold authority over any male CCO members, although in 1977, a nonvoting female was added to the Pastors' Council as a representative of the unmarried female members. The increasing differentiation and stratification of the group, coupled with the new move to single-family dwellings (which counteracts the tendency Kanter noted for communal living to break down sex role differentiation), may work together to stop further evolution in this important area of group life. Thus, although there has been an attempt to bring behavior in line with group theology and to provide a less repressive role for women, the basic role structure of CCO remains the same. A functional analysis of the role structure of this group and the expectations associated with these roles would indicate many system-maintaining characteristics, but the members and leaders would claim that women engage in certain activities because "it's the Lord's will." And so far, at least, their fundamentalist view of the "Lord's will" has prevailed.

In closing this section, we would like to present a direct quote from one key informant, who disagrees somewhat with our interpretation of the inherent sexism in CCO. This brief account will add balance and also bring in some additional information. The written statement was given to us after this leader read early drafts of some of the chapters of the book in summer 1977.

The male is NOT superior to the female in our ideology. They are equal. However, we believe certain social roles are prescribed—namely that the husband is head over the wife and the wife over the children. This does not mean that every man is head over every woman. One man is head over one woman, his wife. In the context of the whole church, women are not to hold line authority over men nor teach doctrine to other believers. I know this sounds absurd in the light of the women's movement. But I think it is important to see through the intellectual climate of the day to what we are saying and not saying. We are not saying that women can't have a career. They can. Some hold advisory authority in the organization, are department heads over other women, edit our magazine, run our medical program, preschools, Sunday schools, etc. We encourage women to teach "unbelievers" and be evangelists recognizing that the first evangelist was the woman at the well in the Gospel of John and that Mary Magdalene was the first to see Jesus after his resurrection. We see no limits imposed by the scripture on secular careers for women. In our minds, the scriptural social role taboos are very specific:

(1) The wife must submit to her husband (with the exception that she not submit to instruction to sin, such as murder, etc.). In exchange, the husband is to love her as described in I Corinthians 13.
(2) The woman is not to hold "line" authority over men in the church. (Men do not have automatic authority over women. Indeed the scripture says to submit one to another in love. This clearly implies to me that men also "submit" to women.)
(3) A woman is not to teach "doctrine" to the entire church. It is acceptable for her to teach women, children, or unbelievers (male or female) or "secular" subjects.

Please note, in our theology, *wives* are to be "subservient" to husbands as their leaders. Reciprocally, husbands are to "lay down their lives" for their wives. The supreme example of laying down your life is Christ himself on the cross, and is the example a husband is to follow in loving his wife. This is not the same as women subservient to all or any men.

Notes

1. Food at The Farm was quite unexciting by normal middle-class standards, and during our research trips, we supplemented our diets by eating food brought with us. Particularly the breakfasts were difficult to eat, as they were commonly made from government surplus oatmeal or such. The only really enjoyable thing about such food was the homemade bread used at all meals—bread made from surplus flour furnished by the federal government. Any special liquid with a meal was unusual, and water was the typical fare. One day during our second major visit, the research team chipped in personal funds to purchase enough milk for one meal for the entire camp, an action not done from any desire to ingratiate, but which was greatly appreciated by residents. As has been noted elsewhere, the diet of CCO members has improved markedly in recent times, as a direct function of increased group prosperity.

2. During the second major visit, we had an opportunity to observe the situation in which for about the first time that season the work crew of The Farm was being hired out to a neighborhood farmer. The Farm crops were still a few days from being ready to pick, so most of the crew was available for reassignment on a temporary basis. Particularly interesting was the justification given by CCO leaders to the work crew for hiring them out, at an obvious financial advantage to organization coffers. Workers were told that God had furnished them with an opportunity to practice picking, so that a better job could be done when the crops of The Farm were ready. Also, it was pointed out that by working hard for the neighboring farmer, the group could witness to him about the truth of their beliefs. With that as an explanation, the crew then rode several miles on a flatbed trailer pulled by a pickup over dusty roads and worked for several hot days eight to ten hours a day. And from every appearance, the workers, many of whom had never done such hard physical labor before, enjoyed their work immensely.

References

Kanter, Rosabeth Moss. *Community and Commitment: Communes and Utopias in Sociological Perspective.* Cambridge, Mass.: Harvard University Press, 1973.

Nordhoff, Charles. *The Communistic Societies of the United States.* New York: Dover, 1966.

Zablocki, Benjamin. *The Joyful Community.* Baltimore: Penguin, 1971.

R E A D I N G   9 . 3

est and Ethics: Rule-Egoism in Middle-Class Culture

Steven M. Tipton

Erhard Seminars Training (*est*) describes itself as an educational corporation that trains its clients "to transform your ability to experience living so that the situations you have been trying to change or have been putting up with clear up just in the process of life itself."[1] The standard training program takes over sixty hours spread across four days on two consecutive weekends. A single trainer delivers it in a hotel ballroom to groups of 200–250 persons who are mostly urban, middle-class young adults, at a cost of $400 per person. "Graduates" of this program are encouraged to attend ongoing graduate seminars, occupationally specialized workshops, and mass special events in order to enhance the training's effects.

Werner Erhard gave the first *est* training in a friend's borrowed apartment in 1971. Ten years later the *est* organization is a model bureaucracy, molded by a former Harvard Business School professor and Coca-Cola execu-

Steven M. Tipton is Professor of Sociology at the Candler School of Theology, Emory University, Atlanta.

Reprinted from Steven M. Tipton, *Getting Saved from the Sixties* (Berkeley: University of California Press, 1982), with permission.

tive, which coordinates the efforts of some 300 paid employees and 25,000 volunteers in twenty-nine cities. At a rate peaking above 6,000 per month, *est* trained roughly 270,000 persons through 1980, a third of whom are concentrated in California. In the San Francisco Bay Area, where *est* is based, one out of every nine college-educated young adults has taken the training. *est* grossed $25 million in 1980, its revenues sheltered by a network of trusts, foundations, and licensing arrangements that stretches to Switzerland.[2]

Werner Erhard was born in 1935 in Philadelphia as John Paul (Jack) Rosenberg, grandson of an immigrant tailor and son of a small-restaurant manager who left Judaism for a Baptist mission before joining his wife in the Episcopal Church. Erhard married and went into sales work after finishing high school. In 1960 he disappeared from his family, changed his name, and moved west, eventually remarrying. From 1961 to 1971 he managed and trained door-to-door salesmen of encyclopedias. To this task he applied more than a decade's eclectic study of self-help and psychic disciplines like positive thinking and hypnosis, Scientology and Mind Dynamics, psychologies like Gestalt, and eastern religions like Zen. At the end of this period, says Erhard, he had a sudden experience "outside of space and time" of "getting it" while driving along the freeway, and he began *est* shortly afterward to serve others by enabling them to share this enlightening experience.[3]

The *est* training consists alternatively of three sorts of activity. Participants listen to the trainer present the "data" of *est*'s view of reality and interact with him by questioning this material and responding to it. They do "processes," in which the trainer instructs them to close their eyes and mentally "create" or visualize various experiences: opening a space in different parts of their bodies, relaxing at the beach, reliving past incidents associated with unwanted emotions and psychosomatic symptoms, feeling terrified of the

person next to them, confronting their parents, intuiting the personality of a stranger. Finally, participants "share" their experience of the processes with the group as a whole.

Participants sit theater-style facing the trainer on a low stage throughout most of the training, except for a few hours of processes done standing or lying on the floor. They are not allowed to touch or talk to each other, take notes, smoke, leave their chairs, or address the group without the trainer's recognition. Participants are encouraged but not required to talk in front of the group and to the trainer. At least a quarter of them never do. A smaller proportion of the group does most of the talking, acknowledged by the compulsory applause of the rest, who report coming to identify with the talkers. Each day usually lasts sixteen or more hours, punctuated by one meal break and two or three brief water and bathroom breaks. Almost all participants report physical tension, fatigue, and mental strain in the course of the training, which they attribute to its long hours and circumstantial restrictions (*est* has been called "the no-piss training"), and to the upsetting character of the trainer's behavior, the data and processes, and others' sharing.

What goes on in the *est* training? *est* informs participants beforehand that they need not figure out, remember, or believe in the training for it to work. They need only be present, follow instructions, and experience whatever comes up. "You have the opportunity to replace believing with experiencing," says *est*. What they will experience is "what is really so for you . . . your natural ability . . . the part of [you] that is truly able, and perfect."[4] Comparing records of several trainings shows the uniform appearance of a few central tenets and techniques in all of them, redundancy in each in developing these tenets, and variation between trainings in the detailed discussion and argument of these tenets and their demonstration by psychological and dramatic enactment. What follows is a quick summary of the few hours' conceptual script from which each trainer improvises sixty hours of psycho-theater.[5]

On the training's first day its procedural rules are announced, and the trainees are instructed to agree to them by sitting still. "Your lives don't work, assholes. Otherwise you wouldn't be here," the trainer begins irrefutably. Instead of feeling alive, people believe they are right. Instead of "accepting, observing, realizing, sharing, and sourcing" their experience at its cause, people are at its effect in "hoping, deciding, helping, and being reasonable" about their experience. Their received and psychologically conditioned beliefs of how life could or should be block their experience of how it actually is in the present and preclude their effective response to it. In this sense each person is the *total cause* of all his own problems, a fact that he must acknowledge in order to take responsibility for his life, give up his "act," and clear up his problems. After hours of restriction and felt attack as this message is driven home, trainees usually have aching muscles and heads. These aches are "experienced out"—progressively relaxed and caused to disappear—by directing nonevaluative, visualized attention at them in several "body processes" at the end of the first day.[6] "Just observe and be with whatever's bothering you," directs the trainer. "Just let it be, and it will disappear." Mind states alter body states, according to such demonstration, confirming that the individual is the cause of his own world. "You're perfect," the trainer explains, "but your barriers block you from experiencing it. You try to change them or control them, but you can't. That's because resisting something makes it persist. Re-creating your experience of it makes it disappear."

On the second day, in "the anatomy of an experience," trainees are told that their problems take the form of physical sensations and emotional feelings ("upsets") psychologically associated with situational behavior, attitudes, points of view, and ideas anchored in mental images of past experience. They are

directed to locate, connect, and experience out these problematic "items," as they did their headaches of the night before, with the trainer's therapeutically detached, firm, and perceptive "assistance." Some trainees undergo and share intense abreactive experiences in public confrontations with the trainer. For example, the sensation of a clenched jaw is tied to feelings of anger and fear, tied to self-righteousness in marital strife, tied to an abusive parent in childhood: these elements of a psychic item are all recalled, vividly reexperienced, and apparently relieved. Others report strong feelings of identification in response to such exemplary cases, which they then follow out on their own in the "truth process." "If you can't re-create the experience and make it disappear, it's running you," warns the trainer. "And if you can make it disappear, then who's responsible for it, huh?" Semantically and mentally, trainees create their own problems by putting coexistent facts into conflict using *but:* "I want to go to the beach, *and* I don't have the time," is no problem at all. Trainees are next required to stand motionless, expressionless, and silent before the group, demonstrating that beneath the "act" of a composed social persona lie self-uncertainty and compelling fears of other persons and, beneath that, their true self. "Drop your shitty act," commands the trainer in the "danger process." "We can see right through it, and there's nothing behind it." Next, in the "fear process" trainees are instructed to enact their fears in terrified screams, and then reverse them into terrifying roars. "Who do you think everyone's afraid of?" asks the trainer. "They're afraid of you." By fully "experiencing your experience" in this way, trainees stuck at its effect come to be at its cause.

On the third day a pop Newtonian definition of reality, based on the "physicalness" of objects, is rejected and reversed to a Humean definition, based on the subjectivity of individual experience. "You are the one and only source of your experience. You created it." I experience, therefore I am, and so is my world. So goes the "suchness" of reality, which requires empathic, nonjudgmental "communication" if individuals are really to relate. Each must "harmoniously recreate the experience of another, intentionally." To this end trainees next experience out their embarrassment at looking foolish, a barrier to self-expression and communication, by histrionically enacting nonsensical and sex-role-reversed skits before one another. Women play tough he-men, for example, and men play cute little girls. They next visualize and enact the building of an "inner center" for communicating with their parents and significant others, wiring its modern audio-visual equipment to their own "wish switch." Finally they touch, taste, smell, and look at physical objects—cubes of pine and steel, a stone, strawberry, tomato, lemon slice, and daisy. Then they subjectively recreate and transform these objects in eyes-closed guided fantasies climaxed by a Mexican hat dance on the petal of a sixty-foot daisy.

On the fourth day the "anatomy of the mind" is exposed. "The mind is a linear arrangement of multisensory, total records of successive moments of now." It is an associative stimulus-response machine conditioned by birth and the chain of successively traumatizing and repressed experiences of pain that make human beings feel upset and act compulsively. The mind's "design function" is its own survival, a purpose it pursues by endlessly trying to prove itself right. In the training's final reversal this deterministic realization in itself proves humans to be self-aware, and thus unlike machines. "Enlightenment is knowing you're a machine." This insight leaves a person free to choose his conditioned responses consciously, experience them out, and thus dissolve his conditioning. "Whatever happens, choose it, and your life will clear up," concludes the trainer. "You *have* a mind that's a machine. And you *are* the perfect being that created it all." Experiencing this paradoxical fact constitutes "get-

ting it": "I am. I am the context of my being me. I am the cause of my experience." After getting it, one can experience life and oneself in all their satisfying aliveness in a world without objectively fixed meaning, judgment, or purpose. The trainer unfolds the nature of reality from this viewpoint: Life is a game played for experiencing aliveness, not for believing you are right. Human choice is not reasonable, no more than choosing to eat chocolate instead of vanilla ice cream. "You choose it because you choose it. *You* cause choice, reasons don't." Successful activity consists of first *being* whatever you wish to be by mentally experiencing it, then *doing* it, then *having* it. (For example, first think of yourself being a millionaire, then borrow and invest, then have a million dollars.) There follows "everything you need to know" about sex ("When you're hot, you're hot. When you're not, you're not."), romantic love (a fantasy overlaid on a self-reinforcing cycle of interaction, affect, and sentiment), and truly "powerful relationships" (persons exchange power supporting each other's achievement of individual goals). At last the trainees graduate by intuitively "profiling" the personality and interests of strangers biographically sketched to them, thereby confirming their newly realized powers of experience and communication.

est graduates typically affirm that "*est* works!" and that "the training had value for me," although they may also complain of feeling manipulated by it. Several psychological surveys find graduates reporting positive changes in health and well-being, especially in psychological outlook, minor psychosomatic symptoms, and level of satisfaction. To date, only preliminary studies, without control groups or evidence besides retrospective self-reports, have investigated the training's results, largely bypassing its ideational content in the process.[7] No consistent correlation has been found between reported changes and use of *est* training processes. Nor, in fact, does *est* itself call for the repetitive practice of these processes outside the training, in contrast to TM or Zen Buddhist injunctions to meditate persistently. Instead *est* seems, as described, to employ these techniques to induce experiences that demonstrate to trainees the accuracy of its tenets, notably that the individual's consciousness creates her experience of the world and herself and is totally responsible for it, even at the level of physical sensation.[8] Like most human potential and therapeutic movements, *est* understands itself to be communicating epistemological, psychological, and psychosomatic facts about human existence, not teaching religious beliefs or moral systems; and doing so via experience, not ideas. Says Erhard, "The Training isn't a set of precepts or concepts or notions; it isn't anything we tell people. . . . It is the experience that the person has of himself."[9] The analysis to follow will suggest that *est* may be practically important to at least some of its participants, particularly sixties youth, for the system of moral norms, values, and attitudes it transmits to them.

Who are *est*'s clients? "Media coverage will sometimes imply that certain types of people take the training," cautions *est*'s president, "when in truth, *people* take the training."[10] These people are almost entirely white by race, middle-class by education, job, and income, and urbanized by outlook and residence.[11] Compared to the larger population, *est* numbers proportionately more women and fewer men, more divorced and fewer married persons, more young adults and fewer persons under twenty or over forty. The mean age of *est* graduates is 33.7 with sixties youth (now twenty-five to thirty-four) comprising nearly half their total. This is more than double their fraction of the Bay Area's population and four times that of the nation's. They also provide the bulk of *est*'s volunteer assistants. Many sixties youth in *est* saw themselves as members of the counterculture while going to college and for several years afterward, often living in modestly hip, dropout style during this time (living com-

munally, working intermittently at casual jobs, using marijuana regularly and psychedelics occasionally). They have moved into apartments and tapered off their drug use since entering full-time white-collar jobs, around which their lives are now organized.

Caucasions make up 88 percent of *est*'s clientele; blacks comprise 1.3 percent. Minority members are usually upwardly mobile middle-class young adults. *est* graduates span the range of the middle class, with their educational level higher than average but their income lower. Nine out of ten graduates began college; less than six (57 percent) finished. More majored in psychology than in any other single discipline. Four out of ten began graduate or professional school; less than two (18 percent) hold advanced degrees or certificates.[12] Relatively few *est* graduates hold jobs as technically specialized professionals or blue-collar workers, perhaps 10 percent in each case. Only 0.4 percent of all graduates are lawyers, 1.4 percent are physicians, and 0.8 percent are laborers, for example, as opposed to 11.7 percent in clerical work—the largest single occupational category.[13] The great majority of *est* graduates (some 70 percent) work primarily with other people, not physical objects or abstractions. They do mainly white-collar work—clerical, sales, managerial, official, educational, and social work. They also do semiprofessional and professional work that puts a premium on interpersonal skills—as media and public relations professionals, executives and administrators, counselors and therapists. Their mean income was somewhere between $7,893 and $12,796 per year in 1974. Sixties youth in *est* tend to work in lower-status, nonprofessional jobs, earn less, and switch jobs more frequently than do older graduates, who switch jobs frequently themselves.[14]

Almost two-thirds of all *est* graduates are now unmarried. More than a quarter have never been married. Another quarter are presently divorced or separated, a rate three times that of San Franciscans and seven times that of Americans generally. Some 26.7 percent of *all* graduates, four out of ten ever married, have gone through such breakups within the year before or after taking *est*. The unreliably fluid, short-lived pattern of graduates' marital relationships carries over among sixties youth in *est*, whom one most commonly finds in nonexclusive, sexually active dating relationships or "living with someone," often for short periods in series and sometimes in tandem with outside dating. The pervasive sense in which *est* graduates live in a singles milieu, not isolated but moving rapidly among loose and shifting ties, is also suggested by the fact that fully half of them report having "different close friends" a year after the training as compared to the year before.[15] Most young graduates live alone with a lover or roommate in an urban apartment, changing addresses every few years. They rarely live in the same city as their parents, whom they see no more than a few times per year.

One out of three *est* graduates is affiliated with a conventional religious denomination, but less than one of ten participates weekly. Conventional religious affiliation among sixties youth in *est* is almost nonexistent. Many of them, however, are involved in spiritual and therapeutic disciplines (macrobiotics, yoga, TM, aikido, encounter groups), with which they tend to keep up after the training.[16] Roughly 60 percent of all *est* clients are women, who generally report themselves more influenced by the training than do men. . . .[17]

Social Responsibility: Making the World Work

Controversy over *est*'s ethic grows sharpest in discussions of its implications for social and political responsibility. Youthful graduates usually disapprove of radical politics and liberal reformism of sixties vintage as inevitably vain attempts to force persons to change or to "help" them, instead of accepting them as they are and "creating the space" for them to transform themselves abreactively. What sort of concrete social activity is implied by the latter ideal? Graduates' views vary in reply. Some justify exemplary responsibility for oneself and for those with whom one normally interacts as sufficient. Most point to participation in *est* itself as the most effective contribution one can make to the future of American society, namely the transformation of its members and institutions in *est*'s image. They cite the growing number of educators, doctors, therapists, clergy, and other professionals who have taken the training, along with special trainings given for schools, prisons, and local governments, to show that progress toward such institutional transformation is already underway. Traditional forms of political participation and voluntarism are supported as secondary ways of "taking responsibility for the system, since you created it the way it is." Graduates often point to *est*'s nonpartisan voter registration drive among its members as an example of the latter sort of social concern, along with its Hunger Project. Since 1977 the Project has enrolled 1.7 million persons and raised 5.7 million dollars to publicize the idea that it is now possible "to end world hunger in twenty years."[18] (See n. 18 for a discussion of the Hunger Project, n. 27 regarding prison trainings, and n. 28 regarding psychiatric criticism of *est*.)

One young graduate, a veteran of antiwar demonstrations and campus politics though never arrested or affiliated with any radical political organization, characterizes his past and present political involvement in terms of *est*'s idea of responsibility:

During the sixties where did you stand on radical politics?

I was for it. I demonstrated. I marched on Washington in '68 at Nixon's inauguration. You know, "There ought to be a Revolution. Off the President. Kick the sonuvabitch out. Change the system. It's worthless, junk it. Let's take over, and start a whole new thing."

How did you see American society in the sixties?

I always pointed the finger at the system. "This is wrong. That's wrong." I blamed the establishment, while I played the victim. I never took responsibility for anything. I wasn't responsible for the rules, I wasn't responsible for the laws. I wasn't responsible for the Vietnam War. I wasn't responsible for politics. I didn't own any of that shit. I didn't take responsibility for my choices. There I was trying to make the world work, and my own life didn't work. I couldn't even make a commitment to be on time before the training.

How does the system look to you now?

Totally different. Now I feel that the system is perfectly fine. What doesn't work is the people, because they don't take responsibility for it. Now I'm taking responsibility. I'm assisting [at *est*]. I'm gonna vote, because the system's set up to vote and it's my system, so I'm gonna take responsibility for it and vote.

What's responsibility then?

Owning my choices. Being more active, dealing with the system *in* the system, under the system. To me what's more important is conscious awareness, awakening. First you have to take responsibility for yourself, and from there it's an easy step to taking responsibility for the people around you and the whole system.

Sixties radicalism, which blamed and opposed the established sources of political power for conditions of social injustice, is now interpreted as self-righteous abnegation of one's own responsibility for these conditions. The graduate sees this to be especially hypocritical in view of his own irresponsibility in his personal life. He sees participation in *est* and cooperation with conventional politics at present to mark acceptance of responsibility for the existing social system. Its failures are due not to external structural conditions or to the concerted efforts of par-

ticular interest groups or classes, but to the universal unwillingness of individuals, first of all oneself, to take *est*'s kind of responsibility for themselves and the society as a whole. Typically, the young graduate has shifted from an attitude of outright alienation from the established social order during the sixties to mediated identification with it at present, from activities of overt opposition (more hip than radical in tenor) to modest participation. His present position is grounded less in any new faith in the established political structure than in commitment to *est*'s ideology of therapeutic change through abreactive acceptance, and the institutional promise *est* offers for the transformation of society from the inside out.

During the 1960s young *est* graduates shared the countercultural perception that American society was fundamentally wrong and in need of change. They usually subscribed to the hip view that America's "screwed-up values," more than its social structure, were to blame for its problems, which were approaching solution through cultural changes already underway. Many youths sympathized with political activists, some accepted radical diagnoses of what was wrong, why, and how it was to be changed. But virtually none committed themselves to enacting any such programs of change.[19] "I hung on the sidelines and watched the political game," concedes one. "I was interested but I wasn't ready to play it." *est*'s picture of society accounts for the futility of the hippie's version of a psychedelic utopia, while retracing its postmillennial shape in more conventional colors.

est agrees that American society is fundamentally faulty, but it blames the individual graduate. The trainer stresses,

When you see why your lives don't work, you'll see why this whole fucking country doesn't work. Look at General Motors. That's the best this country can do. And look at one of their fucking cars. It's a piece of shit! I'm not blaming GM. I'm blaming you for being so stupid that you think it works.... Sure, you *understand* all the problems, you *want* things to get better. But not if it costs *you* anything, not if *you* have to take responsibility for it.[20]

The country is criticized for not working, just as its corporate representative is criticized for the inefficiency of its machinery, not for its mode of ownership and operation, its political influence or ecological impact. Such criticism leads to the conclusion that what must be done is to make the system work by accepting it as it is, acknowledging oneself as its cause, and participating in it according to its rules. Political activists failed in trying to make the system over by resisting it, blaming others for causing it, and dropping out of it, all according to their own rules. "How did the War end, anyway?" the trainer demands. "Did the kids running around with their little banners end it? No! All they did was get everyone else pissed off at them. What ended it was millions of ordinary people in this country going to the polls and voting it out."[21] est argues that the paradox of its psychological theory of change ("Trying to change an experience makes it persist, accepting it and being with it makes it disappear.") applies as powerfully to social institutions as to the individual mind. By heeding it first with themselves, then others, then everyone, individuals can "transubstantiate" social institutions, altering their essence while leaving their structural accidents unchanged. Thus psychologism defines both the mode and sequence of social change.

Transformation and Social Change

est presents itself as an agent of societal transformation whose success will enable "the institutions of man to deliver on their promises," in Erhard's phrase. "What I want is for the world to work," he says. "The organizing principle of est is: 'whatever the world is doing, get it to do that.'"[22] est is already acting to this end along two avenues. First, it is transforming an ever-increasing number of individuals, who will eventually make up a "critical mass" of the entire population, triggering its transformation by a chain reaction. A longtime est volunteer reports:

There's a cumulative effect from graduates changing personally. They create the space for other people to get it. It's Werner's intention to give the training to forty million people in America, which would be like a critical mass. Everybody will be giving the training to everybody else just by living with them day by day.

By transforming individuals est is transforming society conceived as a collection of individuals. In this postmillennial vision no heroic efforts by a small elite of morally perfected Christians or enlightened Buddhists will be required to remake American society after it has been destroyed by divine or ecological catastrophes. Instead, the new age has already dawned and is now advancing, its continuous progress charted by the swelling curve of est's mass membership.[23] In the process of its numerical growth est is "creating a context" to transform society, just as its Hunger Project is "creating a context" to end starvation. Project literature makes clear that "the process by which a context is created is communication and enrollment, communication and enrollment, communication and enrollment;"[24] while est points out that "numerical growth and international trainings represent, however, only one dimension of est's development as a force for transformation in the world."[25]

Second, est is transforming the larger society's institutions of socialization—educational, therapeutic, medical, legal-penal, religious, governmental, and familial. They will take over the training's functions as their members assimilate its ethic, eventually permitting est itself to wither away. Erhard states that "the real thrust and goal of est is to put est in education. est will cease to exist somewhere along the pike. We've already begun to make inroads, we've already made good plans, we've demonstrated our effectiveness to the world, people will listen to us. We are starting to get into the education system. . . ."[26] Although *est* has yet to win over any institutional establishment, its pre-1976 graduates already included 9 percent of all "educators" in the San Francisco School District.[27] The University of California has offered academic credit for a course entitled "The *est* experience: Implications for Educators," with the training as a prerequisite. A California state college has given credit for the training itself, conducted on campus.[28] *est*'s advisory board numbers a score of distinguished doctors and professors, including educators who have formerly been president of Oberlin College, chancellor of the University of California at San Francisco and HEW assistant secretary, and a Harvard Business School assistant dean. It also includes entertainers John Denver, Valerie Harper, Suzy Chaffee, and a vice-president of the National Broadcasting Company.[29]

Asked about *est*'s potential for transforming American institutions, a young graduate replies with confidence, "It seems like it could happen. *est* is growing faster than anything else and graduates are strategically located. *est* doesn't make anything else wrong, so it can get along with anything. It doesn't give you any answers, so its answers can't be proved wrong. It just gives you a more open, useful viewpoint." The utility of *est*'s ethic for bureaucratic work and social relations, the psychological content of its doctrine (high on epistemology, low on cosmology), and its streamlined delivery (weekend scheduling without "touchie-feelie" or religious props) do indeed make *est* more appealing across the range of secular middle-class life than such human potential competitors as Scientology and Arica, let alone conservative Christian or neo-Oriental religion.

est's modest millennialism fits the social situation of its young graduates. Compared to their counterparts in the Christian sect and the Zen center, they have dropped back in

closer to the middle of mainstream work and personal life. In fact, they had not dropped out so far nor burned their bridges back so drastically in the first place. They did not use drugs so heavily, reject school so vehemently, nor so commit themselves to countercultural careers as drug dealers, rock musicians, hustlers, artists, craftsmen, communards, or political activists. Nonetheless they shared countercultural hopes whose disappointment was not painless for them. *est*'s ethic has responded to the frustration and helplessness felt by college-educated youths now stuck in white-collar jobs within the system they had hoped to change. Says one resignedly,

When I look at what we're doing in the world, it makes me feel helpless. There's nothing I can do about it, except accept it. *est* has shown me that's OK. At least after training I felt a big burden of guilt removed toward people who were having problems, whatever they were, because I got that *they* were responsible in a way.

Why do you think it looked different to you in the sixties?

We were all going to college then. The real world was outside. You could be outrageous, because you didn't have to deal with it. In college everyone was young like me. They all did dope like me, wore long hair, and pointed out there at "them," the ones who were screwing everything up.

But then when I got out and started working, I found myself being one of "them." I wanted to get more for my efforts, you know, get ahead. I guess I'd gotten my hands dirty, so I wasn't so interested anymore in sitting around trying to figure out if it was left-wing dirt or right-wing dirt. [laughing] I found out you can't worry about saving the world. You have to just live your own life.

While it represents a reaction to cooled-off politics and a tightened economy in America since the 1960s, this shift of outlook—from seeking to understand the society to surviving in it, from making it over to making one's way in it—cannot be separated from the subject's age-related shift of position in the society: from studying in an age-segregated youth setting while being supported by others to working in an age-integrated adult setting to support oneself.

Following the line of such shifts of position, *est*'s ethic has also sustained hopes for social change, outside the context of radical or liberal politics, in a form compatible with a conventional career and lifestyle. A graduate seeking his first job as a corporate lawyer doing *pro bono* environmental work on the side suggests how closely *est*'s ideology suits his own situation:

When I was an undergrad I was involved in mildly radical politics. The War was a great rallying point for me, although I couldn't swallow the revolutionary rhetoric. I was coming from the place of "What you're doing, America, is wrong. You can't do that. It's evil." Which was absolutely ineffective. I was flailing around with my eyes closed.

Now instead of saying, "No, no, no," I say, "Yes, you're doing that." I'm seeing and dealing with what is, instead of wishing it were different. I'm coming to a place of acknowledging how things actually work, what the facts are, whether I like it or not, because it is what it is. It's not right or wrong.

In the past few years I've become more involved in my relationship to myself, the people around me, the earth. Social concern is there, but it's not the big issue. It's a question of putting it on a smaller scale, trying to change the energy instead of resisting it. *est* is like that. It's less defensive and more accepting than the radicals. And it's very centered and clear about where I am individually. You can accept opposition and not feel threatened about it. You can communicate with other people and see the world through their eyes, and then maybe you can do something better. It's like Werner saying,

The way it is,
is enough.
Who you are is enough.
The only thing you have to do
is be.[30]

I feel OK with a wait-and-see position on *est* and society, since I already see so much value in *est* for individuals.

For many who came of age in the sixties, *est*'s ethic of taking responsibility for the existing social order while pursuing one's own interests within it sounds sensible and straightforward. For many of their elders, once caught in the middle between the establishment and the kids, *est* has opened up a new middle ground. An older businessman reflects on what *est* has meant to him:

Where once I saw a bloated capitalist, an exploiter of the masses, now I see a man in a Lincoln.
Where once I saw radical, hippie freaks, now I see four bearded men in a battered van. . . .
When I had to understand everything, I didn't understand anything. When I needed to judge, I had no standards of my own.
. . . When I knew what the world was supposed to be like, that's the way it was, whether I liked it or not, and I usually didn't.
Since *est*, the world can be any way it wants. Fine with me. Here I am, then, with a wife who pats me on the leg, customers who want more work than I have time to do. I ride along the freeway and kids flash the peace sign, girls wave and two guys in the back of a pickup truck offer me a beer.
So I don't understand it.
So what?[31]

A social world that could not be understood or justified before can now be accepted. A society that could not be changed through politics, can now be "transformed" through *est*. . . .

Notes

1. From "What is the purpose of the *est* training?" a four-page pamphlet published by *est* (#680-3, 13 January 1976).

2. *est* began and is based in San Francisco. It expanded first to Los Angeles, Honolulu, and Aspen, Colorado; then to New York, Washington, D.C., and Chicago. By 1978 it was offering trainings in eighteen of the nation's top twenty-five population areas. *est* estimates that in the San Francisco Bay Area one out of every nine persons aged twenty-five to thirty-nine who are college graduates has taken the training. In Los Angeles, one in twenty; in New York, one in thirty-three. (*est, The Graduate Review*, February 1978, p. 3.)

est grossed $9.3 million in 1975, $10.9 million in 1976, $13.2 million in 1977, $16 million in 1978, $20 million in 1979, and $25 million in 1980, according to *est* trainers V. Gioscia and K. Anbender. Graduate volunteers effectively tripled the size of *est*'s staff by contributing some 20,000 hours per week in 1977 (*est, The Graduate Review*, June 1978, p. 2), mostly in recruiting, logistical, and administrative services. See "A Report on the Legal and Financial Structure of *est*" (a fourteen-page document published by *est* in June 1976) for a description of *est*'s corporate structure in detail sufficient to engross a tax lawyer without disclosing its overall assets and profitability, or the extent of Erhard's effective ownership. Compare Arnold Levison, "Where Erhard Launders the Money," *Mother Jones*, December 1978, pp. 52–53. In essence, Erhard sold his "body of knowledge" to an overseas holding and licensing corporation, to which *est* pays a maximal portion of its gross income in the form of pretax royalties. Now located in the Netherlands, this holding corporation pays 7 percent in Dutch taxes and then sends all its profits to the tax-exempt "Werner Erhard Foundation for *est*" in Switzerland, which owns the holding corporation outright. *est*, meanwhile, pays 30 percent in American taxes on its minimal postroyalty income. All the remaining profits go to The Werner Erhard Charitable Settlement, a tax-exempt trust on the Isle of Jersey, which owns *est*. Devised on the pattern of tax shelters common among high-profit, low-overhead entrepreneurs like bestselling authors, this arrangement is justified by Erhard on the grounds that "you maximize your assets in an organization by paying the least amount of taxes." (Suzanne Gordon, "Let Them Eat *est*," *Mother Jones*, December 1978, p. 54.) It has so far withstood the IRS, which had six income tax cases lined up against *est* and Erhard in the U.S. Tax Court in 1978, pending the outcome of pretrial negotiations.

3. Erhard has described his experience as follows: "I had a direct experience of myself. That means I no longer identified myself with my body or my personality or my past or my future or my situation or my circumstances or my feelings or my thoughts or my notion of myself or my image or my—I think that covers it. (*San Francisco Chronicle*, 3 December 1974.) Note the resemblance between this negative definition and that of enlightenment in the Buddhist Heart Sutra, especially stanza 4. . . . Erhard calls Zen Buddhism the "essential" one of all the disciplines he has studied. (Adelaide Bry, *est—60 Hours That Will Transform Your Life*, p. 99.) Persons involved in Scientology and Mind Dynamics call much of *est*'s data and processes direct copies of their material. (See Mark Brewer, "We're Gonna Tear You Down and Put You Back Together," *Psychology Today*, August 1975, p. 88; and R. C. D. Heck and J. L. Thompson, "*est:* Salvation

or Swindle?" *San Francisco*, January 1976, p. 70.) Erhard was an instructor in Mind Dynamics (a now-defunct program devised by autodidact Alexander Everett to teach people how to control their minds more efficiently, reportedly through self-hypnosis and visualization) immediately before starting *est*, and his delivery of the Mind Dynamics course closely resembled *est*, according to some clients of both. (See Ornstein, p. 11, cited in n. 7 below.) Various observers of *est* have traced its ideas to Zen, Vedanta, and Christian perfectionism; behaviorist determinism, Freud, Maslow, Rogers, and Perls; Korzybski's *General Semantics;* Norman Vincent Peale's *The Power of Positive Thinking;* Napoleon Hill's *Think and Grow Rich*, and the self-image psychology of Maxwell Maltz's *Psycho-Cybernetics*. Its methods have been traced to hypnosis, autosuggestion, revivalism, psychodrama, encounter, Gestalt therapy, and behavior modification; Subud and yoga; military, monastic, and penal institutions; sales and business motivation courses. An *est* staff member describes Erhard's pragmatic use of such sources: "Werner has done just about every discipline and religion and philosophy there is to do. He took the part of each one that really works and cut out the trappings. . . . Once back when Werner was training businessmen, he asked the boss of this company if he could use Zen on them. 'Just as long as it's not blatantly illegal,' the guy said, 'and you don't get any on the walls.' (D. Percy, *est* guest seminar, Palo Alto, California, December 1974; also Bry, *60 Hours*, p. 153.) Erhard managed door-to-door salespersons for the *Encyclopedia Britannica*'s Great Books Program, then for a division of *Parents' Magazine* and later for a subsidiary of the Growth Corporation, both of which marketed "child development materials" for parents to read to their preschool and early-grade school children. (See William W. Bartley, *Werner Erhard: The Transformation of Jack Rosenberg*, Part II, for an account of Erhard's pre-*est* studies and employment.)

4. From "What is the purpose of the *est* training?"

5. For official descriptions of the *est* training see Werner Erhard and Victor Gioscia, "The *est* Standard Training," *Biosciences Communication* 3 (1977): 102–122, and "*est:* Communication in a Context of Compassion," *Current Psychiatric Therapies* 18 (1978): 117–125. For an enthusiastic description of the *est* training by a non-staff member see Bry, *60 Hours*. For an appreciative, Zen-slanted description see Luke Rhinehart, *The Book of est*. For a critical description of the training as para psychology, see Sheridan Fenwick, *Getting It*. For a critical description of the training as "brainwashing" see Brewer, "Tear You Down." I have compared these descriptions with a 100-page account of my own training and detailed taped accounts of several interviewees in trainings other than my own.

6. *est* holds that upsetting physical sensations and

emotions are linked to memories of painful experiences in the past that have not been fully experienced. During the training these memories, along with their physical and emotional symptoms, come up to be experienced. Once fully experienced, they disappear. The entire psychic and psychosomatic constellation can be "experienced out" by directing non-evaluative, all-accepting attention to the symptoms and then to their causes, that is, by "accepting it, being with it, observing it." This model resembles Freud's notion of abreaction: If repressed memories of traumatic past events are recalled and vividly reexperienced, their associated psychic and psychosomatic conditions will be relieved. (See Ornstein, p. 58, cited in n. 7 below.)

7. Robert Ornstein (principal investigator), Charles Swencionis (project director), Arthur Deikman, Ralph Morris (consultants), *A Self-Report Survey: Preliminary Study of Participants in Erhard Seminars Training* (The *est* Foundation, 1975), hereafter cited as Ornstein. In 1972 Behaviordyne, Inc. of Palo Alto, Ca. conducted psychological testing for personality changes among a smaller group of graduates, concluding, "the psychological picture that emerges is that of a happier, psychologically sounder, and more responsible person" (quoted in Bry, *60 Hours*, p. 213). These studies have not been able to weigh the hypothesized influence on their self-reported results of the placebo effect (participants feel better after completing a therapeutic program, regardless of its content, because they expect to) or the phenomenon of regression on the mean (persons tend to seek therapy at some low point in their lives and subsequently to report feeling closer to the mean, regardless of the therapy's content). Expectations of positive change are widespread among those enrolling in the training. Such expectations are vigorously encouraged by promotional and application procedures designed by *est* and by those enthused members of each wave of graduates instrumental in recruiting the following wave. Many if not all of the persons delivering the training share these expectations. Perhaps most significantly, the training's own tenets and techniques appear to mobilize the placebo effect by affirming and demonstrating the power of expectations (states of consciousness and choice, perhaps mediated by the autonomic nervous system) to determine outcomes (experience, particularly its psychological and psychosomatic dimensions). (See Ornstein, pp. 8, 15, 17, 62, 63.) Graduates' retrospective self-reports show no neat correlation between precisely what and how much they expected to improve beforehand, and what and how much they afterward felt to have improved. (Earl Babbie and Donald Stone, "What Have You Gotten After You 'Get It':" Paper presented to the American Psychiatric Association, 13 May 1976, in Miami Beach.) This does not, however, preclude inferring that the placebo effect may be at

work, since the data indicate that diffuse prior expectations of positive change and subsequent self-reports of it are consistently high.

8. Ornstein, pp. 6–9, 62. Also Donald M. Baer and Stephanie B. Stolz, "A Description of the Erhard Seminars Training (*est*) in the Terms of Behavior Analysis," *Behaviorism* 1, 1 (1978): 45–70, esp. 52–54, 56–58.

9. *est*, "Werner Erhard: 'All I Can Do Is Lie,' " reprinted from an interview in the *East-West Journal*, September 1974, p. 2.

10. Donald Cox, *est* mailing, p. 2, par. 2, of a 1976 letter announcing establishment of an "*est* Public Information Office."

11. These data are drawn from Ornstein, pp. 25–27, 34–36, 59; supplemented by reference to Ornstein data sets in File SYS8, 10/11/74, Variables W29–88; and to twenty sixties youths formally interviewed by the writer. . . . The Ornstein sample (surveyed in 1973) showed an average age of 35.1 years; *est*'s own records showed the average age of all graduates falling to 33.7 by 1978. Only 25 percent of all graduates were then over forty. (*est*, *The Graduate Review*, February 1978, p. 3.) Persons twenty-five to thirty-four years of age comprise 46.7 percent of *est*'s clientele and 19 percent of the San Francisco population, a ratio of 2.45 to 1. By the author's informal count of volunteers at *est* graduate seminars, guest seminars, special events, and the like, at least 70–80 percent range from twenty-five to thirty-four in age. (See Brewer, "Tear You Down," p. 36, for a corroborating observation.) Youths interviewed averaged 30.3 years of age, as calculated in 1978, were equally divided by sex, and were all Caucasians. Eighteen of twenty had used marijuana, fourteen LSD. Nine had been in political demonstrations. Eleven of twenty had lived communally; three now did so. Fifteen of twenty had worked irregularly since school; three were now unemployed, one by choice. Ornstein's 1973 sample shows that 39.5 percent of *all* *est* graduates had used marijuana, but only 14.4 percent had used LSD. Since *est*, 49.8 percent reported using less marijuana and 56 percent reported using less LSD. (File SYS8, 11/22/74, pp. 27–30.)

12. Ornstein File SYS8, Variable W85, pp. 69–71. Teaching credentials far outnumbered any other category of "graduate degree" held by *est* clients; for example, eighty-five credentials versus twenty Ph.D's. Psychology majors accounted for 6.4 percent of all college-educated *est* clients. Then came Education, 6.1 percent, and Business Administration, 5.7 percent; "Liberal Arts" or "Two Majors" made up 8.1 percent. Few majored in technical or preprofessional areas: Premedicine, 2.2 percent; Engineering, 2.9 percent; Law, 1 percent; Economics, 1 percent. Interestingly, nonpsychology majors close to *est*'s subject matter are among those least represented: Philosophy, 0.3 percent; Religion, 0.3 percent; Theology, 0.1 percent.

13. Occupational data come from Ornstein File SYS8, Variable W88, pp. 76–78. This file includes sixty occupational categories in six groupings: professional, technical, busines, arts and media, trades, and labor. From these data I estimate that 69.3 percent work mainly with other persons (including students and housewives; excluding them, the estimate is 61.8 percent), as opposed to physical things or abstractions. White-collar workers make up the largest grouping of occupational categories, some 32.7 percent of *all* graduates (including students, housewives, retirees): clerical workers, 11.7 percent; "executives," 9.7 percent; non-college teachers or instructors, 7.4 percent; business owners, 4.4 percent; salesmen, 4.3 percent; media and arts, 6.9 percent. Students made up 9.6 percent of all graduates and housewives 8.6 percent. Professionals comprise roughly 10 percent of all *est* graduates, including: college teachers, 1.8 percent; architects, 1 percent; clinical psychologists, 0.3 percent; psychiatrists, 0.3 percent; clergy, 0.5 percent. Less educated therapists or counselors make up 3.3 percent. Persons working with things make up less than 10 percent of all *est* graduates. They include: artisans and skilled manual workers, 4.7 percent; general service workers, 3.2 percent; and unskilled labor, 0.8 percent.

14. Ornstein, pp. 25, 36, 59. The lower figure for mean income in Ornstein takes in all nonresponses to the question as equaling zero; the higher figure simply excludes them. . . . Nearly half of all *est* graduates reported increased job satisfaction since *est*, and half of this number—one quarter of the entire Ornstein sample—attributed it to getting a new job since the training (an average of eleven months previous). (Ornstein, p. 25.) Of twenty interviewees, fifteen had switched, left, or entered a job within a year of taking the training. Only three such moves constituted a clear-cut advancement or promotion. Interviewees earned an average of $8,150 in 1975. Interviewees were employed as follows:

retail clerk	elementary schoolteacher (M.Ed.)
corporate sales representative	psychiatric social worker (M.S.W.)
shoe salesman	dentist (D.D.S.)
store manager	educational administrator (Ed.D.)
2 secretaries (1 part-time)	lawyer (unemployed by choice)(J.D.)
office clerk	law student (J.D.)
office manager	housepainter/carpenter (self-employed)
car rental agent (unemployed)	nurse (R.N.)
purchasing agent	custodial services manager
assistant buyer (unemployed)	

15. Ornstein, pp. 27, 36, 59. . . . Forty-seven percent of 1,063 respondents reported different close friends, with only seventy-five admitting to having none at all (Ornstein, p. 27). Regarding marital status:

6.2 percent of graduates divorced the year before *est* (n=1,138)

8.5 percent separated the year before *est* (n=1,065)

4.3 percent divorced the year after *est* (n=1,130)

7.7 percent separated the year after *est* (n=1,050)

26.7 percent divorced or separated in this two-year period, yet only 19–22 percent . . . are presently divorced or separated, suggesting a rapid remarriage rate (and/or re-cohabitation rate for those living with someone) as well. No exact figures for those who have *ever* divorced are available; but in light of the existing data, they should be sizable. (See Ornstein, pp. 27, 36.) Fourteen percent of all *est* graduates report themselves "living with someone." (Ornstein, p. 36.) Thirty percent of the sixties youths interviewed were living with someone, with four of the six couples maintaining exclusive sexual relations. Two were married, one with a single child. Another four were previously divorced. Four persons were regularly dating one other person, two of them to the exclusion of others; five were dating two or more persons at once. Three reported dating only occasionally. Fifteen of the twenty had lived with someone for at least several months at some time in the past, and only two were still living with their first such partner. (According to surveys reported in *Time*, 10 January 1977, p. 43, more California residents aged twenty-one to thirty are now living together than are married.) Twelve of the twenty had changed their residence within a year of taking the training. Six had moved to San Francisco within a year before *est*, and one within a year after taking *est* elsewhere.

16. See Ornstein, pp. 35–36. Religious affiliation of all graduates (n=1,188): Protestant 17.8 percent; Catholic 10.5 percent; Jewish 6.4 percent. Religious participation: never 65.6 percent; several times a year 20.2 percent; monthly 6.4 percent; weekly 7.8 percent. Mean number of disciplines practiced: before *est* 1.24; after *est* 0.95. Twelve of twenty interviewees practiced macrobiotics, Rolfing (massage), yoga, aikido, or the like both before and after the training. Afterwards one person took up TM and another started going to a Protestant church for the first time since leaving home, both attributed to ambivalent experiences of *est*. A third interviewee had earlier experimented with Zen meditation, "got" that it was unnecessary in the training, and then stopped it. No other interviewees reported any religious affiliation or participation.

17. According to the Behaviordyne study of *est* (see Bry, *60 Hours*, p. 213). My interviewees support this finding, as does the differential response rate by sex to mailed questionnaires in the Ornstein survey: of re-

spondents 58.7 percent were women, 41.3 percent men (n=1,113); of nonrespondents 52.6 percent were women, 47.4 percent men (n=576). (Ornstein, p. 61.)

18. In February 1977, Erhard declared, "I take responsibility for ending starvation within 20 years," to members of the est Foundation. The Foundation then granted $100,000 to begin The Hunger Project, incorporated independently of est but largely housed in est offices, staffed by est personnel and graduate volunteers, and indebted to est for a $400,000 interest-free loan. In the fall of 1977 Erhard presented the Project in eleven cities (at a cost of $518,000 to the Project) to 40,000 persons, most of them est graduates, and thus to the media and to the public. By 1979, 180,000 persons had enrolled in the Project, two-thirds of them nongraduates. (See *Graduate Review*, September 1977, p. 2; also The Hunger Project, "A Shift in the Wind," *The Hunger Project Newspaper*, 1, May 1978.) "Ultimately, the Hunger Project is about transformation of Self as Humanity—about making the world work," writes Erhard. "It is about creating the end of hunger on our planet as an idea whose time has come." (*Graduate Review*, September 1977, p. 5.) What does this mean in organizational terms? "The Hunger Project is not about feeding people," explains one official. "All the Hunger Project does," says its Boston chairman, "is enroll more people. What we are doing is using money to create growth." (Mac Margolis and R. Hornung, "An Idea on Every Plate," in *Nightfall*, October 1978, pp. 15–22, quoted from p. 18.) Project literature states, "Your donation will be used for the project. The project is not about researching new technical solutions, growing food, or feeding people directly—but rather creating a context of commitment to eliminate starvation on the planet in two decades. The process by which a context is created is communication and enrollment, communication and enrollment, communication and enrollment." (The Hunger Project, "It's Our Planet," p. 5.) The idea of "creating the context to end hunger" is thus identified with the action of "communicating" about and "enrolling" in The Hunger Project. By 1979, each of 180,000 enrollees had been asked to donate at least five dollars to the Project, enroll others, volunteer for its staff, and fast for a day. By this time, the Hunger Project had raised $880,000 and spent over a million, gaining recognition from the media, government officials, and established hunger organizations. Some experts and officials have welcomed the Project's publicity for the issue of world hunger. Others adopted a wait-and-see attitude, or expressed uncertainty about what the Project actually does. Critics have charged that it does little besides publicize itself and recruit new members, thereby performing the same functions for est itself. Such critics point to the Project's initial budget:

57.6 percent ($518,000) went to pay for Erhard's presentations; about 26.6 percent ($238,000) went to produce Project literature and films; 15 percent ($135,250) went for the Project's own administrative, organizational, and miscellaneous expenses. This left 0.8 percent ($7,500) to support other hunger organizations, which actually feed people. Critics also point to reports of nongraduate Project volunteers being pressured by its est-trained staff and assistants to take the training. (See Suzanne Gordon, "Let Them Eat est," *Mother Jones*, December 1978, pp. 42, 44, 50.) Through 1980 the Hunger Project enrolled 1.7 million persons and raised $5.7 million, according to est trainer K. Anbender.

19. If we define the committed political activist by such indicators as leading or regularly participating in radical political activity, being arrested for so doing, belonging to a radical organization, mastering its formal ideology, resisting the draft or filing for CO status, then none of those formally interviewed could be classified as a committed activist. Of thirty additional graduates informally interviewed, only one, an early sixties civil-rights worker and CORE member now turned massage teacher, would qualify, the case of est graduate Jerry Rubin notwithstanding. Seventeen of twenty interviewees reported sympathizing during the sixties with the view that American society seems fundamentally in the wrong; only four of the seventeen accepted a full-blown radical political analysis of what was wrong, and none acted on it.

20. R. McNamara, day 1.

21. Ibid., day 3.

22. Bartley, *Erhard*, p. 221.

23. This postmillennial optimism began to fade in 1975–76 among insiders aware of est's slowing rate of recruitment and profit in its original Western markets, and a rash of related problems. These included defections and discontent among est's staff, IRS investigation of its finances, and media criticism of its "authoritarian" organization and founder. In a videotaped staff meeting in March, 1976, Erhard acknowledged that est's goals of training forty million persons and transforming American society might not, after all, be possible within one generation. est subsequently reincorporated itself more effectively and entered large urban markets in the eastern United States. est's enrollment and profits rebounded after 1976, and its organization stabilized. (See Jesse Kornbluth, "The Führer over est," *New Times*, 19 March 1976; and *Graduate Review*, November, 1976.)

24. The Hunger Project, "It's Our Planet-It's Our Hunger Project," (a 10-page brochure, published May 1978), p. 5.

25. *Graduate Review*, July 1978, p. 16.

26. est, "Werner Erhard: All I Can Do Is Lie," (an undated reprint of an interview published in the *East-West Journal*, September 1974), p. 5.

27. *est* has had mixed success with professionals, winning the loyalty of some individuals, notably clinical psychologists and physicians, but not the approval of any professional establishment. *est has* won over elements of the middle echelons of certain educational, business, and administrative institutions, in which its ethic is particularly applicable. At the end of 1975 *est* claimed 8.83 percent of all "educators" in the San Francisco Unified School District among its graduates. (R. C. Devon Heck and J. L. Thompson, *San Francisco*, January 1976, p. 22.) Disproportionately women, schoolteachers must present themselves to large groups, motivate their efforts through interpersonal means, and manage their behavior within the constraints of a bureaucratized setting, to which youngsters are especially resistant. Special *est* trainings have reportedly had the clearest institutional impact in prisons. Because these prison trainings are often cited to counter indications that *est* appeals predominantly to middle-class whites, it is worth noting that prison inmates—though predominantly poor, black, and male—can be particularly receptive to rule-egoism. They usually hold an individualistic ethic overtly antagonistic to the conventions and rules of "straight" bureaucratic society, yet they find themselves imprisoned within the most totally constraining of all bureaucratic institutions. They are there for trying to beat the system by bucking it. Being there offers strong evidence that their attempts have been unsuccessful. Now the system is beating them, sometimes literally. Rule-egoism sensibly advises that the only way to beat the system, in one's own interests, is to go along with it. One inmate translates *est*'s ethic to another: "What the man is tellin' you is that you don't need to get your head knocked doin' what you're gonna end up doin' anyway." ("The *est* Standard Training at San Quentin Prison," *est* publication #1391, November 1976.) Dropout rates in prison trainings appear to be way above the 3–5 percent middle-class average outside. From Bry, *60 Hours*, p. 125, it seems that 67 percent of those who signed up for the Lompoc Prison training did not complete its first delivery there. Similarly, more than one-third of the prisoner-trainees at San Quentin dropped out by the end of day 3; sixty-one remained of ninety-four who had begun, including eight prison staff members. (*Graduate Review*, September 1976, pp. 1–7.)

28. Robert W. Fuller and Zara Wallace, *A Look at est in Education* (San Francisco: *est*, 1975), pp. 62–63. The sharpest institutional debate over *est*'s meaning and effects has so far occurred among psychiatrists, centered around the possibility of harm raised by apparently rare but nonetheless serious cases of post-*est* psychotic episodes. Several psychiatrists treating such persons concluded: "We are impressed that an authoritarian, confrontational, aggressive leadership style coupled with psychologic deprivation fosters an 'identification with the aggressor.' The inability of this defense mechanism to contain overwhelming anxiety aroused by the process may lead to fusion with the leader, ego fragmentation, and psychotic decompensation." (Leonard L. Glass, M. Kirsch, F. Parris, "Psychiatric Disturbances Associated with Erhard Seminars Training: I. A Report of Cases," *Am. J. Psychiatry* 134 (1977): 245–257.) *est* responded by (1) denying any "causal relationship between taking the *est* training and the occurrence of psychotic problems"; (2) arguing that the incidence of psychotic episodes after the *est* training is 0.8 percent, "less than the number of people having episodes in college classrooms or just walking the street"; (3) citing *est* policy to screen from the training all persons ever in a mental hospital or not currently "winning" in therapy. (*est*, "Statement on article in the *American Journal of Psychiatry*," 1977.) Four of the five psychotic cases reported in the Glass article had no histories of psychiatric disturbance or treatment. Neither side in the debate touched on the apparent congruity between the cognitive content of the psychiatric symptoms reported—grandiosity, paranoia, delusions of influence and reference—and those of *est* tenets. Yet in one case a person, convinced he could live without air, jumped into a swimming pool and tried to breathe under water. Another, convinced "nothing was real," put his hand through a window and severed tendons in his wrist. A third was convinced he could read others' minds, and feared they could control his own mind. These symptoms appear to dramatize, however extremely, such familiar *est* ideas as the omnicausal yet entirely determined self, creating his experience of others yet being created by them, accomplishing all things without "efforting" or "trying." . . .

29. *Graduate Review*, June 1978, pp. 15–17.

30. *est* "Special Guest Seminar" announcement, February 13, 1976.

31. *Graduate Review*, June 1976, p. 11.

S E L E C T I O N   9 . C

The Tnevnoc Cult

David G. Bromley and Anson D. Shupe, Jr.

The 1970s have witnessed a profusion of new religious movements ranging from the traditional Christian-based "Jesus Freaks" to groups of oriental origin such as the International Society for Krishna Consciousness (Hare Krishna), Guru Maharaj Ji's Divine Light Mission, and Sun Myung Moon's Unification Church. As these groups have grown in size and wealth there has been a parallel spread of alarm at the tactics by which they recruit and hold members. Allegations of deception, seduction, drugging, hypnosis and brainwashing have been leveled at these groups both by distraught parents of members and former members who have "escaped" or been deprogrammed and told their horror stories (Edwards, 1979; Thielmann, 1979; Mills, 1979). A number of behavioral scientists and other investigators have lent their support to these accusations and have attempted to formulate explanations for these swift and seemingly bizarre "conversions" (Conway and Siegelman, 1978; Patrick and Dulack, 1976; Stoner and Parke, 1977).

It is the issue of manipulative "mind control" which has been the single most inflammatory allegation running through this popular literature. These accusations create the impression that these new religions have innovated or rediscovered techniques of indoc-

trination which transform otherwise normal individuals into followers who resemble robots or automatons in their slavish zeal, unquestioning obedience, and lack of individuality/free will. However, in the course of our own research (Shupe and Bromley, 1979; Shupe, Spielmann and Stigall, 1977), which has included an historical examination of the social context of these groups, we have discovered several past cases which are remarkably similar in many respects to these new religious groups.

This paper will attempt to demonstrate that what is currently termed the "cult menace" (particularly as it relates to recruitment, socialization and social organization) is not a novel development on the American religious scene. On the contrary, throughout our history the appearance of new religious movements has aroused very similar fears and accusations. Specifically, we shall examine the recruitment and indoctrination practices of the Tnevnoc Cult, a communal, sectarian group affiliated with a large and powerful international religious organization. Tnevnocs and the larger parent body were targets of social repression in America during the nineteenth and early twentieth centuries. Since we are concerned primarily with recruitment and socialization in relation to contemporary charges of manipulation and mind control, we shall focus only on the parallels between the Tnevnocs and such contemporary groups as the Unification Church and Hare Krishna, not on the larger traditions or parent bodies of the groups of either era. The Tnevnocs no longer are as visible or as controversial as they once were due to a gradual trend toward accommodation both by the movement and by powerful institutions within American so-

David G. Bromley is Professor of Sociology at Virginia Commonwealth University.

Anson D. Shupe, Jr. is Professor of Sociology at the University of Texas, Arlington.

This paper is the product of a joint effort. The order of authorship is random and does not imply any difference in the importance of contributions. The authors wish to thank Jeffrey Hadden, Theodore Long, Patrick McNamara and Horace Miner for their contributions to the development of this paper.

Reprinted from *Sociological Analysis* 40 (1979), with permission.

ciety. However, as we document in the ethnographic composite which follows, many of the recruitment and socialization practices of even the accommodated twentieth century Tnevnocs are remarkably similar to those of the current "new religions." Because the Tnevnocs were rigidly segregated by sex and our data deal only with the female Tnevnoc component, we make no claim to generalize to the entire movement.

A Brief Ethnography of the Tnevnoc Cult

Like their modern-day counterparts in the current "cult explosion," such as the Unification Church and the Divine Light Mission, the Tnevnocs made a point of attempting to recruit members when they were still in their teenage and young adult years. This age cohort, Tnevnoc leaders recognized, was the least encumbered by domestic and occupational responsibilities, and its members were, not surprisingly, highly susceptible to idealistic, altruistic appeals. Much of this recruitment was openly conducted in schools and on campuses. On the basis of limited contacts with cult members, young girls were induced to commit themselves totally to the cult. If the cult succeeded in gaining control over them, it subjected them to such thorough indoctrination that they became totally dependent on the cult and in many cases lacked the will to free themselves from it.

Once a girl had been induced to join the cult she was immediately subjected to totalistic control. Like the Hare Krishna and the Children of God, members were forced to surrender all aspects of their former lives. Virtually all personal possessions were taken away, and individuals were prohibited from developing any outside involvements and commitments. Indeed, members were required to devote literally all of their time and energies to cult activities. The round of cult life was relentless and consuming. Members were routinely wakened at 4:30 A.M. to face

an arduous day of menial labor interspersed with long hours of prayer, meditation, mind-numbing chanting, and compulsory religious ceremonies. Like Hare Kirshna sect members who always carry prayer beads in cloth sacks attached to their wrists, Tnevnocs carried such beads which they used in their repetitive, monotonic chanting. Members gathered in candlelit, incense-filled rooms closed to outsiders for a variety of special rituals involving chanting and meditation. One particularly bizarre observance was a type of love unity feast involving ritualistic cannibalism. Members consumed food which they were told symbolically represented parts of the dead father's body.

The time not taken up with such rituals was devoted almost entirely to menial labor such as washing clothes, preparing food, and scrubbing floors. Indeed, only one hour of "free time" was allowed each day, but even during this brief period members were forbidden to be alone or in unsupervised groups, being required to remain together and monitored by cult leaders. All luxuries and even basic amenities were eliminated. For example, members slept each night on wooden planks with only thin straw mats as mattresses. They subsisted on a bland, spartan diet; food deprivation was even more severe than the meager diet implies, members being permitted to eat sweets only once a year and often being placed under considerable pressure to fast periodically. This combination of limited sleep, draining physical labor, and long hours of compulsory group rituals and worship, all supported by a meager subsistence-level diet, left members without sufficient time or energy to preserve even their own senses of individual identity.

All the members' former sources of emotional support also were severed upon joining the cult. During the first year members were forbidden to leave the communal (and often remote rural) setting in which their training took place and could receive no outside visitors beyond one family visitation. It thus became virtually impossible for parents and friends to maintain regular and frequent contact with members. For example, members were permitted to write only a minimal four letters per year. Further, just as do Unification Church leaders, Tnevnoc cult leaders deliberately disrupted family ties by creating a fictive kinship system in which they assumed parental roles intended to replace members' natural parents and siblings. Any other relationships which threatened cult control were also strictly forbidden. For example, sexual attachments of any kind were, without exception, tabooed. Lone Tnevnocs were never allowed in the presence of individuals of the opposite sex and they were forbidden to maintain close personal friendships with each other or even to touch physically. All loyalty had to be channeled to the cult, and its leaders, in authoritarian fashion, enforced those strictures. Leaders went so far as to assert that they were God's direct representatives on earth and therefore due absolute obedience by all members. This subservience was formalized in each member's written promise of absolute obedience for three years, after which time individuals often were led to make similar commitments for the remainder of their lives.

Perhaps most striking was the emergence of cult-induced personality changes. This began with the alteration of each individual's exterior appearance. Like the Hare Krishna, Tnevnoc cult members immediately upon joining had their hair cut off and were dispensed long flowing garments specifically designed to render members indistinguishable from one another. This concerted effort to wipe out any sense of individuality was carried to such extremes that members were never permitted to own or even look into mirrors. The cult literally attempted to destroy the old individual, her identity, and her former life's associations by assigning a new cult name and designating the date of her entry into the group as the individual's "real" birthdate. Of course such identity changes were more difficult to

monitor than behavioral conformity. One way cult leaders maintained close surveillance over the most private aspects of members' lives was to require members to reveal publicly and to record in diaries even the most minor infractions of elaborate cult rules, as well as improper thoughts and wishes.

This totalistic environment, with its rigid, all-encompassing code of behavior that individuals could not possibly follow without some minor infractions, engendered within members constant and inescapable feelings of inadequacy, self-doubt, anxiety and guilt. Cult leaders deliberately exacerbated these nagging feelings by instituting a series of humiliating, ego-destructive punishments for even the most trivial infractions of cult rules. For example, daydreaming or entertaining "improper" thoughts, however fleetingly, called down upon members ceremonies of public degradation. Members were forced to prostrate themselves in front of cult leaders and kiss their feet or, alternately, were denied food and reduced to crawling from member to member on their knees begging for the dregs of other member's meals. Such punishments became more severe as time went on, and members were expected to punish themselves regularly for these deviations. The cult went so far as to issue each member a ring to which were attached several lengths of chain with barbed points on the ends. Members were required to return alone to their beds at night at regular intervals and flagellate themselves with this cruel device as atonement for their infractions.

Not surprisingly, the grueling demands of cult membership and the everpresent feelings of guilt and anxiety created the potential for members to "give up" or defect. In addition to the docility created by the harsh conditions of the daily round of cult life, members were constantly pressured by cult leaders for greater personal sacrifice and evidence of complete commitment. Indeed, members competed with one another to express total selflessness and dedication. These constant exhortations and punishments designed to destroy any vestiges of individuality were reinforced by ceremonies intended to bind the individual inextricably to the group. One particularly ghoulish example was a macabre nuptial ceremony in which members were required to become the living brides of the dead cult leader. Overall these extreme and often bizarre tactics were extremely successful. Although on occasion individuals did manage to extricate themselves from the cult, most were permanently stripped of their individuality and autonomy and lived out their lives in subservient obedience.

Cults—Historical and Contemporary

Two important limitations of the preceding ethnographic composite of the Tnevnocs deserve mention. First, as no analogy is perfect, there are some differences between the Tnevnocs of the nineteenth century and the new religions of the present. For example, the Tnevnocs recruited children from families which were part of the larger international organization while most new religions recruit virtually all their members from families of other religious persuasions. Hence individual Tnevnoc members did not encounter the same hostility and resistance from their own families as did their latter day counterparts in the new religions. Too, in the Tnevnoc's case much (but certainly not all) of the social repression was directed against the larger parent organization rather than specifically against the Tnevnocs themselves. Further, the Tnevnocs were organizationally more reclusive and did not arouse public antagonism by espousing programs for revolutionary social change, as have many of the new religions such as the Unification Church.

Second, the foregoing description of the Tnevnocs actually constitutes a caricature of the group insofar as it fails to convey the sense of majesty, purpose, personal fulfillment and belonging that Tnevnocs experi-

enced individually and collectively. It also ignores the order, harmony, stability and integration of Tnevnoc communal organization. However, these same details also are missing from most contemporary accounts of new religious movements. It is precisely this lack of personal and organizational context and purpose which creates a sense that some of their practices are illegitimate and destructive (Bromley, Shupe and Ventimiglia, 1979).

What have been conveyed fairly accurately in our description of the Tnevnocs are some of the recruitment and socialization techniques by which both they and modern religious movements have sought to create and maintain deep commitment among their members. Certain types of groups historically have tried to harness all of their members' personal energies on a voluntary basis. These include not only the Tnevnocs but also elite military training units, communes, monasteries and social movements seeking to effect radical social change (Kanter, 1972; Coser, 1974; Dornbusch, 1955). In order to gain control over all the members' time and energy such groups must develop high levels of commitment to them. In our research on the Unification Church and other new religious movements we have found that intense commitment can be generated and maintained to the extent that individuals' interest and group interests become *congruent*, that is, to the extent that individuals *wish to act as they are required* to act (Bromley and Shupe, 1979a, 1979b). This process involves totally immersing individuals in a set of activities which render them unavailable for other lines of action and constructing a symbolic system which provides a rationale and meaning for involvement in those activities. In a dynamic sense the process of building total commitment involves a *detachment* of individuals from former involvements and lifestyles, sources of emotional support and bases of personal identity, and *attachment* to new social roles, sources of affective support, and identity bases.

There is, in short, a simultaneous process of *desocialization,* and *resocialization* (McHugh, 1966). The extensiveness and intensity of desocialization and resocialization depends in part on the selectivity groups can exercise in their recruitment activities (e.g., how readily they can attract individuals who already possess characteristics they require). However, since most newly formed groups and movements such as "new religions" have both low selectivity and high needs for member commitment, intense socialization practices usually are socially imperative.

Thus, if the practices of promoting total commitment in members are similar for various historical and contemporary religious groups, the different societal reactions to them cannot be explained solely in terms of those practices. Instead, societal response depends on the *degree of legitimacy,* defined in terms of the number and power of supporting groups, accorded a given religious body. The lower a group's legitimacy, the less resistance it can muster to counter social repression and the less control it has over its own public image. The major difference between the current societal reactions to the Tnevnocs and the Moonies, Hare Krishnas or Children of God, then, is that the Tnevnocs have now been accorded legitimacy, the persistence of at least some of the commitment maintenance practices described in this paper notwithstanding, while the latter groups have not.

Yet, as even a cursory review of American history reveals, virtually every major denomination and religious body was met initially with some degree of skepticism, ostracism or persecution. Indeed, the parallels with contemporary religious groups are striking. Much as the Unification Church, Hare Krishna, Children of God, and People's Temple are currently labeled "cults," the Tnevnocs once were perjoratively lumped together with groups such as the Mormons and Masons despite their enormous doctrinal and organizational diversity. The stereotypes and litany of charges leveled against contemporary "new religions" also are remarkably reminiscent of allegations against the earlier "new religions": political subversion, unconditional loyalty of members to authoritarian leaders, brutalizing of members, sexual indiscretions, and possession of mysterious, extraordinary powers (Sawatsky, 1978; Davis, 1960; Miller, 1979). And the atrocity stories told by apostates from earlier groups (Hopkins, 1830: Monk, 1836; Young, 1875) read much like the lurid tales told by former members of contemporary "new religions."

It is not our intent to argue that all of the accusations leveled against contemporary "new religions" are false. Groups with lofty ideals frequently assume airs of moral superiority and engage in duplicity and deception on the assumption that "the ends justify the means." But it also is true that groups which seek to initiate sweeping social change become the focus of hysterical reactions well out of proportion to the real threat they present. It is easy to be drawn into simplistic calls for repressing current religious "cults," either through anti-cult legislation or more vigilante-style actions such as "deprogramming," on the basis of caricatures like that presented here. Yet it should be kept in mind that contemporary scholars view the repression of religious movements during the nineteenth century as the result of undisguised xenophobic zeal and religious bigotry rather than as a legitimate response to any serious threat. It should also be kept in mind that all social movements encounter enormous pressure, both internal and external, to accommodate to the larger society. While it is premature to forecast the nature and degree of the accommodation of the latest group of "new religions," the past history of now established religious groups, the existing literature in the sociology of religious organizations (Weber, 1964; Niebuhr, 1929; Wilson, 1978) and already emerging trends within the new religions themselves (Bromley and Shupe, 1979a; Wallis, 1977) suggest that these groups may follow a parallel accommodationist course. One of the factors which would be most likely to impede this process would be prolonged, severe social repression. Thus not only does the current anti-cult movement constitute an abrogation of American religious pluralism, but ironically, it also may well have the effect of blocking the opportunity for these movements to follow the very course of accommodation which the anti-cultists profess to support.

References

Bromley, David G., Anson D. Shupe, Jr., and Joseph C. Ventimiglia. 1979. "The role of atrocities in the social construction of evil." Paper presented at the annual meeting of the *American Sociological Association.* Boston, August, 1979. In James T. Richardson (ed.), *Deprogramming Controversy: Sociological, Psychological, Legal, and Historical Perspectives.* Transaction Press, 1982.

Bromley, David G. and Anson D. Shupe, Jr. 1979a. "Moonies" in America: Cult, Church and Crusade. Beverly Hills: Sage.

1979b. " 'Just a few years seem like a lifetime': a role theory approach to participation in religious movements." In Louis Kriesberg (ed.), *Research in Social Movements,* Conflict and Change. Greenwich: Jai Press.

Conway, Flo and Jim Siegelman. 1978. Snapping. New York: Free Press.

Coser, Lewis A. Greedy Institutions. 1974. New York: Free Press.

Davis, David. 1960. "Some themes of counter-subversion: an analysis of anti-Masonic, anti-Catholic, and anti-Mormon literature." *The Mississippi Valley Historical Review* 47:205–24.

Dornbusch, Sanford. 1955. "The military academy as an assimilating institution." *Social Forces* 33:316–21.

Edwards, Christopher. 1979. Crazy for God. Englewood Cliffs: Prentice-Hall.

Hopkins, Hiram. 1830. Renunciation of Free Masonry. Boston.

Kanter, Rosabeth. 1972. Commitment and Community: Communes and Utopias in Sociological Perspective. Cambridge: Harvard.

McHugh, Peter. 1966. "Social disintegration as a requisite of resocialization." *Social Forces* 44:355–63.

Miller, Donald. 1979. "Deprogramming in historical perspective." In James T. Richardson (ed.), *The Deprogramming Controversy: Sociological, Psychological, Legal, and Historical Perspectives.* Transaction Press, 1982.

Mills, Jeannie. 1979. Six Years with God. New York: A&W Publishers.

Monk, Maria. 1836. (1962). Awful Disclosures of the Hotel Dieu Nunnery. Handen: Anchor.

Niebuhr, H. Richard. 1929. The Social Sources of Denominationalism. New York: Holt.

Patrick, Ted and Tom Dulack. 1976. Let Our Children Go. New York: E. P. Dutton.

Reed, Rebecca T. 1835. Six Months in a Convent. New York: Arno Press.

Sawatsky, Rodney. 1978. "Moonies, Mormons and Mennonites: Christian heresy and religious toleration." Pp. 20–40 in M. D. Bryant and H. W. Richardson (eds.), *A Time for Consideration: A Scholarly Appraisal of the Unification Church.* New York: Edwin Mellen Press.

Shupe, Anson D., Jr. and David G. Bromley. 1979. "Witches, Moonies and evil." In Thomas Robbins and Dick Anthony (eds.), *In Gods We Trust: New Patterns of American Religious Pluralism.* Transaction Press, 1981.

Shupe, Anson D., Jr., Roger Spielmann, and Sam Stigall. 1977. "Deprogramming: the new exorcism." *American Behavioral Scientist* 20:941–56.

Stoner, Carroll and Jo Anne Parke. 1977. All God's Children. Radnor: Chilton.

Thielmann, Bonnie. 1979. The Broken God. Elgin: David C. Cook.

Wallis, Roy. 1977. The Road to Total Freedom: A Sociological Analysis of Scientology. New York: Columbia.

Weber, Max. 1964. The Theory of Social Economic Organization. Translated by A. M. Henderson and T. Parsons (eds.). New York: Free Press.

Wilson, John. 1978. Religion in American Society: The Effective Presence. Englewood Cliffs: Prentice-Hall.

Young, Ann. 1875. Wife No. 19: Or, the Story of a Life in Bondage, Being a Complete Expose of Mormonism. Hartford.

A D D I T I O N A L   R E A D I N G S

Articles

Bainbridge, William S., and Stark, Rodney, "Church and Cult in Canada." *Canadian Journal of Sociology* 7 (1982): 351–66.

Bromley, David G., and Shupe, Anson D., Jr. "Financing the New Religions: A Resource Mobilization Approach." *Journal for the Scientific Study of Religion* 19 (1980): 227–39. Religious movements use public solicitation to obtain funds from societies whose values and structures they regard as corrupt. Yet public solicitation is not the only source of funds. See James T. Richardson, "Financing the New Religions: Comparative and Theoretical Considerations." *Journal for the Scientific Study of Religion* 21 (1982): 255–68.

Lynch, Frederick R. " 'Occult Establishment' or 'Deviant Religion'? The Rise and Fall of a Modern Church of Magic." *Journal for the Scientific Study of Religion* 18 (1979): 281–98. Analyzes the world view, social structure, and practices of a modern "Church of Magic," testing two sociological perspectives. The author finds Lofland and Stark's model of conversion to a deviant perspective especially useful.

Richardson, James T. "People's Temple and Jonestown." *Journal for the Scientific Study of Religion* 19 (1980): 239–55. Why People's Temple cannot be viewed in any sense as a "typical cult" and what factors help account for the terrible tragedy of its self-extinction.

Woodrum, Eric. "Religious Organizational Change: An Analysis based on the TM Movement." *Review of Religious Research* 24 (1982):89–103. Traces the Transcendental Meditation movement through three periods, culminating in the 1970-to-present years in which TM is billed as a scientifically validated technique for producing personal and social benefits.

See also the following issues of *Sociological Analysis*, which feature wholly or in considerable part articles on the new religions: 39 (1978); 40 (1979); 41 (1980).

Books

Shupe, Anson D., Jr. *Six Perspectives on New Religions: A Case Study Approach.* New York: Edwin Mellen, 1981. Utilizing several theoretical perspectives, the author examines "fringe religions" whose doctrines and practices are at odds with the value systems of American culture.

Shupe, Anson D., and Bromley, David G. *The New Vigilantes: Deprogrammers, Anti-Cultists, and the New Religions.* Beverly Hills: Sage, 1980. A thoughtful, well-documented study emphasizing the techniques and rationale of deprogramming members of cults; the authors also maintain a critical posture toward the "Anti-Cult Movement" (ACM).

Several major volumes of essays that focus on the new religions include:

Glock, Charles Y., and Bellah, Robert N., eds. *The New Religious Consciousness.* Berkeley: University of California Press, 1976.

Needleman, Jacob, and Baker, George, eds. *Understanding the New Religions.* New York: Seabury, 1978.

Robbins, Thomas, and Anthony, Dick, eds. *In Gods We Trust: New Patterns of Religious Pluralism in America.* New Brunswick, N.J.: Transaction Books, 1981.

Zaretsky, Irving, and Leone, Mark P., eds. *Religious Movements in Con-*

temporary America. Princeton: Princeton University Press, 1974. This slightly older but very valuable collection includes religious groups of a more traditional nature.

Besides the monographs already mentioned in this chapter, the following are noteworthy:

Bainbridge, William Sims. *Satan's Power: Ethnography of a Deviant Psychotherapy Cult.* Berkeley: University of California Press, 1978.

Bromley, David G., and Shupe, Anson D., Jr. *"Moonies" in America: Cult, Church and Crusade.* Beverly Hills: Sage, 1980.

Burnham, Kenneth E. *God Comes to America: Father Divine and the Peace Mission Movement.* Boston: Lambeth Press, 1979.

Damrell, Joseph. *Seeking Spiritual Meaning: The World of Vedanta.* Beverly Hills: Sage, 1977.

Judah, J. Stillson. *Hare Krishna and the Counterculture.* New York: John Wiley, 1974.

Cross-cultural References

Jules-Rosette, Bennetta, ed. *The New Religions of Africa.* Norwood, N.J.: Ablex, 1979. An excellent collection of essays on various new sects and cults in various African countries. The role of women is a notable feature of several studies.

Religion: What Does the Future Hold?

Does religion have a future? Is it declining, or does it show signs of vitality and promise of growth? There can be no immediate yes or no to these questions, for we have seen in Chapter 1 the importance of defining religion before discussing its present or future. For the moment, let us consider only traditional Judeo-Christian *beliefs* and *practices*. If we turn to sociology's founding fathers, we find them sharing the skepticism of their contemporaries. Traditional religion was on the decline, a decline that would continue with advances in science and increasing education. Industrial society had broken up the small communities in which traditional religion thrived, and it could not be brought back again. Auguste Comte saw religion as the victim of a cultural evolution in which scientific thinking replaced earlier stages of theological and metaphysical speculation; Durkheim looked for some "new ideas and new formulae," convinced that "religious faith would become increasingly subject to the influence and the authority of the sciences."[1] Yet both Comte and Durkheim strongly felt that religion's *expressive* side—its rituals and its liturgies, however changed in content—were vital as "cement" by which men and women could express their solidarity and feel their unity with tribe, group, or nation. For Karl Marx, religion was false consciousness; it would wither, as rational thinking and revolutionary praxis exposed religious beliefs and practices for what they really were—superstition, blindness, and ignorance. Freud believed that religion was a massive illusion from which humankind might eventually save itself by becoming aware of religion's roots in the perpetuation of infantile dependence upon a father figure. It was Max Weber who most minutely investigated the impact of religious ideals and practices (of both Western and Eastern religions) on a

345

wide range of human behavior; but even Weber was an agnostic for whom religious beliefs had no validity that could be rationally, systematically sustained. One's values were, in the last analysis, one's personal choices.

This skeptical legacy found its way into modern sociology under the concept of *secularization*, generally defined as the historical process by which religion's influence diminishes throughout the major institutions of society—the political, economic, and educational—as each institution develops its own set of norms and achieves independence from religious guidance. Religion mainly survives in the private sphere of individual and family life. It has little to say about the direction of major sectors of public life or about the operation and direction of modern industrialized societies, influential though it may continue to be in "less-developed" nations. Secularization can be approached in *two* major ways:

1. *Individual religiosity.* Recall a major distinction developed in Chapter 1. A theorist defining religion *inclusively* will tend to see religion persisting under different forms, for human beings "need" ultimate meaning systems by which to guide their lives. The research of J. Milton Yinger, reviewed in the introduction to Chapter 1, suggests that people in different cultures share the same set of major concerns about life, death, suffering, and moral meaning, and have ways of coping with these major challenges. Secularization in this perspective means only that *traditional* religious beliefs, practices, and world views may be in decline, but not religion itself. A person abandoning a Methodist, Buddhist, Islamic, or Baha'i upbringing will still find some interpretive scheme for dealing with "the major challenges." If we leap to a broader, societal framework, structural-functionalists usually hold that any society, if it is to cohere, needs a set of ultimate values on which its members generally agree. Otherwise disunity, even chaos, results. For the inclusivist, then, the major research task is to *trace the changes* from one or more meaning systems to others, or to another set.[2]

Those who prefer an *exclusive* definition of religion, on the other hand, postulate the supernatural or supraempirical as part of their definition; if they adhere to the secularization hypothesis, they will look for *indicators* to measure decline or growth in religion. Thus survey research enters their picture, along with the various dimensional aspects of religion. Has *practice*, for example as measured by weekly attendance, gone up or down over time? Have *beliefs* diminished in vigor? Has the amount of per capita giving to churches declined or increased? Are more or fewer persons married under religious auspices? Are more or fewer persons members of churches? Much discussion accompanies the almost annual production of statistics of this sort.[3] Evidence in the United States and Canada shows that attendance, for example, was high in the 1950s, dropped off in the latter half of the 1960s, and leveled off in the late

1970s and early 1980s. As pointed out in our Chapter 3 readings, evidence also shows that some churches have gained or lost more than others. The widest patterns show that North Americans are generally considerably more "religious," in the sense of practice, than Western Europeans or Latin Americans. Again, the significance attached to these figures depends upon how one defines religion.

2. *Institutional religiosity.* Here one looks at churches or other religious groupings as *institutions* and asks whether they are gaining or losing influence on the societal institutions mentioned (political, economic, educational). Though public opinion polling is somewhat useful here—for example, by asking people whether they *think* religion (or the churches) are gaining or losing influence—the tack taken by most theorists is to cite *structural differentiation* as a major cause of loss of influence. Major institutions have divested themselves of religious authority. The nation-state no longer permits itself to be influenced in any substantial way by religious bodies. Its own bureaucratic apparatus and legal structure develop and function without reference to religious norms. The development of capitalism means that economies proceed under the dynamic of the profit motive; the market has its own mechanisms of guidance, more or less regulated by the state, and sees no need for religious guidance. The loss of traditional community accompanying the rise of industrial cities, and the population movements that uprooted and thrust people into impersonal conditions, have made religion's influence less salient. In contemporary terms, secular schooling is the norm in most modern societies; religion has little influence on selection of teachers or curriculum. In personal terms, people choose their friends less on religious grounds and more on the basis of similar occupational and educational backgrounds. Even some issues of morality, such as those arising from new technological developments (test-tube babies, for example) seem to be first discussed in the public arena and only later by theologians.[4]

One of the most articulate spokespersons for the second thesis (religious *institutions* lose influence) is British sociologist Bryan Wilson. According to Wilson, "irrelevance" is not too strong a term to describe the churches' nonrole in modern societies. Religion is present, he argues, but carries little import for the society as a whole:

The impact of religion on the operation of society, once great, is now negligible, and this change has been determined by technical, economic, and political factors. Religion becomes privatized. In a consumer society it becomes just another consumer good, a leisure-time commodity, no longer affecting the centres of power or the operations of the system—even at the level of social control, socialization, and the organization of the emotions and of motivations. Religion becomes a matter of choice, but whatever religion is chosen is of no consequence to the operation of the social system.[5]

But what about the so-called "new religions" seen in Chapter 9? Are not they a sign of the revival of the sacred in modern society, an indicator that religion persists under whatever changing forms? Posing this question opens the door to an important debate in contemporary sociology of religion. Wilson flatly views the new religions as further evidence of secularization. He acknowledges that earlier religious revivals (such as the American "great awakenings" and John Wesley's preaching to England's industrial proletariat) helped reintegrate individuals into the social order. Virtues such as sobriety, family responsibility, thrift, and so on were positively functional for the efficient operation of an industrial labor force or for the continued dynamic of Western expansion in North America.

The new religions, however, are a far cry from the old revivals. While protesting the impersonality of modern society, "the new cults propose to take the individual out of his society, and to save him by the wisdom of some other, wholly exotic body of belief and practice."[6] In seeking mystical union and not continual involvement in the rational processes of industrial society, these religions further the historical tendency by which traditional religion ceases to have any impact on society at large. Society is left to the mercy, as it were, of technical, economic, and political factors. Immersion in sect or cult will benefit individuals, perhaps, in their quests for personal fulfillment. But it will not affect the direction or operation of culture and society.

The other side of the debate finds expression in a reflective essay by researchers Dick Anthony and Thomas Robbins, who have specialized in the study of the new religions.[7] They point out that some of the new religious groupings and movements are far from culturally or politically neutral. They openly attempt to influence American society in certain directions. Examples are the Unification Church (popularly known as the "Moonies"), with its world view of a morally permissive, corrupt America threatened by godless world communism. "Young converts see themselves as fighting selflessly for universal ideals of love and harmony and world unity in a world permeated by relativism, cynicism, and selfish egoism."[8] The ill-fated People's Temple at Jonestown saw itself as locked in a struggle to the end with a hostile environment symbolized in the capitalistic, racist society of the West but as finally unable to defeat its enemies. "Mass suicide became a means of realizing a form of immortality."[9]

These forms of the new religions, then, are best viewed not as turning adherents away from society into their own privatistic worlds, as Wilson would have it; but as "civil religion sects" with a mission to reform the worlds about them. Anthony and Robbins believe that civil religion is a more useful concept than secularization or loss of community, consensus, and so on. Religious and political symbols have been intertwined throughout American history—to this extent, they agree with Robert N. Bellah (see Bellah's "Civil Religion in America," Chapter 2 in this book). But they believe that Bellah in *The Broken Covenant* (1975) poses too sharp a break between what he terms "Puritan absolutism" on the one hand and utilitarian individualism on the other. Anthony and Robbins see these two tendencies in a kind of synthesis used as a legitimation of American-style capitalism. One could pursue private goals of amassing wealth and justify this effort as conducive to the common welfare (a better, stronger America); and yet, through the legacy of the Puritan tradition, one could also legitimate one's wealth by pointing to a life free of vice and even of "conspicuous consumption." One could be "ascetic" in one's personal life yet drive hard bargains in the economic realm of laissez-faire enterprise. Undergirding both tendencies is a premise of moral responsibility: You can choose whether to be virtuous or not; you are responsible for your behavior and your success or failure in your work or business as well as in your private life.

But both of these principles have been cast into ambiguity and confusion by two developments in the political economy of late twentieth-century capitalism: (1) a planned and managed economy honeycombed with bureaucratic regulations and "government interference," making the ideals of achieving individuals and entrepreneurs much more difficult to attain; and (2) a "permissive" culture, coming into full bloom in the late 1960s, aided and abetted by a consumer economy that merchandises the new morality and encourages spending for any and all pleasures. This thrust is totally antithetical to the Puritan legacy of ascetic control over impulses and the seeking of personal pleasure. Pleasures that were once off-limits, including sex, consumption of liquor, and so on, are taken-for-granted aspects of new life-styles. Finally the tragedy of Vietnam further "de-legitimated" for many Americans the hitherto unquestioned assumption of faith in America's global power.

These societally relevant new religions can be grouped analytically, then, with such "Christian new right" political movements as that described by Louise J. Lorentzen in Chapter 7. Such movements attempt to restore the image of America as a chosen nation with a mission—but in a context of what Anthony and Robbins call a "dualism" of serving God or mammon, Christianity or communism, good or evil, as manifested in the challenges from "the growth of communism, pornography, homosexuality, false gurus, and secular humanism."[10] America must be recalled to its original purposes and destiny. A prophetic form of civil religion is at work.

Other movements, such as the Meher Baba cult, represent yet another response to the ambiguities just mentioned. "Monistic relativism" of such cults emphasize individual consciousness and discovering one's inner self. Thus they repudiate traditional American (or any other) civil religion, urging detachment from all such ideologies and systems. At the same time, in ways pointed out by Anthony and Robbins, their very emphasis on detachment enables them to encourage involvement in bureaucratic institutions and routines that they now envision as harmless because the personal identity is located elsewhere, not in occupational roles.

A parallel essay by W. Clark Roof, focusing on the mainline churches today, acknowledges the same tendencies analyzed by Anthony and Robbins. The established churches are languishing, with fewer people joining them, particularly among younger adults, in the late 1970s and early 1980s. And who gains?

On the one hand, conservative religious belief and ideology flourish, advocating traditional morality and life-styles; evangelical and fundamentalist faiths are the most rapidly growing religious expressions in America. On the other hand, growth is also evident in the various nontraditional, often non-Christian religious movements and in related quasi-religious movements concerned with spiritual therapies. These movements are largely outside of the churches and synagogues, although they include participants from the established institutions. While conservative and nontraditional religious forms prosper, the institutions in the middle—the more liberal mainline Protestant, Catholic, and Jewish bodies—are losing appeal and support.[11]

Roof therefore asks if the "middle ground" occupied by traditional mainline North American churches is collapsing. Survey research shows that gains among those who say they belong to no religion—the "nones"—are made at the expense of the more liberal denominations of the Protestant establishment. Similar realignments seem to be occurring within American Judaism, the Conservative branch losing members, "with the larger, less traditional component moving to the Reform or ceasing to affiliate denominationally, and the smaller, more traditional component moving into the Orthodox."[12]

Attempting to avoid any simplistic notions of "secularization" as an overall explanation, Roof points to demographic change, value changes, institutional policies (such as the continuing divisiveness caused by the involvement of many liberal churches in such causes as civil rights, assistance for draft evaders, community organization, and antiwar efforts), and religious styles and identity (such as the critique of Dean M. Kelley that growing faiths seem to "stand for something," whereas mainline Christianity seems to lack clear identity). Mainline churches are thus composed of diverse constituencies, "liberals" as well as "conservatives," and offer a variety of activities and programs. Instead of growth resulting from these efforts, however, decline has been the outcome. In times of cultural change such as our own, the major churches seem to alternate between prophetic stances and more accommodating ones, again reflecting the diversity of their membership. Can they achieve or regain a "bridging role" as mediators between culturally conflictive groups? Such acutely controversial issues arising in the late 1970s as abortion, homosexuality, and ordination of women resulted in pressures from conservative elements to "adopt a theology of personal and self-fulfillment tailored to private religious tastes."[13] Pressures from liberal constituencies urge the churches toward direct involvement with, and specific stands on, controversial issues, with a risk of making the church seem "too political." One way of coping with this dilemma is through more ecumenical efforts to ally with other churches, helping to buffer some of the internal pressures experienced in attempting to be "relevant" to the world.

What bears close watching in the 1980s and perhaps into the following decade is the apparently increasing tendency of several mainline Protestant churches, as well as the Roman Catholic, to take stands antithetical (at least in some important respects) to policies of the national government. Positions on nuclear deterrence, on human rights policies both at home and abroad, and even a stand critical of exploitative tendencies of contemporary capitalism are bound to arouse intense debate and opposition. How saliently will the opposition mobilize? Will church leaders be heard and be given moral authority to speak on behalf of any considerable proportion of the laity? Or has church authority, both in mainline Protestantism and Catholicism, eroded enough so that believers will continue to go their own ways, for all practical purposes regarding their leaders as just another pressure group? While it certainly marks a change for large churches to go on record *against* national policies, critics such as Bryan Wilson will doubtless inquire how much actual *influence* such stands will have on public policy. To be truly relevant means more than issuing pastoral letters and church statements; it means having genuine impact on what is decided. Measuring such impact is a major challenge for sociologists of religion as we move into the troubled world of the later twentieth century.

Notes

1. Emile Durkheim, *The Elementary Forms of the Religious Life* (New York: Collier, 1961), p. 475; Steven Lukes, *Emile Durkheim: His Life and Work* (New York: Penguin, 1975), p. 476.

2. For a contemporary example of such research, see Daniel Yankelovich, *New Rules: Searching for Self-Fulfillment in a World Turned Upside Down* (New York: Random House, 1981).

3. Statistics on church membership, growth, attendance, and so on are found in the annual report of the Princeton Religion Research Center and the Gallup Organization, Inc., entitled *Religion in America;* and in the *Yearbook of American and Canadian Churches* (Nashville: Abingdon Press).

4. For an excellent discussion of secularization from both viewpoints discussed here, see John Wilson, *Religion in American Society: The Effective Presence* (Englewood Cliffs, N.J.: Prentice-Hall, 1978), Chapters 18 and 19.

5. Bryan Wilson, "The Return of the Sacred," *Journal for the Scientific Study of Religion* 18 (1979), p. 277.

6. Bryan Wilson, *Contemporary Transformations of Religion* (London: Oxford University Press, 1976), p. 98.

7. Dick Anthony and Thomas Robbins, "Spiritual Innovation and the Crisis of American Civil Religion," *Daedalus* 111 (1982), pp. 215–34. Quotations used with permission.

8. Ibid., p. 224.

9. Ibid., p. 225.

10. Ibid., p. 272.

11. W. Clark Roof, "America's Voluntary Establishment: Mainline Religion in Transition," *Daedalus* 111 (1982), p. 172. Quotations used with permission.

12. Ibid., p. 172.

13. Ibid., p. 182.

ADDITIONAL READINGS

Articles

Bourg, Carroll J. "Politics and Religion." *Sociological Analysis* 41 (1980):297–316. Issues of war and peace, energy shortages, and structural unemployment offer opportunities for religion to move out of the private sphere and into publicly debated issues—but will the opportunities be accepted as challenges?

Hastings, Philip K., and Hoge, Dean R. "Religious Trends among College Students, 1948–1979." *Social Forces* 60 (1981): 517–31. Fluctuations are apparent in religious beliefs and practices over the time period in question, but rejection of other societal institutions does not carry with it rejection of the institutional church.

Johnson, Benton. "Taking Stock: Reflections on the End of Another Era." *Journal for the Scientific Study of Religion* 21 (1982):189–200. Mainline churches are currently in a "great depression." Only renewed emphases on theology, history, and the cure of souls can reverse this decline.

Wilson, Bryan. "The Return of the Sacred." *Journal for the Scientific Study of Religion* 18 (1979):268–80. A brief statement of the author's frequently stated thesis that the forces of economic rationalization in modern societies leave room only for privatized versions of religion, that religion no longer has any general meaning for society as a whole.

Patterns of church dropping out and of denominational switching, showing which groups gain at whose expense, have been minutely examined in recent years. This emphasis reflects availability of trend data over a considerable time period. An excellent collection of articles is a special edition of *Review of Religious Research* 21 (Supplement 1980), "The Unchurched American," by Dean R. Hoge and David A. Roozen, guest editors.

Books

Greeley, Andrew M. *Unsecular Man: The Persistence of Religion.* New York: Schocken Books, 1972. A strong counterstatement to secularization theorests such as Wilson. Greeley marshals evidence to show that the sacred persists in modern societies. For a recent restatement of his viewpoint in much more theoretically elaborated form, see *Religion: A Secular Theory.* New York: Free Press, 1982.

Wilson, Bryan. *Religion in Sociological Perspective.* New York: Oxford University Press, 1982. Wilson's most comprehensive statement of his major theses concerning the secularization of modern societies.

N A M E   I N D E X

SUBJECT INDEX